Oxford Resources for IB
Diploma Programme

2023 EDITION

CHEMISTRY

Geoffrey Neuss

STUDY GUIDE

OXFORD
UNIVERSITY PRESS

Great Clarendon Street, Oxford, OX2 6DP, United Kingdom

Oxford University Press is a department of the University of Oxford.
It furthers the University's objective of excellence in research, scholarship, and education by publishing worldwide. Oxford is a registered trade mark of Oxford University Press in the UK and in certain other countries.

First published in 2023

British Library Cataloguing in Publication Data
Data available

9781382016568

9781382016575 (ebook)

10 9 8 7 6 5 4 3 2 1

Paper used in the production of this book is a natural, recyclable product made from wood grown in sustainable forests.

The manufacturing process conforms to the environmental regulations of the country of origin.

Printed in China by Golden Cup.

Acknowledgements

The publisher and authors would like to thank the following for permission to use photographs and other copyright material:

Photos: p68: Oxford University Press.

Artwork: Q2A Media, Six Red Marbles, and Oxford University Press.

Every effort has been made to contact copyright holders of material reproduced in this book. Any omissions will be rectified in subsequent printings if notice is given to the publisher.

Contents

Introduction

This Study Guide is written specifically for students studying chemistry for the International Baccalaureate Diploma Programme, although many students following their own national systems will also find it helpful. This is now the fourth edition of the guide and it has been completely updated so that it comprehensively covers the new programme that will be examined from 2025 onwards. All the information required for each topic is set out in separate boxes with clear titles.

This guide contains all the necessary subject content in one easily accessible and compact format. IB chemistry is, of course, much more than just the final examinations and I encourage you to read widely around the subject to further your knowledge and understanding as well as increase your enjoyment of chemistry.

Dr Geoffrey Neuss

How to use this book

Overall syllabus

The full IB chemistry guide is published by the IB. It is intended for teachers and covers what should be taught and how it will be examined in the context of the IB as a whole. Ask your teacher to provide you with a copy of the parts of the guide that contains the detailed syllabus content relating to your specific Standard or Higher Level course.

It is important to note that the way in which the syllabus content is set out in the guide is not a teaching plan or order. It details what can be assessed externally at the end of the course and internally during the course.

Chemistry is essentially the study of the make-up of materials and how materials can interact with other materials to form new substances. Although many pre-university courses separate chemistry into modules, such as atomic structure, stoichiometry, periodicity, bonding and structure, energetic, kinetics etc., chemistry is a holistic subject so that none of the topics exists in a vacuum as they all relate and overlap with each other. The current IB Diploma syllabus is set out differently. It essentially splits chemistry into two main divisions – Structure and Reactivity – with the aim of integrating concepts, topic content and the Nature of Science through inquiry. Chemistry is a holistic subject and you are expected to be able to think critically and make links between different topics.

Syllabus breakdown

Structure and Reactivity are each then split down into three smaller topics, named S1, S2 etc. These main topics are then broken down into sub-topics e.g. S1.1, S1.2, S1.3 etc. Throughout the book you will find a dark grey box in the top corner of each page. This box contains a reference to the sub-topic covered by the content on that page. This will allow you and your teacher to match the content to the IB guide and keep track of what you know.

S2.1

In the IB guide, each of the sub-topics has its own heading and starts with a Guiding Question. The Guiding Question is an overarching question to frame the topic. After you have studied the sub-topic in this book you should be able to answer the Guiding Question.

The material that you need to know in the IB guide is provided as Understandings, Skills, and Guidance. This is all split into Standard Level content and Additional Higher Level (AHL) content. In this book, an 'AHL' tag in a dashed box next to the heading, or a dashed outline to the box indicates that that part of the book covers additional higher level content.

AHL

Coverage of the syllabus

The first twelve chapters of this Study Guide cover all the underlying chemistry theory and everything in the syllabus essentially as it is laid out in the guide. For the most part the Study Guide follows the syllabus order. Your teacher may not follow the order of the IB guide in their teaching because sometimes it's important to know concepts covered later in the syllabus to help you understand an earlier concept. Similarly, there are a few places in this book where the content is covered in a different order to make it easier for you to learn and understand the concepts.

Linking questions

The IB guide also provides Linking Questions throughout. These provide ideas of links to other parts of the syllabus. This includes the tools for chemists, inquiry skills and Nature of Science. Their aim is to encourage thinking and/or problem solving beyond the immediate content. The ones given in the syllabus are examples and you are also encouraged to make your own linking questions.

As part of your revision or to test your understanding, have a look at the linking questions in the IB guide and see if you can answer them. Then have a go at making your own linking questions and links.

Practice questions

At the end of each chapter there are several pages of practice questions. There are multiple choice questions and short-answer questions. Try answering these questions to test your understanding and practice for the exams. Then check your answers using the answers at the back of the book. These answers are not necessarily the full 'model' answers but they do contain all the information needed to score each possible mark.

Worked examples

Worked examples are provided within the chapters where they are appropriate. For example, there are worked examples for calculations you'll need to be able to complete. Worked examples are marked with a darker header so that you can find them easily. Have a go at completing the example yourself and then carefully follow the steps of the worked example to see a model example of how to do it.

Tools for chemists

The first twelve chapters of this book deal with all the chemistry concepts and details required by the syllabus. To understand and apply chemistry fully a good chemist also needs tools. Some of these are specific for a particular task and others are more general and can be used in a wide variety of applications. They will be assessed either directly or indirectly both in the written final examinations and in the internally assessed report. The IB chemistry guide lists the tools required under three different types of heading: Experimental techniques, technology and mathematical skills. These tools are covered in Chapter 13 of this book.

Underlying philosophy

Chapter 14 takes you through the underlying philosophy of the IB Diploma chemistry course. It explains how all the topics are intimately linked to each other, and also to the Nature of Science and International Mindedness. There are also several pages of holistic short-answer questions that pull together content from across the course and link it to the underlying philosophy.

Obtaining a higher grade

To help you, the student, achieve the highest possible grade, Chapter 16 gives you advice on how to study and prepare for the final external examinations and how to excel at your internally assessed Individual Scientific Investigation. For those who opt for chemistry as the subject for their Extended Essay the final chapter gives advice and guidance on how to choose the topic, formulate the research question and write your Essay. A comprehensive checklist is included to help you gain bonus points towards your IB Diploma.

Introduction to the particulate nature of matter

Elements

All substances are made up of one or more elements. An element cannot be broken down by any chemical process into simpler substances. There are 118 known elements. A full list of all 118 elements can be found in section 6 of the IB data booklet. The smallest part of an element is called an atom.

▼ Names of the first 20 elements

Atomic number	Name	Symbol	Relative atomic mass
1	hydrogen	H	1.01
2	helium	He	4.00
3	lithium	Li	6.94
4	beryllium	Be	9.01
5	boron	B	10.81
6	carbon	C	12.01
7	nitrogen	N	14.01
8	oxygen	O	16.00
9	fluorine	F	19.00
10	neon	Ne	20.18
11	sodium	Na	22.99
12	magnesium	Mg	24.31
13	aluminium	Al	26.98
14	silicon	Si	28.09
15	phosphorus	P	30.97
16	sulfur	S	32.07
17	chlorine	Cl	35.45
18	argon	Ar	39.95
19	potassium	K	39.10
20	calcium	Ca	40.08

Compounds

Some substances are made up of a single element, although there may be more than one atom of the element in a particle of the substance. For example, oxygen is diatomic: a molecule of oxygen contains two oxygen atoms and has the formula O_2. A compound contains more than one element combined chemically in a fixed ratio. For example, a molecule of water contains two hydrogen atoms and one oxygen atom. It has the formula H_2O. Water is a compound, not an element, because it can be broken down chemically into its constituent elements: hydrogen and oxygen. Compounds have different chemical and physical properties from their component elements.

Mixtures

The components of a mixture may be elements or compounds. These components are not chemically bonded together and are not in a fixed ratio. Because they are not chemically combined, the components of a mixture retain their individual properties. If all the components of a mixture are in the same phase, the mixture is said to be **homogeneous**. Air is an example of a gaseous homogeneous mixture. If the components of a mixture are in different phases, the mixture is said to be **heterogeneous**. There is a physical boundary between two phases. A solid and a liquid is an example of a two-phase system. It is possible to have a single state but two phases. For example, two immiscible liquids, such as oil and water, form a heterogeneous mixture.

Separation of mixtures

Because the components of a mixture are not chemically bonded, they can be separated by physical means. Properties to consider when determining the best method to separate the components of a mixture include solubility (in water or other solvents), melting points and boiling points of the components, and whether the mixture is homogeneous or heterogeneous. Common techniques include solvation (e.g. $CuSO_4$ combining with water to form $CuSO_4.5H_2O$), filtration, evaporation, distillation and paper or thin-layer chromatography.

1. Filtration

Filtration is used to separate an insoluble solid from a liquid. The mixture is poured through a filter, and the liquid (the filtrate) passes through to a container below, while the insoluble solid (the residue) is left on the filter paper. If the solid particles are very small, the process can be carried out under reduced pressure, in a Buchner flask, using a vacuum pump.

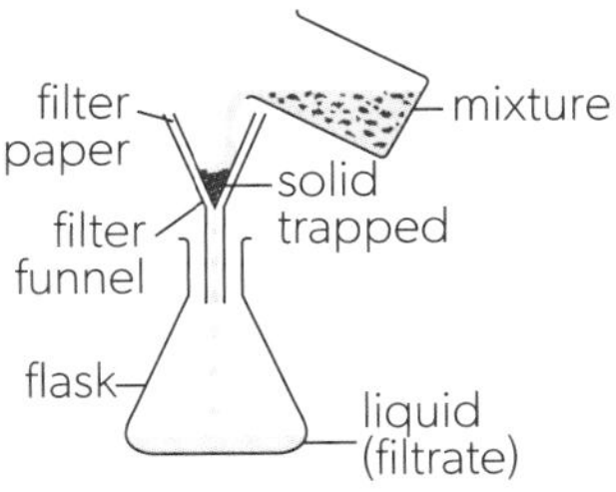

▲ Normal filtration

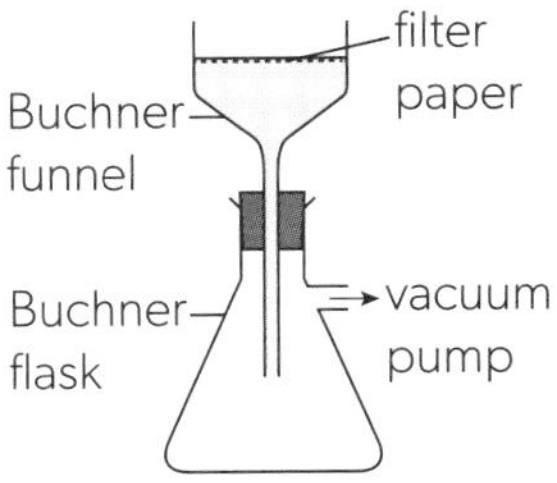

▲ Vacuum filtration

Separation of mixtures

2. Evaporation and recrystallization

If only one of the components of a mixture is soluble in a solvent such as water or ethanol, or in a non-polar solvent such as hexane, the mixture can be warmed with the solvent to dissolve the soluble component. The resulting solution is then filtered to remove any undissolved solid particles and the solvent is evaporated to leave the solute behind. This solid can be purified by dissolving in a minimum quantity of a heated solvent and then leaving the solution to stand so that crystals are formed and any impurities remain in the solution. After filtering, the crystals can be washed with a small amount of the cold solvent and then dried.

3. Separatory funnel

A separatory (or separating) funnel can be used to separate two immiscible liquids. The mixture is shaken with the stopper on, then allowed to stand. Once two layers have formed, the stopper is removed and the more dense lower layer run off by opening the tap.

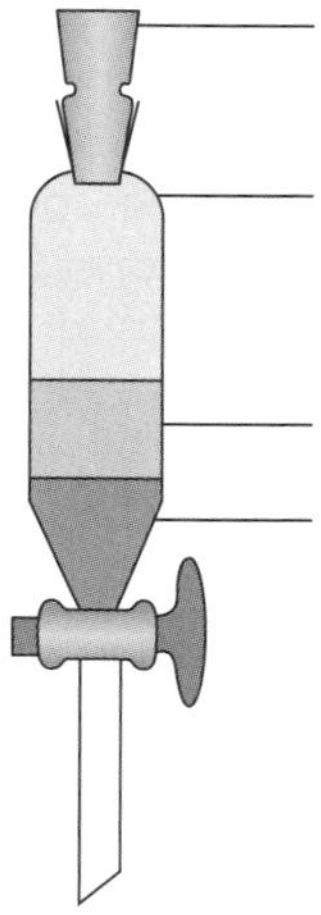

▲ Separatory funnel

4. Distillation (and reflux)

A solvent can be obtained pure from a mixture (such as sea-water) by distillation. The volatile solvent boils to form a gas, which is then condensed and collected. The same apparatus can be rearranged to form a reflux apparatus. This is not for separating mixtures but is used to allow volatile compounds to react together when heated for a period of time, with no loss of compounds through evaporation or boiling.

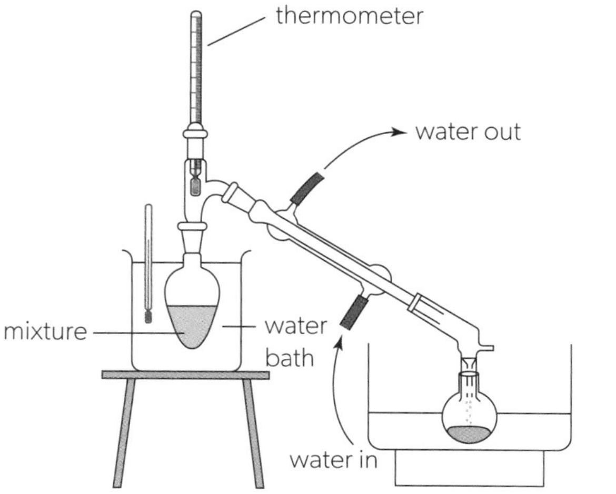

▲ Distillation apparatus

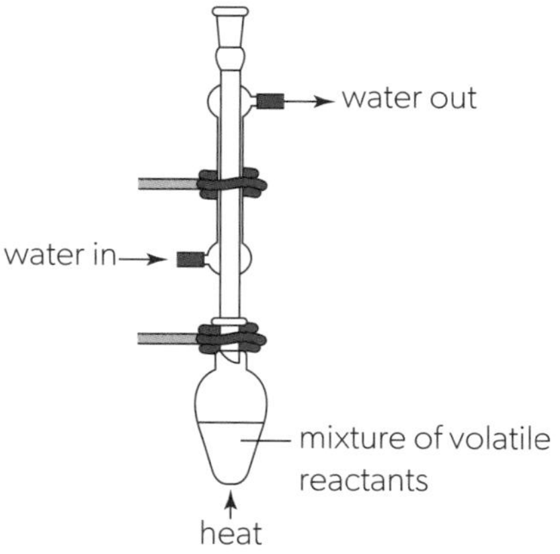

▲ Reflux apparatus

5. Melting point determination

Once a solid has been obtained, its purity can be checked by determining its melting point. Pure substances normally have a fixed sharp melting point and the value can be compared with the literature value. If the substance is impure, it will have a lower melting point and tend to melt over a wider temperature range. The sample is placed in a small melting point tube and the melting point is determined either by using commercial melting point apparatus or by attaching it to a thermometer in an oil bath that is gradually heated.

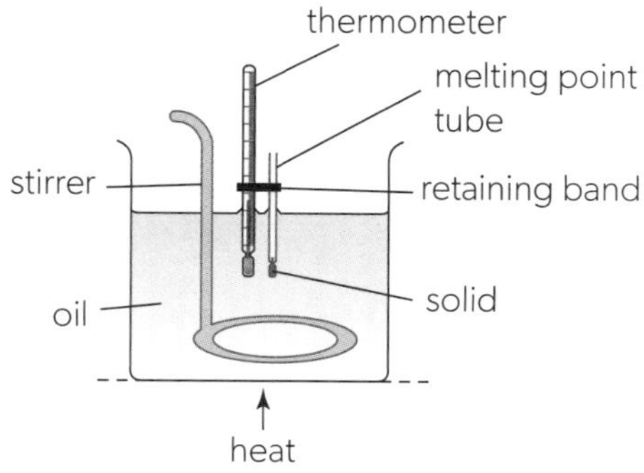

▲ Melting point apparatus

Chromatography

Introduction to chromatography

Chromatography can be used to separate mixtures containing very small amounts of the individual components. Coupled with other techniques, such as mass spectrometry, chromatography can be used to separate and identify complex mixtures, both quantitatively and qualitatively. It can also be used to determine how pure a substance is. There are several types of chromatography, including paper and thin-layer chromatography. In each case, there are two phases: a stationary phase that stays fixed and a mobile phase that moves. Chromatography relies upon the fact that the components in a mixture have different tendencies to adsorb onto a surface or dissolve in a solvent. This provides a way of separating them.

Paper chromatography

The simplest type of chromatography is paper chromatography. When black ink is placed on blotting paper, the different colours in the ink move at different rates so it quickly separates into several colours. Paper consists largely of cellulose fibres. These contain a large number of hydroxyl groups, making the paper quite polar. Water molecules hydrogen bond to these groups so that a sheet of "dry" paper actually contains about 10% water. It is this water that acts as the stationary phase. The mobile phase is a solvent, either water itself or a polar organic liquid such as ethanol, propanone or ethanoic acid. Normally, a small amount of the mixture is spotted onto the paper about 1.0 cm from its base. The paper is then suspended in a small quantity of the solvent (known as the eluent) in a closed container. (The container is closed to saturate the atmosphere and prevent evaporation of the solvent from the paper, to give better and faster separation.) As the solvent rises up the paper, the components in the mixture partition between the two phases depending on their relative solubility. As the solvent nears the top of the paper, a mark is made to record the level and the paper is removed and dried. Coloured components can be seen with the naked eye. Other components can be made visible by staining (e.g. with iodine) or by irradiating with an ultraviolet lamp.

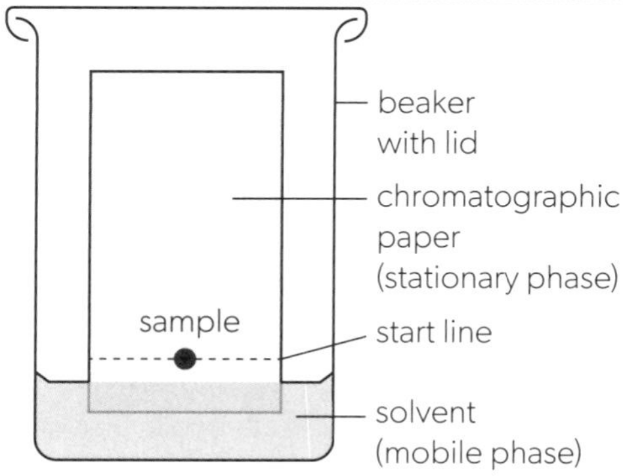

As with all equilibria, the partition of a solute between the two phases is constant at a fixed temperature, so the solute will always move the same fraction of the distance moved by the solvent. Each solute has a particular retardation factor (R_F) for a given eluent. It is obtained by measuring the distance from the original spot both to the centre of the particular component and to the solvent front.

$$R_F = \frac{\text{distance moved by solute}}{\text{distance moved by solvent (eluent)}} = \frac{x}{y}$$

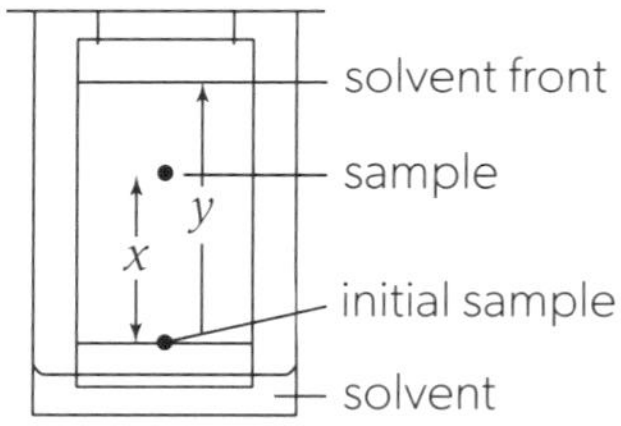

Substances can be identified by their R_F values. If two substances have similar R_F values in one solvent, the paper can be turned 90° and a different solvent used. This is known as two-way chromatography and is often used to separate a mixture of amino acids.

Thin-layer chromatography

Thin-layer chromatography is similar to paper chromatography but uses a thin layer of a solid, such as alumina, Al_2O_3, or silica, SiO_2, on an inert support such as glass. When absolutely dry it works by adsorption but, like paper, alumina and silica have a high affinity for water so the separation occurs more by partition with water as the stationary phase. The choice of a suitable solvent depends on, for example, the polarity of the components of the sample. One real advantage of thin-layer chromatography over paper chromatography is that each of the separated components can be recovered pure. The section containing the component is scraped off the glass and then dissolved in a suitable solvent. The solution is filtered to remove the solid support and the solvent can then be evaporated to leave just the pure component.

Kinetic molecular theory and changes of state

Kinetic molecular theory

The kinetic molecular theory of matter is a model to explain the physical properties of matter (solids, liquids, and gases) and changes of state.

- All matter is made up of particles that are constantly moving.
- The energy of the particles depends upon the absolute temperature.
- A change of state may occur when the energy of the particles is changed.
- The average amount of empty space between particles generally increases as matter moves from the solid to the liquid and gas phases.
- There are forces of attraction between particles which become stronger as the particles move closer together.

States of matter

sublimation (solid → gas)

Solid state (s)
- Fixed shape
- Fixed volume
- Particles held together, in fixed positions, by intermolecular forces
- Particles vibrate about a fixed point but do not have translational velocity

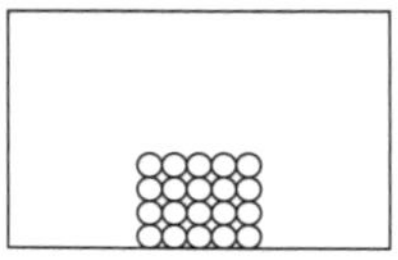

melting (solid → liquid) / freezing (liquid → solid)

Liquid state (l)
- Fixed volume
- Takes up shape of container
- Particles held closely together by intermolecular forces
- Particles have translational velocity so diffusion can occur

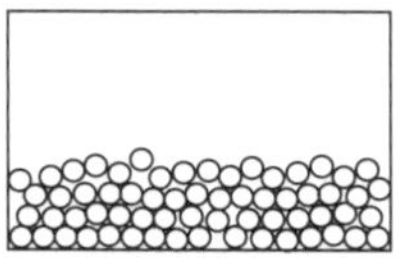

boiling/vaporizing/evaporating (liquid → gas) / condensing (gas → liquid)

Gaseous state (g)
- Widely spaced particles completely fill container
- Pressure of gas due to gaseous particles colliding with the walls of the container
- Negligible intermolecular forces between particles
- Volume occupied by molecules themselves negligible compared with total volume of gas
- Particles move with rapid, random motion so diffusion can occur

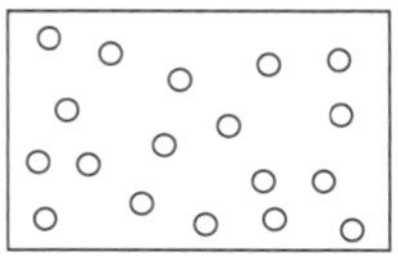

deposition (gas → solid)

Changes of state

When heat is continually supplied to a substance, the following changes take place.

- The solid particles increase in temperature as the kinetic energy increases due to greater vibration of the particles about a fixed position.
- When the vibration is sufficient to overcome the forces holding the lattice together, the solid melts.
- During melting, the temperature does not rise as the heat energy (enthalpy of fusion) is needed to overcome these attractive forces.
- Once all the solid has melted, the liquid particles move faster and the temperature increases.
- Some particles move faster than others and escape from the surface of the liquid to form a vapour.
- Once the pressure of the vapour is equal to the pressure above the liquid, the liquid boils.
- During boiling, the temperature remains constant as the heat is used to overcome the intermolecular forces of attraction (enthalpy of vaporization).
- When all the liquid has turned into a gas, the temperature continues to increase as the particles move ever faster.

A cooling curve shows this process in reverse.

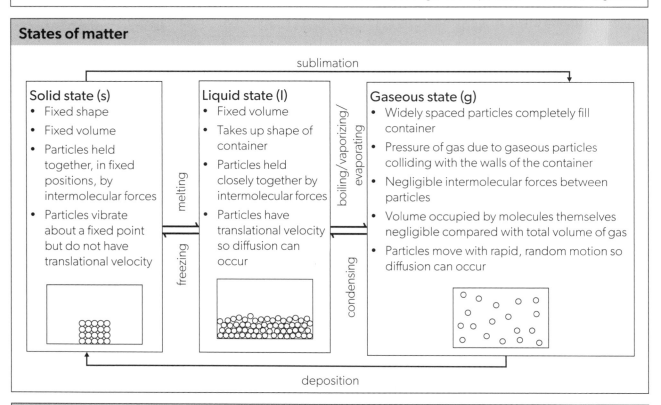

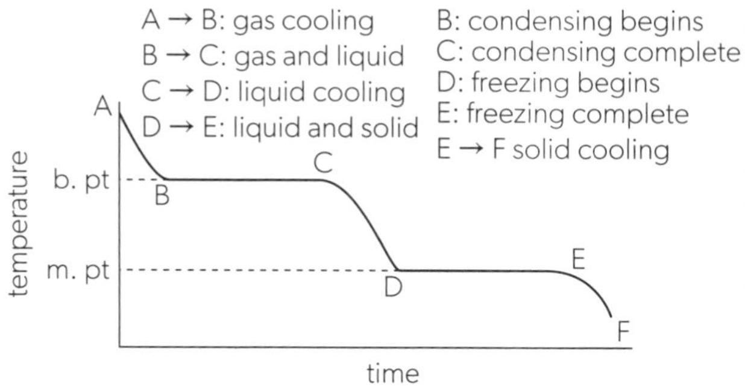

▲ A cooling curve

Distribution of molecular velocities

Maxwell–Boltzmann distribution

The moving particles in a gas or liquid do not all travel with the same velocity. Some are moving very fast and others are moving much more slowly. The faster they move, the more kinetic energy they possess. The distribution of kinetic energies is shown by a Maxwell–Boltzmann curve.

When a liquid evaporates it is the faster-moving particles that escape, so the average kinetic energy of the remaining particles is lower. This explains why a volatile liquid feels cold as it is evaporating.

At higher temperatures, the area under the curve does not change as the total number of particles remains constant. More particles have a very high velocity, resulting in an increase in the average kinetic energy. This leads to a broadening of the curve.

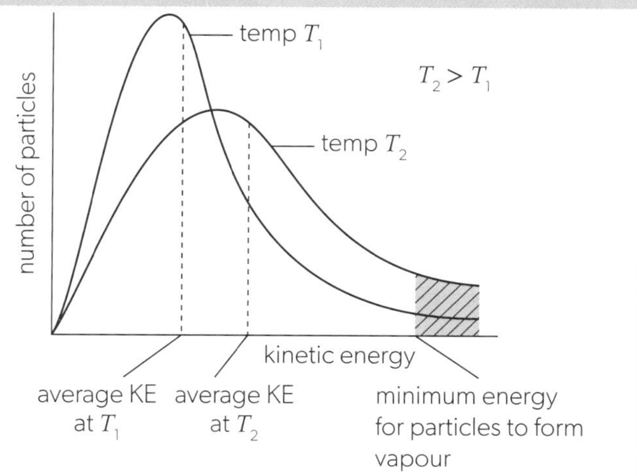

Temperature

The absolute temperature of a substance is proportional to its average kinetic energy (½ mass × velocity²). The SI unit for absolute temperature is kelvin (K). A difference of 1 K is the same as a difference of 1 °C. Absolute zero, 0 K = −273 °C, so to convert temperature values from °C to K add 273. Water freezes at 273 K and boils at 373 K.

Evaporation and boiling

In an open system, all liquids will eventually evaporate as the faster-moving particles have sufficient energy to escape from the surface of the liquid. As the temperature increases, more particles have the necessary energy to escape and the vapour pressure above the liquid increases. When the vapour pressure is equal to the external pressure the liquid boils. Boiling points of liquids are normally quoted for when the external pressure is equal to 101 325 Pa (1.01×10^5 Pa) which is commonly known as 1 atmosphere. Water boils at a higher temperature than 373 K (100 °C) at pressures above 1.01×10^5 Pa and has a lower boiling point when the external pressure is less than 1 atmosphere. For example, on the summit of Mount Everest (8 848 m), where the atmospheric pressure is 3.4×10^4 Pa, water boils at about 344 K (71 °C).

Different liquids have different boiling points as their vapour pressure depends on the strength of the attractive forces between the particles. The weaker the attractive forces, the lower the boiling point.

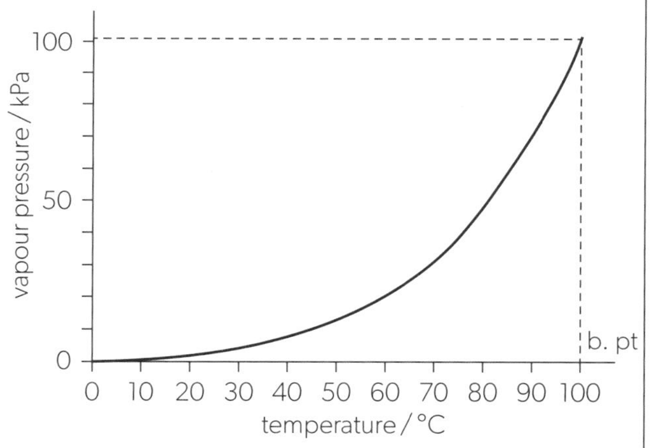

▲ Saturated vapour pressure of water

Multiple-choice questions—Models of the particulate nature of matter

1. Which is a homogeneous mixture?
   - **A.** smoke
   - **B.** salt solution
   - **C.** oil and vinegar
   - **D.** soil

2. Which of the following is NOT a characteristic property of gases?
   - **A.** They can expand without limit.
   - **B.** They readily diffuse.
   - **C.** They are easily compressed.
   - **D.** They have high densities.

3. What changes occur when ice is converted into liquid water at its melting point?
   - **I.** Movement of the molecules increases.
   - **II.** The distance between the molecules decreases.
   - **III.** The density increases.
   - **A.** I and II only
   - **B.** I and III only
   - **C.** II and III only
   - **D.** I, II, and III

4. Which of the following changes gives out heat?
   - **A.** evaporation
   - **B.** deposition
   - **C.** melting
   - **D.** sublimation

5. Which is a compound?
   - **A.** air
   - **B.** steel
   - **C.** water
   - **D.** silicon

6. The boiling points of four hydrocarbons are given. Which pair will mix most readily at the temperature specified?

	T_b / K
cyclohexane	354
cyclooctane	421
cycloheptane	392
cyclononane	444

   - **A.** cyclohexane and cycloheptane at 380 K
   - **B.** cycloheptane and cyclooctane at 390 K
   - **C.** cyclooctane and cyclononane at 460 K
   - **D.** cyclononane and cyclohexane at 420 K

7. Which best explains why gases can be easily compressed?
   - **A.** The volume occupied by the gas is much greater than the volume occupied by its molecules.
   - **B.** The attractive forces between the molecules of the gas are negligible.
   - **C.** Collisions between the gaseous molecules are elastic.
   - **D.** The average kinetic energy of the gaseous molecules is proportional to the absolute temperature of the gas.

8. Which technique would be best to use to obtain pure salt from sea-water?
   - **A.** paper chromatography
   - **B.** distillation
   - **C.** evaporation followed by recrystallization
   - **D.** filtration

9. The diagram shows a developed chromatogram.

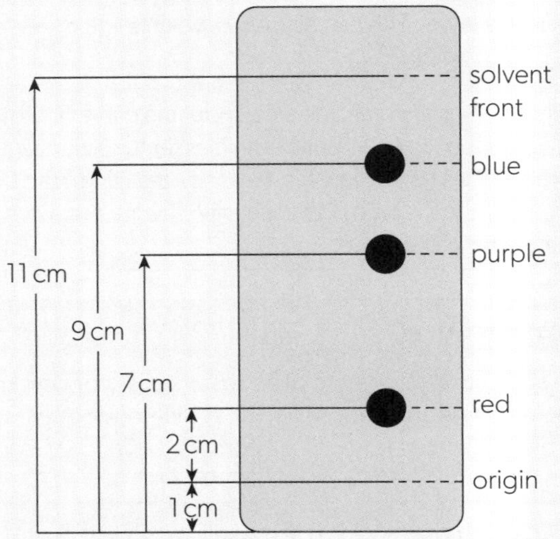

What is the R_F value of the purple component?
   - **A.** 7/10
   - **B.** 7/11
   - **C.** 6/11
   - **D.** 6/10

10. What is the correct name for the R_F value used in paper chromatography?
   - **A.** retardation factor
   - **B.** reproduction factor
   - **C.** retention figure
   - **D.** ratio factor

11. Which is composed of diatomic molecules?
   - **A.** neon gas
   - **B.** nitrogen gas
   - **C.** steam
   - **D.** carbon dioxide

12. The boiling point of ethanol, C_2H_5OH, is 78.4 °C.

The boiling point of uranium hexafluoride, UF_6, is 56.5 °C.

Which is a correct statement at 50 °C?
   - **A.** The forces of attraction between UF_6 molecules are stronger than the forces of attraction between C_2H_5OH molecules.
   - **B.** The average kinetic energy of UF_6 molecules is greater than the average kinetic energy of C_2H_5OH molecules.
   - **C.** The vapour density of the gas above the liquid is lower for UF_6 than it is for C_2H_5OH.
   - **D.** The average velocity of C_2H_5OH molecules is greater than the average velocity of UF_6 molecules.

S1.2 2. Atomic structure

The nuclear atom

Composition of atoms

The smallest part of an element is an atom. It used to be thought that atoms are indivisible but it is now known that they can be broken down into sub-atomic particles. All atoms, except hydrogen, are made up of three fundamental sub-atomic particles—protons, neutrons and electrons.

The simplest atom—hydrogen—contains just one proton and one electron. The data booklet value (section 2) for the mass of a proton is 1.673×10^{-24} g but it is assigned a relative value of 1.
The mass of a neutron is virtually identical and also has a relative value of 1. Compared with a proton or neutron, an electron has negligible mass with a relative mass of only 1/2 000. Neutrons are neutral particles. An electron has a charge of 1.602×10^{-19} coulombs, which is assigned a relative value of −1. A proton carries the same charge but an opposite sign so has a relative value of +1. All atoms are neutral so must contain equal numbers of protons and electrons.

Summary of relative mass and charge

Particle	Relative mass	Relative charge
proton	1	+1
neutron	1	0
electron	5×10^{-4}	−1

Size and structure of atoms

Atoms have a radius in the order of 10^{-10} m. Most of the mass of an atom is concentrated in the nucleus, which has a very small radius in the order of 10^{-14} m. All the protons and neutrons (collectively called nucleons) are in the nucleus. Electrons are found in energy levels or shells surrounding the nucleus. Much of the atom is empty space. Shorthand notation for an atom or ion is shown below.

Shorthand notation for an atom or ion

$${}^{A}_{Z}\mathrm{X}^{n+/n-}$$

Mass number, A: Equal to the number of protons and neutrons in the nucleus.

Atomic number, Z: Equal to the number of protons in the nucleus and to the number of electrons in the atom. This number defines which element the atom belongs to and gives its position in the periodic table.

Charge: Atoms have no charge so $n = 0$ and this is left blank. Atoms can become positive ions by losing electrons, or negative ions by gaining electrons.

Examples

Symbol	Atomic number	Mass number	Number of protons	Number of neutrons	Number of electrons
${}^{9}_{4}\mathrm{Be}$	4	9	4	5	4
${}^{40}_{20}\mathrm{Ca}^{2+}$	20	40	20	20	18
${}^{37}_{17}\mathrm{Cl}^{-}$	17	37	17	20	18

Isotopes

All atoms of the same element must contain the same number of protons; however, they may contain different numbers of neutrons. Such atoms are known as isotopes. Chemical properties are related to the number of electrons, so isotopes of the same element have identical chemical properties. Since their masses are different, their physical properties, such as density and boiling point, are different.

Examples of isotopes: ${}^{1}_{1}\mathrm{H}$ ${}^{2}_{1}\mathrm{H}$ ${}^{3}_{1}\mathrm{H}$ ${}^{12}_{6}\mathrm{C}$ ${}^{14}_{6}\mathrm{C}$ ${}^{35}_{17}\mathrm{Cl}$ ${}^{37}_{17}\mathrm{Cl}$

Relative atomic mass

The mass of an atom depends on the number of nucleons in the nucleus. Therefore, helium atoms, ${}^{4}_{2}He$, are four times heavier than hydrogen atoms, ${}^{1}_{1}H$, and carbon atoms, ${}^{12}_{6}C$, are twelve times heavier than hydrogen atoms. For relative atomic masses of all of the elements, $\frac{1}{12}$ of ${}^{12}_{6}C$ is taken as the reference point rather than the mass of hydrogen.

Because elements are made up of different isotopes, the relative atomic mass is the weighted average of the different isotopes. For example, the two isotopes of chlorine occur in the ratio 3 : 1. For every 100 atoms of naturally occurring chlorine, 75 are ${}^{35}_{17}Cl$ and 25 are ${}^{37}_{17}Cl$.

So the weighted mean relative mass of chlorine is

$$\frac{(75\times35)+(25\times37)}{100}=35.5$$

Accurate relative atomic mass values (to 2 d.p.) for all the elements are given in the IB data booklet. These values must be used when performing calculations in the examinations.

AHL Relative atomic mass and mass spectroscopy

Mass spectrometer

Relative atomic masses can be determined using a mass spectrometer. A vaporized sample is injected into the instrument. Atoms of the element are ionized by being bombarded with a stream of high-energy electrons in the ionization chamber. In practice, the instrument is set so that only ions with a single positive charge are formed. The resulting unipositive ions pass through holes in parallel plates under the influence of an electric field where they are accelerated. The ions are then deflected by an external magnetic field. The amount of deflection depends on both the mass of the ion and its charge. The smaller the mass and the higher the charge, the greater the deflection. Ions with a particular mass/charge ratio are then recorded by a detector that measures both the mass and the relative amounts of all the ions present. This information can then be used to calculate the relative atomic mass.

Worked example: the mass spectrum of naturally occurring lead

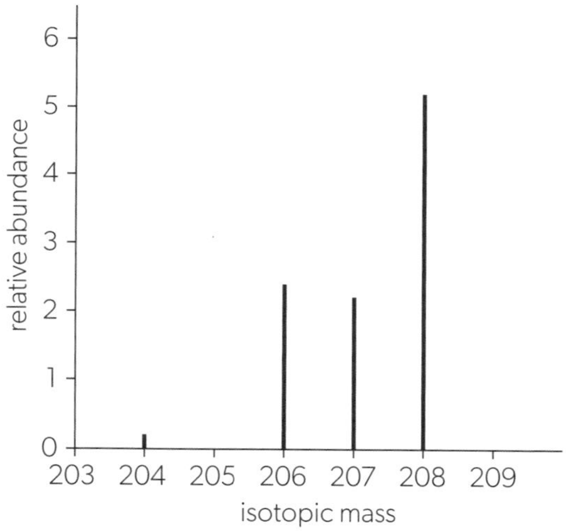

The relative atomic mass of lead can be calculated from the weighted average.

Isotopic mass	Relative abundance	% relative abundance
204	0.2	2
206	2.4	24
207	2.2	22
208	5.2	52

$$\text{relative atomic mass} = \frac{(2\times204)+(24\times206)+(22\times207)+(52\times208)}{100} = 207.2$$

Emission spectra

The electromagnetic spectrum

Electromagnetic waves can travel through space and, depending on the wavelength, also through matter. The velocity of travel c is related to its wavelength λ and its frequency f. Velocity is measured in $m\,s^{-1}$, wavelength in m, and frequency in s^{-1} so it is easy to remember the relationship between them:

$$c\,(m\,s^{-1}) = \lambda\,(m) \times f(s^{-1})$$

Electromagnetic radiation is a form of energy. The smaller the wavelength (and thus the higher the frequency) the more energy the wave possesses. Electromagnetic waves have a wide range of wavelengths, ranging from low-energy radio waves to high-energy γ-radiation. Visible light occupies a very narrow part of the spectrum, with the colours ranging from red (low energy) to violet (high energy).

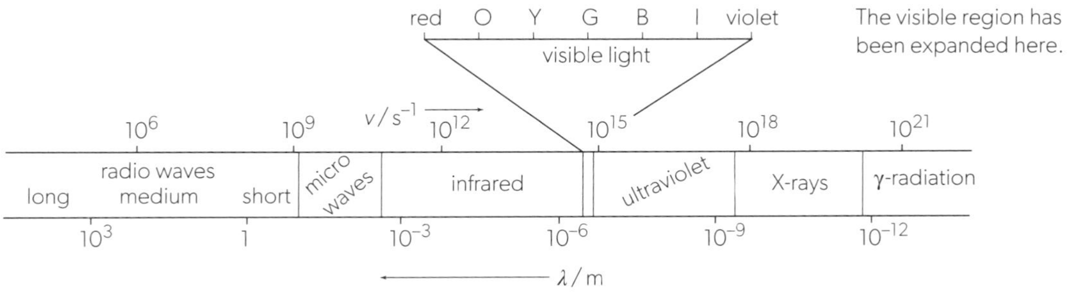

Continuous and line emission spectra

White light is made up of all the colours of the spectrum. When it is passed through a prism, a **continuous spectrum** of all the colours can be obtained.

When energy is supplied to individual elements, they emit a spectrum which only contains emissions at particular wavelengths. Each element has its own characteristic spectrum; this is known as a **line spectrum** as it is not continuous. For example, the visible hydrogen spectrum is shown here.

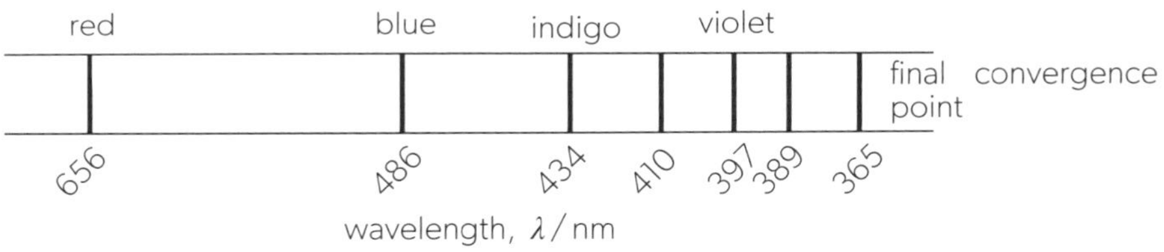

The hydrogen spectrum consists of discrete lines and the lines converge towards the high energy (violet) end of the spectrum. A similar series of lines at even higher energy occurs in the ultraviolet region of the spectrum and several other series of lines at lower energy can be found in the infrared region of the spectrum.

Explanation of emission spectra

When energy is supplied to an atom, electrons are excited (gain energy) from their lowest (ground) state to an excited state. Electrons can only exist in certain fixed energy levels. When electrons drop from a higher level to a lower level, they emit photons of energy. This energy corresponds to a particular wavelength and shows up as a line in the spectrum. When the excited electrons in hydrogen return to the first level ($n = 1$) the series of lines occurs in the ultraviolet region as this involves the largest energy change. The visible region spectrum is formed by electrons dropping back to the $n = 2$ level and the first series in the infrared is due to electrons falling to the $n = 3$ level. The lines in the spectrum converge because the energy levels themselves converge.

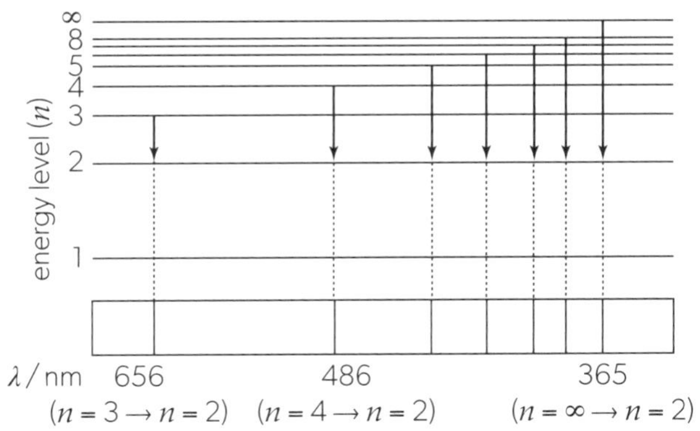

Electron configurations

Main energy levels, sublevels and orbitals

The maximum number of electrons that can occupy an energy level is given by the relationship $2n^2$, where n is known as the principal quantum number. Each energy level can be divided into sublevels: s, p, d and f. Electrons exist within orbitals in these sublevels, with each orbital containing a maximum of two electrons. The s sublevels contain one orbital; the p sublevels contain three orbitals; the d sublevels contain five orbitals; and the f sublevels contain seven orbitals. The first energy level ($n = 1$) contains only one s orbital. The second energy level ($n = 2$) contains one s sublevel and one p sublevel (i.e. three p orbitals all of equal energy), making a maximum total of eight electrons. The third energy level ($n = 3$) contains s, p and d sublevels and the fourth energy level ($n = 4$) contains s, p, d and f sublevels. This is summarized in the following table.

Principal level (shell)	Number of each type of orbital				Maximum number of electrons in level
n	s	p	d	f	$2n^2$
1	1	–	–	–	2
2	1	3	–	–	8
3	1	3	5	–	18
4	1	3	5	7	32

The relative position of all the sublevels for the first four main energy levels can be shown like this.

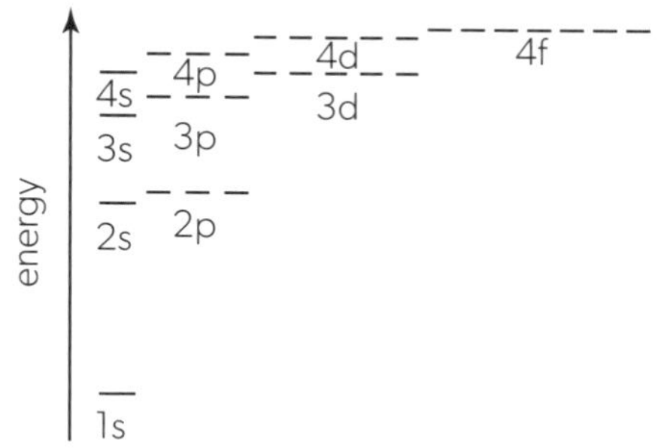

▲ Relative energies of sublevels within an atom

Note that the 4s sublevel is below the 3d sublevel, which explains why the third main energy level is sometimes stated to hold eight or eighteen electrons.

Shapes of orbitals

An electron has the properties of both a particle and a wave. **Heisenberg's uncertainty principle** states that it is impossible to know the exact position of an electron at a precise moment in time. An orbital describes the three-dimensional shape where there is a high probability that the electron will be located.

s orbitals are spherical and the three p orbitals are orthogonal (at right angles) to each other.

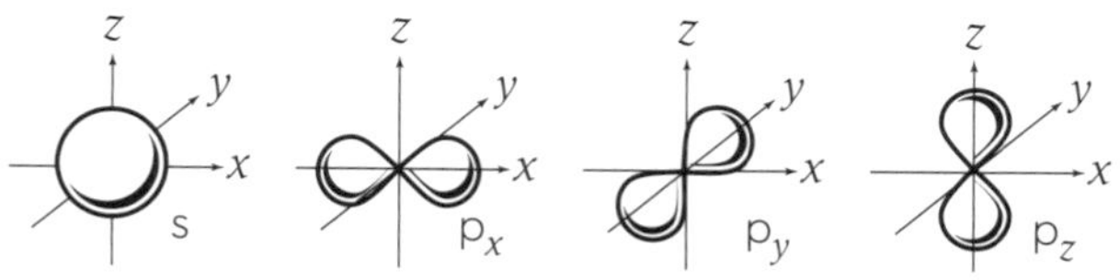

Electron configurations

The electron configuration can be determined by following the **Aufbau principle** for building up electrons. This is based on the **Pauli exclusion principle**, which dictates how many orbitals there are in each sublevel and requires that the two electrons in each filled orbital in the atom must spin in the opposite direction to each other.

The orbitals with the lowest energy are filled first. Orbitals within the same sublevel are filled singly first—known as **Hund's rule**. Using these principles and rule you need to be able to deduce the electron configuration of elements and ions up to $Z = 36$. For example:

H $1s^1$	Li $1s^22s^1$	Na $1s^22s^22p^63s^1$	K $1s^22s^22p^63s^23p^64s^1$
He $1s^2$	Be $1s^22s^2$	Mg $1s^22s^22p^63s^2$	Ca $1s^22s^22p^63s^23p^64s^2$
	B $1s^22s^22p^1$	Al $1s^22s^22p^63s^23p^1$	Sc $1s^22s^22p^63s^23p^64s^23d^1$
	C $1s^22s^22p^2$	Si $1s^22s^22p^63s^23p^2$	Ti $1s^22s^22p^63s^23p^64s^23d^2$
	N $1s^22s^22p^3$	P $1s^22s^22p^63s^23p^3$	V $1s^22s^22p^63s^23p^64s^23d^3$
	O $1s^22s^22p^4$	S $1s^22s^22p^63s^23p^4$	
	F $1s^22s^22p^5$	Cl $1s^22s^22p^63s^23p^5$	
	Ne $1s^22s^22p^6$	Ar $1s^22s^22p^63s^23p^6$	

To save writing out all the lower levels, the configuration may be shortened by building on the last noble gas configuration. For example, continuing on from titanium, vanadium can be written $[Ar]4s^23d^3$, then Cr as $[Ar]4s^13d^5$, Mn as $[Ar]4s^23d^5$, Fe as $[Ar]4s^23d^6$, etc.

The electron configurations of the transition metals show two irregularities. When it is possible for the d sublevel to become half-full or completely full, this takes precedence over completely filling the 4s level first. So chromium has the configuration $[Ar]4s^13d^5$ (rather than $[Ar]4s^23d^4$) so that the 3d sublevel is half full. Copper has the configuration $[Ar]4s^13d^{10}$ (rather than $[Ar]4s^23d^9$) so that the 3d sublevel is completely full.

The full electronic configuration for krypton is $1s^22s^22p^63s^23p^64s^23d^{10}4p^6$; this can be shortened to $[Ar]4s^23d^{10}4p^6$. When writing electronic configurations check that, for a neutral atom, the sum of the superscripts adds up to the atomic number of the element.

When positive ions are formed, the electron(s) are lost from the highest energy level first, so both Na^+ and Mg^{2+} have the electron configuration $1s^22s^22p^6$. For transition elements, the 4s electrons are removed first so the electron configuration of Fe^{2+} is $[Ar]3d^6$.

Orbital diagrams

Sometimes boxes are used to represent orbitals and these then show the electron configuration visually. These are sometimes called "arrow-in-box diagrams". They can be used to easily show the number of unpaired electrons, e.g.

C $1s^22s^22p^2$

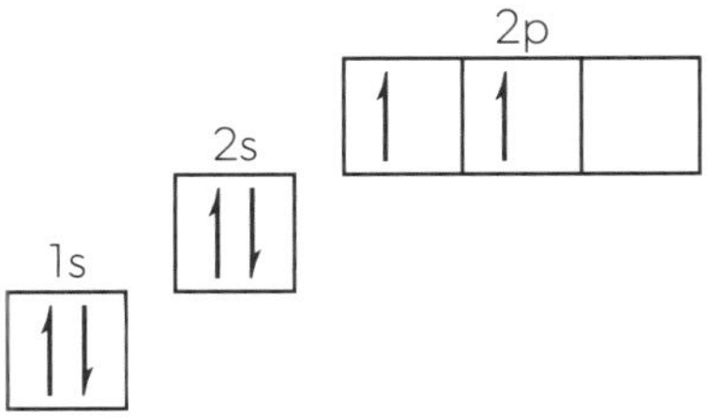

or Cr [Ar]

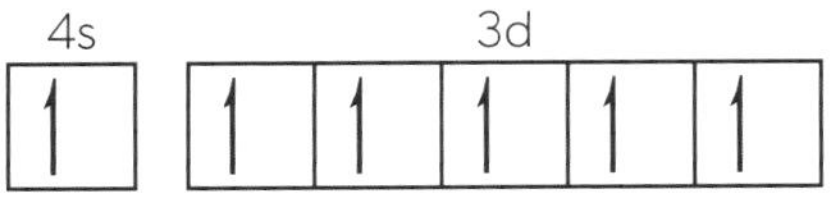

AHL Ionization energies

Evidence from ionization energies

The first ionization energy (IE) of an element is defined as the energy required to remove one electron from an atom in its gaseous state. It is measured in kJ mol^{-1}.

$X(g) \rightarrow X^{+}(g) + e^{-}$

A graph of first ionization energies plotted against atomic number shows a repeating pattern.

The highest value is for helium, an atom that contains two protons and two electrons. The two electrons are in the lowest level and are held tightly by the two protons. For lithium it is relatively easy to remove an electron, which suggests that the third electron in lithium is in a higher energy level than the first two. The value then generally increases until element 10, neon, before it drops sharply for sodium. This graph suggests that the levels can contain different numbers of electrons before they become full.

Electrons with opposite spins tend to repel each other. When orbitals of the same energy (degenerate) are filled, the electrons go singly into each orbital first , to minimize repulsion. They do not pair up until all orbitals contain one electron. This explains why there is a regular increase in the first ionization energies going from B to N as the three 2p orbitals each gain one electron. Then there is a slight decrease between N and O as one of the 2p orbitals gains a second electron , followed by a regular increase again.

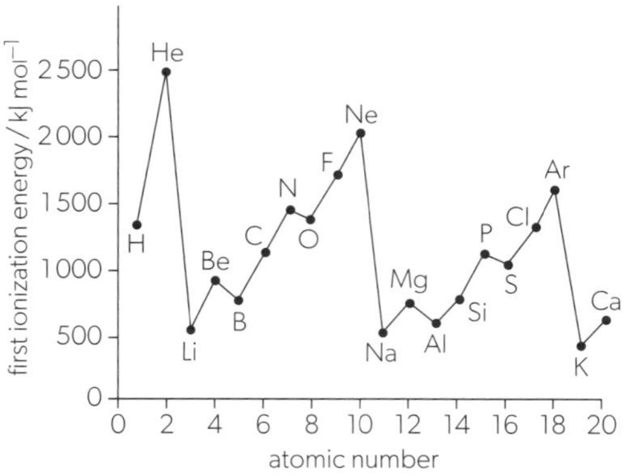

▲ First ionization energies for the first 20 elements

Evidence for sublevels

The graph above shows the first ionization energy for the first 20 elements. Successive ionization energies for the same element can also be measured, e.g. the second ionization energy is given by

$X^{+}(g) \rightarrow X^{2+}(g) + e^{-}$

As more electrons are removed, the pull of the protons holds the remaining electrons more tightly so increasingly more energy is required to remove them; hence a logarithmic scale is usually used. A graph of the successive ionization energies for potassium (right) also provides evidence of the number of electrons in each main level.

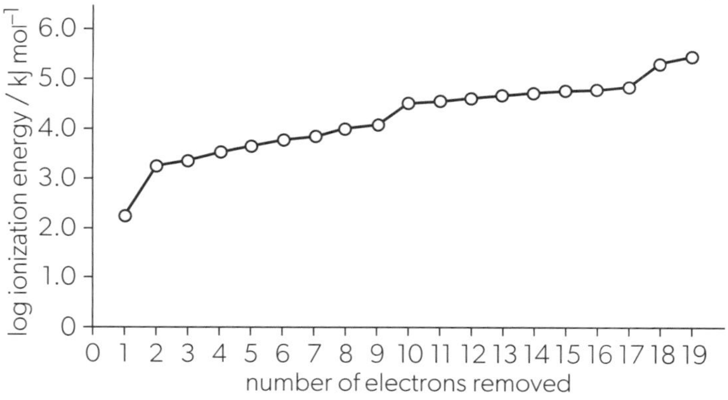

▲ Graph of successive ionization energies for potassium

By looking to see where the first "large jump" occurs in successive ionization energies, you can determine the number of valence electrons (and hence the group in the periodic table to which the element belongs).

If you examine the graph for first ionization energies more closely, you can see that the values do not increase regularly. This provides evidence that the main levels are split into sublevels.

Ionization energies from emission spectra

It can be seen from the emission spectrum of hydrogen that the energy levels converge—this is known as the convergence limit. Hydrogen contains just one electron, which is in the lowest energy level in its ground state. If sufficient energy is supplied, it can be promoted to the infinite level—it is removed from the atom and the atom is ionized to form an H^{+} ion. This amount of energy corresponds to the energy emitted if the electron falls back from $n = \infty$ to $n = 1$, producing a line in the ultraviolet region of the spectrum at a wavelength of 91.2 nm. You can use this value to calculate the energy involved.

Wavelength and frequency are related by the expression $c = \lambda f$ where c is the velocity of light. Energy and frequency are related by the expression $E = hf$ where h is Planck's constant and has the value 6.63×10^{-34} J s.

The energy to remove one electron $= hf = \frac{hc}{\lambda} = \frac{6.63\times10^{-34}\,\text{J s}\times3.00\times10^{8}\,\text{m s}^{-1}}{91.2\times10^{-9}\,\text{m}} = 2.18\times10^{-18}\,\text{J}$

For one mole of electrons, you multiply by Avogadro's constant (6.02×10^{23}) to give 1.312×10^{6} J mol^{-1} or 1312 kJ mol^{-1}. This is the experimentally determined value for the first ionization energy of hydrogen.

Multiple-choice questions—Atomic structure

1. Which of the following particles contain more neutrons than electrons?

   I. $^{1}_{1}H^{+}$ II. $^{79}_{35}Br^{-}$ III. $^{23}_{11}Na^{+}$

   A. I and II only C. II and III only

   B. I and III only D. I, II, and III

2. Which one of the following sets represents a pair of isotopes?

   A. $^{31}_{15}P$ and $^{32}_{15}P$ C. diamond and C_{60}

   B. $^{24}_{12}Mg$ and $^{24}_{12}Mg^{2+}$ D. $^{40}_{18}Ar$ and $^{40}_{20}Ca$

3. Which species contains 16 protons, 17 neutrons, and 18 electrons?

   A. $^{32}S^{-}$ C. $^{34}S^{-}$

   B. $^{33}S^{2-}$ D. $^{35}S^{2-}$

4. Which quantities are the same for all atoms of chlorine?

   I. number of protons

   II. number of electrons

   III. number of neutrons

   A. I and II only C. II and III only

   B. I and III only D. I, II, and III

5. A sample of zinc has the following composition:

Isotope	% abundance
^{64}Zn	55
^{66}Zn	40
^{68}Zn	5

   What is the relative atomic mass of the zinc in this sample?

   A. 64.5 C. 65.9

   B. 65.0 D. 66.4

6. In the electromagnetic spectrum, which will have the shortest wavelength and the greatest energy?

	Shortest wavelength	Greatest energy
A.	ultraviolet	ultraviolet
B.	infrared	infrared
C.	ultraviolet	infrared
D.	infrared	ultraviolet

7. Which electronic transition in a hydrogen atom releases the most energy?

   A. $n = 1 \rightarrow n = 2$ C. $n = 6 \rightarrow n = 7$

   B. $n = 7 \rightarrow n = 6$ D. $n = 2 \rightarrow n = 1$

8. Which shows the sublevels in order of increasing energy in the fourth energy level of an atom?

   A. f < d < p < s C. d < f < p < s

   B. p < d < f < s D. s < p < d < f

9. What is the electron configuration of copper?

   A. $[Ar]4s^{2}3d^{9}$

   B. $1s^{2}2s^{2}2p^{6}3s^{2}3p^{6}3d^{10}$

   C. $1s^{2}2s^{2}2p^{6}3s^{2}3p^{6}4s^{1}3d^{10}$

   D. $[Ar]3d^{9}$

10. How many unpaired electrons are present in an atom of sulfur in its ground state?

    A. 1 C. 4

    B. 2 D. 6

AHL

11. Which is the correct definition for the second ionization energy of carbon?

    A. $C(s) \rightarrow C(s) + e^{-}$ C. $C^{+}(s) \rightarrow C^{2+}(s) + e^{-}$

    B. $C(g) \rightarrow C(g) + e^{-}$ D. $C^{+}(g) \rightarrow C^{2+}(g) + e^{-}$

12. The first five ionization energies, in $kJ\,mol^{-1}$, for a certain element are 577, 1980, 2960, 6190 and 8700, respectively. Which group in the periodic table does this element belong to?

    A. 1 C. 13

    B. 2 D. 14

13. Which transition in the hydrogen emission spectrum corresponds to the first ionization energy of hydrogen?

    A. $n = \infty \rightarrow n = 1$ C. $n = \infty \rightarrow n = 2$

    B. $n = 2 \rightarrow n = 1$ D. $n = 4 \rightarrow n = 2$

14. Which ionization requires the most energy?

    A. $B(g) \rightarrow B^{+}(g) + e^{-}$ C. $N(g) \rightarrow N^{+}(g) + e^{-}$

    B. $C(g) \rightarrow C^{+}(g) + e^{-}$ D. $O(g) \rightarrow O^{+}(g) + e^{-}$

15. Which of the following factors does NOT affect the value of the ionization energy of an atom?

    A. mass of the atom

    B. charge on the nucleus

    C. size of the atom

    D. main energy level from which the electron is removed

16. This graph shows the first four ionization energies of four elements A, B, C and D.

    Which element is magnesium?

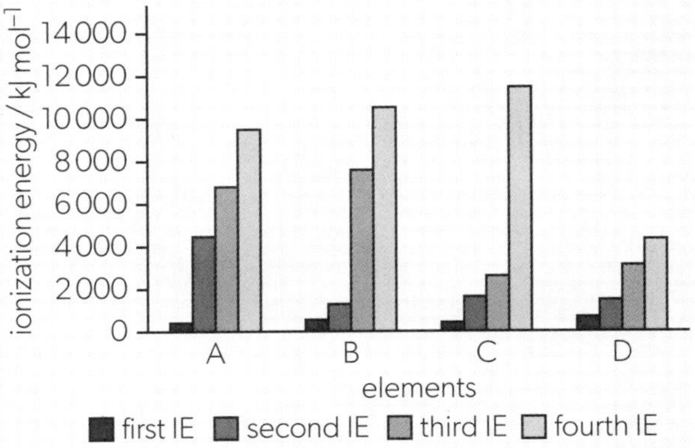

1. a) Define the term relative atomic mass, A_r. [1]
   b) The relative atomic mass of naturally occurring chlorine is 35.45. Calculate the abundances of ^{35}Cl and ^{37}Cl in naturally occurring chlorine. [2]
   c) (i) State the electron configuration of chlorine. [1]
   (ii) State the electron configuration of a chloride ion, Cl^-. [1]
   d) Explain how ^{35}Cl and ^{37}Cl differ in their chemical properties. [2]

2. a) Explain why the relative atomic mass of cobalt is greater than the relative atomic mass of nickel, even though the atomic number of nickel is greater than the atomic number of cobalt. [1]
   b) Deduce the numbers of protons and electrons in the Co^{2+} ion. [1]
   c) (i) Deduce the electron configuration of the Co atom. [1]
   (ii) Deduce the electron configuration of the Co^{2+} ion. [1]

3. $^{43}_{99}Tc$ is a radioactive isotope of technetium.
   a) (i) Define the term isotope. [1]
   (ii) Determine the number of neutrons in one atom of technetium-99. [1]
   (iii) Technetium-99 is used as a tracer in medicine. Suggest a reason why it is potentially dangerous. [1]
   b) Carbon in living organisms consists of two isotopes, ^{12}C and ^{14}C, in a fixed ratio. This ratio remains constant in a living organism as the carbon is constantly being replaced. Once an organism dies, the ^{14}C slowly decays to ^{14}N with a half-life of 5 300 years.
   (i) Identify the number of protons, neutrons and electrons in carbon-12 and in carbon-14. [2]
   (ii) Discuss how the decay of carbon-14 can be used in carbon dating. [2]

4. Annotate the 2s and 2p boxes, using ↑ or ↓ to represent a spinning electron, to complete the electron configuration for an oxygen atom. [1]

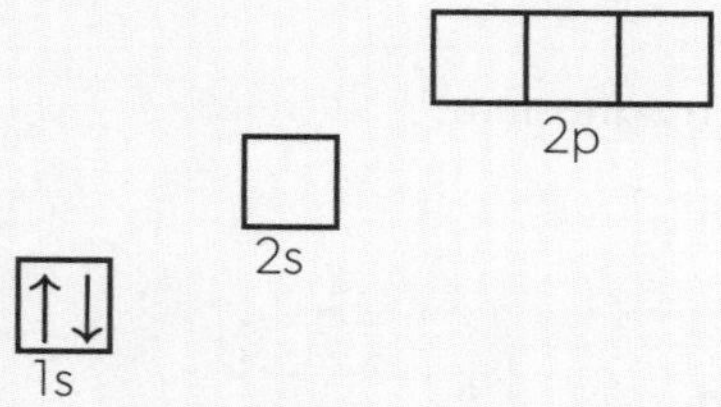

5. Draw and label an energy level diagram for the hydrogen atom. In your diagram show how the series of lines in the ultraviolet and visible regions of its emission spectrum are produced, clearly labelling each series. [4]

6. The electron configuration of chromium can be expressed as $[Ar]4s^x3d^y$.
   a) Explain what the square brackets around argon, [Ar], represent. [1]
   b) State the values of x and y. [1]
   c) Annotate the diagram below showing the 4s and 3d orbitals for a chromium atom using an arrow, ↑ or ↓, to represent a spinning electron. [1]

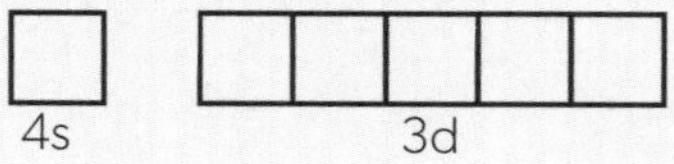

AHL

7. The graph below shows the first ionization energy plotted against atomic number for the first 20 elements.

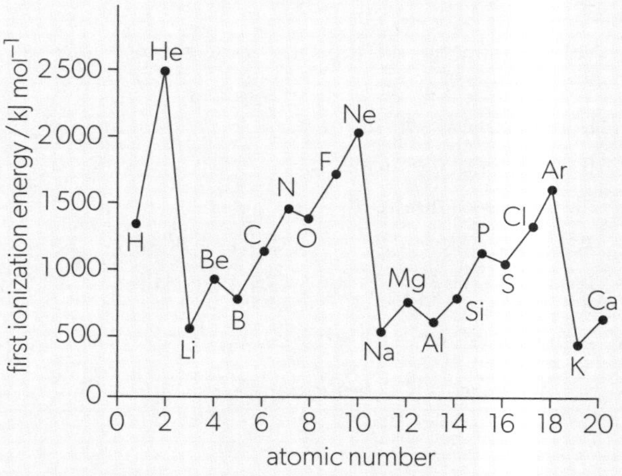

   a) Define the term first ionization energy. [2]
   b) Explain:
   (i) why there is a general increase in the value for the first ionization energy across period 2 from Li to Ne [2]
   (ii) why the first ionization energy of neon is higher than that of sodium [2]
   (iii) why the first ionization energy of beryllium is higher than that of boron [2]
   (iv) why the first ionization energy of sulfur is lower than that of phosphorus. [2]
   c) Predict how the graph for the second ionization energy plotted against atomic number for the first 20 elements differs from the graph shown above. [3]

8. Electrons are much too small to ever be "seen". Discuss the evidence that electrons exist in fixed energy levels and that these levels can be split into sublevels. [5]

9. The first ionization energy of hydrogen is 1 312 kJ mol^{-1}. Determine the frequency and wavelength of the convergence line in the ultraviolet emission spectrum of hydrogen. (Use information given in sections 1 and 2 of the IB data booklet.) [3]

Counting particles by mass: the mole

The mole concept and the Avogadro constant

A single atom of an element has an extremely small mass. For example, an atom of carbon-12, ^{12}C, has a mass of 1.993×10^{-23} g. Atoms are far too small to weigh or count individually. The number of ^{12}C atoms in exactly 12.00 g of ^{12}C is equal to 6.02×10^{23}. This number is known as the Avogadro constant. In the same way that a pair is two or a dozen is twelve, a mole is 6.02×10^{23}. One **mole** of any substance contains exactly the Avogadro constant number of particles of that substance. A mole (mol) is the SI unit of the amount of substance. The Avogadro constant (N_A) has the units mol^{-1}. A particle (elementary entity) may be an atom, a molecule, an ion, an electron, or any other specified group.

Relative masses

The **relative atomic mass** of an element is the weighted mean of the masses of all the naturally occurring isotopes of the element relative to ^{12}C. This is why the values for relative atomic masses are not always whole numbers. Relative atomic masses of elements, A_r, and **relative formula masses** for compounds, M_r, have no units.

Molar mass

The mass of one mole of any substance is known as the **molar mass** and has the symbol M. For example, hydrogen-1 atoms, ^1H, have $\frac{1}{12}$ of the mass of ^{12}C atoms, so one mol of ^1H atoms contains 6.02×10^{23} ^1H atoms and has a mass of 1.00 g. The units of molar mass are $g\ mol^{-1}$.

Be careful to distinguish between the words **mole** and **molecule**. A molecule of hydrogen gas contains two atoms of hydrogen and has the formula H_2. A mole of hydrogen gas contains 6.02×10^{23} molecules of hydrogen made up of 2 mol (1.20×10^{24}) of naturally occurring hydrogen atoms ($A_r = 1.01$) and has a mass of 2.02 g.

To find the molar mass of a compound, simply add the atomic masses of all the atoms in the compound. For example, the molar mass of methane is $CH_4 = 12.01 + (4 \times 1.01) = 16.05\ g\ mol^{-1}$.

Empirical formula

An **empirical formula** is a formula obtained by experiment. It shows the simplest whole number ratio of atoms of each element in a particle of a substance. It can be obtained either by knowing the mass of each element in the compound or from the percentage composition by mass of the compound. The percentage composition can be converted directly into masses by assuming 100 g of the compound is present.

For example, a compound contains 40.00% carbon, 6.73% hydrogen and 53.27% oxygen by mass. Determine the empirical formula.

	Amount / mol	Ratio
C	$\frac{40.00}{12.01} = 3.33$	1
H	$\frac{6.73}{1.01} = 6.66$	2
O	$\frac{53.27}{16.00} = 3.33$	1

Empirical formula = CH_2O

Molecular formula

For molecules, the molecular formula is much more useful as it shows the actual number of atoms of each element in a molecule of the substance.

Methanal, CH_2O ($M_r = 30$), ethanoic acid, $C_2H_4O_2$ ($M_r = 60$) and glucose, $C_6H_{12}O_6$ ($M_r = 180$), are different substances with different molecular formulas but all with the same empirical formula: CH_2O.

You can obtain the molecular formula from the empirical formula if you also know the molar mass of the compound. For example, if you know that the M_r is 60 and the empirical formula is CH_2O ($M_r = 30$), then $\frac{60}{30} = 2$ so the molecular formula is double the empirical formula, giving $C_2H_4O_2$.

Note that subscripts are used to show the number of atoms of each element in the compound.

Experimental determination of an empirical formula

The empirical formula of magnesium oxide can be determined simply in the laboratory. A coil of magnesium ribbon about 10 cm long is placed in a pre-weighed crucible and its mass is recorded. The crucible is placed on a clay triangle and heated strongly. When the magnesium ribbon starts to burn, the lid is lifted slightly to allow more air to enter and the heating is continued until all the magnesium has burned. After cooling, the crucible, its lid and its contents are reweighed.

This table shows some typical raw quantitative data.

	Mass / g (± 0.001 g)
Mass of crucible + lid	30.911
Mass of crucible + lid + magnesium	31.037
Mass of crucible + lid + magnesium oxide	31.106

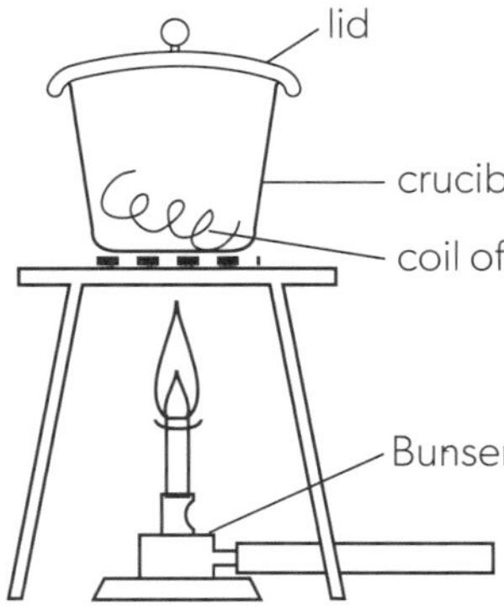

Mass of magnesium = 31.037 – 30.911 = 0.126 g

Mass of magnesium oxide = 31.106 – 30.911 = 0.195 g

Mass of oxygen combining with magnesium = 0.195 – 0.126 = 0.069 g

Amount of magnesium = $\frac{0.126}{24.31} = 5.2 \times 10^{-3}$ mol

Amount of oxygen = $\frac{0.069}{16.00} = 4.3 \times 10^{-3}$ mol

Ratio of Mg to O = $5.2 \times 10^{-3} : 4.3 \times 10^{-3} = 1.2 : 1$

Convert to whole number ratio = 6 : 5

Empirical formula of magnesium oxide as determined by this experiment is Mg_6O_5.

Molar concentration and solutions

Volume is usually used for solutions. 1.000 litre = 1.000 dm^3 = 1000 cm^3

Concentration is the amount of **solute** (dissolved substance) in a known volume of **solution** (solute plus **solvent**). It is expressed either in g dm^{-3} or, more usually, in mol dm^{-3}. A solution of known concentration is known as a **standard solution**.

Since concentration (c) = amount (mol) divided by volume (V) it leads to the expression $c = \frac{n}{V}$ or, as it is given in the data booklet, $n = cV$.

Worked example

To prepare a 1.00 mol dm^{-3} solution of sodium hydroxide, dissolve 1 mol (40.0 g) of solid sodium hydroxide in distilled water and then make the total volume up to 1.00 dm^3.

Concentration is often represented by square brackets, e.g.

[NaOH(aq)] = 1.00 mol dm^{-3}

A 25.0 cm^3 sample of this solution contains

$1.00 \times \frac{25.0}{1000} = 2.50 \times 10^{-2}$ mol of NaOH

Chemical reactions and equations

Chemical equations

Chemical reactions can be represented by chemical equations. Reactants are written on the left-hand side and products on the right-hand side. The number of moles of each element must be the same on both sides in a balanced chemical equation. As an example, consider the reaction of nitric acid (one of the acids present in acid rain) with calcium carbonate (the main constituent of marble statues).

$CaCO_3(s)$	+	$2HNO_3(aq)$	→	$Ca(NO_3)_2(aq)$	+	$CO_2(g)$	+	$H_2O(l)$
calcium carbonate		nitric acid		calcium nitrate		carbon dioxide		water
REACTANTS				PRODUCTS				

State symbols

The physical state that the reactants and products are in can affect both the rate of the reaction and the overall energy change. For this reason, it is good practice to include state symbols in the equation.

(s) = solid; (l) = liquid; (g) = gas; (aq) = in aqueous solution

Use of arrows (→ or ⇌)

A single arrow → is used if the reaction goes to completion. Sometimes the reaction conditions are written on the arrow:

e.g. $C_2H_4(g) + H_2(g) \xrightarrow{\text{Ni catalyst, 180 °C}} C_2H_6(g)$

Reversible arrows ⇌ are used for reactions where both the reactants and products are present in the equilibrium mixture:

e.g. $3H_2(g) + N_2(g) \underset{\text{250 atm}}{\overset{\text{Fe(s), 550 °C}}{\rightleftharpoons}} 2NH_3(g)$

Coefficients and molar ratio

A coefficient is a number in front of a reactant or product in an equation. The coefficients give information about the molar ratio. In the first example above, two moles of nitric acid react with one mole of calcium carbonate to produce one mole of calcium nitrate, one mole of carbon dioxide, and one mole of water. In the reaction between hydrogen and nitrogen above, three moles of hydrogen gas react with one mole of nitrogen gas to produce two moles of ammonia gas.

In a balanced chemical equation, there is a fixed relationship between the number of particles of reactants and products resulting in no overall change in mass; this is known as the **stoichiometry** of the reaction.

Ionic equations

Because ionic compounds are completely dissociated in solution, it is sometimes better to use ionic equations. For example, when silver nitrate solution is added to sodium chloride solution a precipitate of silver chloride is formed.

$Ag^+(aq) + NO_3^-(aq) + Na^+(aq) + Cl^-(aq) \rightarrow AgCl(s) + Na^+(aq) + NO_3^-(aq)$

$Na^+(aq)$ and $NO_3^-(aq)$ are **spectator ions** and do not take part in the reaction. So, the ionic equation becomes:

$Ag^+(aq) + Cl^-(aq) \rightarrow AgCl(s)$

From this you can deduce that any soluble silver salt will react with any soluble chloride to form a precipitate of silver chloride.

Ideal gases

An ideal gas

Gases consist of rapidly moving particles that occupy a large space compared with the volume of the particles themselves. In an **ideal gas**, all collisions between particles are perfectly elastic and there are no attractive forces between the particles, which occupy negligible space compared to the volume of the gas. The temperature of the gas is proportional to the average kinetic energy of its particles and the pressure is due to collisions of the particles with the vessel walls.

A real gas

Real gases do have some attractive forces between the particles and the particles themselves do occupy some space, so they do not exactly obey the ideal gas laws. If real gases did behave as ideal gases, they could never condense into liquids. A real gas behaves most like an ideal gas at high temperatures and low pressures. The differences between a real gas and an ideal gas are most noticeable at low temperatures and high pressures.

Changing the variables for a fixed mass of an ideal gas

$P \propto \frac{1}{V}$, or PV = constant

At **constant temperature**: as the volume decreases the concentration of the particles increases, resulting in more collisions with the container walls. The increase in pressure is inversely proportional to the decrease in volume, i.e. doubling the pressure halves the volume.

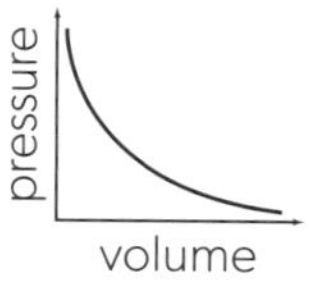

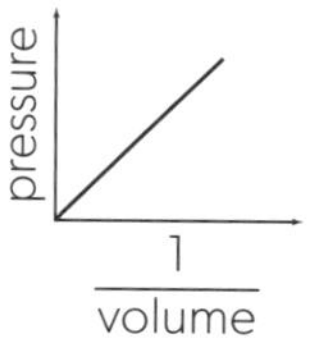

$P \propto T$, or $\frac{P}{T}$ = constant

At **constant volume**: increasing the temperature increases the average kinetic energy, so the force with which the particles collide with the container walls increases. Hence pressure increases and is directly proportional to the absolute temperature, i.e. doubling the absolute temperature doubles the pressure.

$V \propto T$, or $\frac{V}{T}$ = constant

At constant pressure: at higher temperatures the particles have a greater average velocity so individual particles collide with the container walls with greater force. To keep the pressure constant there must be fewer collisions per unit area so the volume of the gas must increase. The increase in volume is directly proportional to the absolute temperature, i.e. doubling the absolute temperature doubles the volume.

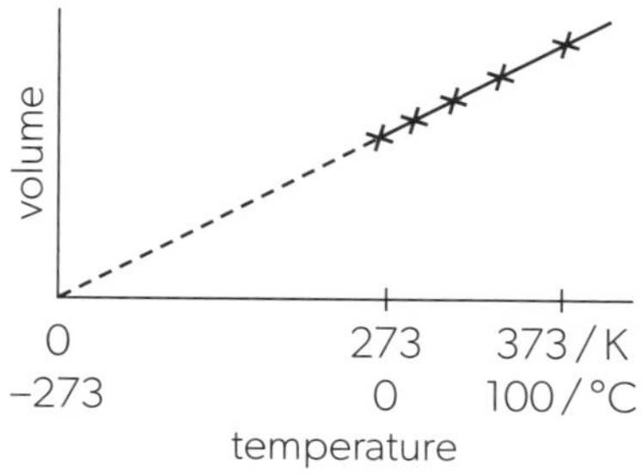

Extrapolating the graph to zero volume gives the value for absolute zero.

Ideal gas equation

The different variables for a gas are all related by the ideal gas equation.

$PV = nRT$

The ideal gas equation and the value of R are given in the IB data booklet.

P = pressure in Pa ($N\,m^{-2}$) (1 atm = 1.013×10^5 Pa)
T = absolute temperature in K
V = volume in m^3 ($1\,cm^3 = 1 \times 10^{-6}\,m^3$)
n = number of moles
R = gas constant = $8.31\,J\,K^{-1}\,mol^{-1}$

Avogadro's law and molar volume of a gas

The ideal gas equation depends on the amount of gas (the number of moles) but not on the nature of the gas. Avogadro's law states that equal volumes of different gases at the same temperature and pressure contain the same number of moles. It follows that one mole of any gas will occupy the same volume at the same temperature and pressure. This is known as the molar volume of a gas. At 273 K and 1.00×10^5 Pa, this volume is $22.7 \times 10^{-2}\,m^3$ ($22.7\,dm^3$ or $22\,700\,cm^3$).

When the mass of a particular gas is fixed, then nR is constant. This gives a useful expression to convert the pressure, temperature and volume under one set of conditions (shown by subscript "1") to another set of conditions (shown by subscript "2") since both $\frac{P_1V_1}{T_1}$ and $\frac{P_2V_2}{T_2} = nR$: $\frac{P_1V_1}{T_1} = \frac{P_2V_2}{T_2}$

This is known as the **combined gas law**. There is no need to convert to SI units as long as the same units for pressure and volume are used on both sides of the equation. Do not forget that T refers to the absolute temperature and must be in kelvin.

Calculations using limiting and excess reagents

Limiting reagents and calculations from equations

Work methodically.

Step 1. Write down the correct formulas for all the reactants and products.

Step 2. Balance the equation to obtain the correct stoichiometry of the reaction.

Step 3. If the amounts of all reactants are known, work out which are in **excess** and which one is the **limiting reagent**. If you know the limiting reagent, you can determine the maximum **theoretical yield** of any of the products.

Step 4. Work out the amount (in mol) of the substance required.

Step 5. Convert the amount (in mol) into a mass or volume.

Step 6. Express the answer to the correct number of significant figures and include the appropriate units.

Worked example 1

Calculate the volume of hydrogen gas evolved at 273 K and 1.00×10^5 Pa when 0.623 g of magnesium reacts with 27.3 cm^3 of 1.25 mol dm^{-3} hydrochloric acid.

Equation: $Mg(s) + 2HCl(aq) \rightarrow H_2(g) + MgCl_2(aq)$

A_r for Mg = 24.31.

Amount of Mg present $= \frac{0.623}{24.31} = 2.56 \times 10^{-2}$ mol

Amount of HCl present $= 1.25 \times \frac{27.3}{1000} = 3.41 \times 10^{-2}$ mol

From the equation, $2 \times 2.56 \times 10^{-2} = 5.12 \times 10^{-2}$ mol of HCl would be required to react with all of the magnesium. Therefore, the magnesium is in excess and the limiting reagent is the hydrochloric acid.

The maximum amount of hydrogen produced =

$\frac{3.41 \times 10^{-2}}{2} = 1.705 \times 10^{-2}$ mol

Volume of hydrogen at 273 K and 1.00×10^5 Pa $= 1.705 \times 10^{-2} \times 22.7 = 0.387$ dm^3 (or 387 cm^3)

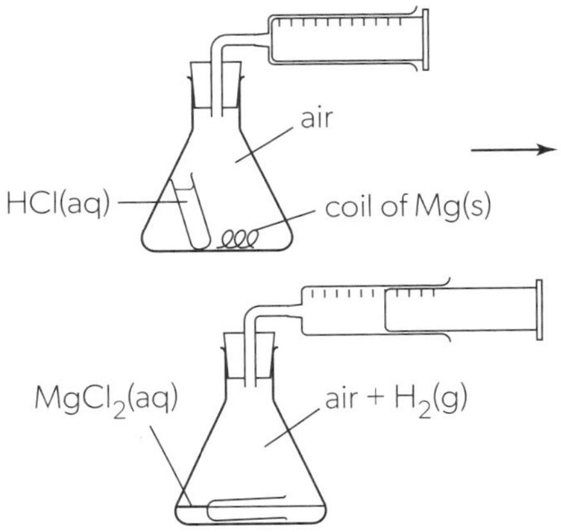

Worked example 2

Calculate the volume occupied by the hydrogen evolved in Worked example 1 if it had been collected at 22 °C and a pressure of 1.12×10^5 Pa.

Step 1. Express the temperature as an absolute temperature

22 °C = 295 K

Step 2. Apply the ideal gas equation $pV = nRT$

$1.12 \times 10^5 \times V = 1.705 \times 10^{-2} \times 8.314 \times 295$

$$V = \frac{1.705 \times 10^{-2} \times 8.314 \times 295}{1.12 \times 10^5} = 3.73 \times 10^{-4}\ m^3\ (373\ cm^3)$$

This could also be solved using $\frac{P_1V_1}{T_1} = \frac{P_2V_2}{T_2}$

$$V_2 = V_1 \times \frac{P_1}{P_2} \times \frac{T_2}{T_1} = 0.387 \times \frac{1.00 \times 10^{-5}}{1.12 \times 10^{-5}} \times \frac{295}{273} = 0.373\ m^3$$

(373 cm^3)

Worked example 3

The actual volume of hydrogen collected under the conditions stated in Worked example 1 was 342 cm^3. Determine the percentage yield.

Step 1. Use the mole ratio from the equation and the amounts of the reactants to determine the limiting reagent and hence the theoretical maximum yield. From Worked example 1, theoretical yield = 387 cm^3

Step 2. Apply the relationship:

$$\text{percentage yield} = \frac{\text{experimental yield}}{\text{theoretical yield}} \times 100$$

$$\text{percentage yield} = \frac{342}{387} \times 100 = 88.4\%$$

Titration and atom economy

Determining an unknown concentration by titration

Titration is a useful technique to find the concentration of a solution of unknown concentration by reacting it with a stoichiometric amount of a standard solution. A known accurate volume of one of the solutions is placed in a conical flask using a pipette. A burette is then used to add the other solution dropwise until the reaction is complete. This can be seen when one drop causes the solution to just change colour. For acid–base titrations, it is usual to add an indicator. However, this is not necessary for some other types of titration, e.g. in redox titrations using acidified potassium permanganate, as the reactant itself causes the colour change.

It is usual to obtain at least two accurate readings, which should be within 0.15 cm^3 of each other.

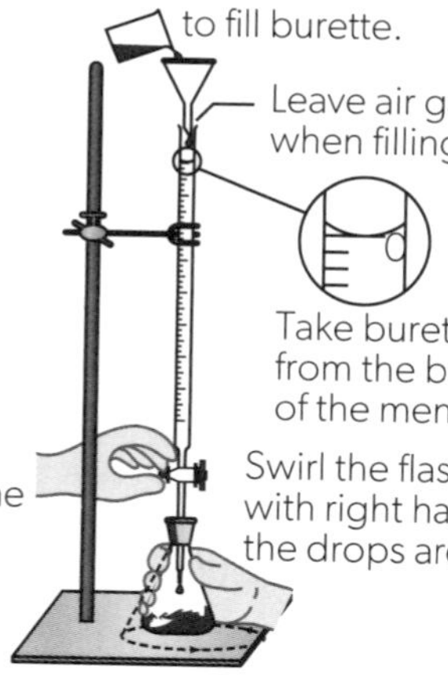

Use a beaker and funnel to fill burette.
Leave air gap when filling.
Take burette reading from the bottom of the meniscus.
Use left hand to control the flow rate.
Swirl the flask with right hand while the drops are being added.

Worked example 1

25.00 cm^3 of a solution of sodium hydroxide of unknown concentration required 23.65 cm^3 of 0.100 mol dm^{-3} hydrochloric acid solution for complete neutralization. Calculate the concentration of the sodium hydroxide solution.

Equation for the reaction: $NaOH(aq) + HCl(aq) \rightarrow NaCl(aq) + H_2O(l)$

Amount of hydrochloric acid present in 23.65 cm^3 = $\frac{23.65}{1000} \times 0.100 = 2.365 \times 10^{-3}$ mol

Since one mol of NaOH reacts with one mol of HCl:

Amount of sodium hydroxide present in 25.00 cm^3 = 2.365×10^{-3} mol

Concentration of sodium hydroxide = $2.365 \times 10^{-3} \times \frac{1000}{25.00} = 0.0946$ mol dm^{-3}

Worked example 2

50.0 cm^3 of 1.00 mol dm^{-3} hydrochloric acid solution, HCl(aq), was added to some egg shell (a mass of 2.016 g). After all the egg shell had reacted, the resulting solution was put into a 100 cm^3 volumetric flask and the volume was made up to the mark with distilled water. 10.0 cm^3 of this solution required 11.40 cm^3 of 1.00×10^{-1} mol dm^{-3} sodium hydroxide solution, NaOH(aq), for complete neutralization. Calculate the percentage of calcium carbonate in the egg shell.

Titration equation:

$NaOH(aq) + HCl(aq) \rightarrow NaCl(aq) + H_2O(l)$

Amount of sodium hydroxide present in 11.40 cm^3 =
$\frac{11.40}{1000} \times 1.00 \times 10^{-1} = 1.140 \times 10^{-3}$ mol

Since one mol of NaOH reacts with one mol of HCl:

Amount of dilute excess hydrochloric acid in the 10.0 cm^3 sample = 1.140×10^{-3} mol

Amount of excess hydrochloric acid in 100 cm^3 = $(1.140 \times 10^{-3}) \times 10 = 1.140 \times 10^{-2}$ mol

Initial amount of hydrochloric acid added to egg shell =
$\frac{50.0}{1000} \times 1.00 = 5.00 \times 10^{-2}$ mol

Amount of hydrochloric acid reacting with egg shell = $(5.00 \times 10^{-2}) - (1.140 \times 10^{-2}) = 3.860 \times 10^{-2}$ mol

Equation for reaction:

$CaCO_3(s) + 2HCl(aq) \rightarrow CaCl_2(aq) + CO_2(g) + H_2O(l)$

Amount of $CaCO_3$ that reacted with the acid = $\frac{1}{2} \times 3.860 \times 10^{-2} = 1.930 \times 10^{-2}$ mol

$M_r(CaCO_3) = 40.08 + 12.01 + (3 \times 16.00) = 100.09$

Mass of $CaCO_3$ in egg shell = $100.09 \times 1.930 \times 10^{-2}$
= 1.932 g

Percentage of calcium carbonate in the egg shell =
$\frac{1.932}{2.016} \times 100 = 95.8\%$

Worked example 3

Crystalline oxalic acid contains water of crystallization and has the formula $(COOH)_2.xH_2O$. It is a dibasic acid, so one mol of the acid reacts with two mol of sodium hydroxide. 17.267 g of oxalic acid crystals were dissolved in distilled water and the volume of the solution made up to exactly 250 cm^3. 25.00 cm^3 of this solution required 27.40 cm^3 of 0.100 mol dm^{-3} NaOH(aq) for complete neutralization. Determine the value of x.

Amount of NaOH in 27.40 cm^3 $= \dfrac{27.40}{1000} \times 0.100 = 0.0274$ mol

Since 2 mol of NaOH neutralize 1 mol of oxalic acid,

amount of oxalic acid in 25.00 cm^3 $= \dfrac{0.0274}{2} = 0.0137$ mol

Amount of oxalic acid in 250 cm^3 = 0.137 mol

Mass of oxalic acid crystals in 250 cm^3 = 17.267 g

$M(\text{oxalic acid}) = \dfrac{17.267}{0.137} = 126.06\ \text{g mol}^{-1}$

$M(\text{oxalic acid}) = ((2 \times 12.01) + (4 \times 16.00) + (4 \times 1.10)) + ((2 \times 1.01) + 16.00)x$

$= 90.04 + 18.02x\ \text{g mol}^{-1}$

$18.02x = 126.06 - 90.04$

$x = \dfrac{36.04}{18.02} = 2$

Atom economy

As well as trying to achieve high yields in industrial processes, chemists try to increase the conversion efficiency of a chemical process. This is known as **atom economy**. Ideally, no atom is wasted in a chemical process. The atom economy is a measure of the amount of starting materials that become useful products. A high atom economy means that fewer natural resources are used and less waste is created. The atom economy can be calculated by using the following steps.

Step 1. Write the balanced equation for the reaction taking place.

Step 2. Calculate the relative molecular mass of each product and then the total mass of each product formed, assuming molar quantities. Note that this is the same as the total mass of the reactants.

Step 3. Calculate the relative molar mass of each desired product and then the total mass of each desired product formed, assuming molar quantities.

Step 4. $\text{atom economy} = \dfrac{\text{total mass of desired product(s)}}{\text{total mass of all products}} \times 100$

Worked example 4

Consider the production of iron by the reduction of iron(III) oxide using the thermite reaction.

$2Al(s) + Fe_2O_3(s) \rightarrow 2Fe(s) + Al_2O_3(s)$

The total mass of products formed = 2 × 55.85 + [(2 × 26.98) + (3 × 16.00)] = 213.66 g

The total amount of iron (the desired product) formed = 2 × 55.85 = 111.70 g

The atom economy for this reaction is $\dfrac{111.70}{213.66} \times 100 = 52.3\%$

Obviously, if all the aluminium oxide produced can be used, then the atom economy for this reaction will increase to 100%.

Multiple-choice questions—Quantitative chemistry

1. How many oxygen atoms are in 0.100 mol of $CuSO_4.5H_2O$?
   A. 5.42×10^{22} C. 2.41×10^{23}
   B. 6.02×10^{22} D. 5.42×10^{23}

2. Which is **NOT** a true statement?
   A. One mole of methane contains four moles of hydrogen atoms.
   B. One mole of ^{12}C has a mass of 12.00 g.
   C. One mole of hydrogen gas contains 6.02×10^{23} atoms of hydrogen.
   D. One mole of methane contains 75% carbon by mass.

3. A pure compound contains 24 g of carbon, 4 g of hydrogen and 32 g of oxygen. No other elements are present. What is the empirical formula of the compound?
   A. $C_2H_4O_2$ C. CH_4O
   B. CH_2O D. CHO

4. What is the mass in grams of one molecule of ethanoic acid, CH_3COOH?
   A. 0.1 C. 1×10^{-22}
   B. 3.6×10^{25} D. 60

5. What is the relative molar mass, M_r, of carbon dioxide, CO_2?
   A. 44.01 g mol^{-1} C. 44.01 kg mol^{-1}
   B. 44.01 mol g^{-1} D. 44.01

6. A 100 cm^3 sample of an ideal gas is at 50 °C. Which change will increase the volume to 200 cm^3?
   A. Doubling the pressure and raising the temperature to 100 °C.
   B. Halving the pressure and keeping the temperature the same.
   C. Raising the temperature to 100 °C and keeping the pressure the same.
   D. Lowering the temperature to 25 °C and keeping the pressure the same.

7. What is the empirical formula for the compound $C_6H_5(OH)_2$?
   A. C_6H_6O C. C_6H_7O
   B. $C_6H_5O_2H_2$ D. $C_6H_7O_2$

8. Phosphorus burns in oxygen to produce phosphorus pentoxide, P_4O_{10}. What is the sum of the coefficients in the balanced equation?

   $\_P_4(s) + \_O_2(g) \rightarrow \_P_4O_{10}(s)$

   A. 3 C. 6
   B. 5 D. 7

9. Magnesium reacts with hydrochloric acid according to the following equation:

   $Mg(s) + 2HCl(aq) \rightarrow MgCl_2(aq) + H_2(g)$

   What mass of hydrogen will be obtained if 100 cm^3 of 2.00 mol dm^{-3} HCl is added to 4.86 g of magnesium?
   A. 0.2 g C. 0.8 g
   B. 0.4 g D. 2.0 g

10. Butane burns in oxygen according to the equation below.

    $2C_4H_{10}(g) + 13O_2(g) \rightarrow 8CO_2(g) + 10H_2O(l)$

    If 11.6 g of butane is burned in 11.6 g of oxygen, which is the limiting reagent?
    A. butane C. neither
    B. oxygen D. oxygen and butane

11. Four identical containers under the same conditions are filled with gases, as shown below. Which container and contents will have the highest mass?

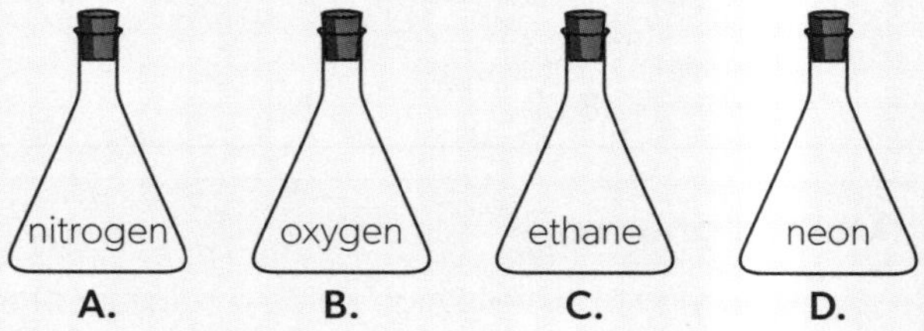

12. What is the amount, in moles, of sulfate ions in 100 cm^3 of 0.020 mol dm^{-3} $FeSO_4(aq)$?
    A. 2.0×10^{-3} C. 2.0×10^{-1}
    B. 2.0×10^{-2} D. 2.0

13. 300 cm^3 of water is added to 200 cm^3 of a 0.5 mol dm^{-3} solution of sodium chloride. What is the concentration of sodium chloride in the new solution?
    A. 0.05 mol dm^{-3} C. 0.2 mol dm^{-3}
    B. 0.1 mol dm^{-3} D. 0.3 mol dm^{-3}

14. Separate samples of two gases, each containing a pure substance, are found to have the same density under the same conditions of temperature and pressure. Which statement about these two samples must be correct?
    A. They have the same volume.
    B. They have the same relative molecular mass.
    C. There are equal numbers of moles of gas in the two samples.
    D. They condense at the same temperature.

15. The graph below represents the relationship between two variables in a fixed amount of gas.

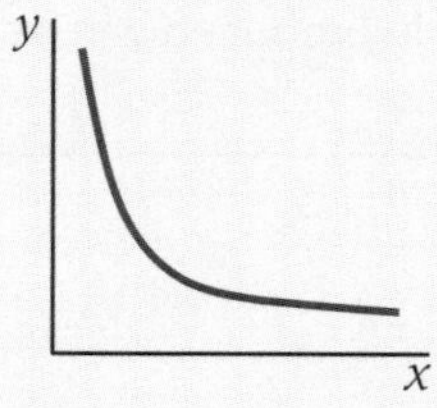

Which variables could be represented by each axis?

	x-axis	*y*-axis
A.	pressure	temperature
B.	volume	temperature
C.	pressure	volume
D.	temperature	volume

16. Sulfuric acid and sodium hydroxide react together according to the equation:

$H_2SO_4(aq) + 2NaOH(aq) \rightarrow Na_2SO_4(aq) + 2H_2O(l)$

What volume of 0.250 mol dm^{-3} NaOH is required to neutralize exactly 25.0 cm^3 of 0.125 mol dm^{-3} H_2SO_4?

A. 25.0 cm^3 C. 50 cm^3
B. 12.5 cm^3 D. 6.25 cm^3

17. What will be the units of the gas constant, R, if pressure is measured in Pa, temperature is measured in K, volume is measured in m^3 and amount is measured in mol?

A. J K^{-1} mol^{-1} C. Pa m^{-1} K mol
B. Pa m^{-3} K^{-1} mol^{-1} D. Pa m^3 K mol^{-1}

18. How many hydrogen atoms are present in one molecule of methane, CH_4?

A. 6.02×10^{23} C. 2.41×10^{23}
B. 2.41×10^{24} D. 4

19. Which contains the greatest amount of nitrogen atoms?

A. 1.00 dm^3 of 0.050 mol dm^{-3} $NH_3(aq)$
B. 0.100 mol of $NaNO_3(s)$
C. 500 cm^3 of 0.10 mol dm^{-3} $HNO_3(aq)$
D. 0.04 mol of $N_2(g)$

20. Which is correct when 0.05 mol magnesium metal is added to 500 cm^3 of 0.10 mol dm^{-3} hydrochloric acid?

$Mg(s) + 2HCl(aq) \rightarrow MgCl_2(aq) + H_2(g)$

	Limiting reagent	Theoretical maximum yield of $H_2(g)$ / mol
A.	Mg(s)	0.050
B.	HCl(aq)	0.050
C.	Mg(s)	0.025
D.	HCl(aq)	0.025

21. Which graph shows the relationship between pressure and volume for a fixed mass of an ideal gas at a constant temperature?

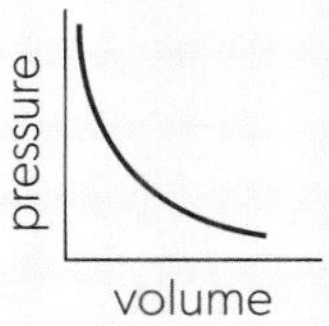

A.

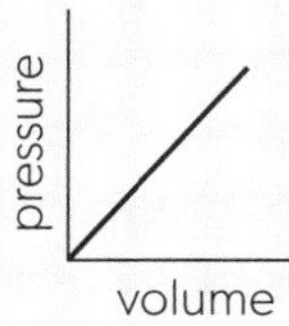

C.

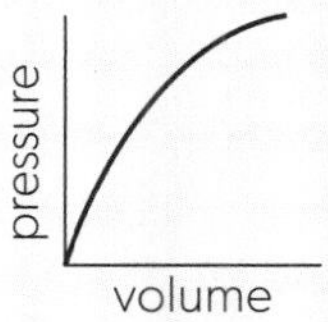

B.

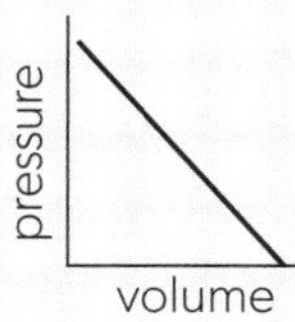

D.

22. What is the atom economy when limestone is converted into calcium oxide and the carbon dioxide produced is lost to the atmosphere?

$CaCO_3(s) \rightarrow CaO(s) + CO_2(g)$

A. 44% C. 56%
B. 100% D. 12%

23. When 6 mol of hydrogen was reacted with 2 mol of nitrogen under certain conditions the percentage yield of ammonia obtained was 10%. What mass of ammonia was obtained in this reaction?

$3H_2(g) + N_2(g) \rightarrow 2NH_3(g)$

A. 10 g C. 6.8 g
B. 1.7 g D. 3.4 g

24. 200 cm^3 of 0.5 mol dm^{-3} NaOH(aq) was mixed with 300 cm^3 of 0.8 mol dm^{-3} NaOH(aq). What is the concentration (in mol dm^{-3}) of the new solution?

A. 0.65 C. 0.70
B. 0.68 D. 0.66

25. An ideal gas occupies 40.0 cm^3 at 20.0 °C and 1.2×10^5 Pa pressure. Which calculation gives the volume (in cm^3) that the same amount of the gas will occupy at 40 °C and 1.5×10^5 Pa pressure?

A. $(40.0 \times 293 \times 1.5) \div (317 \times 1.2)$
B. $(40.0 \times 317 \times 1.5) \div (293 \times 1.2)$
C. $(40.0 \times 293 \times 1.2) \div (317 \times 1.5)$
D. $(40.0 \times 317 \times 1.2) \div (293 \times 1.5)$

26. When 30.0 cm^3 of a hydrocarbon is combusted completely it produces 60.0 cm^3 of gaseous carbon dioxide and 90.0 cm^3 of water vapour. Assuming that all the volumes are measured at the same temperature and pressure, what is the molecular formula of the hydrocarbon?

A. C_3H_8 C. C_2H_6
B. C_3H_6 D. C_2H_3

27. Which reaction produces a precipitate?

A. $Ba(NO_3)_2(aq) + Na_2SO_4(aq) \rightarrow 2NaNO_3(aq) + BaSO_4(s)$
B. $Zn(s) + 2HCl(aq) \rightarrow ZnCl_2(aq) + H_2(g)$
C. $2KOH(aq) + H_2SO_4 \rightarrow K_2SO_4(aq) + 2H_2O(l)$
D. $NaHCO_3(aq) + HCl(aq) \rightarrow NaCl(aq) + CO_2(g) + H_2O(l)$

28. Which compound has a different molecular formula to the other three?

A. butanone, $C_2H_5COCH_3$
B. butan-2-ol, $CH_3CH_2CH(OH)CH_3$
C. ethoxyethane, $C_2H_5OC_2H_5$
D. 2-methylpropan-2-ol, $(CH_3)_3COH$

Short-answer questions—Quantitative chemistry

1. Aspirin, $C_9H_8O_4$, is made by reacting ethanoic anhydride, $C_4H_6O_3$ (M_r = 102.1), with 2-hydroxybenzoic acid (M_r = 138.1), according to the equation:

$$2C_7H_6O_3 + C_4H_6O_3 \rightarrow 2C_9H_8O_4 + H_2O$$

   a) If 15.0 g of 2-hydroxybenzoic acid is reacted with 15.0 g of ethanoic anhydride, determine the limiting reagent in this reaction. [3]

   b) Calculate the maximum mass of aspirin that could be obtained in this reaction. [2]

   c) If the mass obtained in this experiment was 13.7 g, calculate the percentage yield of aspirin. [1]

2. 14.48 g of a metal sulfate with the formula M_2SO_4 was dissolved in water. Excess barium nitrate solution was added in order to precipitate all the sulfate ions in the form of barium sulfate. 9.336 g of precipitate was obtained.

   a) Calculate the amount (in mol) of barium sulfate, $BaSO_4$, precipitated. [2]

   b) Determine the amount of sulfate ions present in the 14.48 g of M_2SO_4. [1]

   c) Deduce the relative molar mass of M_2SO_4. [1]

   d) Calculate the relative atomic mass of M and hence identify the metal. [2]

3. A student added 7.40×10^{-2} g of magnesium ribbon to 15.0 cm^3 of 2.00 mol dm^{-3} hydrochloric acid. The hydrogen gas produced was collected using a gas syringe at 20.0 °C and 1.00×10^5 Pa.

   a) State the equation for the reaction between magnesium and hydrochloric acid. [1]

   b) Determine the limiting reactant. [3]

   c) Calculate the theoretical yield of hydrogen gas:

      (i) in mol [1]

      (ii) in cm^3, under the stated conditions of temperature and pressure. [2]

   d) The actual volume of hydrogen measured was lower than the calculated theoretical volume. Suggest two reasons why the volume of hydrogen gas obtained was less. [2]

4. In 1921 Thomas Midgley discovered that the addition of a lead compound could improve the combustion of hydrocarbons in automobile (car) engines. This was the beginning of the use of leaded gasoline (petrol).

   The percentage composition, by mass, of the lead compound used by Midgley is Pb: 64.052%, C: 29.703%, and H: 6.245%.

   a) (i) Determine the empirical formula of the lead compound. [3]

      (ii) Leaded gasoline has been phased out because the lead(IV) oxide, PbO_2, produced as a side product in the combustion reaction may cause brain damage in children.

      0.01 mol of Midgley's lead compound produces 0.01 mol of lead(IV) oxide. Deduce the molecular formula of Midgley's compound. [1]

      (iii) Determine the equation for the complete combustion of Midgley's compound. [2]

   b) The combustion of unleaded gasoline still produces pollution, with both local and global consequences. Identify one exhaust gas that causes local pollution and one exhaust gas that causes global pollution. [2]

5. A large flask full of air was fitted with a bung and weighed. Gas was then blown into the flask to displace the air, the bung replaced, and the flask reweighed. This was repeated until there was no further change in mass. The flask was then filled with water and the water poured into a measuring cylinder to determine the volume of the flask. The following data was obtained during the experiment.

   Mass of flask + air = 739.50 g

   Mass of flask + gas = 742.10 g

   Volume of flask = 4043 cm^3

   Temperature = 19.0 °C

   Pressure = 1.01×10^5 Pa

   Assuming air is 80% nitrogen, N_2(g), and 20% oxygen, O_2(g), determine the relative molar mass of the gas. [5]

6. Copper metal may be produced by the reaction of copper(I) oxide and copper(I) sulfide according to the equation:

$$2Cu_2O(s) + Cu_2S(s) \rightarrow 6Cu(s) + SO_2(g)$$

   A mixture of 10.0 kg of copper(I) oxide and 5.00 kg of copper(I) sulfide was heated until no further reaction occurred.

   a) Determine the limiting reagent in this reaction. [3]

   b) Calculate the maximum mass of copper that could be obtained from these masses of reactants. [2]

   c) Assuming that the reaction to produce copper goes to completion according to the equation, deduce the atom economy for this reaction. [3]

7. The empirical formula of magnesium oxide is MgO. Suggest four assumptions that were made in the experiment detailed on page 16 that may not be true and which might account for the wrong result being obtained. [4]

8. The percentage composition by mass of a hydrocarbon is C: 85.6% and H: 14.4%.

   a) Calculate the empirical formula of the hydrocarbon. [2]

   b) A 1.00 g sample of the hydrocarbon at a temperature of 273 K and a pressure of 1.00×10^5 Pa has a volume of 0.405 dm^3.

      (i) Calculate the molar mass of the hydrocarbon. [2]

      (ii) Deduce the molecular formula of the hydrocarbon. [2]

   c) Explain why the incomplete combustion of hydrocarbons is harmful to humans. [2]

The ionic model

Ionic bond

Ionic compounds are formed when electrons are transferred from one atom to another to form ions with complete outer shells of electrons. In an ionic compound the positive and negative ions (cations and anions, respectively) are attracted to each other by strong electrostatic forces, and build up into a strong lattice. Ionic compounds have high melting points as considerable energy is required to overcome these forces of attraction.

The charge carried by an ion depends on the number of electrons the atom needs to lose or gain to achieve a full outer shell. Transition elements can form more than one ion. For example, iron can form Fe^{2+} and Fe^{3+} and copper can form Cu^{+} and Cu^{2+}.

Cations			Anions		
Group 1	Group 2	Group 3	Group 15	Group 16	Group 17
+1	+2	+3	−3	−2	−1
Li^{+}, Na^{+}, K^{+}	Mg^{2+}, Ca^{2+}	Al^{3+}	N^{3-}, P^{3-}	O^{2-}, S^{2-}	F^{-}, Cl^{-}, Br^{-}

Formulas of ionic compounds

Binary ionic compounds (comprising just two different elements) are named with the cation first, followed by the anion. The anion adopts the suffix "-ide". It is easy to find the correct formula as the overall charge must be zero.

lithium fluoride $Li^{+}F^{-}$
magnesium chloride $Mg^{2+}Cl^{-}{}_2$
aluminium bromide $Al^{3+}Br^{-}{}_3$
sodium oxide $Na^{+}{}_2O^{2-}$
calcium sulfide $Ca^{2+}S^{2-}$
iron(III) oxide $Fe^{3+}{}_2O^{2-}{}_3$
potassium nitride $K^{+}{}_3N^{3-}$
calcium phosphide $Ca^{2+}{}_3P^{3-}{}_2$
iron(II) oxide $Fe^{2+}O^{2-}$

Note: the formulas above have been written to show the charges carried by the ions. Unless you are specifically asked to do this, it is common practice to omit the charges and simply write LiF, $MgCl_2$, etc.

Ions containing more than one element (polyatomic ions)

In ions formed from more than one element, the charge is often spread (delocalized) over the whole ion. An example of a positive ion (a cation) is the ammonium ion NH_4^{+}, in which all four N–H bonds are identical. Negative ions (anions) are sometimes known as acid radicals as they are formed when an acid loses one or more H^{+} ions.

hydroxide OH^{-}
carbonate CO_3^{2-} (from carbonic acid, H_2CO_3)
nitrate NO_3^{-} (from nitric acid, HNO_3)
hydrogencarbonate HCO_3^{-}
sulfate SO_4^{2-} (from sulfuric acid, H_2SO_4)
ethanoate CH_3COO^{-} (from ethanoic acid, CH_3COOH)
hydrogensulfate HSO_4^{-}
phosphate PO_4^{3-} (from phosphoric acid H_3PO_4)

The formulas of these ionic compounds are obtained in exactly the same way as before. Note: brackets are used to show that the subscript covers all the elements in the ion, e.g. sodium nitrate, $NaNO_3$, ammonium sulfate, $(NH_4)_2SO_4$, and calcium phosphate, $Ca_3(PO_4)_2$.

Ionic compounds and their properties

Ionic compounds are formed between metals on the left of the periodic table and non-metals on the right of the periodic table; that is, between elements in groups 1, 2, and 3 with a low electronegativity (electropositive elements) and elements with a high electronegativity in groups 15, 16, and 17. Generally the difference between the electronegativity values needs to be greater than about 1.8 for ionic bonding to occur. Electronegativity values can be found in section 9 of the IB data booklet.

Ions in solid ionic compounds are held in a three-dimensional lattice structure. The ionic bond is the sum of all the electrostatic attractions (and repulsions) within the lattice. A large amount of energy is required to break the lattice, so ionic compounds tend to have high melting points. Many are soluble in water as the energy given out when the ions become hydrated (hydration energy) provides the energy to overcome the forces holding the ions together in the lattice (lattice enthalpy). The smaller the ions and the greater their charge, the greater the lattice enthalpy. Solid ionic compounds cannot conduct electricity as the ions are held in fixed positions. When molten, the ions are free to move and conduct electricity. They are chemically decomposed at the respective electrodes.

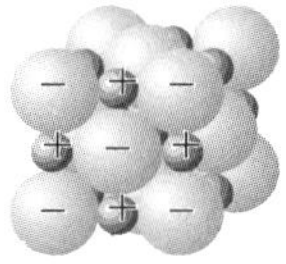

NaCl

▲ Sodium chloride (melting point 801°C); ions held strongly in an ionic lattice

The covalent model

Covalent bonds

Covalent bonding involves the sharing of one or more pairs of electrons so that each atom in the molecule achieves a noble gas configuration. The simplest covalent molecule is hydrogen. Each hydrogen atom has one electron in its outer shell. The two electrons are shared and attracted electrostatically by both positive nuclei, resulting in a directional bond between the two atoms to form a molecule. When one pair of electrons is shared, the resulting bond is known as a single covalent bond. Another example of a diatomic molecule with a single covalent bond is chlorine, Cl_2.

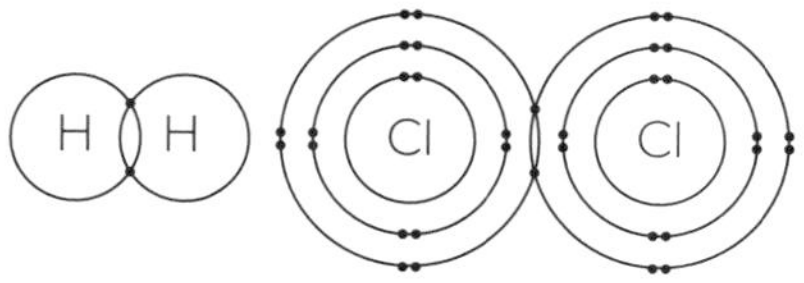

The octet rule

Most atoms, other than hydrogen, try to gain a share of eight electrons in their valence (outer) shell. This is known as the "octet rule". In structural formulas, a shared pair of electrons is represented by a line between the two bonded atoms. For example:

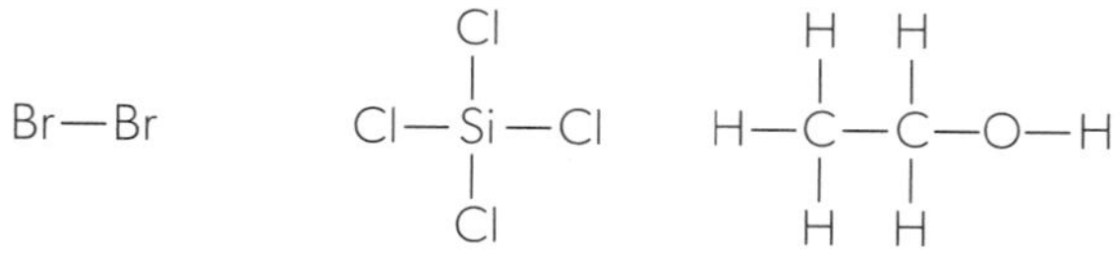

$$Br-Br$$

bromine, Br_2

$$Cl-\underset{\underset{Cl}{|}}{\overset{\overset{Cl}{|}}{Si}}-Cl$$

silicon tetrachloride, $SiCl_4$

$$H-\underset{\underset{H}{|}}{\overset{\overset{H}{|}}{C}}-\underset{\underset{H}{|}}{\overset{\overset{H}{|}}{C}}-O-H$$

ethanol, C_2H_5OH

There are some exceptions where the central atom has less than an octet of outer electrons, e.g. $BeCl_2$ and BF_3. There are also some compounds, e.g. sulfur hexafluoride, SF_6, where the "octet" is expanded to contain more than eight electrons.

Coordination bonds

Both the electrons in the shared pair can originate from the same atom. This is known as a coordination bond or coordinate covalent bond. In these diagrams, an arrow indicates a coordination bond.

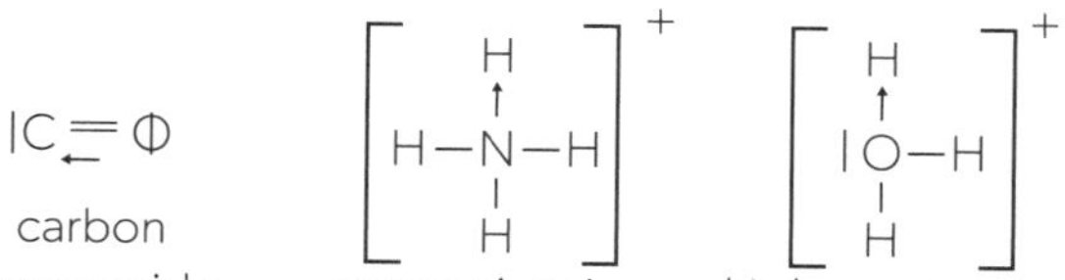

carbon monoxide

ammonium ion

hydroxonium ion

Sulfur dioxide and sulfur trioxide may be shown as having a coordination bond between sulfur and oxygen, or they may be shown as having double bonds between the sulfur and the oxygen.

8 valence electrons around S

10 valence electrons around S

2 coordination bonds, 8 valence electrons around S

12 valence electrons around S

> **AHL** Coordination bonding also occurs in transition element complexes where small molecules or ions such as water, H_2O, ammonia, NH_3, and chloride ions, Cl^-, use a non-bonding pair of electrons to bond to the metal ion, e.g. $[Fe(H_2O)_6]^{2+}$, $[Cu(NH_3)_4]^{2+}$, and $[CuCl_4]^{2-}$.

Lewis formulas

The structures of bromine, silicon tetrachloride, and ethanol (shown above) only show the bonded pair of electrons, whereas Lewis formulas (also known as Lewis structures or electron dot structures) show all the valence electrons. There are various methods of depicting the electrons. The simplest method involves using a line to represent one pair of electrons. It is also acceptable to represent single electrons by dots, crosses, or a combination of the two. The four methods below are all correct ways of showing the Lewis formula of fluorine.

Single covalent bonds

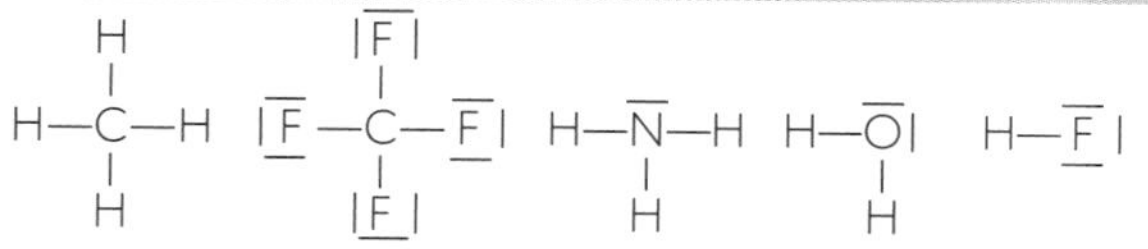

methane   tetrafluoro-   ammonia   water   hydrogen
           methane   fluoride

The carbon atom (electron configuration $1s^2 2s^2 2p^2$) has four electrons in its outer shell and requires a share in four more electrons. It forms four single bonds with elements that only require a share in one more electron, such as hydrogen or chlorine. Nitrogen (electron configuration $1s^2 2s^2 2p^3$) forms three single bonds with hydrogen, forming ammonia, and leaving one non-bonded pair of electrons (also known as a lone pair). In water there are two non-bonded pairs and in hydrogen fluoride there are three non-bonded pairs.

Multiple covalent bonds

In some compounds, atoms can share more than one pair of electrons to achieve a noble gas configuration. If a bond involves two shared pairs of electrons, it is called a double bond. If it involves three shared pairs of electrons, it is called a triple bond.

oxygen   nitrogen   carbon dioxide

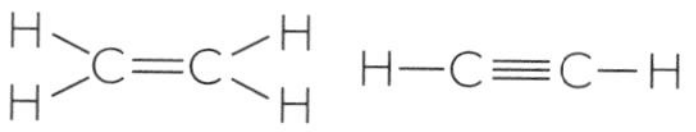

ethene

ethyne

Shapes of simple molecules and ions

The VSEPR model

The shapes of simple molecules and ions can be determined by using the valence shell electron pair repulsion (VSEPR) theory. This states that pairs of electrons arrange themselves around the central atom so that they are as far apart from each other as possible. There is greater repulsion between non-bonded pairs of electrons than between bonded pairs, which affects the bond angles in the molecule or ion. Since all the electrons in a multiple bond must lie in the same direction, double and triple bonds count as one pair of electrons in this theory. Strictly speaking, the theory refers to electron domains, but for most molecules this equates to pairs of electrons.

This results in five basic shapes, depending on the number of pairs. For five and six electron domains, the octet needs to be expanded and this can only happen if there are readily available d orbitals present that can also be utilized. For Standard Level, only two, three, and four electron domains need to be considered.

No. of electron domains	Shape	Name of shape	Bond angles(s)
2	O—O—O	Linear	180°
3	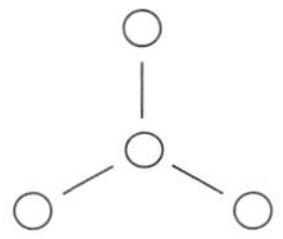	Trigonal planar	120°
4	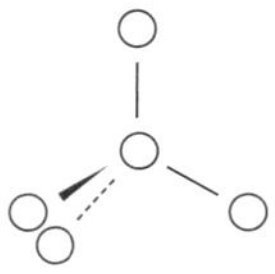	Tetrahedral	109.5°
5	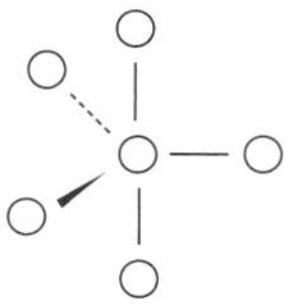	Trigonal bipyramidal	90°, 120°, 180°
6	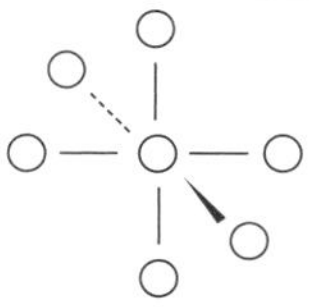	Octahedral	90°, 180°

AHL Five and six electron domains

5 and 6 negative charge centres

trigonal bipyramidal

octahedral

square planar: non-bonding pairs as far apart as possible above and below plane

distorted tetrahedral

Two electron domains

Cl—Be—Cl O=C=O H—C≡C—H H—C≡N

double bond counts as one pair   triple bond counts as one pair

Three electron domains

3 bonding pairs—trigonal planar

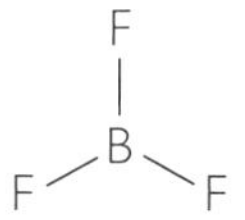

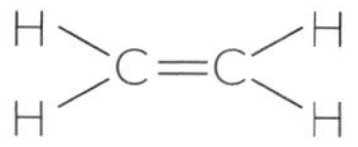

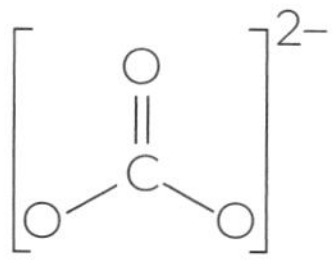

carbonate ion

2 bonding pairs, 1 non-bonded pair—bent or V-shaped

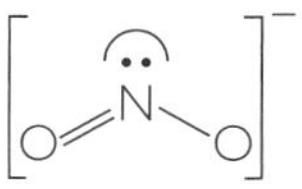

nitrite ion

Four electron domains

4 bonding pairs—tetrahedral

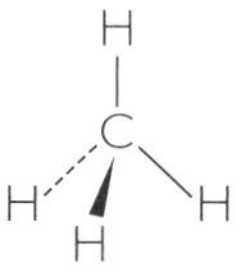

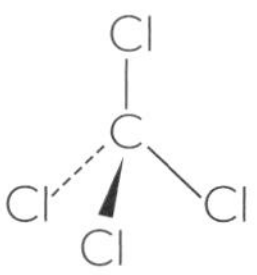

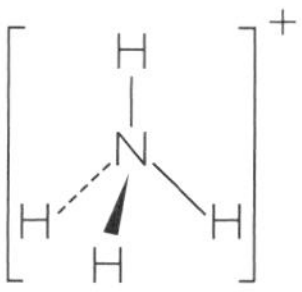

ammonium ion

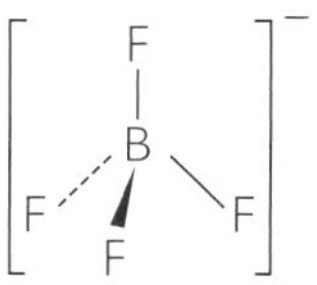

tetrafluoroborate ion

3 bonding pairs, 1 non-bonding pair—trigonal pyramidal

ammonia

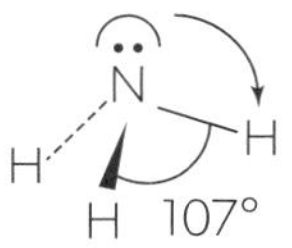

greater repulsion by non-bonding pair, so bond angle smaller than 109.5°

2 bonding pairs, 2 non-bonding pairs—bent or V-shaped

water

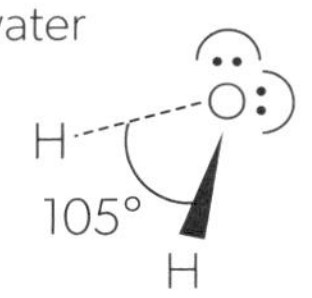

even greater repulsion by two non-bonding pairs, so bond angle even smaller

Working out the actual shape

To work out the actual shape of a molecule, calculate the number of pairs of electrons around the central atom, then work out how many are bonding pairs and how many are non-bonding pairs. (For ions, the number of electrons that equate to the charge on the ion must also be included when calculating the total number of electrons.)

Bond strength and polarity

Bond length and bond strength

The strength of attraction that the two nuclei have for the shared electrons affects both the length and strength of the bond. There is considerable variation in the bond lengths and strengths of single bonds in different compounds, while double bonds are generally much stronger and shorter than single bonds. The strongest covalent bonds are shown by triple bonds.

		Length / nm	Strength / kJ mol^{-1}
Single bonds	Cl–Cl	0.199	242
	C–C	0.154	346
Double bonds	C=C	0.134	614
	O=O	0.121	498
Triple bonds	C≡C	0.120	839
	N≡N	0.110	945

These are the bond lengths in ethanoic acid:

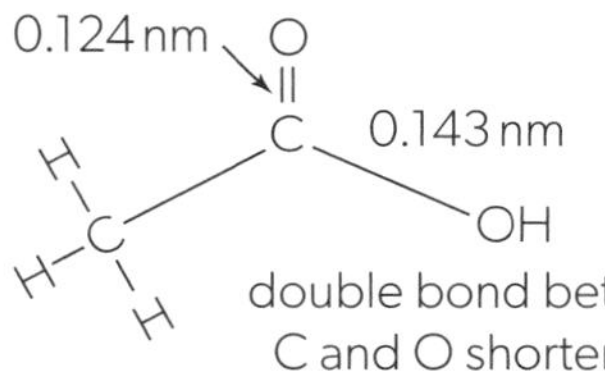

double bond between C and O shorter and stronger than single bond

Bond polarity

In diatomic molecules containing the same element (e.g. hydrogen, H_2, oxygen, O_2, or nitrogen, N_2) the electron pair(s) will be shared equally as both atoms exert an identical attraction. However, when the atoms are different the more electronegative atom exerts a greater attraction for the electron pair(s). One end of the bond will thus be more electron rich than the other end, resulting in a bond dipole (polar bond). The relatively small difference in charge is represented by using δ+ and δ−, or by using a vector, ⟼ with the arrow pointing to the negative pole. Electronegativity values for each element can be found in section 9 of the IB data booklet. Generally, the values increase across a period and decrease down a group. Carbon has a slightly higher value than hydrogen but the difference is quite small, so the C−H bond has little polarity.

Molecular polarity

Whether a molecule is polar, or not, depends both on the relative electronegativities of the atoms in the molecule (bond polarity) and on its shape. If individual bonds are polar, then it does not necessarily follow that the molecule will be polar. There may be no resultant dipole as all the individual dipoles may cancel out.

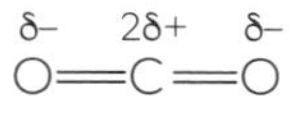

non-polar
(resultant dipole zero)

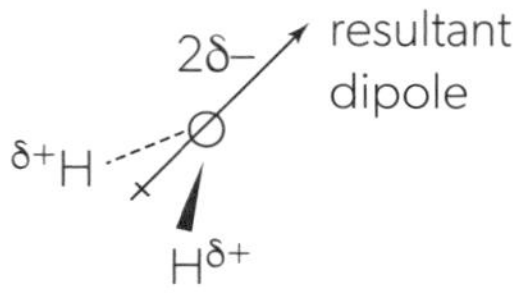

polar

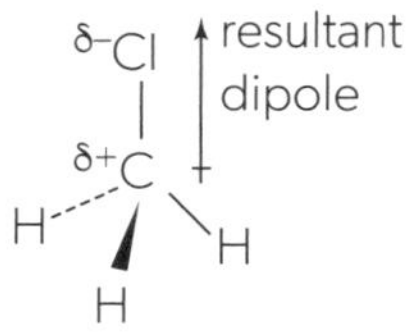

polar

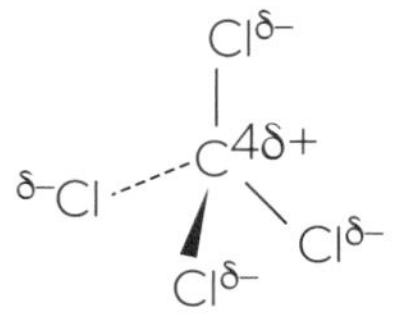

non-polar
(resultant dipole zero)

Covalent network structures of carbon and silicon

Allotropes of carbon

Allotropes occur when an element can exist in different crystalline forms. Because they have different bonding and structural patterns, allotropes of the same element have different chemical and physical properties. Allotropes of carbon include diamond, graphite, fullerenes, and graphene.

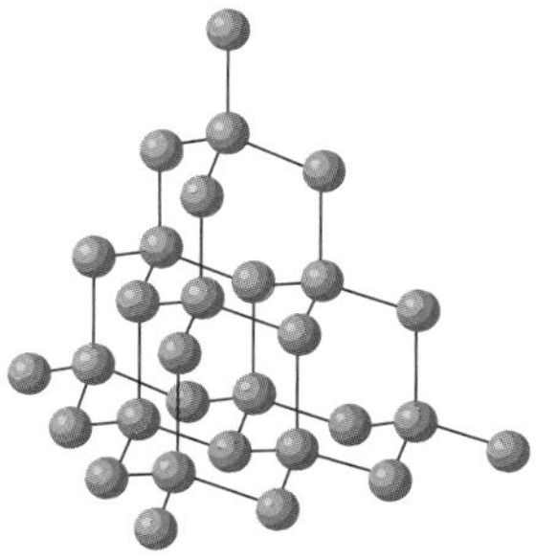

▲ diamond

In diamond, each carbon atom forms four single covalent bonds to four other carbon atoms to form a giant tetrahedral covalent structure, with bond angles of 109.5°. The C–C bond length is 1.54×10^{-10} m. All the bonds are equally strong, so diamond is exceptionally hard and has a very high melting point. All the electrons in diamond are localized, so it does not conduct electricity.

In graphite, each carbon atom has three very strong bonds to three other carbon atoms to give layers of hexagonal rings where the bond angle between the carbon atoms is 120° and the C–C bond length is 1.42×10^{-10} m. There are only very weak attractive forces between the layers and the distance between the layers is 3.41×10^{-10} m. The layers can slide over each other, so graphite is an excellent lubricant and feels waxy to the touch. Like diamond, graphite has a very high melting point. The electrons between the layers are delocalized, so graphite is a good conductor of electricity.

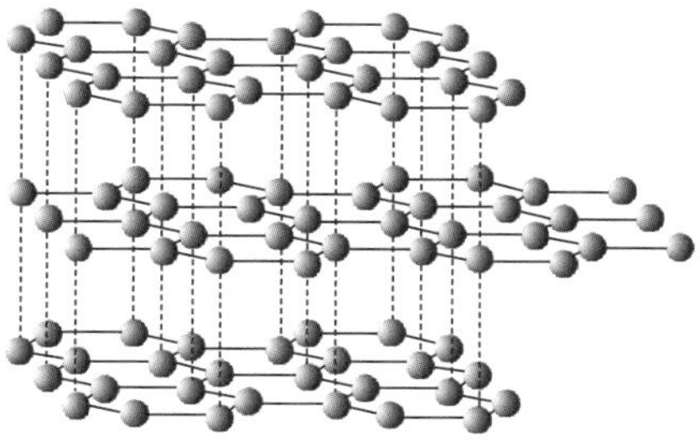

▲ graphite

Graphene is a single layer of hexagonally arranged carbon atoms, i.e. it is essentially a form of graphite which is just one atom thick. It is extremely light, functions as a semiconductor, and is 200 times stronger than steel. In 2012, the Nobel Prize for Physics was awarded for discovering graphene and, more recently, chemists have developed a new magnetic form of graphene which is called graphone.

Fullerenes are large spheroidal molecules consisting of a hollow cage of sixty or more carbon atoms. For example, the first fullerene discovered was buckminsterfullerene, C_{60}. Buckminsterfullerene consists of sixty carbon atoms arranged in hexagons and pentagons to give a geodesic spherical structure similar to a football. The branch of science looking at fullerenes is called nanotechnology.

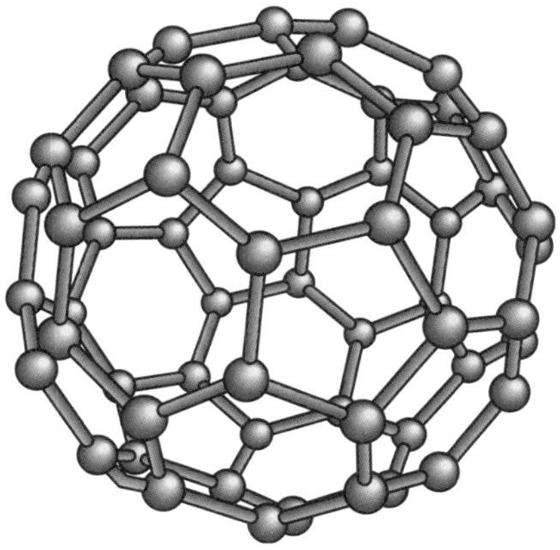

▲ buckminsterfullerene, C_{60}

Silicon and silicon dioxide

Like carbon, silicon is also in group 14 and contains four valence electrons. It is a crystalline solid with a blue-grey metallic lustre and has the same giant tetrahedral covalent structure as diamond. The Si–Si bond length is 2.32×10^{-10} m and silicon is a hard brittle solid with a high melting point (although this is lower than that of diamond). Silicon is a metalloid and acts as a semiconductor.

Silicon dioxide, SiO_2, which is also known as silica, is found in nature as quartz, and is the main component of sand. Silicon dioxide can form a giant tetrahedral covalent structure similar to diamond and silicon. It is also very hard and has a high melting point. As it contains no delocalized electrons, it does not conduct electricity.

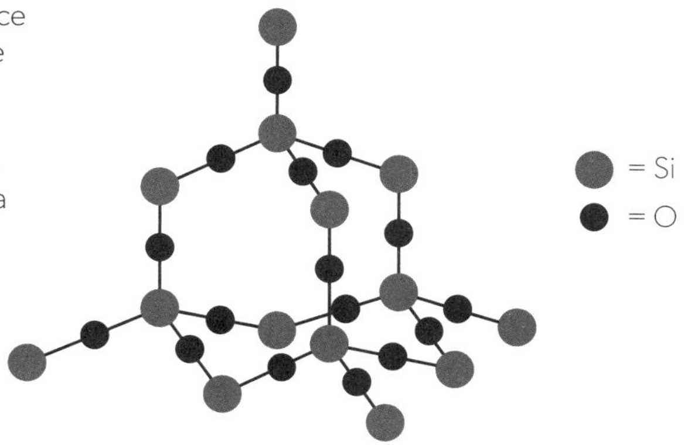

▲ silicon dioxide, SiO_2

Intermolecular forces

Van der Waals forces

The covalent bonds between atoms *within* a molecule are very strong. The forces of attraction *between* the molecules are much weaker. The strength of these intermolecular forces depends upon the size and polarity of the molecules. Be careful with the terminology. The weakest intermolecular forces are called London dispersion forces. This description refers to instantaneous induced dipole–induced dipole forces that exist between any atoms or groups of atoms and should only be used to describe the attractive forces between non-polar entities. A more general, more inclusive, term is van der Waals forces, which include dipole–induced dipole and dipole–dipole forces of attraction as well as London dispersion forces.

London dispersion forces

Even in non-polar molecules, the electrons can at any one moment be unevenly spread. This produces a temporary instantaneous dipole which can induce another dipole in a neighbouring particle, resulting in a weak attraction between the two particles. London dispersion forces increase with increasing mass.

	F_2	Cl_2	Br_2	I_2
M_r	38.0	70.9	160	254
B. pt / °C	−188	−34.0	58.0	183

increasing London dispersion forces →

	CH_4	C_2H_6	C_3H_8	C_4H_{10}
M_r	16.0	30.0	44.0	58.0
B. pt / °C	−162	−88.6	−42.2	−0.5

Dipole–dipole forces

Polar molecules are attracted to each other by electrostatic forces. Although still relatively weak, the attraction is stronger than London dispersion forces.

non-polar polar

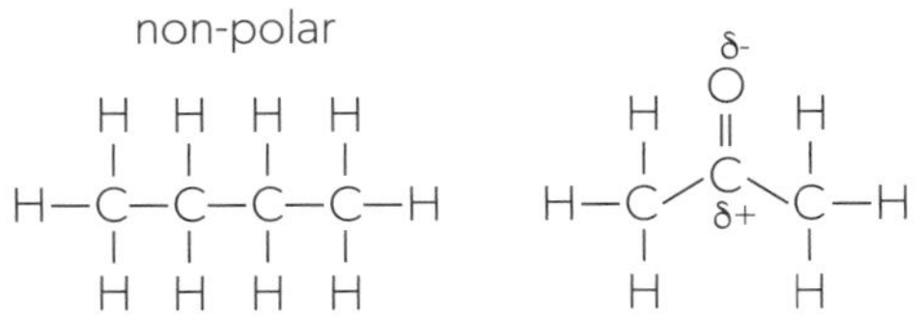

butane M_r = 58
b. pt −0.5°C

propanone M_r = 58
b. pt 56.2°C

identical masses (different intermolecular forces)

Dipole–induced dipole forces

Dipole–induced dipole attractive forces are weak attractive forces that occur between a polar molecule and a non-polar molecule. The polar molecule (such as water) disturbs the arrangement of electrons in the non-polar molecule, inducing a temporary dipole. Dipole–induced dipole forces are generally stronger than London dispersion forces but weaker than dipole–dipole forces of attraction.

Hydrogen bonding

Hydrogen bonding occurs when hydrogen is covalently bonded directly to a small highly electronegative element, such as fluorine, oxygen, or nitrogen. As the electron pair is drawn away from the hydrogen atom by the electronegative element, all that remains is the proton in the nucleus, as hydrogen has no inner electrons. The proton attracts a non-bonding pair of electrons from the F, N, or O atom, resulting in a much stronger dipole–dipole attraction. Water has a much higher boiling point than the other group 16 hydrides because the hydrogen bonding between water molecules is much stronger than the dipole–dipole bonding in the other hydrides.

A similar trend is seen in the hydrides of group 15 and group 17.

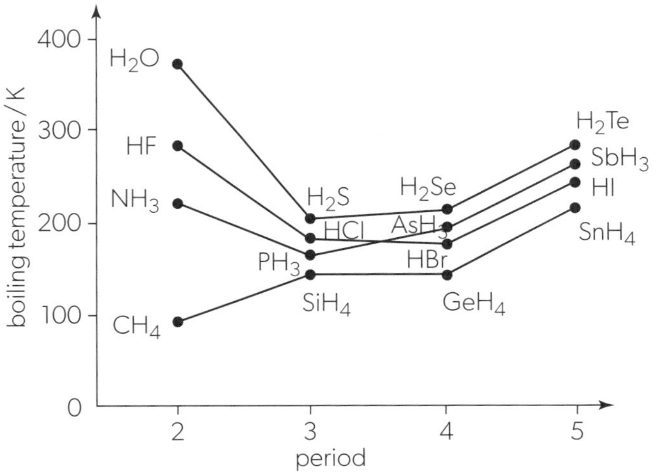

Hydrogen bonds between the molecules in ice result in a very open structure. When ice melts the molecules can move closer to each other, so that water has its maximum density at 4°C.

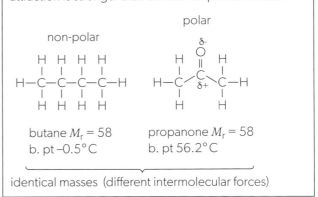

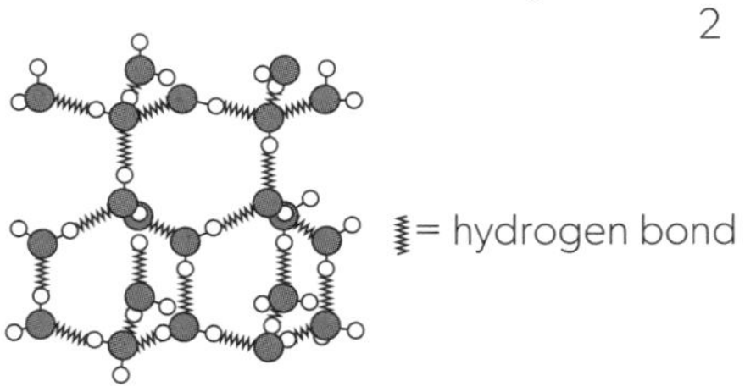

the ice lattice

Physical properties of covalent compounds

Melting and boiling points

When a liquid turns into a gas, the attractive forces between the particles are completely broken. This means that boiling point is a good indication of the strength of intermolecular forces. When solids melt, the crystal structure is broken down, but there are still some attractive forces between the particles. Melting points do give an indication of the strength of intermolecular forces but they are also determined by the way the particles are packed in the crystal state and they are affected by impurities. Impurities weaken the structure and result in lower melting points.

Covalent bonds are very strong, so macromolecular covalent structures have extremely high melting and boiling points. For example, diamond, which has a giant tetrahedral structure, melts in the region of 4000°C and silicon dioxide, SiO_2, which has a similar structure, melts at over 1600°C. Graphite has very strong bonds between the carbon atoms in its hexagonal layers and has a similar melting point to diamond.

The melting and boiling points of simple covalent molecules depend on the type of forces of attraction between the molecules. These follow the order: hydrogen bonding > dipole–dipole > London dispersion forces

The weaker the attractive forces, the more volatile the substance. For example, propane, ethanal, and ethanol have similar molar masses but there is a considerable difference in their melting points.

Compound	propane 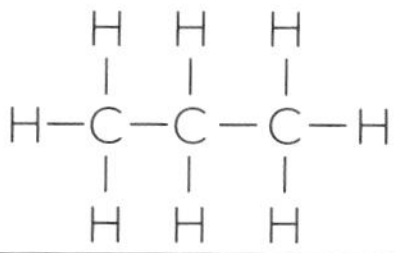	ethanal 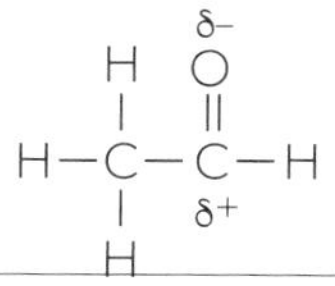	ethanol 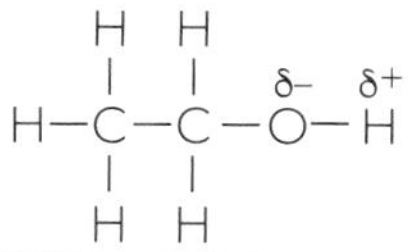
M_r	44	44	46
M. pt / °C	–42.2	20.8	78.5
Polarity	non-polar	polar	polar
Bonding type	London dispersion	dipole–dipole	hydrogen bonding

Solubility

"Like tends to dissolve like". Polar substances tend to dissolve in polar solvents, such as water, whereas non-polar substances tend to dissolve in non-polar solvents, such as heptane or tetrachloromethane. Organic molecules often contain a polar head and a non-polar carbon chain tail. As the non-polar carbon chain length increases in a homologous series, the molecules become less soluble in water.

CH_3OH
C_2H_5OH
C_3H_7OH
C_4H_9OH
↓ decreasing solubility in water

Ethanol is a good solvent for other substances as it contains both polar and non-polar ends. Ethanol is completely miscible with water as it can hydrogen bond to water molecules.

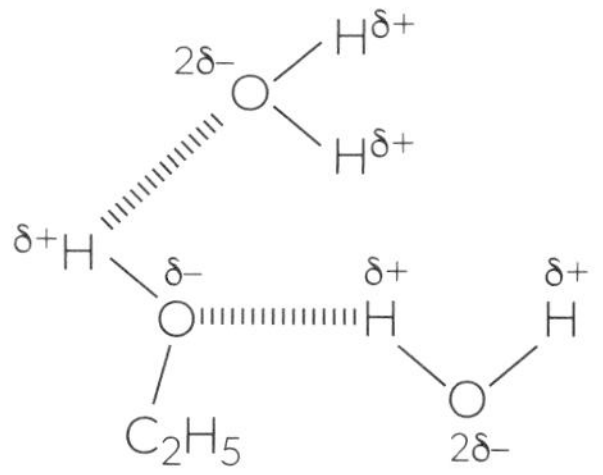

Conductivity

For conduction to occur, the substance must possess electrons or ions that are free to move. Covalent compounds, with a few exceptions such as graphite, are poor conductors as the electrons are generally not free to move. Metals (and graphite) contain delocalized electrons and are excellent conductors. Molten ionic salts also conduct electricity, but are chemically decomposed in the process. If all the electrons are held in fixed positions (as in diamond) or in simple molecules, no electrical conductivity occurs.

When a potential gradient is applied to a metal, the delocalized electrons can move towards the positive end of the potential gradient, carrying charge.

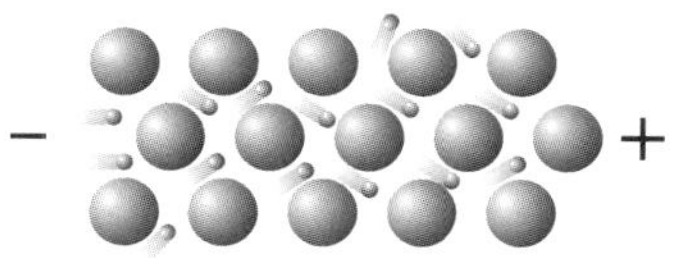

When an ionic compound melts, the ions are free to move to oppositely charged electrodes. Note: in molten ionic compounds, ions carry the charge, not free electrons.

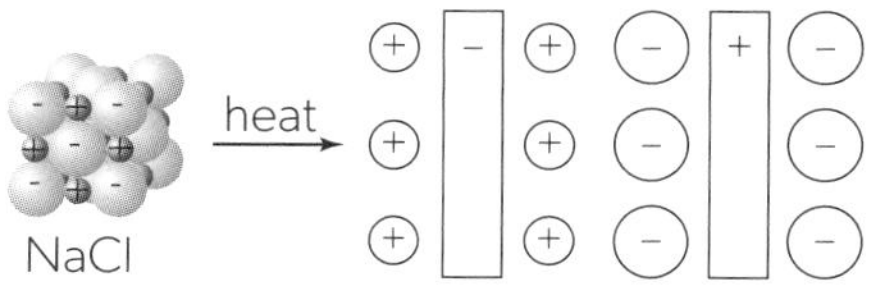

The metallic model

Metallic bonding

The valence electrons in metals become detached from the individual atoms so that a metal consists of a closely packed lattice of positive ions (cations) in a "sea" of delocalized electrons. A metallic bond is the attraction that two neighbouring positive ions have for the delocalized electrons between them.

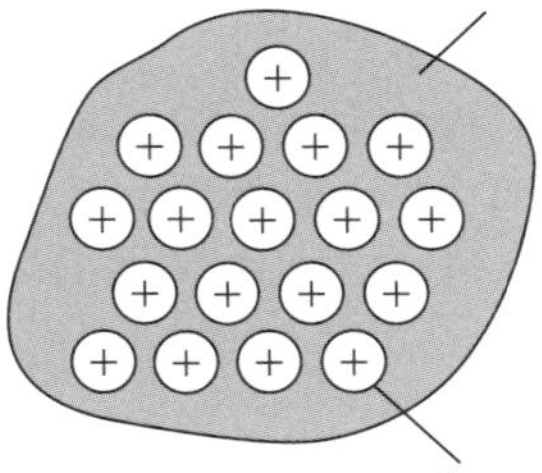

Generally, the strength of a metallic bond depends on the charge of the ions and the radius of the metal ion.

Metals are malleable, that is, they can be bent and reshaped under pressure. They are also ductile, which means that they can be drawn out into a wire.

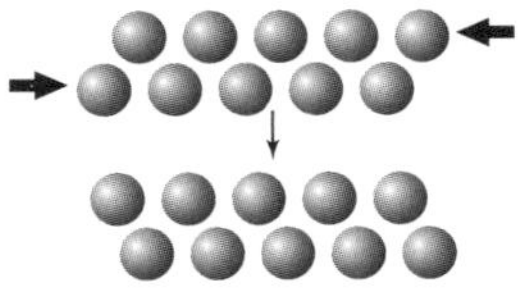

Metals are malleable and ductile because the closely packed layers of positive ions can slide over each other without breaking more bonds than are made.

Melting point of metals

Although most metals tend to have quite high melting points, mercury is a liquid at room temperature and the group 1 elements (alkali metals) all melt below 181°C. The trend in group 1 clearly follows the pattern that the smaller the metal ion formed when the valence electrons delocalize, the stronger the metallic bond and the higher the melting point.

	Li	Na	K	Rb	Cs
M. pt / °C	180.5	97.79	63.38	39.30	28.44

However, this logic holds true for only part of period 3 (Na to Al), even though the charge on the ion is increasing at the same time as the size of the ion is decreasing.

	Na	Mg	Al
M. pt / °C	97.79	650.0	660.3

The trend breaks down in group 14 as tin, which has a smaller ionic radius than lead, has a lower boiling point.

	Sn	Pb
M. pt / °C	231.9	327.5

This is because the melting point does not only depend on the electron density (the size and charge of the ion formed) when the valence electrons are delocalized but also on the way in which the atoms are arranged in the solid metal.

AHL Transition elements

Transition elements (sometimes referred to as transition metals) are covered more fully in the chapter on Periodicity. They have several distinguishing properties, such as the ability to exhibit variable oxidation states. They are all metals and contain an incomplete d level in one or more of their oxidation states. When they become ionized, they lose their ns electron(s) before they lose their $(n-1)$d electrons, so their first few ionization energies are relatively low. This means that, compared with many other metals, there are more electrons available to become delocalized. The radius of the ion formed is also relatively small, so the attraction between the charged metal ions and the delocalized electrons in the metal is high. This explain why they tend to have much higher melting points than metals in groups 1, 2, 13, and 14. The presence of delocalized electrons, which can move through the metal, also explains why they are good conductors of both heat and electricity.

▼ Melting points of first row transition elements

	(Sc)	Ti	V	Cr	Mn	Fe	Co	Ni	Cu
Electron configuration [Ar]	$4s^23d^1$	$4s^23d^2$	$4s^23d^3$	$4s^13d^5$	$4s^23d^5$	$4s^23d^6$	$4s^23d^7$	$4s^23d^8$	$4s^13d^{10}$
M. pt / °C	1541	1670	1910	1907	1246	1538	1495	1455	1085

AHL Resonance structures and benzene

Resonance structures

When writing the Lewis formulas for some molecules or ions, it is possible to write more than one correct structure. For example, ozone can be written as:

These two structures are known as resonance structures. They are extreme forms of the true structure, known as a **resonance hybrid structure**, which lies somewhere between the two. Evidence that this is true comes from bond lengths, as the bond lengths between the oxygen atoms in ozone are both the same and are intermediate between the length of an O=O double bond and an O–O single bond. Resonance structures are usually shown with a double headed arrow between them. Other common compounds that can be written using resonance structures are shown here.

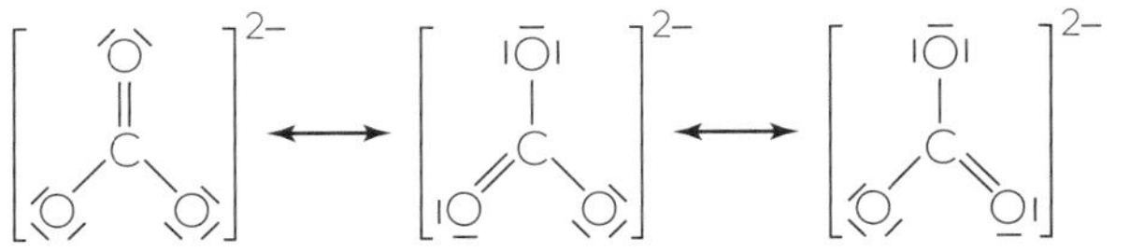

carbonate ion

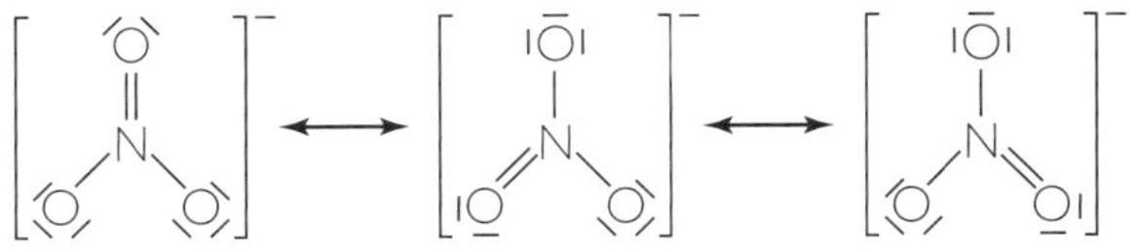

nitrate ion

ethanoate ion

Evidence for resonance structure of benzene

The simplest aromatic compound (arene) is benzene, C_6H_6. The Kekulé structure of benzene (cyclohexa-1,3,5-triene) contains three double bonds (see right).

There is both physical and chemical evidence to support the fact that benzene does not contain three separate double bonds but exists as a resonance hybrid structure with delocalized electrons. The two resonance structure forms are shown on the right.

1. The C–C bond lengths are all the same and have a value of 0.140 nm, which lies between the values for C–C (0.154 nm) and C=C (0.134 nm).

2. The enthalpy of hydrogenation of cyclohexene is –120 kJ mol^{-1}.

   $$+ H_2 \xrightarrow[180\,°C]{Ni} \qquad \Delta H^\ominus = -120 \text{ kJ mol}^{-1}$$

   If benzene simply had the cyclohexa-1,3,5-triene structure with three double bonds, the enthalpy change of hydrogenation of benzene would be expected to be equal to three times the enthalpy change of hydrogenation of cyclohexene, i.e. –360 kJ mol^{-1}.

   However, the experimentally determined value for benzene is –210 kJ mol^{-1}.

   The difference of 150 kJ mol^{-1} is the extra energy associated with the delocalization. This is known as the delocalization energy or the resonance energy.

   $$+ 3H_2 \longrightarrow \qquad \Delta H^\ominus = -210 \text{ kJ mol}^{-1}$$

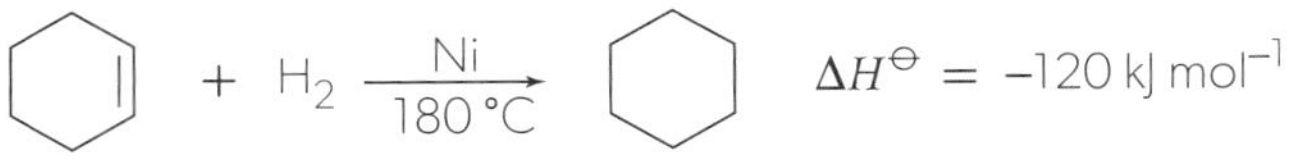

3. Only one isomer exists for 1,2-disubstituted benzene compounds. If there were simply alternate double bonds, then two isomers would exist.

   ◀ The two isomers of 1,2-dichlorobenzene which would be expected if benzene has the cyclohexa-1,3,5-triene structure

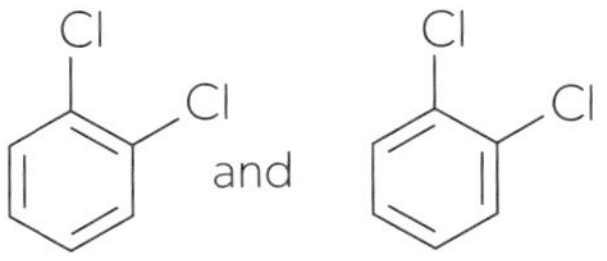

4. If benzene had three normal double bonds, it would be expected to readily undergo addition reactions. In fact, it will only undergo addition reactions with difficulty and more commonly undergoes substitution reactions. For example, with bromine it forms bromobenzene and hydrogen bromide rather than 1,2-dibromobenzene.

   $$+ Br_2 \xrightarrow{AlBr_3 \text{ catalyst}} \qquad + HBr$$

The actual bonding in benzene is best described by the delocalization of electrons. For this reason, benzene is often represented by a hexagonal ring with a circle in the middle of it.

AHL Formal charge and molecular orbitals

Formal charge

Formal charge is a technique used in chemistry which is based on a false assumption but can be useful for determining which of several potential Lewis formulas is preferred when two or more are possible. It assumes that all atoms in a molecule or ion have the same electronegativity (the false assumption).

Formal charge = (number of valence electrons) – (number of non-bonding electrons) – ½ (number of bonding electrons)

FC = V – N – ½B. Note that this formula is not given in the IB data booklet.

The preferred formula (or structure) is the one where the individual atoms have the lowest possible formal charge.

For example, consider two possible structures for carbon dioxide, both of which obey the octet rule.

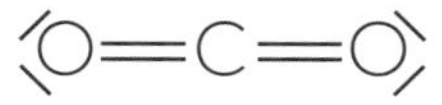

(0) (0) (0)

(+1) (0) (−1)

Formal charges

C = 4 – 0 – (½ × 8) = 0
O = 6 – 4 – (½ × 4) = 0

C = 4 – 0 – (½ × 8) = 0
O = 6 – 2 – (½ × 6) = +1 (O with triple bond)
O = 6 – 6 – (½ × 2) = –1 (O with single bond)

Both give a total formal charge of zero, but the preferred formula is the first one with the two double bonds as the individual atoms have the lowest formal charges.

Combination of atomic orbitals to form molecular orbitals

Although the Lewis representation is a useful model to represent covalent bonds, it does make the false assumption that all the valence electrons are the same. A more advanced model of bonding considers the combination of atomic orbitals to form **molecular orbitals**.

σ bonds

A σ (sigma) bond is formed when two atomic orbitals on different atoms overlap along a line drawn through the two nuclei. This occurs when two s orbitals overlap, an s orbital overlaps with a p orbital, or when two p orbitals overlap "head on".

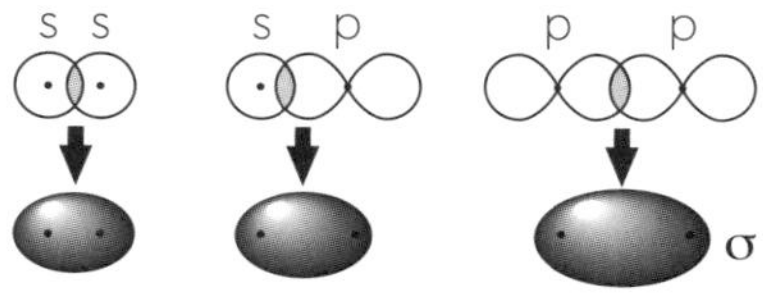

π bonds

A π (pi) bond is formed when two p orbitals overlap "sideways on". The overlap now occurs above and below the line drawn through the two nuclei. A π bond is made up of two regions of electron density.

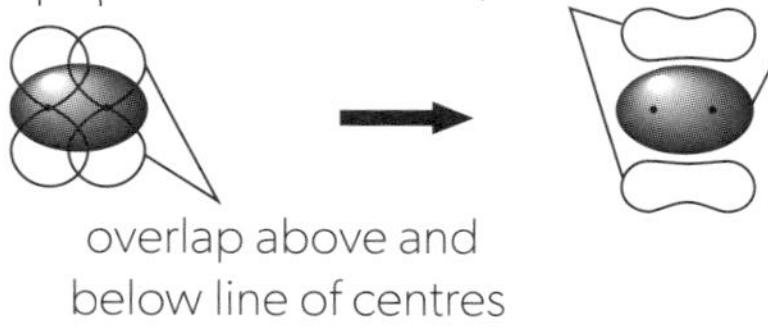

Delocalization of electrons

Resonance can also be explained by the delocalization of electrons. For example, in the ethanoate ion the carbon atom and the two oxygen atoms each have a p orbital containing one electron after the σ bonds have been formed. Instead of forming just one double bond between the carbon atom and one of the oxygen atoms, the electrons can delocalize over all three atoms. This is energetically more favourable than forming just one double bond.

Delocalization can occur whenever alternate double and single bonds occur between carbon atoms, such as in benzene.

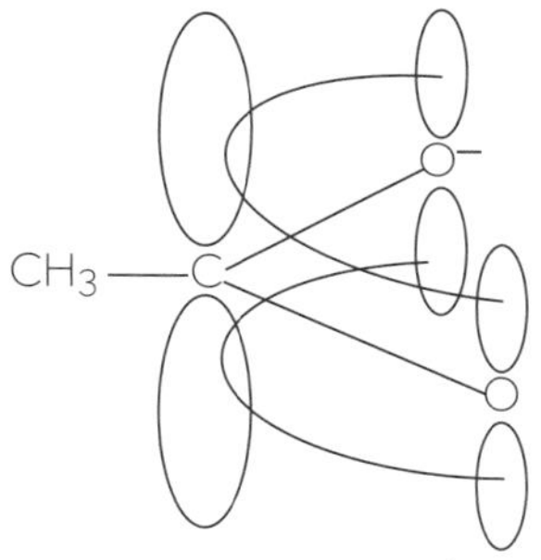

ethanoate ion shown as

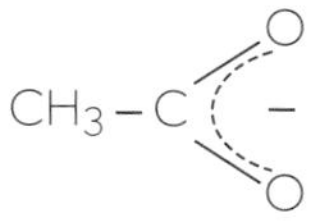

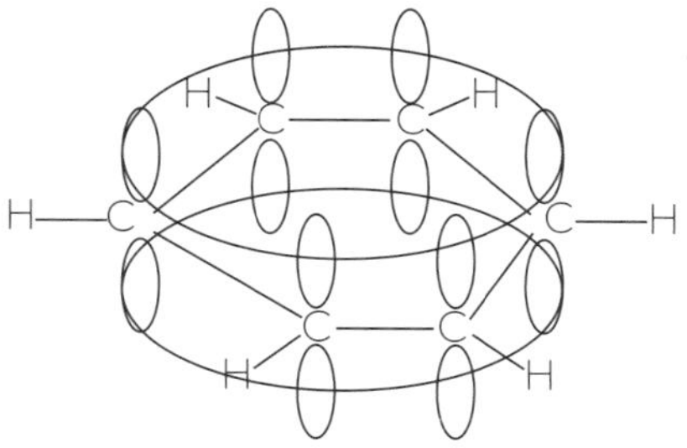

benzene ring shown as

AHL Hybridization (1)

sp^3 hybridization

Methane provides a good example of sp^3 hybridization. Methane contains four equal C–H bonds pointing towards the corners of a tetrahedron with bond angles of 109.5°. A free carbon atom has the configuration $1s^2 2s^2 2p^2$. It cannot retain this configuration in methane. Not only are there only two unpaired electrons, but the p orbitals are at 90° to each other and will not give bond angles of 109.5° when they overlap with the s orbitals on the hydrogen atoms.

When the carbon atom in methane bonds, one of its 2s electrons is promoted to a 2p orbital and then the 2s and three 2p orbitals hybridize to form four new hybrid orbitals. These four new orbitals arrange themselves to be as mutually repulsive as possible, i.e. tetrahedrally. Four equal σ bonds can then be formed with the four hydrogen atoms.

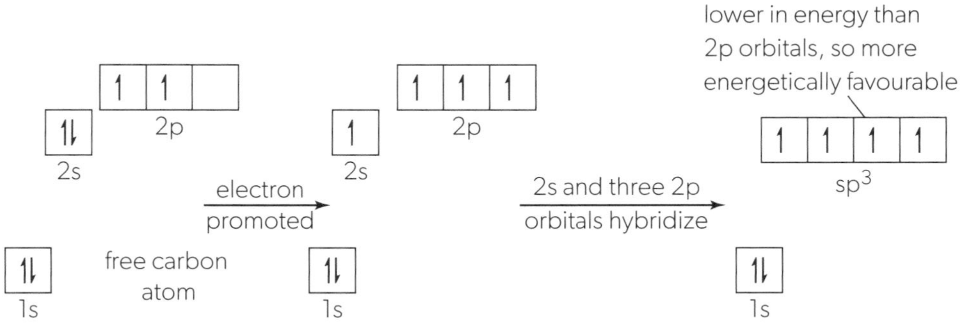

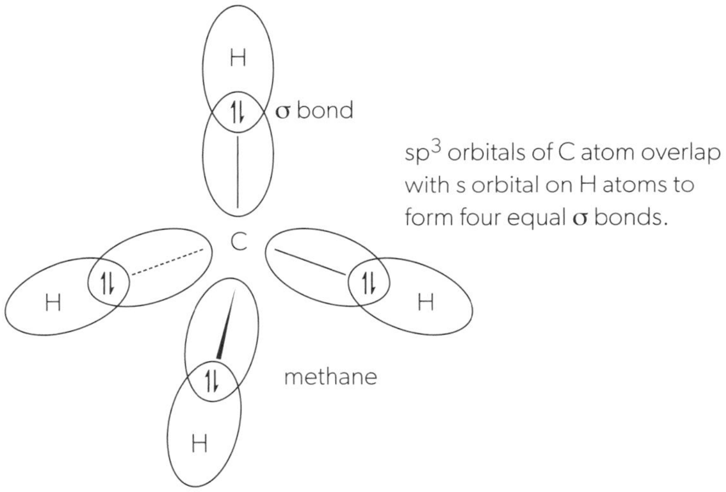

sp^2 hybridization

sp^2 hybridization occurs in ethene (C_2H_4). After a 2s electron on the carbon atom is promoted, the 2s orbital hybridizes with two of the 2p orbitals to form three new planar hybrid orbitals with a bond angle of 120° between them. These can form σ bonds with the hydrogen atoms and also a σ bond between the two carbon atoms. Each carbon atom now has one electron remaining in a 2p orbital. These can overlap to form a π bond. Ethene is thus a planar molecule with a region of electron density above and below the plane.

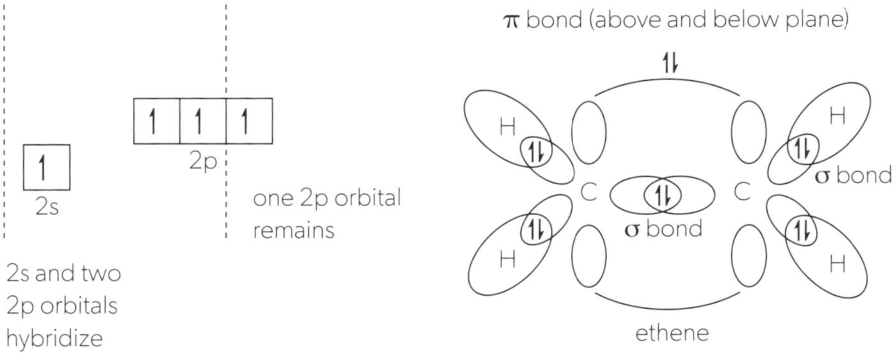

AHL Hybridization (2)

sp hybridization

sp hybridization occurs when the 2s orbital hybridizes with just one of the 2p orbitals to form two new linear sp hybrid orbitals with an angle of 180° between them. The remaining two p orbitals on each carbon atom then overlap to form two π bonds. An example of a molecule with sp hybridization is ethyne.

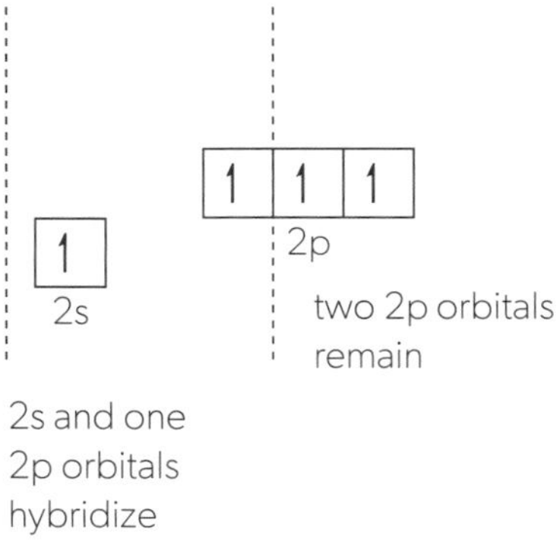

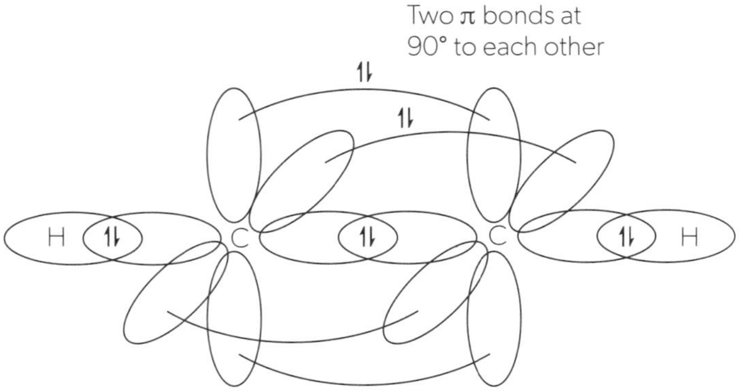

Predicting the type of bonding and hybridization in molecules

In carbon compounds containing single, double, or triple bonds, the numbers of each different type of bond (σ or π) and the type of hybridization shown by each carbon atom can be deduced.

For example, Vitamin A contains 5 C=C double bonds, 15 C–C bonds, 29 C–H bonds, 1 C–O bond, and 1 O–H bond.

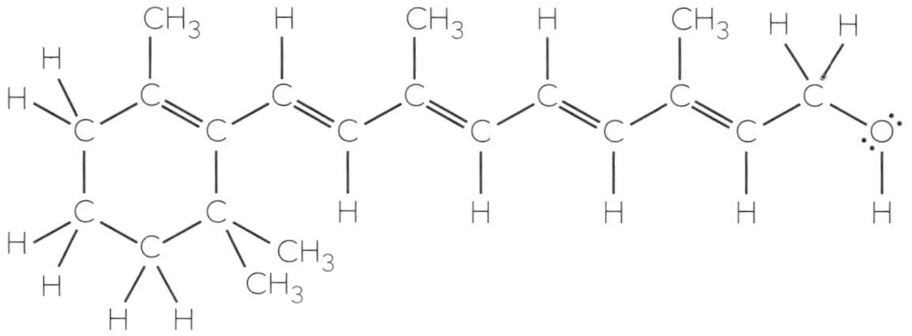

Each single bond is a σ bond and each double bond contains one σ and one π bond, so there is a total of 51 σ bonds and 5 π bonds in the molecule. Each carbon atom either side of a double bond is sp^2 hybridized, so 10 of the carbon atoms are sp^2 hybridized. The remaining 10 carbon atoms are sp^3 hybridized. The oxygen atom, which has four pairs of electrons around it, is also sp^3 hybridized.

Relationship between type of hybridization, Lewis formula and molecular shapes

Molecular shapes can be determined either by using the VSEPR theory or by knowing the type of hybridization. Hybridization can take place between any s and p orbital in the same energy level and is not restricted to carbon compounds. If the shape and bond angles are known from using Lewis formulas, then the type of hybridization can be deduced. Similarly, if the type of hybridization is known, the shape and bond angles can be deduced.

Hybridization	Regular bond angle	Examples
sp^3	109.5°	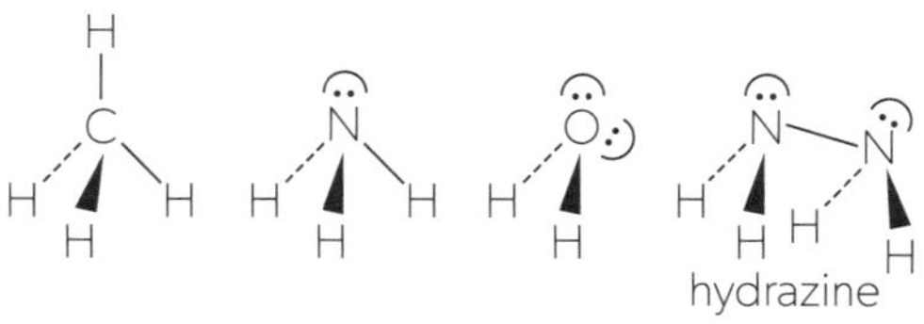
sp^2	120°	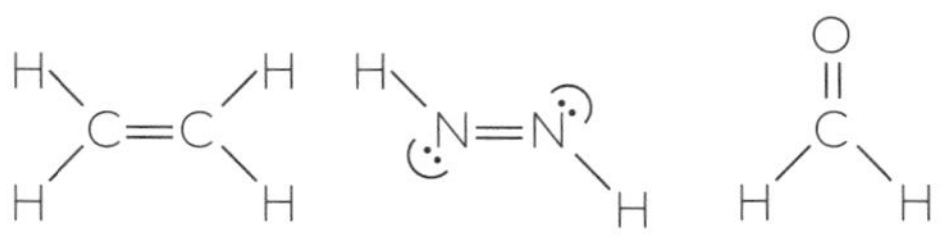
sp	180°	H—C≡C—H (:N≡N:)

Bonding in materials

Triangular bonding diagrams

The key to understanding the macroscopic properties of a material is the identity of the type or types of bonding present in the material. Metallic substances tend to have very different properties to non-metals and the properties of ionic compounds differ greatly from covalent compounds. The degree of covalent, ionic, or metallic character in a compound can be deduced from its position on a triangular bonding diagram—also known as a Van Arkel–Ketelaar diagram. In reality, the chemical bonding in compounds is generally a continuum between different bonding types. Bond triangles show the three extremes of bonding in terms of electronegativity difference (ionicity) plotted against the average electronegativity (localization) for binary compounds. The three extreme cases of types of bonding—ionic, covalent, and metallic—are found at the vertices of an equilateral triangle.

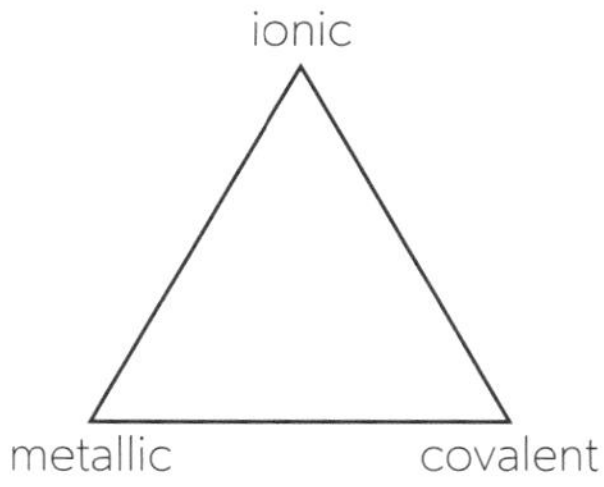

These three extreme cases are characterized by caesium (metallic), fluorine (covalent), and caesium fluoride (ionic). Other materials can be placed around the triangle based on their differences in electronegativities. The bottom side of the triangle, from metallic (low electronegativity) to covalent (high electronegativity) is for elements and compounds with varying degrees of delocalization and directionality in the bond. Pure metals with only delocalized bonding occur on the extreme left (metallic corner) and, at the other extreme, are covalent compounds where all the electron orbitals overlap in a particular direction. The left side of the triangle (from ionic to metallic) is for delocalized bonds with varying electronegativity difference and the right side shows the change from covalent to ionic. The diagram below shows that compounds such as silicon tetrachloride and carbon dioxide are very much covalent. Silicon dioxide is polar covalent but a compound such as aluminium chloride lies very close to the border between covalent and ionic. Similarly, lithium oxide has a high degree of ionic character, whereas lithium hydride lies close to the border between ionic and metallic.

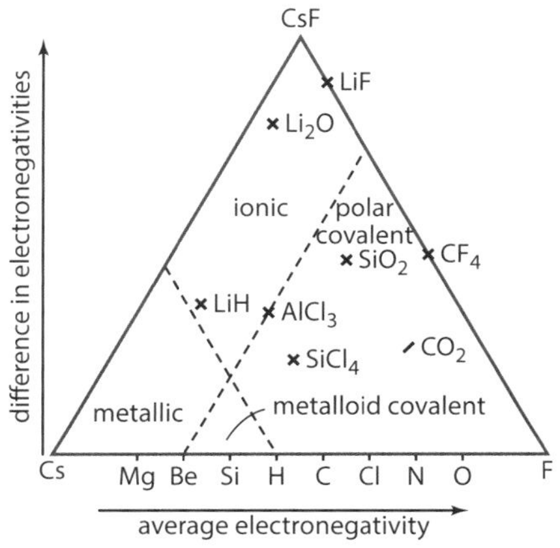

Alloys

Alloys are sometimes termed metallic solid solutions. They are homogeneous mixtures that are usually made up of two or more metals, although steel is an alloy of iron and carbon. Some common alloys are brass, bronze, solder, pewter, and amalgams.

Alloy	Principal metal	Added metal(s)
brass	copper	zinc
bronze	copper	tin
solder	lead	tin (some may have more tin than lead)
pewter	tin	copper, antimony, bismuth, or lead
amalgams	mercury	e.g. tin, silver, gold, or sodium

The addition of another metal to a metallic element alters its properties. The added metals are likely to have a different radius and may have a different charge and so distort the structure of the original metal as the bonding is less directional. One obvious example of this is that alloys may have lower melting points than their component metals. For example, before copper and plastic were used for water piping, lead tended to be used (the origin of the word plumber). Lead melts at 328 °C and, when pipes were being joined or repaired, there was a danger of melting the actual pipe if too much heat was employed. Solder has a much lower melting point (typically 180–190 °C) and can be used to weld lead pipes together or to secure wires to terminals in an electrical circuit.

Generally, alloys are less ductile and less malleable than pure metals as the added impurities disturb the lattice. This also tends to make alloys harder than the pure metals they are derived from. For example, aluminium is a soft, ductile, and malleable metal. When it is alloyed with another soft metal, such as copper, the resulting aluminium alloy is much harder and stronger and yet still retains much of its low density. Small amounts of carbon added to iron produce steel, an alloy with a high tensile strength. If chromium is also added, the alloy is stainless steel, which has a much increased resistance to corrosion.

Polymers

Types of polymer and structural features

Polymers consist of many repeating units (monomers) joined together to form macromolecules with high molar masses. This theory was first proposed by Herman Staudinger in 1920 and has since been substantiated by X-ray diffraction and scanning tunnelling electron microscopy. By understanding the molecular structure of polymers, chemists have been able to manipulate their properties and develop new polymers.

Polymers can be subdivided into thermoplastics and thermosets. Many alkenes polymerize to form thermoplastics, which soften when heated and harden when cooled so that they can be remoulded each time they are heated. Thermosetting polymers, such as Bakelite, polyurethanes, and vulcanized rubber, form prepolymers in a soft solid or viscous state. These change irreversibly into hardened thermosets by curing so that, once shaped, they cannot be remoulded. Some polymers, such as rubber, are flexible polymers known as elastomers. Elastomers can be deformed under force but return to nearly their original shape once the stress is released. Generally, the longer the chain length of a polymer, the higher the strength and melting point; cross-linking (or branching) and the orientation of the substituent groups can also affect particular properties.

Addition polymers

Under certain conditions, ethene can undergo addition reactions with itself to form a long-chain polymer containing many thousands (typically 40 000 to 800 000) of carbon atoms. See page 134 for more on addition reactions.

ethene — poly(ethene) (also known as polythene)

These addition reactions can be extended to other substituted alkenes to give a wide variety of different addition polymers.

e.g.

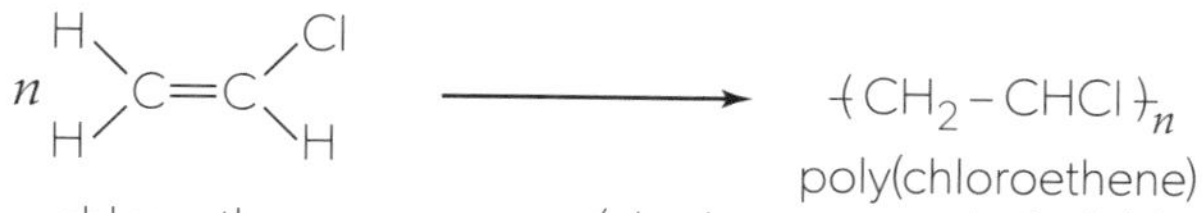

chloroethene — poly(chloroethene) (also known as polyvinylchloride, PVC)

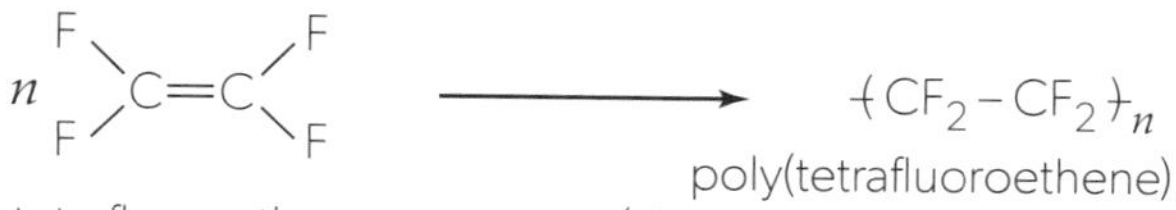

tetrafluoroethene — poly(tetrafluoroethene), PTFE (also known as Teflon or "non-stick")

Two other examples of addition polymers are poly(2-methylpropene) and poly(styrene). Poly(2-methylpropene), which is also known as butyl rubber or polyisobutylene, is a good elastomer with many uses, such as car tyre inner tubes and cling film.

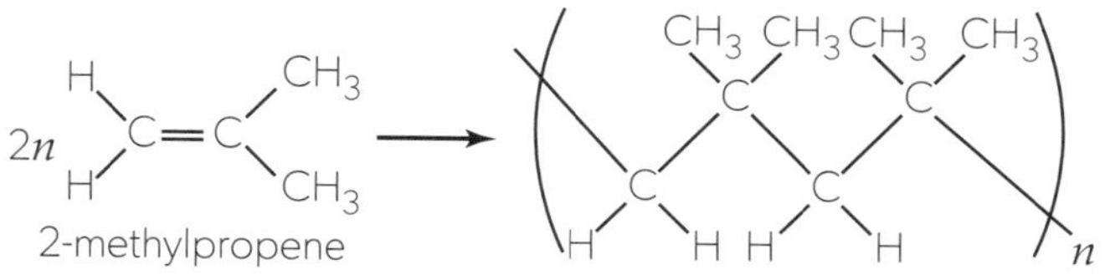

2-methylpropene — poly(2-methylpropene)

Expanded polystyrene, which contains air trapped in the polymer, is a light material that is a good thermal insulator. It is also used in packaging as it has good shock absorbing properties.

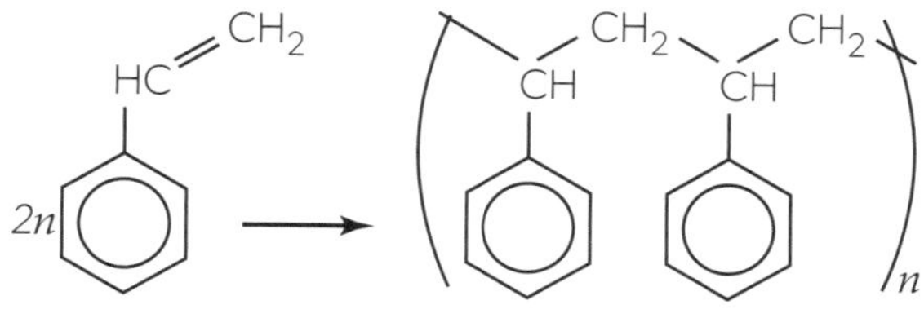

styrene — polystyrene

AHL Condensation polymers

Formation of condensation polymers

Addition polymers are usually made from alkenes whereas condensation polymers are made from monomers that contain at least two reactive functional groups (or the same functional group at least twice). When the monomers condense to form the polymer, small molecules, such as water or hydrogen chloride, are also produced and released.

Polyamides and polyesters are examples of condensation polymers. Nylon is a polyamide, which can be made by condensing diamines with dicarboxylic acids to form an amide link (also known as a peptide bond).

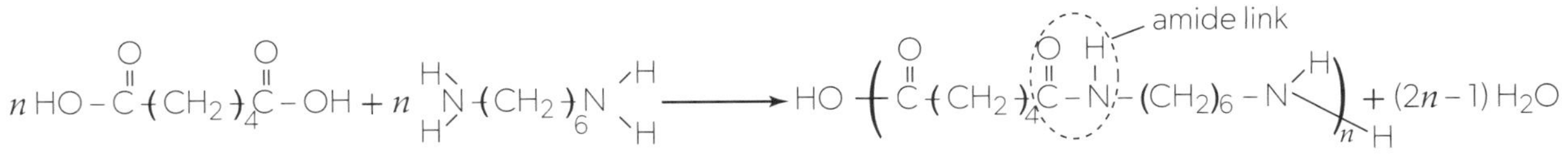

hexane-1, 6-dioic acid 1,6-diaminohexane repeating unit nylon 6,6
(6, 6 because each monomer contains 6 carbon atoms)

Another example of a polyamide is Kevlar, the material from which lightweight bullet-proof vests, composites for motorcycle helmets, and armour are made. It is manufactured by condensing 1,4-diaminobenzene with benzene-1,4–dicarbonyl chloride.

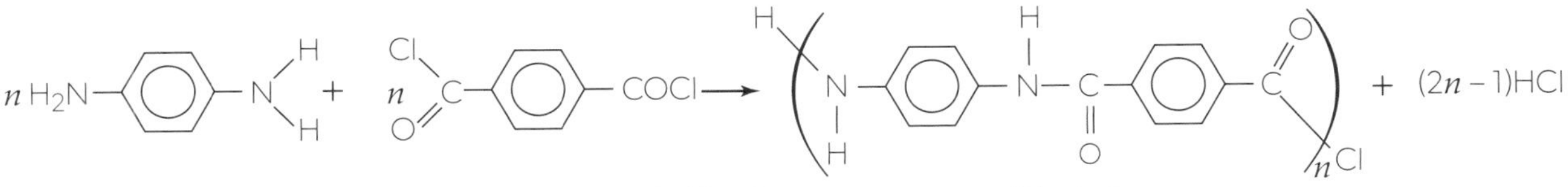

1,4-diaminobenzene benzene-1,4-dicarbonyl chloride "Kevlar"

Because the H atom on the amine group can form hydrogen bonds with the O atom on the carbonyl group it can form cross-links between the polymer chains which explains its considerable protective strength.

An example of a polyester is polyethene terephthalate (known as Terylene or Dacron), which is made from benzene-1,4-dicarboxylic acid and ethane-1,2-diol. It is used for textiles.

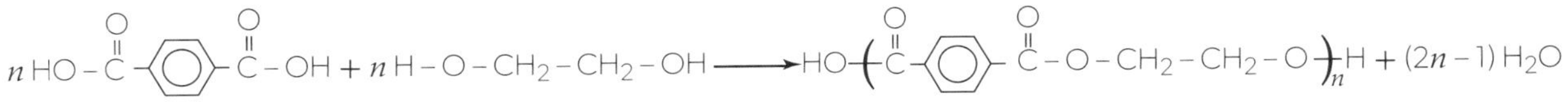

benzene-1,4-dicarboxylic acida ethane-1,2-diol repeating unit "Terylene" or "Dacron"

Biological condensation polymers

Starch and proteins are both examples of condensation polymers that occur in nature. Starch is formed by the condensation of sugar molecules. Proteins are large macromolecules formed by the condensation reactions of 2-amino acids. Each 2-amino acid molecule contains a carboxyl group and an amino group both bonded to the same carbon atom.

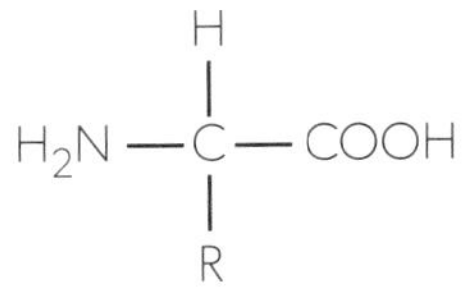

2-amino acid

There are about twenty 2-amino acids that occur naturally. When two 2-amino acids condense, they form a dipeptide. For example, when alanine, $H_2N–CHCH_2–COOH$, and cysteine, $H_2N–CH(CH_2SH)–COOH$, react they can form two different dipeptides and water.

Each dipeptide also contains two reactive groups, so they can undergo further condensation reactions to produce polypeptides. The reactions can be reversed by hydrolysis with water in acidic or alkaline solution.

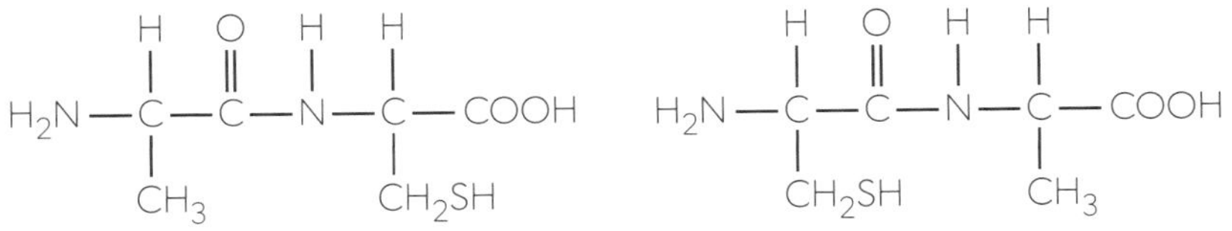

H_2N-Ala-Cys-COOH H_2N-Cys-Ala-COOH

Multiple-choice questions—Bonding and structure

1. What are the correct formulas of the following ions?

	Nitrate	Phosphate	Carbonate	Ammonium
A.	NO_3^-	PO_4^{3-}	CO_3^-	NH_3^+
B.	NO_3^{2-}	PO_3^{2-}	CO_3^{2-}	NH_3^+
C.	NO_3^-	PO_4^{3-}	CO_3^{2-}	NH_4^+
D.	NO_3^{2-}	PO_3^{2-}	CO_3^{2-}	NH_4^+

2. Which is the correct Lewis formula for ethene?

A. 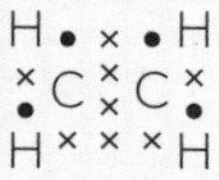

C. 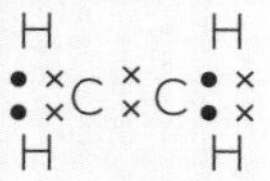

B. 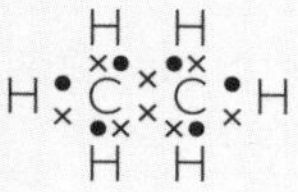

D. 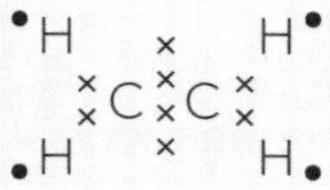

3. Given the following electronegativities, H = 2.2, N = 3.0, O = 3.5, F = 4.0, which bond would be the most polar?

A. O–H in H_2O
C. N–O in NO_2
B. N–F in NF_3
D. N–H in NH_3

4. Which substance is made up of a lattice of positive ions and free-moving electrons?

A. graphite
C. sulfur
B. sodium chloride
D. sodium

5. When CH_4, NH_3, and H_2O, are arranged in order of **increasing** bond angle, what is the correct order?

A. CH_4, NH_3, H_2O
C. NH_3, CH_4, H_2O
B. NH_3, H_2O, CH_4
D. H_2O, NH_3, CH_4

6. Which order is correct when the following compounds are arranged in order of **increasing** melting point?

A. $CH_4 < H_2S < H_2O$
C. $CH_4 < H_2O < H_2S$
B. $H_2S < H_2O < CH_4$
D. $H_2S < CH_4 < H_2O$

7. Which species contain a coordination covalent bond?

I. HCHO
II. CO
III. H_3O^+

A. I and II only
C. II and III only
B. I and III only
D. I, II, and III

8. Which is the correct order for **decreasing** H–N–H bond angles in the species NH_2^-, NH_3, and NH_4^+?

A. NH_3, NH_2^-, NH_4^+
C. NH_2^-, NH_4^+, NH_3
B. NH_4^+, NH_3, NH_2^-
D. NH_2^-, NH_3, NH_4^+

9. Which is the correct order for **increasing** intermolecular forces of attraction?

A. covalent bonds, hydrogen bonds, dipole–dipole, London dispersion forces
B. London dispersion forces, dipole–dipole, hydrogen bonds, covalent bonds
C. London dispersion forces, hydrogen bonds, dipole–dipole, covalent bonds
D. covalent bonds, dipole–dipole, hydrogen bonds, London dispersion forces

10. Which statement best explains why alloys tend to be less malleable than pure metals?

A. The added metal has more valence electrons, which increases the amount of delocalization.
B. The added metal prevents the layers from being drawn out into a wire.
C. The added metal disturbs the lattice so that the layers are less able to slide over each other.
D. The added metal acts as an impurity and so lowers the melting point.

11. Chloroethene, CH_2CHCl, can be polymerized to form poly(chloroethene), which is also known as PVC. Which represents the repeating unit of PVC?

A. –[CHCl–CHCl]–
C. –[CH_2–CHCl]–
B. –[CH=CCl]–
D. –[CH_2–CHCl–CHCl–CH_2]–

12. Which compound has the shortest carbon–carbon bond length?

A. ethane, C_2H_6
C. ethyne, C_2H_2
B. ethene, C_2H_4
D. ethanol, CH_3CH_2OH

13. What is the formula of copper(I) sulfate?

A. Cu_2SO_4
C. $Cu(SO_4)_2$
B. $CuSO_4$
D. CuS

14. Which compound has the lowest boiling point?

A. H_2O
C. HF
B. CH_4
D. NH_3

15. Which does **not** contain a bond angle of 120°?

A. graphene
C. graphite
B. boron trifluoride
D. nitrogen trichloride

16. Which three species are located at the three corners of the bonding triangle?

A. Na, NaCl, and Cl_2
C. K, KF, and F_2
B. Cs, CsF, and F
D. Na, K, and Cs

AHL

17. Which of the following species contains at least one atom that is sp^2 hybridized?
   A. hydrogen cyanide, HCN
   B. 2-methylpropane, $CH_3CH(CH_3)CH_3$
   C. propanone, CH_3COCH_3
   D. ethanol, CH_3CH_2OH

18. How many σ and π bonds are present in propanal, CH_3CH_2CHO?
   A. 8σ and 2π
   B. 8σ and 1π
   C. 5σ and 1π
   D. 9σ and 1π

19. Which species have delocalized electrons?

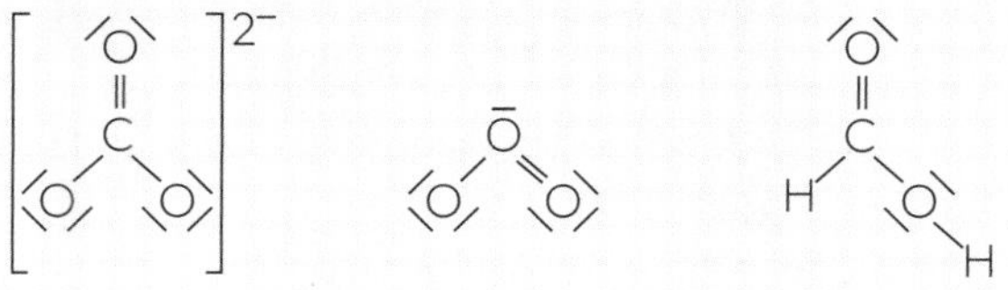

I II III

   A. I and II only
   B. I and III only
   C. II and III only
   D. I, II, and III

20. What is the formal charge on the oxygen atom in the hydronium ion, H_3O^+?
   A. −2
   B. −1
   C. 0
   D. +1

21. Which describes the shape of the SF_4 molecule?
   A. tetrahedral
   B. seesaw
   C. square planar
   D. trigonal bipyramidal

22. Which statements about graphene are correct?
   I. It can be considered as a single layer of graphite.
   II. The hybridization of the carbon atoms is sp^2.
   III. It is an allotrope of carbon.
   A. I and II only
   B. I and III only
   C. II and III only
   D. I, II, and III

23. Which can condense together to form a polyamide?
   I. $HOOC–CH_2–NH_2$ and $HOOC–CH(CH_3)–NH_2$
   II. $H_2N–(CH_2)_6–NH_2$ and $HOOC–(CH_2)_6–COOH$
   III. $HO–(CH_2)_4–OH$ and $HOOC–CH_2–CH_2–COOH$
   A. I and II only
   B. I and III only
   C. II and III only
   D. I, II, and III

24. What are the bond angles in XeF_4?
   A. 90° only
   B. 90° and 180°
   C. 109° only
   D. 90° and 120°

25. Styrene can be polymerized to make polystyrene. What type(s) of hybridization is/are present in polystyrene?

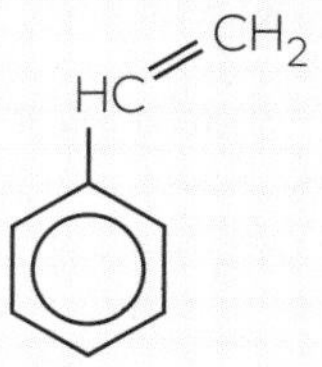

styrene

   A. sp^2 only
   B. sp^3 only
   C. sp^2 and sp^3
   D. sp^2 and sp

26. Which compound contains only atoms that obey the octet rule?
   A. $BeCl_2$
   B. PF_5
   C. SF_6
   D. H_2S

27. Which can be represented fully by two resonance Lewis formulas?
   I. NO_3^-
   II. NO_2^-
   III. CH_3COO^-
   A. I and II only
   B. I and III only
   C. II and III only
   D. I, II, and III

28. Which atomic orbitals combine to give a π bond?
   A. s and p_x
   B. s and s
   C. p_x and p_z
   D. p_y and p_y

29. Which is correct?

	Atom	Hybridization	Number of electron domains	Bond angle
A.	N in NH_3	sp^3	4	109.5°
B.	F in HF	sp	2	180°
C.	C in C_2H_6	sp^3	3	109.5°
D.	C in C_6H_6	sp^2	4	120°

30. How many sigma (σ) and pi (π) bonds are present in one molecule of caffeine?

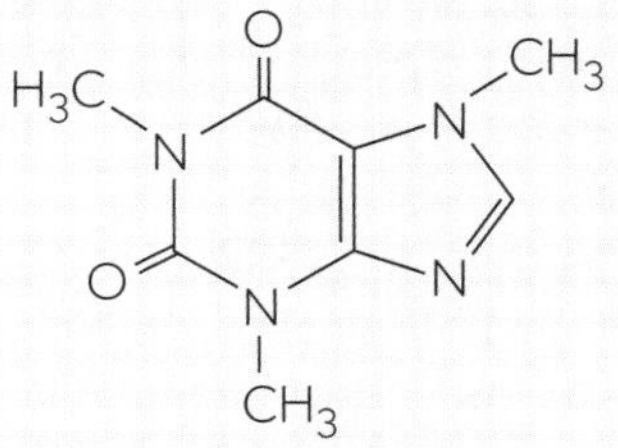

caffeine

   A. 14σ and 4π
   B. 25σ and 4π
   C. 25σ and 2π
   D. 10σ and 4π

1. PF_3, SF_2, and SiF_4 have different shapes. Draw their Lewis formulas and use the VSEPR theory to predict the name of the electron domain geometry and the molecular shape of each molecule. [8]

2. a) (i) Draw the Lewis formula of NH_3, state its molecular shape, and deduce and explain the H–N–H bond angle in NH_3. [4]

(ii) The graph below shows the boiling points of the hydrides of group 15. Discuss the variation in the boiling points. [4]

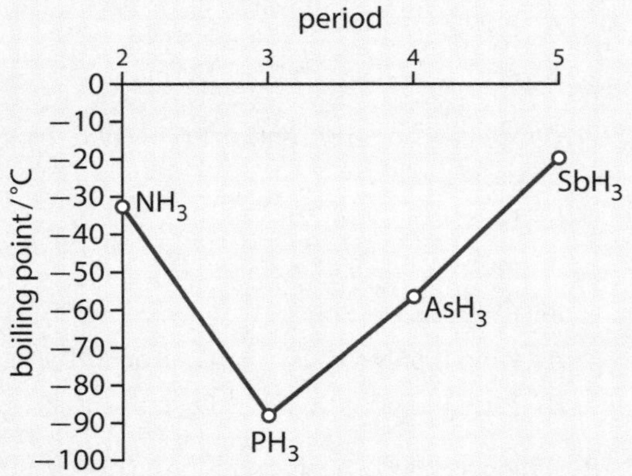

b) Explain, using diagrams, why CO and NO_2 are polar molecules but CO_2 is a non-polar molecule. [5]

3. Ethane, C_2H_6, and disilane, Si_2H_6, are both hydrides of group 14 elements. They have similar structures but different chemical properties.

a) Deduce the Lewis (electron dot) formula for Si_2H_6, showing all valence electrons. [1]

b) State and explain the H–Si–H bond angle in Si_2H_6. [2]

c) State which of the bonds, Si–H or C–H, is more polar. Explain your choice. [2]

d) Predict, with an explanation, the polarity of the two molecules. [2]

e) Explain why disilane has a higher boiling point than ethane. [2]

4. a) State and explain which of propan-1-ol, $CH_3CH_2CH_2OH$, and methoxyethane, $CH_3OCH_2CH_3$, is more volatile. [3]

b) Propan-1-ol, $CH_3CH_2CH_2OH$, and hexan-1-ol, $CH_3(CH_2)_4CH_2OH$, are both alcohols. State and explain which compound is more soluble in water. [2]

c) Graphite is used as a lubricant and is an electrical conductor. Diamond is hard and does not conduct electricity. Explain these statements in terms of the structure and bonding of these allotropes of carbon. [6]

5. a) State the **full** and the **condensed** electron configurations for chlorine. [2]

b) Deduce the orbital diagram for silicon using a box □ to represent an orbital and ↑ and ↓ to represent electrons with opposite spins. [2]

c) Explain why chlorine forms an ionic compound with sodium but a covalent compound with silicon. [2]

AHL

6. a) Ozone and sulfur hexafluoride are greenhouse gases.

(i) Draw the Lewis formula of sulfur hexafluoride. [1]

(ii) Explain why sulfur can expand its octet whereas oxygen cannot. [1]

(iii) Deduce the electron domain geometry for both ozone and sulfur hexafluoride and deduce their molecular shape. [2]

(iv) Deduce the bond angles in ozone and sulfur hexafluoride. [2]

b) Deduce the molecular geometry of dichlorodifluoromethane. [2]

7. Two Lewis formulas that obey the octet rule can be proposed for the nitronium ion, NO_2^+.

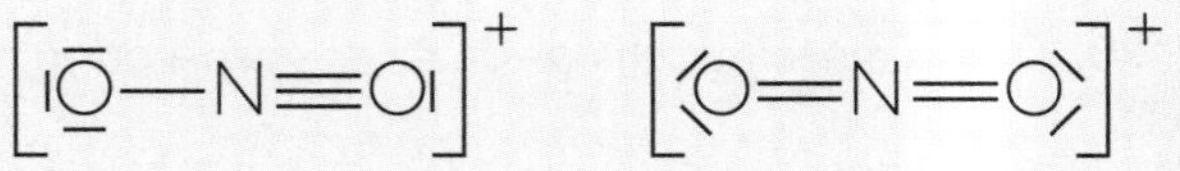

I II

Deduce the formal charge for each atom in both of the two proposed structures and determine which structure is more likely. [4]

8. a) Describe the bonding within the carbon monoxide molecule. [2]

b) Describe the delocalization of π (pi) electrons and explain how this can account for the structure and stability of the carbonate ion, CO_3^{2-}. [3]

c) Explain the meaning of the term hybridization. State the type of hybridization shown by the carbon atoms in carbon dioxide, diamond, graphite, and the carbonate ion. [5]

d) (i) Explain the electrical conductivity of molten sodium oxide and liquid sulfur trioxide. [2]

(ii) Samples of sodium oxide and solid sulfur trioxide are added to separate beakers of water. Deduce the equation for each reaction and predict the electrical conductivity of each of the solutions formed. [3]

9. Halogens can combine with themselves or with other halogens to give interhalogen molecules or ions. Four such species are ICl_4^+, ICl_4^-, I_3^-, and BrF_3.

a) For each of the four species, determine the number of electron domains around each central atom and hence the number of bonding and non-bonding pairs of electrons. [4]

b) Deduce the molecular geometry of each of the four species. [4]

The periodic table: classification of elements

The periodic table

group number

s-block (groups 1–2); d-block (groups 3–12); p-block (groups 13–18)

Key: atomic number / **element**

period number (n)	1	2	3	4	5	6	7	8	9	10	11	12	13	14	15	16	17	18
1	1 H																	2 He
2	3 Li	4 Be											5 B	6 C	7 N	8 O	9 F	10 Ne
3	11 Na	12 Mg											13 Al	14 Si	15 P	16 S	17 Cl	18 Ar
4	19 K	20 Ca	21 Sc	22 Ti	23 V	24 Cr	25 Mn	26 Fe	27 Co	28 Ni	29 Cu	30 Zn	31 Ga	32 Ge	33 As	34 Se	35 Br	36 Kr
5	37 Rb	38 Sr	39 Y	40 Zr	41 Nb	42 Mo	43 Tc	44 Ru	45 Rh	46 Pd	47 Ag	48 Cd	49 In	50 Sn	51 Sb	52 Te	53 I	54 Xe
6	55 Cs	56 Ba	57 * La	72 Hf	73 Ta	74 W	75 Re	76 Os	77 Ir	78 Pt	79 Au	80 Hg	81 Tl	82 Pb	83 Bi	84 Po	85 At	86 Rn
7	87 Fr	88 Ra	89 * Ac*	104 Rf	105 Db	106 Sg	107 Bh	108 Hs	109 Mt	110 Ds	111 Rg	112 Cn	113 Nh	114 Fl	115 Mc	116 Lv	117 Ts	118 Og

f-block

*	58 Ce	59 Pr	60 Nd	61 Pm	62 Sm	63 Eu	64 Gd	65 Tb	66 Dy	67 Ho	68 Er	69 Tm	70 Yb	71 Lu
**	90 Th	91 Pa	92 U	93 Np	94 Pu	95 Am	96 Cm	97 Bk	98 Cf	99 Es	100 Fm	101 Md	102 No	103 Lr

Features of the periodic table

- In the periodic table, elements are placed in order of increasing atomic number.
- Elements are arranged into four blocks associated with the four sub-levels: s, p, d, and f.
- The period number (n) is the outer energy level that is occupied by electrons. A "period" is a row in the periodic table.
- Elements in the same vertical column are called groups, numbered 1 to 18. Elements in a group contain the same number of electrons in the outer energy level.
- Certain groups have their own name. For example, group 1 is known as the alkali metals, group 17 as the halogens, and group 18 as the noble gases.
- The number of the principal energy level and the number of valence electrons in an atom can be deduced from its position in the periodic table. This can then be used to deduce the full electron configuration.
- The periodic table shows the positions of metals, non-metals, and metalloids. Metals are on the left and in the centre of the table and non-metals are on the right (distinguished by the thick line). Metalloids, such as boron, silicon, and germanium, have properties intermediate between those of a metal and a non-metal.
- The d-block elements (groups 3 to 12) are known as the transition metals. The f-block elements form two distinct groups: the lanthanoids (from La to Lu) and the actinoids (from Ac to Lr).

Electron configuration and the periodic table

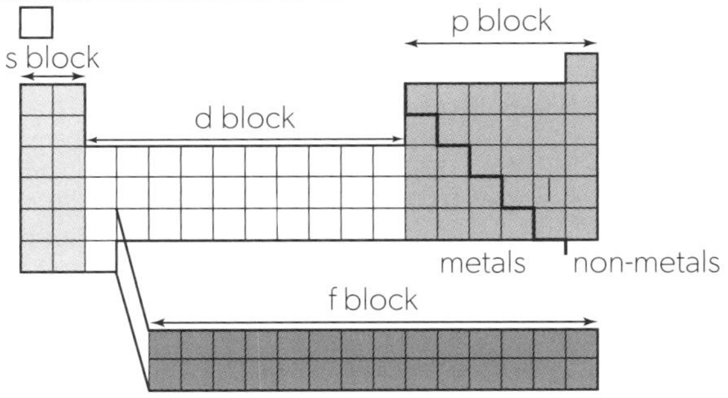

An element's position in the periodic table is related to its valence electrons, so the electronic configuration of any element can be deduced from the table, e.g. iodine ($Z = 53$) is a p-block element. Iodine is in group 17 so its configuration will contain ns^2np^5. If one takes H and He as being the first period, then iodine is in the fifth period, so $n = 5$. The full configuration for iodine will therefore be:

$1s^2 2s^2 2p^6 3s^2 3p^6 4s^2 3d^{10} 4p^6 5s^2 4d^{10} 5p^5$ or $[Kr]5s^2 4d^{10} 5p^5$

Periodic trends (1)

Periodicity

Elements in the same group tend to have similar chemical and physical properties. There is a change in chemical and physical properties across a period. The repeating pattern of physical and chemical properties shown by the different periods is known as **periodicity**.

These periodic trends can be seen clearly in atomic radii, ionic radii, ionization energies, electronegativities, electron affinities, and melting points.

Atomic radius

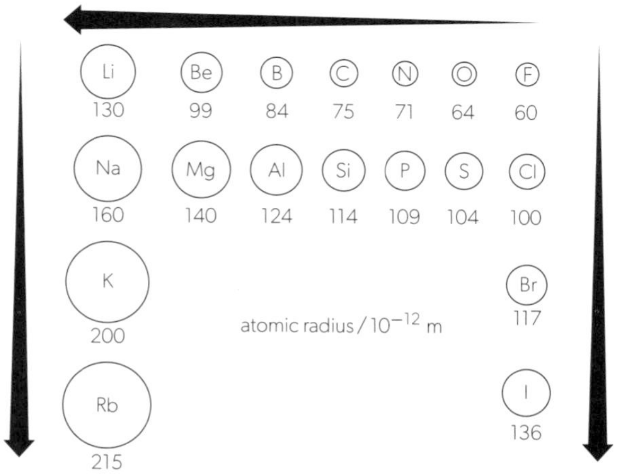

The atomic radius is the distance from the nucleus to the outermost electron. Since the position of the outermost electron can never be known precisely, the atomic radius is usually defined as half the distance between the nuclei of two bonded atoms of the same element.

- As you go down a group, the outermost electron is in a higher energy level, which is further from the nucleus, so the radius increases.
- As you go across a period, electrons are being added to the same energy level, but the number of protons in the nucleus also increases. This attracts the energy level closer to the nucleus, so the atomic radius decreases across a period.

Ionic radius

It is important to distinguish between positive ions (cations) and negative ions (anions). Both cations and anions increase in size down a group as the outer level gets further from the nucleus.

Cations contain fewer electrons than protons, so the electrostatic attraction between the nucleus and the outermost electron is greater and the ion is smaller than the parent atom. It is also smaller because the number of electron shells has decreased by one. Across a period, the ions contain the same number of electrons (**isoelectronic**), but an increasing number of protons, so the ionic radius decreases.

Anions contain more electrons than protons so are larger than the parent atom. Across a period, the size decreases because the number of electrons remains the same but the number of protons increases.

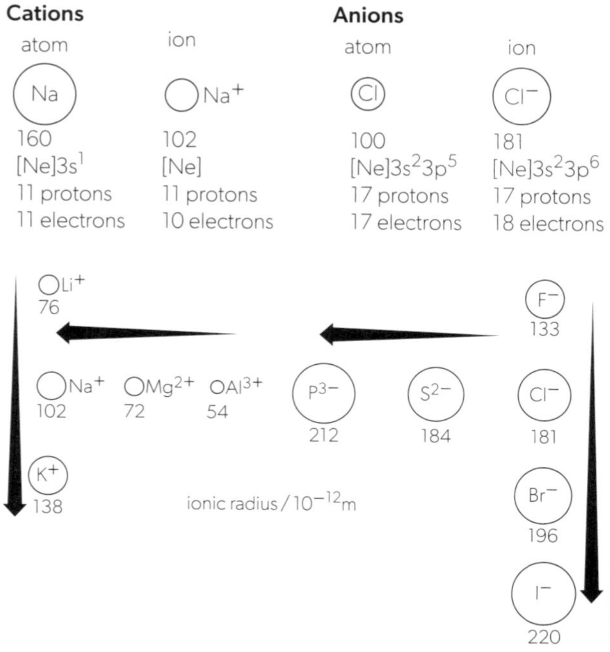

Periodic trends (2)

Melting points

Melting points depend both on the structure of the element and on the type of attractive forces holding the atoms together. Using period 3 (Na to Ar) as an example:

- At the left of the period, elements exhibit metallic bonding (Na, Mg, and Al), which increases in strength as the number of valence electrons increases.
- Silicon, the metalloid, in the middle of the period, has a macromolecular covalent structure, with very strong bonds, which results in a very high melting point.
- Elements in groups 15, 16, and 17 (P_4, S_8, and Cl_2) show simple molecular structures with weak forces of attraction between the molecules.
- The noble gas Ar exists as **monatomic molecules** (single atoms) with extremely weak forces of attraction between the atoms.

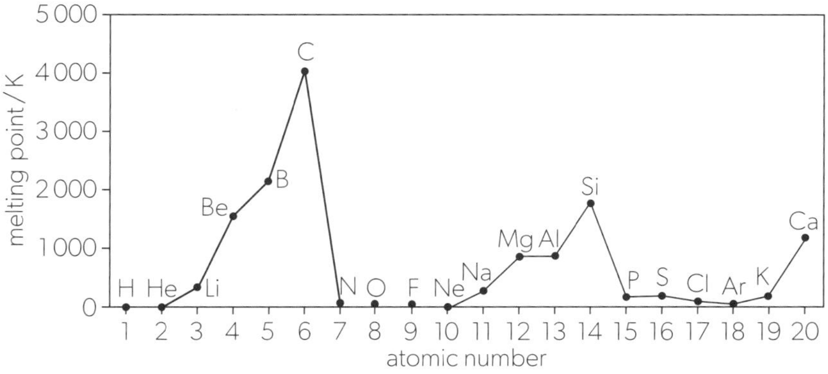

Within groups, there are also clear trends:

- In group 1, the melting point decreases down the group as the atoms become larger and the strength of the metallic bond decreases.

	Li	Na	K	Rb	Cs
M. pt / K	454	371	336	312	302

- In group 17, the attractive forces between the diatomic molecules increase down the group, so the melting points increase.

	F_2	Cl_2	Br_2	I_2
M. pt / K	53	172	266	387

First ionization energy

The definition of first ionization energy and a graph showing the values for the first 20 elements are given on page 12. The values decrease down each group as the outer electron is further from the nucleus and therefore less energy is required to remove it, e.g. for the group 1 elements, Li, Na, and K:

Element	Li	Na	K
Electron configuration	$1s^22s^1$	$[Ne]3s^1$	$[Ar]4s^1$
First ionization energy (kJ mol^{-1})	520	496	419

Generally, the values increase across a period because the extra electrons fill the same energy level and the extra protons in the nucleus attract this energy level more closely, making it harder to remove an electron.

The values do not increase regularly across a period because new sub-levels are being filled. The p sub-level is higher in energy than the s sub-level. This explains why the value for B ($1s^22s^22p^1$) is slightly lower than the value for Be ($1s^22s^2$) and the value for Al ($[Ne]3s^23p^1$) is slightly lower than Mg ($[Ne]3s^2$). There is also a drop in value between N ($1s^22s^22p^3$) and O ($1s^22s^22p^4$) and between P ($[Ne]3s^23p^3$) and S ($[Ne]3s^23p^4$). This is because when electrons pair up in an orbital there is increased repulsion, so the paired electron is easier to remove compared with when the three electrons are all unpaired, one each in the three separate p orbitals.

Electronegativity

Electronegativity was discussed in Chapter 4. As the atomic radius decreases, the attraction to the shared pair of electrons increases, so the electronegativity value increases across a period and down a group. The three most important electronegative elements are fluorine, oxygen, and nitrogen.

Electron affinity

The electron affinity is the energy change when an electron is added to an isolated atom in the gaseous state, i.e. $X(g) + e^- \rightarrow X^-(g)$

Atoms "want" an extra electron, so electron affinity values are negative for the addition of the first electron. However, when oxygen forms the O^{2-} ion, the overall process is endothermic:

$$O(g) + e^- \rightarrow O^-(g) \qquad \Delta H^\ominus = -141\ \text{kJ mol}^{-1}$$

$$O^-(g) + e^- \rightarrow O^{2-}(g) \qquad \Delta H^\ominus = +753\ \text{kJ mol}^{-1}$$

$$\text{overall} \quad O(g) + 2e^- \rightarrow O^{2-}(g) \qquad \Delta H^\ominus = +612\ \text{kJ mol}^{-1}$$

Chemical properties of elements

Group 1: the alkali metals

Li
Na
K
Rb
Cs
↓ increasing reactivity

Lithium, sodium, and potassium all contain one electron in their outer shell. They are all reactive metals and are stored under liquid paraffin to prevent them reacting with air. They react by losing their outer electron to form the metal ion. Because they can readily lose an electron, they are good reducing agents. The reactivity increases down the group as the outer electron is in successively higher energy levels and less energy is required to remove it.

They are called alkali metals because they all react with water to form an alkaline solution of the metal hydroxide and hydrogen gas. Lithium floats and reacts quietly; sodium melts into a ball which darts around on the surface; and the heat generated from the reaction with potassium ignites the hydrogen.

$2Li(s) + 2H_2O(l) \rightarrow 2Li^+(aq) + 2OH^-(aq) + H_2(g)$

$2Na(s) + 2H_2O(l) \rightarrow 2Na^+(aq) + 2OH^-(aq) + H_2(g)$

$2K(s) + 2H_2O(l) \rightarrow 2K^+(aq) + 2OH^-(aq) + H_2(g)$

The alkali metals also react readily with chlorine, bromine, and iodine to form ionic salts, e.g.

$2Na(s) + Cl_2(g) \rightarrow 2Na^+Cl^-(s)$

$2K(s) + Br_2(l) \rightarrow 2K^+Br^-(s)$

$2Li(s) + I_2(g) \rightarrow 2Li^+I^-(s)$

Group 17: the halogens

F_2
Cl_2
Br_2
I_2
↑ increasing reactivity

The halogens react by gaining one more electron to form halide ions. They are good oxidizing agents. The reactivity decreases down the group as the outer shell is at increasingly higher energy levels and further from the nucleus. This, together with the fact that there are more electrons between the nucleus and the outer shell, decreases the attraction for an extra electron.

Chlorine is a stronger oxidizing agent than bromine, so can remove the electron from bromide ions in solution to form chloride ions and bromine. Similarly, both chlorine and bromine can oxidize iodide ions to form iodine.

$Cl_2(aq) + 2Br^-(aq) \rightarrow 2Cl^-(aq) + Br_2(aq)$

$Cl_2(aq) + 2I^-(aq) \rightarrow 2Cl^-(aq) + I_2(aq)$

$Br_2(aq) + 2I^-(aq) \rightarrow 2Br^-(aq) + I_2(aq)$

Test for halide ions

The presence of halide ions in solution can be detected by adding silver nitrate solution. The silver ions react with the halide ions to form a precipitate of the silver halide. The silver halides can be distinguished by their colour. These silver halides react with light to form silver metal. This is the basis of old-fashioned film photography.

$Ag^+(aq) + X^-(aq) \rightarrow AgX(s)$ where X = Cl, Br, or I

$$AgX(s) \xrightarrow{\text{light}} Ag(s) + \tfrac{1}{2}X_2$$

AgCl white

AgBr cream

AgI yellow

The metallic and non-metallic nature of the elements

Metals tend to be shiny and are good conductors of heat and electricity. Sodium, magnesium, and aluminium all conduct electricity well. Silicon is a semiconductor and is called a metalloid as it possesses some of the properties of a metal and some of a non-metal. Phosphorus, sulfur, chlorine, and argon are non-metals and do not conduct electricity.

Metals can also be distinguished from non-metals by their chemical properties. Metal oxides tend to be basic, whereas non-metal oxides tend to be acidic. Metallic properties increase down a group and metals and non-metals can exist in the same group. In group 14, for example, carbon is a non-metal, silicon and germanium are metalloids, and tin and lead are metals.

Sodium oxide and magnesium oxide are both basic and react with water to form hydroxides:

$Na_2O(s) + H_2O(l) \rightarrow 2NaOH(aq)$

$MgO(s) + H_2O(l) \rightarrow Mg(OH)_2$

Aluminium is a metal but its oxide is amphoteric, that is, it can be either basic or acidic depending on whether it is reacting with an acid or a base.

Some important non-metal oxides are those of sulfur and carbon. Sulfur trioxide, SO_3, reacts with water to form sulfuric acid. Sulfur dioxide, SO_2, and oxides of nitrogen, such as NO_2, are the main gases responsible for the formation of acid rain. Carbon dioxide, CO_2, is also acidic. It dissolves in rain water forming carbonic acid, but carbonic acid is too weak an acid to cause acid rain, which is defined as having a pH below 5.6. (Acid rain is covered in more detail on page 109.) However, increasing atmospheric levels of carbon dioxide are responsible for ocean acidification, which affects marine life such as coral.

$SO_3(g) + H_2O(l) \rightarrow H_2SO_4(aq)$

$SO_2(g) + H_2O(l) \rightarrow H_2SO_3(aq)$

$CO_2(g) + H_2O(l) \rightarrow H_2CO_3(aq)$

Oxidation states and naming ionic compounds

Rules for determining oxidation states

The oxidation state of an atom or ion in a compound is the number assigned to that atom to show the number of electrons transferred in forming a bond. If the compound was composed of ions, the oxidation state would be the charge on that atom. Oxidation states can be a useful tool to identify which species has been oxidized and which reduced in a redox reaction. They are also useful to help determine the correct formula and name for ionic compounds.

Oxidation states are assigned according to a set of rules.

1. In an ionic compound between two elements, the oxidation state of each element is equal to the charge carried by the ion, e.g.

   Na^+Cl^- Na = +1, Cl = −1

   $Ca^{2+}Cl^-_2$ Ca = +2, Cl = −1

2. For covalent compounds, assume that the compound is ionic, with the more electronegative element forming the negative ion, e.g.

   CCl_4 C = +4, Cl = −1

   NH_3 N = −3, H = +1

3. The algebraic sum of all the oxidation states in a compound equals zero, e.g.

   CCl_4 $(+4) + 4 \times (-1) = 0$

   H_2SO_4 $2 \times (+1) + (+6) + 4 \times (-2) = 0$

4. The algebraic sum of all the oxidation states in an ion equals the charge on the ion, e.g.

   SO_4^{2-} $(+6) + 4 \times (-2) = -2$

   MnO_4^- $(+7) + 4 \times (-2) = -1$

   NH_4^+ $(-3) + 4 \times (+1) = +1$

5. Elements not combined with other elements have an oxidation state of zero, e.g.

   O_2; P_4; S_8.

6. Oxygen, when combined, always has an oxidation state of −2 except in peroxides (e.g. H_2O_2) when it has an oxidation state of −1.

7. Hydrogen, when combined, always has an oxidation state of +1 except in certain metal hydrides (e.g. NaH) when it has an oxidation state of −1.

Many elements can show different oxidation states in different compounds, e.g. nitrogen in:

NH_3	N_2H_4	N_2	N_2O	NO	NO_2	NO_3^-
−3	−2	0	+1	+2	+4	+5

Naming of ionic compounds

Metals in groups 1, 2, and 13 are straightforward as they form positive ions (cations) with oxidation states of +1, +2, and +3, respectively, so it is not usual to indicate this in the name. Examples include:

Na_2O	MgS	$AlCl_3$	CaF_2
sodium oxide	magnesium sulfide	aluminium chloride	calcium fluoride

Transition metals (and some other metals, such as tin and lead) form more than one ion as they have variable oxidation states. In the past, these had separate names, e.g. cuprous, cupric, ferrous, and ferric for Cu^+, Cu^{2+}, Fe^{2+}, and Fe^{3+}, respectively. Now the oxidation number is used. Roman numerals are used for oxidation numbers so the names of the two oxides of copper are copper(I) oxide, Cu_2O, and copper(II) oxide, CuO. Note that there is no gap between the oxidation number and the species it refers to.

Oxyanions are formed when oxygen combines with another element to form a complex ion. In the past, these were given different names to distinguish between them. Examples include sulfate, SO_4^{2-}, sulfite, SO_3^{2-}, nitrate, NO_3^-, and nitrite, NO_2^-. These names are still in common usage even though, technically, they should now all have the suffix "-ate". SO_4^{2-} is the sulfate(VI) ion to distinguish it from the sulfate(IV) ion, SO_3^{2-}. Other common examples include nitrate(V) and nitrate(III) for NO_3^- and NO_2^-; manganate(VII) for the permanganate ion, MnO_4^-, and manganate(VI) for the manganate ion, MnO_4^{2-}. The IB tends to use oxidation numbers when naming most compounds, for example, potassium dichromate(VI) rather than just potassium dichromate, $K_2Cr_2O_7$. However, it still also uses the common name for many compounds and ions, e.g. water is still water, and not hydrogen(I) oxide.

Note that IUPAC rules state that oxidation states have + or − in front of an Arabic numeral (except for elements, which are zero) and oxidation numbers use just the number which is a Roman numeral. However, the two are often used interchangeably and either term is acceptable in an assessment.

AHL The transition metals

The first row transition elements

Element	(Sc)	Ti	V	Cr	Mn	Fe	Co	Ni	Cu	(Zn)
Electron configuration [Ar]	$4s^23d^1$	$4s^23d^2$	$4s^23d^3$	$4s^13d^5$	$4s^23d^5$	$4s^23d^6$	$4s^23d^7$	$4s^23d^8$	$4s^13d^{10}$	$4s^23d^{10}$

A transition element is defined as an element that possesses an incomplete d sub-level in one or more of its oxidation states. Scandium is not a typical transition metal as its common ion, Sc^{3+}, has no d electrons. Zinc is not a transition metal as it contains a full d sub-level in all its oxidation states. (Note: for Cr and Cu it is more energetically favourable to half fill or completely fill the d sub-level, respectively, so that they contain only one 4s electron.)

Transition elements have high melting points, variable oxidation states, form complex ions with ligands, have coloured compounds, and display catalytic and magnetic properties.

Variable oxidation states

The 3d and 4s sub-levels are very similar in energy. When transition metals lose electrons they lose the 4s electrons first. All transition metals can show an oxidation state of +2. Some of the transition metals can form the +3 or +4 ion (e.g. Fe^{3+}, Mn^{4+}) as the values of the ionization energies are such that up to two d electrons as well as the 4s electrons can be lost relatively easily. The Mn^{4+} ion is rare and, in the higher oxidation states, the element is usually found not as the free metal ion but is either covalently bonded or as an oxyanion, such as MnO_4^-.

Some common examples of variable oxidation states in addition to +2 are:

Cr(+3)	$CrCl_3$	chromium(III) chloride
Cr(+6)	$Cr_2O_7^{2-}$	dichromate(VI) ion
Mn(+4)	MnO_2	manganese(IV) oxide
Mn(+7)	MnO_4^-	manganate(VII) ion
Fe(+3)	Fe_2O_3	iron(III) oxide
Cu(+1)	Cu_2O	copper(I) oxide

Catalytic behaviour

Many transition elements and their compounds are very efficient catalysts: that is, they increase the rate of chemical reactions. This helps to make industrial processes more efficient and economical. Platinum and palladium are used in catalytic converters fitted to cars to reduce carbon monoxide and nitrogen oxide emissions by catalysing their conversion into carbon dioxide and nitrogen, respectively. Other common uses of catalysts include:

Iron in the Haber process to manufacture ammonia

$$3H_2(g) + N_2(g) \xrightleftharpoons{Fe(s)} 2NH_3(g)$$

Vanadium(V) oxide in the Contact process to manufacture sulfuric acid

$$2SO_2(g) + O_2(g) \xrightleftharpoons{V_2O_5(s)} 2SO_3(g)$$

Nickel in hydrogenation reactions

$$C_2H_4(g) + H_2(g) \xrightarrow{Ni(s)} C_2H_6(g)$$

Manganese(IV) oxide with hydrogen peroxide

$$2H_2O_2(aq) \xrightarrow{MnO_2(s)} 2H_2O(l) + O_2(g)$$

Magnetic properties

Transition metals and their complexes that contain unpaired electrons can exhibit magnetism. Iron metal and some other metals (e.g. nickel and cobalt) show **ferromagnetism**. This is a permanent type of magnetism. In this type of magnetism, the unpaired electrons align parallel to each other in domains, irrespective of whether an external magnetic or electric field is present. This property of iron has been utilized for centuries to make compasses, which align with the Earth's magnetic field to point north.

Many complexes of transition metals contain unpaired electrons. Unlike paired electrons, where the spins cancel each other out, the spinning unpaired electrons create a small magnetic field and will line up in an applied electric or magnetic field to make the transition metal complex weakly magnetic when the field is applied, i.e. they reinforce the external magnetic field. This type of magnetism is known as **paramagnetism**. The more unpaired electrons there are in the complex, the more paramagnetic the complex will be.

When all the electrons in a transition metal complex are paired up, the complex is said to be **diamagnetic**.

AHL Transition metal complexes

Formation of complex ions

because of their small size, d-block ions act as Lewis acids and attract species that are rich in electrons. Such species are known as **ligands**. Ligands are neutral molecules or anions that contain a non-bonding pair of electrons and which act as Lewis bases. These electron pairs can form coordination covalent bonds with the metal ion to form **complex ions**.

Water is a common ligand and most (but not all) transition metal ions exist as hexahydrated complex ions in aqueous solution, e.g. $[Fe(H_2O)_6]^{3+}$. Ligands can be replaced by other ligands. A typical example is the addition of ammonia to an aqueous solution of copper(II) sulfate to give the deep blue colour of the tetraaminecopper(II) ion. Similarly, if concentrated hydrochloric acid is added to a solution of $Cu^{2+}(aq)$ the yellow tetrachlorocopper(II) anion is formed. Note: the overall charge on this ion is –2 as the four ligands each have a charge of –1.)

$$[CuCl_4]^{2-} \underset{H_2O}{\overset{Cl^-}{\rightleftharpoons}} [Cu(H_2O)_6]^{2+} \underset{H_2O}{\overset{NH_3}{\rightleftharpoons}} [Cu(NH_3)_4]^{2+}$$

The number of lone pairs bonded to the metal ion is known as the **coordination number**. Compounds with a coordination number of six are octahedral in shape; those with a coordination number of four are tetrahedral or square planar; and those with a coordination number of two are usually linear.

Coordination number	6	4	2
Examples	$[Fe(CN)_6]^{3-}$	$[CuCl_4]^{2-}$	$[Ag(NH_3)_2]^+$
	$[Fe(OH)_3(H_2O)_3]$	$[Cu(NH_3)_4]^{2+}$	

Polydentate ligands

Ligands such as water and cyanide ions are known as **monodentate ligands** as they utilize just one non-bonding pair to form a coordination covalent bond to the metal ion. Some ligands contain more than one non-bonding pair and can form two or more coordination bonds to the metal ion. Three common examples are ethylenediamine, $H_2NCH_2CH_2NH_2$, and oxalate ions, $(COO^-)_2$, both of which can use two non-bonding pairs to form **bidentate ligands**, and EDTA (ethylenediaminetetraacetic acid) or its ion, $EDTA^{4-}$, which can act as **hexadentate ligands**.

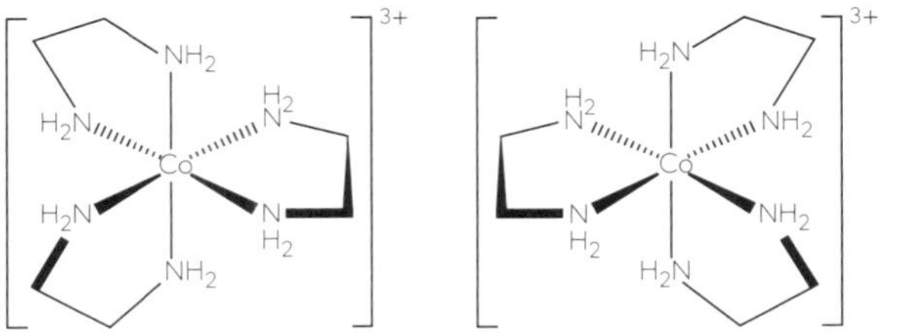

The Co^{3+} ion can form two different stereoisomers (mirror images) with the three separate ethylenediamine molecules acting as bidentate ligands. The coordination number is six. Although each metal ion is surrounded by only three ligands the metal ion forms a total of six coordination bonds with the ligands.

$EDTA^{4-}$ can also act as a hexadentate ligand with a transition metal, M, to form a complex such as $[Cu(EDTA)]^{2-}$ (right). Note that the coordination number is still six even though only one ligand surrounds the metal ion.

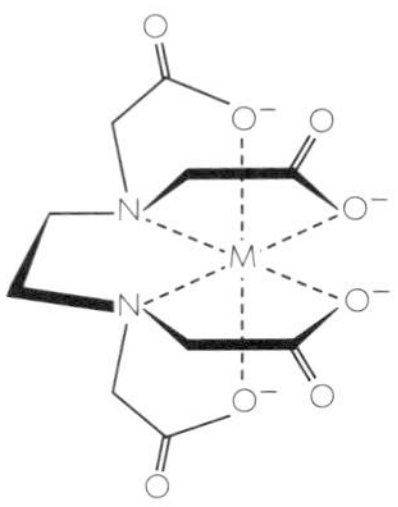

Factors affecting the colour of transition metal complexes

Transition metals are known for their formation of coloured compounds.

Compounds of Sc^{3+}, which have no d electrons, and of Cu^+ and Zn^{2+}, which both have complete d sub-shells, are colourless. This strongly suggests that the colour of transition metal complexes is related to an incomplete d level. The actual colour is determined by four different factors.

1. The nature of the transition element. For example, $Mn^{2+}(aq)$ and $Fe^{3+}(aq)$ both have the configuration $[Ar]3d^5$. $Mn^{2+}(aq)$ is pink whereas $Fe^{3+}(aq)$ is yellow.
2. The oxidation state. $Fe^{2+}(aq)$ is green whereas $Fe^{3+}(aq)$ is yellow.
3. The identity of the ligand. $[Cu(H_2O)_6]^{2+}$ (sometimes shown as $[Cu(H_2O)_4]^{2+}$), is blue; $[Cu(NH_3)_4(H_2O)_2]^{2+}$ (sometimes shown as $[Cu(NH_3)_4]^{2+}$), is blue/violet; and $[CuCl_4]^{2-}$ is yellow (green in aqueous solution).
4. The stereochemistry of the complex. The colour is also affected by the shape of the molecule or ion. In the above example, $[Cu(H_2O)_6]^{2+}$ is octahedral whereas $[CuCl_4]^{2-}$ is tetrahedral. (Note that for the IB only octahedral complexes in aqueous solution will be considered.)

AHL

Colour of transition metal complexes

Splitting of the d orbitals

In the free ion, the five d orbitals are all of equal energy, so they are called **degenerate**.

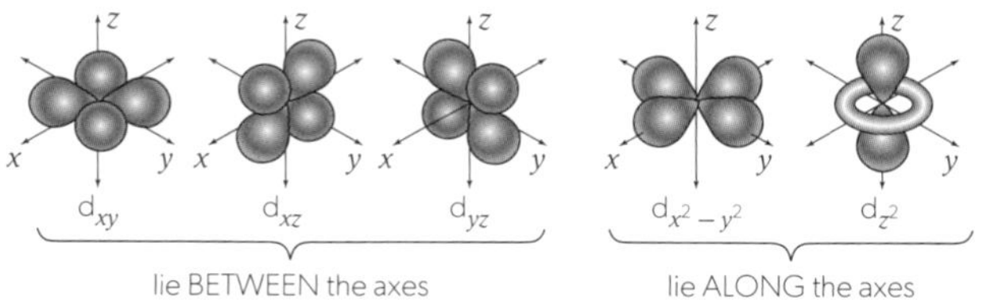

Note that three of the orbitals (d_{xy}, d_{xz}, and d_{yz}) lie between the axes, whereas the other two ($d_{x^2-y^2}$ and d_{z^2}) lie along the axes.

Ligands act as Lewis bases and donate a non-bonding pair of electrons to form a coordination bond. As the ligands approach the metal along the axes to form an octahedral complex, the non-bonding pairs of electrons on the ligands repel the $d_{x^2-y^2}$ and d_{z^2} orbitals, causing the five d orbitals to split, three to lower energy and two to higher energy. The difference in energy between the two levels, ΔE, corresponds to wavelengths of visible light.

When white light falls on the aqueous solution of the complex, the colour corresponding to ΔE is absorbed as an electron is promoted, and the transmitted light will be the complementary colour. For example, $[Cu(H_2O)_6]^{2+}$ absorbs red light so the compound appears blue. The amount that the d orbitals are split determines the exact colour. Changing the transition metal changes the number of protons in the nucleus, which affects the levels. Similarly, changing the oxidation state affects the splitting as the number of electrons in the levels is different. Different ligands also cause different amounts of splitting, depending on their electron density.

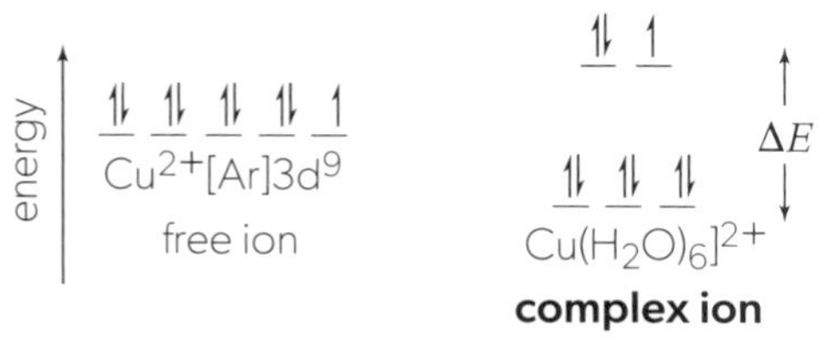

The spectrochemical series

Ligands can be arranged in order of their ability to split the d orbitals in octahedral complexes.

$I^- < Br^- < S^{2-} < Cl^- < F^- < OH^- < H_2O < SCN^- < NH_3 < CN^- < CO$

This order is known as the **spectrochemical series**. Iodide ions cause the smallest splitting and the carbonyl group, CO, causes the largest splitting. The energy of light absorbed increases when, for example, ammonia is substituted for water in Cu^{2+} complexes as the splitting increases, i.e. in going from $[Cu(H_2O)_6]^{2+}$ to $[Cu(NH_3)_4(H_2O)_2]^{2+}$. This means that the wavelength of the light absorbed decreases and this is observed in the colour of the transmitted light, which changes from blue to a blue-violet (purple) colour.

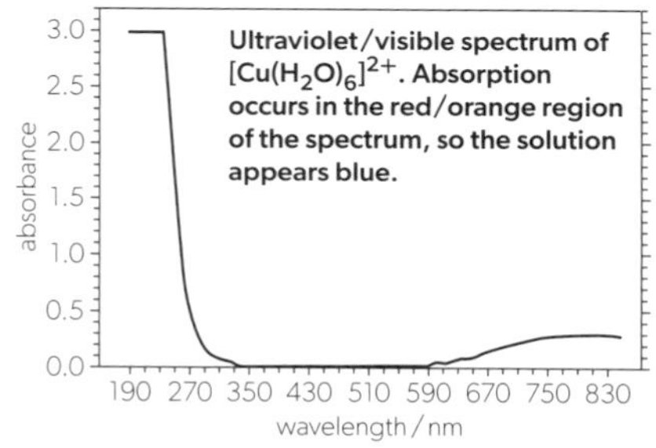

Ultraviolet/visible spectrum of $[Cu(H_2O)_6]^{2+}$. Absorption occurs in the red/orange region of the spectrum, so the solution appears blue.

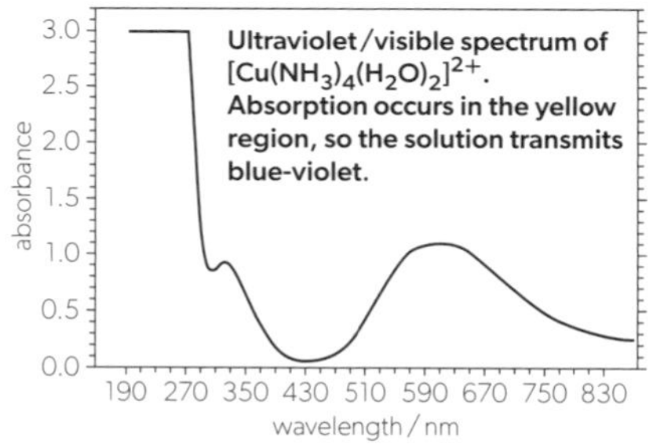

Ultraviolet/visible spectrum of $[Cu(NH_3)_4(H_2O)_2]^{2+}$. Absorption occurs in the yellow region, so the solution transmits blue-violet.

Complementary colours

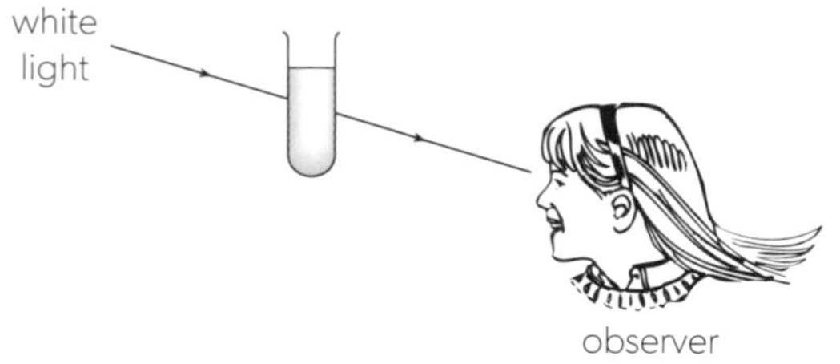

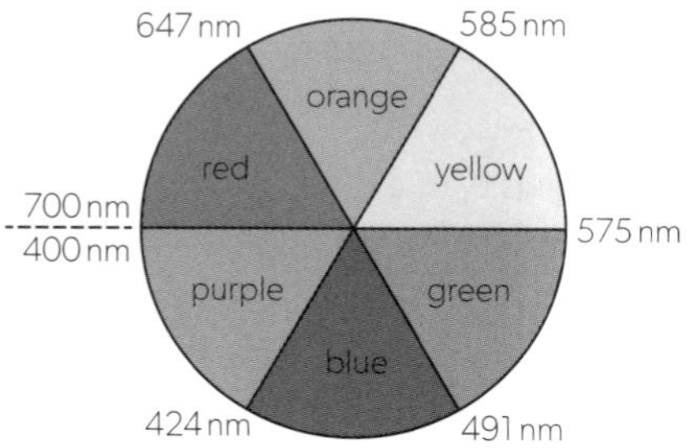

If red/orange light is absorbed, the solution appears blue-green as that is the transmitted complementary colour. Complementary colours are opposite each other in this "colour wheel".

Multiple-choice questions—Periodicity

1. Where in the periodic table would the element with the electronic structure $1s^2 2s^2 2p^6 3s^2 3p^6 4s^2 3d^{10} 4p^2$ be located?
   A. s block
   B. p block
   C. d block
   D. lanthanoids

2. Which property decreases with increasing atomic number in group 17 (the halogens)?
   A. melting point
   B. electronegativity
   C. atomic radius
   D. ionic radius of the negative ion

3. Which property increases with increasing atomic number for both the halogens and the alkali metals?
   A. reactivity with water
   B. electronegativity
   C. electron affinity
   D. atomic radius

4. Which one of the following series is arranged in order of increasing size?
   A. P^{3-}, S^{2-}, Cl^-
   B. Cl, Ar, K
   C. Na^+, Mg^{2+}, Al^{3+}
   D. H^+, H, H^-

5. Which element has the lowest electronegativity value?
   A. potassium
   B. fluorine
   C. iodine
   D. hydrogen

6. Which statements about the periodic table are correct?
   I. The elements Mg, Ca, and Sr have similar chemical properties.
   II. Elements in the same period have the same number of main energy levels.
   III. The oxides of Na, Mg, and P are basic.
   A. I and II only
   B. I and III only
   C. II and III only
   D. I, II, and III

7. The *x*-axis of the graph below represents the atomic number of the elements in period 3.

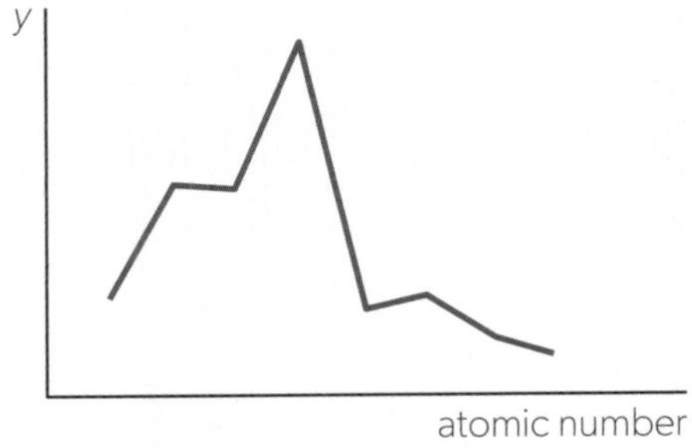

   Which variable could the *y*-axis represent?
   A. melting point
   B. electronegativity
   C. ionic radius
   D. atomic radius

8. Which is the correct definition for the electron affinity of element X?
   A. $X(s) + e^- \rightarrow X^-(s)$
   B. $X(s) \rightarrow X^+(s) + e^-$
   C. $X(g) + e^- \rightarrow X^-(g)$
   D. $X(g) \rightarrow X^+(g) + e^-$

9. Which oxide will react with water to give a solution with a pH greater than 7?
   A. NO_2
   B. P_4O_{10}
   C. MgO
   D. SiO_2

10. Which reaction does not occur readily?
   A. $Cl_2(aq) + 2Br^-(aq) \rightarrow Br_2(aq) + 2Cl^-(aq)$
   B. $2Na(s) + H_2O(l) \rightarrow 2NaOH(aq) + H_2(g)$
   C. $Na_2O(s) + H_2O(l) \rightarrow 2NaOH(aq)$
   D. $I_2(aq) + 2Br^-(aq) \rightarrow Br_2(aq) + 2I^-(aq)$

11. Which reaction is endothermic (takes in energy)?
   A. $Li(g) + e^- \rightarrow Li^-(g)$
   B. $O(g) + 2e^- \rightarrow O^{2-}(g)$
   C. $O(g) + e^- \rightarrow O^-(g)$
   D. $F(g) + e^- \rightarrow F^-(g)$

12. What is the oxidation state of nitrogen in HNO_3?
   A. +3
   B. −3
   C. +5
   D. −5

13. What is the correct name for MnO_2?
   A. manganese oxide
   B. manganese(II) oxide
   C. manganese (III) oxide
   D. manganese(IV) oxide

14. Which gas does **not** cause acid rain?
   A. CO_2
   B. SO_3
   C. SO_2
   D. NO_2

15. Which species can react with bromide ions to form bromine?
   A. NaCl(aq)
   B. Cl_2(aq)
   C. NaI(aq)
   D. I_2(aq)

16. Which element is a metalloid?
   A. aluminium
   B. phosphorus
   C. sulfur
   D. silicon

17. Which family of elements is associated with the d block?
   A. transition metals
   B. lanthanoids
   C. alkali metals
   D. halogens

18. Which complex ion is colourless in aqueous solution?
A. $[Mn(H_2O)_6]^{2+}$
B. $[Zn(H_2O)_4]^{2+}$
C. $[Cu(NH_3)_4]^{2+}$
D. $[CuCl_4]^{2-}$

19. A certain element has the electron configuration $1s^2 2s^2 2p^6 3s^2 3p^6 4s^2 3d^3$. What oxidation state(s) is this element most likely to show?
A. +2 only
B. +3 only
C. +2 and +5 only
D. +2, +3, +4, and +5

20. What is the overall charge on the complex ion formed by Fe(III) and six CN^- ligands?
A. +3
B. −6
C. −3
D. +6

21. Which statements about transition metal complexes are correct?
I. The colour of the complex is due to light being emitted when an electron falls from a higher split d sub-level to a lower split d sub-level.
II. The difference in energy between the split d sub-levels depends on the nature of the surrounding ligands.
III. The colour of the complex is influenced by the oxidation state of the metal.
A. I and II only
B. I and III only
C. II and III only
D. I, II, and III

22. What is the electron configuration of the Mn^{2+} ion?
A. $1s^2 2s^2 2p^6 3s^2 3p^6 3d^5$
B. $1s^2 2s^2 2p^6 3s^2 3p^6 4s^2 3d^5$
C. $1s^2 2s^2 2p^6 3s^2 3p^6 4s^2 3d^3$
D. $1s^2 2s^2 2p^6 3s^2 3p^6 4s^1 3d^4$

23. Which statement is true for all polydentate ligands?
A. They contain more than one pair of non-bonding electrons.
B. They can form only one coordination bond with a transition metal ion.
C. They do not affect the size of the splitting of the d sub-level.
D. They can only form complexes with transition metal ions.

24. Which species will be paramagnetic?
A. Ca^{2+}
B. Zn^{2+}
C. Cu^+
D. Cr^{3+}

25. Which best explains why the first ionization energy of oxygen is lower than the first ionization energy of nitrogen?
A. Ionization energies increase across a period.
B. A half-filled energy level confers stability.
C. The electron to be removed in O is spin paired, whereas in N all three p electrons are unpaired.
D. The 3p sub-level is higher in energy than the 3s sub-level.

26. Which is a correct statement about Sc^{3+}?
A. It forms coloured complex ions.
B. It contains no d electrons.
C. It has a lower ionization energy than Ti^{3+}.
D. The formula of its nitrate is $Sc(NO_2)_3$.

27. Which species contains the metal in the highest oxidation state?
A. MnO_4^-
B. VO_3^-
C. $Cr_2O_7^{2-}$
D. CrO_4^{2-}

28. Which has no effect on the colour of transition metal complexes?
A. the oxidation state of the metal ion
B. the shape of the complex ion
C. the isotopic mixture of the ions
D. the identity of the ligands

29. The order of three ligands in the spectrochemical series is $Cl^- < H_2O < NH_3$. Which statements can be deduced correctly from this information?
I. Complexes containing Cl^- ligands absorb light of a higher frequency than those containing H_2O ligands.
II. NH_3 ligands split the d orbitals more than H_2O ligands.
III. All the ligands are Lewis bases.
A. I and II only
B. I and III only
C. II and III only
D. I, II, and III

30. Which is the best hydrogenation catalyst?
A. V_2O_5
B. $Pb(C_2H_5)_4$
C. MnO_2
D. Ni

Short-answer questions—Periodicity

1. Carbon, silicon, and tin belong to the same group in the periodic table.
   a) Distinguish between the terms "group" and "period" in terms of electron configuration. [2]
   b) State in which block of the periodic table (s, p, d, or f) these three elements are located. [1]
   c) Explain why the first ionization energy of silicon is lower than that of carbon. [2]
   d) Describe a simple experiment to measure the conductivity of carbon, silicon, and tin and state what would be observed for each element. [3]

2. a) The maximum number of electrons in each energy level is determined by the expression $2n^2$, where n is the number of the level. Explain why the third level is sometimes said to contain eight electrons and sometimes said to contain eighteen electrons. [2]
   b) In terms of electron configuration, describe the essential difference between the lanthanoids and the actinoids. [2]

3. a) Describe how the acid–base nature of the oxides changes across period 3 (Na to Cl). [3]
   b) State the equation for the reaction of water with:
      (i) sodium oxide, Na_2O [1]
      (ii) calcium oxide, CaO [1]
      (iii) sulfur(VI) oxide, SO_3. [1]
   c) Explain why oxides of nitrogen and oxides of sulfur cause damage to many types of buildings. Include relevant equations in your explanation. [4]

4. a) State the electron configuration for the P^{3-} ion. [1]
   b) Explain why the ionic radius of the S^{2-} ion is smaller than that of the P^{3-} ion. [2]
   c) Potassium and bromine are in the same period. Explain why the atomic radius of bromine is considerably smaller than the atomic radius of potassium. [2]
   d) Suggest a reason why no value is given for the atomic radius of neon in the IB data booklet. [1]

5. The periodic table shows the relationship between electron configuration and the properties of elements and is a valuable tool for making predictions in chemistry.
   a) (i) Identify the property used to arrange elements in the periodic table. [1]
      (ii) Outline **two** reasons why electronegativity increases across period 3 in the periodic table and **one** reason why noble gases are not assigned electronegativity values. [3]
   b) (i) Define the term first ionization energy of an atom. [2]
      (ii) Explain the general increasing trend in the first ionization energies of the period 2 elements, Li to Ne. [2]
      (iii) Explain why the first ionization energy of boron is lower than that of beryllium. [2]
   c) Explain why sodium conducts electricity but phosphorus does not. [2]

6. In many cities around the world, public transport vehicles use diesel, a liquid hydrocarbon fuel, which often contains sulfur impurities and undergoes incomplete combustion. All public transport vehicles in New Delhi, India, have been converted to use compressed natural gas (CNG) as their fuel. Suggest **two** ways in which this improves air quality, giving a reason for your answer. [3]

AHL

7. Transition elements, such as iron, have many characteristic properties and uses.
   a) State and explain, in terms of acid–base properties, the type of reaction that occurs between Fe^{2+} ions and water to form $[Fe(H_2O)_6]^{2+}$. [2]
   b) Explain why the colour of $[Fe(H_2O)_6]^{2+}$ is different from that of $[Fe(H_2O)_6]^{3+}$. [2]
   c) Explain why iron metal is magnetic and why some of its complexes, such as $[Fe(H_2O)_6]^{2+}$, are paramagnetic whereas others, such as $[Fe(CN)_6]^{4-}$, are diamagnetic. [4]
   d) The Haber process to form ammonia is exothermic. Explore the economic significance of using an iron catalyst. [3]

8. The diagram shows the $[Cu(EDTA)]^{2-}$ ion.

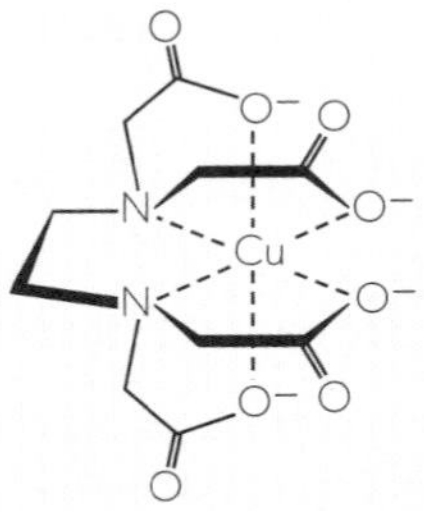

   a) Deduce the formula mass of this complex ion. [2]
   b) State the coordination number and the shape of the ion. [2]
   c) Explain how the $EDTA^{4-}$ ion is able to bond to the Cu^{2+} ion. [3]

9. Ligands can be listed in terms of their ability to split the d orbitals. This is known as the spectrochemical series.
   a) Suggest a reason why different ligands cause the d orbitals to be split by different amounts. [2]
   b) Ammonia molecules are higher in the spectrochemical series (cause greater splitting) than water molecules. Explain why the light blue colour of $[Cu(H_2O)_6]^{2+}$ changes to a more purple colour when excess ammonia is added to copper(II) sulfate solution to form the $[Cu(NH_3)_4(H_2O)_2]^{2+}$ ion. [3]
   c) Explain why aqueous solutions of scandium(III) compounds are not coloured. [2]

IUPAC naming

Uniqueness of carbon

Carbon is unique in that it forms more compounds than are known of all the other elements in the periodic table put together. Many millions of organic compounds have been identified or synthesized and it is worth considering why carbon is so different when compared with all the other elements.

1. *Carbon can form multiple bonds with itself and with atoms of other elements.*

Carbon can form single bonds, C–C, double bonds, C=C, and triple bonds, C≡C, to itself. As well as forming single bonds, it can form double bonds and triple bonds with other elements, such as oxygen in ethanoic acid, CH_3COOH, and nitrogen in hydrogen cyanide, HCN.

2. *The strength of the C–C single bond and the C–H bond.*

The strength of the C–C bond means that it is thermally quite stable, particularly when compared with the single bond formed between two atoms of other elements in group 14 of the periodic table.

Bond	C–C	Si–Si	Ge–Ge	Sn–Sn
Average bond enthalpy / kJ mol^{-1}	348	226	188	151

The single covalent bond that carbon forms with hydrogen is also very strong, 412 kJ mol^{-1}, compared with the silicon to hydrogen bond, 318 kJ mol^{-1}. This contributes to the thermal stability of carbon compounds.

3. *Carbon can form chains and rings.*

The ability of carbon to form strong bonds to itself means that it can form long chains of carbon atoms. In some polymers, there can be well over one thousand carbon atoms in a single chain. The chains can also link to themselves to form cyclic or ring compounds, such as cyclohexane, C_6H_{12}, and benzene, C_6H_6. This ability to form chains and rings is known as **catenation**.

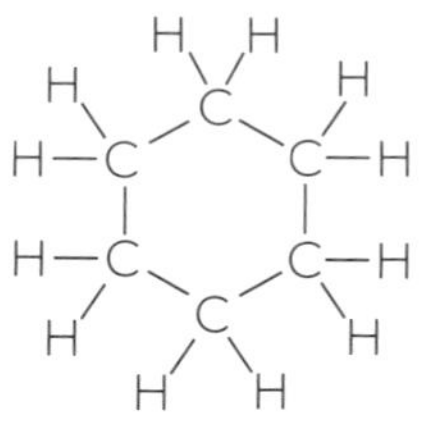

cyclohexane, C_6H_{12}

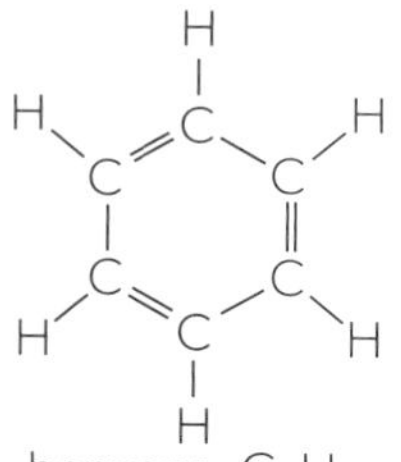

benzene, C_6H_6

4. *Carbon cannot expand its octet of valence electrons.*

When it is bonded, a carbon atom has a share in a full octet of electrons and the outer shell cannot expand to include any more electrons, so it cannot form any more bonds. Silicon, the element below carbon in group 14, also has a full octet when it is bonded to four other atoms, but this octet can be expanded. This makes silicon compounds much less stable kinetically. The most striking example of this is the comparison between carbon tetrachloride (tetrachloromethane, CCl_4) and silicon tetrachloride (tetrachlorosilane, $SiCl_4$). Carbon tetrachloride is completely immiscible in water and does not react. Silicon tetrachloride reacts vigorously in water to produce hydrochloric acid. This is because a non-bonding pair of electrons on an oxygen atom in a water molecule is able to expand the octet on the silicon atom during the reaction.

Naming organic compounds

Initially, as new carbon compounds were discovered or synthesized, they were given names which were individual and often not very systematic. As it became apparent that many compounds contained similar features or fitted a particular general formula, a more systematic way of naming organic compounds evolved. This is called "IUPAC nomenclature" after the set of rules determined by the International Union of Pure and Applied Chemistry.

The main rules are:

1. *Identify the longest carbon chain.*

   1 carbon = **meth-**
   2 carbons = **eth-**
   3 carbons = **prop-**
   4 carbons = **but-**
   5 carbons = **pent-**
   6 carbons = **hex-**
   7 carbons = **hept-**
   8 carbons = **oct-**

2. *Identify the type of bonding in the chain or ring.*
   All single bonds in the carbon chain = **-an-**
   One double bond in the carbon chain = **-en-**
   One triple bond in the carbon chain = **-yn-**

3. *Identify the functional group joined to the chain or ring.*
   This may come at the beginning or end of the name, e.g.
   alkane: only hydrogen (–H) joined to chain = **-e**
   hydroxyl: –OH = **-ol**
   amino: $-NH_2$ = **amino-**
   carboxyl: —C(=O)—OH = **-oic acid**
   ester: —C(=O)—OR = **-oate**

(Functional groups are explained further on the next page.)

4. *Numbers are used to give the position of groups or bonds along the chain.*
   The lowest number possible is used, so counting can start at either end of the longest chain.
   e.g. both $CH_3CH(OH)CH_2CH_2CH_3$ and $CH_3CH_2CH_2CH(OH)CH_3$ are pentan-2-ol (or 2-pentanol).

Homologous series and functional groups

Homologous series

The alkanes form a series of compounds all with the general formula C_nH_{2n+2}, e.g.

methane, CH_4 propane, C_3H_8

ethane, C_2H_6 butane, C_4H_{10}

If one of the hydrogen atoms is removed, what is left is known as an alkyl radical R– (e.g. methyl, CH_3–; ethyl, C_2H_5–). When other atoms or groups are attached to an alkyl radical, they can form a different series of compounds. The attached atoms or groups are known as functional groups and the series formed are all homologous series.

Homologous series have the same general formula, with neighbouring members of the series differing by –CH_2–. For example, the general formula of alcohols is $C_nH_{2n+1}OH$. The chemical properties of the individual members of a homologous series are similar and they show a gradual change in physical properties.

Functional groups

A functional group is a specific grouping of atoms that forms part of an organic compound and which is responsible for the characteristic chemical reactions and physical properties of that compound. In addition to the alkyl group, –R (formed by loss of a hydrogen atom from an alkane), and the phenyl group, –C_6H_5 (formed by loss of a hydrogen atom from benzene), the IB lists eight other specific functional groups that you need to be able to recognize and identify.

hydroxyl: –OH = **-ol**

carbonyl:

$$\begin{array}{c} O \\ \| \end{array}$$
aldehyde —C—H = **-al**, when on the end of a chain

$$\begin{array}{c} O \\ \| \end{array}$$
ketone —C— = **-one**, when not on the end of the chain

halogeno: –X = **chloro-**, **bromo-**, or **iodo-**

alkoxy: –OR = **methoxy-**, **ethoxy-**, etc.

amino: –NH_2 = **amino-**

$$\begin{array}{c} O \\ \| \end{array}$$
carboxyl: —C—OH = **-oic**

$$\begin{array}{c} O \\ \| \end{array}$$
ester: —C—OR = **-oate**

$$\begin{array}{c} O \\ \| \end{array}$$
amido: —C—NH_2 = **amido-**

Class of organic compound

Different compounds that all contain the same functional group are divided into classes. Sometimes the name of the class is the same as the functional group, but sometimes it is different. For example, the name of the class is the same for all **esters** that contain the ester functional group (–COOR), but it is different for all **alcohols** that contain the hydroxyl (–OH) functional group. The carbonyl functional group is –CO–, where the carbon atom is joined by a double bond to the oxygen atom. Several classes of compounds contain this functional group, as it depends upon what else is bonded to the carbon atom. For example, if H is bonded to the carbon atom, then they are known as aldehydes (–COH), whereas if an alkyl group is bonded to the carbon atom, then they are known as ketones (–COR). The –COOH functional group is known as the carboxyl group and the class of compounds containing this group is called carboxylic acids. Compounds containing an amino group are known as amines, whereas compounds containing an amido group, –$CONH_2$ are known as amides. Compounds containing a halogeno group are known as halogenoalkanes (or, more specifically, chloroalkanes, bromoalkanes, or iodoalkanes).

Classification of alcohols, halogenoalkanes, and amines

Alcohols and halogenoalkanes may be classified according to how many –R groups are bonded to the carbon atom containing the functional group. Similar logic applies to amines, but now it is the number of –R groups attached to the nitrogen atom of the amino functional group.

Primary, with one –R group bonded to the C or N atom:

$$R-\underset{\underset{H}{|}}{\overset{\overset{H}{|}}{C}}-OH \qquad R-\underset{\underset{H}{|}}{\overset{\overset{H}{|}}{C}}-Br \qquad R-\underset{}{\overset{\overset{H}{|}}{N}}-H$$

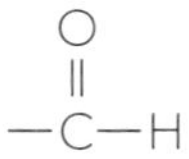

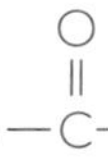

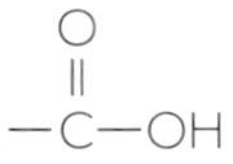

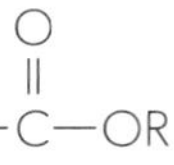

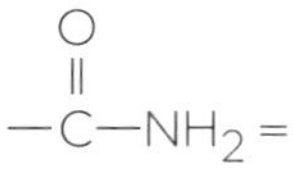

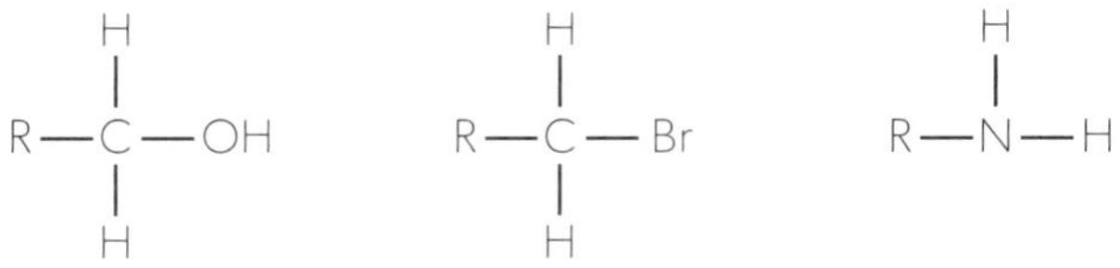

Secondary, with two –R groups bonded to the C or N atom. R′ may be the same as R or may be different:

$$R-\underset{\underset{R'}{|}}{\overset{\overset{H}{|}}{C}}-OH \qquad R-\underset{\underset{R'}{|}}{\overset{\overset{H}{|}}{C}}-Br \qquad R-\underset{}{\overset{\overset{H}{|}}{N}}-R'$$

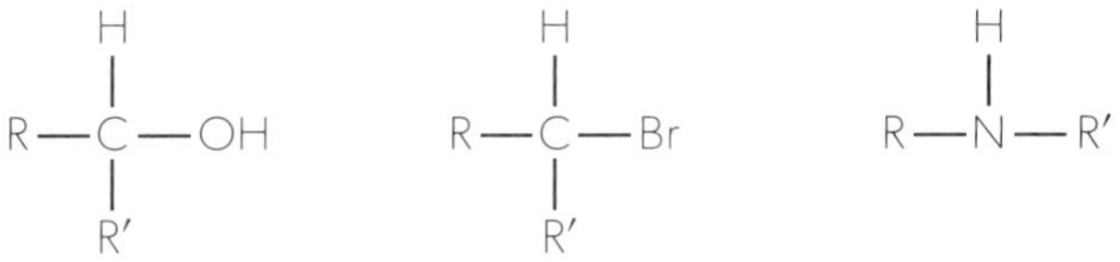

Tertiary, with three –R groups bonded to the C or N atom. R″ may be the same as R′ or R, or may be different:

$$R-\underset{\underset{R'}{|}}{\overset{\overset{R''}{|}}{C}}-OH \qquad R-\underset{\underset{R'}{|}}{\overset{\overset{R''}{|}}{C}}-Br \qquad R-\underset{}{\overset{\overset{R''}{|}}{N}}-R'$$

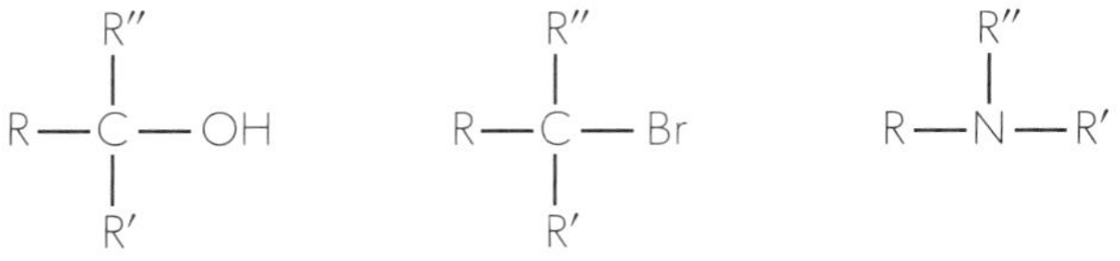

Common classes of organic compounds

Formula	Name	Examples
R—H	alkane	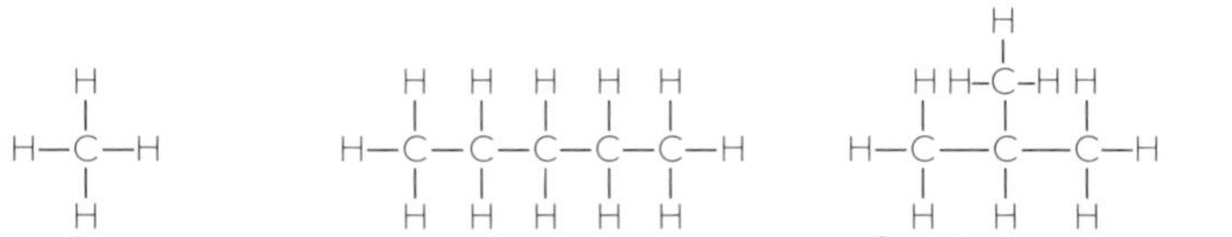 methane, butane, 2-methylpropane
$>C{=}C<$	alkene functional group: alkenyl	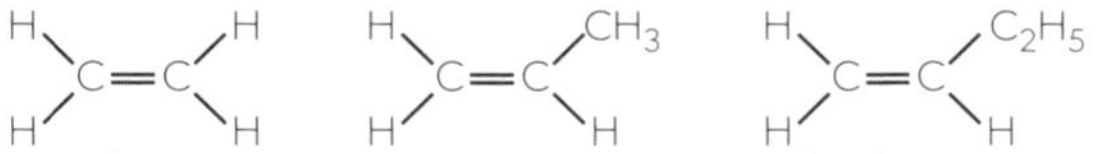 ethene, propene, but-1-ene
—C≡C—	alkyne functional group: alkynyl	H—C≡C—H ethyne H—C≡C—CH_3 propyne
R—OH	alcohol functional group: hydroxyl	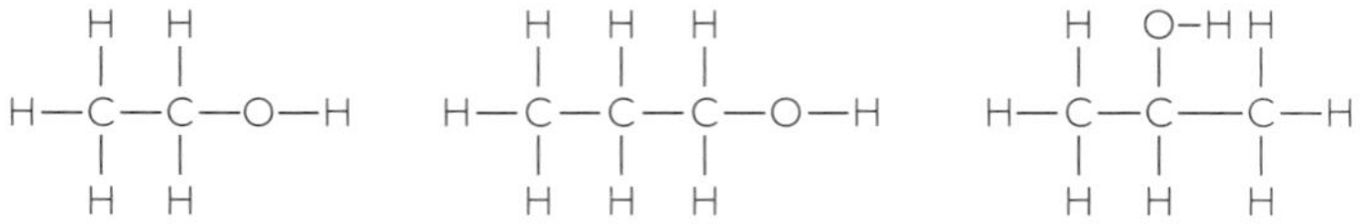 ethanol, propan-1-ol, propan-2-ol
R—NH_2	amine	 ethanamine (ethylamine), 2-butanamine (2-aminobutane)
R—X (X = F, Cl, Br, or I)	halogenoalkane	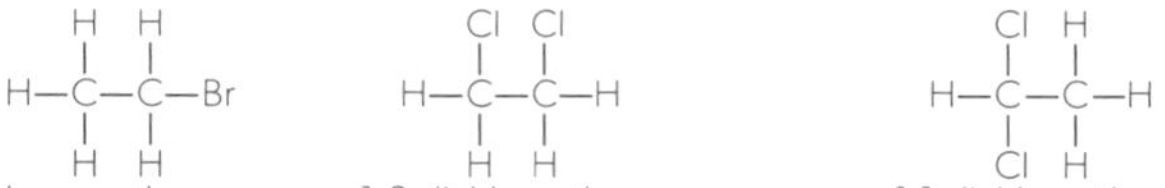 bromoethane, 1,2-dichloroethane, 1,1-dichloroethane
R—C(=O)—H	aldehyde	 ethanal, propanal
R—C(=O)—R′ (R′ may be the same as or different from R)	ketone	H_3C—C(=O)—CH_3 propanone H_3C—C(=O)—CH_2—CH_2—CH_3 pentan-2-one H_3C—CH_2—C(=O)—CH_2—CH_3 pentan-3-one
R—C(=O)—OH	carboxylic acid functional group: carboxyl	 methanoic acid, propanoic acid
R—C(=O)—OR′	ester	 ethyl ethanoate, propyl methanoate
R—C(=O)—NH_2	amide functional group: amido	CH_3—C(=O)—NH_2 ethanamide C_2H_5—C(=O)—NH_2 propanamide
R—O—R′	ether functional group: alkoxy	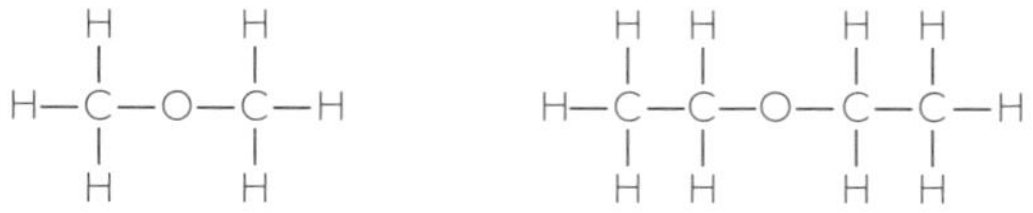 methoxymethane, ethoxyethane
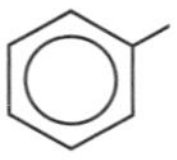	(C_6H_5–) benzene ring functional group: phenyl	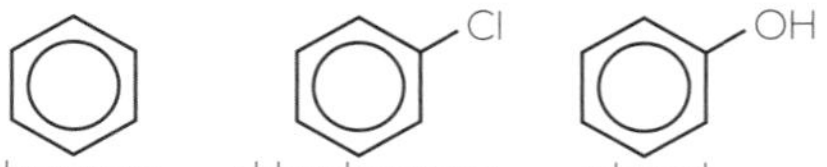 benzene, chlorobenzene, phenol

Structural formulas

Structural formulas

The differences between the empirical and molecular formulas of a compound have already been covered in Chapter 3. Because the physical and chemical properties of a compound are determined by the functional group and the arrangement of carbon and other atoms within the molecule, the structural formulas for organic compounds are often used.

These may be shown in a variety of different ways, but all ways should show unambiguously how the atoms are bonded together. When drawing full structural formulas with lines representing bonds and the symbol of the element representing atoms, all the hydrogen atoms must also be included in the diagram. This is because a skeletal formula does not include any symbols for the elements and the end of a line represents a methyl group unless another atom is shown attached. Although you should understand skeletal formulas, they are not normally used for simple formulas except where benzene is involved. Note that, unless specifically asked for, Lewis formulas, showing all the valence electrons, are not necessary.

The bonding must be clearly indicated. Structures may be shown using lines as bonds or in their shortened form, e.g. $CH_3CH_2CH_2CH_2CH_3$ or $CH_3–(CH_2)_3–CH_3$ for pentane. This is sometimes known as a semi-structural formula or condensed structural formula: unlike the molecular formula, C_5H_{12}, it still shows how the atoms are bonded together.

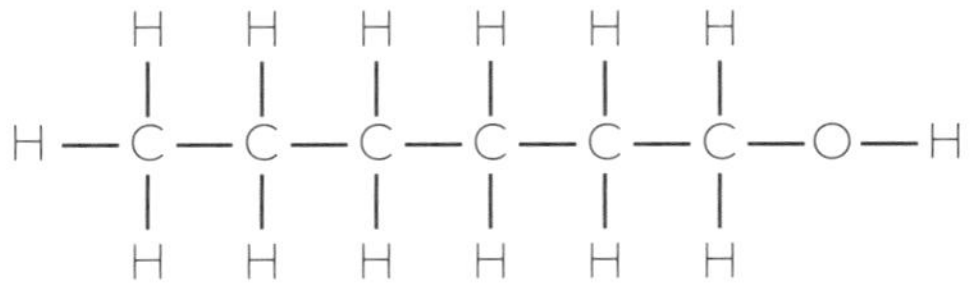

▲ Full structural formula for hexan-1-ol

Other acceptable structural formulas for hexan-1-ol are $CH_3CH_2CH_2CH_2CH_2CH_2OH$ and $CH_3(CH_2)_4CH_2OH$

▲ Skeletal formula of hexan-1-ol

Structural formulas of hydrocarbons

Isomers of alkanes

Each carbon atom in an alkane has four single bonds, to give a saturated compound. There is only one possible structure for each of methane, ethane, and propane; however, two structures of butane are possible.

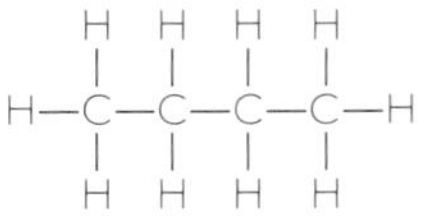

butane

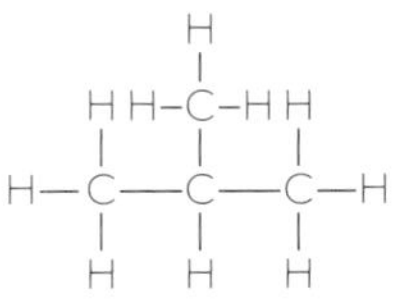

2-methylpropane

These are examples of structural isomers. **Structural isomers** have the same molecular formula but a different structural formula. They normally have similar chemical properties, but their physical properties may be slightly different. There are three structural isomers of pentane.

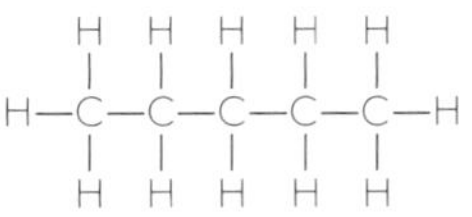

pentane

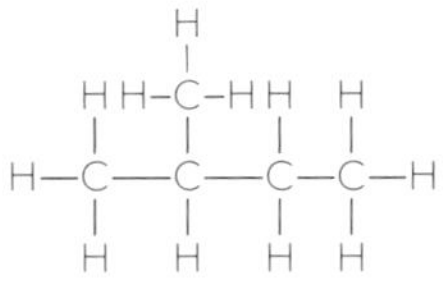

2-methylbutane

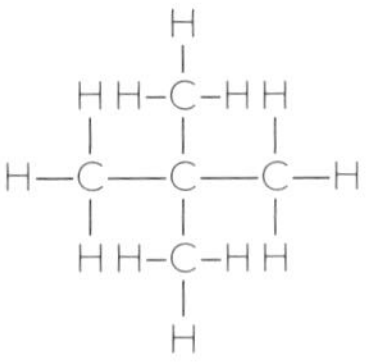

2,2-dimethylpropane

Isomers of alkenes and alkynes

Alkenes and alkynes are unsaturated.

The alkenes ethene and propene each have only one possible structure but butene has three structural isomers.

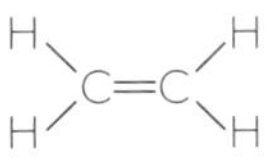

ethene

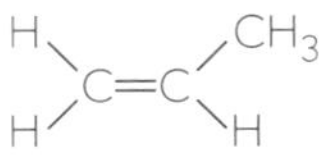

propene

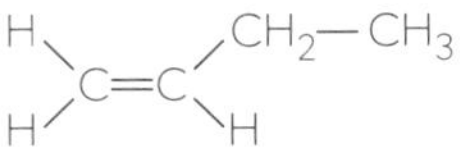

but-1-ene

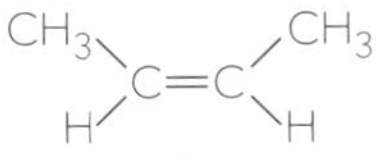

but-2-ene

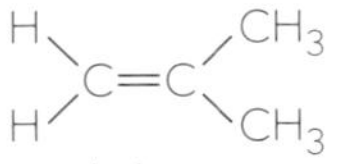

2-methylpropene

Similarly, the alkynes ethyne and propyne each have only one possible structure but butyne has two.

$H—C\equiv C—H$ ethyne

$H—C\equiv C—CH_3$ propyne

$H—C\equiv C—CH_2—CH_3$ but-1-yne

$CH_3—C\equiv C—CH_3$ but-2-yne

Types and names of structural isomers

Types of structural isomers

Structural isomers are molecules that have the same molecular formula but different connectivities. They can be divided into three sub-groups.

1. Chain isomers

Structural isomers may be either straight chain or branched. The three isomers of pentane illustrated on page 57 exemplify this. All three have the same molecular formula, C_5H_{12}. One is the straight-chain isomer, $CH_3CH_2CH_2CH_2CH_3$; one has a methyl group substituted on the second carbon atom of butane, so it is 2-methylbutane, $CH_3CH(CH_3)CH_2CH_3$; and the third has two methyl groups substituted on the second carbon atom of propane, so it is 2,2-dimethylpropane, $C(CH_3)_4$.

2. Position isomers

Position isomers have the same basic carbon skeleton, but the functional group is located on a different carbon atom. Examples include propan-1-ol and propan-2-ol, and pentan-2-one and pentan-3-one.

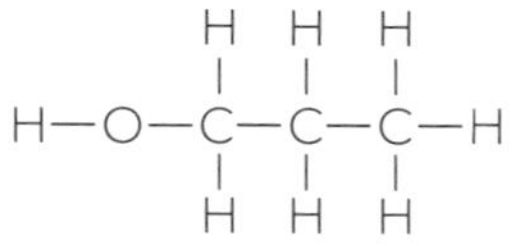
propan-1-ol

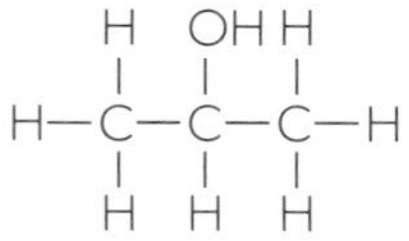
propan-2-ol

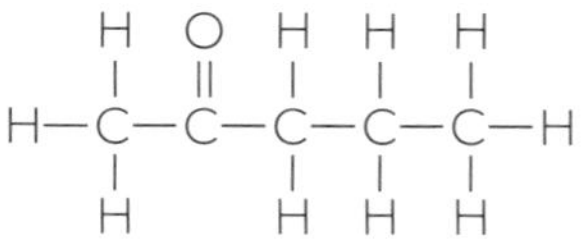
pentan-2-one

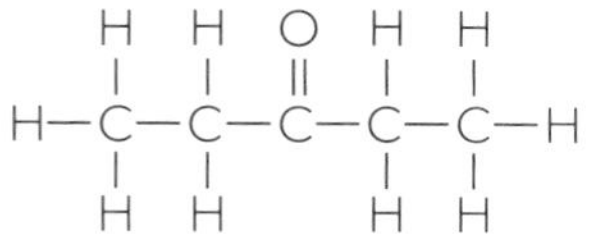
pentan-3-one

3. Functional group isomers

Functional group isomers may have very different chemical and physical properties as they contain completely different functional groups. A simple example is compounds with the molecular formula C_2H_6O. This could either be an alcohol, CH_3CH_2OH, or an ether CH_3OCH_3.

$H_3C–CH_2–OH$	$H_3C–O–CH_3$
ethanol	methoxymethane
(alcohol)	(ether)

Another simple example is $C_3H_4O_2$. This could either be a carboxylic acid or an ester.

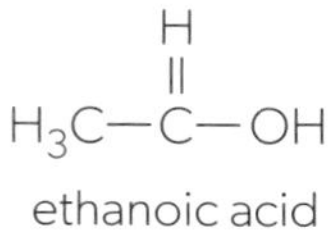
ethanoic acid
(carboxylic acid)

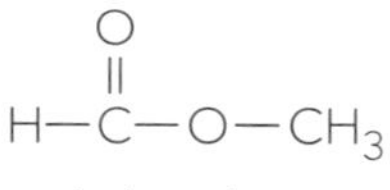
methyl methanoate
(ester)

Naming structural isomers

The IB requires you to be able to apply the IUPAC nomenclature to saturated or mono-unsaturated compounds having up to six carbon atoms in the parent chain and containing one type of the following functional groups: halogeno, hydroxyl, carbonyl, and carboxyl.

For example, four different structural isomers with the molecular formula $C_6H_{12}O$ are shown.

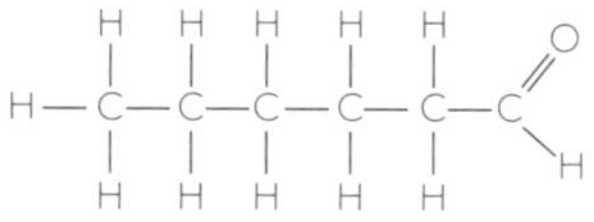
or $CH_3CH_2CH_2CH_2CH_2CHO$
hexanal

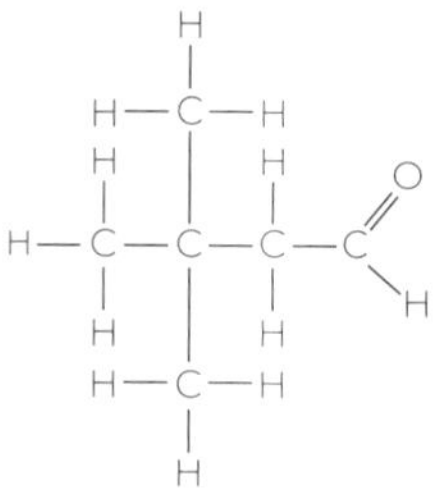
$CH_3C(CH_3)_2CH_2CHO$
3, 3-dimethylbutanal

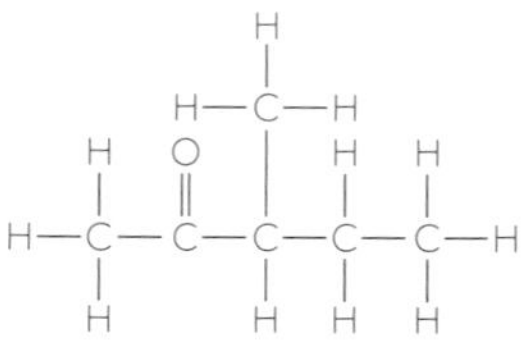
$CH_3COCH(CH_3)CH_2CH_3$
3-methylpentan-2-one

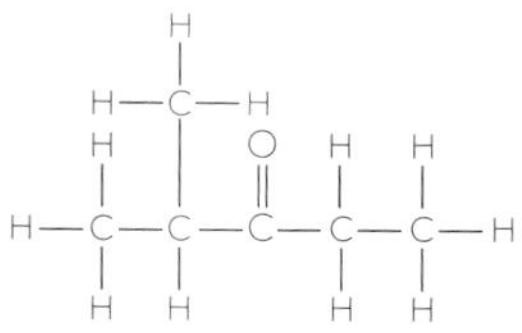
$CH_3CH(CH_3)COCH_2CH_3$
2-methylpentan-3-one

3D models of structural formulas

3D representations

To help to distinguish between isomers, and because the chemical and physical properties of molecules depend upon their shape and the types of bonds and functional groups they contain, it is helpful to be able to visualize structures in three dimensions. Two-dimensional display diagrams of alkanes, for example, wrongly suggest that the H–C–H bond angles are 90° instead of 109.5°. The traditional way in which chemists have approached this is to use a full "wedge" to show an atom coming out of the two-dimensional page and a dotted line to show it going behind the page.

The very best way to "see" molecular structures in three dimensions is to use a molecular modelling kit and build the models for yourself. This can be particularly helpful when distinguishing between isomers and understanding bond angles. Two common ways to represent molecules in 3D are "ball and stick" models and space-fill models. You can also see virtual 3D representations using apps on your laptop, smart phone, or tablet, and these are also able to show the molecules rotating.

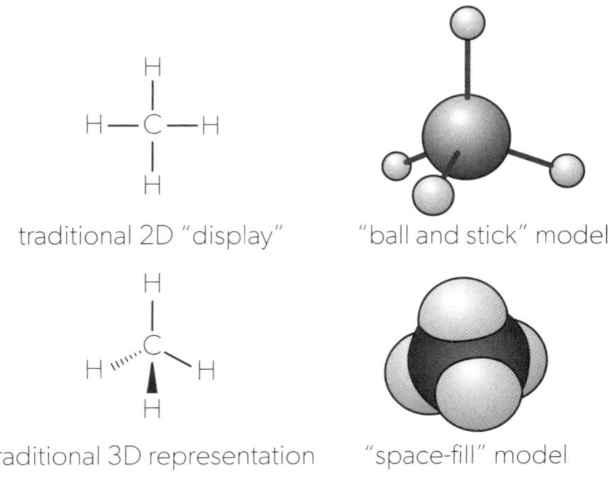

▲ Some models of the structure of methane

Identifying functional groups in molecules from virtual 3D models

As well as recognizing different functional groups within more complex molecules from their structural formulas, you should also be able to recognize them from virtual 3D representations.

The illustrated molecules—aspirin, paracetamol (acetaminophen), and ibuprofen—are all mild pain killers. As you can see, they all contain a phenyl group, although this is a phenol in paracetamol as the phenyl group is directly bonded to a hydroxyl group. Aspirin and ibuprofen contain a carboxyl group (carboxylic acid); aspirin also contains an ester group and paracetamol contains an amido group.

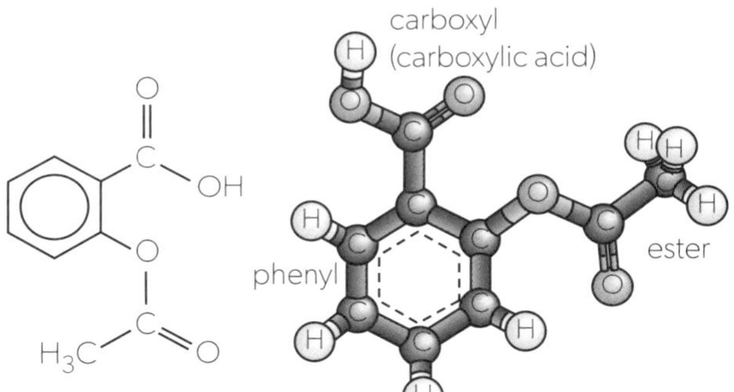

aspirin

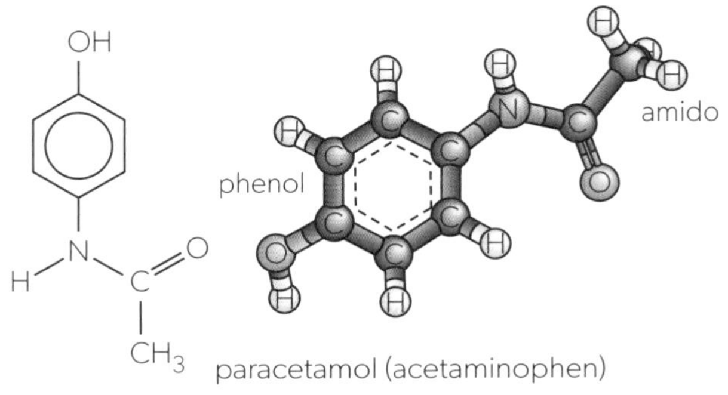

paracetamol (acetaminophen)

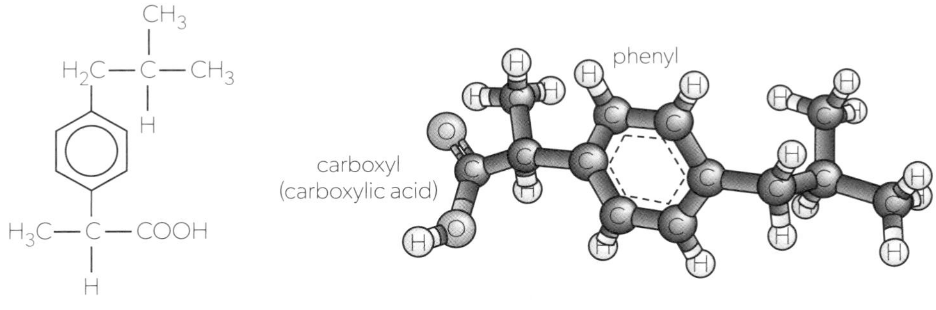

ibuprofen

Properties of different homologous series

Boiling points

As the carbon chain in the homologous series of alkanes increases, the London dispersion forces of attraction increase and hence the boiling points and melting points also increase. A plot of boiling point against number of carbon atoms shows a sharp increase at first, as the percentage increase in mass is high, but, as successive $-CH_2-$ groups are added, the rate of increase in boiling point decreases.

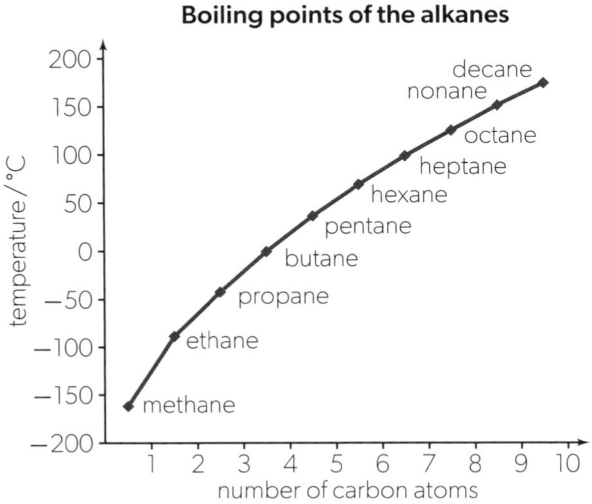

When branching occurs, the molecules become more spherical in shape, which reduces the contact surface area between different molecules and lowers the boiling point.

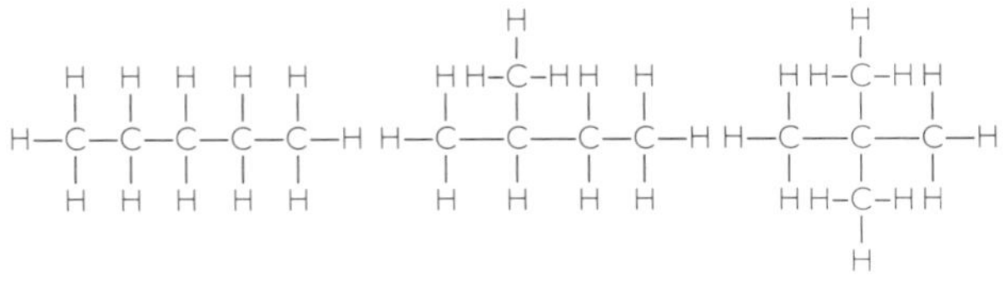

pentane (b. pt 36.3 °C) 2-methylbutane (b. pt 27.9 °C) 2,2-dimethylpropane (b. pt 9.5 °C)

Other homologous series show similar trends, but the actual temperatures at which the compounds boil will depend on the types of attractive forces between the molecules. The volatility of the compounds also follows the same pattern. The lower members of the alkanes are all gases as the attractive forces are weak, and the next few members are volatile liquids. Methanol, the first member of the alcohols, is a liquid at room temperature, due to the presence of hydrogen bonding. Methanol is classed as volatile as its boiling point is 64.5 °C, but when there are four or more carbon atoms in the chain the boiling points exceed 100 °C so the higher alcohols have low volatility.

Compound	Formula	M_r	Class of compound	Strongest type of attraction	B. pt / °C
butane	C_4H_{10}	58	alkane	London dispersion forces	−0.5
but-1-ene	C_4H_8	56	alkene	London dispersion forces	−6.5
but-1-yne	C_4H_6	54	alkyne	London dispersion forces	8.1
methyl methanoate	$HCOOCH_3$	60	ester	dipole–dipole	31.5
propanal	CH_3CH_2CHO	58	aldehyde	dipole–dipole	48.8
propanone	CH_3COCH_3	58	ketone	dipole–dipole	56.2
propanamine (aminopropane)	$CH_3CH_2CH_2NH_2$	59	amine	hydrogen bonding	48.6
propan-1-ol	$CH_3CH_2CH_2OH$	60	alcohol	hydrogen bonding	97.2
ethanoic acid	CH_3COOH	60	carboxylic acid	hydrogen bonding	118

Solubility in water

Whether or not an organic compound is soluble in water depends on the polarity of the functional group and on the length of the hydrocarbon chain. The lower members of alcohols, amines, aldehydes, ketones, and carboxylic acids are all water soluble. However, as the length of the non-polar hydrocarbon chain increases, the solubility in water decreases. For example, ethanol and water mix in all proportions, but hexan-1-ol is only slightly soluble in water. Compounds with non-polar functional groups, such as alkanes and alkenes, do not dissolve in water but are soluble in other non-polar solvents. Propan-1-ol is a good solvent because it contains both polar and non-polar groups and can, to some extent, dissolve both polar and non-polar substances.

AHL Stereoisomerism (1)

Types of isomerism

Isomers are compounds that are composed of the same elements in the same proportions but differ in properties because of differences in the arrangement of atoms. Structural isomers share the same molecular formula but have different structural formulas: that is, their atoms are bonded in different ways. Stereoisomers have the same structural formulas but differ in their spatial arrangement. Stereoisomers can be sub-divided into two classes: conformational isomers, which interconvert by rotation about a σ bond, and configurational isomers, which interconvert only by breaking and reforming a bond. The IB syllabus on stereoisomerism is concerned with configurational isomers, which can be further sub-divided into *cis–trans* isomers (are also known as *E/Z* isomers, and which together used to be known by the now obsolete term of geometrical isomers) and optical isomers.

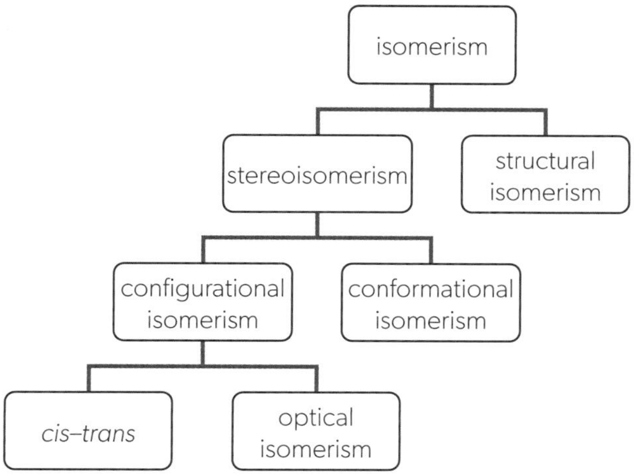

Cis–trans isomerism

Cis–trans isomerism occurs when rotation about a bond is restricted or prevented. The classic examples of *cis–trans* isomerism occur with asymmetric non-cyclic alkenes of the type RR′C=CRR′. A *cis* isomer is one in which the substituents are on the same side of the double bond. In a *trans* isomer the substituents are on opposite sides of the double bond. For example, consider *cis*-but-2-ene and *trans*-but-2-ene.

cis- *trans-*

When there is a single bond between two carbon atoms, free rotation about the bond is possible. However, the double bond in an alkene is made up of a σ bond and a π bond. The π bond is formed from the combination of two p orbitals, one from each of the carbon atoms. These two p orbitals must be in the same plane to combine. Rotating the bond would cause the π bond to break, so rotation is not possible.

Cis–trans isomerism will always occur in alkenes when the two groups X and Y attached to each of the two carbon atoms are different.

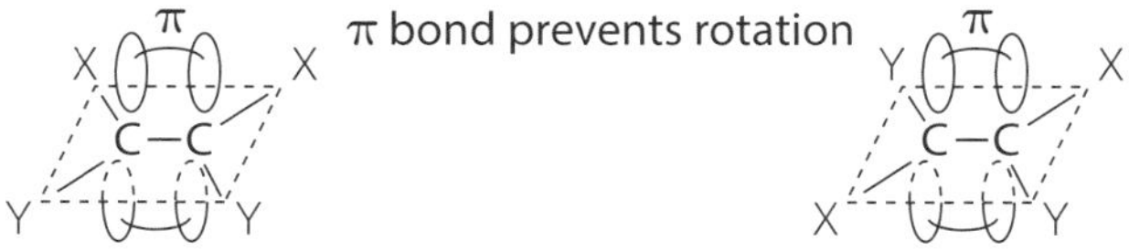

cis- trans-

Cis–trans isomerism can also occur in disubstituted cycloalkanes. The rotation is restricted because the C–C single bond is part of a ring system. Examples include 1,2-dichlorocyclopropane and 1,3-dichlorocyclobutane.

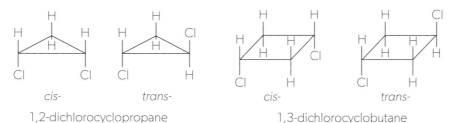

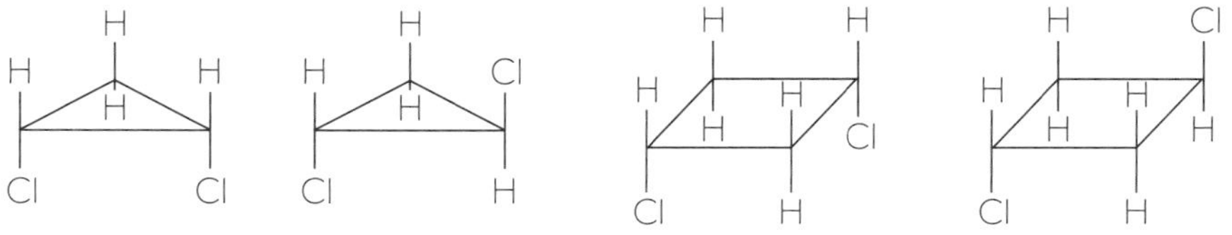

cis- *trans-*
1,2-dichlorocyclopropane

cis- *trans-*
1,3-dichlorocyclobutane

AHL Stereoisomerism (2)

Physical and chemical properties of *cis–trans* isomers

The chemical properties of *cis–trans* isomers tend to be similar but their physical properties are different. For example, the boiling point of *cis*-1,2-dichloroethene is 60.3 °C whereas *trans*-1,2-dichloroethene boils at the lower temperature of 47.5 °C. Sometimes there can be a marked difference in both chemical and physical properties. This tends to occur when there is some sort of chemical interaction between the substituents. *cis*-but-2-ene-1,4-dioic acid melts with decomposition at 130–131 °C. However, *trans*-but-2-ene-1,4-dioic acid does not melt until 286 °C. In the *cis* isomer, the two carboxylic acid groups are closer together and so intramolecular hydrogen bonding is possible between them. In the *trans* isomer, these groups are too far apart to attract each other, so there are stronger intermolecular forces of attraction between different molecules, which results in a higher melting point.

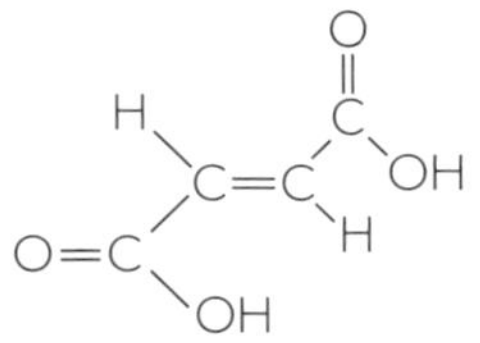

trans-but-2-ene-1,4-dioic acid

heat

cannot form cyclic acid anhydride when heated

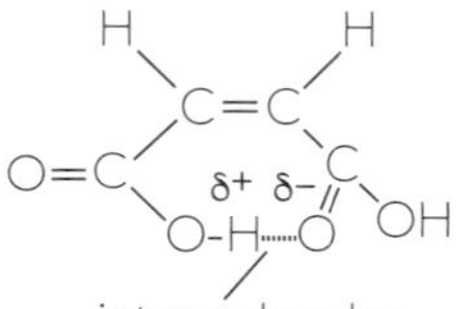

intramolecular hydrogen bonding

cis-but-2-ene-1,4-dioic acid

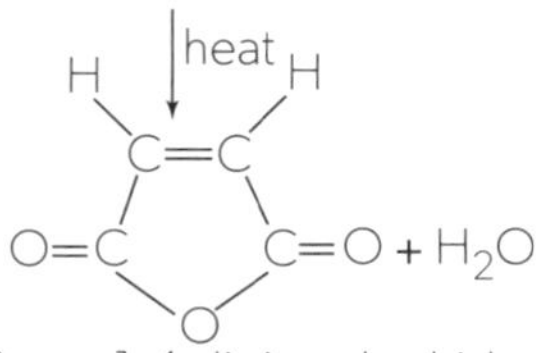

cis-but-2-ene-1,4-dioic anhydride

The *cis* isomer reacts when heated, losing water and forming a cyclic acid anhydride. The *trans* isomer cannot undergo this reaction.

Limitations of *cis–trans* nomenclature

Although the IB only requires you to be able to use *cis–trans* nomenclature, this only works when the two substituents R and R′ (or X and Y) occur on either side of the carbon to carbon double bond. Most chemists now use *E*/*Z* nomenclature (rather than *cis–trans*) as this covers every case, i.e. for RR′C=CR′′R′′′ (where R ≠ R′, R′′ ≠ R′′′ and where neither R nor R′ need be different from R′′ or R′′′).

E/*Z* works on a priority system. The higher the atomic number of the atoms attached to each carbon atom, the higher the priority. Consider 1,2-dichloroethene. Chlorine has a higher atomic number than hydrogen, so has a higher priority. If the atoms / groups lie on the same side, the isomer is *Z*; if they lie on opposite sides, the isomer is *E*. In this simple case, *Z* is the *cis* form and *E* is the *trans* form.

Both highest priorities lie on the same side, so *Z* isomer.

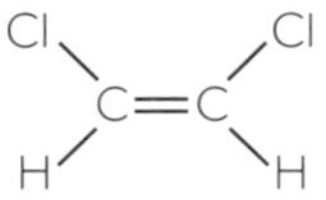

cis-1,2-dichloroethene
(*Z*)-1,2-dichloroethene

Highest priorities lie on opposite sides, so *E* isomer.

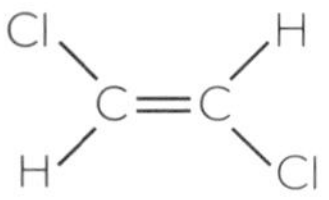

trans-1,2-dichloroethene
(*E*)-1,2-dichloroethene

Cis–trans nomenclature does not work at all when all the groups are different so, although not required by the IB, *E*/*Z* must be used. For example it is not obvious which would be the *cis* and *trans* forms in 2-bromo-1-chloro-2-iodoethene. Using the *E*/*Z* priority system, the *E* and *Z* forms can easily be determined.

Both highest priorities lie on the same side so *Z* isomer.

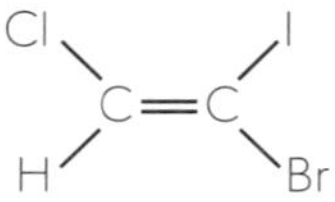

(*Z*)-2-bromo-1-chloro-2-iodoethene

Highest priorities lie on opposite side so *E* isomer.

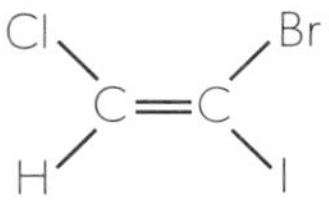

(*E*)-2-bromo-1-chloro-2-iodoethene

AHL Stereoisomerism (3)

Optical isomerism

Optical isomerism is shown by all compounds that contain at least one asymmetric or chiral carbon atom within the molecule. A chiral carbon atom is one that contains four different atoms or groups bonded to it; also known as a stereocentre. The two isomers are known as enantiomers and are mirror images of each other. Examples include butan-2-ol, $CH_3CH(OH)C_2H_5$, 2-hydroxypropanoic acid (lactic acid), $CH_3CH(OH)COOH$, and all amino acids (except glycine, NH_2CH_2COOH).

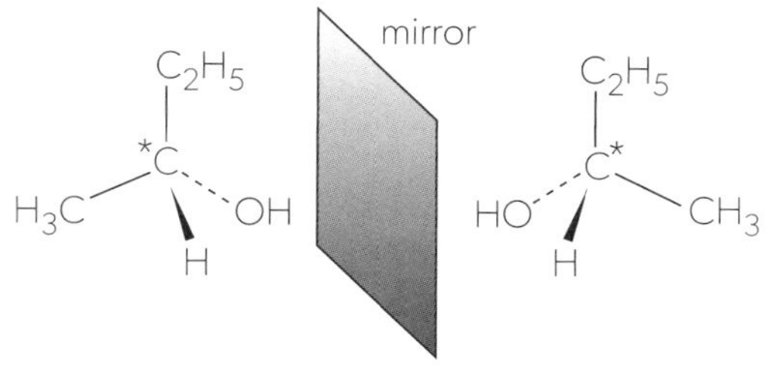

enantiomers of butan-2-ol
(* asymmetric carbon/chiral carbon/stereocentre)

The two different isomers are optically active with plane-polarized light. Normal light consists of electromagnetic radiation that vibrates in all planes. When it is passed through a polarizing filter, the waves vibrate in only one plane and the light is said to be plane polarized.

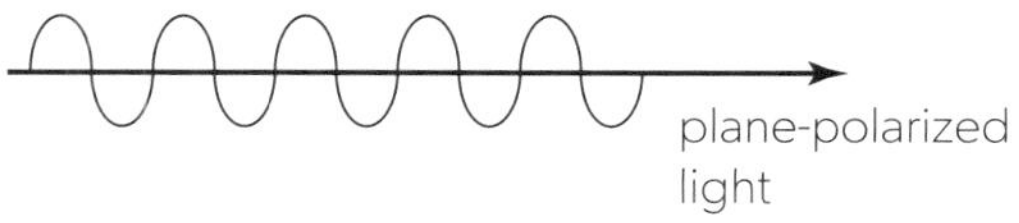

The two enantiomers both rotate the plane of plane-polarized light. One of the enantiomers rotates it to the left and the other rotates it by the same amount to the right. Apart from their behaviour towards plane-polarized light, enantiomers have identical physical properties. Their chemical properties are identical too except when they interact with other optically active substances. This is often the case in the body where the different enantiomers can have completely different physiological effects. For example one of the enantiomers of the amino acid asparagine $H_2NCH(CH_2CONH_2)COOH$ tastes bitter whereas the other enantiomer tastes sweet.

If a molecule contains two or more stereocentres, then several different stereoisomers are possible. They are known as enantiomers if they are mirror images and as diastereomers if they are not mirror images of each other. Diastereomerism occurs when two or more stereoisomers of a compound have different configurations at one or more (but not all) of the equivalent stereocentres. This is particularly important with many sugars and some amino acids. Diastereomers have different physical properties and different chemical reactivity.

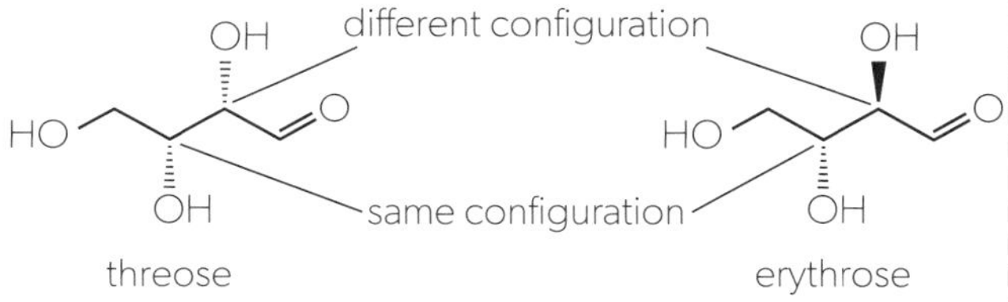

diastereomers of 2,3,4-trihydroxybutanal

Racemic mixtures

The optical activity of enantiomers can be detected and measured by an instrument called a polarimeter. It measures the angle by which plane-polarized light is rotated by a pure sample of the enantiomer, either clockwise (dextrorotatory) or anticlockwise (laevorotatory) to give light of maximum intensity.

The two enantiomers rotate the plane of plane-polarized light by the same amount but in opposite directions. If both enantiomers are present in equal amounts, then the two rotations cancel each other out and the mixture appears to be optically inactive. Such a mixture is known as a **racemic mixture** or **racemate**.

AHL Spectroscopic identification of organic compounds: mass spectrometry (MS)

Information from different analytical techniques

The classical way to determine the structure of an organic compound was to determine both its empirical formula and relative molar mass experimentally, then deduce the nature of the functional groups from its chemical reactivity. However, modern well-equipped laboratories now employ a variety of instrumental techniques, which, if used in combination, are able to unambiguously determine the exact structural formula. They can also be used to determine the composition of the components in a mixture and to determine purity. These techniques are becoming ever more refined and some of them (e.g. mass spectrometry) can be used on extremely small samples. Before analysis can usually take place, it is important to separate any mixture into its individual components—hence the need for chromatography. Often information is not obtained from a single technique but from a combination of several of them. Some examples are:

- Infrared spectroscopy: organic structural determination, information on the strength of bonds, information about the secondary structure of proteins, measuring the degree of unsaturation of oils and fats, and determining the level of alcohol in the breath.
- Mass spectrometry: organic structural determination, isotopic dating (e.g. ^{14}C dating).
- Proton nuclear magnetic resonance spectroscopy (^1H NMR): organic structural determination, body scanning (known as MRI).
- Chromatography: drug testing in the blood and urine, food testing, and forensic science.

Mass spectrometry

The principles of mass spectroscopy and its use to determine relative atomic masses have already been explained in Chapter 2. It can be used in a similar way with organic compounds. However, in addition to giving the precise molecular mass of the substance, mass spectroscopy gives considerable information about the actual structure of the compound from the fragmentation patterns.

When a sample is introduced into the machine, the vaporized sample becomes ionized to form the molecular ion $M^+(g)$. Inside the mass spectrometer, some of the molecular ions break down to give fragments, which are also deflected by the external magnetic field and which then show up as peaks on the detector. By looking at the difference in mass from the parent peak, it is often possible to identify particular fragments:

e.g. $(M_r - 15)^+$ = loss of CH_3

$(M_r - 17)^+$ = loss of OH

$(M_r - 18)^+$ = loss of H_2O

$(M_r - 28)^+$ = loss of C_2H_4 or CO

$(M_r - 29)^+$ = loss of C_2H_5 or CHO

$(M_r - 31)^+$ = loss of CH_2OH

$(M_r - 45)^+$ = loss of COOH

This can provide a useful way of distinguishing between structural isomers.

The mass spectra of propan-1-ol and propan-2-ol both show a peak at 60 due to the molecular ion, $C_3H_8O^+$. However, the mass spectrum of propan-1-ol shows a strong peak at 31 due to the loss of $-C_2H_5$, and this peak is absent in the mass spectrum of propan-2-ol. There is a strong peak at 45 in the spectrum of propan-2-ol as it contains two different methyl groups, which can fragment.

Mass spectrum of propan-1-ol $CH_3-CH_2-CH_2-OH$

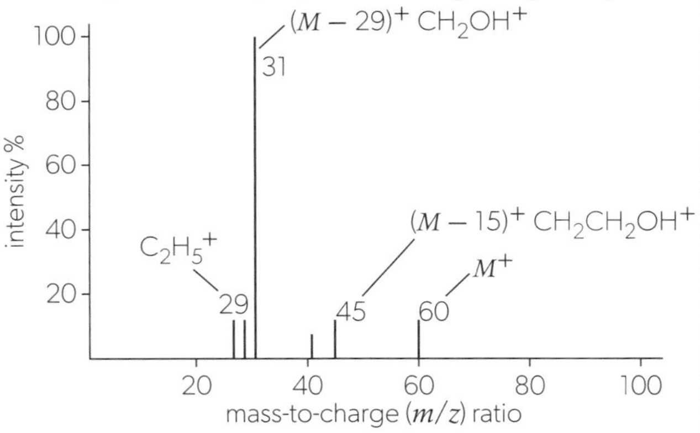

Mass spectrum of propan-2-ol $CH_3-CH(OH)-CH_3$

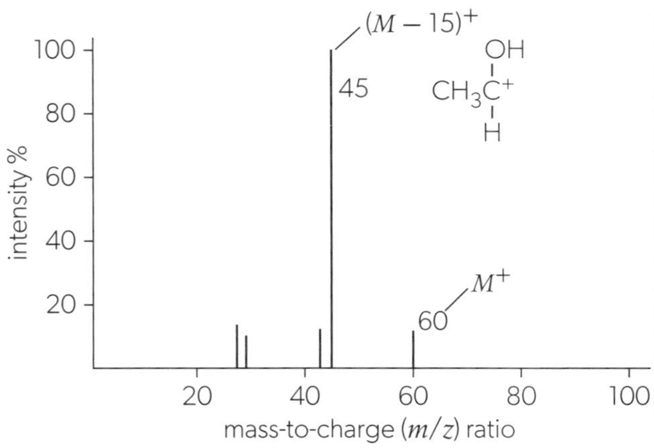

AHL

Spectroscopic identification of organic compounds: IR spectroscopy

Infrared (IR) spectroscopy

When molecules absorb energy in the infrared region of the spectrum they vibrate (i.e. the bonds stretch and bend). The precise value of the energy they absorb depends on the particular bond and, to a lesser extent, on the other groups attached to the two atoms forming the bond. When infrared radiation is passed through a sample, the spectrum shows characteristic absorptions, which confirm that particular bonds are present in the molecule. Some absorptions, e.g. those due to C–H, are not particularly useful, as they are shown by most organic compounds. However, other absorptions give a very clear indication of a particular functional group.

In addition to these particular absorptions, infrared spectra also possess a "fingerprint" region. This is a characteristic pattern around 1400–400 cm^{-1} that is specific to a particular compound. It is often possible to identify an unknown sample by comparing the fingerprint region with a library of spectra of known compounds. Note that "wavenumber" (in cm^{-1}) is the reciprocal of wavelength (in cm).

▼ A simplified correlation chart

Bond	Wavenumber / cm^{-1}
C–Cl	600–800
C–O	1050–1410
C=C	1620–1680
C=O	1700–1750
C≡C	2100–2260
O–H (in carboxylic acids)	2500–3000
C–H	2850–3090
O–H (in alcohols)	3200–3600

Infrared spectrum of ethanol CH_3CH_2OH

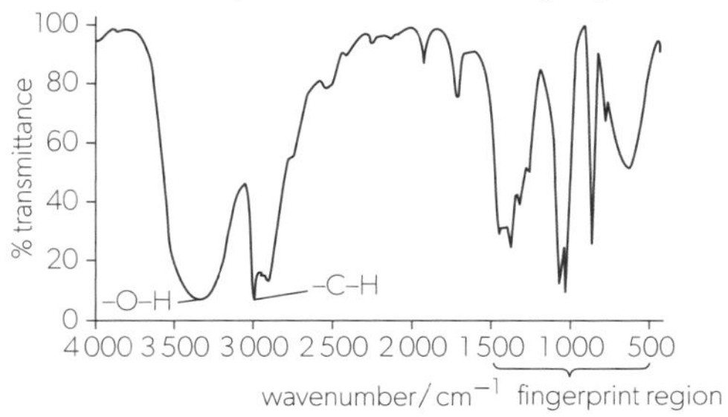

Infrared spectrum of ethyl ethanoate $CH_3-C(=O)-O-C_2H_5$

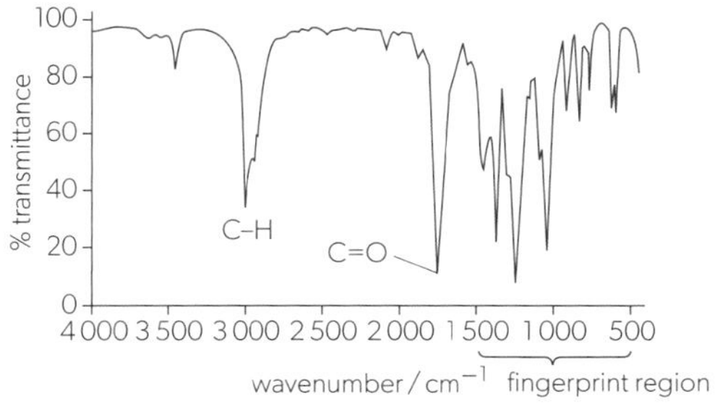

Bond vibrations and greenhouse gases

For simple molecules such as H–Cl there is only one type of vibration, bond stretching, where the atoms alternately move further apart and then closer together. For vibrations to absorb infrared radiation, there must be a change in the dipole moment (molecular polarity) so diatomic molecules containing only one element, such as the gases O_2 and N_2 found in the atmosphere, do not absorb infrared radiation. For other more complex molecules found in the air, such as carbon dioxide and water, bending vibrations can also occur and those vibrations that involve a dipole change will absorb infrared radiation.

Vibrations of H_2O and CO_2

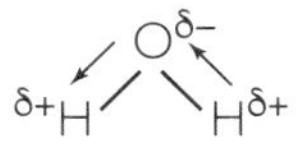

asymmetrical stretching; IR active

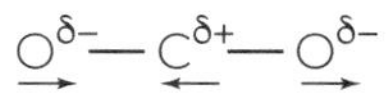

asymmetrical stretching; IR active

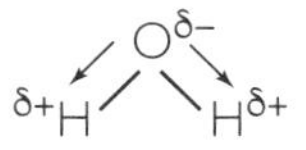

symmetrical stretching; IR active

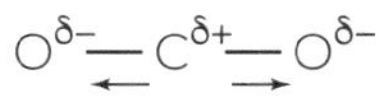

symmetrical stretching; no change in dipole moment, so IR inactive

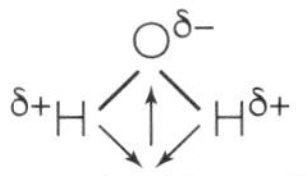

symmetrical bending; IR active

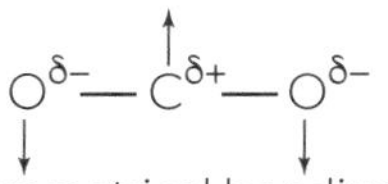

symmetrical bending; two modes at right angles; IR active

The mean average temperature of the Earth is a result of the equilibrium that exists between the energy reaching the Earth from the Sun and the energy reflected back by the Earth into space. Some of the shorter wavelength incoming radiation (visible and ultraviolet radiation) is reflected back into space and some is absorbed by the atmosphere before it reaches the Earth's surface. The energy reflected back from the Earth's surface is longer wavelength infrared radiation. Not all the radiation escapes. Greenhouse gases such as water and carbon dioxide allow the passage of the incoming shortwave radiation but absorb some of the longer wave reflected infrared radiation and re-radiate it back to the Earth's surface, which increases the Earth's temperature. The contribution to global warming made by different greenhouse gases depends on their concentration in the atmosphere and on their ability to absorb infrared radiation. Apart from water, carbon dioxide contributes about 50% to global warming and methane contributes 18%. Other greenhouse gases such as chlorofluorocarbons (CFCs), N_2O, and SF_6 are many times better at absorbing infrared radiation compared with carbon dioxide but have much lower concentrations, so their effect is more limited.

AHL Spectroscopic identification of organic compounds: ^{1}H NMR spectroscopy (1)

Proton nuclear magnetic resonance spectroscopy (^{1}H NMR)

Whereas infrared spectroscopy gives information about the types of bonds in a molecule, ^{1}H NMR spectroscopy provides information on the chemical environment of all the hydrogen atoms in the molecule. The nuclei of hydrogen atoms possess spin and can exist in two possible states of equal energy. If a strong magnetic field is applied, the spin states may align themselves either with the magnetic field, or against it, and there is a small energy difference between these alignments. The nuclei can absorb a photon of energy when transferring from the lower to the higher spin state. The photon's energy is very small and occurs in the radio region of the spectrum. The precise energy difference depends on the chemical environment of the hydrogen atoms.

The position in the ^{1}H NMR spectrum where the absorption occurs for each hydrogen atom in the molecule is known as the **chemical shift**, and is measured in parts per million (ppm). The area under each signal corresponds to the number of hydrogen atoms in that particular environment. A full list of chemical shifts for different proton environments is given in the IB data booklet (along with mass spectral fragments and infrared absorptions). A simplified list is given below.

▼ Some common proton shift values

Type of proton	Chemical shift / ppm
R–CH_3	0.9–1.0
–CH_2–R	1.3–1.4
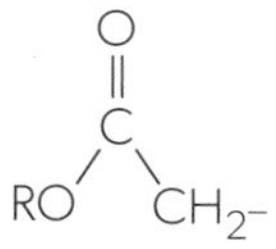	2.0–2.5
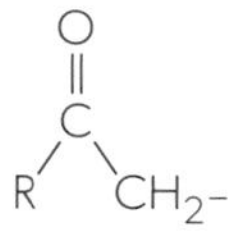	2.2–2.7
R–O–H	1.0–6.0 (note the large range)
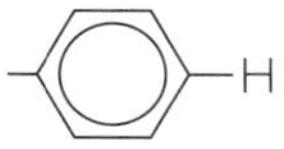	6.9–9.0
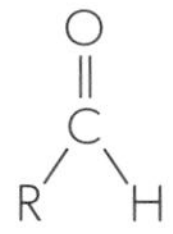	9.4–10.0

^{1}H NMR spectrum of ethyl ethanoate

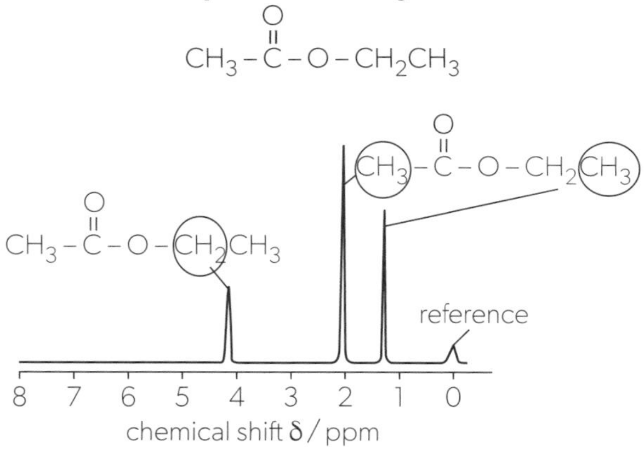

To see the areas under each signal more clearly, an integration trace is usually added. The vertical height of each section of the trace is proportional to the number of hydrogen atoms in each chemical environment.

^{1}H NMR spectrum of ethanol CH_3CH_2OH

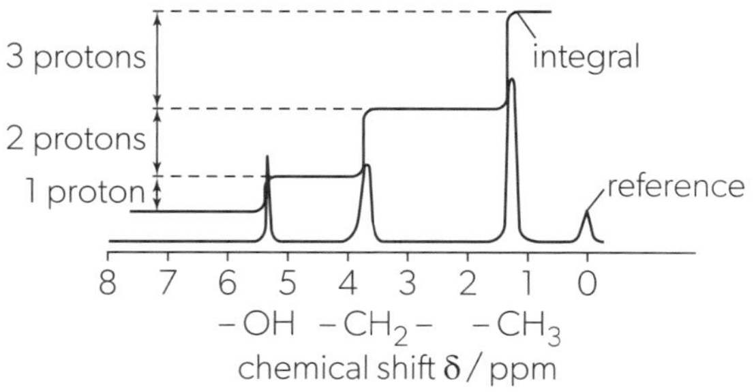

AHL Spectroscopic identification of organic compounds: ^{1}H NMR spectroscopy (2)

The main features of ^{1}H NMR spectra

1. *The number of different absorptions (signals)*

Each proton in a particular chemical environment absorbs at a particular frequency. The number of signals thus gives information about the number of different chemical environments occupied by the protons.

2. *The area under each signal*

The area under each absorption signal is proportional to the number of hydrogen atoms in that particular chemical environment. Normally, each area is integrated and the heights of the integrated traces can be used to obtain the ratio of the number of hydrogen atoms in each environment.

3. *The chemical shift*

Because spinning electrons create their own magnetic field, the surrounding electrons of neighbouring atoms can exert a shielding effect. The greater the shielding, the lower the frequency for the resonance to occur. The chemical shift (δ) of each absorption is measured in parts per million (ppm) relative to a standard. The normal standard is tetramethylsilane (TMS), which is assigned a value of 0 ppm. A table of chemical shifts can be found in the IB data booklet.

4. *Splitting pattern*

In ^{1}H NMR spectroscopy, the chemical shift of protons within a molecule is slightly altered by protons bonded to adjacent carbon atoms. This spin–spin coupling shows up in high-resolution ^{1}H NMR as splitting patterns. If the number of adjacent equivalent protons is equal to n, then the signal will be split into $(n + 1)$ signals.

TMS as the reference standard

The advantages of using tetramethylsilane $Si(CH_3)_4$ as the reference standard are:

- All the protons are in the same environment so it gives a strong single signal.
- It is not toxic and is very unreactive (so does not interfere with the sample).
- It absorbs upfield well away from most other protons.
- It is volatile (has a low boiling point) so can easily be removed from the sample.

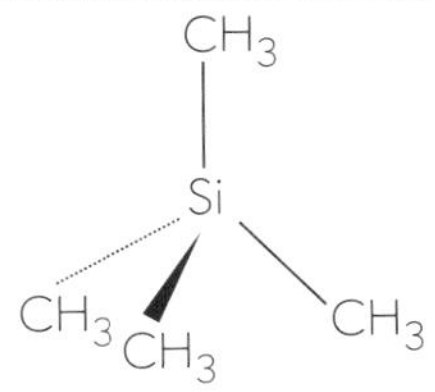

Spin–spin coupling

Splitting patterns are due to spin–spin coupling. For example, if there is one proton ($n = 1$) adjacent to a methyl group, then it will line up either with the magnetic field or against it. The methyl protons will thus experience one slightly stronger and one slightly weaker external magnetic field, which results in an equal splitting of the signal. This is known as a doublet ($n + 1 = 2$).

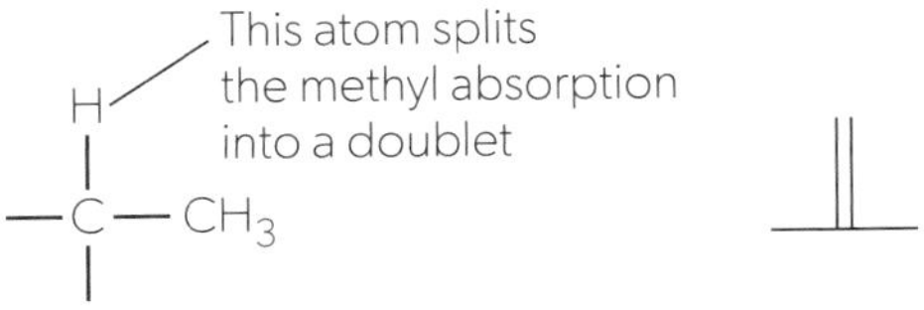

This atom splits the methyl absorption into a doublet

If there is a $-CH_2-$ group ($n = 2$) adjacent to a methyl group, then there are three possible energy states available.

1. Both proton spins are aligned with the field. ↑↑
2. One is aligned with the field and one is against it (two combinations). ↑↓ ↓↑
3. Both are aligned against the field. ↓↓

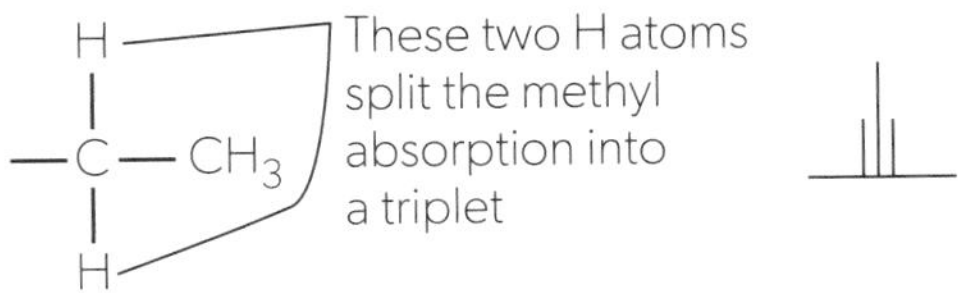

These two H atoms split the methyl absorption into a triplet

This results in a triplet with signals in the ratio 1:2:1.

The pattern of splitting can always be predicted using Pascal's triangle to cover all possible combinations.

Number of adjacent protons (n)	Splitting pattern	Type of splitting
0	1	singlet
1	1 1	doublet
2	1 2 1	triplet
3	1 3 3 1	quartet
4	1 4 6 4 1	quintet

Thus a methyl group ($n = 3$) next to a proton will result in the absorption for that proton being split into a quartet with signals in the ratio 1:3:3:1.

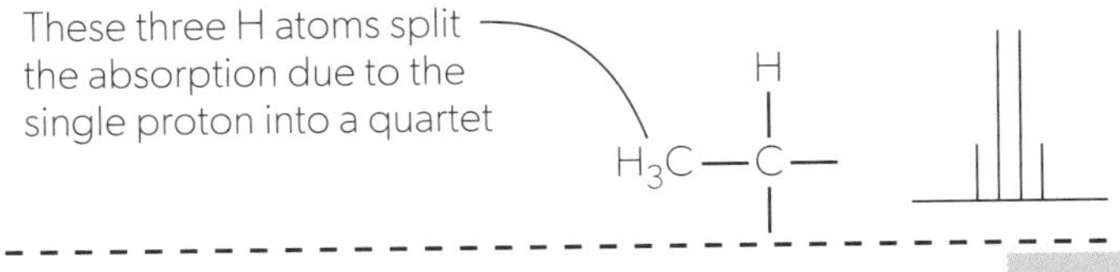

These three H atoms split the absorption due to the single proton into a quartet

AHL Spectroscopic identification of organic compounds: ¹H NMR spectroscopy (3)

Interpreting ¹H NMR spectra

¹H NMR spectrum of butanone

$CH_3-\overset{\overset{O}{\|}}{C}-CH_2-CH_3$

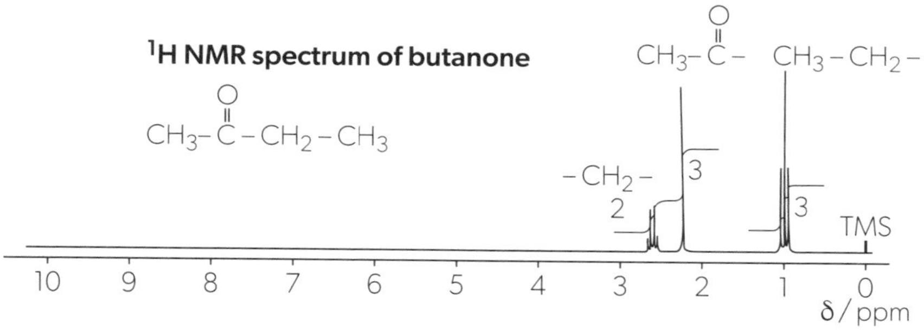

1. The three different signals show that the hydrogen atoms within the molecule are in three different chemical environments.

2. The integrated trace shows that the hydrogen atoms are in the ratio 2:3:3.

3. The chemical shifts of the three signals identify them as R–CH₃ at 0.9 ppm, $CH_3-\overset{\overset{O}{\|}}{C}-$ at 2.0 ppm, and

   $R-CH_2-\overset{\overset{O}{\|}}{C}-$ at 2.3 ppm.

4. The –CH₂– group has three adjacent protons so is split into a quartet ($n + 1 = 4$).

   The $CH_3-\overset{\overset{O}{\|}}{C}-$ protons contain no adjacent protons so no splitting occurs.

   The CH₃– group next to the –CH₂– group is split into a triplet ($n + 1 = 3$).

Further examples of ¹H NMR spectra involving splitting patterns

¹H NMR spectrum of phenylpropanone $C_6H_5-\overset{\overset{O}{\|}}{C}-CH_2-CH_3$

¹H NMR spectrum of 1,1-dichloroethane CHCl₂CH₃

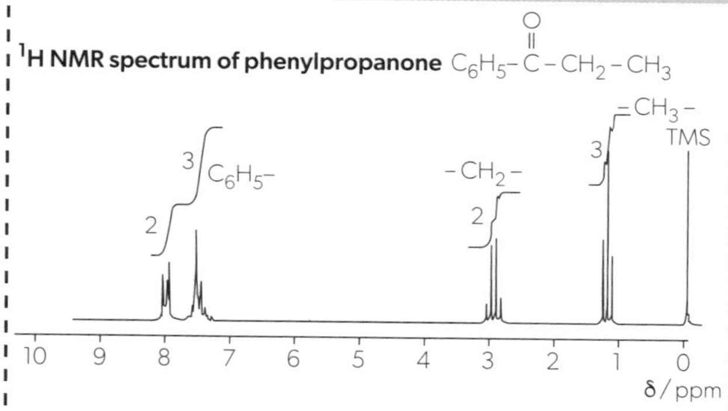

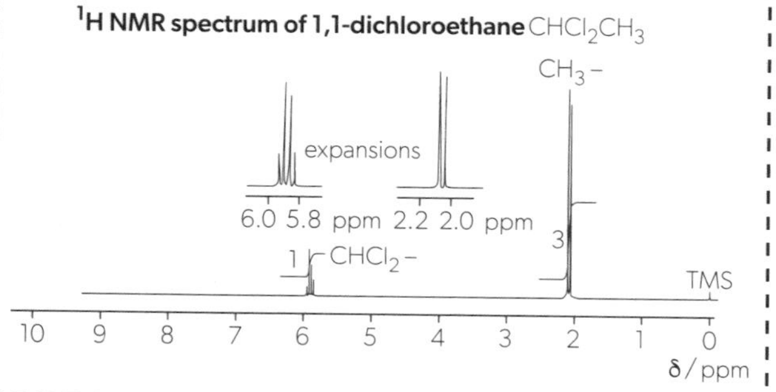

Uses of NMR spectroscopy

1. Structural determination

¹H NMR is a particularly powerful tool in structural determination as it enables information to be gained on the precise chemical environment of all the protons in the molecule. Similarly, ¹³C and other forms of NMR can also provide very detailed structural information including, for example, distinguishing between *cis* and *trans* isomers in organometallic compounds.

2. Medicinal uses

NMR is particularly useful in medicine as the energy of the radio waves involved is completely harmless and there are no known side effects. ¹H NMR is used in body scanning. The whole body of the patient can be placed inside the magnet of a large NMR machine. Protons in water, lipids, and carbohydrates give different signals so that an image of the body can be obtained. This is known as MRI (magnetic resonance imaging). The image can be used to diagnose and monitor conditions such as cancer, multiple sclerosis, and hydrocephalus.

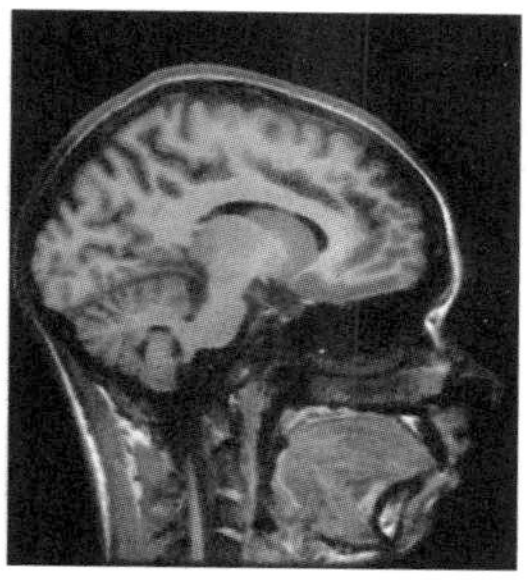

▲ An MRI image of the human brain

AHL Combination of techniques to determine structure

Elemental analysis

Compound X was found to contain 48.63% carbon, 8.18% hydrogen, and 43.19% oxygen by mass.

From this information, the empirical formula of the compound can be deduced as $C_3H_6O_2$. The calculation below assumes a 100 g sample of Compound X.

Element	Amount / mol	Simplest ratio
C	$\frac{48.63}{12.01} = 4.05$	3
H	$\frac{8.18}{1.01} = 8.10$	6
O	$\frac{43.19}{16.00} = 2.70$	2

Infrared spectroscopy

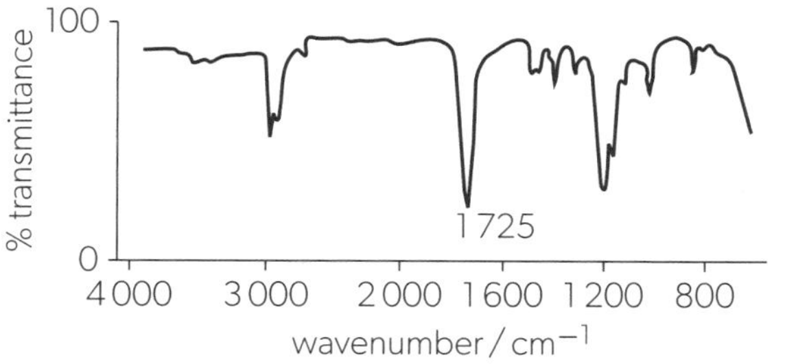

Information from the infrared spectrum of Compound X:

- Absorption at 2980 cm^{-1} due to presence of C–H.
- Absorption at 1725 cm^{-1} due to presence of C=O.
- Absorption at 1200 cm^{-1} due to presence of C–O.
- Absence of broad absorption at 3300 cm^{-1} indicates that Compound X does not contain O–H.

Mass spectrometry

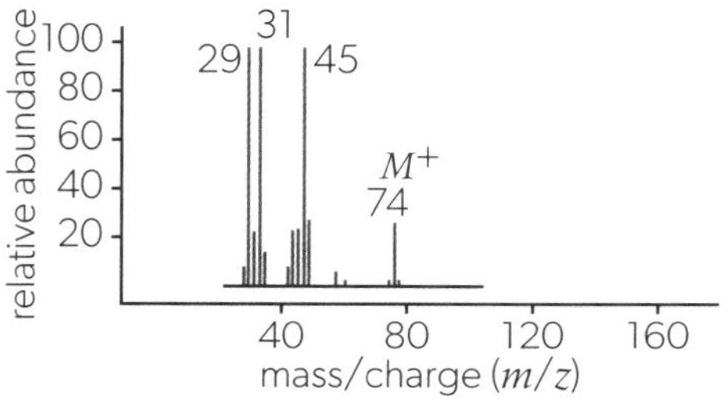

Information from the mass spectrum of Compound X:

- Since M^+ occurs at 74, the relative molecular mass of Compound X = 74.
- From this and the empirical formula, it can be deduced that the molecular formula of Compound X is $C_3H_6O_2$.
- Fragment at 45 due to $(M-29)^+$, so Compound X may contain C_2H_5– and/or CHO–.
- Fragment at 31 due to $(M-43)^+$, so Compound X may contain C_2H_5O.
- Fragment at 29 due to $(M-45)^+$, so Compound X may contain HOOC– or H—C(=O)—O—.
- Peak at 75 due to the presence of ^{13}C.

^{1}H NMR spectroscopy

Information available from the ^{1}H NMR spectrum:

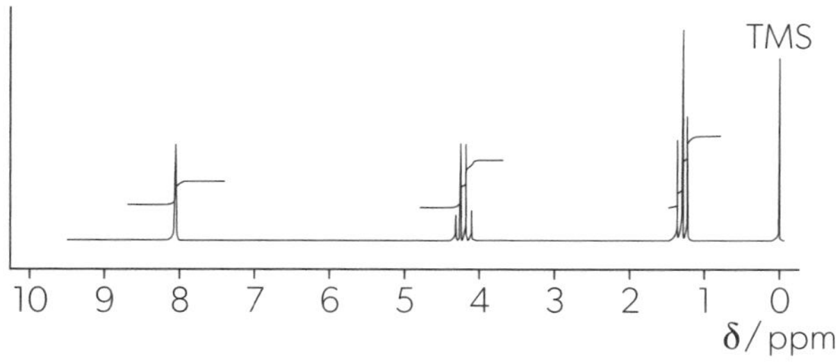

- Three separate signals, so Compound X contains hydrogen atoms in three chemical environments.
- From the integration trace, the hydrogen atoms are in the ratio 3 : 2 : 1 for the signals at 1.3, 4.2 and 8.1 ppm, respectively. Since there are six hydrogen atoms in the molecule, this is the actual number of protons in each environment.
- From the IB data booklet:

1.3 ppm	R–CH_3 (cannot be R–CH_2–R as it is for three protons)
4.2 ppm	R—C(=O)—O—CH_2—R
8.1 ppm	not in the IB data booklet but consistent with H—C(=O)—O—R

- From the splitting patterns, the number of adjacent hydrogen atoms can be determined.

1.3 ppm	triplet: two adjacent hydrogen atoms
4.2 ppm	quartet: three adjacent hydrogen atoms
8.1 ppm	singlet: no adjacent hydrogen atoms

Identification

All the above information is consistent with only one definitive structure.

Compound X is ethyl methanoate. H—C(=O)—O—CH_2CH_3

Multiple-choice questions—Classification of organic compounds

1. Which two compounds both belong to the same homologous series?
   A. C_2H_4 and C_2H_6
   B. C_2H_5OH and C_3H_7OH
   C. C_2H_5Br and $C_2H_4Br_2$
   D. H_3CCOOH and $HCOOCH_3$

2. How many different structural isomers of C_5H_{12} exist?
   A. 1
   B. 2
   C. 3
   D. 4

3. Applying IUPAC nomenclature, what is the name of the molecule below?

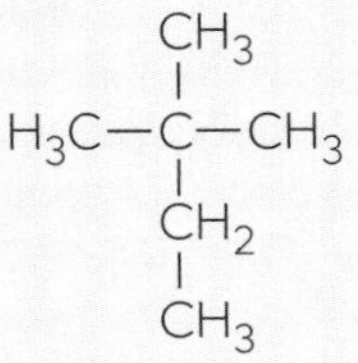

   A. 2-methyl-2-ethylpropane
   B. 2,2-dimethylbutane
   C. hexane
   D. 2-methylpentane

4. Which compound is an ether?
   A. CH_3COOH
   B. CH_3COCH_3
   C. CH_3CHO
   D. CH_3OCH_3

5. Which compound is a secondary halogenoalkane?
   A. $CH_3CH_2CH_2CH_2I$
   B. $(CH_3)_3CBr$
   C. $CH_3CHClCH_2CH_3$
   D. $(CH_3)_2CHCH_2Br$

6. Which pair of compounds are functional group structural isomers?
   A. $HCOOCH_2CH_3$ and CH_3CH_2COOH
   B. $CH_3CH_2COCH_3$ and CH_3COOCH_3
   C. $CH_3CH_2COOCH_3$ and $CH_3COOCH_2CH_3$
   D. $CH_3CH(OH)CH_2CH_3$ and $CH_3CH_2CH_2CH_2OH$

7. Which compound has the lowest boiling point?
   A. $CH_3CH_2CH_2CH_2CH_3$
   B. $C(CH_3)_4$
   C. $CH_3CH(CH_3)CH_2CH_3$
   D. They are all the same.

8. Which functional group appears in the compound below?

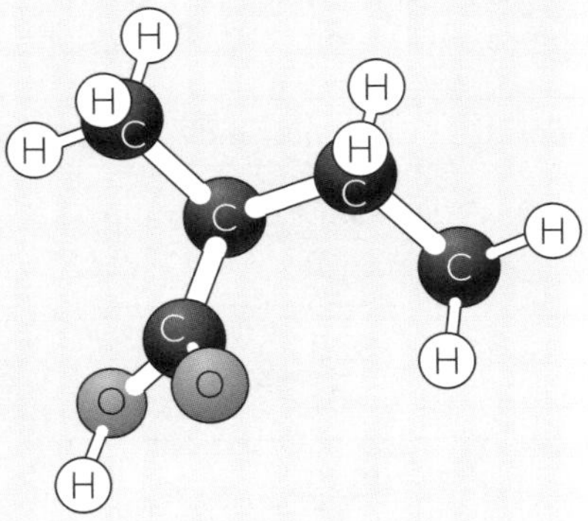

   A. ester
   B. alkoxy
   C. hydroxyl
   D. carboxyl

9. What is the molecular formula of ibuprofen, shown in the diagram below?

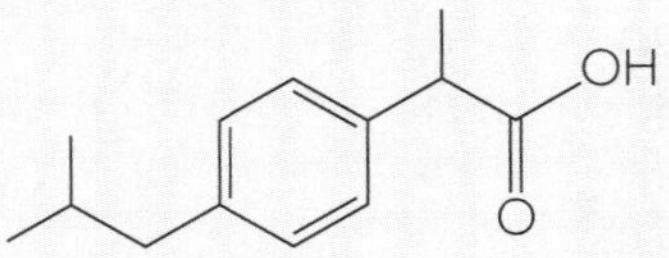

ibuprofen

   A. $C_{13}H_{18}O_2$
   B. $C_{10}H_{12}O_2$
   C. $C_{13}H_{20}O_2$
   D. $C_{10}H_{14}O_2$

AHL

10. How many four-membered ring isomers are there of dichlorocyclobutane, $C_4H_6Cl_2$?
A. 3
B. 4
C. 5
D. 6

11. Which molecule contains a chiral carbon atom?
A. $CH_3CHBrCH_2CH_3$
B. $CH_3COCH_2CH_3$
C. $CH_3CH_2CH_2CH_2Br$
D. $CH_3COOCH_2CH_3$

12. What information can be obtained from the number of signals in the ^1H NMR spectrum of a compound?
A. The number of different chemical environments occupied by the protons in one molecule of the compound.
B. The number of hydrogen atoms in one molecule of the compound.
C. The number of different functional groups in one molecule of the compound.
D. The number of carbon atoms in one molecule of the compound.

13. The mass spectrum of a compound includes peaks with m/z values of 88, 73, 59, and 43. Which compound could give this spectrum?
A. $HCOCH_2CH_2CH_3$
B. $CH_3CH_2COOCH_2CH_3$
C. $CH(CH_3)_2COOH$
D. $CH_3CH_2CH_2COOH$

14. Which compound gives this ^1H NMR spectrum?

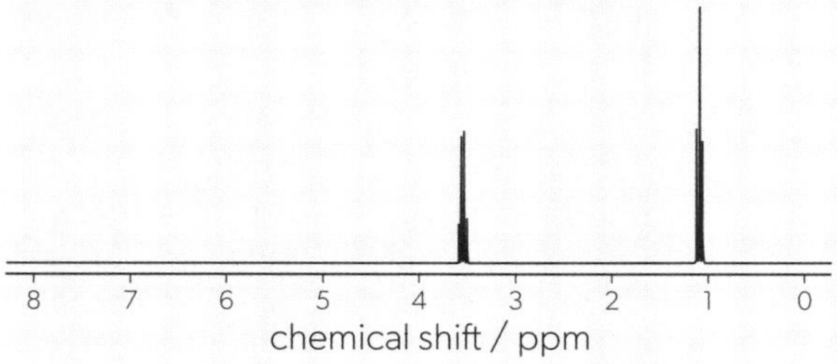

A. $CH_3CH_2CH_2OH$
B. $CH_3CH_2OCH_3$
C. CH_3COOCH_3
D. $CH_3CH_2OCH_2CH_3$

15. The ^1H NMR spectrum of a particular compound shows three separate signals. The relative height of each integration trace and the splitting patterns are:

Signal number	Integration trace	Splitting pattern
1	3	triplet
2	2	quartet
3	1	singlet

Which compound could give this spectrum?
A. $HCOOCH_2CH_3$
B. $CH_3CH_2CH_2COOH$
C. $CH_3CH_2COOCH_3$
D. $CH_3CH(OH)CH_3$

16. Which are advantages for using tetramethylsilane as a standard reference in ^1H NMR?
I. All its protons are in the same chemical environment.
II. It is chemically unreactive.
III. It does not absorb energy in the same region as most other protons.
A. I and II only
B. I and III only
C. II and III only
D. I, II, and III

17. Which compound will contain a peak with a triplet splitting pattern in its ^1H NMR spectrum?
A. CH_3OH
B. CH_3CH_2COOH
C. $CH_3CHClCOOH$
D. $(CH_3)_3COH$

Short-answer questions—Classification of organic compounds

1. The following is a three-dimensional computer-generated representation of aspirin. Each carbon, oxygen, and hydrogen atom has been given a unique number.

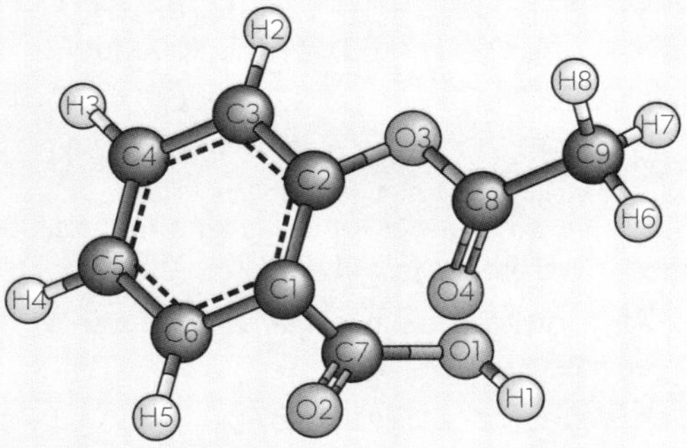

   a) Identify one carbon atom that is part of:
      (i) the phenyl functional group
      (ii) the carboxylic functional group
      (iii) the ester functional group. [3]

   b) Explain why the bond between C8 and O3 is longer than the bond between C8 and O4. [2]

   c) Compare the length of the bond between C1 and C6 with the bond between C1 and C7. [2]

2. Isobutylene is used to make synthetic rubber.

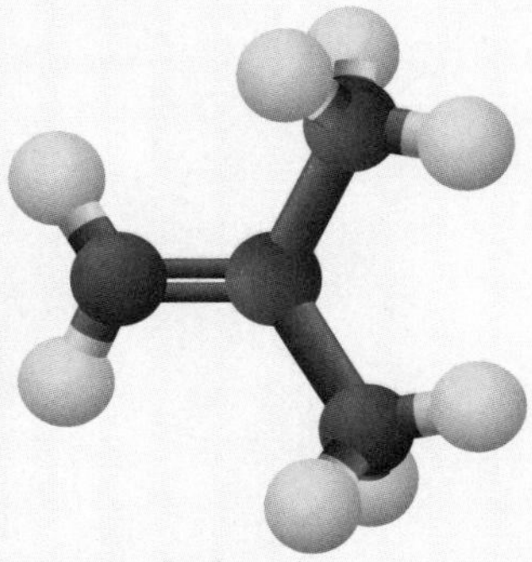

isobutylene

   a) (i) State the IUPAC name of isobutylene. [1]
      (ii) State the general formula of the homologous series to which isobutylene belongs. [1]
      (iii) Draw a section, showing three repeating units, of the polymer that can be formed from isobutylene. [1]

   b) Compound **X** is a structural isomer of isobutylene.

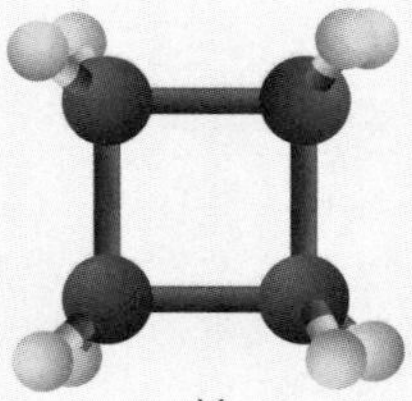

X

   State the name of the type of structural isomerism involved. [1]

   c) Explain why the boiling points of isobutylene and **X** are low and why both are insoluble in water. [2]

AHL

3. Consider alkenes with the molecular formula C_5H_9Br.

   Give structural formulas for one isomer that shows:
   (a) no stereoisomerism [1]
   (b) optical isomerism but no *cis–trans* isomerism [1]
   (c) optical isomerism and *trans* isomerism [1]
   (d) optical isomerism and *cis* isomerism [1]
   (e) *trans* isomerism but no optical isomerism [1]
   (f) *cis* isomerism but no optical isomerism. [1]

4. The ^1H NMR spectrum of an unknown compound is given below:

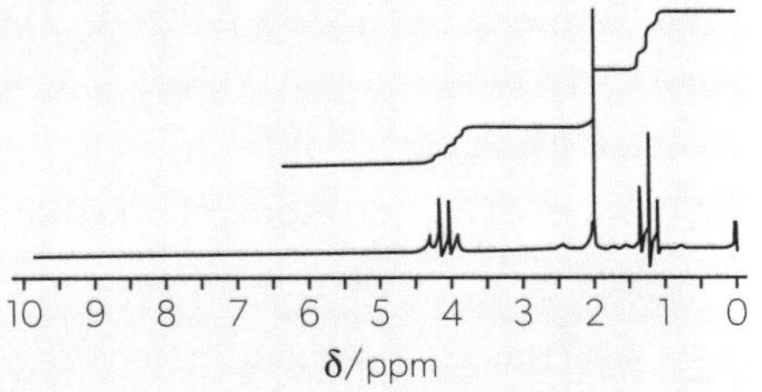

   a) Why is tetramethylsilane used in ^1H NMR spectroscopy? [1]

   b) What word is used to describe the multiplicity of the signals centred at 4.1 ppm? [1]

   c) What is the ratio of the number of hydrogen atoms responsible for the chemical shifts centred at 1.2, 2.0, and 4.1 ppm? [1]

   d) Two structures that have chemical shifts centred at 4.1 ppm are $RCOOCH_2R$ and $C_6H_5OCOCH_3$. From consideration of the rest of the spectrum, only one of these general structures is possible. Identify which one and explain your reasoning. [2]

   Below is the infrared spectrum of the same compound:

   e) Identify which particular vibrations are responsible for the peaks labelled A, B, and C. [3]

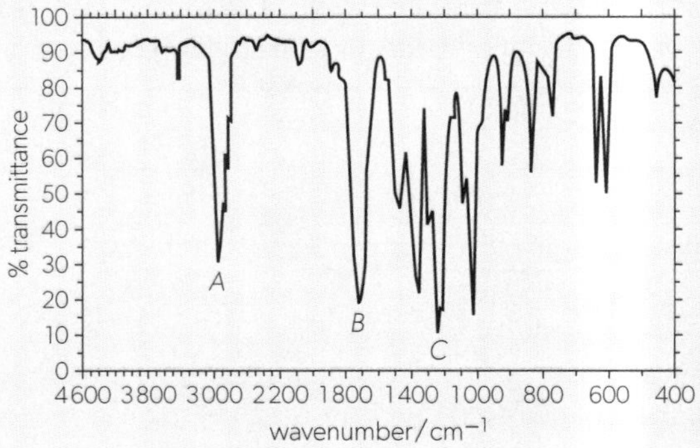

   f) The mass spectrum of the same compound shows a molecular ion peak at $m/z = 88\ m/z$. The fragmentation pattern shows peaks at $m/z = 73$ and 59 among others. Identify the ions responsible for these peaks. [3]

   g) Give the name and structural formula of the compound. [2]

Measuring enthalpy changes

Exothermic and endothermic reactions

In a chemical reaction energy is required to break the bonds in the reactants, and energy is given out when new bonds are formed in the products. The most important type of energy in chemistry is heat. If the bonds in the products are stronger than the bonds in the reactants, then the product(s) will be more energetically stable than the reactant(s). The heat that is given out is transferred to the surroundings and the reaction is said to be **exothermic**. Examples of exothermic processes include combustion and neutralization.

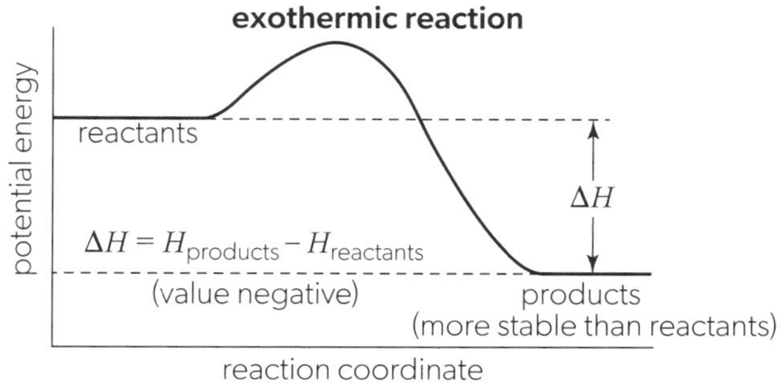

In **endothermic** reactions, heat is absorbed from the surroundings because the bonds in the reactants are stronger than the bonds in the products.

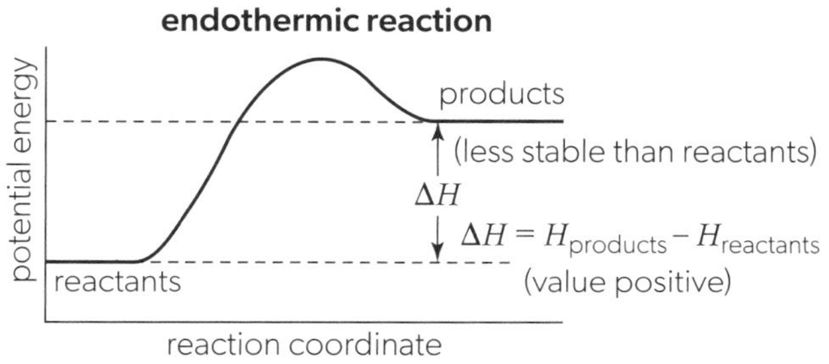

The internal energy stored in the reactants is known as its **enthalpy**, H. The absolute value of the enthalpy of the reactants cannot be known, nor can the enthalpy of the products. However, what can be measured is the difference between them, ΔH, which is the amount of heat transferred to or from the surroundings. By convention, ΔH has a negative value for exothermic reactions and a positive value for endothermic reactions. ΔH is normally measured under standard conditions of 100 kPa pressure at a temperature of 298 K. The **standard enthalpy change of a reaction** is denoted by $\Delta H^{\ominus}$.

Temperature and heat

It is important to be able to distinguish between heat and temperature as the terms are often used loosely.

- Heat is a measure of the total energy in a given amount of substance and therefore depends on the amount of substance present.
- Temperature is a measure of the "hotness" of a substance. It represents the average kinetic energy of the substance, but is independent of the amount of substance present.

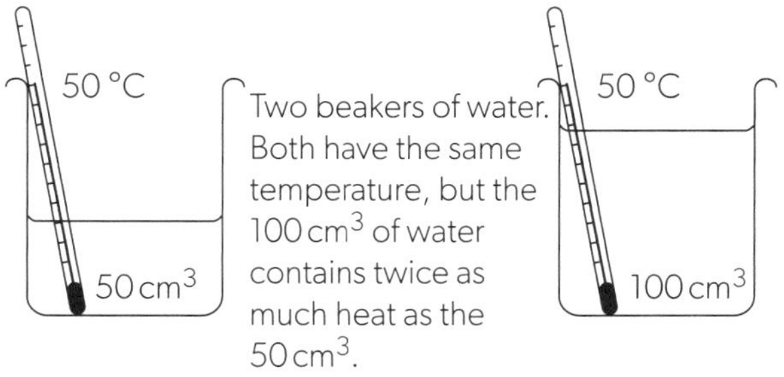

ΔH calculations from calorimetry

Calorimetry

The enthalpy change for a reaction can be measured experimentally by using a calorimeter. In a simple calorimeter, all the heat evolved in an exothermic reaction is used to raise the temperature of a known mass of water. For endothermic reactions, the heat transferred from the water to the reaction can be calculated by measuring how much the temperature of a known mass of water falls.

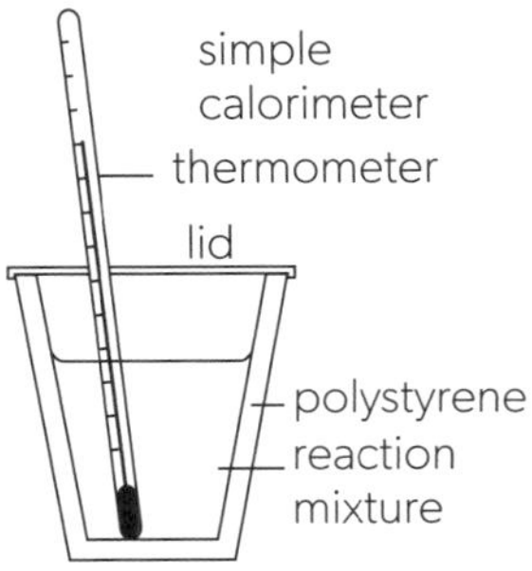

To compensate for the heat lost to the surroundings from the water as an exothermic reaction proceeds, a plot of temperature against time can be drawn. By extrapolation, it is possible to calculate the temperature rise that would have taken place had the reaction been instantaneous.

T_0 = initial temperature of reactants

T_1 = highest temperature actually reached

T_2 = temperature that would have been reached if no heat lost to surroundings

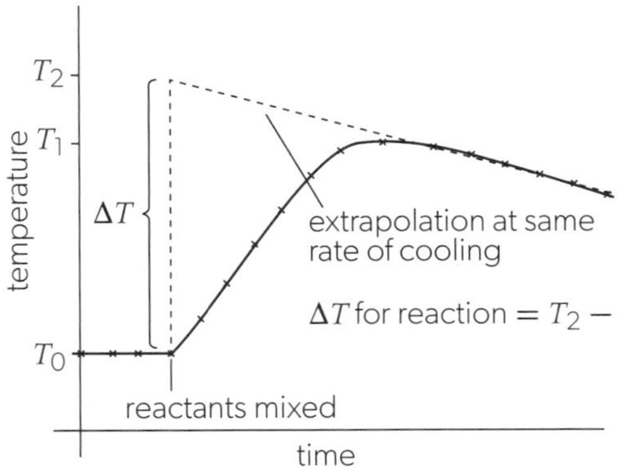

Calculation of enthalpy changes

The heat involved in changing the temperature of any substance can be calculated from the equation:

heat energy, Q = mass (m) × specific heat capacity (c) × temperature change (ΔT)

The specific heat capacity of water is 4.18 kJ kg^{-1} K^{-1}. That is, it requires 4.18 kilojoules of energy to raise the temperature of one kilogram of water by one kelvin. This value is given in the data booklet.

Enthalpy changes are normally quoted in kJ mol^{-1}, for either a reactant or a product, so it is also necessary to work out the amount (in moles) involved in the reaction that produces the heat change in the water. So:

enthalpy change, $\Delta H = -\dfrac{\text{heat energy, } Q}{\text{moles, } n}$

Worked example 1

50.0 cm^3 of 1.00 mol dm^{-3} hydrochloric acid solution was added to 50.0 cm^3 of 1.00 mol dm^{-3} sodium hydroxide solution in a polystyrene beaker. The initial temperature of both solutions was 16.7 °C. After stirring and accounting for heat loss, the highest temperature reached was 23.5 °C. Calculate the enthalpy change for this reaction.

Step 1. Write equation for reaction:

$HCl(aq) + NaOH(aq) \rightarrow NaCl(aq) + H_2O(l)$

Step 2. Calculate molar quantities:

Amount of HCl $= \dfrac{50.0}{1000} \times 1.00 = 5.00 \times 10^{-2}$ mol

Amount of NaOH $= \dfrac{50.0}{1000} \times 1.00 = 5.00 \times 10^{-2}$ mol

Therefore the heat evolved will be for 5.00×10^{-2} mol.

Step 3. Calculate heat evolved:

Total volume of solution = 50.0 + 50.0 = 100 cm^3

Assume the solution has the same density and specific heat capacity as water. Then:

Mass of "water" = 100 g = 0.100 kg

Temperature change = 23.5 – 16.7 = 6.8 °C = 6.8 K

Heat evolved in reaction, $Q = mc\Delta T$

$= 0.100 \times 4.18 \times 6.8$

$= 2.84$ kJ (for 5.00×10^{-2} mol)

ΔH for reaction $= -\dfrac{Q}{n} = -\dfrac{2.84}{5.00 \times 10^{-2}} = -56.8$ kJ mol^{-1}

(a negative value as the reaction is exothermic)

Worked example 2

A student used a simple calorimeter to determine the enthalpy change for the combustion of ethanol.

$C_2H_5OH(l) + 3O_2(g) \rightarrow 2CO_2(g) + 3H_2O(l)$

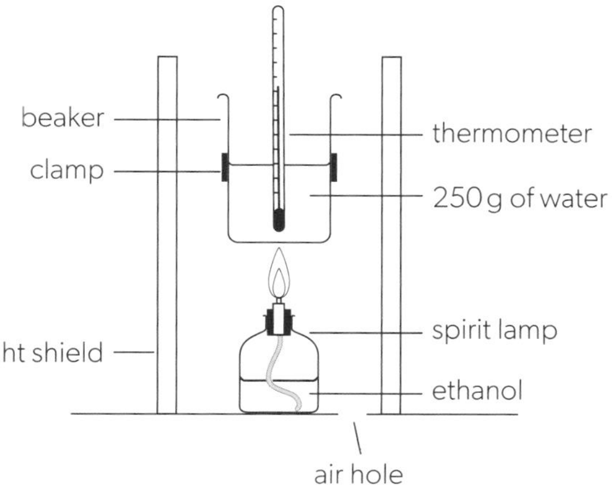

When 0.690 g (0.015 mol) of ethanol was burned it produced a temperature rise of 13.2 K in 250 g of water. Calculate ΔH for the reaction.

Heat evolved by 0.015 mol

$$= \frac{250}{1000} \times 4.18 \times 13.2$$

$$= 13.79 \text{ kJ}$$

$$\Delta H = -\frac{13.79}{0.015} = -920 \text{ kJ mol}^{-1}$$

Note: the IB data booklet value is -1371 kJ mol^{-1}. Reasons for the discrepancy include the fact that not all the heat produced is transferred to the water, the water loses some heat to the surroundings, and there is incomplete combustion of the ethanol.

Worked example 3

50.0 cm^3 of 0.200 mol dm^{-3} copper(II) sulfate solution was placed in a polystyrene cup. After two minutes 1.20 g of powdered zinc was added. The temperature was taken every 30 seconds and the graph shown below (right) was obtained.

Calculate the enthalpy change for the reaction taking place.

Step 1. Write the equation for the reaction:

$Cu^{2+}(aq) + Zn(s) \rightarrow Cu(s) + Zn^{2+}(aq)$

Step 2. Determine the limiting reagent:

Amount of $Cu^{2+}(aq) = \frac{50.0}{1000} \times 0.200 = 0.0100$ mol

Amount of $Zn(s) = \frac{1.20}{65.37} = 0.0184$ mol

$\therefore Cu^{2+}(aq)$ is the limiting reagent,

Step 3. Extrapolate the graph to compensate for heat loss and determine ΔT (see right):

$\Delta T = 10.4$ °C

Step 4. Calculate the heat evolved in the experiment for 0.0100 mol of reactants:

Heat evolved, $Q = \frac{50.0}{1000} \times 4.18 \times 10.4\,°C = 2.17$ kJ

Step 5. Express this as the enthalpy change for the reaction:

$$\Delta H = -\frac{2.17}{0.0100} = -217 \text{ kJ mol}^{-1}$$

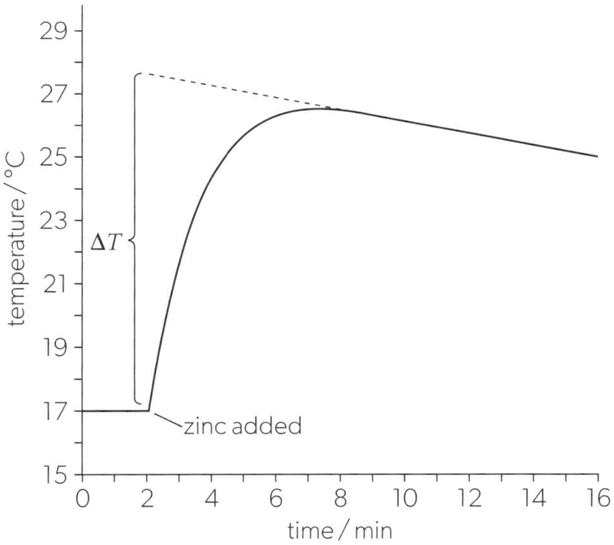

Bond enthalpies

Bond enthalpies

Enthalpy changes can also be calculated directly from bond enthalpies. The **bond enthalpy** is defined as the enthalpy change for the process:

X–Y(g) ⇌ X(g) + Y(g) Note the gaseous state.

For bond formation, the value is negative as energy is evolved. For bond breaking, energy has to be put in so the value is positive. If the bond enthalpy values are known for all the bonds in the reactants and products, then the overall enthalpy change can be calculated.

Some bond enthalpies and average bond enthalpies

H–H 436	C=C 614	C≡C 839
C–C 346	O=O 498	N≡N 945
C–H 414		
O–H 463		
N–H 391		
N–N 158		

All values are in kJ mol^{-1}. Average bond enthalpy values are given in section 12 of the IB data booklet.

Limitations

For simple diatomic molecules, the bond enthalpies can be known precisely. However, for bonds such as the C–H bond there are many compounds containing a C–H bond, and the value can differ slightly depending upon the surrounding atoms. The term **average bond enthalpy** is used. This is defined as the energy needed to break one mole of a bond in a gaseous molecule averaged over similar compounds. In practice, the energy of a particular bond will vary in different compounds. For this reason, ΔH values calculated using average bond enthalpies are not necessarily very accurate.

Bond enthalpies can only be used on their own if all the reactants and products are in the gaseous state. If, for example, water was a liquid product in a reaction, then even more heat would be evolved since the enthalpy change of vaporization of water would also need to be included in the calculation.

Worked example 1

Combustion of hydrazine in oxygen (this reaction has been used to power spacecraft)

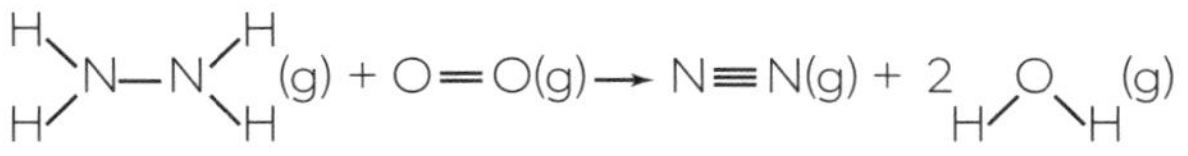

energy absorbed:

N—N 158
4N—H 4 × 391
O=O 498
} 2 220 kJ

energy released:

N≡N 945
4O—H 4 × 463
} 2 797 kJ

$\Delta H = -(2\,797 - 2\,220) = -577$ kJ mol^{-1}

Worked example 2

Hydrogenation of ethene

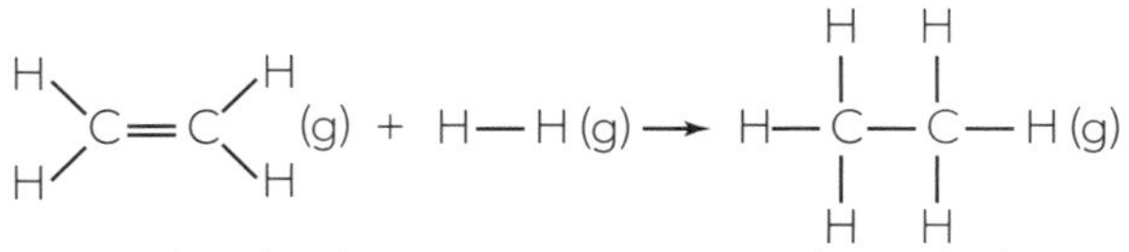

energy absorbed to break bonds:

C=C 614
4C—H 4 × 414
H—H 436
} 2 706 kJ

energy released when bonds are formed:

C—C 346
6C—H 6 × 414
} 2 830 kJ

$\Delta H = -(2\,830 - 2\,706) = -124$ kJ mol^{-1} so the reaction is exothermic.

Worked example 3

Chlorination of methane in ultraviolet light.

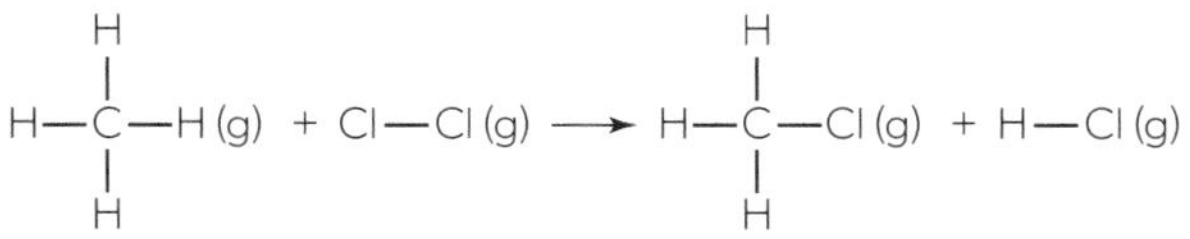

Just considering the actual bonds broken and formed

$\Delta H = -(656 - 755) = -99$ kJ

energy absorbed			energy released		
C–H	414	656 KJ	C–Cl	324	755 KJ
Cl–Cl	242		H–Cl	431	

Enthalpies of formation and combustion

Reasons to use enthalpies of formation and combustion

The limitations of using just average bond enthalpies are illustrated by the determination of the enthalpy change of combustion of methane using bond enthalpies. The equation for the reaction using bond enthalpies is:

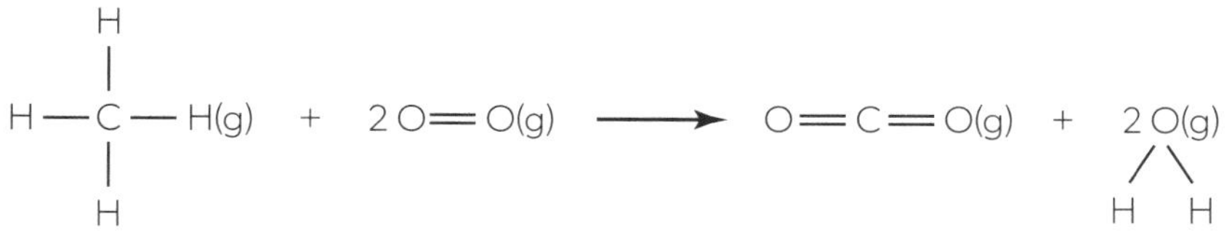

Energy taken in / $kJ\,mol^{-1}$	Energy given out / $kJ\,mol^{-1}$
4 × C–H = 4 × 414 = +1656	2 × C=O = 2 × (–804) = –1608
2 × O=O = 2 × 498 = +996	4 × O–H = 4 × (–463) = –1852
Total = +2652	Total = –3460

The calculated enthalpy change for the reaction using just bond enthalpies is therefore –808 $kJ\,mol^{-1}$. This is considerably different from the value of –891 $kJ\,mol^{-1}$ given in the IB data booklet. This difference arises because the definition of enthalpy of combustion states that the reactants and products should be in their normal states under standard conditions; therefore, you need to consider the extra 2 × 44 $kJ\,mol^{-1}$ of energy given out when the two moles of gaseous water product turn to liquid water. This brings the enthalpy of combustion value to –896 $kJ\,mol^{-1}$. This is much closer to –891 $kJ\,mol^{-1}$ with a difference of about 0.5%. This difference is due to the fact that average bond enthalpies have been used throughout: the bond enthalpy for C=O in carbon dioxide, where there are two double bonds to oxygen on the same carbon atom, may be different from the average C=O enthalpy.

AHL Standard enthalpy changes of formation $\Delta H_f^\ominus$ and combustion $\Delta H_c^\ominus$

The **standard enthalpy change of formation** of a compound, $\Delta H_f^\ominus$, is the enthalpy change when one mole of the compound is formed from its elements in their standard states at standard pressure (100 kPa). The temperature should be specified but normally it is 298 K. From this it follows that $\Delta H_f^\ominus$ for an element in its standard state will be zero.

The **standard enthalpy change of combustion**, $\Delta H_c^\ominus$, is the enthalpy change when one mole of a substance is completely combusted in oxygen under standard conditions (100 kPa).

You can calculate the standard enthalpies of reactions using:

$\Delta H^\ominus$ reaction = $\Sigma(\Delta H_f^\ominus$ products) – $\Sigma(\Delta H_f^\ominus$ reactants)

$\Delta H^\ominus$ reaction = $\Sigma(\Delta H_c^\ominus$ products) – $\Sigma(\Delta H_c^\ominus$ reactants)

Hess's law

Hess's law

Hess's law states that the enthalpy change for a reaction depends only on the difference between the enthalpy of the products and the enthalpy of the reactants. The enthalpy change is independent of the reaction pathway.

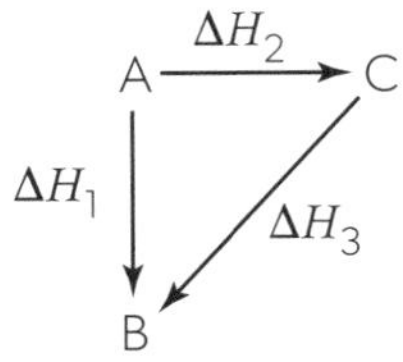

$$\Delta H_1 = \Delta H_2 + \Delta H_3$$

The enthalpy change going from A to B is the same whether the reaction proceeds directly to B or whether it goes via an intermediate (C).

This law is a statement of the law of conservation of energy. It can be used to determine enthalpy changes that cannot be measured directly.

For example, the enthalpy of combustion of both carbon and carbon monoxide to form carbon dioxide can easily be measured directly, but the enthalpy of combustion of carbon to form carbon monoxide cannot. These enthalpies can be represented by an energy cycle.

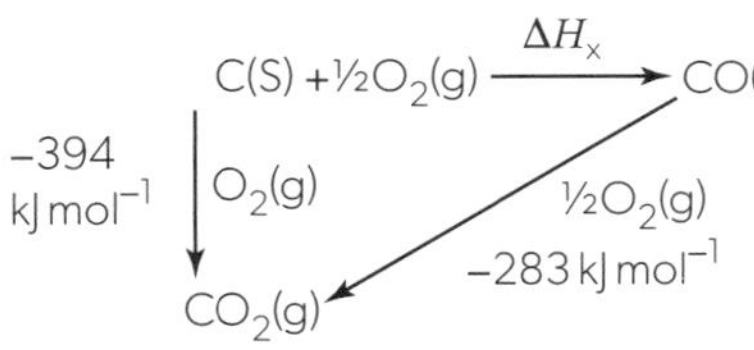

$-394 = \Delta H_x + (-283)$

$\Delta H_x = -394 + 283 = -111\ \text{kJ mol}^{-1}$

Hess's law problems can also be solved using simultaneous equations. Write the equations that are known and then manipulate them to arrive at the required equation. For example,

I	$C(s) + O_2(g) \rightarrow CO_2(g)$	$\Delta H = -394\ \text{kJ mol}^{-1}$
II	$CO(g) + \frac{1}{2}O_2(g) \rightarrow CO_2(g)$	$\Delta H = -283\ \text{kJ mol}^{-1}$

Subtract II from I:

$C(s) + \frac{1}{2}O_2(g) - CO(g) = 0$ $\quad\Delta H = -394 - (-283)\ \text{kJ mol}^{-1}$

Rearrange equation:

$C(s) + \frac{1}{2}O_2(g) \rightarrow CO(g)$ $\quad\Delta H = -111\ \text{kJ mol}^{-1}$

Worked example 1

The enthalpy change for the formation of methane cannot be obtained experimentally as many different hydrocarbons may be formed when carbon and hydrogen combine directly. However, Hess's law can be used to find the value from the enthalpy changes when carbon, hydrogen and methane are combusted. The standard enthalpies of combustion, $\Delta H_c^{\ominus}$, of carbon, hydrogen, and methane are −394, −286, and −890 kJ mol−1, respectively.

Step 1. Write the equation for the enthalpy change with the unknown $\Delta H^{\ominus}$ value. Call this value $\Delta H_x^{\ominus}$:

$$C(s) + 2H_2(g) \xrightarrow{\Delta H_x^{\ominus}} CH_4(g)$$

Step 2. Construct an energy cycle showing the different routes to the products (in this case, the products of combustion):

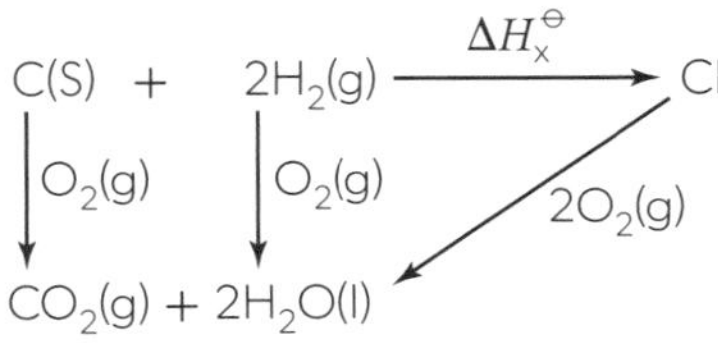

Step 3. Use Hess's law to equate the energy changes for the two different routes:

$$\underbrace{\Delta H_c^{\ominus}(C) + 2\Delta H_c^{\ominus}(H_2)}_{\text{direct route}} = \underbrace{\Delta H_x^{\ominus} + \Delta H_c^{\ominus}(CH_4)}_{\text{route via methane}}$$

Step 4. Rearrange the equation and substitute the values to give the answer:

$$\Delta H_x^{\ominus} = \Delta H_c^{\ominus}(C) + 2\Delta H_c^{\ominus}(H_2) - \Delta H_c^{\ominus}(CH_4)$$

$$= -394 + (2 \times -286) - (-890)\ \text{kJ mol}^{-1}$$

$$= -76\ \text{kJ mol}^{-1}$$

Worked example 2

The standard enthalpy change of formation of ethanol, $C_2H_5OH(l)$, cannot be determined directly but an accurate value can be obtained indirectly by using the experimental values (in kJ mol−1) for the standard enthalpy changes of combustion of carbon (−393.5), hydrogen (−285.8), and ethanol (−1 371). Although this could be solved using simultaneous equations, it is neater to show the energy cycle. Hess's law is then applied by equating the energy changes involved in combusting carbon and hydrogen directly with the energy changes involved when they are first combined to form ethanol and then the ethanol is combusted.

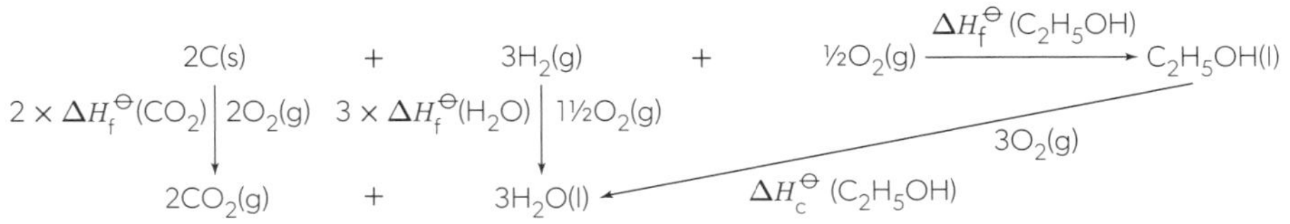

By Hess' law: $\Delta H_f^{\ominus}(C_2H_5OH) = 2 \times \Delta H_f^{\ominus}(CO_2) + 3 \times \Delta H_f^{\ominus}(H_2O) - \Delta H_c^{\ominus}(C_2H_5OH)$

Substituting the relevant values: $\Delta H_f^{\ominus}(C_2H_5OH) = (2 \times -393.5) + (3 \times -285.8) - (-1371) = -273.4\ \text{kJ mol}^{-1}$

AHL Energy cycles

Born–Haber cycles

Born–Haber cycles are energy cycles for the formation of ionic compounds. The enthalpy change of formation of sodium chloride can be considered to occur through a number of separate steps. (Ionization energy is explained on page 12 and electron affinity on page 45.)

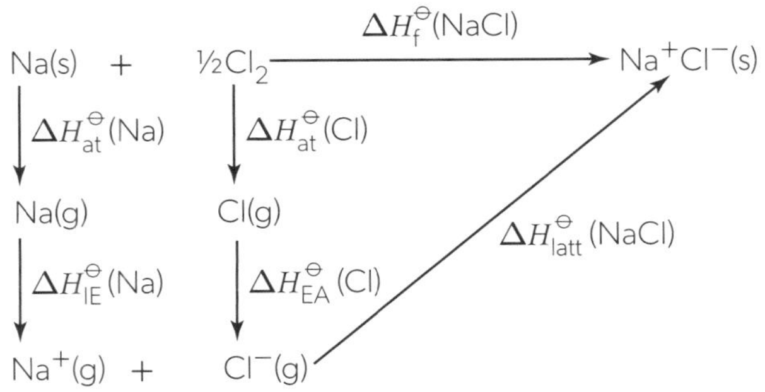

Using Hess's law:

$\Delta H_f^\ominus$(NaCl) = $\Delta H_{at}^\ominus$(Na) + $\Delta H_{IE}^\ominus$(Na) + $\Delta H_{at}^\ominus$(Cl) + $\Delta H_{EA}^\ominus$(Cl) + $\Delta H_{latt}^\ominus$(NaCl)

Substituting the relevant values:

$\Delta H_f^\ominus$(NaCl) = +108 + 496 + 121 − 349 − 790

= −414 kJ mol−[1]

Note: it is the large lattice enthalpy that mainly compensates for the endothermic processes and leads to the enthalpy of formation of ionic compounds having a negative value.

Sometimes Born–Haber cycles are written as energy level diagrams with the arrows for endothermic processes in the opposite direction to the arrows for exothermic processes.

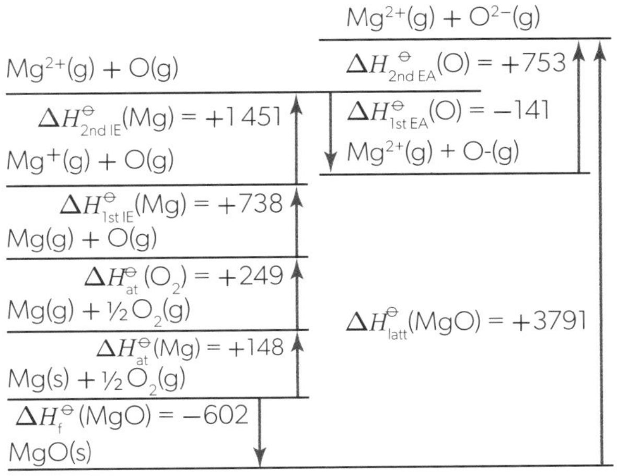

Enthalpy of atomization

The **standard enthalpy of atomization**, $\Delta H_{at}^\ominus$, is the standard enthalpy change when one mole of gaseous atoms is formed from an element in its standard state under standard conditions. For diatomic molecules, the atomization energy is therefore equal to half of the bond enthalpy as two moles of gaseous atoms are formed from one mole of the diatomic molecule when the bond dissociates.

½Cl_2(g) → Cl(g) $\Delta H_{at}^\ominus$ = +121 kJ mol^{-1}

Lattice enthalpy

The **lattice enthalpy** relates either to the endothermic process of turning a crystalline solid into its gaseous ions or to the exothermic process of turning gaseous ions into a crystalline solid.

MX(s) ⇌ M^+(g) + X^-(g)

The sign of the lattice enthalpy indicates whether the lattice is being formed (–) or broken (+).

The magnitude of the lattice enthalpy depends both on the size of the ions and on the charge carried by the ions. The smaller the ion and the greater the charge, the higher the lattice enthalpy.

	cation size increasing →			anion size increasing →			charge on cation increasing →		charge on anion increasing →	
Cation or anion	LiCl	NaCl	KCl	NaCl	NaBr	NaI	NaCl	$MgCl_2$	$MgCl_2$	MgO
Lattice enthalpy / kJ mol^{-1}	864	790	720	790	754	705	790	2 540	2 540	3 791

Energy from fuels

Chemical sources of energy

Both living organisms and society need energy to function. Apart from tidal energy and nuclear energy, the Sun is the ultimate source of energy on the planet. A fuel is a source of chemical energy, that is, any compound that releases energy when it is oxidized. Fuels are either renewable, that is, they are naturally replenished (e.g. biofuels), or non-renewable, that is, finite (e.g. fossil fuels).

Combustion reactions

Reactive metals, non-metals, and organic compounds undergo combustion reactions when heated in oxygen with the evolution of heat. For example:

$Mg(s) + ½O_2(g) \rightarrow MgO(s)$ $\Delta H_c^\ominus = -602\,kJ\,mol^{-1}$

$C(s) + O_2(g) \rightarrow CO_2(g)$ $\Delta H_c^\ominus = -394\,kJ\,mol^{-1}$

$CH_4(g) + 2O_2(g) \rightarrow CO_2(g) + 2H_2O(l)$ $\Delta H_c^\ominus = -891\,kJ\,mol^{-1}$

$C_2H_5OH(l) + 3O_2(g) \rightarrow 2CO_2(g) + 3H_2O(l)$ $\Delta H_c^\ominus = -1367\,kJ\,mol^{-1}$

$C_8H_{18}(l) + 12½O_2(g) \rightarrow 8CO_2(g) + 9H_2O(l)$ $\Delta H_c^\ominus = -5470\,kJ\,mol^{-1}$

In all of these combustion reactions, oxygen is the oxidizing agent as it is being reduced. The oxidation state of oxygen changes from 0 to −2. The substance burning (the fuel) is being oxidized so it is acting as a reducing agent and its oxidation state increases.

Choice of fuel

Several factors determine the choice of fuel, including availability, ease of extraction and storage, the environmental and social effects of extracting and using the energy, and physical factors. An important physical factor is the specific energy.

$$\text{specific energy} = \frac{\text{energy released from the fuel}}{\text{mass of fuel consumed}}$$

For example, compare ethanol (a biofuel) and gasoline (a fossil fuel).

	Ethanol, C_2H_5OH	Gasoline (octane), C_8H_{18}
M_r	46.08	114.26
$\Delta H_c^\ominus$ / $kJ\,mol^{-1}$	−1 367	−5 470
Specific energy / $kJ\,kg^{-1}$	29 670	47 890

Weight for weight, gasoline produces about 1.6 times as much energy as ethanol and about 1.4 times by volume, as the energy density (the energy released by burning one litre of the fuel) of octane is more than the energy density of ethanol. Both produce carbon dioxide (a greenhouse gas) when burned. Gasoline adds to the total amount of carbon dioxide in the atmosphere as it is a fossil fuel, whereas ethanol is formed from crops grown now so does not significantly alter the amount of carbon dioxide in the atmosphere, making it more environmentally friendly. Weighed against this is the fact that the large scale use of ethanol uses up land to grow crops that could otherwise be used to grow food.

Incomplete combustion

The equations given above assume that the fuel has been combusted completely in oxygen. Often when fuels burn, particularly in air or in a limited supply of oxygen, partial or incomplete combustion occurs. This is particularly the case with carbon-containing compounds, e.g. carbon itself, hydrocarbons, and alcohols. Incomplete combustion of organic compounds made up of carbon and hydrogen or carbon, hydrogen, and oxygen produces carbon monoxide and carbon as well as carbon dioxide and water. The precise amounts of each product depend upon the ratio of oxygen to fuel and the reaction conditions, i.e. the degree of incomplete combustion. Some typical incomplete combustion equations are:

$2C(s) + O_2(g) \rightarrow 2CO(g)$

$C_4H_{10}(g) + 5O_2(g) \rightarrow 2CO_2(g) + 5H_2O(l) + CO(g) + C(s)$

$C_2H_5OH + 2O_2(g) \rightarrow CO_2(g) + C(s) + 3H_2O(l)$

When incomplete combustion occurs less heat energy is evolved. The more carbon atoms there are in a compound, the more likely it is that incomplete combustion will occur as a greater amount of oxygen is required for complete combustion. Incomplete combustion tends to produce a more smoky, yellow flame and both carbon monoxide and soot are pollutants.

Carbon monoxide is poisonous as it can bind irreversibly to haemoglobin, preventing blood from carrying oxygen. Soot forms particulates in the atmosphere, which can actually have the opposite effect to greenhouse gases such as carbon dioxide, as they can scatter the short wave radiation from the Sun and reflect some of it back into space. Particulates are poisonous to humans as they can cause damage to the lungs and the heart.

Fossil fuels

Photosynthesis

Approximately 5.6×10^{21} kJ of energy reaches the surface of the planet from the Sun each year. About 0.06% of this is used to store energy in plants. This is achieved through **photosynthesis**—a complex process summarized by the reaction of carbon dioxide and water to form carbohydrates in the presence of chlorophyll.

$$6CO_2(g) + 6H_2O(l) \rightarrow C_6H_{12}O_6(s) + 6O_2(g)$$

This process, the biological fixing of carbon, is endothermic, requiring 2 816 kJ of energy per mole of glucose. The green pigment chlorophyll contains an extended system of alternating single and multiple bonds known as **conjugation**. Substances such as chlorophyll and α-carotene that contain extended conjugation are able to absorb visible light by exciting an electron within this conjugated system. The energy absorbed by chlorophyll when it interacts with light is able to drive photosynthesis. The products of photosynthesis are used as food to provide energy for animals through the reverse process—**respiration**. Wood is mainly cellulose—a polymer made up of repeating glucose units.

Formation of fossil fuels

Coal is fossilized plant material containing mainly carbon together with hydrogen, nitrogen, and sulfur. Most coal was formed during the Carboniferous period (286–360 million years ago). The action of pressure and heat through geological forces converted the plant material in stages from peat to lignite to bituminous soft coal to hard coal (anthracite). At each stage, the percentage of carbon increases. Coal contains between 80 and 90% carbon by mass.

Crude oil was formed from the remains of marine organisms mainly during the Paleozoic era, up to 600 million years ago. Thick sediments built up on top of the organic layers and, under the action of high pressures and biochemical activity, crude oil was formed. The oil migrated through rocks due to Earth movements and collected in traps. Crude oil is a complex mixture of straight-chain, branched, cyclic, and aromatic hydrocarbons, although it consists mainly of alkanes.

Natural gas was formed at the same time as crude oil and the two are often found together, although natural gas may occur on its own or with coal. It consists mainly of methane (85–95%) with varying amounts of ethane, propane, butane, and other gases such as hydrogen sulfide.

Relative advantages and disadvantages of fossil fuels

Fossil fuel	Advantages	Disadvantages
Coal	1. Present in large quantities and distributed throughout the world. 2. Can be converted into synthetic liquid fuels and gases. 3. Feedstock for organic chemicals. 4. Has the potential to yield vast quantities of energy compared with renewable sources and is safer than nuclear power. 5. Longer lifespan (350 years?) compared with oil or gas.	1. Contributes to acid rain and global warming. 2. Not so readily transported (no pipelines). 3. Coal waste (slag heaps) lead to ground acidity and visual and chemical pollution. 4. Mining is dangerous: cave-ins, explosions, and long-term effect of coal dust on miners. 5. Dirty (produces dust, smoke, and particulates).
Oil	1. Easily transported in pipelines or by tankers. 2. Convenient fuel for use in cars, lorries, etc. 3. Feedstock for organic chemicals.	1. Contributes to acid rain and global warming. 2. Limited lifespan (30–50 years?) and uneven distribution worldwide. 3. Risk of pollution associated with transportation by tankers.
Natural gas	1. Clean fuel. 2. Easily transported in pipelines and pressurized containers. 3. Does not contribute to acid rain. 4. Releases a higher quantity of energy per kg than coal or oil.	1. Contributes to global warming. 2. Limited lifespan (30 years?) and uneven distribution worldwide. 3. Greater risk of explosions due to leaks.

Atmospheric carbon dioxide and biofuels

Contribution to atmospheric carbon dioxide

Assuming complete combustion, the amount of carbon dioxide ($M_r = 44.01$) released when fossil fuels burn can be calculated. Weight for weight, 1 kg of coal containing 90% carbon releases $0.9 \times 44.01 \times \frac{1000}{12.01} = 3.30$ kg. Assuming natural gas is 100% methane ($M_r = 16.05$), 1 kg of methane releases $44.01 \times \frac{1000}{16.05} = 2.74$ kg.

The amount of carbon dioxide in the atmosphere has been monitored for the past 60 years. It has increased by almost 30% in that time and continues to rise. It is now generally recognized that there is a clear link between greenhouse gas emissions and global warming. This is because greenhouse gases allow higher energy radiation from the Sun to pass though the Earth's atmosphere but absorb some of the lower energy radiation radiated back from the Earth. Many countries are now actively trying to reduce carbon emissions. The consequences of global warming are hard to predict accurately but are likely to involve changes in agriculture and biodiversification as well as rising sea-levels due to thermal expansion and the melting of polar ice caps and glaciers.

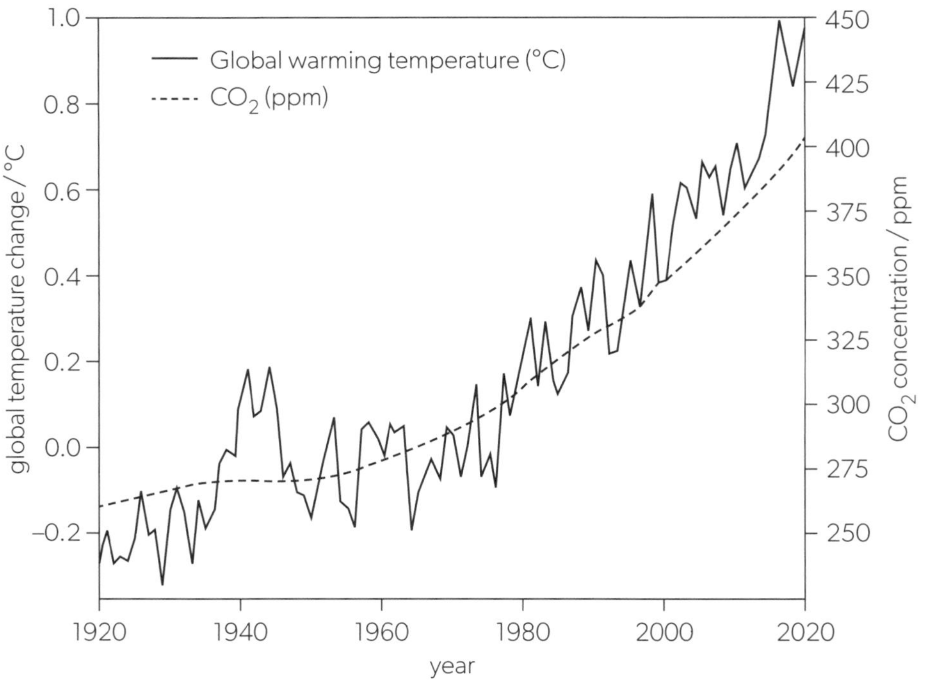

Coal and oil also contribute to acid rain as the sulfur content forms sulfur dioxide during the combustion process.

Biofuels

Biofuels release the energy that has been stored relatively recently by the fixation of carbon through photosynthesis and hence are a renewable source of energy. There is a range of ways in which biofuels can be used.

1. Direct combustion of plant material or combustion of waste material derived from plants, such as animal dung.

   e.g. $C_6H_{12}O_6(s) + 6O_2(g) \rightarrow 6CO_2(g) + 6H_2O(l)$ $\Delta H^\ominus = -2\,816\ \text{kJ mol}^{-1}$

2. Biogas. The anaerobic decay of organic matter by bacteria produces a mixture of mainly methane and carbon dioxide known as biogas. The manure from farm animals can generate enough methane to provide the heating, cooking, and refrigeration needs of rural communities.

3. Fermentation to produce ethanol. Carbohydrates can be fermented by enzymes in yeast.

   $C_6H_{12}O_6(s) \rightarrow 2C_2H_5OH(l) + 2CO_2(g)$

   The ethanol can then be burned to produce energy.

   $C_2H_5OH(l) + 3O_2(g) \rightarrow 2CO_2(g) + 3H_2O(l)$ $\Delta H^\ominus = -1\,371\ \text{kJ mol}^{-1}$

By combining ethanol with gasoline a fuel called **gasohol** can be produced. This can be used by unmodified cars, which makes them less reliant on the supply and cost of pure gasoline (petrol).

Biofuels are renewable, readily available, and relatively non-polluting. In many hot countries animal dung is dried and used as a fuel for heating and cooking. Garbage consisting of animal and vegetable waste is burned in incinerators in several cities to provide heat and electricity. This has the added advantage of reducing the amount of waste that has to be dumped in landfill sites. However, disadvantages of biofuels include the fact that they are widely dispersed, they take up land where food crops can be grown, and they remove nutrients from the soil.

Fuel cells

A **hydrogen fuel cell** utilizes the reaction between oxygen and hydrogen to produce water. Unlike combustion, a fuel cell converts chemical energy directly to electrical energy rather than first emitting it as heat. As reactants are used up, more are added so a fuel cell can give a continuous supply of electricity. Hydrogen fuel cells are used in spacecraft as, unlike rechargeable batteries, they do not need an external source of electricity for recharging. The electrolyte is aqueous sodium hydroxide. It is contained within the cell using porous electrodes that allow the passage of water, hydrogen, and oxygen. The half-equations are:

Oxidation at anode (−): $H_2 + 2OH^- \rightarrow 2H_2O + 2e^-$

Reduction at cathode (+): $O_2 + 2H_2O + 4e^- \rightarrow 4OH^-$

Hydrogen fuel cells can also be made using phosphoric acid as the electrolyte. Then the half-equations are:

Oxidation at anode (−): $H_2 \rightarrow 2H^+ + 2e^-$

Reduction at cathode (+): $O_2 + 4H^+ + 4e^- \rightarrow 2H_2O$

In both cases, energy is given out and the overall equation is: $2H_2(g) + O_2(g) \rightarrow 2H_2O(l)$

Other fuels apart from hydrogen can be used. For example, the **methanol fuel cell** produces carbon dioxide and water as the products.

Oxidation at anode (−): $CH_3OH + H_2O \rightarrow CO_2 + 6H^+ + 6e^-$

Reduction at cathode (+): $\frac{3}{2}O_2 + 6H^+ + 6e^- \rightarrow 3H_2O$

An advantage of a hydrogen fuel cell is that it does not pollute, as water is the only product.

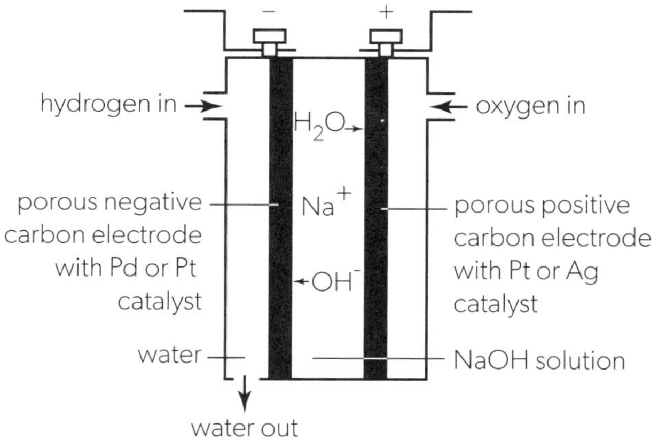

▲ Hydrogen–oxygen fuel cell with an electrolyte of NaOH

AHL Entropy and spontaneity

Entropy

Entropy (S) refers to the distribution of available energy among the particles in a system. The more ways the energy can be distributed, the higher the entropy. This is used as a measure of the disorder of a system. In nature, systems naturally tend towards an increase in entropy. An increase in entropy (disorder) can result from:

- mixing different types of particles, e.g. the dissolving of sugar in water
- a change in state where the distance between the particles increases, e.g. liquid water → steam
- the increased movement of particles, e.g. heating a liquid or gas
- increasing the number of particles, e.g. $2H_2O_2(l) \rightarrow 2H_2O(l) + O_2(g)$

The greatest increase in disorder is usually found where the number of particles in the gaseous state increases.

The change in the disorder of a system is known as the **entropy change**, ΔS. The more disordered the system becomes, the more positive the value of ΔS becomes. Systems which become more ordered will have negative ΔS values.

$NH_3(g) + HCl(g) \rightarrow NH_4Cl(s)$ $\Delta S = -284\,J\,K^{-1}\,mol^{-1}$

(2 moles of gas) (1 mole of solid)

Absolute entropy values

The standard entropy of a substance is the entropy change per mole that results from heating the substance from 0 K to the standard temperature of 298 K. Unlike enthalpy, absolute values of entropy can be measured. The standard entropy change for a reaction can then be determined by calculating the difference between the entropy of the products and the entropy of the reactants.

$\Delta S^{\ominus} = S^{\ominus}(\text{products}) - S^{\ominus}(\text{reactants})$

For example, for the formation of ammonia:

$3H_2(g) + N_2(g) \rightleftharpoons 2NH_3(g)$

The standard entropies of hydrogen, nitrogen, and ammonia are, respectively, 131, 192, and 192 J K^{-1} mol^{-1}.

Therefore, per mole of reaction:

$\Delta S^{\ominus} = 2 \times 192 - [(3 \times 131) + 192] = -201\,J\,K^{-1}\,mol^{-1}$

(or, per mole of ammonia, $\Delta S^{\ominus} = \frac{-201}{2} = -101\,J\,K^{-1}\,mol^{-1}$)

Spontaneity and Gibbs energy

A reaction is said to be **spontaneous** if it causes a system to move from a less stable state to a more stable state. This will depend both upon the enthalpy change and the entropy change, where the entropy change takes into account not only the direct entropy change from the chemicals taking part in the reaction but also the indirect entropy change resulting from the transfer of heat energy to or from the surroundings.

These two factors can be combined and expressed as the **Gibbs energy change**, ΔG.

The standard energy change, $\Delta G^{\ominus}$, is defined as:

$\Delta G^{\ominus} = \Delta H^{\ominus} - T\Delta S^{\ominus}$

where all the values are measured under standard conditions. The units of $\Delta G^{\ominus}$ are kJ mol^{-1}. For a reaction to be spontaneous it must be able to do work, that is, $\Delta G^{\ominus}$ must have a negative value.

Note: the fact that a reaction is spontaneous does not necessarily mean that it will proceed without any input of energy. For example, the combustion of coal is a spontaneous reaction and yet coal is stable in air. It will only burn after it has received some initial energy so that some of the molecules have the necessary activation energy for the reaction to occur.

$\Delta S^{\ominus}$ and the position of equilibrium

As a reaction proceeds, the composition of the reactants and products is continually changing and the Gibbs energy change moves closer to zero. The position of equilibrium corresponds to a maximum value of entropy and a minimum value of the Gibbs energy change, i.e. at equilibrium, ΔG = zero. The reaction will not proceed any further at this point, i.e. the rate of the forward reaction will equal the rate of the reverse reaction. The equilibrium composition of an equilibrium mixture thus depends upon the value of ΔG. From this it can also be deduced that the equilibrium constant for the reaction, K_c, will also depend upon the value of ΔG (see page 102).

Interpreting the sign of ΔG

Some reactions will always be spontaneous. If $\Delta H^{\ominus}$ is negative or zero and $\Delta S^{\ominus}$ is positive, then $\Delta G^{\ominus}$ must always have a negative value. Conversely, if $\Delta H^{\ominus}$ is positive or zero and $\Delta S^{\ominus}$ is negative, then $\Delta G^{\ominus}$ must always be positive and the reaction will never be spontaneous.

For some reactions, whether or not they will be spontaneous depends upon the temperature. If $\Delta H^{\ominus}$ is positive or zero and $\Delta S^{\ominus}$ is positive, then $\Delta G^{\ominus}$ will only become negative at high temperatures when the value of $T\Delta S^{\ominus}$ exceeds the value of $\Delta H^{\ominus}$.

Type	$\Delta H^{\ominus}$	$\Delta S^{\ominus}$	$T\Delta S^{\ominus}$	$\Delta H^{\ominus} - T\Delta S^{\ominus}$	$\Delta G^{\ominus}$	Example
1	0	+	+	(0) – (+)	–	Mixing two gases is always spontaneous.
2	0	–	–	(0) – (–)	+	Gases do not unmix of their own accord.
3	–	+	+	(–) – (+)	–	The decomposition of ammonium dichromate is spontaneous at all temperatures. $(NH_4)_2Cr_2O_7(s) \rightarrow N_2(g) + Cr_2O_3(s) + 4H_2O(g)$
4	+	–	–	(+) – (–)	+	The formation of hydrazine from its elements will never be spontaneous. $N_2(g) + 2H_2(g) \rightarrow N_2H_4(g)$
5	+	+	+	(+) – (+)	– or +	The decomposition of calcium carbonate is only spontaneous at high temperature. $CaCO_3(s) \rightarrow CaO(s) + CO_2(g)$
6	–	–	–	(–) – (–)	+ or –	The hydration of ethene ceases to be spontaneous above a certain temperature. $C_2H_4(g) + H_2(g) \rightarrow C_2H_6(g)$

Determining the value of $\Delta G^{\ominus}$

The precise value of $\Delta G^{\ominus}$ for a reaction can be determined from $\Delta G_f^{\ominus}$ values using an energy cycle.

Worked example 1

You can find the standard Gibbs energy of combustion of methane given the standard Gibbs energies of formation of methane, carbon dioxide, water, and oxygen.

$$CH_4(g) + 2O_2 \xrightarrow{\Delta G_x^{\ominus}} CO_2(g) + 2H_2O(l)$$

$$C(s) + 2O_2(g) + 2H_2(g)$$

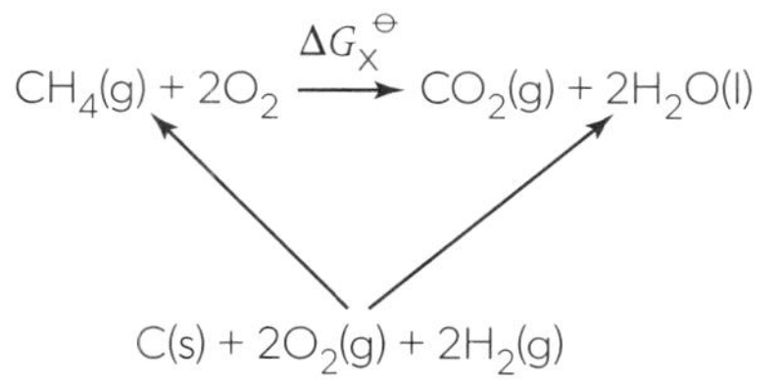

By Hess's law:

$\Delta G_x^{\ominus} = [\Delta G_f^{\ominus}(CO_2) + 2\Delta G_f^{\ominus}(H_2O)] - [\Delta G_f^{\ominus}(CH_4) + 2\Delta G_f^{\ominus}(O_2)]$

Substituting the actual values: $\Delta G_x^{\ominus} = [-394 + 2 \times (-237)] - [-50 + 2 \times 0] = -818\ kJ\ mol^{-1}$

$\Delta G^{\ominus}$ values can also be calculated using the equation

$\Delta G^{\ominus} = \Delta H^{\ominus} - T\Delta S^{\ominus}$

Worked example 2

For the thermal decomposition of calcium carbonate (Type 5 in the table) the values for $\Delta H^{\ominus}$ and $\Delta S^{\ominus}$ are +178 kJ mol^{-1} and +165.3 J K^{-1} mol^{-1}, respectively. Note that the units of $\Delta S^{\ominus}$ are different from those of $\Delta H^{\ominus}$.

At 25 °C (298 K) the value for $\Delta G^{\ominus} = 178 - (298 \times \dfrac{165.3}{1000}) = +129\ kJ\ mol^{-1}$

This means that the reaction is not spontaneous. The reaction will become spontaneous when $T\Delta S^{\ominus} > \Delta H^{\ominus}$.

$T\Delta S^{\ominus} = \Delta H^{\ominus}$ when $T = \dfrac{\Delta H^{\ominus}}{\Delta S^{\ominus}} = \dfrac{178}{165.3/1000}$
$= 1077\ K\ (804\ °C)$

Therefore above 804 °C the reaction will be spontaneous.

Note: this calculation assumes that the entropy value is independent of temperature, which is not strictly true.

Multiple-choice questions—Energetics

1. Which statement about the reaction below is correct?

$2NO(g) + O_2(g) \rightarrow 2NO_2(g) \qquad \Delta H^\ominus = -114\,kJ$

A. 114 kJ of energy is absorbed for every mole of NO reacted.

B. 114 kJ of energy is released for every mole of NO reacted.

C. 57 kJ of energy is absorbed for every mole of NO reacted.

D. 57 kJ of energy is released for every mole of NO reacted.

2. When an aqueous solution of sulfuric acid is added to an aqueous solution of potassium hydroxide the temperature increases. Which describes the reaction taking place?

	Type	Sign of $\Delta H^\ominus$
A.	exothermic	+
B.	exothermic	–
C.	endothermic	–
D.	endothermic	+

3. A student measured the temperature of a reaction mixture over time using a temperature probe. By considering the graph, which of the following deductions can be made?

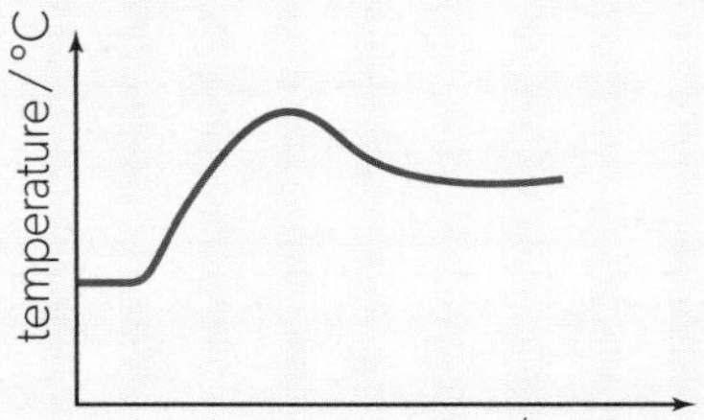

I. The reaction is exothermic.

II. The products are more stable than the reactants.

III. The reactant bonds are stronger than the product bonds.

A. I and II only
B. I and III only
C. II and III only
D. I, II, and III

4.

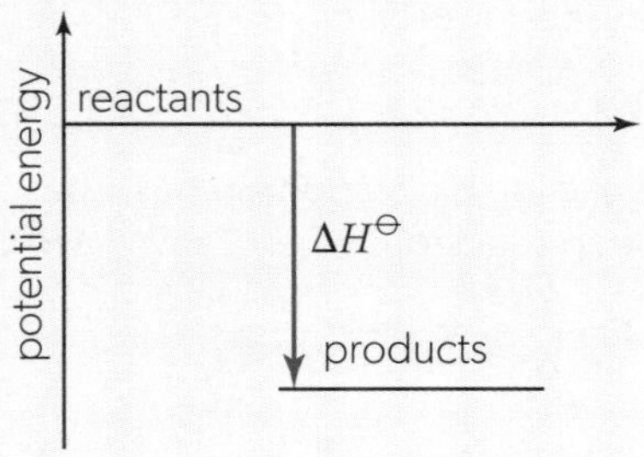

What can be deduced about the relative stability of the reactants and products and the sign of ΔH from the enthalpy level diagram above?

	Relative stability	Sign of $\Delta H^\ominus$
A.	Products more stable	–
B.	Products more stable	+
C.	Reactants more stable	–
D.	Reactants more stable	+

5. Consider the following reactions.

$CH_4(g) + O_2(g) \rightarrow HCHO(l) + H_2O(l) \qquad \Delta H^\ominus = x$

$HCHO(l) + \tfrac{1}{2}O_2(g) \rightarrow HCOOH(l) \qquad \Delta H^\ominus = y$

$2HCOOH(l) + \tfrac{1}{2}O_2(g) \rightarrow (COOH)_2(s) + H_2O(l) \qquad \Delta H^\ominus = z$

What is the enthalpy change of the reaction below?

$2CH_4(g) + 3\tfrac{1}{2}O_2(g) \rightarrow (COOH)_2(s) + 3H_2O(l)$

A. $x + y + z$
B. $2x + y + z$
C. $2x + 2y + z$
D. $2x + 2y + 2z$

6. Which equation represents the H–F bond enthalpy?

A. $2HF(g) \rightarrow H_2(g) + F_2(g)$
B. $HF(g) \rightarrow H^+(g) + F^-(g)$
C. $HF(g) \rightarrow H^-(g) + F^+(g)$
D. $HF(g) \rightarrow H(g) + F(g)$

7.

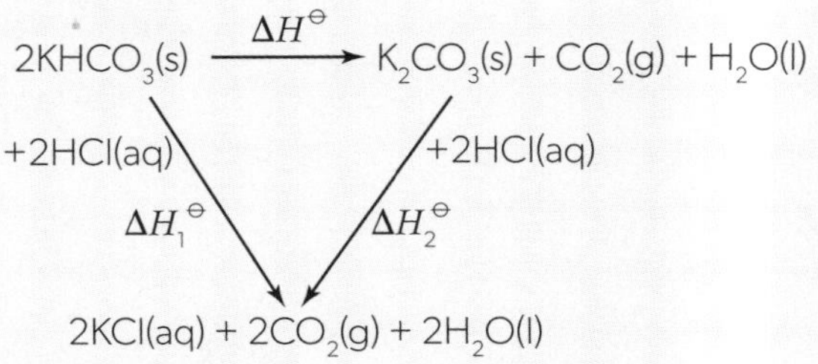

This cycle may be used to determine $\Delta H^\ominus$ for the decomposition of potassium hydrogencarbonate.

Which expression can be used to calculate $\Delta H^\ominus$?

A. $\Delta H^\ominus = \Delta H_1^\ominus + \Delta H_2^\ominus$

B. $\Delta H^\ominus = \Delta H_1^\ominus - \Delta H_2^\ominus$

C. $\Delta H^\ominus = \tfrac{1}{2}\Delta H_1^\ominus - \Delta H_2^\ominus$

D. $\Delta H^\ominus = \Delta H_2^\ominus - \Delta H_1^\ominus$

8. Which process is endothermic?

A. $HNO_3(aq) + NaOH(aq) \rightarrow NaNO_3(aq) + H_2O(l)$

B. $Cl(g) + e^- \rightarrow Cl^-(g)$

C. $H_2O(l) \rightarrow H_2O(g)$

D. $C_2H_5OH(l) + 3O_2(g) \rightarrow 2CO_2(g) + 3H_2O(l)$

9. Which reaction occurs at the negative electrode (anode) in a methanol fuel cell?

A $CH_3OH + H_2O \rightarrow CO_2 + 6H^+ + 6e^-$

B. $CH_3OH + H_2O + 2e^- \rightarrow CH_3COOH + 2H^+$

C. $O_2 + 4H^+ + 4e^- \rightarrow 2H_2O$

D. $H_2 + 2OH^- \rightarrow 2H_2O + 2e^-$

10. During the incomplete combustion of methane the following reaction occurs.

$2CH_4(g) + 3O_2(g) \rightarrow 2CO(g) + 4H_2O(g)$

Which expression is correct for the enthalpy change, $\Delta H^{\ominus}$, for this reaction (in kJ mol^{-1}) using the bond enthalpy data given?

Bond	Average bond enthalpy / kJ mol^{-1}
C–H	w
O–H	x
O=O	y
C≡O	z

A. $(2z + 8x) - (8w + 3y)$
B. $(8w + 3y) - (2z + 8x)$
C. $(2z + 4x) - (2w + 3y)$
D. $(2w + 3y) - (2z + 4x)$

11. Carbohydrates such as glucose can be combusted to produce energy:

$C_6H_{12}O_6(s) + 6O_2(g) \rightarrow 6CO_2(g) + 6H_2O(l)$

$\Delta H^{\ominus} = -2\,816$ kJ mol^{-1}

or they can first be converted into ethanol by fermentation:

$C_6H_{12}O_6(s) \rightarrow 2C_2H_5OH(l) + 2CO_2(g)$

and then the ethanol is combusted to produce energy:

$C_2H_5OH(l) + 3O_2(g) \rightarrow 2CO_2(g) + 3H_2O(l)$

$\Delta H^{\ominus} = -1\,371$ kJ mol^{-1}

What is the enthalpy of fermentation of glucose to ethanol in kJ mol^{-1}?

A. +1445
B. +74
C. −1445
D. −74

12. Which is a correct statement about heat and temperature?

A. When 1.0 kg of water cools from 21 °C to 20 °C it gives out 4.18 kJ of heat.
B. 50 g of water at 20 °C contains the same amount of energy as 100 g of water at 20 °C.
C. Heat and temperature are both a measure of the total kinetic energy of the particles.
D. Heat and temperature are both forms of energy.

AHL

13. Which is a correct definition of lattice enthalpy?

A. It is the enthalpy change that occurs when an electron is removed from 1 mol of gaseous atoms.
B. It is the enthalpy change that occurs when 1 mol of a compound is formed from its elements.
C. It is the enthalpy change that occurs when 1 mol of solid crystal changes into a liquid.
D. It is the enthalpy change that occurs when 1 mol of solid crystal is formed from its gaseous ions.

14. The diagram represents the Born–Haber cycle for the lattice enthalpy of sodium chloride.

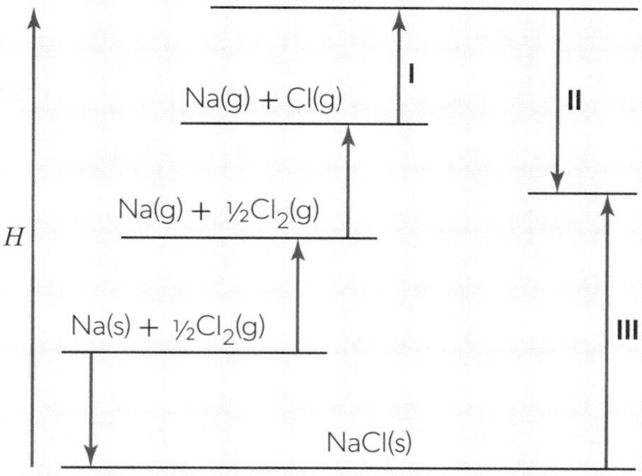

What are the names of the enthalpy changes I, II, and III?

	I	II	III
A.	ionization energy of Na	electron affinity of Cl	lattice enthalpy of NaCl
B.	lattice enthalpy of NaCl	ionization energy of Na	electron affinity of Cl
C.	electron affinity of Cl	ionization energy of Na	lattice enthalpy of NaCl
D.	ionization energy of Na	lattice enthalpy of NaCl	electron affinity of Cl

15. Which reaction has the largest increase in entropy?

A. $H_2(g) + Cl_2(g) \rightarrow 2HCl(g)$
B. $Al(OH)_3(s) + NaOH(aq) \rightarrow Al(OH)_4^-(aq) + Na^+(aq)$
C. $Na_2CO_3(s) + 2HCl(aq) \rightarrow 2NaCl(aq) + CO_2(g) + H_2O(l)$
D. $BaCl_2(aq) + Na_2SO_4(aq) \rightarrow BaSO_4(s) + 2NaCl(aq)$

16. Which statements about entropy for the following reaction at 298 K are correct?

$2NO(g) + O_2(g) \rightarrow 2NO_2(g)$

I. $S^{\ominus}(O_2) = 0$
II. $\Delta S^{\ominus} = 2S^{\ominus}(NO_2) - 2S^{\ominus}(NO) - S^{\ominus}(O_2)$
III. $\Delta S^{\ominus} < 0$

A. I and II only
B. I and III only
C. II and III only
D. I, II, and III

17. Which ionic compound has the highest lattice enthalpy value?

A. NaCl
B. MgS
C. MgO
D. NaI

18. Which is a correct statement?

A. If $\Delta H > 0$, then a reaction can never be spontaneous.
B. If $\Delta H < 0$, then a reaction can never be spontaneous.
C. If $\Delta S > 0$, then a reaction can be spontaneous if the temperature is low enough.
D. If $\Delta S < 0$, then a reaction can be spontaneous if the temperature is low enough.

19. Which is correct for the signs of the entropy change associated with this physical change?

$C_2H_5OH(g) \rightarrow C_2H_5OH(l)$

	ΔS_{system}	$\Delta S_{surroundings}$
A.	−	−
B.	−	+
C.	+	−
D.	+	+

20. Calcium carbonate decomposes into calcium oxide and carbon dioxide.

$CaCO_3(s) \rightarrow CaO(s) + CO_2(g)$ $\quad \Delta H^\ominus = +178\,kJ\,mol^{-1}$

$\Delta S^\ominus = +165\,J\,K^{-1}\,mol^{-1}$

Above what temperature will this reaction become spontaneous?

A. (178 ÷ 165) °C

B. (178 ÷ 0.165) °C

C. (178 ÷ 0.165) K

D. (178 ÷ 165) K

21. When solid ammonium nitrate, NH_4NO_3, dissolves in distilled water, the temperature of the solution decreases. What are the signs of $\Delta H^\ominus$, $\Delta S^\ominus$, and $\Delta G^\ominus$ for this spontaneous process?

	$\Delta H^\ominus$	$\Delta S^\ominus$	$\Delta G^\ominus$
A.	+	+	+
B.	+	+	−
C.	−	−	−
D.	+	−	+

Short-answer questions—Energetics

1. In an experiment to measure the enthalpy change of combustion of ethanol, a student heated a copper calorimeter containing 100 cm^3 of water with a spirit lamp and collected the following data.

Initial temperature of water: 20.0 °C

Final temperature of water: 55.0 °C

Mass of ethanol burned: 1.78 g

Density of water: 1.00 g cm^{-3}

a) Use the data to calculate the heat evolved (in kJ) when the ethanol was combusted. [2]

b) Calculate the enthalpy change of combustion per mole of ethanol. [2]

c) Suggest two reasons why the result is not the same as the value in the IB data booklet. [2]

2. Ethanol is used as a component in fuel for some vehicles. One fuel mixture contains 10% by mass of ethanol in unleaded petrol (gasoline). This mixture is often referred to as Gasohol E10.

a) Assume that the other 90% by mass of Gasohol E10 is octane. 1.00 kg of this fuel mixture was burned.

$CH_3CH_2OH(l) + 3O_2(g) \rightarrow 2CO_2(g) + 3H_2O(l)$

$\Delta H^\ominus = -1\,367\,kJ\,mol^{-1}$

$C_8H_{18}(l) + 12\frac{1}{2}O_2(g) \rightarrow 8CO_2(g) + 9H_2O(l)$

$\Delta H^\ominus = -5\,470\,kJ\,mol^{-1}$

(i) Calculate the mass, in g, of ethanol and octane in 1.00 kg of the fuel mixture. [1]

(ii) Calculate the amount, in mol, of ethanol and octane in 1.00 kg of the fuel mixture. [1]

(iii) Calculate the total amount of energy, in kJ, released when 1.00 kg of the fuel mixture is completely burned. [3]

b) If the fuel blend was vaporized before combustion, predict whether the amount of energy released would be greater, less, or the same. Explain your answer. [2]

3. The data shown are from an experiment to measure the enthalpy change for the reaction of aqueous copper(II) sulfate, $CuSO_4(aq)$, and zinc, Zn(s).

$Cu^{2+}(aq) + Zn(s) \rightarrow Cu(s) + Zn^{2+}(aq)$

$50.0\,cm^3$ of $1.00\,mol\,dm^{-3}$ copper(II) sulfate solution was placed in a polystyrene cup and zinc powder was added after 100 seconds. The temperature–time data was taken from a data-logging software program. The table shows the initial 19 readings.

	A	B	C	D	E	F	G	H
1	time / s	temperature / °C						
2	0.0	24.8						
3	1.0	24.8						
4	2.0	24.8						
5	3.0	24.8						
6	4.0	24.8						
7	5.0	24.8						
8	6.0	24.8						
9	7.0	24.8						
10	8.0	24.8						
11	9.0	24.8						
12	10.0	24.8						
13	11.0	24.8						
14	12.0	24.8						
15	13.0	24.8						
16	14.0	24.8						
17	15.0	24.8						
18	16.0	24.8						
19	17.0	24.8						
20	18.0	24.8						
21								
22								
23								
24								

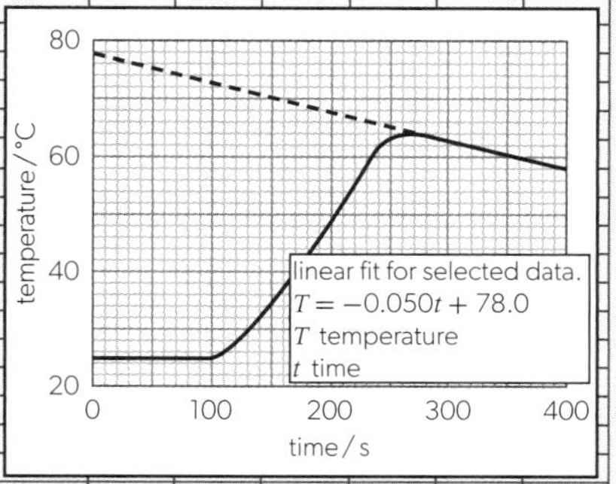

A straight line has been drawn through some of the data points. The equation for this line is given by the data-logging software as $T = -0.050t + 78.0$

a) The heat produced by the reaction can be calculated from the temperature change, ΔT, using the expression:

heat change = volume of $CuSO_4(aq)$ × specific heat capacity of $H_2O \times \Delta T$

Describe two assumptions made in using this expression to calculate heat changes. [2]

b) (i) Use the data presented by the data-logging software to deduce the temperature change, ΔT, which would have occurred if the reaction had taken place instantaneously with no heat loss. [2]

(ii) State the assumption made in part b) (i). [1]

(iii) Calculate the heat, in kJ, produced during the reaction using the expression given in part a). [1]

c) The colour of the solution changed from blue to colourless. Deduce the amount, in moles, of zinc that reacted in the polystyrene cup. [1]

d) Calculate the enthalpy change, in $kJ\,mol^{-1}$, for this reaction. [1]

AHL

4. The standard enthalpy change of three combustion reactions is given below in kJ.

$2C_2H_6(g) + 7O_2(g) \rightarrow 4CO_2(g) + 6H_2O(l)$

$\Delta H^\ominus = -3120$

$2H_2(g) + O_2(g) \rightarrow 2H_2O(l)$

$\Delta H^\ominus = -572$

$C_2H_4(g) + 3O_2(g) \rightarrow 2CO_2(g) + 2H_2O(l)$

$\Delta H^\ominus = -1411$

a) Based on this information, calculate the standard change in enthalpy, $\Delta H^\ominus$, for the following reaction.

$C_2H_6(g) \rightarrow C_2H_4(g) + H_2(g)$ [4]

b) Predict, stating a reason, whether the sign of $\Delta S^\ominus$ for the above reaction would be positive or negative. [2]

c) Discuss why the above reaction is non-spontaneous at low temperature but becomes spontaneous at high temperatures. [2]

d) Using bond enthalpy values, calculate $\Delta H^\ominus$ for the following reaction.

$C_2H_6(g) \rightarrow C_2H_4(g) + H_2(g)$ [3]

e) Suggest, with a reason, why the values obtained in parts a) and d) are different. [1]

5. "Synthesis gas" is produced by the following reaction.

$CH_4(g) + H_2O(g) \rightarrow 3H_2(g) + CO(g) \qquad \Delta H^\ominus = +210\,kJ$

For this reaction $\Delta S^\ominus = +216\,J\,K^{-1}$.

a) Explain why this reaction is not spontaneous at 298 K. [2]

b) Calculate the temperature at which this reaction becomes spontaneous. [2]

The rate of chemical change

Rate of reaction and kinetics

Chemical kinetics is the study of the factors affecting the rate of a chemical reaction. The rate of a chemical reaction can be defined either as the increase in the concentration of one of the products per unit time or as the decrease in the concentration of one of the reactants per unit time. It is measured in mol $dm^{-3}\,s^{-1}$.

The change in concentration can be measured by using any property that differs between the reactants and the products. Common methods include mass or volume changes when a gas is evolved, absorption using a spectrometer when there is a colour change, pH changes when there is a change in acidity, and electrical conductivity when there is a change in the ionic concentrations. Data loggers could be used for all these methods. A graph of concentration against time is then usually plotted. The rate at any point in time is the **gradient** of the graph at that time. You can find the gradient at any point using a tangent to the curve. Rates of reaction usually decrease with time as the reactants are used up.

The reaction of hydrochloric acid with calcium carbonate can be used to illustrate three typical curves that could be obtained depending on whether the concentration of reactant, the volume of the product, or the loss in mass due to the carbon dioxide escaping is followed.

$CaCO_3(s) + 2HCl(aq) \rightarrow CaCl_2(aq) + H_2O(l) + CO_2(g)$

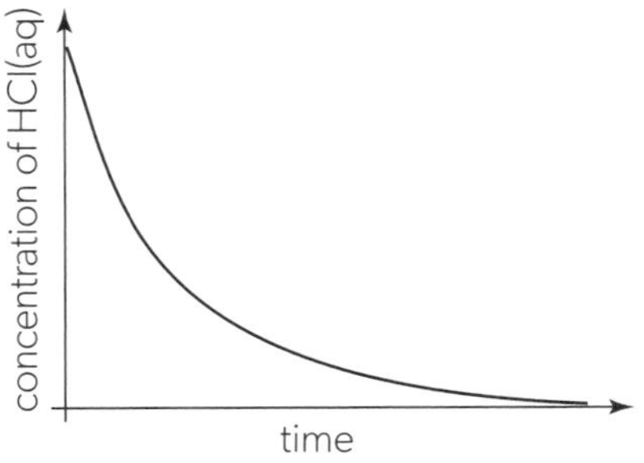

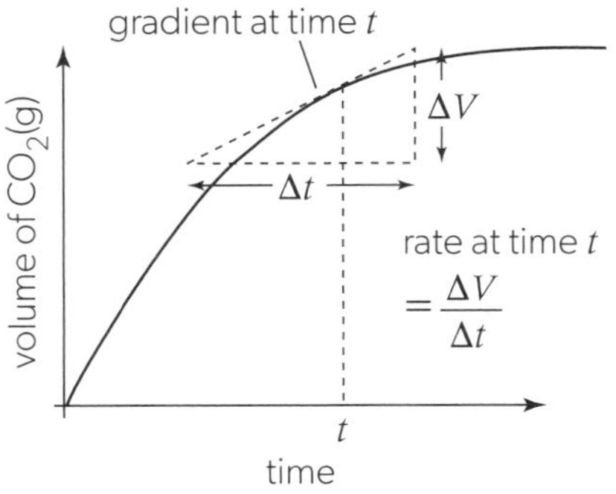

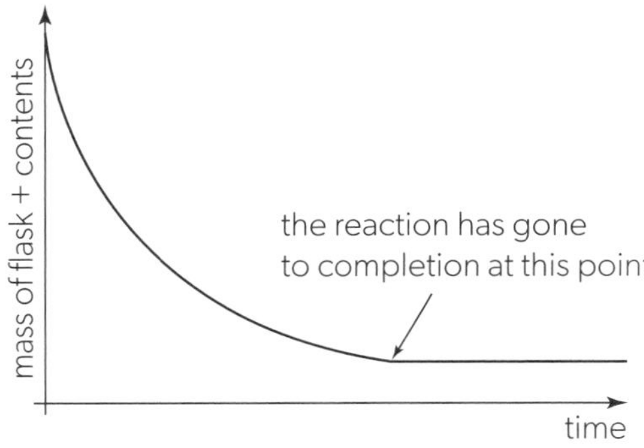

Collision theory

For a reaction between two particles to occur, three conditions must be met.

- The particles must collide.
- They must collide with the appropriate geometry or orientation so that the reactive parts of the particles come into contact with each other.
- They must collide with sufficient kinetic energy to bring about the reaction.

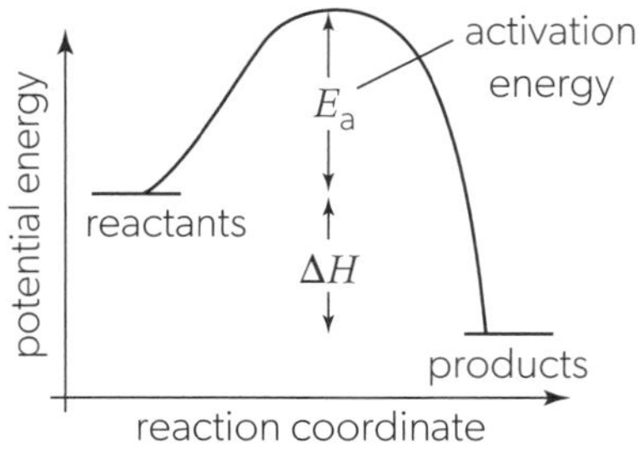

This minimum amount of energy required is known as the **activation energy**, E_a. Any factor that either increases the frequency of the collisions or increases the energy with which the particles collide will make the reaction go faster.

Factors affecting the rate of reaction

Temperature

The Maxwell–Boltzmann curve discussed on page 5 shows that, as the temperature increases, the particles move faster with increased energy, so there will be more collisions between reactant particles per second. However, the main reason why an increase in temperature increases the rate is that more of the colliding particles possess the necessary activation energy, so more of the collisions are successful. As a rough rule of thumb, an increase of 10 °C doubles the rate of a chemical reaction.

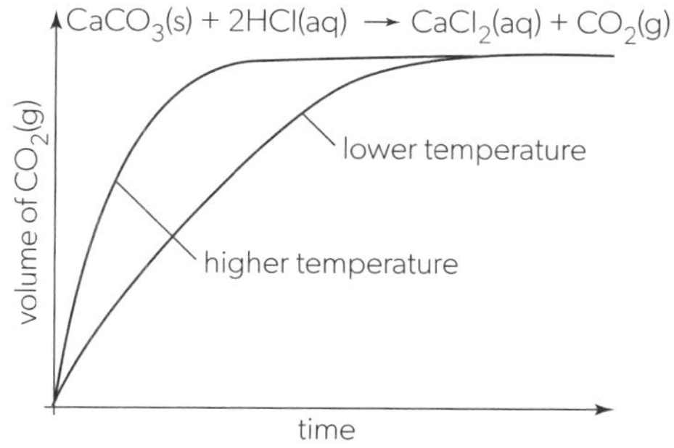

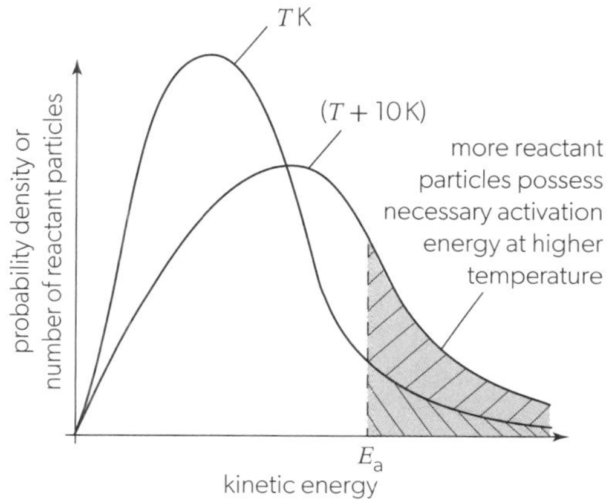

Surface area

In a solid substance, only the particles on the surface can come into contact with a surrounding reactant. If the solid is powdered, then the surface area increases dramatically and the rate increases correspondingly.

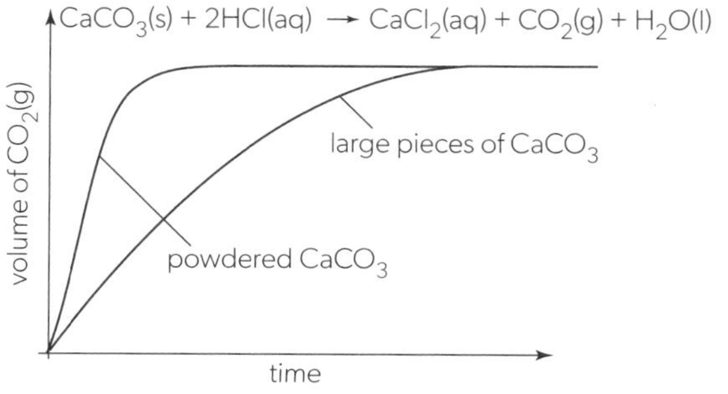

Concentration

The more concentrated the reactants, the more collisions there will be per second per unit volume. (For gases, concentration is related to pressure, as the more particles are present in a fixed volume of a gas, the higher the pressure.) As the reactants are used up, their concentration decreases. This explains why the rate of most reactions gets slower as the reaction proceeds.

Note that some exothermic reactions do initially speed up if the heat that is given out more than compensates for the decrease in concentration.

Note: this graph assumes that calcium carbonate is the limiting reagent or that equal amounts (mol) of acid have been added.

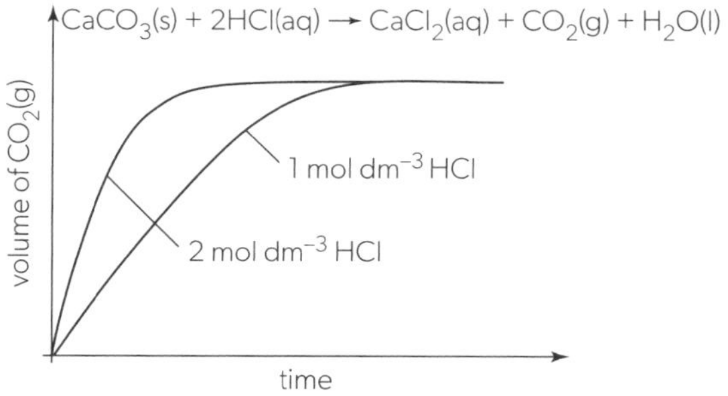

Catalysts

Catalysts increase the rate of a chemical reaction without themselves being chemically changed at the end of the reaction. A brief explanation of how catalysts work is that they bring the reactive parts of the reactant particles into close contact with each other. This provides an alternative pathway for the reaction with a lower activation energy. More of the reactants will possess this lower activation energy, so the rate increases.

Enzymes are biological catalysts, but they only function efficiently at ambient temperatures as they are denatured at higher temperatures.

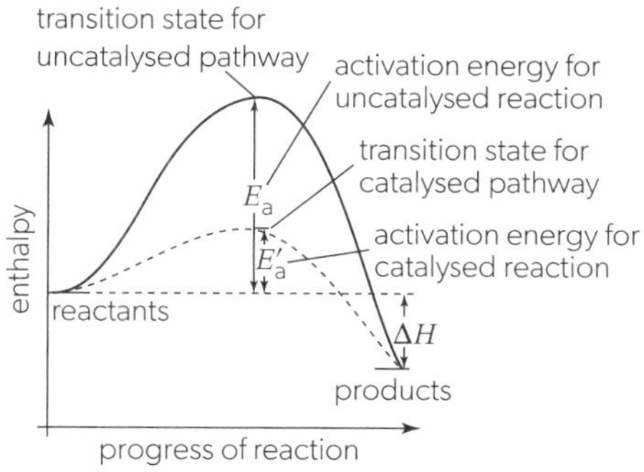

▲ Energy profile for an exothermic reaction

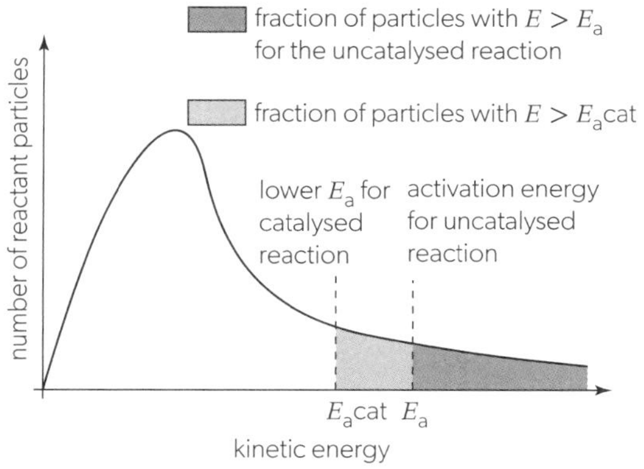

AHL Rate expression and order of reaction

Rate expressions

The rate of reaction between two reactants, A and B, can be followed experimentally. The rate will be found to be proportional to the concentration of A raised to a power and also to the concentration of B raised to a power. If square brackets are used to denote concentration, this can be written as rate $\propto [A]^x$ and rate $\propto [B]^y$. These statements can be combined to give the rate expression: rate $= k[A]^x[B]^y$

where k is the constant of proportionality and is known as the **rate constant**.

x is known as the **order of the reaction** with respect to A.

y is known as the order of the reaction with respect to B.

The overall order of the reaction $= x + y$.

Note: the order of the reaction and the rate expression can only be determined experimentally. They cannot be deduced from the balanced equation for the reaction.

Graphical representations of reactions

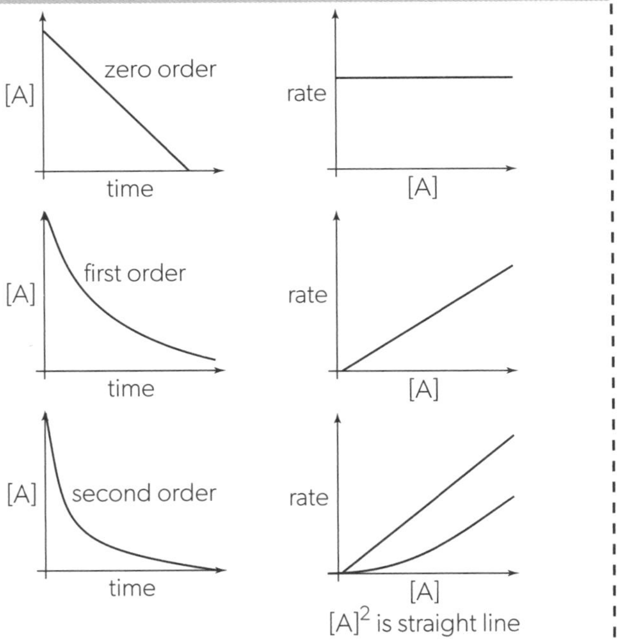

Units of rate constant

The units of the rate constant depend on the overall order of the reaction.

First order: rate $= k[A]$

$$k = \frac{\text{rate}}{[A]} = \frac{\text{mol dm}^{-3}\,\text{s}^{-1}}{\text{mol dm}^{-3}} = \text{s}^{-1}$$

Second order: rate $= k[A]^2$ or $k = [A][B]$

$$k = \frac{\text{rate}}{[A]^2} = \frac{\text{mol dm}^{-3}\,\text{s}^{-1}}{(\text{mol dm}^{-3})^2} = \text{dm}^3\,\text{mol}^{-1}\,\text{s}^{-1}$$

Third order: rate $= k[A]^2[B]$ or rate $= k[A][B]^2$

$$k = \frac{\text{rate}}{[A]^2[B]} = \frac{\text{mol dm}^{-3}\,\text{s}^{-1}}{(\text{mol dm}^{-3})^3} = \text{dm}^6\,\text{mol}^{-2}\,\text{s}^{-1}$$

Deriving a rate expression from experimental data

Below is some experimental data obtained from the reaction between hydrogen and nitrogen monoxide at 1073 K:

$2H_2(g) + 2NO(g) \rightarrow 2H_2O(g) + N_2(g)$

Experiment	Initial concentration of H_2(g) / mol dm^{-3}	Initial concentration of NO(g) / mol dm^{-3}	Initial rate of formation of N_2(g) / mol dm^{-3} s^{-1}
1	1×10^{-3}	6×10^{-3}	3×10^{-3}
2	2×10^{-3}	6×10^{-3}	6×10^{-3}
3	6×10^{-3}	1×10^{-3}	0.5×10^{-3}
4	6×10^{-3}	2×10^{-3}	2.0×10^{-3}

From experiments 1 and 2, doubling $[H_2]$ doubles the rate, so rate $\propto [H_2]$.

From experiments 3 and 4 doubling [NO] quadruples the rate, so rate $\propto [NO]^2$.

Rate expression is rate $= k[H_2][NO]^2$.

The rate is first order with respect to hydrogen, second order with respect to nitrogen monoxide, and third order overall. The value of k can be found by substituting the values from any one of the four experiments:

$$k = \frac{\text{rate}}{[H_2][NO]^2} = 8.33 \times 10^4\,\text{dm}^6\,\text{mol}^{-2}\,\text{s}^{-1}$$

AHL Reaction mechanisms and activation energy

Reaction mechanisms

Many reactions do not go in one step. This is particularly true when there are more than two reactant molecules, as the chance of a successful collision between three or more particles is extremely small. When there is more than one step, then each step will proceed at its own rate. The overall rate of the reaction depends only on the slowest step, no matter how fast the other steps are. This slowest step is known as the **rate-determining step**.

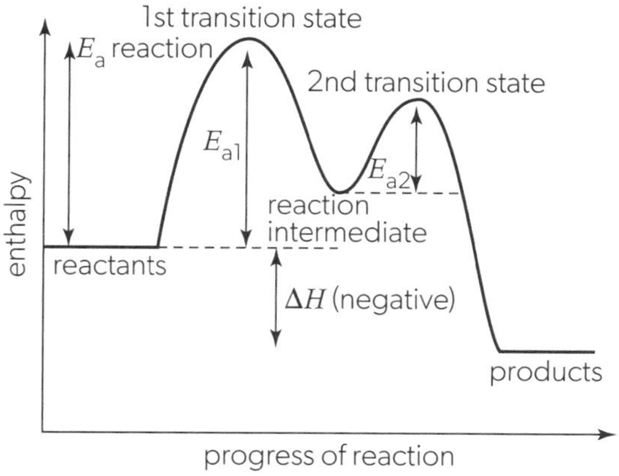

▲ Energy profile for a two-step exothermic reaction

In each single step of a reaction, the activation energy is the minimum energy required to reach the transition state before the products are formed. A transition state is not a chemical substance that can be isolated but consists of an association of the reacting particles in which bonds are in the process of being broken and formed; it then either breaks down to form the products or reverts back to the original reactants. In a two-step reaction in which an intermediate is formed (such as the S_N1 reactions of halogenoalkanes), there are two transition states, each with its own activation energy. However, the overall activation energy, E_a, is not the sum of the individual activation energies ($E_{a1} + E_{a2}$). Instead, it is the difference in energy between the reactant state and the highest energy transition state. The slow step will be the step that has the highest activation energy.

When the separate steps in a chemical reaction are analysed, there are essentially only two types of process. Either a single species can break down into two or more products by what is known as a **unimolecular process**, or two species can collide and interact by a **bimolecular process**. Termolecular reactions are rare and involve three reacting species.

The number of species taking part in any specified step in the reaction is known as the **molecularity**. In most cases, the molecularity refers to the slowest step, that is, the rate-determining step.

In the reaction between nitrogen monoxide and hydrogen, discussed on the previous page, the stoichiometry of the reaction involves two molecules of hydrogen and two molecules of nitrogen monoxide. Any proposed mechanism must be consistent with the rate expression.

The proposed mechanism is:

$$NO(g) + NO(g) \xrightarrow{\text{fast}} N_2O_2(g)$$

$$N_2O_2(g) + H_2(g) \xrightarrow{\text{slow}} N_2O(g) + H_2O(g)$$

rate-determining step

$$N_2O(g) + H_2(g) \xrightarrow{\text{fast}} N_2(g) + H_2O(g)$$

Overall: $2NO(g) + 2H_2(g) \rightarrow N_2(g) + 2H_2O(g)$

If the first step was the slowest step, the rate expression would be rate = $k[NO]^2$ and the rate would be zero order with respect to hydrogen. The rate for the second step depends on $[H_2]$ and $[N_2O_2]$. However, the concentration of N_2O_2 depends on the first step. So the rate expression for the second step becomes rate = $k[H_2][NO]^2$, which is consistent with the experimentally determined rate expression. The molecularity of the reaction is two, as two reacting species are involved in the rate-determining step.

Arrhenius equation

The rate constant for a reaction is only constant if the temperature remains constant. As the temperature increases, the reactants possess more energy and the rate constant increases. The relationship between rate constant and absolute temperature is given by the Arrhenius equation:

$$k = Ae^{(-E_a/RT)}$$

where E_a is the activation energy and R is the gas constant. A is known as the Arrhenius factor (or frequency factor) and is indicative of the frequency of collisions with the correct orientation for the reaction to occur. This equation is often expressed in its logarithmic form:

$$\ln k = \frac{-E_a}{RT} + \ln A$$

The equation can be used to determine both the Arrhenius factor and the activation energy for the reaction. This can be done either by substitution using simultaneous equations or by plotting $\ln k$ against $\frac{1}{T}$ to give a straight-line graph. The gradient of the graph will be equal to $\frac{-E_a}{R}$, from which the activation energy can be calculated. Extrapolating the graph back to the $\ln k$ axis will give an intercept with a value equal to $\ln A$.

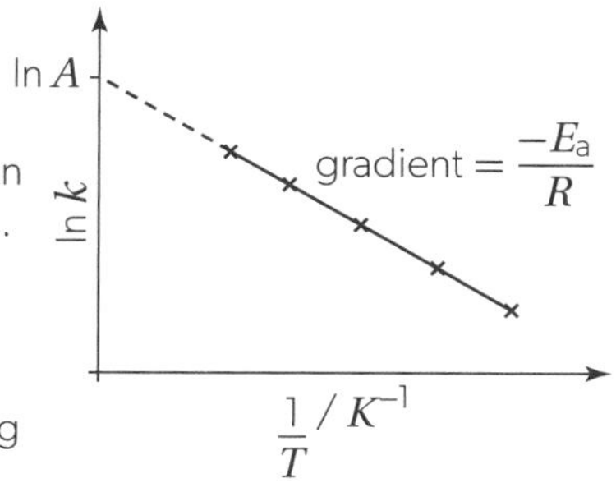

Multiple-choice questions —Chemical kinetics

1. A piece of zinc was added to aqueous nitric acid and the volume of hydrogen gas produced was measured every minute. The results are plotted on the graph below.

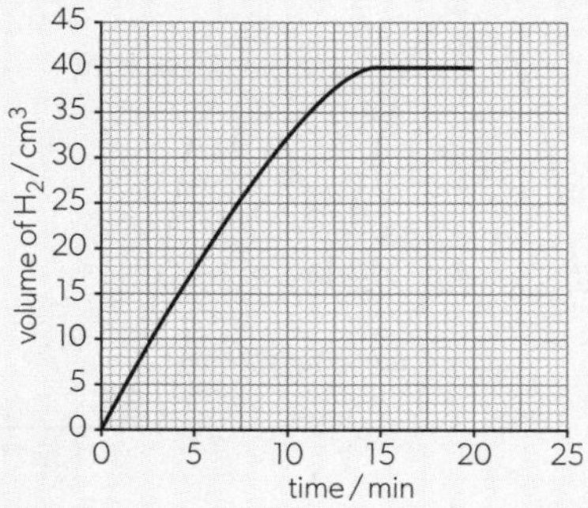

Which graph would you expect if the same mass of powdered zinc was added to nitric acid with the same concentration?

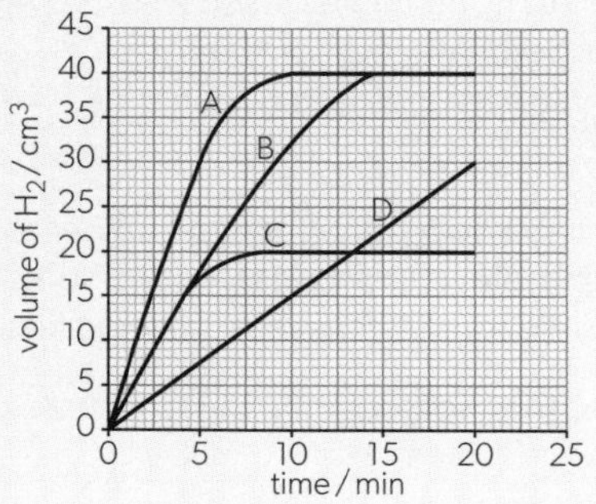

2. Which changes increase the rate of the reaction below?

$C_4H_{10}(g) + Cl_2(g) \rightarrow C_4H_9Cl(l) + HCl(g)$

I. Increase of pressure

II. Increase of temperature

III. Removal of HCl(g)

A. I and II only C. II and III only

B. I and III only D. I, II, and III

3. The reaction between excess calcium carbonate and hydrochloric acid can be followed by measuring the volume of carbon dioxide produced with time. The results of one such reaction are shown below. How does the rate of this reaction change with time and what is the main reason for this change?

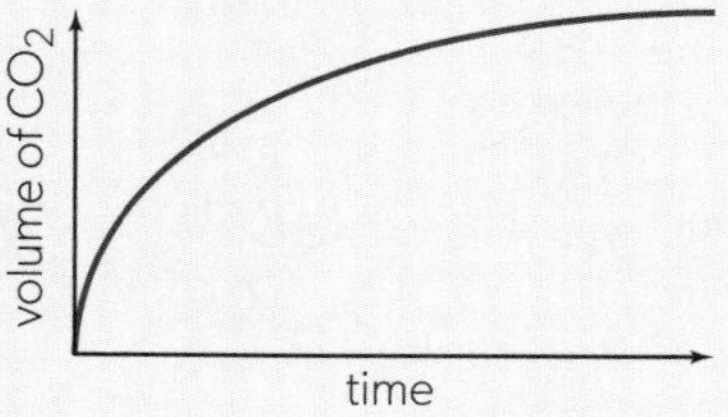

A. The rate increases with time because the calcium carbonate particles get smaller.

B. The rate increases with time because the acid becomes more dilute.

C. The rate decreases with time because the calcium carbonate particles get smaller.

D. The rate decreases with time because the acid becomes more dilute.

4. Hydrochloric acid is reacted with large pieces of calcium carbonate. The reaction is then repeated using calcium carbonate powder. How does this change affect the activation energy and the collision frequency?

	Activation energy	Collision frequency
A.	increases	increases
B.	stays constant	increases
C.	increases	stays constant
D.	stays constant	stays constant

5. Which statement is true about using sulfuric acid as a catalyst in the following reaction?

$$CH_3–CO–CH_3(aq) + I_2(aq) \xrightarrow{H^+(aq)} CH_3–CO–CH_2–I(aq) + HI(aq)$$

I. The catalyst increases the rate of reaction.

II. The catalyst lowers the activation energy for the reaction.

III. The catalyst has been consumed at the end of the chemical reaction.

A. I and II only C. II and III only

B. I and III only D. I, II, and III

6. Which are appropriate units for the rate of a reaction?

A. $mol\ dm^{-3}\ s$ C. $mol\ dm^{-3}$

B. $mol\ dm^{-3}\ s^{-1}$ D. s

7. The following enthalpy level diagram shows the effect of the addition of a catalyst to a chemical reaction. What do m, n, and o represent?

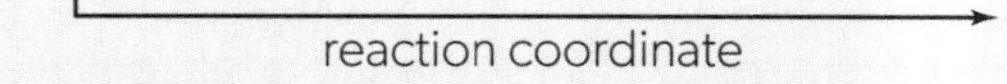

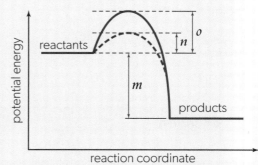

	m	n	o
A.	ΔH	E_a (without a catalyst)	E_a (with a catalyst)
B.	E_a (with a catalyst)	ΔH	E_a (without a catalyst)
C.	E_a (with a catalyst)	E_a (without a catalyst)	ΔH
D.	ΔH	E_a (with a catalyst)	E_a (without a catalyst)

8. Consider the reaction between magnesium and hydrochloric acid. Which factors will affect the reaction rate?

I. The collision frequency of the reactant particles

II. The number of reactant particles with $E \geq E_a$

III. The number of reactant particles that collide with the appropriate geometry

A. I and II only
C. II and III only
B. I and III only
D. I, II, and III

9. What is the best definition of rate of reaction?

A. The time it takes to use up all the reactants
B. The rate at which all the reactants are used up
C. The increase in concentration of a product per unit time
D. The time it takes for one of the reactants to be used up

10. At 25 °C, 200 cm³ of 1.0 mol dm⁻³ nitric acid is added to 5.0 g of magnesium powder. If the experiment is repeated using the same mass of magnesium powder, which conditions will result in the same initial reaction rate?

	Volume of HNO_3 / cm^3	Concentration of HNO_3 / mol dm^{-3}	Temperature / °C
A.	200	2.0	25
B.	200	1.0	50
C.	100	2.0	25
D.	100	1.0	25

11. The dotted line graph represents the volume of carbon dioxide evolved when excess sodium hydrogencarbonate is added to 1.00 mol dm^{-3} hydrochloric acid.

Which graph will show the evolution of carbon dioxide when excess sodium hydrogencarbonate is added to the same volume of 2.00 mol dm^{-3} hydrochloric acid?

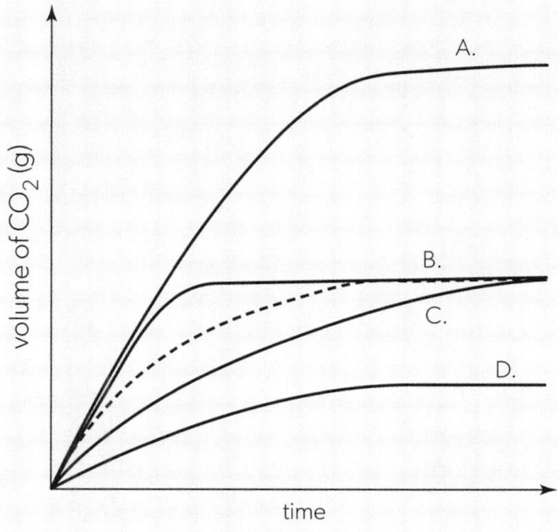

12. Which are correct labels for the axes of a Maxwell–Boltzmann energy distribution curve?

	x-axis	*y*-axis
A.	kinetic energy	probability density
B.	potential energy	probability density
C.	probability density	kinetic energy
D.	kinetic energy	reaction pathway

13. Which factors can alter the rate of a chemical reaction?

I. Pressure of a gaseous reactant

II. Surface area of a solid reactant

III. Concentration of a reactant in solution

A. I and II only
C. I and III only
B. II and III only
D. I, II, and III

14. The graph shows the distribution of molecular speeds for identical amounts of two different gases X and Y in two different identical containers both at 100 °C and 1.00 kPa pressure. What is the difference between the two gases?

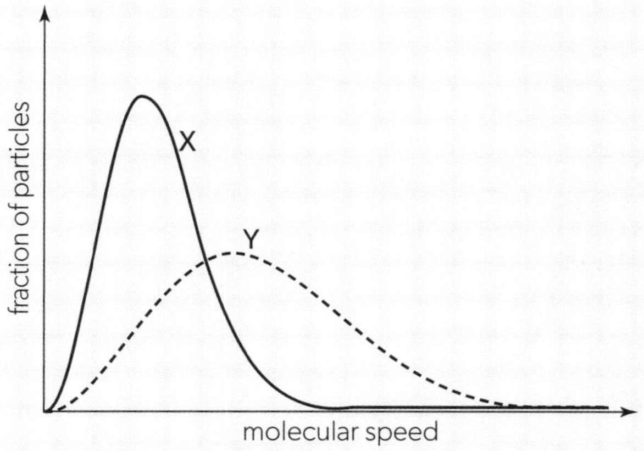

A. *M*X > *M*Y
B. *M*Y > *M*X
C. Y has the higher average kinetic energy
D. X has the higher average kinetic energy

15. Which methods could be used to follow the progress of the reaction between zinc metal and hydrochloric acid?

I. Change in mass of the reaction mixture

II. Change in volume of gas evolved

III. Change in colour of the reaction mixture

A. I and II only
C. I and III only
B. II and III only
D. I, II, and III

16. Which of the following are important in determining how fast a reaction occurs?

I. Energy of the molecules

II. Orientation of the molecules

III. The number of collisions between reactant particles

A. I and II only
B. II and III only

C. I and III only
D. I, II, and III

17. The decomposition of N_2O_5 occurs according to the following equation.

$2N_2O_5(g) \rightarrow 4NO_2(g) + O_2(g)$

The reaction is first order with respect to N_2O_5. What combination of variables could the axes represent on the graph below?

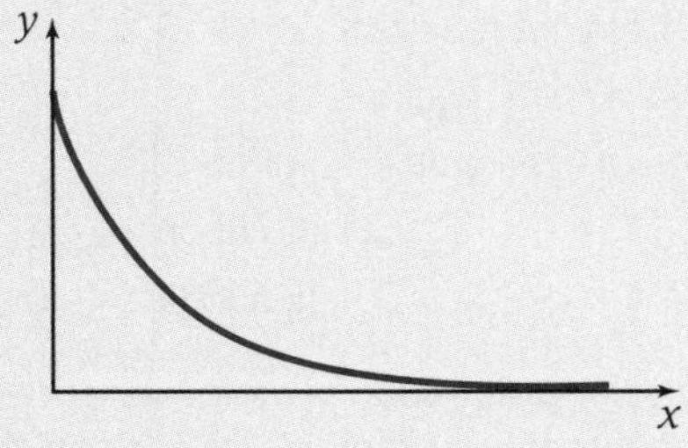

	x-axis	*y*-axis
A.	time	$[N_2O_5]$
B.	$[N_2O_5]$	time
C.	$[N_2O_5]$	rate of reaction
D.	rate of reaction	$[N_2O_5]$

18. Which graph represents a reaction that is second order with respect to X for the reaction X → products?

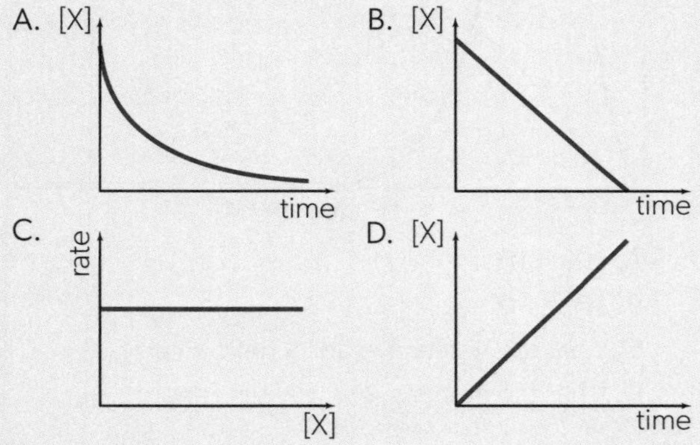

19. Consider the reaction:

$2NO(g) + Br_2(g) \rightarrow 2NOBr(g)$

One suggested mechanism is:

$NO(g) + Br_2(g) \rightleftharpoons NOBr_2(g)$ fast

$NOBr_2(g) + NO(g) \rightarrow 2NOBr(g)$ slow

Which statements are correct?

I. $NOBr_2(g)$ is an intermediate.
II. The second step is the rate-determining step.
III. rate = $k[NO]^2[Br_2]$

A. I and II only
C. II and III only
B. I and III only
D. I, II, and III

20. Consider the following reaction.

$2P + Q \rightarrow R + S$

This reaction occurs according to the following mechanism.

$P + Q \rightarrow X$ slow

$P + X \rightarrow R + S$ fast

What is the rate expression?

A. rate = $k[P]$
C. rate = $k[P][Q]$
B. rate = $k[P][X]$
D. rate = $k[P]^2[Q]$

21. The data refers to the initial rate for the reaction between fluorine and nitrogen dioxide at different concentrations of reactants at a fixed temperature.

$[F_2(g)]$ / mol dm^{-3}	$[NO_2(g)]$ / mol dm^{-3}	Initial rate / mol dm^{-3} min^{-1}
0.2	0.15	0.10
0.2	0.30	0.40
0.4	0.15	0.20

What is the rate equation for this reaction?

A. rate = $k[NO_2(g)][F_2(g)]$
B. rate = $k[NO_2(g)]^2[F_2(g)]$
C. rate = $k[NO_2(g)][F_2(g)]^2$
D. rate = $k[NO_2(g)]^2$

22. Which is correct when a graph of ln *k* is plotted against $1/T$?

$$\ln k = -\frac{E_a}{RT} + \ln A$$

	Intercept on *y*-axis	Gradient
A.	$-\ln A$	$-\frac{E_a}{R}$
B.	$-\frac{E_a}{R}$	$-\ln A$
C.	$\ln A$	$-\frac{E_a}{R}$
D.	$-\frac{E_a}{R}$	$\ln A$

23. Which statements are both correct?

	Effect of decreasing temperature on rate constant	Units of third-order rate constant
A.	no effect	dm^6 mol^{-2} s^{-1}
B.	decreases	dm^3 mol^{-1} s^{-1}
C.	no effect	dm^3 mol^{-1} s^{-1}
D.	decreases	dm^6 mol^{-2} s^{-1}

Short-answer questions—Chemical kinetics

1. a) (i) Draw a graph that shows the distribution of molecular energies in a sample of a gas at two different temperatures, T_1 and T_2, such that T_2 is greater than T_1. [2]

   (ii) Define the term activation energy. [1]

   (iii) State and explain the effect of a catalyst on the rate of an endothermic reaction. [2]

   b) (i) Magnesium is added to a solution of hydrochloric acid. Sketch a graph of acid concentration on the y-axis against time on the x-axis to illustrate the progress of the reaction. [1]

   (ii) Describe how the slope of the line changes with time. [1]

   (iii) Use the collision theory to state and explain the effect of decreasing concentration on the rate of the reaction. [2]

2. Hydrogen peroxide, $H_2O_2(aq)$, releases oxygen gas, $O_2(g)$, as it decomposes according to the equation:

$$2H_2O_2(aq) \rightarrow 2H_2O(l) + O_2(g)$$

50.0 cm³ of hydrogen peroxide solution was placed in a boiling tube, and a drop of liquid detergent was added to create a layer of bubbles on the top of the hydrogen peroxide solution as oxygen gas was released. The tube was placed in a water bath at 75 °C and the height of the bubble layer was measured every 30 seconds. A graph was plotted of the height of the bubble layer against time.

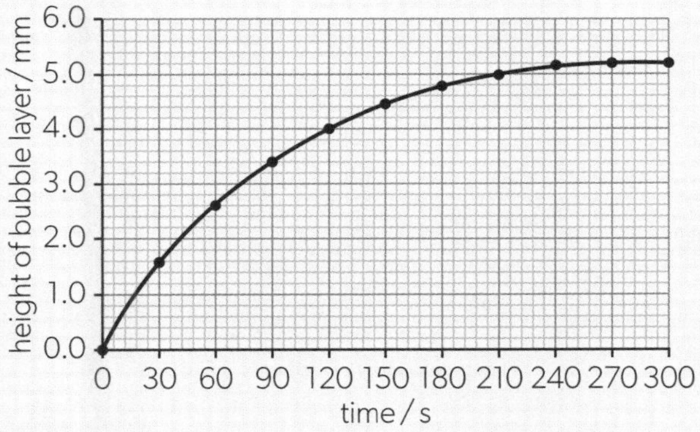

a) Explain why the curve reaches a maximum. [1]

b) Use the graph to calculate the rate of decomposition of hydrogen peroxide at 120 s. [3]

c) The experiment was repeated using solid manganese(IV) oxide, $MnO_2(s)$, as a catalyst.

   (i) Draw a curve on the graph above to show how the height of the bubble layer changes with time when manganese(IV) oxide is present. [1]

   (ii) Explain the effect of the catalyst on the rate of decomposition of hydrogen peroxide. [2]

AHL

3. Hydrogen and nitrogen(II) oxide react together exothermically as follows.

$$2H_2(g) + 2NO(g) \rightarrow 2H_2O(g) + N_2(g)$$

The rate of this reaction was investigated in a series of experiments carried out at the same temperature, the results of which are shown below.

Experiment	Initial $[H_2(g)]$ / mol dm^{-3}	Initial $[NO(g)]$ / mol dm^{-3}	Initial rate of reaction / mol dm^{-3} s^{-1}
1	2.0×10^{-3}	4.0×10^{-3}	4.0×10^{-3}
2	4.0×10^{-3}	4.0×10^{-3}	8.0×10^{-3}
3	6.0×10^{-3}	4.0×10^{-3}	
4	2.0×10^{-3}	2.0×10^{-3}	1.0×10^{-3}
5	2.0×10^{-3}	1.0×10^{-3}	

a) Explain how the results from Experiments 1 and 2 can be used to deduce that the order of reaction with respect to hydrogen is 1. [1]

b) Deduce the order of reaction with respect to nitrogen(II) oxide. Give a reason for your answer. [2]

c) Use your answers from parts **a)** and **b)** to deduce the rate expression for the reaction. [1]

d) Calculate the rate of reaction for each of Experiments 3 and 5. [2]

e) Use the results from Experiment 1 to determine the value of, and the units for, the rate constant, k, for the reaction. [2]

f) Suggest a mechanism for the reaction that is consistent with the rate expression. [2]

g) The reaction is faster in the presence of a heterogeneous catalyst. Explain the meaning of the term heterogeneous as applied to a catalyst. Draw a labelled enthalpy level diagram that shows the effect of the catalyst. [3]

4. a) The reaction between nitrogen(II) oxide and chlorine was studied at 263 K.

$$2NO(g) + Cl_2(g) \rightleftharpoons 2NOCl(g)$$

It was found that the forward reaction is first order with respect to Cl_2 and second order with respect to NO. The reverse reaction is second order with respect to NOCl.

   (i) State the rate expression for the forward reaction. [1]

   (ii) Predict the effect on the rate of the forward reaction and on the rate constant if the concentration of NO is halved. [2]

   b) State two situations when the rate of a chemical reaction is equal to the rate constant. [2]

The extent of chemical change

Dynamic equilibrium

$$A + B \underset{\text{reverse reaction}}{\overset{\text{forward reaction}}{\rightleftharpoons}} C + D$$

Most chemical reactions do not go to completion. Once some products are formed the reverse reaction can take place to re-form the reactants. In a closed system, the concentrations of all the reactants and products will eventually become constant. Such a system is said to be in a state of **dynamic equilibrium**. The forward and reverse reactions continue to occur, but, at equilibrium, the rate of the forward reaction is equal to the rate of the reverse reaction.

(i) (ii)

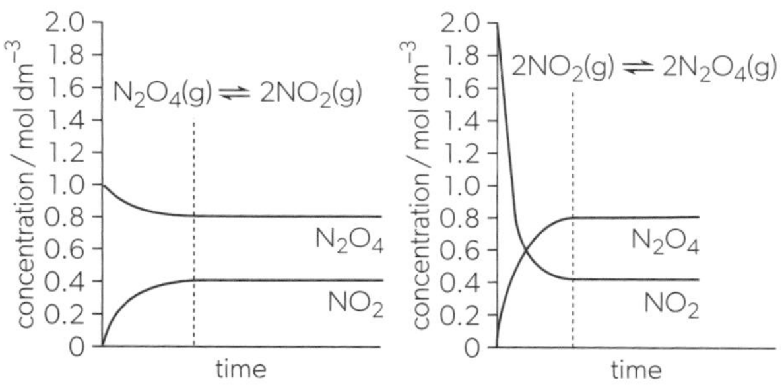

Graph (i) shows the decomposition of N_2O_4. Graph (ii) shows the reverse reaction starting with NO_2. Once equilibrium is reached (shown by the dotted vertical line), the composition of the mixture remains constant and is independent of the starting materials.

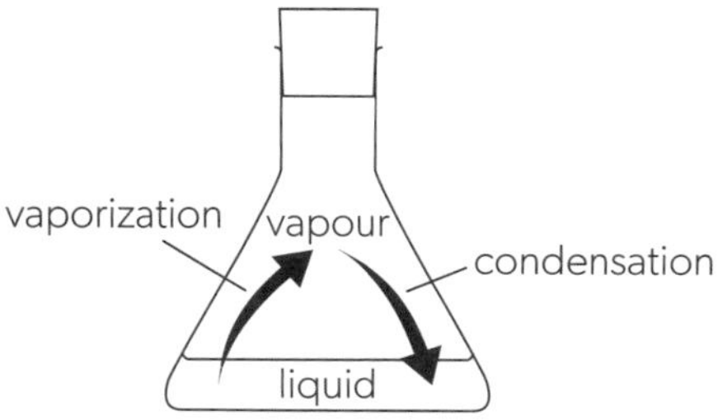

Dynamic equilibrium also occurs when physical changes take place. In a closed flask containing some water, equilibrium will be reached between the liquid water and the water vapour. The faster-moving molecules in the liquid will escape from the surface to become vapour and the slower-moving molecules in the vapour will condense back into liquid. Equilibrium will be established when the rate of vaporization equals the rate of condensation.

$H_2O(l) \rightleftharpoons H_2O(g)$

Closed system

A **closed system** is one in which neither matter nor energy can be lost or gained from the system, that is, the macroscopic properties remain constant. If the system is open, some of the products from the reaction could escape and equilibrium would never be reached.

The equilibrium law and equilibrium constant

Consider the following general reversible reaction in which w moles of A react with x moles of B to produce y moles of C and z moles of D.

$$wA + xB \rightleftharpoons yC + zD$$

As the reaction proceeds, the concentrations of the reactants and products change until the point of equilibrium is reached. At that point, the concentrations of A, B, C, and D remain constant.

The equilibrium law states that for this reaction at a particular temperature the equilibrium constant K_c is:

$$K_c = \frac{[C]^y_{eqm} \times [D]^z_{eqm}}{[A]^w_{eqm} \times [B]^x_{eqm}}$$

Note: K is the general symbol for an equilibrium constant and refers to a stoichiometric equation. However, K_c is the symbol usually used when the expression is written using the concentrations of the reactants and products. Other letters are used for specific cases, e.g. K_a and K_b for acid and base dissociation constants and K_w for the ionic product of water, $H_2O(l) \rightleftharpoons H^+(aq) + OH^-(aq)$, where $K_w = 1 \times 10^{-14}$ at 298 K.

Examples

Formation of sulfur trioxide in the Contact process:

$$2SO_2(g) + O_2(g) \rightleftharpoons 2SO_3(g) \quad K_c = \frac{[SO_3]^2_{eqm}}{[SO_2]^2_{eqm} \times [O_2]_{eqm}}$$

Formation of an ester from ethanol and ethanoic acid:

$$C_2H_5OH(l) + CH_3COOH(l) \rightleftharpoons CH_3COOC_2H_5(l) + H_2O(l)$$

$$K_c = \frac{[CH_3COOC_2H_5]_{eqm} \times [H_2O]_{eqm}}{[C_2H_5OH]_{eqm} \times [CH_3COOH]_{eqm}}$$

In both of these examples, all the reactants and products are in the same phase. In the first example they are all in the gaseous phase and in the second example they are all in the liquid phase. Such reactions are known as **homogeneous** reactions. Another example of a homogeneous system would be where all the reactants and products are in the aqueous phase.

The equilibrium law can also apply to **heterogeneous** systems, for example, $H_2O(l) \rightleftharpoons H_2O(g)$ and the distribution of a solute between two immiscible liquids. However, if a solid is involved, then it does not appear in the equilibrium expression as it has no concentration.

Le Chatelier's principle and factors affecting the position of equilibrium

Le Chatelier's principle

Provided the temperature remains constant, the value for K_c must remain constant. If the concentration of the reactants is increased, or if one of the products is removed from the equilibrium mixture, then more of the reactants must react in order to keep K_c constant, i.e. the position of equilibrium will shift to the right (towards more products). This is the explanation for **Le Chatelier's principle**, which states that if a system at equilibrium is subjected to a small change, the equilibrium tends to shift to minimize the effect of the change.

2. equilibrium shifts to minimize effect

$$A + B \rightleftharpoons C + D$$

1. remove product

Factors affecting the position of equilibrium

Change in concentration

$C_2H_5OH(l) + CH_3COOH(l) \rightleftharpoons CH_3COOC_2H_5(l) + H_2O(l)$

If more ethanoic acid is added, the concentration of ethanoic acid increases so that at the time of addition:

$$K_c \neq \frac{[\text{ester}]\times[\text{water}]}{[\text{acid}]\times[\text{alcohol}]}$$

To restore the system so that the equilibrium law is obeyed, the equilibrium will move to the right, so the concentrations of ester and water increase and the concentrations of acid and alcohol decrease.

Change in pressure

If there is an overall volume change in a gaseous reaction, i.e. a change in the amount (in mol) present, then increasing the pressure will move the equilibrium towards the side with less volume. This shift reduces the total number of molecules in the system at equilibrium and so tends to minimize the pressure.

$2NO_2(g) \rightleftharpoons N_2O_4(g)$

brown colourless

(2 vols) (1 vol)

If the pressure is increased, the mixture will initially go darker, as the concentration of NO_2 increases, and then become lighter as the position of equilibrium is re-established with a greater proportion of N_2O_4.

Adding a catalyst

A catalyst will increase the rate at which equilibrium is reached, as it will speed up both the forward and reverse reactions equally, but it will have no effect on the position of equilibrium and hence on the value of K_c.

Change in temperature

In exothermic reactions, heat is also a product. Taking the heat away will move the equilibrium towards the right, so more products are formed. The forward reaction in exothermic reactions is therefore increased by lowering the temperature.

$2NO_2(g) \rightleftharpoons N_2O_4(g)$ $\quad \Delta H^\ominus = -24\ \text{kJ mol}^{-1}$

brown colourless

Lowering the temperature will cause the mixture to become lighter as the equilibrium shifts to the right.

For an endothermic reaction the opposite will be true.

Unlike changing the concentration or pressure, a change in temperature will also change the value of K_c. For an exothermic reaction the concentration of the products in the equilibrium mixture decreases as the temperature increases, so the value of K_c will decrease. The opposite is true for endothermic reactions.

e.g. $H_2(g) + CO_2(g) \rightleftharpoons H_2O(g) + CO(g)$
$\Delta H^\ominus = +41\ \text{kJ mol}^{-1}$

T / K	K_c
298	1.00×10^{-5}
500	7.76×10^{-3}
700	1.23×10^{-1}
900	6.01×10^{-1}

increase

Heterogeneous equilibria

Solids do not affect the position of equilibrium in heterogenous systems as they have no concentration nor do they exert a gaseous pressure, so they do not appear in the equilibrium expression. When a solid, such as calcium carbonate, decomposes to another solid and a gas upon heating, only the pressure of the gas evolved affects the position of equilibrium.

$CaCO_3(s) \rightleftharpoons CaO(s) + CO_2(g)$

Removing the gas as it forms will move the position of equilibrium to the product side, increasing the decomposition.

Magnitude of the equilibrium constant

Since the equilibrium expression has the concentration of products on the top of the fraction (the numerator) and the concentration of reactants on the bottom (the denominator), it follows that the magnitude of the equilibrium constant is related to the position of equilibrium. When the reaction goes nearly to completion, $K_c \gg 1$. If the reaction hardly proceeds, then $K_c \ll 1$. If the value for K_c lies between about 10^{-2} and 10^2, then both reactants and products will be present in the system in noticeable amounts. The value for K_c in the esterification reaction above is 4 at 100 °C. From this it can be inferred that the concentration of the products present in the equilibrium mixture is roughly twice that of the reactants.

When a reaction is reversed, the equilibrium constant for the reverse reaction will be the reciprocal of the equilibrium constant for the forward reaction, K_c. For example, for the reverse reaction of the Haber process:

$2NH_3(g) \rightleftharpoons N_2(g) + 3H_2(g)$

$$K_c' = \frac{[N_2]\times[H_2]^3}{[NH_3]^2} = \frac{1}{K_c}$$

AHL Equilibrium calculations

The equilibrium law can be used either to find the value for the equilibrium constant, or to find the value of an unknown equilibrium concentration.

Worked example 1

23.0 g (0.50 mol) of ethanol was reacted with 60.0 g (1.0 mol) of ethanoic acid and the reaction allowed to reach equilibrium at 373 K. 37.0 g (0.42 mol) of ethyl ethanoate was found to be present in the equilibrium mixture.

Calculate K_c to the nearest integer at 373 K.

	$C_2H_5OH(l)$ +	$CH_3COOH(l)$ ⇌	$CH_3COOC_2H_5(l)$ +	$H_2O(l)$
Initial amount / mol	0.50	1.00	–	–
Equilibrium amount / mol	(0.50 – 0.42)	(1.00 – 0.42)	0.42	0.42
Equilibrium concentration / mol dm^{-3} (where V = total volume)	$\frac{(0.50-0.42)}{V}$	$\frac{(1.00-0.42)}{V}$	$\frac{0.42}{V}$	$\frac{0.42}{V}$

$$K_c = \frac{[\text{ester}]\times[\text{water}]}{[\text{alcohol}]\times[\text{acid}]} = \frac{(0.42/V)\times(0.42/V)}{(0.08/V)\times(0.58/V)} = 4 \text{ (to the nearest integer)}$$

Worked example 2

1.60 mol of hydrogen and 1.00 mol of iodine are allowed to reach equilibrium at a temperature of 704 K in a 4.00 dm^3 flask. The amount of hydrogen iodide formed in the equilibrium mixture is 1.80 mol. Determine the value of the equilibrium constant at this temperature.

	$H_2(g)$ +	$I_2(g)$ ⇌	$2HI(g)$
Initial amount / mol	1.60	1.00	0
Equilibrium amount / mol	0.70	0.10	1.80
Equilibrium concentration / mol dm^{-3}	0.175	0.025	0.450

$$K_c = \frac{[HI(g)]^2}{[H_2(g)]\times[I_2(g)]} = \frac{0.450^2}{0.175\times0.025} = 46.3 \text{ at 704 K}$$

Worked example 3

What mass of ester will be formed at equilibrium if 2.0 moles of ethanoic acid and 1.0 mole of ethanol are reacted under the same conditions?

Let x moles of ester be formed and let the total volume be V dm^3.

$$K_c = 4 = \frac{[\text{ester}]\times[\text{water}]}{[\text{alcohol}]\times[\text{acid}]} = \frac{x^2/V^2}{(1.0-x/V)\times(2.0-x/V)} = \frac{x^2}{(x^2-3x+2)}$$

$\Rightarrow 3x^2 - 12x + 8 = 0$

This can be solved by substituting into the quadratic expression:

$$x = \frac{-b\pm\sqrt{b^2-4ac}}{2a} \Rightarrow x = \frac{12\pm\sqrt{144-96}}{6}$$

$x = 0.845$ or 3.15, but x cannot be 3.15 as only 1.0 mol of ethanol was taken.

Mass of ester = 0.845 × 88.08 = 74.4 g

(Note: IB Diploma Programme chemistry does not examine the use of the quadratic expression.)

Worked example 4

When the value of the equilibrium constant is very small, i.e. $K_c \ll 1$, unknown concentrations can be found by making an approximation.

The equilibrium constant for the reaction of nitrogen and oxygen to form nitrogen monoxide, NO(g), is 4.1×10^{-4} at 2 273 K. If 1.00 mol of nitrogen and 1.00 mol of oxygen are mixed in a 100 dm^3 container at 2 273 K, what will be the concentration of nitrogen monoxide in the mixture once the position of equilibrium has been reached?

Let the amount of nitrogen dioxide at equilibrium be $2x$ mol.

	$N_2(g)$ +	$O_2(g)$	$\rightleftharpoons 2NO(g)$
Initial amount / mol	1	1	0
Equilibrium amount / mol	$1-x$	$1-x$	$2x$
Equilibrium concentration / mol dm^{-3}	$\frac{1-x}{100}$	$\frac{1-x}{100}$	$\frac{2x}{100}$

$$K_c = 4.1\times10^{-4} = \frac{[NO]^2}{[N_2]\times[O_2]} = \frac{(2x/100)^2}{((1-x)/100)^2} = \frac{4x^2}{(1-x)^2}$$

but since x is very small compared with 1, $(1-x) \approx 1$ and $[\text{reactant}]_{\text{initial}} \approx [\text{reactant}]_{\text{eqm}}$

Therefore: $x^2 = \frac{4.1\times10^{-4}}{4} = 1.025 \times 10^{-4}$

$x = (1.025 \times 10^{-4})^{½} = 0.0101$ mol and $[NO(g)] = \frac{2x}{100} = 2.02 \times 10^{-4}$ mol dm^{-3}

Note that if the approximation had not been made, then:

$4x^2 - ((4.1 \times 10^{-4}) \times (1-x)^2) = 0$

Solving the quadratic gives $x = 0.0100$ or -0.0102, so the approximation is reasonable.

AHL

Reaction quotient, equilibrium constant and free energy

Reaction quotient

The equilibrium expression is stated in terms of the concentrations of the reactants and products once the specified reaction has reached equilibrium. The reaction quotient, Q, uses the same equilibrium expression but uses the non-equilibrium concentrations of reactants and products in a reaction at a particular point in time.

Knowing the reaction quotient enables you to predict the direction in which a reaction is likely to proceed by comparing its value with the value of the equilibrium constant.

If $Q > K$, then the numerator of the equilibrium expression is greater than the denominator so the reaction will proceed in the direction of the reactants as it moves towards equilibrium.

Conversely, if $Q < K$, then the denominator of the equilibrium expression is greater than the numerator so the reaction will proceed in the direction of the products.

If $Q = K$, then the reaction is at equilibrium.

Worked example 1

Consider the water–gas shift reaction, which is a way of making hydrogen from carbon monoxide and water.

$CO(g) + H_2O(g) \rightleftharpoons CO_2(g) + H_2(g)$

At 1100 K, the value of the equilibrium constant K, is 1.00. What will be the value of Q and in what direction will the reaction move when the concentrations of CO, H_2O, CO_2, and H_2 at 1100 K in a sealed vessel are 1.00, 1.50, 1.50, and 2.00 mol dm^{-3} respectively?

$$Q = \frac{[CO_2]\times[H_2]}{[CO]\times[H_2O]} = \frac{1.50\times2.00}{1.00\times1.50} = 2$$

Since Q is greater than K, more of the CO_2 and H_2 will react together to reduce their concentrations and increase the concentrations of CO and H_2O, so the reaction will shift in the direction of the reactants.

Gibbs energy change and the equilibrium constant

The Gibbs energy change for the water–gas shift reaction given above is −28.5 kJ, i.e.

$CO(g) + H_2O(g) \rightleftharpoons CO_2(g) + H_2(g) \quad \Delta G^\ominus = -28.5\text{ kJ}$

This means that the reaction between carbon monoxide and water is spontaneous and the reverse reaction is non-spontaneous. The relationship between Gibbs energy and the reaction quotient at any point in the reaction is:

$$\Delta G = \Delta G^\ominus + RT\ln Q$$

i.e. when only the reactants are present, $Q = 0$ and $\Delta G = \Delta G^\ominus$.

As the forward reaction proceeds towards the products the quantitative value of the Gibbs energy, ΔG, decreases (ΔG becomes less negative). For any reaction, equilibrium occurs when ΔG = zero. At this point, when $Q = K$, the rate of the forward reaction is equal to the rate of the reverse reaction so no net Gibbs energy change occurs and the point of maximum entropy has been reached, i.e. $0 = \Delta G^\ominus + RT\ln K$. Hence the Gibbs energy change, $\Delta G^\ominus$, can be used to determine the value of the equilibrium constant, K, for a reaction as they are related by the equation:

$$\Delta G^\ominus = -RT\ln K$$

(where $\Delta G^\ominus$ is the Gibbs energy change for the forward reaction as it is written to give the equilibrium expression for K, **not** the value of ΔG at equilibrium). These equations are given in the data booklet.

Worked example 2

The relationship between Gibbs energy and the equilibrium constant can be illustrated by the dissociation of water according to the equation:

$H_2O(l) \rightleftharpoons H^+(aq) + OH^-(aq) \quad \Delta H^\ominus = +55.8\text{ kJ mol}^{-1}$

The relevant entropy values are:

	$H_2O(l)$	$H^+(aq)$	$OH^-(aq)$
$S^\ominus$ / J K^{-1} mol^{-1}	+70.0	0	−10.9

Change in entropy:

$\Delta S^\ominus = (\sum S^\ominus \text{ products}) - (\sum S^\ominus \text{ reactants})$
$= (-10.9) - (+70.0) = -80.9\text{ J K}^{-1}\text{ mol}^{-1}$

$\Delta G^\ominus = \Delta H^\ominus - T\Delta S^\ominus = +55.8 \times 1000 - (298 \times -80.9)$
$= +79\,908\text{ J mol}^{-1}$

Using the expression $\Delta G^\ominus = -RT\ln K$:

$$\ln K = \frac{-79\,908}{8.314\times298} = -32.2$$

$K = e^{-32.2} = 1.00 \times 10^{-14}$ at 298 K

This is the value for the equilibrium constant of water at 298 K, known as the ionic product constant for water (K_w), given in Section 2 of the IB data booklet.

Multiple-choice questions—Equilibrium

1. Which statement is true about a chemical reaction at equilibrium?
   A. The reaction has completely stopped.
   B. The concentrations of the products are equal to the concentrations of the reactants.
   C. The rate of the forward reaction is equal to the rate of the reverse reaction.
   D. The concentrations of the products and reactants are constantly changing.

2. What is the equilibrium constant expression, K_c, for the following reaction?

   $2NOBr(g) \rightleftharpoons 2NO(g) + Br_2(g)$

   A. $K_c = \frac{[NO][Br_2]}{[NOBr]}$ C. $K_c = \frac{2[NO]+[Br_2]}{[2NOBr]}$

   B. $K_c = \frac{[NO]^2[Br_2]}{[NOBr]^2}$ D. $K_c = \frac{[NOBr]^2}{[NO]^2[Br_2]}$

3. The following are K_c values for a reaction carried out at different temperatures but with the same starting conditions. Which equilibrium mixture has the highest concentration of products?
   A. 1×10^{-2} C. 1×10^{1}
   B. 1 D. 1×10^{2}

4. What effect will an increase in temperature have on the K_c value and the position of equilibrium in the following reaction?

   $N_2(g) + 3H_2(g) \rightleftharpoons 2NH_3(g)$ $\Delta H = -92$ kJ

	K_c	Equilibrium position
A.	increases	shifts to the right
B.	decreases	shifts to the left
C.	increases	shifts to the left
D.	decreases	shifts to the right

5. Consider the following equilibrium reaction.

   $2SO_2(g) + O_2(g) \rightleftharpoons 2SO_3(g)$ $\Delta H^\ominus = -197$ kJ

   Which change in conditions will increase the amount of SO_3 present when equilibrium is re-established?
   A. Decreasing the concentration of SO_2
   B. Increasing the volume
   C. Decreasing the temperature
   D. Adding a catalyst

6. The Haber process uses an iron catalyst to convert hydrogen gas, $H_2(g)$, and nitrogen gas, $N_2(g)$, to ammonia gas, $NH_3(g)$.

   $3H_2(g) + N_2(g) \rightleftharpoons 2NH_3(g)$

   Which statements are correct for this equilibrium system?

   I. The iron catalyst increases rates of the forward and reverse reactions equally.
   II. The iron catalyst does not affect the value of the equilibrium constant, K_c.
   III. The iron catalyst increases the yield for ammonia gas, $NH_3(g)$.

   A. I and II only C. II and III only
   B. I and III only D. I, II, and III

7. The formation of nitric acid, $HNO_3(aq)$, from nitrogen dioxide, $NO_2(g)$, is exothermic and is a reversible reaction.

   $4NO_2(g) + O_2(g) + 2H_2O(l) \rightleftharpoons 4HNO_3(aq)$

   What is the effect of a catalyst on this reaction?
   A. It increases the yield of nitric acid.
   B. It increases the rate of the forward reaction only.
   C. It increases the equilibrium constant.
   D. It has no effect on the equilibrium position.

8. The value of K_c for the reaction $H_2(g) + Br_2(g) \rightleftharpoons 2HBr(g)$ is 4.0×10^{-2}. What is the value of the equilibrium constant for the reaction $2HBr(g) \rightleftharpoons H_2(g) + Br_2(g)$ at the same temperature?
   A. 4.0×10^{-2} C. 25
   B. 2.0×10^{-1} D. 400

AHL

9. 0.50 mol of $I_2(g)$ and 0.50 mol of $Br_2(g)$ are placed in a closed flask. The following equilibrium is established.

   $I_2(g) + Br_2(g) \rightleftharpoons 2IBr(g)$

   The equilibrium mixture contains 0.80 mol of IBr(g). What is the value of K_c?
   A. 0.64 C. 2.6
   B. 1.3 D. 64

10. A 2.0 dm^3 reaction vessel initially contains 4.0 mol of P and 5.0 mol of Q. At equilibrium, 3 mol of R are present. What is the value of K_c for the following reaction?

    $P(g) + Q(g) \rightleftharpoons R(g) + S(g)$

    A. $\frac{2}{9}$ C. 4.5
    B. $\frac{9}{20}$ D. 9

11. At 35 °C, $K_c = 1.6 \times 10^{-5}$ for the reaction:

    $2NOCl(g) \rightleftharpoons 2NO(g) + Cl_2(g)$

    Which relationship must be correct at equilibrium?
    A. [NO] = [NOCl] C. [NOCl] < $[Cl_2]$
    B. 2[NO] = $[Cl_2]$ D. [NO] < [NOCl]

Short-answer questions—Equilibrium

1. Ethanol can be manufactured by the hydration of ethene, according to the equation below.

   $C_2H_4(g) + H_2O(g) \rightleftharpoons C_2H_5OH(g)$

   a) State the expression for the equilibrium constant, K_c, for this reaction. [1]

   b) Under certain conditions, the value of K_c for this reaction is 3.7×10^{-3}. When the temperature is increased the value is 4.9×10^{-4}.

      (i) State what can be deduced about the position of equilibrium at the higher temperature from these values of K_c. [1]

      (ii) State what can be deduced about the sign of ΔH for the reaction, explaining your choice. [3]

   c) The process used to manufacture ethanol is carried out at high pressure. State and explain two advantages of using high pressure. [4]

2. Ammonia is produced by the Haber process according to the following reaction:

   $N_2(g) + 3H_2(g) \rightleftharpoons 2NH_3(g)$ $\quad\quad$ ΔH is negative

   a) State the equilibrium expression for the above reaction. [1]

   b) Predict, giving a reason, the effect on the position of equilibrium when the pressure in the reaction vessel is increased. [2]

   c) State and explain the effect on the value of K_c when the temperature is increased. [2]

   d) Explain why a catalyst has no effect on the position of equilibrium. [1]

3. Consider the following equilibrium:

   $4NH_3(g) + 5O_2(g) \rightleftharpoons 4NO(g) + 6H_2O(g)$
   $\Delta H^\ominus = -909$ kJ

   a) Deduce the equilibrium constant expression, K_c, for the reaction. [1]

   b) Predict the direction in which the equilibrium will shift when the following changes occur. [4]

      (i) The volume increases.

      (ii) The temperature decreases.

      (iii) $H_2O(g)$ is removed from the system.

      (iv) A catalyst is added to the reaction mixture.

   c) Define the term *activation energy*. [1]

4. An example of a homogeneous reversible reaction is the reaction between hydrogen and iodine.

   $H_2(g) + I_2(g) \rightleftharpoons 2HI(g)$

   a) Outline the characteristics of a homogeneous chemical system that is in a state of equilibrium. [2]

   b) Formulate the expression for the equilibrium constant, K_c. [1]

   c) Predict what would happen to the position of equilibrium and the value of K_c if the pressure was increased from 1 atm to 2 atm. [2]

   d) The value of K_c at 500 K is 160 and the value of K_c at 700 K is 54. Deduce what this information tells you about the enthalpy change of the forward reaction. [1]

   e) Deduce the value of the equilibrium constant, K_c', at 500 K for the following reaction. [1]

   $2HI(g) \rightleftharpoons H_2(g) + I_2(g)$

AHL

5. Consider the two equilibrium systems involving bromine gas illustrated below.

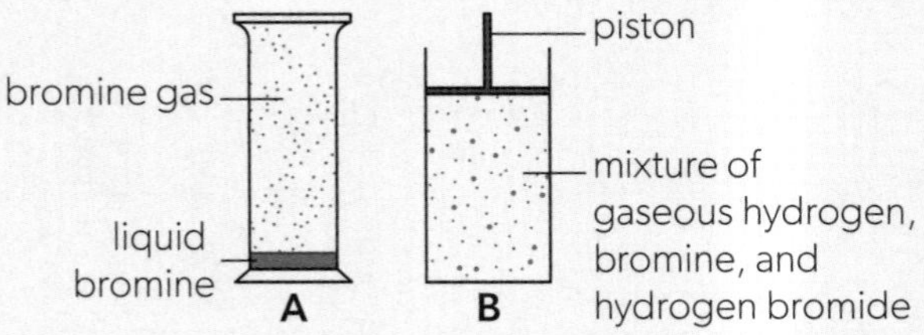

   a) Formulate equations to represent the equilibria in systems **A** and **B** with $Br_2(g)$ on the left-hand side in both equilibria. [2]

   b) (i) Describe what you will observe if a small amount of liquid bromine is introduced into system **A**. [1]

      (ii) Predict what happens to the position of equilibrium if a small amount of hydrogen is introduced into system **B**. [1]

      (iii) State and explain the effect of increasing the pressure in system **B** on the position of equilibrium. [2]

   c) (i) Deduce the equilibrium constant expression, K_c, for the equilibrium in system **B**. [1]

      (ii) State the effect of increasing $[H_2]$ in system **B** on the value of K_c. [1]

6. Ammonia production is important in industry.

   $N_2(g) + 3H_2(g) \rightleftharpoons 2NH_3(g)$ $\quad\quad$ $\Delta H = -92$ kJ

   a) The standard entropy values, $S^\ominus$, at 298 K for $N_2(g)$, $H_2(g)$, and $NH_3(g)$ are 193, 131, and 192 J K^{-1} mol^{-1} respectively. Calculate $\Delta S^\ominus$ for the reaction as shown by the equation above. [2]

   b) Determine $\Delta G^\ominus$ for the reaction at 298 K. [2]

   c) Describe and explain the effect of increasing temperature on the spontaneity of the reaction. [2]

   d) Determine the value of the equilibrium constant at 298 K by using the value of $\Delta G^\ominus$ that you obtained in **b)**. [3]

   e) 0.20 mol of $N_2(g)$ and 0.20 mol of $H_2(g)$ was allowed to reach equilibrium in a 1 dm^3 closed container at a temperature T_2 that is different from 298 K. At equilibrium, the concentration of $NH_3(g)$ was found to be 0.060 mol dm^{-3}. Determine the value of K_c at temperature T_2. [3]

   f) Comment on the two different values for K_c that you have obtained. [2]

What are the mechanisms of chemical change?

The ionic theory

Acids were originally identified by their sour taste. Later, an acid was said to be the oxide of a non-metal combined with water, although hydrochloric acid does not fit into this definition. The ionic theory, which is still commonly used today, states that an **acid** is a substance which produces hydrogen ions, $H^+(aq)$, in aqueous solution, e.g.

$HCl(aq) \rightarrow H^+(aq) + Cl^-(aq)$

In aqueous solution hydrogen ions are hydrated to form hydroxonium ions, $H_3O^+(aq)$. For the IB, it is correct to write either $H^+(aq)$ or $H_3O^+(aq)$ to represent the hydrogen ions in an aqueous solution. Strictly speaking, an acid gives a hydrogen ion concentration in aqueous solution greater than 1.0×10^{-7} mol dm^{-3}. A **base** is a substance that can neutralize an acid. An **alkali** is a base that is soluble in water.

Brønsted–Lowry acids and bases

A Brønsted–Lowry acid is a substance that can *donate* a proton. A Brønsted–Lowry base is a substance that can *accept* a proton.

Consider the reaction between hydrogen chloride gas and water.

$HCl(g) + H_2O(l) \rightleftharpoons H_3O^+(aq) + Cl^-(aq)$

acid base acid base

Under this definition, both HCl and H_3O^+ are acids as both can donate a proton. Similarly, both H_2O and Cl^- are bases as both can accept a proton. Cl^- is said to be the **conjugate base** of HCl, and H_2O is the conjugate base of H_3O^+. The conjugate base of an acid is the species remaining after the acid has lost a proton. Every base also has a **conjugate acid**, which is the species formed after the base has accepted a proton.

Water is behaving as a base in the reaction with hydrogen chloride. Water can also behave as an acid.

$NH_3(g) + H_2O(l) \rightleftharpoons NH_4^+(aq) + OH^-(aq)$

base acid acid base

Substances such as water, which can act both as an acid and as a base by donating or accepting a proton, are described as **amphiprotic**.

Many acids, particularly organic acids, contain one or more non-acidic hydrogen atoms. The location of the acidic hydrogen atom(s) should be clearly identified. For example, ethanoic acid should be written as CH_3COOH, rather than $C_2H_4O_2$, so that the conjugate base can be identified as the carboxylate anion CH_3COO^-, rather than just $C_2H_3O_2^-$.

Neutralization reactions with bases

Here are examples of the reactions of acids with bases:

- with metal hydroxides to form a salt and water, e.g.

  $CH_3COOH(aq) + NaOH(aq) \rightarrow NaCH_3COO(aq) + H_2O(l)$

- with metal oxides to form a salt and water, e.g.

  $H_2SO_4(aq) + CuO(s) \rightarrow CuSO_4(aq) + H_2O(l)$

- with ammonia and amines to form salts, e.g.

  $HCl(aq) + NH_3(aq) \rightarrow NH_4Cl(aq)$

  $HCl(aq) + C_2H_5NH_2 \rightarrow C_2H_5NH_3Cl(aq)$

- with reactive metals (those above copper in the activity series) to form a salt and hydrogen, e.g.

  $2HCl(aq) + Mg(s) \rightarrow MgCl_2(aq) + H_2(g)$

- with carbonates (soluble or insoluble) to form a salt, carbon dioxide, and water, e.g.

  $2HNO_3(aq) + Na_2CO_3(aq) \rightarrow 2NaNO_3(aq) + CO_2(g) + H_2O(l)$

  $2HCl(aq) + CaCO_3(s) \rightarrow CaCl_2(aq) + CO_2(g) + H_2O(l)$

- with hydrogencarbonates to form a salt, carbon dioxide, and water, e.g.

  $HCl(aq) + NaHCO_3(aq) \rightarrow NaCl(aq) + CO_2(g) + H_2O(aq)$

The pH scale

The pH scale

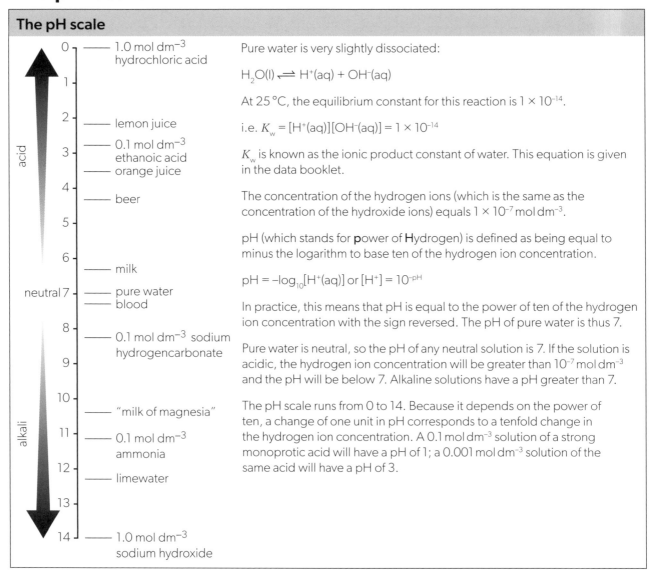

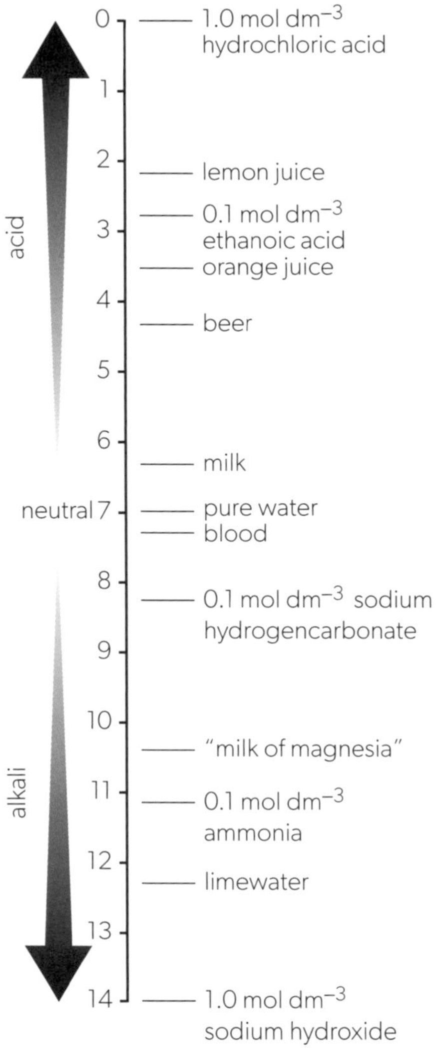

Pure water is very slightly dissociated:

$H_2O(l) \rightleftharpoons H^+(aq) + OH^-(aq)$

At 25 °C, the equilibrium constant for this reaction is 1×10^{-14}.

i.e. $K_w = [H^+(aq)][OH^-(aq)] = 1 \times 10^{-14}$

K_w is known as the ionic product constant of water. This equation is given in the data booklet.

The concentration of the hydrogen ions (which is the same as the concentration of the hydroxide ions) equals 1×10^{-7} mol dm^{-3}.

pH (which stands for **p**ower of **H**ydrogen) is defined as being equal to minus the logarithm to base ten of the hydrogen ion concentration.

$pH = -\log_{10}[H^+(aq)]$ or $[H^+] = 10^{-pH}$

In practice, this means that pH is equal to the power of ten of the hydrogen ion concentration with the sign reversed. The pH of pure water is thus 7.

Pure water is neutral, so the pH of any neutral solution is 7. If the solution is acidic, the hydrogen ion concentration will be greater than 10^{-7} mol dm^{-3} and the pH will be below 7. Alkaline solutions have a pH greater than 7.

The pH scale runs from 0 to 14. Because it depends on the power of ten, a change of one unit in pH corresponds to a tenfold change in the hydrogen ion concentration. A 0.1 mol dm^{-3} solution of a strong monoprotic acid will have a pH of 1; a 0.001 mol dm^{-3} solution of the same acid will have a pH of 3.

Determination of pH

The pH of a solution can be determined in several ways.

1. Using acid–base indicators

Indicators can be used to determine whether or not a solution is acidic. Common indicators include:

Indicator	Colour in acidic solution	Colour in alkaline solution
litmus	red	blue
phenolphthalein	colourless	pink
methyl orange	red	yellow

2. Using a pH meter

A pH meter gives the most accurate and precise readings. The pH meter (or pH probe connected to a data logger) is calibrated using a buffer solution of known pH, then inserted into a solution to measure the pH.

3. Using "universal" indicator

Universal indicator contains a mixture of indicators that give a range of colours at different pH values, as shown in the table below.

pH	$[H^+]$ / mol dm^{-3}	$[OH^-]$ / mol dm^{-3}	Description	Colour of universal indicator
0	1	1×10^{-14}	very acidic	red
4	1×10^{-4}	1×10^{-10}	acidic	orange
7	1×10^{-7}	1×10^{-7}	neutral	green
10	1×10^{-10}	1×10^{-4}	basic	blue
14	1×10^{-14}	1	very basic	purple

The $\log_{10}$ scale and p-scale

Normal scale: the distances between consecutive numbers are equal

–5 –4 –3 –2 –1 0 1 2 3 4 5

Log_{10} scale: the distances between powers of ten are equal

0.00001 0.0001 0.001 0.01 0.1 1 10 100 1000 10000 100000

This can be written as

10^{-5} 10^{-4} 10^{-3} 10^{-2} 10^{-1} 10^{0} 10^{1} 10^{2} 10^{3} 10^{4} 10^{5}

p-scale: sometimes used by chemists to express equilibrium constants and concentration; it is equal to minus the power of ten in the logarithmic scale, so the scale becomes

5 4 3 2 1 0 –1 –2 –3 –4 –5

Strong, concentrated and corrosive

In English, the words "strong" and "concentrated" are often used interchangeably. However, in chemistry they have very precise meanings:

- **strong:** completely dissociated into ions
- **concentrated:** a high number of moles of solute per litre (dm^3) of solution
- **corrosive:** chemically reactive.

Similarly, "weak" and "dilute" also have very different chemical meanings:

- **weak:** only slightly dissociated into ions
- **dilute:** a low number of moles of solute per litre of solution.

Strong and weak acids and bases

A strong acid is completely dissociated (ionized) into its ions in aqueous solution. Similarly, a strong base is completely dissociated into its ions in aqueous solution. Here are some examples of strong acids and bases.

Strong acids	Strong bases
hydrochloric acid, HCl	sodium hydroxide, $NaOH$
nitric acid, HNO_3	potassium hydroxide, KOH
sulfuric acid, H_2SO_4	barium hydroxide, $Ba(OH)_2$

Note: because one mole of HCl produces one mole of hydrogen ions it is known as a **monoprotic** acid. Sulfuric acid is known as a **diprotic** acid as one mole of sulfuric acid produces two moles of hydrogen ions.

Weak acids and bases are only slightly dissociated (ionized) into their ions in aqueous solution. Here are some examples of weak acids and bases.

Weak acids	Weak bases
ethanoic acid, CH_3COOH	ammonia, NH_3
"carbonic acid", H_2CO_3	aminoethane, $C_2H_5NH_2$

The difference can be seen in their reactions with water.

- For a strong acid, the reaction goes to completion:

  $HCl(g) + H_2O(l) \rightarrow H_3O^+(aq) + Cl^-(aq)$

- For a weak acid, the equilibrium lies on the left, i.e. on the side with the weaker conjugate:

  $CH_3COOH(aq) + H_2O(l) \rightleftharpoons CH_3COO^-(aq) + H_3O^+(aq)$

A solution of hydrochloric acid consists only of hydrogen ions and chloride ions in water, whereas a solution of ethanoic acid contains mainly undissociated ethanoic acid molecules with only a very few hydrogen ions and ethanoate ions.

- For a strong base, the reaction goes to completion:

  $KOH(s) \xrightarrow{H_2O(l)} K^+(aq) + OH^-(aq)$

- For a weak base, the equilibrium lies on the left:

  $NH_3(g) + H_2O(l) \rightleftharpoons NH_4^+(aq) + OH^-(aq)$

Strong and weak acids and bases and simple pH calculations

Strong acid and base pH calculations

For pure water the pH must be 7 at 25 °C as the concentration of $H^+(aq)$ is equal to the concentration of $OH^-(aq)$ and $[H^+(aq)] \times [OH^-(aq)] = 1 \times 10^{-14}$. Strong acids are completely dissociated so, for example, the hydrogen ion concentration of 0.100 mol dm^{-3} hydrochloric acid, HCl(aq), will be 0.100 mol dm^{-3} as each mole of acid produces one mole of hydrogen ions when it dissociates (ionizes). The pH of 0.100 mol dm^{-3} HCl(aq) will therefore be equal to $-\log_{10}(0.100) = 1$.

If the acid is diluted ten times, then the new hydrogen ion concentration will be 0.0100 mol dm^{-3} and the pH will be equal to $-\log_{10}(0.0100)$ or $-\log_{10}(1.00 \times 10^{-2}) = 2$.

Sulfuric acid is assumed, for simplicity, to be a strong diprotic acid. The hydrogen ion concentration of 0.0100 mol dm^{-3} $H_2SO_4(aq)$ is therefore 2 × 0.0100 or 2.00×10^{-2} mol dm^{-3} and the pH will equal $-\log_{10}(2.00 \times 10^{-2}) = 1.7$.

Note that pH is a measure of concentration, so 10.0 cm^3 of 0.100 mol dm^{-3} HCl(aq) has the same pH as 100 cm^3 of 0.100 mol dm^{-3} HCl(aq). Also note that $[H^+(aq)] = 10^{-pH}$, so if the pH of an acid is 3, then $[H^+(aq)] = 10^{-3} = 1.0 \times 10^{-3}$ mol dm^{-3}.

To calculate the pH of a strong base, you need to work out the hydroxide concentration first and then calculate the hydrogen ion concentration using the expression $[H^+(aq)] \times [OH^-(aq)] = 1 \times 10^{-14}$.

Worked example 1

Calculate the pH of 0.100 mol dm^{-3} NaOH(aq).

$[OH^-(aq)] = 0.100$ mol dm^{-3}

$$[H^+(aq)] = \frac{1 \times 10^{-14}}{0.100} = 1 \times 10^{-13} \text{ mol dm}^{-3}$$

$pH = -\log_{10}(1.00 \times 10^{-13}) = 13$

Worked example 2

Calculate the pH of 0.100 mol dm^{-3} $Ba(OH)_2(aq)$.

$[OH^-(aq)] = 0.200$ mol dm^{-3}

$$[H^+(aq)] = \frac{1 \times 10^{-14}}{0.200} = 5 \times 10^{-14} \text{ mol dm}^{-3}$$

$pH = -\log_{10}(5.00 \times 10^{-14}) = 13.3$

Experiments to distinguish between strong and weak acids and bases

1. pH measurement

Because a strong acid produces a higher concentration of hydrogen ions in solution than a weak acid with the same concentration, the pH of a strong acid is lower than that of a weak acid. Similarly, a strong base has a higher pH in solution than a weak base with the same concentration.

0.100 mol dm^{-3} HCl(aq)	pH = 1.0
0.100 mol dm^{-3} CH_3COOH	pH = 2.9

2. Conductivity measurement

Strong acids and strong bases in solution give much higher readings on a conductivity meter than **equimolar** (equal concentration) solutions of weak acids or bases, because they contain more ions in solution.

3. Concentration measurement

As the concentration of hydrogen ions is much greater, the rate of reaction of strong acids with metals, metal oxides, metal hydroxides, metal hydrogencarbonates, and metal carbonates is greater than that of weak acids with the same concentration.

Acid rain

Oxides of sulfur, SO_x

Sulfur dioxide occurs naturally from volcanoes. It is produced industrially from the combustion of sulfur-containing fossil fuels and the smelting of sulfide ores.

$S(s) + O_2(g) \rightarrow SO_2(g)$

In the presence of sunlight, sulfur dioxide is oxidized to sulfur trioxide.

$SO_2(g) + \frac{1}{2}O_2(g) \rightarrow SO_3(g)$

These oxides can react with water in the air to form sulfurous acid and sulfuric acid:

$SO_2(g) + H_2O(l) \rightarrow H_2SO_3(aq)$
sulfurous acid

$SO_3(g) + H_2O(l) \rightarrow H_2SO_4(aq)$
sulfuric acid

Oxides of nitrogen, NO_x

Nitrogen oxides occur naturally from electrical storms and bacterial action. Nitrogen monoxide, NO, is produced in the internal combustion engine and in jet engines.

$N_2(g) + O_2(g) \rightarrow 2NO(g)$

Oxidation to nitrogen dioxide occurs in the air.

$2NO(g) + O_2(g) \rightarrow 2NO_2(g)$

The nitrogen dioxide then reacts with water to form nitric acid and nitrous acid:

$2NO_2(g) + H_2O(l) \rightarrow HNO_3(aq) + HNO_2(aq)$
nitric acid nitrous acid

or is oxidized directly to nitric acid by oxygen in the presence of water:

$4NO_2(g) + O_2(g) + 2H_2O(l) \rightarrow 4HNO_3(aq)$

Acid rain

Pure rainwater is naturally acidic, with a pH of 5.65, due to the presence of dissolved carbon dioxide. Carbon dioxide itself is not responsible for acid rain since acid rain is defined as rain with a pH less than 5.6. It is the oxides of sulfur and nitrogen present in the atmosphere which are responsible for **acid deposition**—the process by which acidic particles, gases, and precipitation leave the atmosphere. Wet deposition, due to the acidic oxides dissolving and reacting with water in the air, is known as "**acid rain**" and includes fog, snow, and dew as well as rain. Dry deposition includes acidic gases and particles.

Vegetation

Increased acidity in the soil leaches important nutrients, such as Ca^{2+}, Mg^{2+}, and K^+. Reduced levels of Mg^{2+} can cause a reduction in chlorophyll, lowering the ability of plants to photosynthesize. Many trees have been seriously affected by acid rain. Symptoms include stunted growth, thinning of tree tops, and yellowing and loss of leaves. The main cause is leaching of aluminium from rocks into the soil water. The Al^{3+} ion damages the roots and prevents trees from taking up enough water and nutrients to survive.

Buildings

Stone that contains calcium carbonate, such as marble, is eroded by acid rain. Calcium carbonate reacts with sulfuric acid to form calcium sulfate, which is washed away by rainwater thus exposing more stone to corrosion. Salts can also form within the stone, causing the stone to crack and disintegrate.

$CaCO_3(s) + H_2SO_4(aq) \rightarrow CaSO_4(aq) + CO_2(g) + H_2O(l)$

Lakes and rivers

Increased levels of aluminium ions in water can kill fish. Aquatic life is also highly sensitive to pH. Below pH 6, numbers of sensitive fish, such as salmon and minnow, decline as do insect larvae and algae. Snails cannot survive a pH less than 5.2 and, below pH 5.0, many microscopic animal species disappear. Below pH 4.0 lakes are effectively dead. Nitrates present in acid rain can also lead to eutrophication.

Human health

The acids formed when NO_x and SO_x dissolve in water irritate the mucous membranes and increase the risk of respiratory illnesses, such as asthma, bronchitis, and emphysema. In acidic water, there is more probability of poisonous ions, such as Cu^{2+} and Pb^{2+}, leaching from pipes and high levels of aluminium in water may be linked to Alzheimer's disease.

Methods to lower or counteract the effects of acid rain

1. Reduce amounts of NO_x and SO_x formed, e.g. by improved engine design, using catalytic converters, and removing sulfur before, during, and after combustion of sulfur-containing fuels.
2. Switch to alternative methods of energy production (e.g. wind and solar power) and reduce the amount of fuel burned, e.g. by reducing private transport, increasing public transport, and designing more efficient power stations.
3. Liming of lakes: adding calcium oxide or calcium hydroxide (lime) neutralizes the acidity, increases the amount of calcium ions and precipitates aluminium from solution. This has been shown to be effective in many, but not all, lakes where it has been tried.

pH curves

Data from strong acid–strong base titrations

The method of titration to determine an unknown concentration of either an acid or a base by reacting it with a known concentration of an alkali or an acid has already been discussed on page 20. Normally, for an acid–base titration, an indicator is added. Indicators change colour within certain pH ranges. For example, methyl orange changes colour (from red to yellow) between pH 4.4 and 6.2 whereas phenolphthalein changes colour (from colourless to pink) between pH 8.3 and 10.0. The difference between pH 4.4 and pH 10.0 is large, so indicators are not very accurate for determining the equivalence point. The titration can also be carried out using a pH meter and the change in pH can be monitored. By recording the pH after every cm^3 has been added, enough data can be collected to plot a graph.

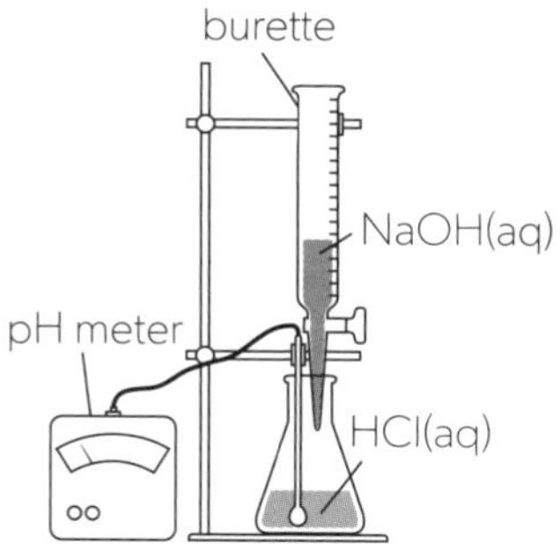

Calculating theoretical pH change

The pH change can also be determined theoretically. Consider starting with 50 cm^3 of 1.00 mol dm^{-3} hydrochloric acid solution, HCl(aq). Since $[H^+(aq)] = 1.00$ mol dm^{-3} the initial pH will be 0. After 49.0 cm^3 of 1.00 mol dm^{-3} sodium hydroxide solution, NaOH(aq), has been added there will be 1.0 cm^3 of the original 1.0 mol dm^{-3} hydrochloric acid solution remaining that has not been neutralized. 1.0 cm^3 of 1.00 mol dm^{-3} hydrochloric acid contains 1.0×10^{-3} mol of $H^+(aq)$ ions. This is in 99 cm^3 of solution (which is almost 100 cm^3) so $[H^+(aq)] = 1.00 \times 10^{-2}$ mol dm^{-3} and the pH is 2. Similar calculations can be made for when further 0.10 cm^3 amounts of 1.00 mol dm^{-3} sodium hydroxide solution are added, to give the following table.

Volume of NaOH added / cm^3	49.0	49.1	49.2	49.3	49.4	49.5	49.6	49.7	49.8	49.9	50.0
pH	2.00	2.05	2.10	2.15	2.22	2.30	2.40	2.52	2.70	3.00	7.00

Volume of NaOH added / cm^3	50.0	50.1	50.2	50.3	50.4	50.5	50.6	50.7	50.8	50.9	51.0
pH	7.00	11.00	11.30	11.48	11.60	11.70	11.78	11.85	11.90	11.95	12.00

Interpreting pH curves

By plotting the data calculated above, or data collected experimentally during a titration, you can interpret the data and determine several important points. This is called a pH curve. The general shape of a pH curve for the reaction between a monoprotic strong acid and a monoprotic strong base is always like the example below:

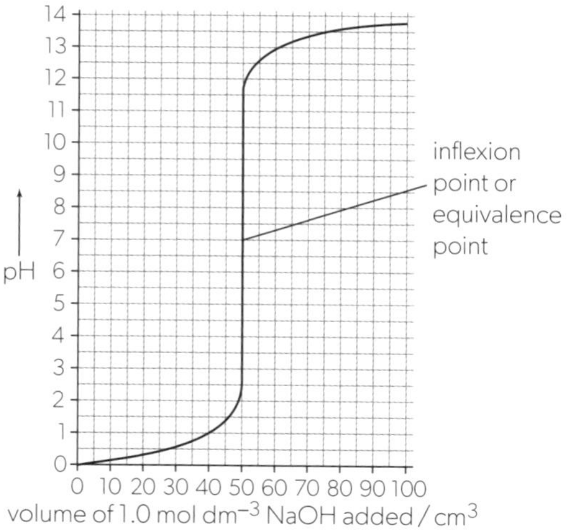

The area on the graph where the pH changes most rapidly and the line is almost vertical is called the inflexion point or equivalence point. It represents the stoichiometric point when equal amounts of acid and base have reacted. The line is almost vertical as the change occurs within a very small change in volume of added NaOH(aq). Almost all acid–base indicators change colour within this region. This means that for a strong acid–strong base titration it does not really matter which indicator is used. The point where the indicator changes colour is known as the end point and is almost identical to the equivalence point. Reading vertically downwards from the equivalence point gives the volume of acid or base needed to reach neutralization.

Similarly, a graph can be plotted when HCl is added to NaOH. The pH is initially around 14 and falls to around 0 after neutralization.

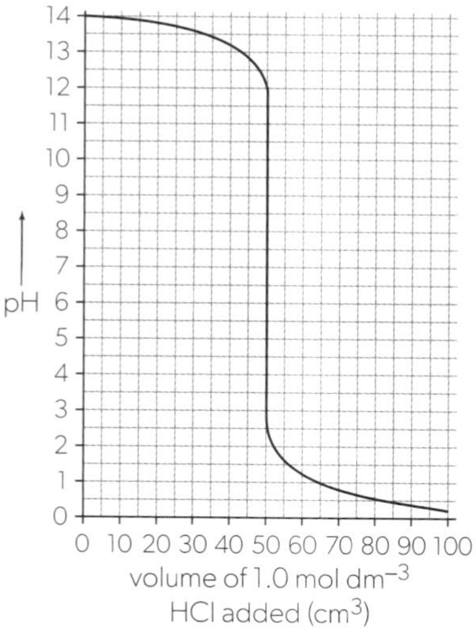

AHL

Calculations involving pH, pOH and pK_w

The ionic product of water

Pure water is very slightly ionized:

$H_2O(l) \rightleftharpoons H^+(aq) + OH^-(aq)$ $\Delta H^\ominus = +57.3\ \text{kJ mol}^{-1}$

$$K_c = \frac{[H^+(aq)] \times [OH^-(aq)]}{[H_2O(l)]}$$

Since the equilibrium lies far to the left, the concentration of water can be regarded as constant so:

$K_w = [H^+(aq)] \times [OH^-(aq)] = 1.00 \times 10^{-14}$ at 298 K

where K_w is known as the ionic product of water.

The dissociation of water into its ions is an endothermic process, so the value of K_w will increase as the temperature is increased.

Variation of K_w with temperature

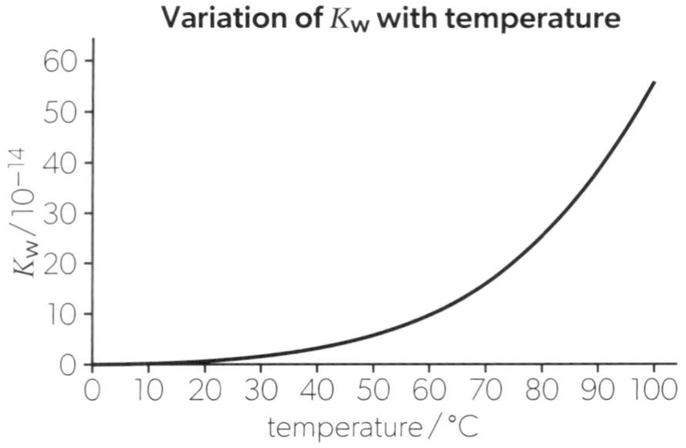

For pure water:

$[H^+(aq)] = [OH^-(aq)] = 1.00 \times 10^{-7}\ \text{mol dm}^{-3}$ at 298 K

From the graph: $K_w = 1.00 \times 10^{-13}$ at 334 K (61 °C)

At this temperature:

$[H^+(aq)] = \sqrt{1.00 \times 10^{-13}} = 3.16 \times 10^{-7}\ \text{mol dm}^{-3}$

pH, pOH and pK_w for strong acids and bases

As stated earlier in this chapter, the pH of a solution depends only upon the hydrogen ion concentration and is independent of the volume of the solution.

$pH = -\log_{10}[H^+(aq)]$

i.e. $[H^+(aq)] = 10^{-pH}$

For strong monoprotic acids, the hydrogen ion concentration is equal to the concentration of the acid. For strong diprotic acids, the hydrogen ion concentration is twice the value of the acid, concentration.

The use of the logarithmic scale can be extended to other values, e.g. pOH and pK_w.

$pOH = -\log_{10}[OH^-(aq)]$ and $pK_w = -\log_{10}K_w$

i.e. $[OH^-(aq)] = 10^{-pOH}$

Taking logarithms to base ten, the expression for the ionic product of water, $K_w = [H^+(aq)] \times [OH^-(aq)]$ becomes:

$\log_{10}K_w = \log_{10}[H^+(aq)] + \log_{10}[OH^-(aq)]$

This can also be written as:

$-\log_{10}K_w = -\log_{10}[H^+(aq)] - \log_{10}[OH^-(aq)]$

$-\log_{10}[H^+(aq)] = pH$ and $-\log_{10}[OH^-(aq)] = pOH$

This leads to the useful expression:

$pK_w = pH + pOH$

At 25 °C, $K_w = 10^{-14}$ and $pH + pOH = 14$

This expression gives another way of calculating the pH of a strong base since the pOH can be determined directly from the hydroxide ion concentration and then be subtracted from 14.

Worked example

Determine the pH of $4.00 \times 10^{-3}\ \text{mol dm}^{-3}$ $Ba(OH)_2$.

$[OH^-(aq)] = 2 \times 4.00 \times 10^{-3} = 8.00 \times 10^{-3}\ \text{mol dm}^{-3}$

$pOH = -\log_{10}(8.00 \times 10^{-3}) = 2.10$

$pH = 14 - 2.10 = 11.9$

AHL Calculations with weak acids and bases

Weak acids

The dissociation of a weak acid, HA, in water can be written as $HA(aq) \rightleftharpoons H^+(aq) + A^-(aq)$.

The equilibrium expression for this reaction is: $K_a = \frac{[H^+]\times[A^-]}{[HA]}$ where K_a is known as the acid dissociation constant.

For example, to calculate the pH of 0.100 mol dm^{-3} CH_3COOH given that $K_a = 1.8 \times 10^{-5}$ mol dm^{-3} at 298 K:

	$CH_3COOH(aq) \rightleftharpoons$	$CH_3COO^-(aq)$ +	$H^+(aq)$
Initial concentration / mol dm^{-3}	0.100	–	–
Equilibrium concentration / mol dm^{-3}	$(0.100 - x)$	x	x

$$K_a = \frac{[CH_3COO^-]\times[H^+]}{[CH_3COOH]} = \frac{x^2}{(0.10-x)} = 1.8 \times 10^{-5}\ \text{mol dm}^{-3} \quad \Rightarrow x^2 + (1.8 \times 10^{-5}x) - 1.8 \times 10^{-6} = 0$$

Solving the quadratic equation gives $x = 1.33 \times 10^{-3}$ mol dm^{-3} $pH = -\log_{10}(1.33 \times 10^{-3}) = 2.88$

If the acids are quite weak, the equilibrium concentration of the acid can be assumed to be the same as its initial concentration. Provided this assumption is stated, it is usual to simplify the expression in calculations to avoid a quadratic equation. In the above example:

$$K_a = \frac{[CH_3COO^-]\times[H^+]}{[CH_3COOH]} = \frac{[H^+]^2}{0.10} = 1.8 \times 10^{-5}\ \text{mol dm}^{-3} \quad \Rightarrow [H^+] = \sqrt{1.8\times10^{-6}} = 1.34 \times 10^{-3}\ \text{mol dm}^{-3}$$

pH = 2.87

Worked examples

1. The pH of a 0.020 mol dm^{-3} solution of a weak acid is 3.9. Find the K_a of the acid.

$$K_a = \frac{[H^+]^2}{(0.020-[H^+])} \approx \frac{10^{-3.9}\times10^{-3.9}}{0.020}$$
$$= 7.92 \times 10^{-7}\ \text{mol dm}^{-3}$$

2. An acid whose K_a is 4.1×10^{-6} mol dm^{-3} has a pH of 4.5. Find the concentration of the acid.

$$[HA] = \frac{[H^+]^2}{K_a} = \frac{10^{-4.5}\times10^{-4.5}}{4.1\times10^{-6}} = 2.44 \times 10^{-4}\ \text{mol dm}^{-3}$$

Note that the weaker the weak acid the smaller the value of K_a and the larger the value of pK_a. Thus ethanoic acid ($pK_a = 4.76$) is a weaker acid than methanoic acid ($pK_a = 3.75$). The same is true with K_b for weak bases.

Weak bases

The reaction of a weak base can be written:

$$B(aq) + H_2O(l) \rightleftharpoons BH^+(aq) + OH^-(aq)$$

Since the concentration of water is constant:

$K_b = \frac{[BH^+]\times[OH^-]}{[B]}$ where K_b is the base dissociation constant.

If one considers the reverse reaction of BH^+ acting as an acid to give B and H^+, then $K_a = \frac{[B]\times[H^+]}{[BH^+]}$

So $K_a \times K_b = \frac{[B]\times[H^+]}{[BH^+]} \times \frac{[BH^+]\times[OH^-]}{[B]}$

$= [H^+] \times [OH^-] = K_w$

$pK_a = -\log_{10}K_a$; $pK_b = -\log_{10}K_b$; and $pK_w = -\log_{10}K_w = 14$, so $pK_a + pK_b = 14$

Worked examples

1. The K_b value for ammonia is 1.8×10^{-5} mol dm^{-3}. Find the pH of a 1.00×10^{-2} mol dm^{-3} solution.

Since $[NH_4^+] = [OH^-]$ then:

$$K_b = \frac{[OH^-]^2}{[NH_3]} \approx \frac{[OH^-]^2}{1.00\times10^{-2}} = 1.8\times10^{-5}$$

$[OH^-] = \sqrt{1.8\times10^{-7}} = 4.24 \times 10^{-4}$ mol dm^{-3}

$\Rightarrow pOH = -\log_{10}(4.24 \times 10^{-4}) = 3.37$

$\Rightarrow pH = 14 - 3.37 = 10.6$

2. The pH of a 3.00×10^{-2} mol dm^{-3} solution of weak base is 10.0. Calculate the pK_b value of the base.

pH = 10.0 so pOH = 4.0

$$K_b = \frac{10^{-4}\times10^{-4}}{3.00\times10^{-2}} = 3.33 \times 10^{-7}\ \text{mol dm}^{-3}$$

$\Rightarrow pK_b = 6.48$

3. The value for the pK_a of methylamine (aminomethane) is 10.66. Calculate the concentration of an aqueous solution of methylamine with a pH of 10.8.

$pK_b = 14 - 10.66 = 3.34$; $pOH = 14 - 10.8 = 3.2$

$$[CH_3NH_2] = \frac{[OH^-]^2}{K_b} = \frac{10^{-3.2}\times10^{-3.2}}{10^{-3.34}}$$
$$= 8.71 \times 10^{-4}\ \text{mol dm}^{-3}$$

AHL Salt hydrolysis, indicators and pH curves

Salt hydrolysis

Sodium chloride is neutral in aqueous solution. It is the salt of a strong acid and a strong base so its ions remain completely dissociated in solution.

Salts made from a weak acid and a strong base, such as sodium ethanoate, are alkaline in solution. This is because the ethanoate ions combine with hydrogen ions from water to form mainly undissociated ethanoic acid, leaving excess hydroxide ions in solution.

$$NaCH_3COO(aq) \longrightarrow Na^+(aq) + CH_3COO^-(aq)$$
$$+$$
$$H_2O(l) \rightleftharpoons OH^-(aq) + H^+(aq)$$

strong base so completely dissociated $CH_3COOH(aq)$

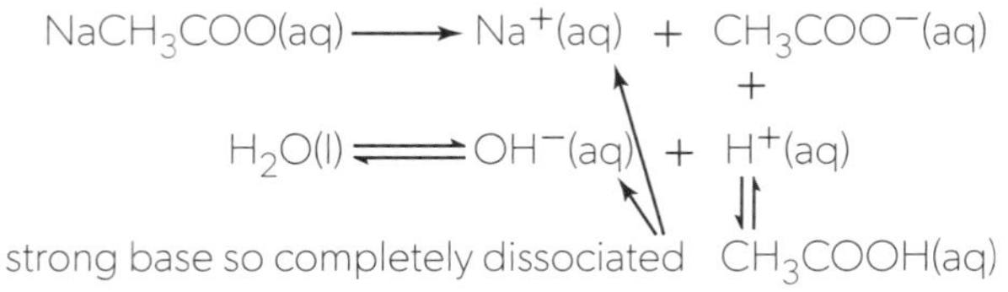

Similarly, salts derived from a strong acid and a weak base will be acidic in solution.

$$NH_4Cl(aq) \longrightarrow NH_4^+(aq) + Cl^-(aq)$$
$$+$$
$$H_2O(l) \rightleftharpoons OH^-(aq) + H^+(aq)$$

strong acid so completely dissociated

$$NH_3(aq) + H_2O(l)$$

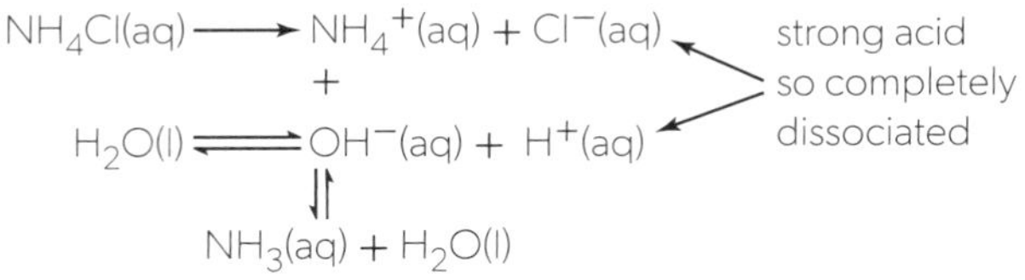

Indicators

An indicator is a weak acid (or weak base) in which the dissociated form is a different colour to the undissociated form.

$$HInd(aq) \rightleftharpoons H^+(aq) + Ind^-(aq)$$

colour A   colour B

(colour in acid solution)   (colour in alkali solution)

$$K_{ind} = [H^+] \times \frac{[Ind^-]}{[HInd]}$$

Assuming the colour changes when $[Ind^-] \approx [HInd]$ then the end point of the indicator will be when $[H^+] \approx K_{ind}$, i.e. when $pH \approx pK_{ind}$. Different indicators have different K_{ind} values and so change colour within different pH ranges.

Indicator	pK_{ind}	pH range	Use
methyl orange	3.7	3.1–4.4	titrations with strong acids
phenolphthalein	9.6	8.3–10.0	titrations with strong bases

An appropriate indicator for a titration has an end point range that coincides with the pH at the equivalence point. Universal indicator is a mixture of many indicators with a wide pH range of colour change.

pH curves for titrations involving weak acids and bases

Consider titrating $50.0 \, cm^3$ of $1.00 \, mol \, dm^{-3}$ CH_3COOH with $1.00 \, mol \, dm^{-3}$ NaOH.

$$CH_3COOH(aq) + NaOH(aq) \rightarrow NaCH_3COO(aq) + H_2O(l)$$

$K_a = 1.8 \times 10^{-5}$. Making the usual assumptions, the initial $[H^+] = \sqrt{K_a \times [CH_3COOH]}$ and pH = 2.37. This means that the y-intercept will be higher than for a strong acid.

When $49.0 \, cm^3$ of the $1.00 \, mol \, dm^{-3}$ NaOH has been added, $[CH_3COO^-] \approx 0.05 \, mol \, dm^{-3}$ and $[CH_3COOH] \approx 1.0 \times 10^{-2} \, mol \, dm^{-3}$.

$$[H^+] = \frac{K_a \times [CH_3COOH]}{[CH_3COO^-]} \approx \frac{1.8 \times 10^{-5} \times 1 \times 10^{-3}}{0.05}$$

$$= 3.6 \times 10^{-7} \, mol \, dm^{-3} \text{ and pH} = 6.44$$

The pH changes more slowly in this region with a weak acid, as a buffer solution forms, so it is sometimes called the buffer region. See page 114.

When $25 \, cm^3$ of alkali have been added, half of the acid has been turned into salt, so $pK_a = pH$.

After the equivalence point, the graph will follow the same pattern as the strong acid–strong base curve as more sodium hydroxide is simply being added to the solution.

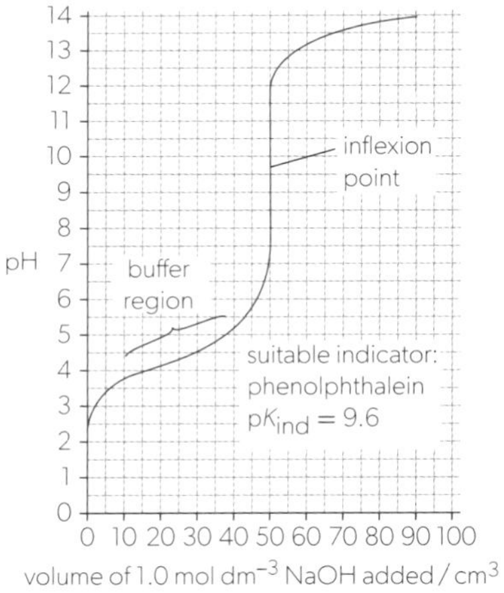

Similar arguments can be used to explain the shapes of pH curves for strong acid–weak base, and weak acid–weak base titrations. Titrations involving weak acids with weak bases should not be used in analytical chemistry since there is no sharp inflexion point.

Strong acid–weak base e.g. HCl(aq) and NH_3(aq)

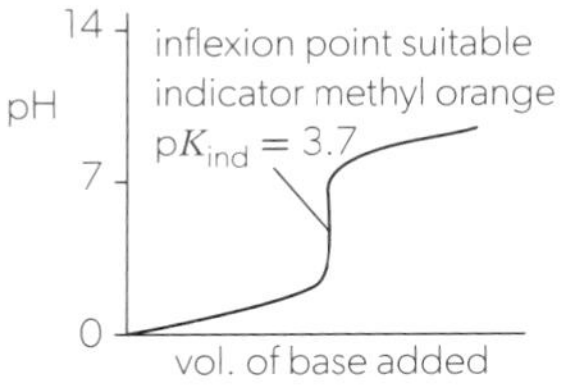

Weak acid–weak base e.g. CH_3COOH(aq) and NH_3(aq)

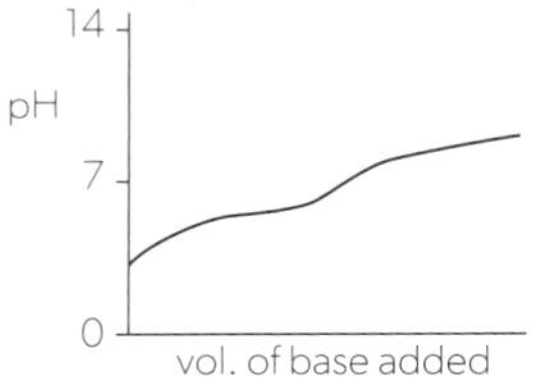

AHL

Buffer solutions

A buffer solution resists changes in pH when small amounts of acid or alkali are added to it.

Acidic buffers

An acidic buffer solution can be made by mixing a weak acid together with the salt of that acid and a strong base. An example is a solution of ethanoic acid and sodium ethanoate. The weak acid is only slightly dissociated in solution, but the salt is fully dissociated into its ions, so the concentration of ethanoate ions is high.

$$NaCH_3COO(aq) \rightarrow Na^+(aq) + CH_3COO^-(aq)$$

$$CH_3COOH(aq) \rightleftharpoons CH_3COO^-(aq) + H^+(aq)$$

If some acid is added, the extra H^+ ions coming from the acid are removed as they combine with ethanoate ions to form undissociated ethanoic acid.

The concentration of H^+ ions remains unaltered.

$$CH_3COO^-(aq) + H^+(aq) \rightleftharpoons CH_3COOH(aq)$$

If some alkali is added, the hydroxide ions from the alkali are removed by their reaction with the undissociated acid to form water, so again the H^+ ion concentration stays constant.

$$CH_3COOH(aq) + OH^-(aq) \rightarrow CH_3COO^-(aq) + H_2O(l)$$

In practice, acidic buffers are often made by taking a solution of a strong base and adding excess weak acid to it, so that the solution contains the salt and the unreacted weak acid.

$$\underset{\text{limiting reagent}}{NaOH(aq)} + CH_3COOH(aq) \rightarrow \underbrace{\underset{\text{salt}}{NaCH_3COO(aq)} + H_2O(l) + \underset{\text{excess weak acid}}{CH_3COOH(aq)}}_{\text{buffer solution}}$$

Alkali buffers

An alkali buffer with a fixed pH greater than 7 can be made from a weak base together with the salt of that base with a strong acid. An example is ammonia with ammonium chloride.

$$NH_4Cl(aq) \rightarrow NH_4^+(aq) + Cl^-(aq)$$

$$NH_3(aq) + H_2O(l) \rightleftharpoons NH_4^+(aq) + OH^-(aq)$$

If H^+ ions are added, they will combine with OH^- ions to form water and more of the ammonia will dissociate to replace them. If more OH^- ions are added, they will combine with ammonium ions to form undissociated ammonia. In both cases, the hydroxide ion concentration and the hydrogen ion concentration remain constant.

Buffer calculations

The equilibrium expression for weak acids also applies to acidic buffer solutions, e.g. ethanoic acid/sodium ethanoate solution.

$$K_a = \frac{[H^+] \times [CH_3COO^-]}{[CH_3COOH]}$$

The essential difference now is that the concentrations of the two ions from the acid will not be equal.

Since the sodium ethanoate is completely dissociated, the concentration of the ethanoate ions in solution will be the same as the concentration of the sodium ethanoate; only a very little will come from the acid.

If logarithms are taken and the equation is rearranged, then:

$$pH = pK_a + \log_{10}\frac{[CH_3COO^-]}{[CH_3COOH]}$$

So,the pH of the buffer does not change on dilution, as the concentration of the ethanoate ions and the undissociated acid will be affected equally.

Also, the buffer will be most efficient when $[CH_3COO^-] = [CH_3COOH]$. At this point, which equates to the half-equivalence point when ethanoic acid is titrated with sodium hydroxide, the pH of the solution will equal the pK_a value of the acid. This is known as the buffer region.

Worked example 1

Calculate the pH of a buffer containing 0.200 mol of sodium ethanoate in 500 cm³ of 0.100 mol dm⁻³ ethanoic acid, given that K_a for ethanoic acid $= 1.8 \times 10^{-5}$ mol dm^{-3}.

$[CH_3COO^-] = 0.400$ mol dm^{-3};
$[CH_3COOH] = 0.100$ mol dm^{-3}

$$K_a \approx \frac{[H^+] \times 0.400}{0.100} = 1.8 \times 10^{-5}\ \text{mol dm}^{-3}$$

$[H^+] = 4.5 \times 10^{-6}$ mol dm^{-3} so, pH = 5.35

Worked example 2

Calculate what mass of sodium propanoate must be dissolved in 1.00 dm³ of 1.00 mol dm⁻³ propanoic acid ($pK_a = 4.87$) to give a buffer solution with a pH of 4.5.

$$[C_2H_5COO^-] = \frac{K_a \times [C_2H_5COOH]}{[H^+]} = \frac{10^{-4.87} \times 1.00}{10^{-4.5}}$$

$$= 0.427\ \text{mol dm}^{-3}$$

Mass of NaC_2H_5COO required $= 0.427 \times 96.07 = 41.0$ g

Multiple-choice questions—Proton transfer reactions: acid–base behaviour

1. Which statement about hydrochloric acid is false?
   A. It can react with copper to give hydrogen.
   B. It can react with sodium carbonate to give carbon dioxide.
   C. It can react with ammonia to give ammonium chloride.
   D. It can react with copper oxide to give water.

2. $1.00\,cm^3$ of a solution has a pH of 3. What is the pH of $100\,cm^3$ of the same solution?
   A. 1 B. 3 C. 5
   D. Impossible to calculate from the data given.

3. Which statement(s) is/are true about separate solutions of a strong acid and a weak acid both with the same concentration?
   I. They both have the same pH.
   II. They both have the same electrical conductivity.
   A. I and II C. II only
   B. I only D. Neither I nor II

4. Identify the correct statement about $25\,cm^3$ of a solution of $0.1\,mol\,dm^{-3}$ ethanoic acid, CH_3COOH.
   A. It will contain more hydrogen ions than $25\,cm^3$ of $0.1\,mol\,dm^{-3}$ hydrochloric acid.
   B. It will have a pH greater than 7.
   C. It will react exactly with $25\,cm^3$ of $0.1\,mol\,dm^{-3}$ sodium hydroxide.
   D. It is completely dissociated into ethanoate and hydrogen ions in solution.

5. What is the pH of $1.0 \times 10^{-4}\,mol\,dm^{-3}$ sulfuric acid, $H_2SO_4(aq)$?
   A. −4 C. 4
   B. between 3 and 4 D. between 4 and 5

6. $NH_3(aq)$, $HCl(aq)$, $NaOH(aq)$, $CH_3COOH(aq)$

   When $1.0\,mol\,dm^{-3}$ solutions of the substances above are arranged in order of decreasing pH, what is the order?
   A. $NaOH(aq)$, $NH_3(aq)$, $CH_3COOH(aq)$, $HCl(aq)$
   B. $NH_3(aq)$, $NaOH(aq)$, $HCl(aq)$, $CH_3COOH(aq)$
   C. $CH_3COOH(aq)$, $HCl(aq)$, $NaOH(aq)$, $NH_3(aq)$
   D. $HCl(aq)$, $CH_3COOH(aq)$, $NH_3(aq)$, $NaOH(aq)$

7. Which statement is true about two solutions, one with a pH of 3 and the other with a pH of 6?
   A. The solution with a pH of 3 is twice as acidic as the solution with a pH of 6.
   B. The solution with a pH of 6 is twice as acidic as the solution with a pH of 3.
   C. The hydrogen ion concentration in the solution with a pH of 6 is one thousand times greater than that in the solution with a pH of 3.
   D. The hydrogen ion concentration in the solution with a pH of 3 is one thousand times greater than that in the solution with a pH of 6.

8. Which of the following is **not** a conjugate acid–base pair?
   A. HNO_3/NO_3^- C. NH_3/NH_2^-
   B. H_2SO_4/HSO_4^- D. H_3O^+/OH^-

9. Which gas cannot lead to acid rain?
   A. CO_2 C. NO
   B. SO_2 D. NO_2

10. Which statement is true during the titration of a known volume of a strong acid with a strong base?
    A. There is a steady increase in pH.
    B. There is a sharp increase in pH around the end point.
    C. There is a steady decrease in pH.
    D. There is a sharp decrease in pH around the end point.

11. What is the pH of $0.001\,mol\,dm^{-3}$ potassium hydroxide solution, $KOH(aq)$?
    A. 1 B. 3 C. 11 D. 13

12. Which statement is correct?
    A. A weak acid is highly dissociated and has a strong conjugate base.
    B. A weak acid is slightly dissociated and has a weak conjugate base.
    C. A weak base is a proton donor and has a strong conjugate acid.
    D. A weak base is a proton acceptor and has a strong conjugate acid.

13. Which will react with hydrochloric acid to give water as one of the products?
    I. magnesium oxide
    II. sodium carbonate
    III. potassium hydrogencarbonate
    A. I and II only C. II and III only
    B. I and III only D. I, II, and III

14. Which solution will have the highest electroconductivity?
    A. $1.00\,mol\,dm^{-3}$ $H_2SO_4(aq)$
    B. $1.00\,mol\,dm^{-3}$ $NaOH(aq)$
    C. $2.00\,mol\,dm^{-3}$ $CH_3COOH(aq)$
    D. $2.00\,mol\,dm^{-3}$ $NH_3(aq)$

15. $5.0\,cm^3$ of aqueous solution of sodium hydroxide with a pH of 11 is mixed with $445.0\,cm^3$ of distilled water. What is the pH of the resulting solution?
    A. 7 C. 9
    B. 8 D. 10

16. Three acids, HA, HB, and HC, have the following K_a values:

$K_a(HA) = 1 \times 10^{-5}$ $K_a(HB) = 2 \times 10^{-5}$ $K_a(HC) = 1 \times 10^{-6}$

What is the correct order of increasing acid strength (weakest first)?

A. HA, HB, HC
B. HC, HB, HA
C. HC, HA, HB
D. HB, HA, HC

17. Which of the following reagents could not be added together to make a buffer solution?

A. $NaOH(aq)$ and $CH_3COOH(aq)$
B. $NaCH_3COO(aq)$ and $CH_3COOH(aq)$
C. $NaOH(aq)$ and $NaCH_3COO(aq)$
D. $NH_4Cl(aq)$ and $NH_3(aq)$

18. Which statement is true when 1.0 cm^3 of a weak acid solution is added to 100 cm^3 of a buffer solution?

A. The volume of the resulting mixture is 100 cm^3.
B. There is almost no change in the pH of the solution.
C. The pH of the solution increases noticeably.
D. The pH of the solution decreases noticeably.

19. Which salt forms an acidic solution in water?

A. CH_3COONa
B. Na_2CO_3
C. $KHCO_3$
D. NH_4NO_3

20. An indicator changes colour in the pH range 8.3–10.0. This indicator should be used when titrating a known volume of:

A. a strong acid with a weak base
B. a weak acid with a weak base
C. a weak base with a strong acid
D. a weak acid with a strong base.

21. Which curve represents the titration of a strong base with a weak acid?

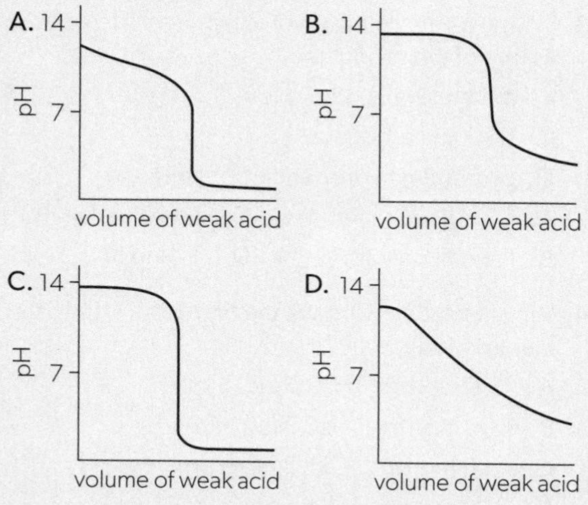

22. What is the pH of the resulting solution when 50.0 cm^3 of 1.0 $mol\,dm^{-3}$ NaOH is added to 100 cm^3 of 1.0 $mol\,dm^{-3}$ ethanoic acid? (pK_a of $CH_3COOH = 4.76$)

A. 4.76
B. between 5 and 7
C. between 2 and 3
D. >7

23. Which combination of reactants is likely to have a pH in the region of 8.5 at the equivalence point?

A. $HCl(aq) + NaOH(aq)$
B. $CH_3COOH(aq) + NaOH(aq)$
C. $CH_3COOH(aq) + NH_3(aq)$
D. $HCl(aq) + NH_3(aq)$

24. What is the order of **increasing** acid strength?

Acid	K_a	pK_a
C_6H_5OH	1.02×10^{-10}	
C_2H_5OH		15.50
$CH_2ClCOOH$	1.35×10^{-3}	
C_6H_5COOH		4.20

A. $CH_2ClCOOH < C_6H_5COOH < C_6H_5OH < C_2H_5OH$
B. $C_2H_5OH < C_6H_5OH < C_6H_5COOH < CH_2ClCOOH$
C. $C_6H_5COOH < CH_2ClCOOH < C_6H_5OH < C_2H_5OH$
D. $C_2H_5OH < C_6H_5COOH < CH_2ClCOOH < C_6H_5OH$

25. Which is the best indicator to use for the acid–base titration shown?

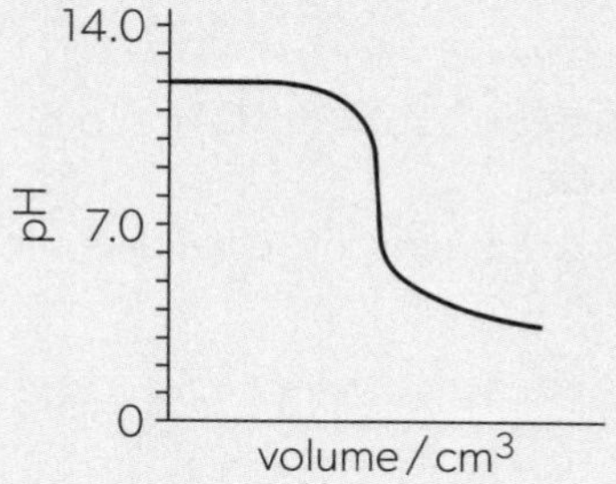

A. methyl red ($pK_a = 5.1$)
B. methyl orange ($pK_a = 3.7$)
C. phenolphthalein ($pK_a = 9.6$)
D. bromophenol blue ($pK_a = 4.2$)

26. The pK_b values for ethylamine, $C_2H_5NH_2$, diethylamine, $(C_2H_5)_2NH$, and triethylamine, $(C_2H_5)_3N$, are 3.35, 3.16, and 3.25, respectively.

Which statements are correct?

I. Diethylamine is the strongest of the three bases.
II. $(C_2H_5)_2NH_2^+ + H_2O \rightleftharpoons (C_2H_5)_2NH + H_3O^+$ $pK_a = 10.84$
III. $C_2H_5NH_2 + H_2O \rightleftharpoons C_2H_5NH_3^+ + OH^-$ $K_b = 10^{-3.35}$

A. I and II only
B. I and III only
C. II and III only
D. I, II, and III

Short-answer questions—Proton transfer reactions: acid–base behaviour

1. a) (i) Define a Brønsted–Lowry base. [1]

   (ii) Deduce the two acids and their conjugate bases in the following reaction:

   $H_2O(l) + HCl(aq) \rightleftharpoons H_3O^+(aq) + Cl^-(aq)$ [2]

   b) Ethanoic acid, CH_3COOH, is a weak acid.

   (i) Explain the difference between a strong acid and a weak acid. [2]

   (ii) State the equation for the reaction of ethanoic acid with aqueous ammonia. [1]

   (iii) Compare and contrast the reactions of 1.00 mol dm^{-3} hydrochloric acid and 1.00 mol dm^{-3} ethanoic acid with excess magnesium metal. [4]

2. a) 1.00 cm^3 of 5.00×10^{-3} mol dm^{-3} sulfuric acid, $H_2SO_4(aq)$, is added to an empty volumetric flask.

   (i) Calculate the pH of the sulfuric acid solution. Assume that it is a strong diprotic acid. [2]

   (ii) Determine the pH of the diluted solution if the total volume is made up to 100 cm^3 with distilled water. [2]

   b) State the equation for the reaction of sulfuric acid with sodium hydroxide solution. [1]

   c) The diluted solution in **a)(ii)** is used to titrate 25.0 cm^3 of 1.00×10^{-4} mol dm^{-3} sodium hydroxide solution.

   (i) Describe what will be observed when the end point is reached if phenolphthalein is used as the indicator for this titration. [2]

   (ii) Determine the volume of acid needed to reach the equivalence point of this titration. [2]

3. When hydrochloric acid is added to a solution of sodium hydrogencarbonate, $NaHCO_3(aq)$, carbon dioxide is evolved.

   a) State the equation for this reaction. [2]

   b) The hydrogencarbonate ion can act either as an acid or a base according to Brønsted–Lowry theory.

   (i) Deduce the formula of the conjugate base if it is behaving as an acid. [1]

   (ii) Deduce the formula of the acid if it is behaving as a conjugate base. [1]

   c) State the equations for the reaction of hydrochloric acid with:

   (i) copper(II) oxide, CuO

   (ii) sodium carbonate, Na_2CO_3. [2]

4. a) Explain why rain water with a pH of 6 is not classified as "acid rain" even though its pH is less than 7? [2]

   b) State the equation for the formation of nitrogen(II) oxide, NO(g), in an internal combustion engine and describe, with equations, how it is converted into nitric acid in the atmosphere. [4]

   c) Explain why marble statues become corroded by acid rain. [2]

   d) Outline why adding calcium hydroxide (lime) to lakes can reduce the effects of acid deposition. [2]

AHL

5. The graph below shows how the ionic product of water, K_w, varies with temperature.

Variation of K_w with temperature

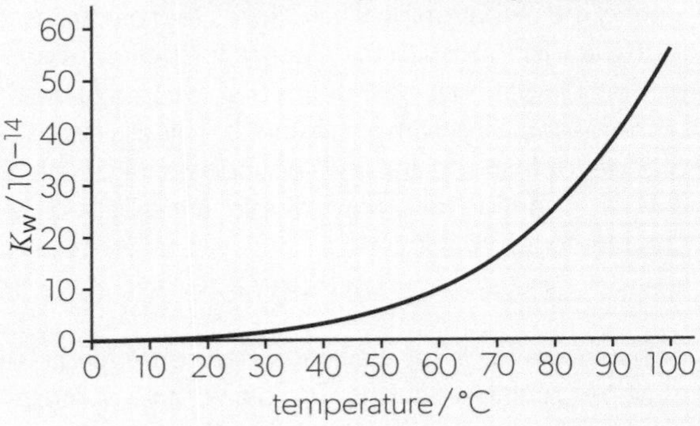

   a) State the equation for the dissociation of water and deduce from the graph whether the reaction is exothermic or endothermic. [2]

   b) Determine the hydrogen ion concentration and the hydroxide ion concentration in pure water at 90 °C and hence deduce the pH of pure water at this temperature. [3]

6. The acid dissociation constant, K_a, for lactic acid, $CH(CH_3)(OH)COOH$, is 1.38×10^{-4} at 298 K.

   a) Explain why lactic acid can exist in two different enantiomeric forms. [1]

   b) Calculate the pH of 0.100 mol dm^{-3} lactic acid solution at 298 K. [3]

   c) Determine the mass of lactic acid that must be added together with 2.00 g of sodium hydroxide to make 500 cm^3 of a buffer solution at 298 K with a pH of 4.00. [4]

7. a) (i) State the equation for the reaction between propanoic acid, $C_2H_5COOH(aq)$, and water and deduce the equilibrium expression. [2]

   (ii) Calculate the pH of a 2.00×10^{-3} mol dm^{-3} solution of propanoic acid ($pK_a = 4.87$). [3]

   (iii) State any assumptions you have made in arriving at your answer to **a)(ii)**. [2]

   b) 25.0 cm^3 of 2.00×10^{-3} mol dm^{-3} sodium hydroxide solution, NaOH(aq), was added to 50 cm^3 of 2.00×10^{-3} mol dm^{-3} propanoic acid.

   (i) Identify all the chemical species present in the resulting solution. [2]

   (ii) Explain how the resulting solution can function as a buffer solution if a small amount of alkali is added. [2]

Redox reactions (1)

Definition of oxidation and reduction

Oxidation used to be narrowly defined as the addition of oxygen to a substance. For example, when magnesium is burned in air the magnesium is oxidized to magnesium oxide.

$$2Mg(s) + O_2(g) \rightarrow 2MgO(s)$$

The electronic configuration of magnesium is [Ne]3s^2. During the oxidation process it loses two electrons to form the Mg^{2+} ion with the electronic configuration of [Ne]. Oxidation is now defined as the loss of one or more electrons from a substance. This is a much broader definition, as it does not necessarily involve oxygen. Bromide ions, for example, are oxidized by chlorine to form bromine.

$$2Br^-(aq) + Cl_2(aq) \rightarrow Br_2(aq) + 2Cl^-(aq)$$

If one substance loses electrons then something else must be gaining electrons. The gain of one or more electrons is called reduction. In the first example, oxygen is reduced as it is gaining two electrons from magnesium to form the oxide ion O^{2-}. Similarly, in the second example, chlorine is reduced as each chlorine atom gains one electron from a bromide ion to form a chloride ion.

Since the processes involve the transfer of electrons, oxidation and reduction must occur simultaneously. Such reactions are known as **redox reactions**. In order to distinguish between the two processes half-equations are often used:

Oxidation	$2Mg(s) \rightarrow 2Mg^{2+}(s) + 4e^-$
Reduction	$O_2(g) + 4e^- \rightarrow 2O^{2-}(s)$
Overall equation	$2Mg(s) + O_2(g) \rightarrow 2MgO(s)$

Oxidation	$2Br^-(aq) \rightarrow Br_2(aq) + 2e^-$
Reduction	$Cl_2(aq) + 2e^- \rightarrow 2Cl^-(aq)$
Overall equation	$2Br^-(aq) + Cl_2(aq) \rightarrow Br_2(aq) + 2Cl^-(aq)$

Understanding that magnesium must lose electrons and oxygen must gain electrons when magnesium oxide, MgO, is formed from its elements is a good way to remember the definitions of oxidation and reduction. Some students prefer to use the mnemonic OILRIG: Oxidation Is the Loss of electrons, Reduction Is the Gain of electrons.

Oxidation and reduction in terms of oxidation states

The rules for assigning oxidation states to elements within a compound and the use of oxidation numbers for naming compounds are covered on page 47. When a redox reaction occurs there is a change in oxidation states.

When an element is oxidized its oxidation state increases:

e.g. $\underset{(0)}{Mg(s)} \rightarrow \underset{(+2)}{Mg^{2+}(aq)} + 2e^-$

When an element is reduced its oxidation state decreases:

e.g. $\underset{(+6)}{SO_4^{2-}(aq)} + 2H^+(aq) + 2e^- \rightarrow \underset{(+4)}{SO_3^{2-}(aq)} + H_2O(l)$

The change in the oxidation state is equal to the number of electrons involved in the half-equation.

Using oxidation states makes it easy to identify whether or not a reaction is a redox reaction.

Redox reactions (change in oxidation states):

$\underset{(+2)}{CuO(s)} + \underset{(0)}{H_2(g)} \rightarrow \underset{(0)}{Cu(s)} + \underset{(+1)}{H_2O(l)}$

$\underset{(+2)}{5Fe^{2+}(aq)} + \underset{(+7)}{MnO_4^-(aq)} + 8H^+(aq) \rightarrow \underset{(+3)}{5Fe^{3+}(aq)} + \underset{(+2)}{Mn^{2+}(aq)} + 4H_2O(l)$

Not redox reactions (no change in oxidation states):

precipitation $\underset{(+1)}{Ag^+(aq)} + \underset{(-1)}{Cl^-(aq)} \rightarrow \underset{(+1)(-1)}{AgCl(s)}$

neutralization $\underset{(+1)(-1)}{HCl(aq)} + \underset{(+1)(-2)(+1)}{NaOH(aq)} \rightarrow \underset{(+1)(-1)}{NaCl(aq)} + \underset{(+1)(-2)}{H_2O(l)}$

Note: reactions where an element is uncombined on one side of the equation and combined on the other side must be redox reactions since there must be a change in oxidation state:

e.g. $Mg(s) + 2HCl(aq) \rightarrow MgCl_2(aq) + H_2(g)$

Redox reactions (2)

Oxidizing and reducing agents

A substance that readily oxidizes other substances is known as an oxidizing agent. Oxidizing agents are thus substances that readily accept electrons. Usually, they contain elements that are in their highest oxidation state, e.g. O_2, Cl_2, F_2, SO_3 (SO_4^{2-} in solution), MnO_4^-, and $Cr_2O_7^{2-}$.

Reducing agents readily donate electrons and include H_2, Na, C, CO, and SO_2 (SO_3^{2-} in solution).

Balancing redox equations

To obtain the overall redox equation, the number of electrons in the oxidation half-equation must balance the number of electrons in the reduction half-equation. For many redox equations this is straightforward. For example, the oxidation of magnesium by silver(I) ions. Write the two half-equations, then double the silver half-equation so that both half-equations involve two electrons. Finally, add them together:

$$2Ag^+(aq) + 2e^- \rightarrow 2Ag(s)$$

$$Mg(s) \rightarrow Mg^{2+}(aq) + 2e^-$$

Overall $2Ag^+(aq) + Mg(s) \rightarrow 2Ag(s) + Mg^{2+}(aq)$

It is less straightforward when there is a change in the number of oxygen atoms in a compound or ion. The rule is that if oxygen atoms need to be accounted for, then water is used and if hydrogen atoms need to be accounted for, then hydrogen ions, $H^+(aq)$, are used. Consider the oxidation of sulfite ions, $SO_3^{2-}(aq)$, to sulfate ions, $SO_4^{2-}(aq,)$ by purple manganate(VII) ions:

$$SO_3^{2-}(aq) \rightarrow SO_4^{2-}(aq)$$

Add the extra O atom by adding water and then ensure that the charges on both sides are equal, so the balanced half-equation becomes:

$$SO_3^{2-}(aq) + H_2O(l) \rightarrow SO_4^{2-}(aq) + 2H^+(aq) + 2e^-$$

The manganate(VII) ions, $MnO_4^-(aq)$, are reduced to very pale pink (virtually colourless) Mn^{2+} ions in the process:

$$MnO_4^-(aq) \rightarrow Mn^{2+}(aq)$$

Add eight H^+ ions to remove the oxygen atoms as water and then ensure that the charges on both sides are equal, so the balanced half-equation becomes:

$$MnO_4^-(aq) + 8H^+(aq) + 5e^- \rightarrow Mn^{2+}(aq) + 4H_2O(l)$$

Note that the number of electrons can also be obtained from the change in oxidation states. S goes from +4 to +6, so two electrons are involved, and Mn goes from +7 to +2, so five electrons are involved.

To ensure that both half-equations have the same number of electrons, multiply the sulfite equation by 5 and the manganate(VII) equation by 2, then obtain the overall redox equation by adding them together to cancel out the ten electrons, and simplify the water and hydrogen ions.

$$2MnO_4^-(aq) + 16H^+(aq) + 10e^- + 5SO_3^{2-}(aq) + 5H_2O(l) \rightarrow 2Mn^{2+}(aq) + 8H_2O(l) + 5SO_4^{2-}(aq) + 10H^+(aq) + 10e^-$$

The overall redox equation simplifies to:

$$2MnO_4^-(aq) + 6H^+(aq) + 5SO_3^{2-}(aq) \rightarrow 2Mn^{2+}(aq) + 3H_2O(l) + 5SO_4^{2-}(aq)$$

This means that acid (H^+ ions) need to be present for the reaction to take place.

Worked example of a redox titration

The colour changes when transition metal ions change oxidation state mean that some redox titrations can be self-indicating. Here is an example.

0.7439 g of hydrated oxalic acid crystals, $(COOH)_2.xH_2O$ was dissolved in water and titrated with 0.100 mol dm^{-3} potassium manganate(VII) solution, $KMnO_4(aq)$. The end point was reached when one drop caused a slight pink colour to remain. It was found that 23.60 cm^3 of the $KMnO_4(aq)$ solution was required to reach the end point. Calculate the value of x.

Half equations:

$(COOH)_2(aq) \rightarrow 2CO_2(g) + 2H^+(aq) + 2e^-$

$MnO_4^-(aq) + 8H^+(aq) + 5e^- \rightarrow Mn^{2+}(aq) + 4H_2O(l)$

Overall reaction: $5(COOH)_2(aq) + 2MnO_4^-(aq) + 6H^+(aq) \rightarrow 10CO_2(g) + 2Mn^{2+}(aq) + 8H_2O(l)$

Amount of MnO_4^- used $= \frac{23.60}{1000} \times 0.100 = 2.360 \times 10^{-3}$ mol

Since 2 mol of MnO_4^- reacts with 5 mol of $(COOH)_2$:

Amount of $(COOH)_2$ in solution $= \frac{5}{2} \times 2.360 \times 10^{-3} = 5.900 \times 10^{-3}$ mol

M of hydrated oxalic acid $= \frac{0.7439}{5.900 \times 10^{-3}} = 126.08$ g mol^{-1}

M of $(COOH)_2.xH_2O = (2 \times 12.01) + (4 \times 16.00) + (2 \times 1.01) + x(18.02)$

$= 90.04 + 18.02x = 126.08$ g mol^{-1}

$x = \frac{(126.08 - 90.04)}{18.02} = 2$. Therefore, the formula of hydrated oxalic acid is $(COOH)_2.2H_2O$

Relative ease of oxidation and reduction

Activity series for metals and hydrogen

Lithium, sodium, and potassium all react with cold water to give similar products but the reactivity increases down the group.

$2M(s) + 2H_2O(l) \rightarrow 2M^+(aq) + 2OH^-(aq) + H_2(g)$
(M = Li, Na, or K)

Slightly less reactive metals react with steam and release hydrogen with dilute acids, e.g.

$Mg(s) + 2H_2O(g) \rightarrow Mg(OH)_2 + H_2(g)$

$Mg(s) + 2HCl(aq) \rightarrow Mg^{2+}(aq) + 2Cl^-(aq) + H_2(g)$

$Fe(s) + H_2SO_4(aq) \rightarrow FeSO_4(aq) + H_2(g)$

In all of these reactions the metal is losing electrons so it is being oxidized and, in the process, it is acting as a reducing agent. You can deduce an activity series of reducing agents by considering the reactivity of metals with water and acids, and the reactions of metals with the ions of other metals.

You can base an activity series on the total energy change that occurs, including the hydration of the ions formed. This has lithium metal at the top. The simplified series follows the order:

Li > K > Ca > Na > Mg > Al > Zn > Fe > Sn > Pb > H > Cu > Ag > Au

Alternatively, if you take into account how vigorously the metals react, the activity series has potassium metal at the top, although from magnesium onwards the orders are the same.

K > Na > Li > Ca > Mg > Al > Zn > Fe > Sn > Pb > H > Cu > Ag > Au

This makes more sense in terms of the observation that potassium metal is much more reactive with water than lithium. It also fits in with the trend in the periodic table that as the group is descended the outer electron is easier to remove. However, ionization energies are measured in the gaseous state and the smaller lithium ion, $Li^+(g)$, has a much larger hydration energy when it forms $Li^+(aq)$ than the potassium ion, $K^+(g)$, does when it forms $K^+(aq)$. The reaction of lithium with water actually gives out more energy than the reaction of potassium with water but over a longer period of time.

Metals higher in the series can displace metal ions lower in the series from solution, e.g. zinc metal can react with copper ions to form zinc ions and precipitate copper metal.

$Zn(s) + Cu^{2+}(aq) \rightarrow Zn^{2+}(aq) + Cu(s)$

$Zn(s) \rightarrow Zn^{2+}(aq) + 2e^-$	Zn loses electrons in preference to Cu
$Cu^{2+}(aq) + 2e^- \rightarrow Cu(s)$	Cu^{2+} gains electrons in preference to Zn^{2+}

This also explains why only metals above hydrogen can react with acids (displace hydrogen ions) to produce hydrogen gas, e.g.

$Zn(s) + 2H^+(aq) \rightarrow Zn^{2+}(aq) + H_2(g)$

Activity series for oxidizing agents

When a metal high in the series displaces metal ions from a metal lower in the activity series, it can be seen that the series lists the metals in terms of their reducing ability. The higher the metal in the series the better the reducing agent, so the alkali metals are excellent reducing agents. At the same time, the metals higher in the series are being oxidized by the ions of metals lower in the series, so copper(II) ions, $Cu^{2+}(aq)$, and silver(I) ions, $Ag^+(aq)$, are good oxidizing agents as they readily gain electrons.

The best oxidizing agents, however, are non-metals. Fluorine is the strongest oxidizing agent of all and is a dangerous substance as it oxidizes most materials it comes into contact with. As can be predicted from their position in the periodic table, the halogens (group 17 elements) readily gain an electron to form the halide ion, so they are all good oxidizing agents. Their oxidizing ability decreases as the group is descended as the outer energy level gets further away from the nucleus.

This means that chlorine, for example, can oxidize both bromide ions and iodide ions. Bromine can oxidize iodide ions and although iodine can oxidize metals such as sodium it cannot oxidize the ions of the other common halogens even though it could be predicted that it could oxidize astatide ions, At^-, and tennesside ions, Ts^-.

Oxidizing ability of the halogens

$I^-(aq) \rightleftharpoons e^- + \frac{1}{2}I_2(aq)$

$Br^-(aq) \rightleftharpoons e^- + \frac{1}{2}Br_2(aq)$

$Cl^-(aq) \rightleftharpoons e^- + \frac{1}{2}Cl_2(aq)$

$F^-(aq) \rightleftharpoons e^- + \frac{1}{2}F_2(aq)$

Increasing oxidizing ability ↓

Oxidizing agents lower in the series gain electrons from species higher in the series e.g.

$Cl_2(aq) + 2Br^-(aq) \rightarrow 2Cl^-(aq) + Br_2(aq)$

Electrochemical cells

Simple voltaic cells

A **half-cell** is simply a metal in contact with an aqueous solution of its own ions. A **primary voltaic cell** consists of two different half-cells, connected together to enable the electrons transferred during the redox reaction to produce energy in the form of electricity. The cells are connected by an external wire and by a **salt bridge**. The salt bridge allows the free movement of ions. A salt bridge is often a filter paper or glass tube with a saturated solution of KNO_3.

A good example of a primary voltaic cell is a zinc half-cell connected to a copper half-cell. Because zinc is more reactive, the electrons flow from the zinc half-cell towards the copper half-cell. To complete the circuit and to keep the half-cells electrically neutral, ions flow through the salt bridge. The voltage produced by a voltaic cell depends on the relative difference between the two metals in the activity series. Thus the voltage from an $Mg(s)/Mg^{2+}(aq)$ half-cell connected to a $Cu(s)/Cu^{2+}(aq)$ half-cell will be greater than that obtained from a $Zn(s)/Zn^{2+}(aq)$ half-cell connected to an $Fe(s)/Fe^{2+}(aq)$ half-cell.

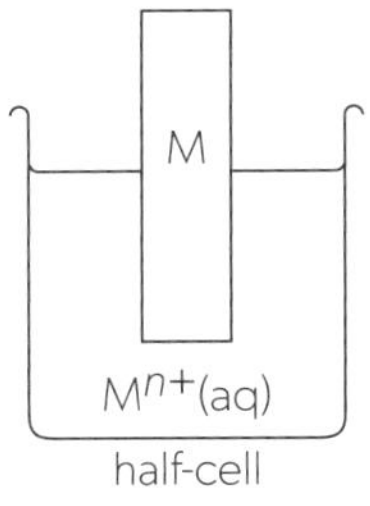

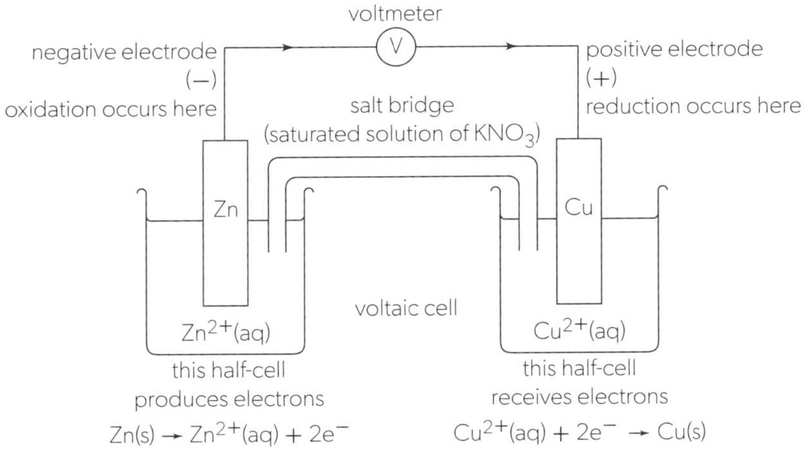

Convention for writing cells

By convention, in a cell diagram the half-cell undergoing oxidation is placed on the left of the diagram and the half-cell undergoing reduction is placed on the right of the diagram. The two aqueous solutions are then placed either side of the salt bridge.

To save drawing out the whole cell, a shorthand notation has been adopted. A half-cell is denoted by a / between the metal and its ions, and two vertical lines are used to denote the salt bridge between the two half-cells.

e.g. $Zn(s)/Zn^{2+}(aq) \,||\, Cu^{2+}(aq)/Cu(s)$

$Cu(s)/Cu^{2+}(aq) \,||\, H^+(aq)/H_2(g)$

$Zn(s)/Zn^{2+}(aq) \,||\, H^+(aq)/H_2(g)$

The words "cathode" and "anode" can also be used to describe the electrodes. The anode is where oxidation occurs and the cathode is where reduction occurs. Note that, for a voltaic cell, the anode is the negative electrode but for an electrolytic cell (see page 123), where the electricity is provided from an external source, the anode is the positive electrode; this can cause some confusion.

Batteries

A battery is a general term for an electrochemical cell in which chemical energy is converted into electrical energy. The electrons transferred in the spontaneous redox reaction taking place in the voltaic cell produce the electricity. Batteries are a useful way to store and transport relatively small amounts of energy. Some batteries (primary cells), such as the carbon–zinc dry cell, can only be used once as the electrochemical reaction taking place is irreversible. Secondary cells can be recharged, as the redox reactions involved can be reversed using electricity. Examples of rechargeable batteries include lead–acid, nickel–cadmium, and lithium-ion batteries. A third type of cell in which the reactants are continually supplied is the fuel cell, which is covered on page 83.

The voltage of a battery is essentially the difference in electrode potential between the two half-cells. It depends only on the nature of the chemical components of the two half-cells. By combining two cells in series, the voltage can be doubled. Three cells in series will triple the voltage, etc. The power of a battery (i.e. the total work that can be obtained from the cell) is the rate at which it can deliver energy and is measured in joules per second. It is affected both by the size of the cell and the physical quantities of the materials present. An electrochemical cell has internal resistance due to the finite time it takes for ions to diffuse. The maximum current of a cell is limited by its internal resistance.

Examples of primary and secondary cells

Primary cell: carbon–zinc dry cell

The common dry cell contains a paste of ammonium chloride and manganese(IV) oxide as the electrolyte. The positive electrode (cathode) is made of graphite (often with a brass cap) and the zinc casing is the negative electrode (anode). A porous separator acts as a salt bridge. When the cell is working, electrons flow from the zinc to the graphite.

Oxidation at anode (–) $Zn \rightarrow Zn^{2+} + 2e^-$

Reduction at cathode (+) $MnO_2 + NH_4^+ + e^- \rightarrow MnO(OH) + NH_3$

The ammonia then reacts with the zinc ions to form $[Zn(NH_3)_4]^{2+}$. This prevents a build up of ammonia gas.

A carbon–zinc dry cell produces 1.5 volts when new. In addition to having to replace the battery when it wears out, it has a poor shelf-life and the acidic ammonium chloride can corrode the zinc casing.

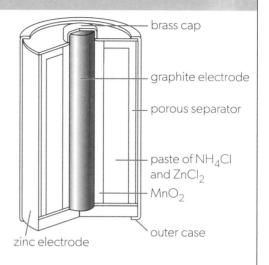

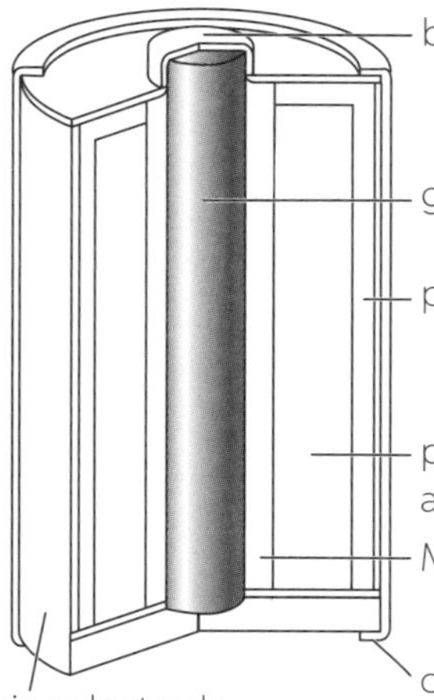

Secondary (rechargeable) cells

Lead–acid battery

The lead–acid battery is used in automobiles and is an example of a secondary cell. Usually, it consists of six cells in series producing a total voltage of 12 V. The electrolyte is an aqueous solution of sulfuric acid. The negative electrodes are made of lead and the positive electrodes are made of lead(IV) oxide.

Oxidation at anode (–) $Pb + SO_4^{2-} \rightarrow PbSO_4 + 2e^-$

Reduction at cathode (+) $PbO_2 + 4H^+ + SO_4^{2-} + 2e^- \rightarrow PbSO_4 + 2H_2O$

The overall reaction taking place is thus:

$Pb + PbO_2 + 4H^+ + 2SO_4^{2-} \rightarrow 2PbSO_4 + 2H_2O$

The reverse reaction takes place during charging. This can be done using a battery charger or through the alternator as the automobile is being driven. As sulfuric acid is used up during discharging, the density of the electrolyte can be measured using a hydrometer to give an indication of the state of the battery. The disadvantages of lead–acid batteries are that they are heavy and both lead and sulfuric acid are potentially polluting.

During recharging, hydrogen and oxygen are evolved from the electrolysis of dilute H_2SO_4, so lead–acid batteries need topping up occasionally with distilled water.

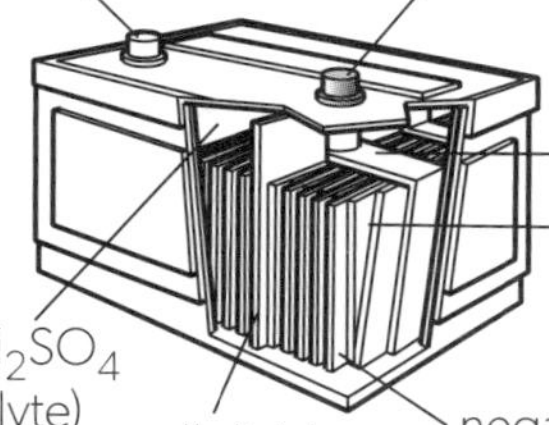

Nickel–cadmium and lithium-ion batteries

Rechargeable nickel–cadmium (NiCd) batteries are used in electronics and toys. They have a cell potential of 1.2 V. The positive electrode is made of nickel hydroxide, which is separated from the negative electrode made of cadmium hydroxide. The electrolyte is potassium hydroxide. During discharge, the following reaction occurs:

$2NiO(OH) + Cd + 2H_2O \rightarrow 2Ni(OH)_2 + Cd(OH)_2$

This process is reversed during charging. One of the disadvantages of NiCd batteries is that cadmium is an extremely toxic heavy metal, so the batteries need to be disposed of responsibly.

Laptops, tablets, smart phones, and other handheld devices often use lithium-ion batteries. These contain lithium atoms complexed to other ions, e.g. Li_xCoO_2, in the positive electrode and it is these ions rather than lithium itself that undergo the redox reactions. The negative electrode is made of graphite. Lithium-ion batteries are much lighter than NiCd batteries and produce a higher voltage, 3.6–4.2 V, but they do not have such a long lifespan.

Electrolytic cells

Electrolytic cells

In a voltaic cell, electricity is produced by the spontaneous redox reaction taking place. Electrolytic cells are used to make non-spontaneous redox reactions occur by providing energy in the form of electricity from an external source. In an electrolytic cell, direct electric current is passed through an electrolyte and electrical energy is converted into chemical energy. An electrolyte is a substance that does not conduct electricity when solid, but does conduct electricity when molten or in aqueous solution and is chemically decomposed in the process. A simple example of an electrolytic cell is the electrolysis of molten sodium chloride.

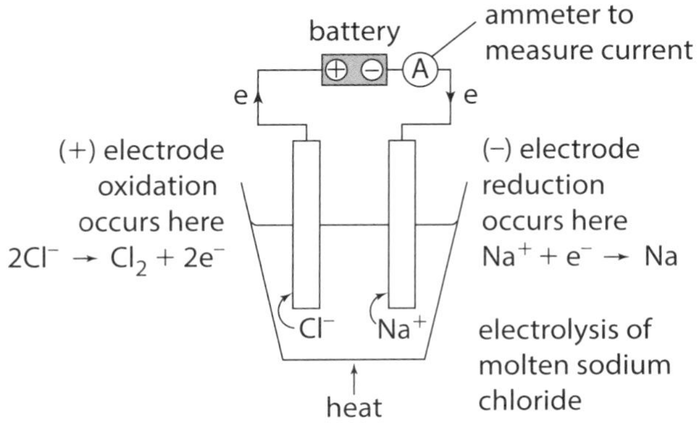

During the electrolysis:

- sodium is formed at the negative electrode (cathode)

  $Na^+(l) + e^- \rightarrow Na(l)$ reduction
- chlorine is formed at the positive electrode (anode)

  $2Cl^-(l) \rightarrow Cl_2(g) + 2e^-$ oxidation
- The current is due to the movement of electrons in the external circuit and the movement of ions in the electrolyte.

Electrolysis is an important industrial process that is used to obtain reactive metals, such as sodium, from their common ores.

AHL

Electroplating and refining

Electrolysis can also be used in industry to coat one metal with a layer of another metal. This process is known as **electroplating**. For example, many metal objects are made shiny and protected from oxidation by coating with a layer of chromium—a process known as chrome plating. The object to be chrome plated is used as the cathode and the anode is made from a piece of chromium metal. The electrolyte used is normally a solution of chromium(III) sulfate or chromium(III) chloride. (A solution of Cr(VI) ions can also be used but Cr(VI) ions are extremely toxic.)

As the electrolysis proceeds, the concentration of the electrolyte remains constant as the chromium metal anode is oxidized to $Cr^{3+}(aq)$ while simultaneously chromium metal is deposited at the cathode to form a thin uniform layer of chromium on the selected object.

Anode reaction: $Cr(s) \rightarrow Cr^{3+}(aq) + 3e^-$

Cathode reaction: $Cr^{3+}(aq) + 3e^- \rightarrow Cr(s)$

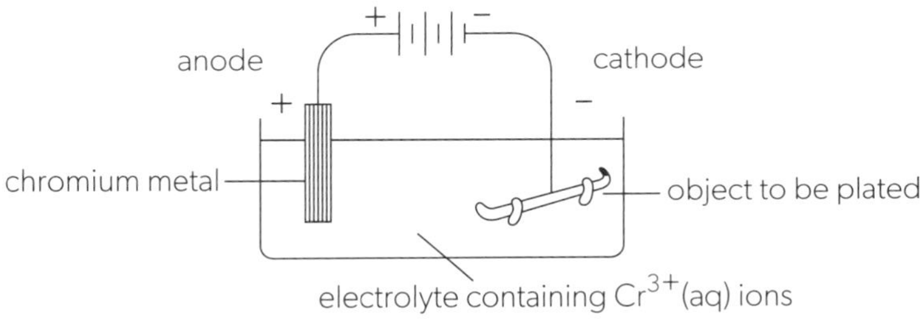

▲ Chrome plating

Similarly, in copper plating, the negative electrode (cathode) is made from the metal to be copper plated. It is placed into a solution of copper(II) sulfate, $CuSO_4(aq)$, together with a positive electrode (anode) made from a piece of copper. As electricity is passed through the solution, the copper anode dissolves in the solution to form $Cu^{2+}(aq)$ ions and the $Cu^{2+}(aq)$ ions in solution are deposited onto the cathode. If the anode is made of impure copper and the cathode from a small piece of pure copper, this process can also be used to purify impure copper. This refining of copper is an important industrial process. One of the main uses of copper is for electrical wiring where purity is important because impure copper has a much higher electrical resistance.

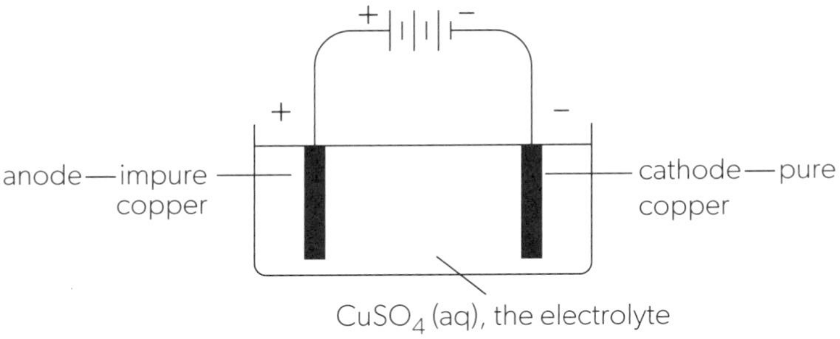

▲ Refining of copper

AHL

Standard electrode potentials and the electrochemical series

Standard electrode potentials, $E^\ominus$

There are two opposing tendencies in a half-cell. The metal may dissolve in the solution of its own ions to leave the metal with a negative potential compared with the solution, or the metal ions may deposit on the metal, which will give the metal a positive potential compared with the solution. It is impossible to measure this potential, as any attempt to do so interferes with the system being investigated. However, the electrode potential of one half-cell can be compared against another half-cell. The hydrogen half-cell is normally used as the standard. Under standard conditions of 100 kPa pressure, 298 K, and 1.0 mol dm^{-3} hydrogen ion concentration, the standard electrode potential, $E^\ominus$, of the hydrogen electrode is assigned a value of zero volts.

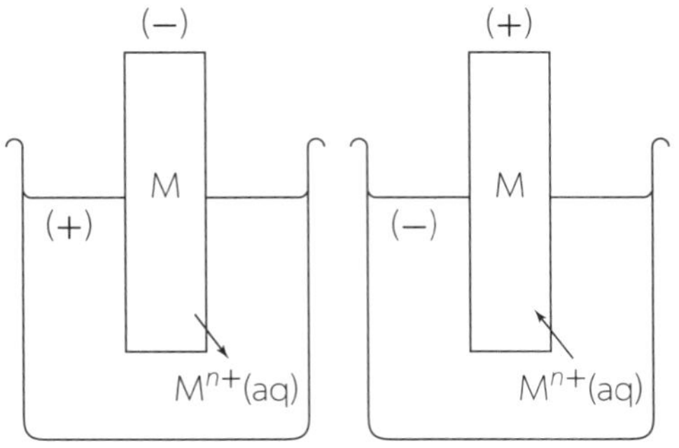

$$H^+(aq) + e^- \rightleftharpoons \tfrac{1}{2}H_2(g) \qquad E^\ominus = 0.00\,V$$

When the half-cell contains a metal above hydrogen in the reactivity series, electrons flow from the half-cell to the hydrogen electrode, and the electrode potential is given a negative value. If the half-cell contains a metal below hydrogen in the reactivity series, electrons flow from the hydrogen electrode to the half-cell, and the electrode potential has a positive value. The standard reduction potentials are arranged in increasing order to form the electrochemical series.

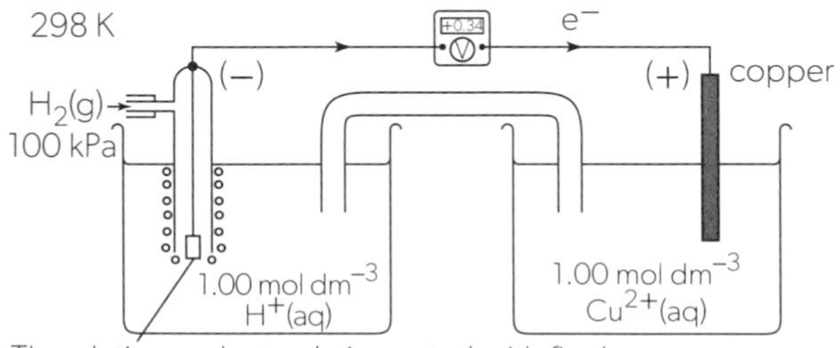

The platinum electrode is coated with finely-divided platinum, which serves as a catalyst for the electrode reaction.

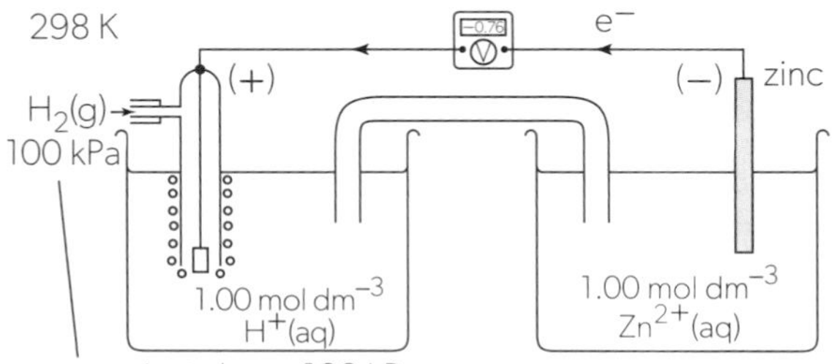

pressure just above 100 kPa so H_2 can escape from electrode

Electrochemical series

Half-cells are listed in the electrochemical series according to the value of their standard reduction potentials. In the IB data booklet, in Table 19, they are listed with a reversible equilibrium arrow between the two species:

e.g. $Mg^{2+}(s) + 2e^- \rightleftharpoons Mg(s) \quad E^\ominus = -2.37\,V$

The oxidized species is written as the reactant and the reduced species as the product. The problem with a reversible equilibrium arrow is that if the reaction is written the other way round, i.e. $Mg(s) \rightleftharpoons Mg^{2+}(s) + 2e^-$, it is tempting to think that the sign of $E^\ominus$ will be reversed so that $E^\ominus = +2.37\,V$. This is not the case, as the value of $E^\ominus$ refers to the value obtained when the half-cell (which consists of both the oxidized and the reduced species) is connected to the standard hydrogen electrode. It is better to think of a magnesium half-cell simply as magnesium in contact with magnesium ions and it is often written either as $Mg(s)/Mg^{2+}(aq)$ or as $Mg^{2+}(aq)/Mg$. What is important is that the metals are listed in order of their reducing ability (i.e. lithium is the strongest reducing agent), whereas at the bottom of the table the oxidized form shows the species in order of increasing oxidizing ability (so fluorine is the strongest oxidizing agent).

Note the position of water and hydrogen ions. $H_2O/\tfrac{1}{2}H_2(g) + OH^-(aq)$ has an $E^\ominus$ value of −0.83 V so only metal/metal ion systems with more negative values than this (i.e. metals including manganese and above) can spontaneously react with water to release hydrogen. Contrast this to the $E^\ominus$ value of 0 V for $H^+(aq)/\tfrac{1}{2}H_2(g)$, which means that all metals with a negative $E^\ominus$ value can react spontaneously with acids to produce hydrogen, whereas copper cannot, as $E^\ominus$ for $Cu(s)/Cu^{2+}(aq)$ is +0.34 V.

AHL Spontaneity of electrochemical reactions

Standard cell potential

The standard cell potential (also known as standard electromotive force, emf) of any cell, $E^\ominus_{cell}$, is simply the difference between the standard reduction potentials of the two half-cells:

e.g. $Zn(s)/Zn^{2+}(aq)$ || $Cu^{2+}(aq)/Cu(s)$

$E^\ominus = -0.76\,V$ $E^\ominus = +0.34\,V$

$E^\ominus_{cell} = 1.10\,V$

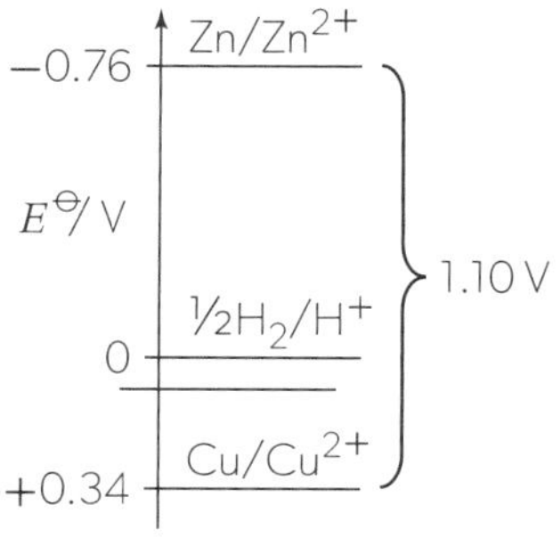

Electron flow, spontaneous reactions and free energy

By using standard potentials, it is easy to see what will happen when two half-cells are connected together. The electrons will always flow from the more negative half-cell to the more positive half-cell. For example, consider an iron half-cell connected to a magnesium half-cell:

e^-

$Mg(s)/Mg^{2+}(aq)$	|| $Fe^{2+}(aq)/Fe(s)$
$E^\ominus = -2.37\,V$	$E^\ominus = -0.45\,V$
more negative	more positive
$Mg \rightarrow Mg^{2+} + 2e^-$	$Fe^{2+} + 2e^- \rightarrow Fe$

Spontaneous reaction:

$Mg(s) + Fe^{2+}(aq) \rightarrow Mg^{2+}(aq) + Fe(s)$ $E^\ominus_{cell} = 1.92\,V$

From the expression $\Delta G^\ominus = -nFE^\ominus$ it can be seen that positive $E^\ominus_{cell}$ values give negative $\Delta G^\ominus$ values, which is obvious as the cell is producing electrical energy that can do work as the reaction is spontaneous. The actual amount of energy can be calculated as F is one faraday, and has a value equal to $9.65 \times 10^4\,C\,mol^{-1}$, and 1 joule = 1 volt × 1 coulomb.

Using the example above, the transfer of two mol of electrons is involved so:

$\Delta G^\ominus = -2\,(mol) \times 9.65 \times 10^4\,(C\,mol^{-1}) \times 1.92\,(V)$
$= -3.71 \times 10^5\,J = -371\,kJ$

The reverse reaction ($Fe(s) + Mg^{2+}(aq) \rightarrow Fe^{2+}(aq) + Mg(s)$) has a negative $E^\ominus_{cell}$ value, which gives a positive value of +371 kJ for $\Delta G^\ominus$. This means that the reaction will not be spontaneous: it will only proceed if an external source of energy is provided greater than 371 kJ, i.e. a voltage greater than 1.92 V is supplied to force the reaction in the opposite direction. It is worth noting that just because a reaction is thermodynamically spontaneous (i.e. has a negative $\Delta G^\ominus$ value) this does not mean it will necessarily proceed: the reaction may have a large activation energy that first needs to be overcome.

Spontaneous redox reactions in acid solution

Standard electrode potentials can be extended to cover any half-equation. The values, which can be found in the IB data booklet, can then be used to determine whether a particular reaction is spontaneous. For example, $Cr_2O_7^{2-}(aq)/Cr^{3+}(aq)$, $E^\ominus = +1.36\,V$, but this only takes place in acid solution, so hydrogen ions and water are required to balance the half-equation. Consider the reaction between acidified dichromate(VI) ions, $Cr_2O_7^{2-}(aq)$, and sulfite ions, $SO_3^{2-}(aq)$. Using standard electrode potentials the cell becomes:

e^-

$SO_3^{2-}(aq)/SO_4^{2-}(aq)$	|| $Cr_2O_7^{2-}(aq)/Cr^{3+}(aq)$
$E^\ominus = +0.17\,V$	$E^\ominus = +1.36\,V$
more negative	more positive
SO_3^{2-} will lose electrons	$Cr_2O_7^{2-}$ will gain electrons
$SO_3^{2-} + H_2O \rightarrow SO_4^{2-} + 2H^+ + 2e^-$	$Cr_2O_7^{2-} + 14H^+ + 6e^- \rightarrow 2Cr^{3+} + 7H_2O$

As previously explained, to obtain the overall equation the number of electrons in both half-equations must be equal. This is achieved by multiplying the sulfite equation by three. The two equations are then added together and the water and hydrogen ions, which appear on both sides, are simplified. This gives:

$Cr_2O_7^{2-}(aq) + 8H^+(aq) + 3SO_3^{2-}(aq)$
$\rightarrow 2Cr^{3+}(aq) + 3SO_4^{2-}(aq) + 4H_2O(l)$ $E^\ominus_{cell} = 1.19\,V$

The acid that is normally added to supply the $H^+(aq)$ ions is sulfuric acid, since acidified dichromate ions cannot oxidize sulfate ions. The standard electrode potential for the $\frac{1}{2}Cl_2(aq)/Cl^-(aq)$ half-cell is +1.36 V. This is exactly the same as the value for the $Cr_2O_7^{2-}(aq)/Cr^{3+}(aq)$ half-cell. Under standard conditions, dichromate ions will not oxidize chloride ions from hydrochloric acid to chlorine but, if the conditions are changed slightly, this may no longer be true. For this reason, hydrochloric acid should never be used to acidify the solution of dichromate ions.

AHL

Electrolysis

Factors affecting the discharge of ions during electrolysis

During the electrolysis of molten salts there are usually only two ions present, so the cation will be discharged at the negative electrode (cathode) and the anion at the positive electrode (anode). However, for aqueous electrolytes there will also be hydrogen ions and hydroxide ions from the water present. There are three main factors that influence which ions are discharged at their respective electrodes.

1. Value of the standard reduction potential

The lower the metal ion is in the electrochemical series, i.e. the more positive its standard reduction potential, the more readily it will gain electrons (be reduced) to form the metal at the cathode. Thus, in the electrolysis of a solution of sodium hydroxide, hydrogen will be evolved at the negative electrode in preference to sodium, whereas in a solution of copper(II) sulfate, copper will be deposited at the negative electrode in preference to hydrogen.

For negative ions, the order of discharge follows $OH^- > Cl^- > SO_4^{2-}$.

2. Concentration

If one of the ions is much more concentrated than another ion, then it may be preferentially discharged. For example, when electricity is passed through an aqueous solution of sodium chloride both oxygen and chlorine are evolved at the positive electrode. For dilute solutions mainly oxygen is evolved, but for concentrated solutions of sodium chloride more chlorine than oxygen is evolved.

3. The nature of the electrode

It is normally safe to assume that the electrodes are inert, i.e. do not play any part in the reaction. However, if copper electrodes are used during the electrolysis of a solution of copper sulfate, then the positive electrode is itself oxidized to release electrons and form copper(II) ions. Since copper is simultaneously deposited at the negative electrode, the concentration of the solution will remain constant throughout the electrolysis.

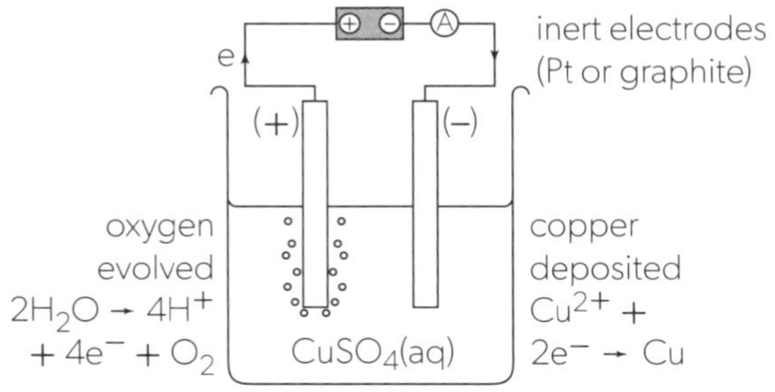

solution loses blue colour and forms sulfuric acid

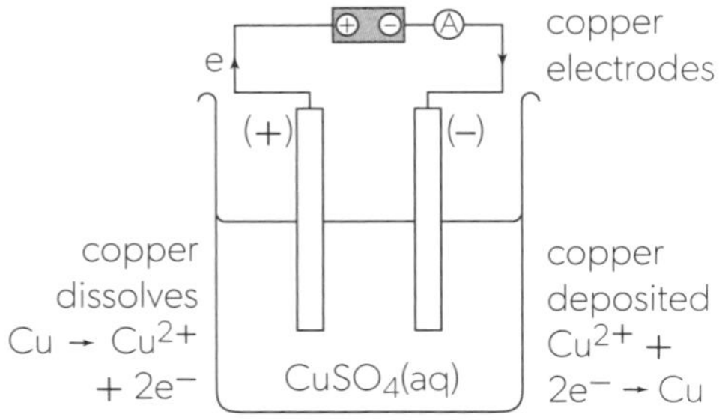

solution retains blue colour

Factors affecting the quantity of products discharged during electrolysis

The amount of substance deposited will depend on the following.

1. The number of electrons flowing through the system, i.e. the amount of charge passed. This, in turn, depends on the current and the time for which it flows. If the current is doubled, then twice as many electrons pass through the system and twice as much product will be formed. Similarly, if the time is doubled, twice as many electrons will pass through the system and twice as much product will be formed.

   charge = current × time

   (1 coulomb = 1 ampere × 1 second)

2. The charge on the ion. To form one mole of sodium in the electrolysis of molten sodium chloride requires one mole of electrons to flow through the cell. However, the formation of one mole of lead during the electrolysis of molten lead(II) bromide requires two moles of electrons.

   $Na^+(l) + e^- \rightarrow Na(l)$ $Pb^{2+}(l) + 2e^- \rightarrow Pb(l)$

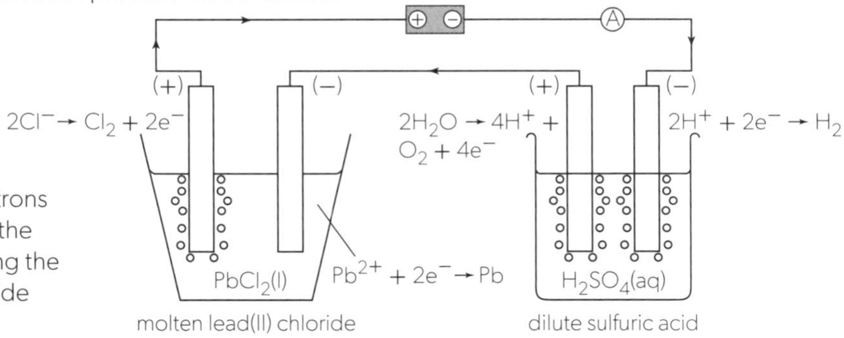

molar ratios of products evolved $2Cl_2 : 2Pb : O_2 : 2H_2$

If cells are connected in series, then the same amount of electricity will pass through both cells and the relative amounts of the products obtained can be determined.

Oxidation of organic functional groups

Combustion

Ethanol is used both as a solvent and as a fuel. Like all alcohols, it combusts completely in a plentiful supply of oxygen to give carbon dioxide and water.

$$C_2H_5OH(l) + 3O_2(g) \rightarrow 2CO_2(g) + 3H_2O(l) \qquad \Delta H^{\ominus} = -1371\ kJ\ mol^{-1}$$

Ethanol is already partially oxidized, so it releases less energy when burned than an alkane of comparable mass. However, it can be obtained by the fermentation of biomass, so in some countries it is mixed with petrol to produce "gasohol", which decreases the dependence on crude oil.

The general equation for any alcohol combusting completely in oxygen is:

$C_nH_{(2n+1)}OH + (2n-1)O_2 \rightarrow nCO_2 + (n+1)H_2O$

Oxidation of alcohols

The oxidation reactions of alcohols can be used to distinguish between primary, secondary, and tertiary alcohols.

In a primary alcohol, the carbon atom bonded to the –OH group is bonded to one alkyl group and two hydrogen atoms. All primary alcohols are oxidized by acidified potassium dichromate(VI), first to aldehydes and then to carboxylic acids.

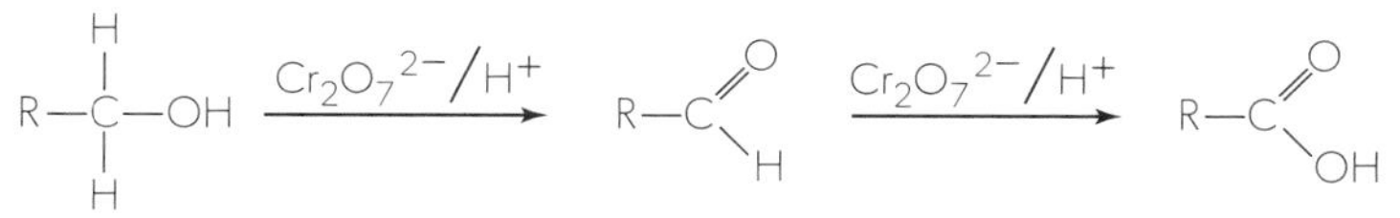

primary alcohol aldehyde carboxylic acid

Secondary alcohols are oxidized to ketones, which cannot undergo further oxidation.

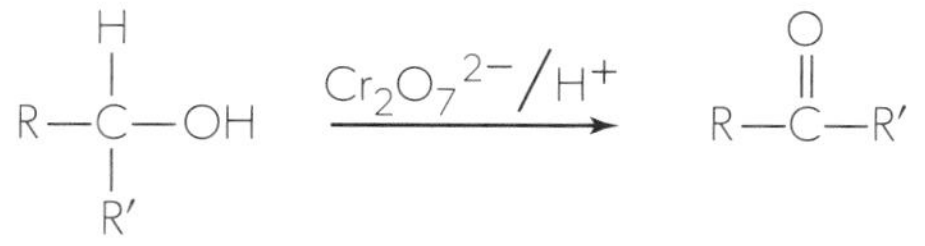

secondary alcohol ketone

Tertiary alcohols cannot be oxidized by acidified dichromate(VI) ions as they have no hydrogen atoms attached directly to the carbon atom containing the –OH group. It is not true to say that tertiary alcohols can never be oxidized, as they burn readily, but when this happens the carbon chain is destroyed.

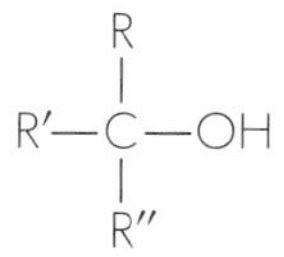

tertiary alcohol

Example: oxidation of ethanol

Ethanol can be readily oxidized by warming with an acidified solution of potassium dichromate(VI). During the process, the orange dichromate(VI) ion, $Cr_2O_7^{2-}$, is reduced from an oxidation state of +6 to the green Cr^{3+} ion. This is utilised in simple breathalyser tests, where a motorist who is suspected of having exceeded the alcohol limit blows into a bag containing crystals of potassium dichromate(VI).

Ethanol is initially oxidized to ethanal.

$3CH_3CH_2OH(aq) + Cr_2O_7^{2-}(aq) + 8H^+(aq) \rightarrow 3CH_3CHO(aq) + 2Cr^{3+}(aq) + 7H_2O(l)$

The ethanal is then oxidized further to ethanoic acid.

$3CH_3CHO(aq) + Cr_2O_7^{2-}(aq) + 8H^+(aq) \rightarrow 3CH_3COOH(aq) + 2Cr^{3+}(aq) + 4H_2O(l)$

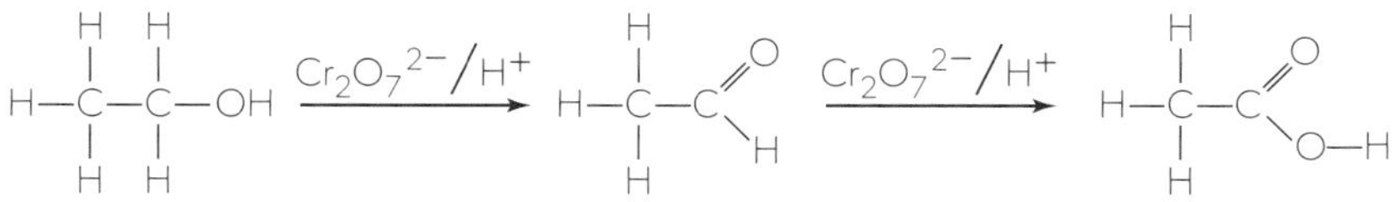

ethanol ("wine") ethanal ethanoic acid ("vinegar")

Unlike ethanol (b. pt 78.5 °C) and ethanoic acid (b. pt 118 °C), ethanal (b. pt 20.8 °C) does not have hydrogen bonding between its molecules, and so has a lower boiling point. To stop the reaction at the aldehyde stage, the ethanal can be distilled from the reaction mixture as soon as it is formed. If the complete oxidation to ethanoic acid is required, then the mixture can be heated under reflux so that none of the ethanal can escape. The experimental set-ups for distillation and reflux are shown on page 2.

Reduction of organic functional groups

Reduction of carbonyl compounds

The reduction reactions of aldehydes and ketones are the reverse of the oxidation reactions of primary and secondary alcohols. Aldehydes are reduced to primary alcohols and ketones are reduced to secondary alcohols.

There are two inorganic reducing agents that are commonly used to reduce carbonyl compounds. These are lithium aluminium hydride (IUPAC name: lithium tetrahydridoaluminate(III)), $LiAlH_4$, and sodium borohydride (IUPAC name: sodium tetrahydridoborate(III)), $NaBH_4$. Both effectively provide a source of H^- (hydride) ions that act as a nucleophile when reacting with the electron-deficient carbon atom of the polar carbonyl group. $LiAlH_4$ is the stronger reducing agent and, unlike $NaBH_4$, can also reduce carboxylic acids to primary alcohols.

Examples

Reduction of an aldehyde to a primary alcohol

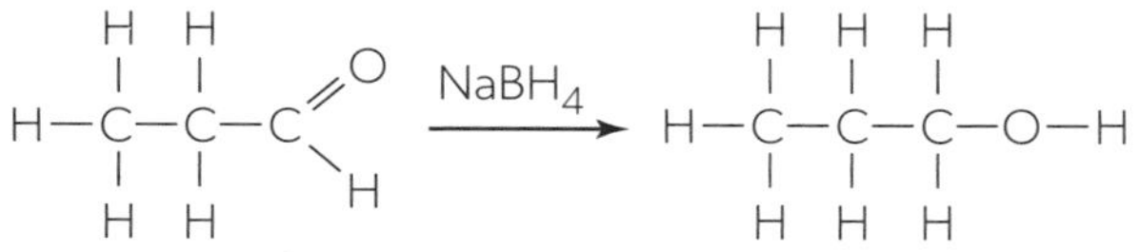

propanal → propan-1-ol

Reduction of a ketone to a secondary alcohol

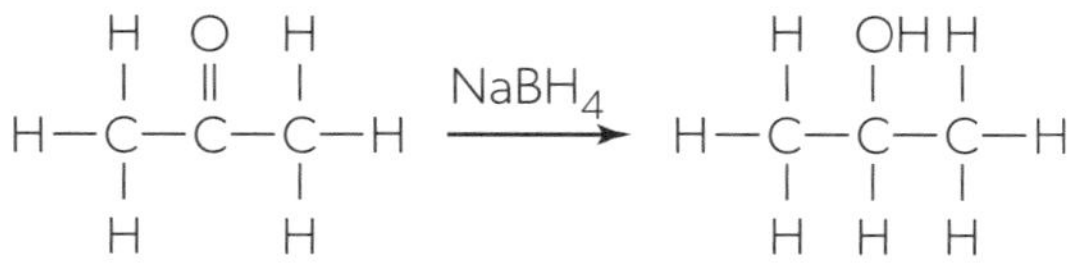

propanone → propan-2-ol

Reduction of a carboxylic acid to a primary alcohol. This reaction goes via the aldehyde.

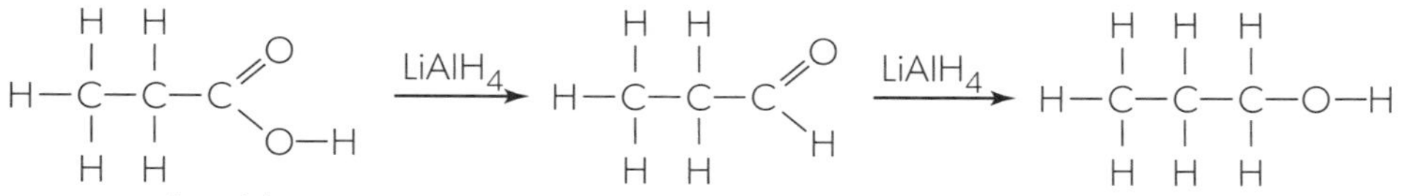

propanoic acid → propanal → propan-1-ol

Reduction of unsaturated compounds

Compounds containing a double or triple carbon to carbon bond, i.e. alkenes and alkynes, can be reduced directly with hydrogen with a nickel catalyst at 180 °C. This is an example of an addition reaction and the process is known as **hydrogenation**.

For example:

propene → propane

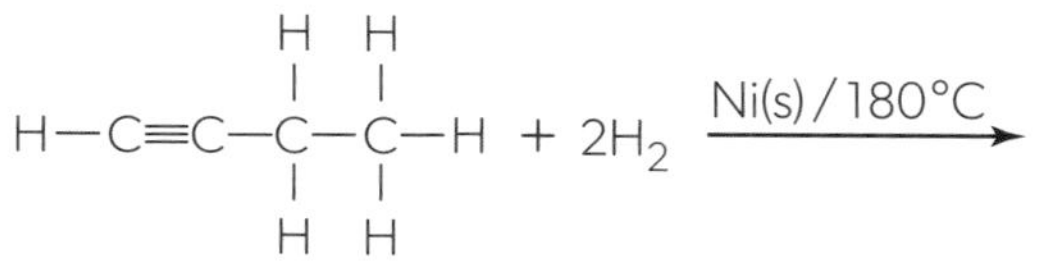

but-1-yne

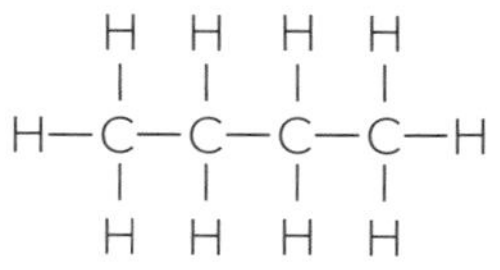

butane

During the process, the compounds have changed from being unsaturated to saturated, i.e. their degree of unsaturation has decreased.

Degree of unsaturation

The degree of unsaturation of a hydrocarbon can be ascertained either from its structural formula or from its molecular formula. Alkanes are saturated, that is, all the bonds around the carbon atoms are single bonds, and they have the general formula C_nH_{2n+2}.

Alkenes containing one double bond have the general formula C_nH_{2n}. Adding one mol of hydrogen, H_2, to one mol of the compound will make it saturated, so the degree of unsaturation is one.

Alkynes have the general formula C_nH_{2n-2} so a hydrocarbon containing one triple bond will have a degree of unsaturation of two as two mol of H_2 can be added to each mol of the hydrocarbon.

It gets a little more complicated when ring systems are involved. Cyclohexane is a cyclic hydrocarbon with the formula C_6H_{12}. If the ring system is broken down, then one mol of H_2 can be added to make it saturated with the formula C_6H_{14}, so the degree of unsaturation of cyclohexane is one. Benzene has the equivalent of three double bonds and is also a ring system, so its degree of unsaturation is four. This can be seen from its molecular formula (C_6H_6) as eight more hydrogen atoms (four mol of H_2) are required to make it saturated.

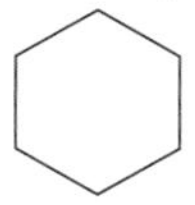

cyclohexane, C_6H_{12} degree of unsaturation = 1

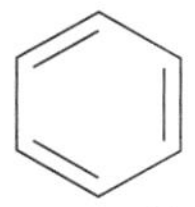

benzene, C_6H_6 degree of unsaturation = 4

Multiple-choice questions—Electron transfer reactions: oxidation–reduction behaviour

1. $5Fe^{2+}(aq) + MnO_4^-(aq) + 8H^+(aq) \rightarrow 5Fe^{3+}(aq) + Mn^{2+}(aq) + 4H_2O(l)$

   Which statement is true about the reaction above?

   A. $Fe^{2+}(aq)$ is the oxidizing agent.

   B. $H^+(aq)$ ions are reduced.

   C. $Fe^{2+}(aq)$ ions are oxidized.

   D. $MnO_4^-(aq)$ is the reducing agent.

2. What are the oxidation states of nitrogen in NH_3, HNO_3, and NO_2, respectively?

   A. −3, −5, +4   C. −3, +5, −4

   B. +3, +5, +4   D. −3, +5, +4

3. Which one of the following reactions is **not** a redox reaction?

   A. $Ag^+(aq) + Cl^-(aq) \rightarrow AgCl(s)$

   B. $2Na(s) + Cl_2(g) \rightarrow 2NaCl(s)$

   C. $Mg(s) + 2HCl(aq) \rightarrow MgCl_2(aq) + H_2(g)$

   D. $Cu^{2+}(aq) + Zn(s) \rightarrow Cu(s) + Zn^{2+}(aq)$

4. Which substance does **not** have the correct formula?

   A. iron(III) sulfate, $Fe_2(SO_4)_3$

   B. iron(II) oxide, Fe_2O

   C. copper(I) sulfate, Cu_2SO_4

   D. copper(II) nitrate, $Cu(NO_3)_2$

5. For which conversion is an oxidizing agent required?

   A. $2H^+(aq) \rightarrow H_2(g)$ C. $SO_3(g) \rightarrow SO_4^{2-}(aq)$

   B. $2Br^-(aq) \rightarrow Br_2(aq)$ D. $MnO_2(s) \rightarrow Mn^{2+}(aq)$

6. Ethanol can be oxidized to ethanal by an acidic solution of dichromate(VI) ions.

   $\_C_2H_5OH(aq) + \_H^+(aq) + \_Cr_2O_7^{2-}(aq) \rightarrow \_CH_3CHO(aq) + \_Cr^{3+}(aq) + \_H_2O(l)$

   What is the sum of all the coefficients in the balanced equation?

   A. 24   C. 28

   B. 26   D. 30

7. Which statement is true when an $Fe(s)/Fe^{2+}(aq)$ half-cell is connected to a $Cu(s)/Cu^{2+}(aq)$ half-cell by a salt bridge and a current is allowed to flow between them?

   A. The electrons will flow from the copper to the iron.

   B. The salt bridge allows the flow of ions to complete the circuit.

   C. The salt bridge allows the flow of electrons to complete the circuit.

   D. The salt bridge can be made of copper or iron.

8. Which statement is true during the electrolysis of molten sodium chloride using platinum electrodes?

   A. Sodium is formed at the negative electrode.

   B. Chlorine is formed at the negative electrode.

   C. Sodium is formed at the positive electrode.

   D. Oxygen is formed at the positive electrode.

9. Which statement is true?

   A. Lead chloride is ionic, so solid lead chloride will conduct electricity.

   B. When a molten ionic compound conducts electricity, free electrons pass through the liquid.

   C. When liquid mercury conducts electricity, mercury ions move towards the negative electrode.

   D. During the electrolysis of a molten salt, reduction will always occur at the negative electrode.

10. The following information is given about reactions involving the metals X, Y, and Z and solutions of their sulfates.

    $X(s) + YSO_4(aq) \rightarrow$ no reaction

    $Z(s) + YSO_4(aq) \rightarrow Y(s) + ZSO_4(aq)$

    When the metals are listed in **decreasing** order of reactivity (most reactive first), what is the correct order?

    A. Z > Y > X   C. Y > X > Z

    B. X > Y > Z   D. Y > Z > X

11. Which statement is correct when a spoon is chromium plated using the spoon as the cathode, a piece of chromium as the anode, and chromium(III) sulfate as the electrolyte?

    A. $[Cr^{3+}(aq)]$ decreases

    B. $Cr^{3+}(aq)$ is converted into $Cr^{2+}(aq)$

    C. $[Cr^{3+}(aq)]$ remains constant

    D. $[Cr^{3+}(aq)]$ increases

12. Which compound has a degree of unsaturation of 2?

    A. hexane   C. hex-1-yne

    B. hex-2-ene   D. cyclohexane

13. Which compound can be oxidized by warming with an acidified solution of potassium dichromate(VI)?

    A. $(CH_3)_3COH$ C. CH_3COCH_3

    B. CH_3CHO D. CH_3COOH

14. Which compound can be reduced to form a secondary alcohol?

    A. $(CH_3)_3COH$ C. CH_3COCH_3

    B. CH_3CHO D. CH_3COOH

15. What is prevented by distilling ethanal as soon as it is formed during its preparation from ethanol?

    A. Conversion of ethanal into ethanoic acid.

    B. Reverting ethanal back into ethanol.

    C. Further reduction of ethanal.

    D. Thermal decomposition of ethanal.

16. A half-cell made of metal X in a solution of its ions, $X^{2+}(aq)$, is connected via an external circuit and a salt bridge to another half-cell made of metal Y in a solution of its ions, $Y^{2+}(aq)$. If metal Y is more reactive than metal X, which is a true statement?

A. A thin layer of metal X will deposit on metal Y.

B. Electrons flow through the salt bridge from the $Y(s)/Y^{2+}(aq)$ half-cell to the $X(s)/X^{2+}(aq)$ half-cell.

C. The reaction occurring at the anode is $X^{2+}(aq) + 2e^- \rightarrow X(s)$

D. Metal Y will decrease in mass.

AHL

17. Which statements are correct for a spontaneous reaction occurring in a voltaic cell?

I. $E^\ominus$ for the cell has a positive value.

II. $\Delta G^\ominus$ for the reaction has a negative value.

III. The reaction must occur under standard conditions.

A. I and II only | C. II and III only

B. I and III only | D. I, II, and III

18. When the same quantity of electricity was passed through a dilute solution of sodium hydroxide and through a molten solution of lead bromide, 0.100 mol of lead was produced. What amount (in mol) of hydrogen gas was evolved?

A. 0.014 | C. 0.100

B. 0.050 | D. 0.200

Use this information for questions 19, 20, and 21.

$Sn^{2+}(aq) + 2e^- \rightleftharpoons Sn(s)$ $E^\ominus = -0.14\,V$

$Sn^{4+}(aq) + 2e^- \rightleftharpoons Sn^{2+}(aq)$ $E^\ominus = +0.15\,V$

$Fe^{2+}(aq) + 2e^- \rightleftharpoons Fe(s)$ $E^\ominus = -0.45\,V$

$Fe^{3+}(aq) + e^- \rightleftharpoons Fe^{2+}(aq)$ $E^\ominus = +0.77\,V$

19. Which is correct under standard conditions?

A. $Sn^{2+}(aq)$ can reduce $Fe^{3+}(aq)$.

B. Fe(s) can oxidize $Sn^{2+}(aq)$.

C. Sn(s) can reduce Fe(s).

D. $Fe^{3+}(aq)$ can reduce $Sn^{4+}(aq)$.

20. A half-cell of $Fe^{2+}(aq)/Fe^{3+}(aq)$ is connected by a salt bridge to a half-cell of $Sn^{2+}(aq)/Sn^{4+}(aq)$ under standard conditions and a current is allowed to flow in an external circuit. What is the total emf of the spontaneous reaction?

A. +0.92 V | C. +0.62 V

B. −0.92 V | D. −0.62 V

21. What is the standard electrode potential for the $Sn(s)/Sn^{2+}(aq)$ half-cell if the normal reference hydrogen electrode is exchanged for a standard $Fe(s)/Fe^{2+}(aq)$ electrode?

A. −0.59 V | C. +0.31 V

B. −0.31 V | D. +0.59 V

22. What are the major products when electricity is passed through a dilute solution of sodium chloride?

	Anode	Cathode
A.	oxygen	chlorine
B.	chlorine	hydrogen
C.	oxygen	hydrogen
D.	chlorine	oxygen

23. $E^\ominus_{cell}$ for the reaction between zinc metal and copper(II) ions in aqueous solution is +1.10 V. What is the value of the standard Gibbs energy change, $\Delta G^\ominus$, for this reaction (in kJ)? ($1\,F = 9.65 \times 10^4\,C\,mol^{-1}$)

A. $-2.20 \times F$ | C. $-1.10 \times 10^{-3} \times F$

B. $-2.20 \times 10^{-3} \times F$ | D. $-1.10 \times F$

24. Consider the two half-equations:

$Mn^{2+}(aq) + 2e^- \rightleftharpoons Mn(s)$ $E^\ominus = -1.18\,V$

$Pb^{2+}(aq) + 2e^- \rightleftharpoons Pb(s)$ $E^\ominus = -0.13\,V$

What is the value of $E^\ominus_{cell}$ (in volts) for the reaction

$Mn(s) + Pb^{2+}(aq) \rightarrow Mn^{2+}(aq) + Pb(s)$?

A. −1.31 B. +1.31 C. −1.05 D. +1.05

25. Which statements are correct when electricity is passed through a solution of copper(II) sulfate using platinum electrodes?

I. Copper is deposited at the cathode.

II. Oxygen is evolved at the anode.

III. As the electrolysis proceeds the solution becomes increasingly acidic.

A. I and II only | C. II and III only

B. I and III only | D. I, II, and III

26. Which statements are correct about the standard hydrogen electrode?

I. The solution is $1.00\,mol\,dm^{-3}\,H_2SO_4(aq)$.

II. The temperature is 298 K.

III. $E^\ominus = 0.00\,V$

A. I and II only | C. II and III only

B. I and III only | D. I, II, and III

27. Consider the two half-cells:

$Ni^{2+}(aq) + 2e^- \rightleftharpoons Ni(s)$ $E^\ominus = -0.26\,V$

$Sn^{2+}(aq) + 2e^- \rightleftharpoons Sn(s)$ $E^\ominus = -0.14\,V$

When the two half-cells are connected together to produce electricity, which species is the oxidizing agent?

A. $Sn^{2+}(aq)$ B. $Ni^{2+}(aq)$ C. Sn(s) D. Ni(s)

28. Two electrolytic cells, both with platinum electrodes, are connected in series. The first cell contains dilute sulfuric acid and the second cell contains molten zinc chloride. If the total amount of oxygen evolved is 1×10^{-2} mol, what amount (in mol) of zinc is formed?

A. 1×10^{-2} | C. 2×10^{-2}

B. 4×10^{-2} | D. 2.5×10^{-3}

Short-answer questions—Electron transfer reactions: oxidation–reduction behaviour

1. The data below is from an experiment used to determine the percentage of iron present in a sample of iron ore. This sample was dissolved in acid and all of the iron was converted to Fe^{2+}. The resulting solution was titrated with a standard solution of potassium manganate(VII), $KMnO_4$. This procedure was carried out three times. In acidic solution, MnO_4^- reacts with Fe^{2+} ions to form Mn^{2+} and Fe^{3+} and the end point is indicated by a slight pink colour.

Titre	1	2	3
Initial burette reading/cm^3	1.00	23.60	10.00
Final burette reading/cm^3	24.60	46.10	32.50

Mass of iron ore/g	3.682×10^{-1}
Concentration of $KMnO_4$ solution/mol dm^{-3}	2.152×10^{-2}

a) Deduce the balanced redox equation for this reaction in acidic solution. [2]

b) Identify the reducing agent in the reaction. [1]

c) Calculate the amount, in moles, of MnO_4^- used in the titration. [2]

d) Calculate the amount, in moles, of Fe present in the 3.682×10^{-1} g sample of iron ore. [2]

e) Determine the percentage by mass of Fe present in the 3.682×10^{-1} g sample of iron ore. [2]

2. Chemical energy can be converted to electrical energy in the voltaic cell below.

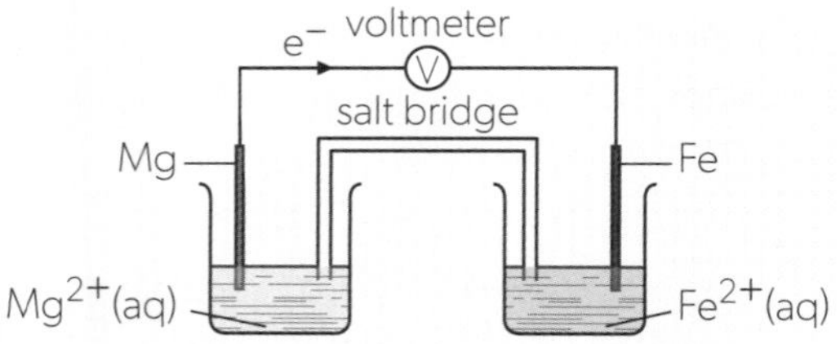

a) Explain how the diagram confirms that magnesium is above iron in the activity series. [2]

b) Identify the positive electrode (anode) of the cell. [1]

c) (i) State the half-equation for the reaction occurring at the iron electrode. [1]

(ii) State the overall equation for the reaction when the cell is producing electricity. [2]

d) Deduce whether the voltage produced by the cell would be greater or less if the iron half-cell was replaced by a copper half-cell. [2]

3. a) Molten sodium chloride can be electrolysed using graphite electrodes.

(i) Draw the essential components of this electrolytic cell and identify the products that form at each electrode. [2]

(ii) State the half-equations for the oxidation and reduction processes and deduce the overall cell reaction, including state symbols. [2]

b) Explain why solid sodium chloride does not conduct electricity. [1]

c) Using another electrolysis reaction, aluminium can be extracted from its ore, bauxite, which contains Al_2O_3. State one electrochemical reason why aluminium is often used instead of iron in many engineering applications. [1]

4. Iodine reacts with thiosulfate ions to form the tetrathionate ion according to the equation

$$I_2(aq) + 2S_2O_3^{2-}(aq) \rightarrow S_4O_6^{2-}(aq) + 2I^-(aq)$$

a) Show that this reaction is a redox reaction. [2]

b) The thiosulfate ion has a structure similar to the sulfate ion, SO_4^{2-}, except that one of the outer oxygen atoms has been replaced by a sulfur atom.

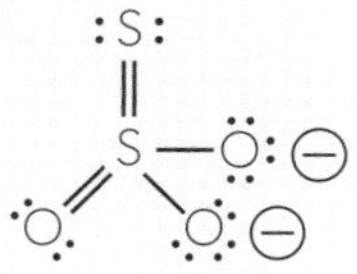

thiosulfate ion

(i) Comment on the difference in the oxidation state of sulfur in the thiosulfate ion compared with the sulfate ion. [2]

(ii) Explore the concept of oxidation state using the tetrathionate ion, $S_4O_6^{2-}$, as an example. [3]

c) Discuss whether the complete combustion of carbon in oxygen to form carbon dioxide can be described as the oxidation of carbon according to all the different definitions of oxidation. [4]

AHL

5. Consider the following two half-equations:

$Ag^+(aq) + e^- \rightleftharpoons Ag(s)$ $\quad E^\ominus = +0.80\,V$

$\frac{1}{2}Cl_2(g) + e^- \rightleftharpoons Cl^-(aq)$ $\quad E^\ominus = +1.36\,V$

a) Deduce the overall equation for the spontaneous reaction that will occur when a silver half-cell is connected to a chlorine half-cell. [2]

b) Identify the direction of electron flow in the external circuit when the cell is operating. [1]

c) Determine the cell potential, $E^\ominus_{cell}$. [1]

d) Calculate the free energy produced by the cell when it is operating under standard conditions. [2]

6. a) Identify the products that will be obtained at the positive (anode) and negative (cathode) electrodes when **(i)** a dilute solution and **(ii)** a concentrated solution of sodium chloride undergo electrolysis. [3]

b) Explain why the electrolysis of a dilute solution of sulfuric acid or a dilute solution of sodium hydroxide are both sometimes described as the electrolysis of water. [3]

c) Describe how you could use electrolysis to coat a spoon made of steel with a thin layer of silver. [2]

Free radical reactions

Homolytic fission

When covalent chemical bonds break, they may break heterolytically or homolytically. In **heterolytic fission** both of the electrons in the shared pair go to one of the atoms, resulting in a negative ion and a positive ion. In **homolytic fission** each of the two atoms forming the bond retains one of the electrons, resulting in the formation of two free radicals. Free radicals contain an unpaired electron and are very reactive. The movement of a pair of electrons can be shown using a "curly arrow". The movement of a single electron can be shown using an arrow with a single head, known as a "fishhook", and a radical is often shown with a dot to signify the unpaired electron.

$$A \overset{\frown}{\underset{x}{\bullet}} B \longrightarrow A^+ + \overset{\bullet}{\underset{x}{}} B^-$$

$$A \overset{\frown}{\underset{x}{\bullet}} B \longrightarrow \overset{\bullet}{\underset{x}{}} A^- + B^+$$

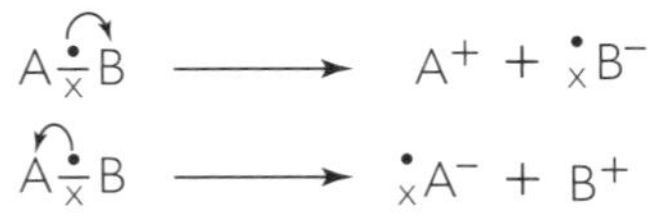

▲ Heterolytic fission: both bonding electrons move to one atom, forming a positive ion and a negative ion.

$$A \overset{\frown \frown}{\underset{x}{\bullet}} B \longrightarrow A^\bullet + B^\bullet$$

▲ Homolytic fission: each of the two bonding atoms retains one of the electrons, resulting in the formation of two free radicals.

Ultraviolet light can often provide the energy required for weaker bonds to break homolytically. For example:

$$Cl_2(g) \xrightarrow{UV} 2Cl\bullet(g)$$

Free radicals can be single atoms or a group of atoms, e.g. the methyl radical, $\bullet CH_3$, or the hydroxyl radical, $\bullet OH$. They can also be ions, such as the superoxide ion radical $O_2\bullet^-$.

Substitution reactions of alkanes

Alkanes tend to be quite unreactive because of their relatively strong C−C and C−H bonds and because they have low polarity. They only readily undergo combustion reactions with oxygen and substitution reactions with halogens in ultraviolet light. Examples of substitution reactions include the reaction of methane with chlorine to form chloromethane and the reaction of ethane with bromine to form bromoethane.

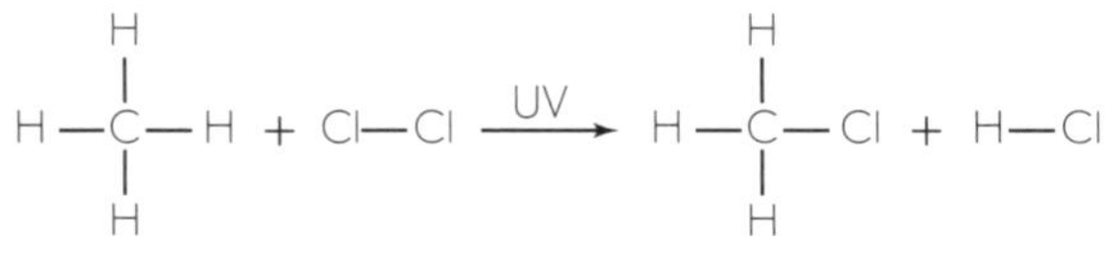

methane   chloromethane

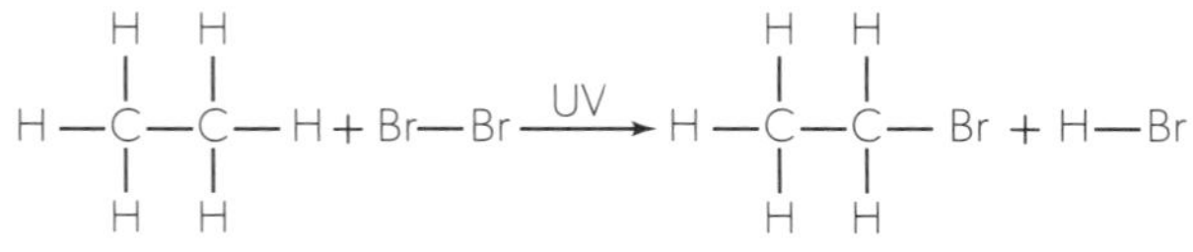

ethane   bromoethane

Mechanism of chlorination of methane

The mechanism for the chlorination of methane occurs in three separate steps.

1. **Initiation step**

The bond between the two halogen atoms is weaker than the C−C or C−H bonds in alkanes and can break homolytically in the presence of ultraviolet light. This initiates the formation of radicals.

$$Cl_2(g) \xrightarrow{UV} 2Cl\bullet(g)$$

2. **Propagation step**

When the highly reactive chlorine free radicals come into contact with a methane molecule they combine with a hydrogen atom to produce hydrogen chloride and a methyl radical.

$$H_3C-H + Cl\bullet \longrightarrow H_3C\bullet + HCl$$

Since a new radical is produced, this stage of the mechanism is called propagation. The methyl free radical is also extremely reactive and reacts with a chlorine molecule to form the product (chloromethane) and regenerate another chlorine radical. This is a further propagation reaction and enables a chain reaction to occur as the process can repeat itself.

$$H_3C\bullet + Cl_2 \longrightarrow H_3C-Cl + Cl\bullet$$

In theory, a single chlorine radical may cause up to 10 000 molecules of chloromethane to be formed.

3. **Termination step**

Termination occurs when two radicals react together to form a non-radical product.

$$\left. \begin{array}{l} Cl\bullet + Cl\bullet \rightarrow Cl_2 \\ H_3C\bullet + Cl\bullet \rightarrow CH_3Cl \\ H_3C\bullet + H_3C\bullet \rightarrow C_2H_6 \end{array} \right\} \text{termination}$$

Further substitution can occur when chlorine radicals react with a substituted product. For example:

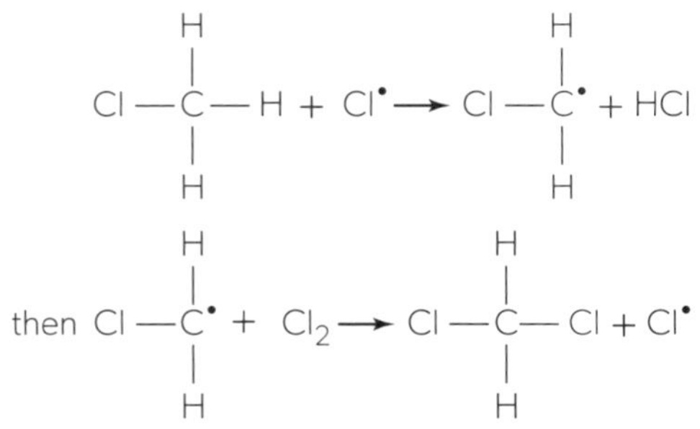

dichloromethane

The substitution can continue even further to produce trichloromethane and then tetrachloromethane.

The overall mechanism is called free radical substitution. [Note that, in this mechanism, hydrogen radicals H$\bullet$ are not formed.]

Nucleophiles and substitution reactions

Definition and examples of nucleophiles

A **nucleophile** is a chemical species that donates a pair of electrons to form a coordination covalent chemical bond with another atom other than hydrogen (its reaction partner). Normally, the term is used in relation to organic reactions. All molecules or ions with at least one non-bonding pair of electrons can act as nucleophiles.

Common ionic nucleophiles include hydroxide ions, $H\ddot{O}^-$, alkoxide ions, $R\ddot{O}^-$, and cyanide ions, $:CN^-$.

Common neutral nucleophiles include water, ammonia, and amines.

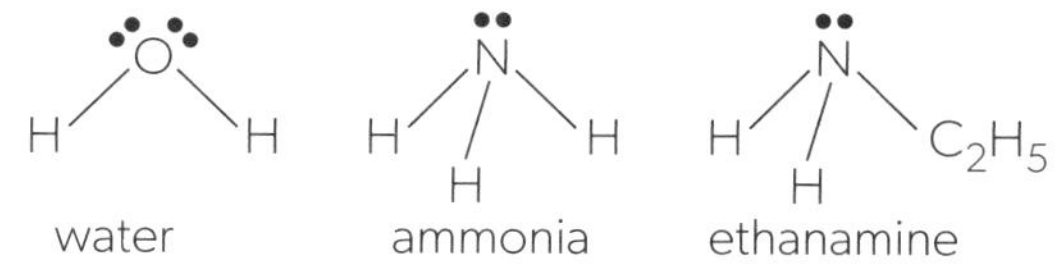

water   ammonia   ethanamine

Nucleophilic substitution reactions

The carbon to halogen bond in halogenoalkanes is polar due to the greater electronegativity of the halogen atom compared with the carbon atom. Nucleophiles are attracted to the electron-deficient $\delta+$ carbon atom, forming a coordination covalent bond to the carbon atom. The bond between the carbon atom and halogen atom breaks, causing the halogen atom (the leaving group) to leave as the halide ion.

The general reaction with a bromoalkane can be shown using Nu^- to represent the nucleophile and double-headed "curly arrows" to show the movement of pairs of electrons. The "curly arrows" show where each pair of electrons originates and where it ends up.

$$Nu^-: \qquad C^{\delta+} \quad Br^{\delta-} \qquad \longrightarrow \qquad C \quad + \quad Br^-$$
$$\qquad\qquad\qquad\qquad\qquad\qquad\qquad Nu$$

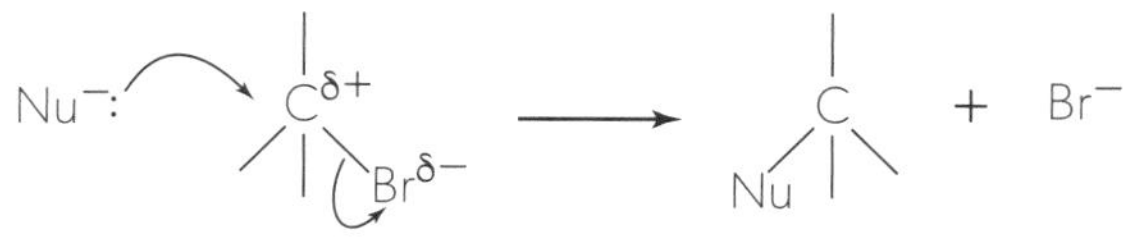

Examples of nucleophilic substitution reactions

A typical example is the formation of alcohols by warming halogenoalkanes with warm dilute sodium hydroxide solution. For example, the reaction of 1-bromopropane with hydroxide ions produces propan-1-ol and sodium bromide.

$$C_3H_7Br + NaOH \rightarrow C_3H_7OH + NaBr$$

The breaking of the carbon to halogen bond during this nucleophilic substitution reaction is an example of heterolytic fission as both of the electrons in the bonding pair end up on the halogen atom, forming the halide ion.

The synthesis of ethanol from ethane neatly illustrates a reaction involving homolytic fission followed by a reaction involving heterolytic fission.

$$C_2H_6 + Br_2 \xrightarrow{\ UV\ } C_2H_5Br + HBr \xrightarrow{\ NaOH(aq)\,/\,warm\ } C_2H_5OH$$

free radical reaction
involves homolytic fission

nucleophilic substitution reaction
involves heterolytic fission

Nucleophilic substitution reactions are particularly useful in organic synthesis as they can be used to make different classes of compounds. When they react with cyanide ions they also provide a way of increasing the number of carbon atoms in the carbon chain.

$$C_2H_5OC_2H_5 + Br^-$$
(ether)

$$\uparrow C_2H_5O^-$$

$$Br^- + C_2H_5CN \xleftarrow{\ CN^-\ } C_2H_5Br \xrightarrow{\ NH_3\ } C_2H_5NH_2 + HBr$$
(amine)

$$\downarrow H^+/H_2O \qquad\qquad \downarrow OH^-$$

$$C_2H_5COOH \qquad C_2H_5OH + Br^-$$
(carboxylic acid)   (alcohol)

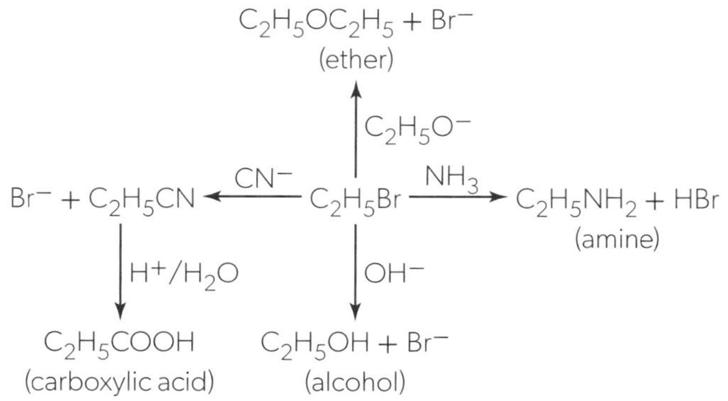

Electrophiles and addition reactions of alkenes

Definition and examples of electrophiles

An electrophile is a reactant that forms a coordination covalent bond to its reaction partner (the nucleophile) by accepting both of the electrons in the bonding pair from that reaction partner. Electrophiles are either positively charged or are neutral but polar, so that the electron-deficient $\delta+$ part of the polar, species is attracted to the nucleophile. The polarity may be permanent or induced as the molecule approaches the nucleophile.

Examples of positively charged electrophiles include H^+, Cl^+, NO_2^+, and CH_3^+. Examples of polar electrophiles include the hydrogen halides such as hydrogen bromide, where the $\delta+$ hydrogen atom acts as the electrophile. Non-polar electrophiles include the halogens, for example, bromine. As the non-polar bromine molecule approaches the electron-rich nucleophile the bonding pair of electrons in the bromine molecule is repelled, causing one of the bromine atoms to become electron deficient so it can act as an electrophile.

Electrophilic addition reactions of alkenes

The bond enthalpy of the C=C double bond has a value of 612 kJ mol^{-1}. This is less than twice the average bond enthalpy for the C−C single bond and accounts for the relative reactivity of alkenes compared to alkanes. The most important reaction of alkenes is addition to form a saturated addition product.

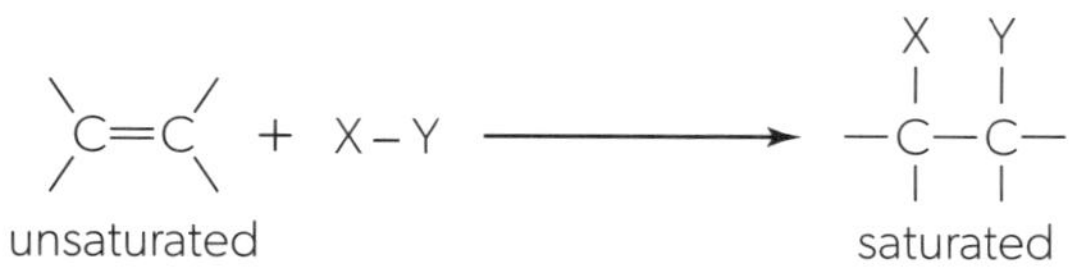

The hydrogenation of alkenes to form alkanes was discussed in Chapter 11 as an example of a redox reaction. The addition reactions of alkenes and substituted alkenes to themselves to form addition polymers such as poly(ethene) and poly(vinyl chloride) were discussed in Chapter 4, under bonding in materials.

The high electron density of the C=C double bond makes it susceptible to attack by electrophiles to bring about saturated addition products. These reactions are known as electrophilic addition reactions. Three examples of electrophilic addition reactions are the reactions of ethene with water, ethene with hydrogen bromide, and ethene with bromine.

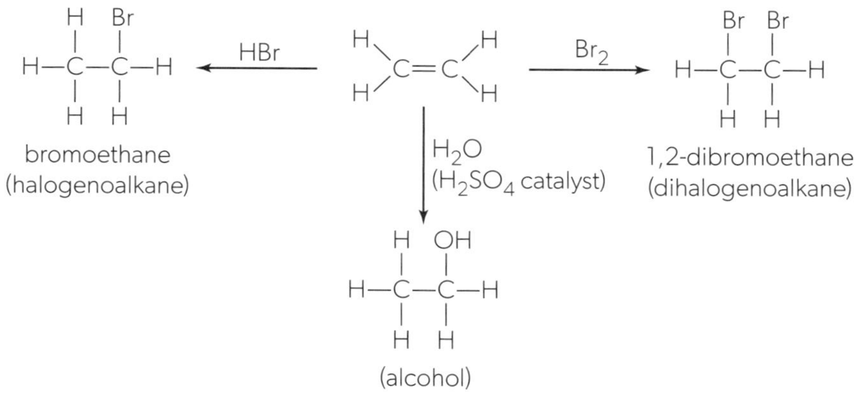

The reaction of bromine water with an alkene provides a useful laboratory test for the presence of an alkene group. Pure bromine is a reddish liquid but it has a distinctive yellow/orange colour in solution. When a solution of bromine is added to an alkene, the bromine solution is quickly decolourized as the organic dibromo-addition product is colourless.

The reaction of an alkene with water to form an alcohol is known as hydration. Ethene is an important industrial product formed during the cracking of oil. Although ethanol can be made by the fermentation of starch and sugars, much industrial ethanol is formed from the addition of steam to ethene.

AHL

Lewis acids and bases

Definitions of Lewis acids and bases

Brønsted–Lowry bases must contain a non-bonding pair of electrons to accept the proton. The Lewis theory gives an alternative definition of acids and bases which takes this further and describes bases as substances that can donate a pair of electrons and describes acids as substances that can accept a pair of electrons. In the process, a coordination covalent bond (both electrons provided by one species) is formed between the base and the acid.

The Lewis theory is all-embracing, so the term Lewis acid is usually reserved for substances that are not also Brønsted–Lowry acids. Many Lewis acids do not even contain hydrogen.

Examples of Lewis acids in inorganic chemistry

BF_3 is a good Lewis acid as there are only six electrons around the central boron atom, which leaves room for two more. Another common Lewis acid is aluminium chloride, $AlCl_3$.

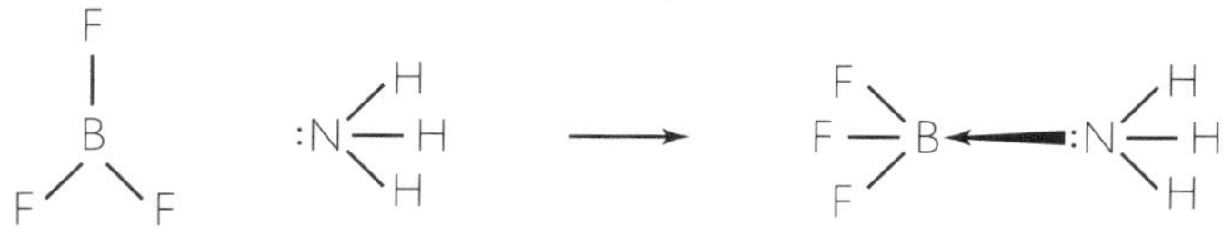

acid base

Transition metal ions in aqueous solution can also accept a pair of electrons from each of six surrounding water molecules, e.g. $[Fe(H_2O)_6]^{3+}$, so these are described as Lewis acids and the ligands are Lewis bases.

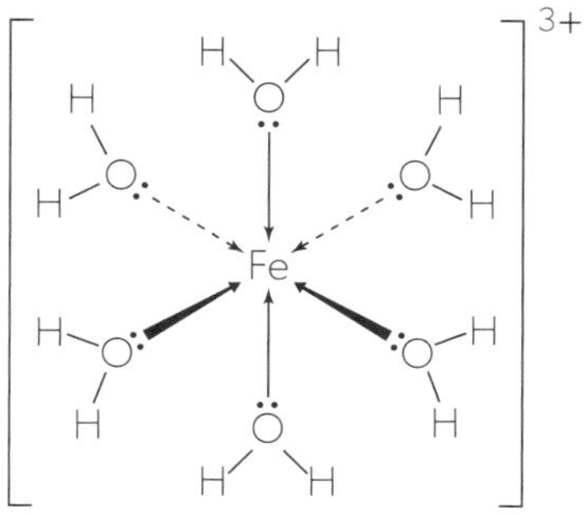

Note that hydrated transition metal ions, such as $[Fe(H_2O)_6]^{3+}$ are acidic in solution as the +3 charge is spread over a very small ion which gives the ion a high charge density. The non-bonded pair of electrons on one of the water molecules surrounding the ion will be strongly attracted to the ion and the water molecule will lose a hydrogen ion in the process. This process can continue until iron(III) hydroxide is formed. The equilibrium can be further moved to the right by adding hydroxide ions, $OH^-(aq)$, or back to the left by adding hydrogen ions, $H^+(aq)$. This is a good example of the ion's amphoteric nature.

$$[Fe(H_2O)_6]^{3+} \underset{H^+}{\overset{-H^+}{\rightleftharpoons}} [Fe(H_2O)_5OH]^{2+} \underset{H^+}{\overset{-H^+}{\rightleftharpoons}} [Fe(H_2O)_4(OH)_2]^{+} \underset{H^+}{\overset{-H^+}{\rightleftharpoons}} Fe(H_2O)_3(OH)_3 \underset{H^+}{\overset{OH^-}{\rightleftharpoons}} [Fe(H_2O)_2(OH)_4]^{-}$$

Examples of Lewis acids in organic chemistry

The Lewis acid and base concept is also used in organic chemistry, in particular to identify reacting species and in the use of "curly arrows" to explain the movement of pairs of electrons in organic reaction mechanisms.

For example, the addition of hydrogen bromide to an alkene proceeds by an electrophilic addition mechanism (see page 138). The $\delta+$ hydrogen atom of the hydrogen bromide molecule acts as the electrophile and accepts a pair of electrons from the double bond of the alkene. Hence, the electrophile is acting as a Lewis acid and the alkene is acting as a Lewis base. Since a "curly arrow" shows the movement of a pair of electrons, the arrow always originates from the Lewis base and the head of the "curly arrow" always points towards the Lewis acid. A second Lewis acid–base reaction occurs when the bromide ion (acting as the Lewis base) donates a pair of electrons to the positive carbon atom in the carbocation intermediate to form the brominated addition product.

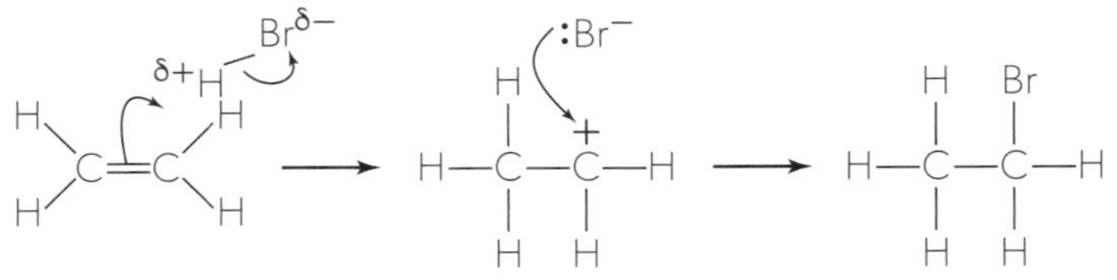

Another good example of Lewis acids in organic chemistry is the function of halogen carriers as catalysts in the electrophilic reactions of benzene (see page 140). Benzene is electron rich due to its delocalized π bond and can react with chlorine to form chlorobenzene. A halogen carrier such as aluminium chloride is added to provide a positive chloride ion which acts as the electrophile. So, in this reaction, aluminium chloride (Lewis acid) and chlorine (Lewis base) undergo a Lewis acid–base reaction and then a second Lewis acid–base reaction occurs between the positive chloride ion (Lewis acid) and the benzene molecule (Lewis base). A third Lewis acid–base reaction occurs when the hydrogen atom (Lewis acid) is removed from the intermediate to form hydrogen chloride and regenerate the aluminium chloride catalyst.

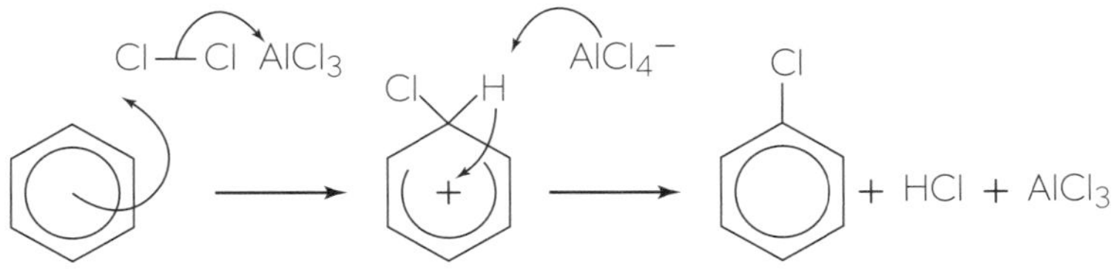

AHL Nucleophilic substitution

Mechanisms of nucleophilic substitution

Primary halogenoalkanes with nucleophiles

A primary halogenoalkane has one alkyl group attached to the carbon atom bonded to the halogen.

For example, the reaction between bromoethane and warm dilute sodium hydroxide solution:

$$C_2H_5Br + OH^- \rightarrow C_2H_5OH + Br^-$$

The experimentally determined rate expression is:

$$\text{rate} = k[C_2H_5Br][OH^-]$$

The proposed mechanism involves the formation of a transition state that involves both of the reactants.

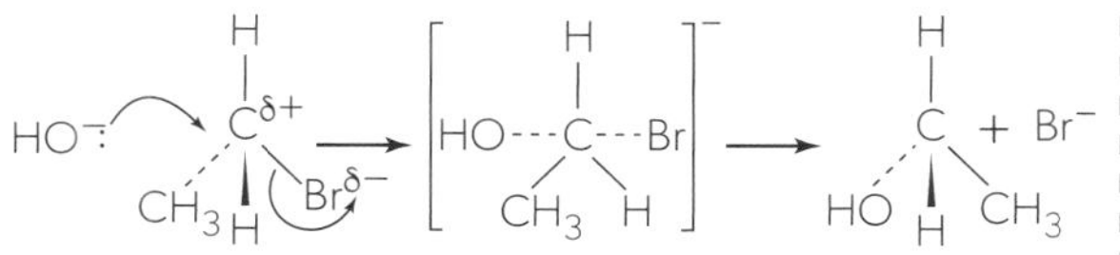

Because the molecularity of this single-step mechanism is two it is known as an S_N2 mechanism (bimolecular nucleophilic substitution).

Note that the S_N2 mechanism is stereospecific, with an inversion of configuration at the central carbon atom.

Primary halogenoalkanes do not contain an asymmetric (chiral) carbon atom. However, when the reactant is a secondary halogenoalkane with a chiral carbon atom, e.g., 2-bromobutane, $C_2H_5CHBrCH_3$, and the reaction proceeds via an S_N2 mechanism the product will rotate the plane of plane-polarized light in the opposite direction. This inversion provides good evidence to support the proposed S_N2 mechanism.

Tertiary halogenoalkanes

A tertiary halogenoalkane has three alkyl groups attached to the carbon atom bonded to the halogen.

For example, the reaction between 2-bromo-2-methylpropane and warm dilute sodium hydroxide solution:

$$C(CH_3)_3Br + OH^- \rightarrow C(CH_3)_3OH + Br^-$$

The experimentally determined rate expression for this reaction is:

$$\text{rate} = k[C(CH_3)_3Br]$$

A two-step mechanism is proposed that is consistent with this rate expression:

$$C(CH_3)_3Br \xrightarrow{\text{slow}} C(CH_3)_3^+$$

$$C(CH_3)_3^+ + OH^- \xrightarrow{\text{fast}} C(CH_3)_3OH$$

In this reaction, the first step—the heterolytic fission of the C–Br bond—is the rate-determining step. The molecularity of this step is one and the mechanism is known as S_N1 (unimolecular nucleophilic substitution).

Secondary halogenoalkanes

The mechanism for the hydrolysis of secondary halogenoalkanes (e.g. 2-bromopropane, $CH_3CHBrCH_3$) is more complicated as they can proceed by either S_N1 or S_N2 pathways or a combination of both.

If the secondary halogenoalkanes are chiral molecules and the reaction proceeds by the S_N2 mechanism then inversion will occur. If the reaction proceeds by the S_N1 mechanism, a racemic mixture of both enantiomers will be formed as the hydroxide ion can add to either side of the planar carbocation intermediate.

Factors affecting the rate of nucleophilic substitution

The nature of the nucleophile

The effectiveness of a nucleophile depends on its electron density. Anions are more electron dense so tend to be more reactive than the corresponding neutral species. This explains why the hydroxide ion is a much better nucleophile than water.

The nature of the halogen

The rate will depend upon how easy it is for the halogen to leave the halogenoalkane. Iodine is a better **leaving group** than either bromine or chlorine as the C−I bond is considerable weaker than the C−Br and C−Cl bonds and therefore requires less energy to break. For both S_N1 and S_N2 reactions iodoalkanes react faster than bromoalkanes which in turn react faster than chloroalkanes.

Bond	Bond enthalpy / $kJ\ mol^{-1}$	
C−Cl	324	↓ Increasing rate of nucleophilic substitution
C−Br	285	
C−I	228	

The nature of the halogenoalkane

Tertiary halogenoalkanes react faster than secondary halogenoalkanes which in turn react faster than primary halogenoalkanes. The S_N1 mechanism, which involves the formation of an intermediate carbocation, is faster than the S_N2 mechanism, which involves a transition state with a relatively high activation energy.

AHL Electrophilic addition reactions (1)

Electrophilic addition to symmetric alkenes

As stated earlier in this chapter, alkenes such as ethene readily undergo addition reactions. With hydrogen bromide, ethene forms bromoethane:

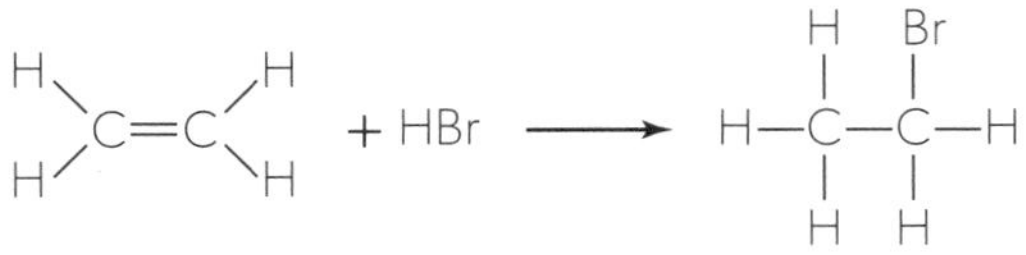

The reaction can occur in the dark, which suggests that a free radical mechanism is not involved. The double bond in the ethene molecule has a region of high electron density above and below the plane of the molecule. Hydrogen bromide is a polar molecule due to the greater electronegativity of bromine compared with hydrogen. The hydrogen atom (which contains a charge of δ+) from the H–Br is attracted to the double bond and the H–Br bond breaks, forming a bromide ion. At the same time the hydrogen atom adds to one of the ethene carbon atoms, leaving the other carbon atom with a positive charge. A carbon atom with a positive charge is known as a carbocation. The carbocation then combines with the bromide ion to form bromoethane. Because the hydrogen bromide molecule is attracted to a region of electron density it is described as an electrophile and the mechanism is described as electrophilic addition.

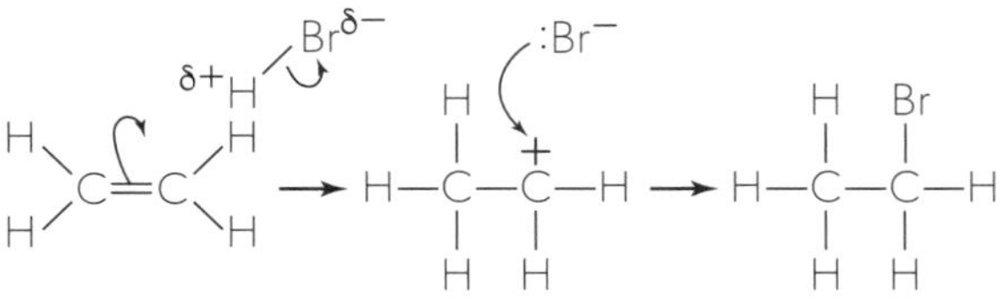

Electrophilic addition also takes place when bromine adds to ethene in a non-polar solvent to give 1,2-dibromoethane. Bromine itself is non-polar but as it approaches the double bond of the ethene an induced dipole is formed by the electron cloud.

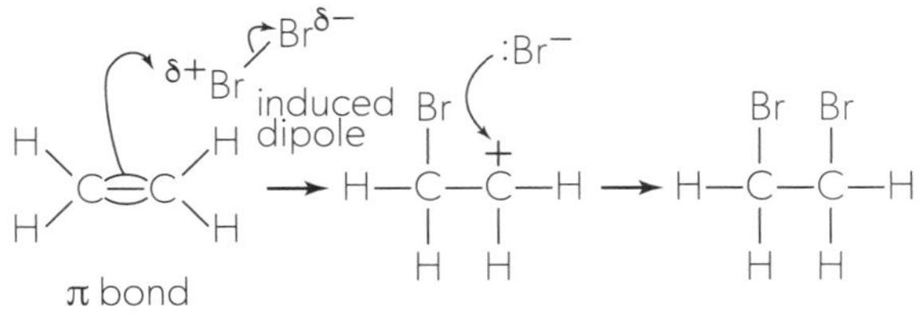

Evidence for this mechanism is that when bromine water is reacted with ethene the main product is 2-bromoethanol not 1,2-dibromoethane. This suggests that hydroxide ions from the water add to the carbocation in preference to bromide ions.

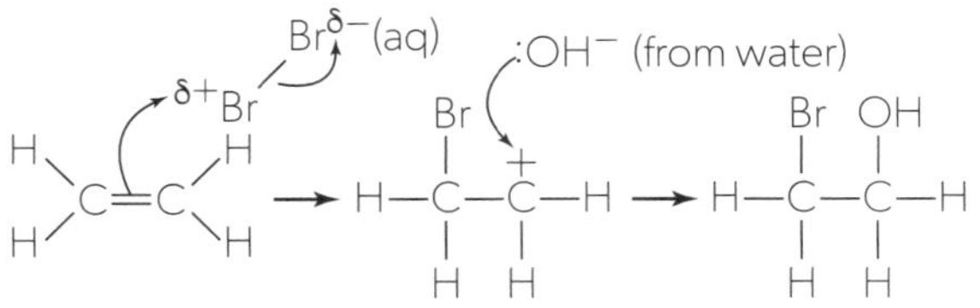

Water adds to alkenes in the presence of an acid catalyst such as sulfuric acid or phosphoric acid. The electrophile is H^+, which dissociates from the strong acid, forming an intermediate carbocation. This carbocation reacts with a non-bonding pair of electrons on the oxygen atom of a water molecule. H^+ is then removed by the acid radical to regenerate the acid catalyst and form the alcohol.

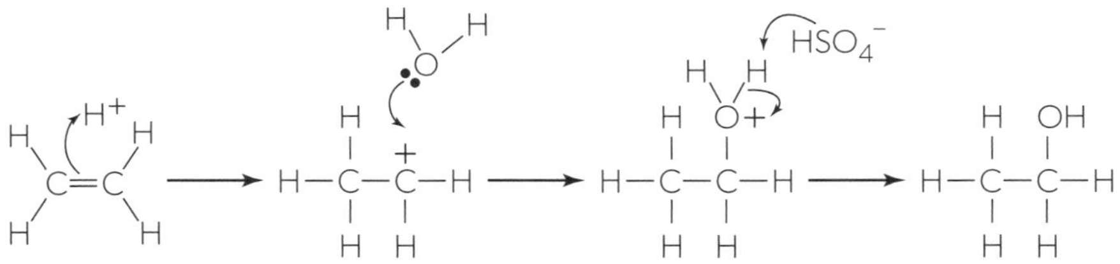

Symmetric and asymmetric alkenes

Asymmetric alkenes contain different groups attached to the carbon atoms of the C=C bond.

Symmetric alkenes

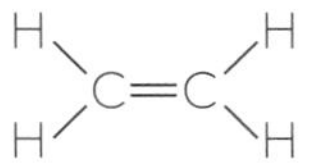
ethene

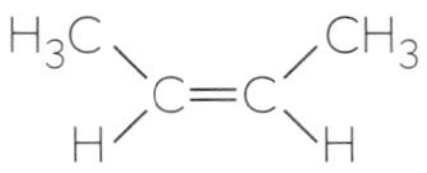
but-2-ene

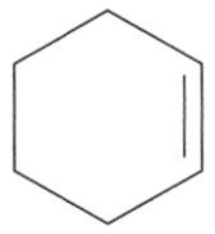
cyclohexene

Asymmetric alkenes

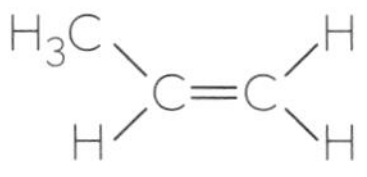
propene

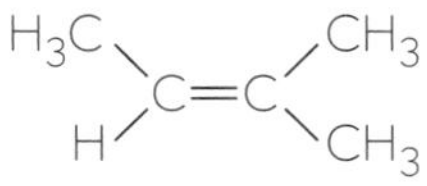
2-methylbut-2-ene

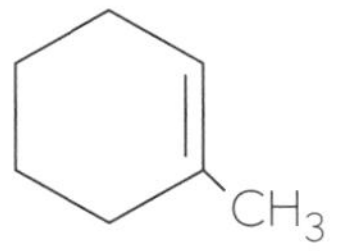
1-methylcyclohexene

AHL Electrophilic addition reactions (2)

Markovnikov's rule

When hydrogen halides add to asymmetric alkenes, two products are possible, depending on which carbon atom the hydrogen atom bonds to. For example, the addition of hydrogen bromide to propene could produce 1-bromopropane or 2-bromopropane.

Markovnikov's rule enables you to predict which isomer will be the major product. It states that the hydrogen atom will add to the carbon atom that already contains the most hydrogen atoms bonded to it. Thus, in the above example, 2-bromopropane will be the major product.

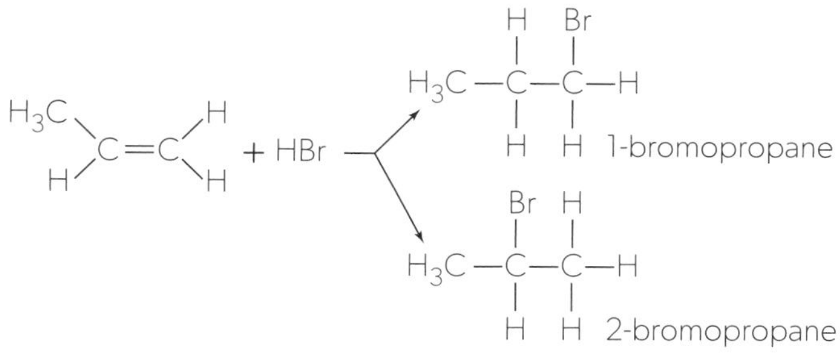

Explanation of Markovnikov's rule

Markovnikov's rule enables the product to be predicted but it does not explain why. It can be explained by considering the nature of the possible intermediate carbocations formed during the reaction.

When hydrogen ions react with propene, two different carbocation intermediates can be formed.

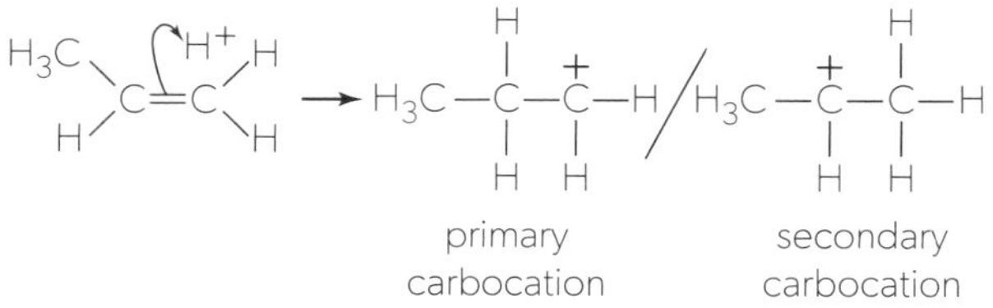

The first one has the general formula RCH_2^+ and is known as a primary carbocation. The second one has two R groups attached to the positive carbon ion R_2CH^+ and is known as a secondary carbocation. A tertiary carbocation has the general formula R_3C^+. The R groups (alkyl groups) tend to push electrons towards the carbon atom they are attached to, which tends to stabilize the positive charge on the carbocation. This is known as a positive inductive effect. This effect is greatest with tertiary carbocations and smallest with primary carbocations.

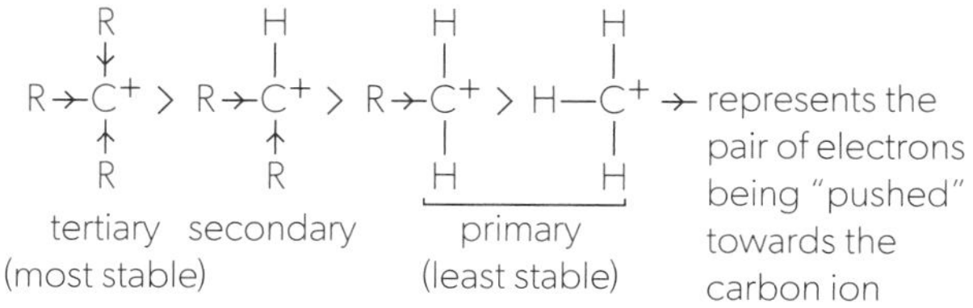

Thus, in the reaction on the left, the secondary carbocation will be preferred as it is more stable than the primary carbocation. This secondary carbocation intermediate leads to the major product, 2-bromopropane.

Understanding this mechanism enables you to predict what will happen when an interhalogen adds to an asymmetric alkene even though no hydrogen atoms are involved. Consider the reaction of iodine chloride, ICl, with but-1-ene. Since iodine is less electronegative than chlorine, the iodine atom will act as the electrophile and add first to the alkene.

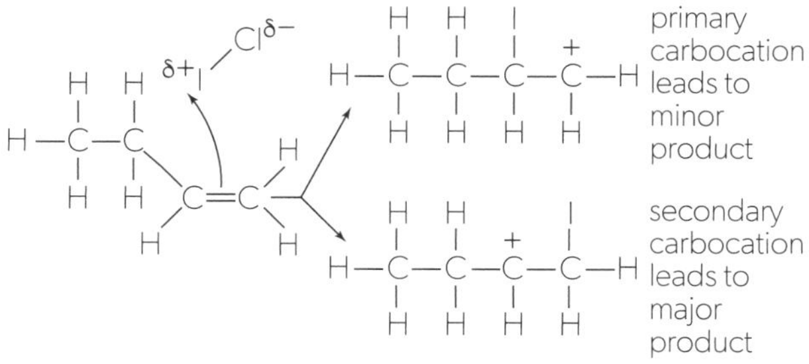

The major product will thus be 2-chloro-1-iodobutane.

Electrophilic substitution reactions

Electrophilic substitution

Benzene reacts with a mixture of concentrated nitric acid and concentrated sulfuric acid when warmed at 50 °C to give nitrobenzene and water. Note that the temperature should not be raised above 50 °C, otherwise, further nitration to dinitrobenzene will occur.

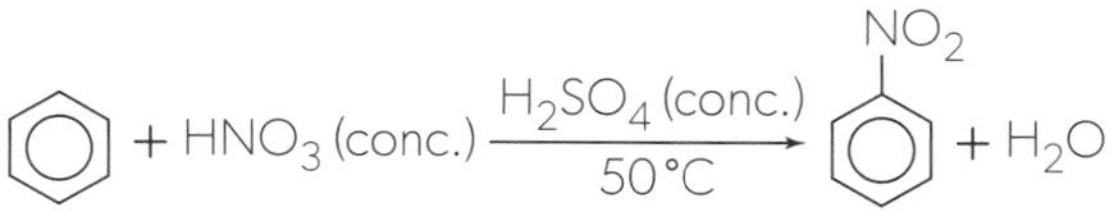

$$\text{benzene} + HNO_3 \text{ (conc.)} \xrightarrow[50\,°C]{H_2SO_4 \text{ (conc.)}} \text{nitrobenzene} + H_2O$$

The electrophile, E^+, is the nitryl cation NO_2^+ (also called the nitronium ion). The concentrated sulfuric acid acts as a catalyst. Its function is to protonate the nitric acid, which then loses water to form the electrophile. In this reaction, nitric acid is acting as a base in the presence of the more acidic sulfuric acid.

$$H_2SO_4 + HNO_3 \rightleftharpoons H_2NO_3^+ + HSO_4^-$$
$$\downarrow$$
$$H_2O + NO_2^+$$

The NO_2^+ is attracted to the delocalized π bond and attaches to one of the carbon atoms. This requires considerable activation energy as the delocalized π bond is partially broken. The positive charge is distributed over the remains of the π bond in the intermediate. The intermediate then loses a proton and energy is evolved as the delocalized π bond is reformed. The proton can recombine with the hydrogensulfate ion to regenerate the catalyst.

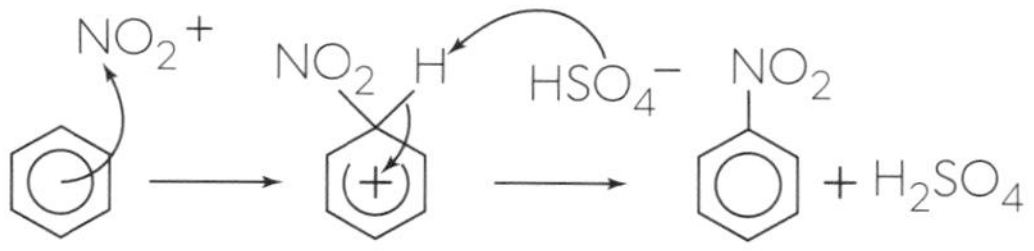

Although it is more correct to draw the intermediate as a partially delocalized π bond, it can sometimes be convenient to show benzene as if it does contain alternate single and double carbon to carbon bonds. In this model, the positive charge is located on a particular carbon atom.

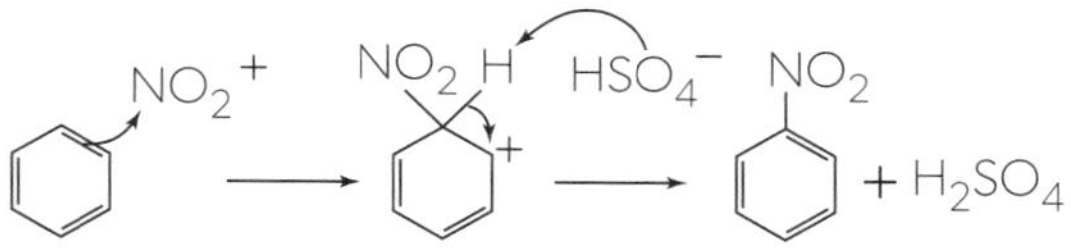

Other electrophilic substitution reactions with benzene include using $AlCl_3$ as a halogen carrier with chlorine to form chlorobenzene, where the electrophile is Cl^+ (see page 136). $AlCl_3$ can also be used with halogenoalkanes (such as chloroethane, where the electrophile is $C_2H_5^+$) to alkylate benzene.

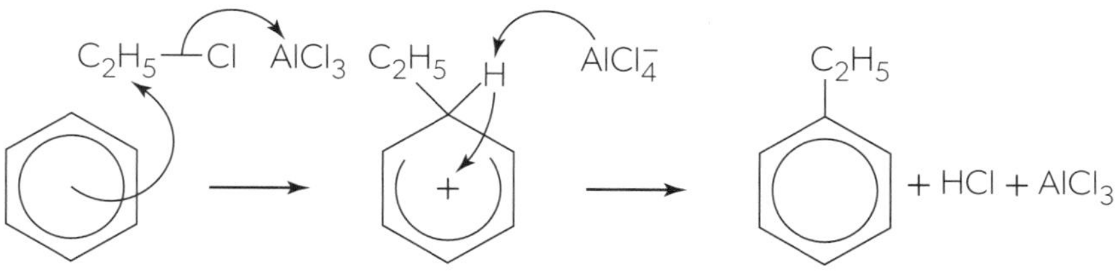

ethylbenzene

Multiple-choice questions—Electron sharing reactions

1. Which statement about the reaction between methane and chlorine is correct?
   A. It involves heterolytic fission and Cl^- ions.
   B. It involves heterolytic fission and Cl• radicals.
   C. It involves homolytic fission and Cl^- ions.
   D. It involves homolytic fission and Cl• radicals.

2. Which formula is that of a secondary halogenoalkane?
   A. $CH_3CH_2CH_2CH_2Br$
   B. $CH_3CHBrCH_2CH_3$
   C. $(CH_3)_2CHCH_2Br$
   D. $(CH_3)_3CBr$

3. What is the reaction between bromine and ethene in the dark an example of?
   A. free radical substitution
   B. esterification
   C. nucleophilic substitution
   D. electrophilic addition

4. Which is a termination step in the reaction between methane and chlorine in ultraviolet light?
   A. $CH_3\bullet + CH_3\bullet \rightarrow C_2H_6$
   B. $CH_3\bullet + H\bullet \rightarrow CH_4$
   C. $CH_3\bullet + Cl_2 \rightarrow CH_3Cl + Cl\bullet$
   D. $CH_3^+ + Cl^- \rightarrow CH_3Cl$

5. Which **cannot** act as a nucleophile?
   A. NH_3
   B. H_2O
   C. Br^-
   D. CH_4

6. Which statements are correct when hydrogen bromide reacts with ethene to form bromoethane?
   I. An intermediate carbocation is formed.
   II. The mechanism is electrophilic substitution.
   III. The C=C double bond acts as a nucleophile.
   A. I and II only
   B. I and III only
   C. II and III only
   D. I, II, and III

7. Which is **not** an electrophilic addition reaction?
   A. $CH_3CHCHCH_3 + H_2 \rightarrow CH_3CH_2CH_2CH_3$
   B. $CH_3CHCHCH_3 + Br_2 \rightarrow CH_3CHBrCHBrCH_3$
   C. $CH_3CHCHCH_3 + HBr \rightarrow CH_3CHBrCH_2CH_3$
   D. $CH_3CHCHCH_3 + H_2O \rightarrow CH_3CHOHCH_2CH_3$

8. Which reaction involves heterolytic fission?
   A. $C_2H_6 + Cl_2 \rightarrow C_2H_5Cl + HCl$
   B. $H^+ + Cl^- \rightarrow HCl$
   C. $C_2H_4 + HCl \rightarrow C_2H_5Cl$
   D. $Cl\bullet + Cl\bullet \rightarrow Cl_2$

AHL

9. Which statements are true about the reactions of halogenoalkanes with warm dilute sodium hydroxide solution?
   I. CH_3I reacts faster than CH_3F.
   II. $(CH_3)_3CBr$ reacts faster than CH_3Br.
   III. $(CH_3)_3CBr$ and $(CH_3)_3CCl$ both react by S_N1 mechanisms.
   A. I and II only
   B. I and III only
   C. II and III only
   D. I, II, and III

10. What is the product from the reaction of iodine monochloride, ICl, with pent-1-ene?
    A. $CH_3CH_2CHICHClCH_3$
    B. $CH_3CH_2CH_2CHICH_2Cl$
    C. $CH_3CH_2CH_2CHClCH_2I$
    D. $CH_3CH_2CHClCHICH_3$

11. Which is an asymmetric alkene?
    A. 2,3-dimethylbut-2-ene
    B. but-2-ene
    C. 2-methylbut-2-ene
    D. hex-3-ene

12. Which **cannot** act as a Lewis acid?
    A. $AlCl_3$
    B. O^{2-}
    C. Fe^{2+}
    D. BF_3

13. Which will react fastest with NaOH(aq)?
    A. $CH_3CHBrCH_3$
    B. $CH_3CH_2CH_2I$
    C. CH_3CHICH_3
    D. $CH_3CH_2CH_2Br$

14. Which statements about ligands are correct?
    I. They are Lewis bases.
    II. Different ligands split the d-sub-level in transition metal ions by different amounts.
    III. Polydentate ligands form more than one coordination bond to transition metal ions.
    A. I and II only
    B. I and III only
    C. II and III only
    D. I, II, and III

15. Which species is the electrophile when bromoethane reacts with benzene in the presence of aluminium bromide to form ethylbenzene?
    A. C_6H_6
    B. $AlBr_3$
    C. Br^+
    D. $C_2H_5^+$

16. Which reactions involve the formation of an intermediate tertiary carbocation?
    I. $CH_3CHBrCH_3 + OH^- \rightarrow CH_3CHOHCH_3 + Br^-$
    II. $(CH_3)_2C{=}CH_2 + HBr \rightarrow (CH_3)_2CBrCH_3$
    III. $(CH_3)_3CBr + OH^- \rightarrow (CH_3)_3COH + Br^-$
    A. I and II only
    B. I and III only
    C. II and III only
    D. I, II, and III

Short-answer questions—Electron sharing reactions

1. a) Bromine reacts with propene.

   (i) Give the equation for the reaction and name the organic product using IUPAC rules. [2]

   (ii) State the name of the type of addition reaction that takes place. [1]

   (iii) Explain why this reaction is also a redox reaction. [2]

   b) Bromine also reacts with propane.

   (i) Give the equation for the reaction and name the organic product using IUPAC rules. [2]

   (ii) State the name of the type of reaction that takes place. [1]

   (iii) Explain with equations the mechanism of this reaction. [4]

   c) Even though bromine reacts with both propene and propane, explain how the reactions can be used to distinguish between propene and propane. [2]

   d) Methylbenzene is a substituted alkane. Draw the structures of the two products formed in the overall reaction when one molecule of bromine reacts with one molecule of methylbenzene in ultraviolet light.

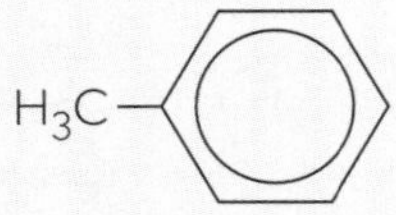

methylbenzene [2]

2. a) State and explain whether the following compounds are primary, secondary, or tertiary halogenoalkanes.

A.

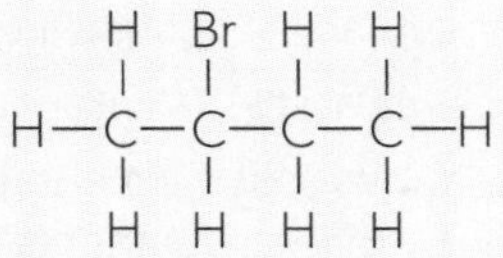

B.

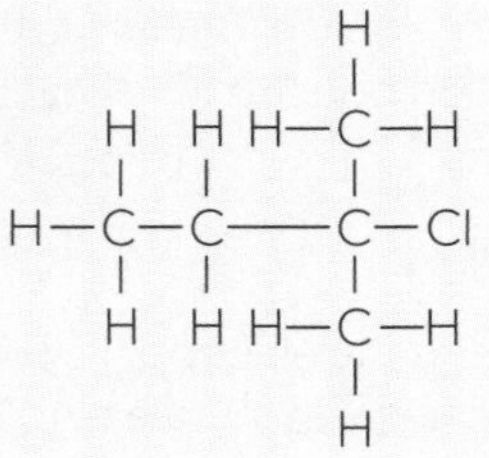

[2]

   b) Both compounds **A** and **B** can react with dilute sodium hydroxide solution.

   (i) Identify how the hydroxide ion is behaving in these two reactions. [1]

   (ii) Name the organic products obtained in these two reactions. [2]

   (iii) Describe and explain how these two products differ in their reaction with an acidified solution of potassium dichromate(VII), $K_2Cr_2O_7$. [4]

   c) Deduce the structure and the class of organic product formed when compound **A** reacts with:

   (i) sodium ethoxide, NaC_2H_5O [2]

   (ii) ammonia. [2]

AHL

3. 1-bromopropane undergoes a substitution reaction with warm aqueous sodium hydroxide solution.

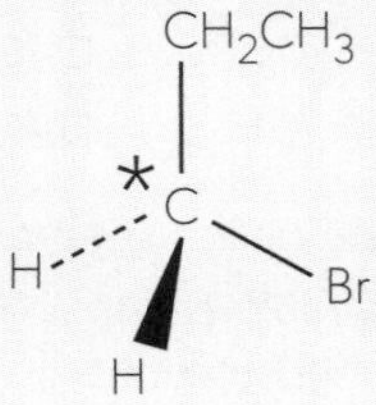

   a) Explain why the substitution occurs on the carbon atom that is marked as *C. [1]

   b) State the rate equation for this reaction and identify the name of the reaction mechanism. [2]

   c) Explain the mechanism of the reaction using curly arrows to represent the movement of electron pairs during the substitution. [4]

   d) Explain how changing the halogenoalkane to 1-chloropropane would affect the rate of the substitution reaction. [2]

4. Benzene can be nitrated to form nitrobenzene by warming with a mixture of concentrated nitric acid and concentrated sulfuric acid. Explain, with any necessary equations, the role of the concentrated sulfuric acid in this reaction. [6]

Experimental techniques

Safety and respect for others

Different countries, local areas within a country, and individual schools will all have their own safety rules and requirements. You should familiarize yourself with them and follow these regulations. Chemistry laboratories and the chemicals and apparatus in them are potentially extremely hazardous. Safe practice and a high level of awareness of potential risks (both immediate and long term) should be maintained consistently at all times. You also need to be aware not only of your own safety but the safety of others. When carrying out practical work you should always wear a laboratory coat or other type of protective clothing, along with safety goggles or a face mask. It is good practice to treat all chemicals with care. Use minimum quantities in well ventilated spaces, always replace stoppers on bottles after use, and clear up any spillages immediately. Look at the label on the bottle or container and make sure you are familiar with the hazard warning and safety signs.

supply symbols

hazard warning signs

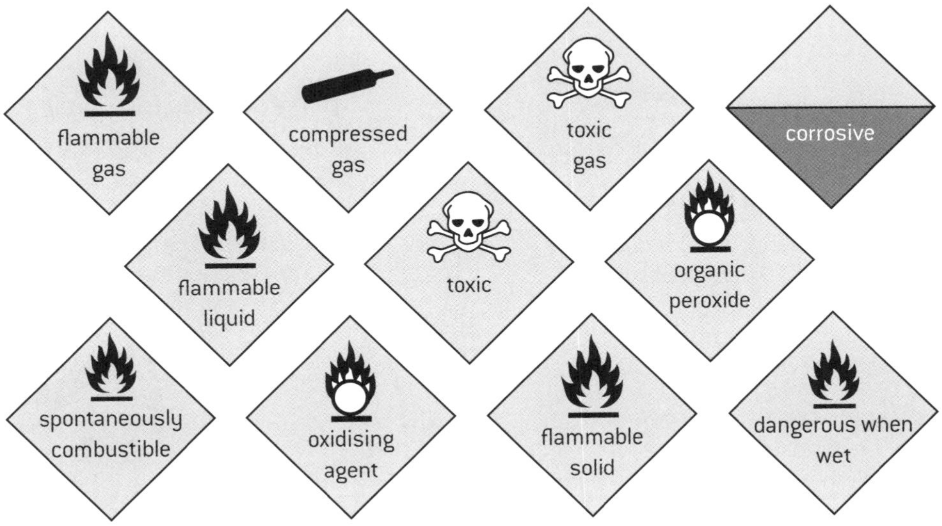

Effect on the environment

All of us have a responsibility to ensure that we respect the environment. Dealing with chemicals poses particular problems; ultimately the only way to be absolutely sure that no environmental damage is caused is to simply not do any practical work. A risk assessment should be done for each laboratory investigation, which takes into account not only the safety aspects but also any environmental risks. Experiments should be designed to keep these effects as small as possible. Any ethical considerations should also be taken into account and addressed if necessary. Quantities of chemicals should be kept to a minimum and waste chemicals placed in appropriately labelled waste containers (e.g. for heavy metals, chlorinated and non-chlorinated organic waste) for proper disposal. Keep the use of distilled water to a minimum, as considerable energy is used in its production and in many cases tap water will do just as well.

Measuring variables

Mass (SI unit: kilogram, kg)

In a school laboratory it is more usual to work in grams rather than the SI unit of kilograms. For accuracy, an analytical electronic balance should be used. These are normally accurate to ±1 of the last unit so an electronic balance weighing to 4 decimal places would be accurate to ±0.0001 g. It is important to include any zeros within the limit of the balance; thus a mass of exactly 1.5 g measured on an analytical balance weighing to 4 decimal places should be recorded as 1.5000 ± 0.0001 g whereas on a balance weighing to 2 decimal places it would be recorded as 1.50 ± 0.01 g.

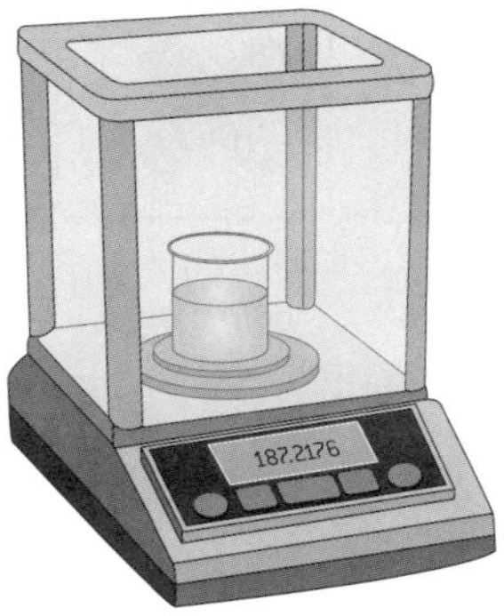

▲ An electronic analytical balance accurate to ± 0.0001 g

Volume (SI derived unit: cubic metre, m^3)

Although the SI derived unit is cubic metres, chemists normally measure volume in cubic centimetres, cm^3 (1 ml) or in cubic decimetres, dm^3.
$1\ dm^3 = 1\ \text{litre} = 1000\ cm^3 = 1 \times 10^{-3}\ m^3$.

▲ The bulb of a 25 cm^3 pipette, showing it is accurate to ±0.03 cm^3

For very approximate measurements a beaker or conical flask can be used. For slightly more accurate measurements use a graduated cylinder (also known as a measuring cylinder). For very accurate measurements, a pipette or burette should be used. A bulb pipette is usually the most accurate for delivering a fixed volume as the exact mark can be made on the narrow neck of the pipette. For variable volumes, a burette is usually better. For distilled water (density 1.00 g cm^{-3}) consider using an accurate electronic balance as the volume in cm^3 will be the same as the mass in g. Most burettes and pipettes have their uncertainty printed on them.

Time (SI unit: second, s)

Most digital timing devices can record to 0.01 s but if you are using them manually then your own reaction time limits this accuracy considerably. Be careful when recording time in other units, e.g. minutes, as you need to make it clear whether 11.40 minutes is 11 minutes and 40 seconds or 11.40 minutes, i.e. 11 minutes and 24 seconds.

Temperature (SI unit: kelvin, K)

Most thermometers and digital devices record the temperature in degrees Celsius rather than kelvin. For temperature differences this is not a problem as a difference of 1 °C is the same as a difference of 1 K. However, for calculations that require the absolute temperature you will need to convert °C to K by adding 273.15. Manual thermometers tend to have a low degree of accuracy, so you should use a digital thermometer wherever possible.

Distance (SI unit: metre, m)

Choose whatever is the most appropriate and accurate instrument for the distance required. Instruments vary from simple rulers and tape measures to laser measurements with a quoted uncertainty of ± 0.002 m in measurements up to 100 m.

pH of solution (no units)

Although pH is a measure of the hydrogen ion concentration it has no units as it is a logarithmic value. Universal indicator solution or paper can be used for approximate values but, for accurate readings, a pH meter (or pH probe connected to a data logger) that has been calibrated using buffer solutions of known pH should be used.

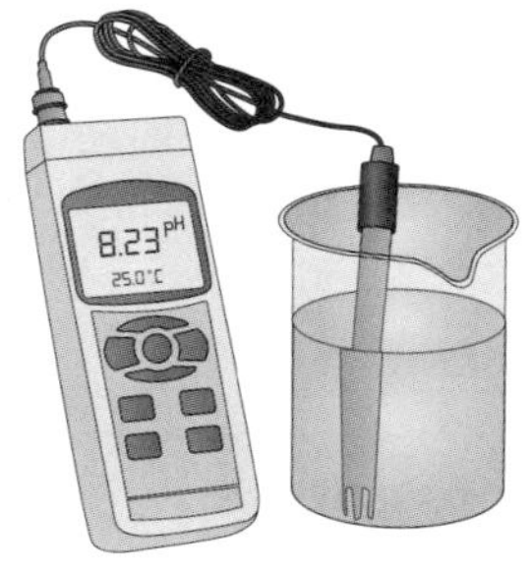

▲ A typical portable pH meter and probe

Current (SI unit: ampere, A) and potential difference (SI derived unit: volt, V)

Current is the flow of electric charge per second. There are several ways to measure current, but the usual way is to use a digital multimeter. This actually measures current indirectly by finding the potential difference (voltage) across a precision resistor. The voltage is then converted into amperes by using Ohm's law, to give the current through the resistor. Voltmeters should be connected in parallel. They should have a high resistance so that they do not use any significant current.

Required practical techniques

You should gain hands on experience of all of the experimental techniques that need to be covered during your two-year practical scheme of work in the laboratory. Some of them are used to obtain substances in a pure state and these are covered in Chapter 1. These include simple distillation and reflux, paper and thin-layer chromatography, filtration of heterogeneous mixtures, determination of melting point, and recrystallization. Acid–base and redox titrations are covered on page 20 in Chapter 3, calorimetry on page 74 in Chapter 7, and electrochemical cells on page 121 in Chapter 11. Some other specific techniques that are required are covered below.

Preparation of a standard solution

A standard solution is a solution of known concentration. The solid should be weighed accurately into a beaker and the solid dissolved in distilled water. All the contents of the beaker should then be transferred to a volumetric flask of known volume. The beaker should be washed with distilled water and all the washings also transferred to the volumetric flask. Distilled water is then added so that the bottom of the meniscus is on the calibration line of the volumetric flask. Finally, the flask is stoppered and shaken to ensure an evenly distributed mixture.

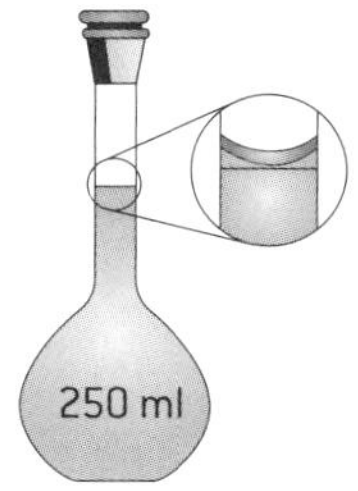

▲ A volumetric flask

Carrying out a dilution

Carrying out a dilution also uses a volumetric flask. A known volume of the solution to be diluted is added to the volumetric flask using a pipette. Washings from the pipette are also added to the flask, to ensure that all the solution has been transferred, and then the volume is made up to the mark using distilled water.

Determining a concentration by colorimetry or spectrophotometry

The concentration of a coloured compound in a solution of unknown concentration can be determined either by UV–vis spectroscopy or by using filters with a fixed wavelength in a colorimeter. From the absorption curve, the wavelength at which maximum absorption occurs, λ_{max}, is determined. A standard solution of the coloured compound is made and diluted successively to give a range of solutions with known concentrations. Measurements of the absorption at the fixed wavelength of λ_{max} for these solutions are obtained. Provided the path length of the light remains the same, i.e. the same cuvette (sample tube) is used, the absorption is directly proportional to the concentration. A calibration curve can then be obtained by using the line of best fit. When the unknown solution is placed in the same cuvette and its absorption measured, the concentration of the solution can be obtained by interpolation of the graph.

Worked example

A student was asked to plan an experiment to determine the concentration of Cu^{2+} in an unknown solution. They were provided with a separate solution of 1.00 mol dm^{-3} copper(II) sulfate.

Using a spectrometer, the student measured the absorbance of a diluted sample of the copper(II) sulfate solution at different wavelengths to obtain the value of 720 nm for λ_{max}. They then carefully diluted the 1.00 mol dm^{-3} solution to give separate solutions with a range of known concentrations. The absorbance at 720 nm for each of these diluted solutions was then measured.

Concentration of $CuSO_4$(aq) / mol dm^{-3}	Absorbance at 720 nm
0.100	0.362
0.150	0.498
0.200	0.798
0.250	0.901
0.300	1.002
0.500	1.751

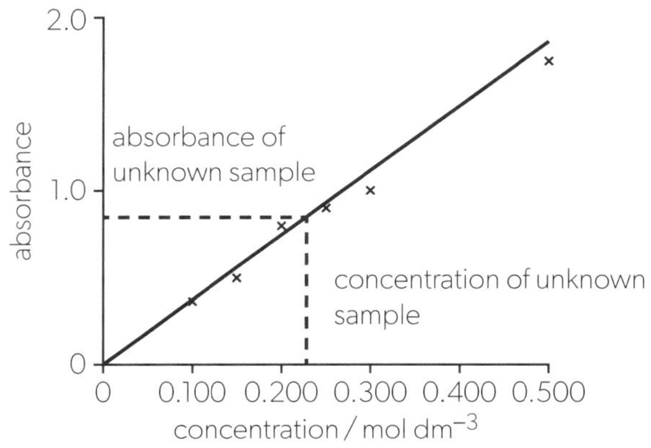

The student used these results to plot a calibration curve using the line of best fit. The absorbance of the unknown solution at 720 nm was then measured. The value was found to be 0.850. From the graph the unknown concentration was determined to be 0.232 mol dm^{-3}.

Technology

Physical molecular modelling

Often physical modelling involves making a smaller representation of an object. In chemistry, physical models of molecules are many magnitudes of ten larger than the molecules they represent. There are different types of modelling kits that can be used, each with their own advantages and disadvantages. For example, wires may be used to hold coloured balls together in an ionic lattice whereas, in reality, they are held by electrostatic forces. Simple covalent molecules can be physically modelled in many different ways, e.g. ball and stick (where one "stick" represents a single bond and two sticks represent a double bond, etc.) or space fill. Most kits provide balls of different colours and sizes to represent different common elements.

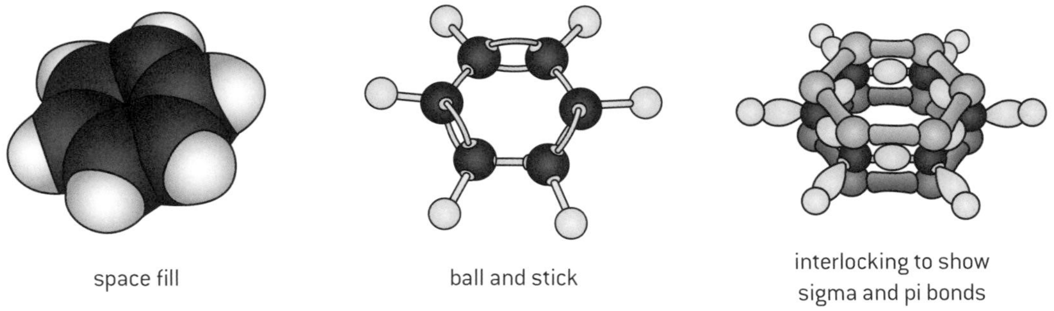

▲ Different ways of modelling benzene

Making physical models helps you to visualize how atoms bond, the relative sizes of atoms, and the distances between them. For instance, you can make a model of phosphorus heptafluoride, PF_7, but if you try to make a model of PI_7 you will not succeed as there is insufficient room to accommodate seven iodine atoms around a central phosphorus atom. Making models of the different shapes that can be obtained from arranging electron domains with either bonding or non-bonding pairs of electrons around a central atom will also help you to understand and apply VSEPR theory.

Digital molecular modelling

There are many apps that you can use to build digital models. These have the advantage that you can quickly switch to different models of the same molecule on your screen.

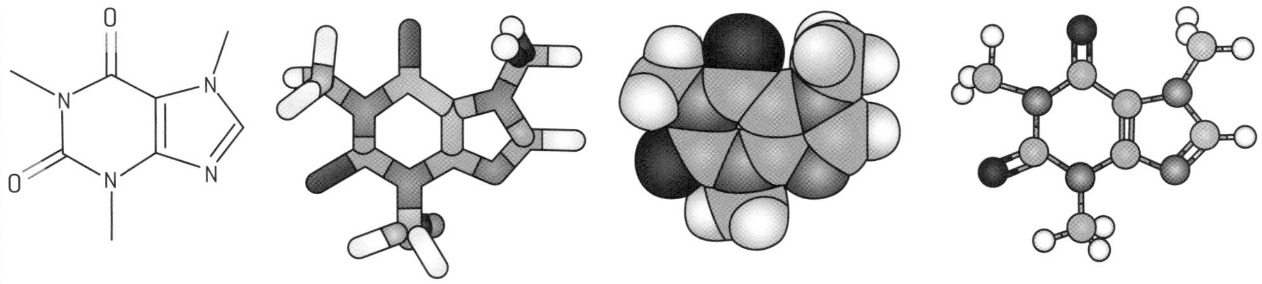

▲ Different models of caffeine, all of which can flip and rotate. These were obtained from an app.

You can obtain precise values for bond lengths and bond angles and also rotate them so that they have a 3D representation. Do remember, though, that unlike physical models they are not actually 3D as you are viewing them on a 2-D flat screen. More sophisticated digital molecular modelling is increasingly being used in medicine and biological systems to design and assess the potential of new drugs and treatments.

Use of data loggers and sensors

A data logger is a piece of equipment that records electronic signals at pre-set intervals over a period of time. They can be used to measure independent or dependent variables electronically and record and store the raw data. There are two real advantages to using data loggers. One is when a large number of readings are required in a short space of time. For example, in fast reactions 100 readings can be recorded each second; this would be impossible to do manually. The second advantage is for reactions that take a long period of time. For example, a data logger could be used to record the pH of the water in a river with readings being taken every hour over several days.

Data loggers can, of course, also be used to take and record readings that can be done easily manually, such as measuring pH changes during a titration. Different types of data logger are available commercially, but they all connect to a variety of different probes (sensors) that can measure pH, temperature, light, conductivity, dissolved oxygen, absorption, etc.

▲ A graphical data logger

Manipulation of data using a spreadsheet

Some data loggers, like the Pasco graphical data logger, can manipulate the raw data for you and put it into graphical form. However, raw data, either from a data logger or extracted from a database, can be recorded onto a spreadsheet program such as Excel. Within the spreadsheet, you should know how to add headers to columns, enter data, fill down a column (and across rows, if necessary), format cells, add a function, and sort columns. Once the raw data has been correctly manipulated, suitable graphs can plotted directly.

This is illustrated by the following simple example.

A student carried out an experiment to find the value of the gas constant. The volume of 1.000 g of oxygen gas was measured at a constant pressure of 1.03×10^5 Pa.

The raw data was recorded onto an Excel spreadsheet.

	A	B
1	Temperature / °C	Volume/cm^3
2	20.0	739
3	31.2	765
4	40.5	778
5	50.3	821
6	62.1	842
7		

In the next column, the temperature was then converted into kelvin by writing "= A2 + 273.1" into the C2 cell and then filling down.

C2 fx = A2 + 273.1

	A	B	C
1	Temperature / °C	Volume/cm^3	Temperature/ K
2	20.0	739	293.1
3	31.2	765	304.3
4	40.5	778	313.6
5	50.3	821	323.4
6	62.1	842	335.2
7			

From the equation $PV = nRT$ it can be seen that if a graph of $\frac{PV}{n}$ is plotted against T, the gradient will give the value of the gas constant, R.

Knowing that the amount of oxygen $= \frac{1.000}{32.02} =$ 0.03123 mol and also knowing that the units of volume need to be in m^3, a new column can then be created that calculates the value of $\frac{PV}{n}$ in J mol^{-1} for each value of T. "= (103000 * B2*0.000001) / 0.03123" is written in cell D2 and then filled down.

D6 fx = (103000*B6*0.000001) / 0.03123

	A	B	C	D
1	Temperature / °C	Volume/cm^3	Temperature/ K	pV / n / J mol^{-1}
2	20.0	739	293.1	2437.3
3	31.2	765	304.3	2523.1
4	40.5	778	313.6	2565.9
5	50.3	821	323.4	2707.7
6	62.1	842	335.2	2777.0

Using the graphing scatter facility the values in columns C and D are chosen and a line graph plotted.

	Temperature / °C	Volume/cm^3	Temperature/ K	pV / n / J mol^{-1}
1	Temperature / °C	Volume/cm^3	Temperature/ K	pV / n / J mol^{-1}
2	20.0	739	293.1	2437.3
3	31.2	765	304.3	2523.1
4	40.5	778	313.6	2565.9
5	50.3	821	323.4	2707.7
6	62.1	842	335.2	2777.0

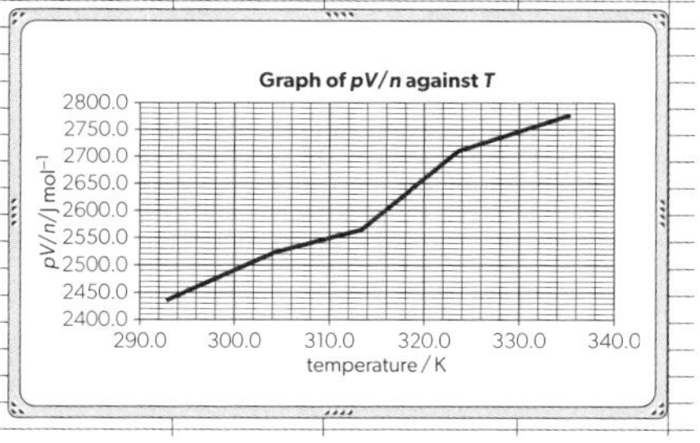

The line of best fit is then added and the equation obtained for the best-fit line. The gradient of 8.35 J K^{-1} mol^{-1} gives the value for R.

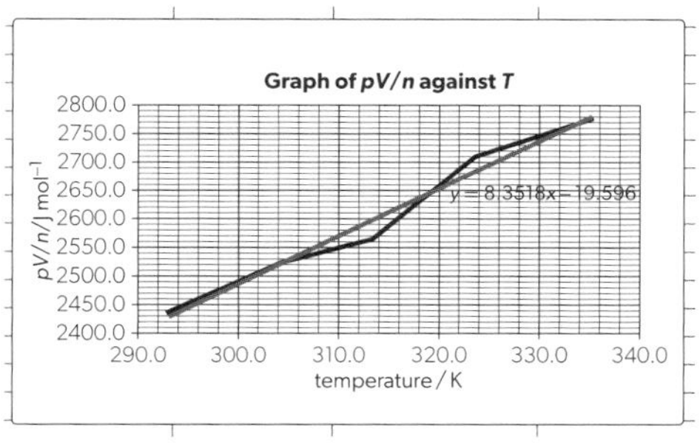

Mathematics

Required mathematical skills

One big advantage of the IB compared with some other systems is that all students study mathematics as one of their six diploma subjects, so the mathematical skills required for IB chemistry should not present you with a problem. Essentially, the skills required concern numeracy and application rather than complex mathematical techniques. These mathematical skills mostly require straightforward application to solve problems and address concepts, but a few have some points worth noting that have particular relevance to chemistry.

Logarithmic calculations

Logarithmic calculations can easily be performed on a graphical calculator. Perhaps because of this some students do not have a good grasp of the underlying concepts.

Logarithms to the base ten are simply the power that 10 is raised to give the number. This is particularly relevant when determining the pH of a solution.

$100 = 10^2$ so $\log_{10} 100 = 2$; $1000 = 10^3$ so $\log_{10} 1000 = 3$

When the number is between 100 and 1000, the logarithm will be between 2 and 3. Similarly, if a number is between 0.1 and 0.01, the logarithm will be between −1 and −2.

$1 = 10^0$ and $10 = 10^1$, so numbers between 1 and 10 have logarithms to the base ten between 0 and 1.

$\log_{10} 2 = 0.30$

$\log_{10} 200 = \log (2 \times 10^2) = \log_{10} 2 + \log_{10} 10^2 = +0.30 + 2.00 = 2.30$

$\log_{10} 0.02 = \log_{10} (2 \times 10^{-2}) = \log_{10} 2 + \log_{10} 10^{-2} = +0.30 - 2.00 = -1.70$

Natural logarithms are to the base e rather than base 10 and are used in expressions such as $\Delta G^\ominus = -RT \ln K$.

Using your calculator

Most calculators are capable of performing functions far beyond the demands of the IB chemistry course. When simple numbers are involved, try to solve problems without using your calculator. Even when the numbers are more complex, try to estimate what the answer will be before using the calculator. This should help to ensure that you do not accept and use a wrong answer because you failed to realize that you pushed the wrong buttons. Don't just give the "calculator answer" but record the answer to the correct number of significant figures.

The IB recommends that for chemistry you use a digital display calculator. Make sure that the calculator you have is one that is approved by the IB, as smart calculators are not allowed. Make sure you know how to use your calculator to work out problems involving logarithms for pH and pK_a. The examples given below are for a TI-84 Plus.

To convert a hydrogen ion concentration of 1.8×10^{-5} mol dm^{-3} into pH.

$pH = -\log_{10} 1.8 \times 10^{-5}$

To obtain the value, press the following keys in sequence:

[(−)] [(] [LOG] [1.8] [×] [10] [^] [(−)] [5] [)] [ENTER]

This will give a value of 4.74.

To convert a pK_a value of 3.75 into a K_a value, press:

[2nd] [10^x] [(−)] [3.75] [ENTER]

to give a value of 1.78×10^{-4}.

Variables

A scientific **variable** is any factor, condition or quantity that can be controlled or changed during a scientific experiment.

For example, consider an experiment to determine the rate constant for the reaction between two different gases, A and B, to produce a product C. Possible variables could include:

- the nature of gas A and the nature of gas B
- the purity of both gases
- the mass (or amount) of both gases
- the temperature of the reaction
- the pressure at which the reaction is carried out
- the nature, amount, and surface area of any catalyst present
- the vessel in which the reaction is carried out
- the method of determining the rate (e.g. change in volume, mass, absorption)
- the presence or otherwise of UV light, etc.

The purpose of a scientific experiment is to determine whether there is a cause and effect relationship between two of the variables. If such a relationship can be established while keeping all the other factors constant, then the experiment can lead to observable and verifiable predictions.

Variables can be classified in several ways, although the main categorization is to identify them as dependent, independent, and controlled variables.

The **independent variable** is the variable that is manipulated or changed and the **dependent variable** is the variable that is observed or measured during the experiment. In order to determine the effect of changing the independent variable, x, on the dependent variable, y, all the other variables need to be kept constant. These are the **controlled variables** (sometimes known as constant variables). Raw data relevant to the dependent variable may be obtained directly, e.g. measuring volume change against time, or the raw data may need to be manipulated to obtain processed data relevant to the independent variable, such the rate of a reaction. Be careful, too, about selecting pH as the dependent variable in a rate experiment, as the logarithmic nature of pH means that calculating the rate of change of pH does not simply relate to the change in concentration of reactants or products.

You need to be able to distinguish between continuous and discrete variables. A **continuous variable** is a variable whose value is obtained by measuring, whereas a **discrete variable** is a variable whose value is obtained by counting. Continuous variables (which are used most often in chemistry) can have an infinite number of possible values between two intervals. An example is the volume of a gas evolved during a reaction. Discrete variables have separate indivisible categories so that no value can exist between neighbouring categories. An example is atomic numbers when plotting a graph of first ionization energy against atomic number.

There may also be a correlation between two variables. Correlation indicates that as one variable changes the other variable tends to change in a specific direction. If they are 100% positively correlated, then the two variables move together by exactly the same percentage and direction. An example is pressure and temperature for a fixed mass of gas at a constant volume. If they are 100% negatively correlated, then the two variables move in opposite directions: for example, pressure and volume for a fixed mass of gas at a constant temperature. *Correlation* indicates that there is a relationship between two variables, but it does not necessarily imply that one variable causes the other to change.

Use of approximation and estimation

Approximation is a useful way to avoid having to solve quadratic expressions in equilibrium calculations provided the equilibrium constant is small, i.e. less than about 1×10^{-3}. This makes it particularly suitable for finding the pH of a weak acid.

For example, calculate the pH of a solution of 0.100 mol dm^{-3} ethanoic acid ($K_a = 1.8 \times 10^{-5}$).

The equation for the dissociation is

$$CH_3COOH(aq) \rightleftharpoons CH_3COO^-(aq) + H^+(aq)$$

$$K_a = \frac{[CH_3COO^-(aq)] \times [H^+(aq)]}{[CH_3COOH(aq)]}$$

If $[H^+(aq)] = x$ at equilibrium, then $[CH_3COOH(aq)] = 0.100 - x$

Then $K_a = 1.8 \times 10^{-5} = \dfrac{x^2}{(0.100 - x)}$

This leads to a quadratic expression to solve in order to find x. However, because x is so small, $(0.100 - x)$ approximates to 0.100, so $1.8 \times 10^{-5} \approx \dfrac{x^2}{0.100}$. So $x = \sqrt{(1.8 \times 10^{-6})} = 1.34 \times 10^{-3}$ and $pH = -\log_{10}(1.34 \times 10^{-3}) = 2.87$

Estimation can be useful when dealing with large or small numbers.

For example, does the Sahara Desert contain more than 1 mole of grains of sand?

The Sahara Desert covers an area of about 4500 km by 1500 km. Assuming the average depth of the sand is 10 m, the volume of sand in the Sahara desert is $4.5 \times 10^6 \times 1.5 \times 10^6 \times 10^1 = 6.75 \times 10^{13}$ m^3.

Assuming that 1.0 cm^3 of sand contains 1000 particles of sand, then 1 m^3 of sand contains 1.0×10^9 particles of sand. This means that the Sahara Desert is estimated to contain 6.75×10^{22} grains of sand, i.e. about 0.1 mol. The fact that there is unlikely to be more than 1 mol of grains of sand in the whole of the Sahara Desert and yet 12 g of carbon contains 1 mol of carbon atoms can help to explain why it is so difficult to visualize the size of Avogadro's constant or how small an atom really is.

Percentage yield

The percentage yield is a measure of the amount of product obtained in a pure state from a specified amount of one of the reactants. To calculate percentage yield the stoichiometric equation is required, so that the theoretical maximum yield can be calculated.

$$\text{percentage yield} = \frac{\text{experimental yield}}{\text{theoretical yield}} \times 100$$

For example, when 8.625 g of 4-aminophenol was reacted with excess ethanoic anhydride, it produced 9.342 g of paracetamol. Calculate the percentage yield.

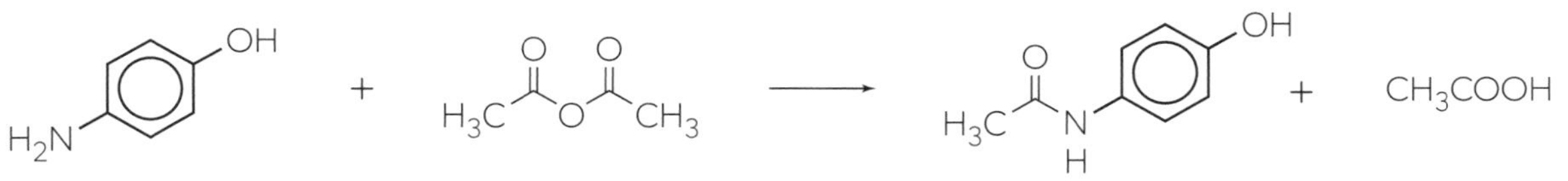

4-aminophenol C_6H_7NO $M_r = 109.13$ | ethanoic anhydride $C_4H_6O_3$ | paracetamol $C_8H_6NO_2$ $M_r = 151.17$ | ethanoic acid $C_2H_4O_2$

1 mol of 4-aminophenol produces 1 mol of paracetamol.

Initial amount of 4-aminophenol $= \dfrac{8.625}{109.13} = 0.07903$ mol

Maximum theoretical yield of paracetamol $= 0.07903 \times 151.17 = 11.948$ g

$$\text{percentage yield} = \frac{9.342}{11.948} \times 100 = 78.2\%$$

SI units and prefixes

The **International System of Units** (also known as the SI system) is accepted officially by almost every country. There are seven base units, which cover time, length, mass, electric current, temperature, amount of substance, and luminous intensity.

▼ The seven SI base units

Quantity	Name	Symbol
time	second	s
length	metre	m
mass	kilogram	kg
electric current	ampere	A
temperature	kelvin	K
amount of substance	mole	mol
luminous intensity	candela	cd

In addition, there are SI derived units. These have their own name but are derived from the base units. Derived units used in chemistry include frequency, force, pressure, energy, electric charge, and potential difference.

▼ Some of the SI derived units used in chemistry

Quantity	Name	Symbol	SI base units
frequency	hertz	Hz	s^{-1}
force	newton	N	$kg\,m\,s^{-2}$
pressure	pascal	Pa	$kg\,m^{-1}\,s^{-2}$ ($N\,m^{-2}$)
energy	joule	J	$kg\,m^2\,s^{-2}$ ($N\,m$)
electric charge	coulomb	C	$s\,A$
potential difference	volt	V	$kg\,m^2\,s^{-3}\,A^{-1}$

Chemistry also uses some coherent units derived from base units. These include area (square metre, m^2), volume (cubic metre, m^3), speed (metre per second, $m\,s^{-1}$), and concentration (mole per cubic metre, $mol\,m^{-3}$).

The same unit can be used to measure very large and very small values by using powers of ten. For example, the radius of an atom is in the order of 1×10^{-10} m whereas the distance from the Earth to the Sun is in the order of 1.5×10^{11} m. Prefixes can be used to take account of the powers of ten. Common prefixes used in chemistry are giga (10^9), mega (10^6), and kilo (10^3) for larger measurements, and deci (10^{-1}), centi (10^{-2}), milli (10^{-3}), micro (10^{-6}), nano (10^{-9}), and pico (10^{-12}) for smaller measurements. For example, there are 1×10^9 micrograms in 1 kilogram.

Symbols

Chemistry makes much use of symbols, the most obvious being the symbols of the 118 elements used as shorthand (abbreviations) for the formulas of compounds, e.g. $CuSO_4.5H_2O$. There are also many other symbols that are frequently used in this guide and in examinations.

- State symbols: solid (s), liquid (l), gas (g), aqueous solution, (aq); and the use of [ ] to express concentration.
- Thermodynamic symbols: enthalpy, H, entropy, S, and Gibbs energy, G; change in enthalpy, ΔH, change in entropy, ΔS, and change in Gibbs energy ΔG. The symbol $\ominus$ is used for thermodynamic measurements made under standard conditions, for example, $\Delta H^{\ominus}$.
- Nuclear symbols: atomic number, Z, mass number, A, molar mass, M, relative atomic mass, A_r, relative molar mass, M_r, and Avogadro's constant, N_A.
- Other symbols: rate constant, k, equilibrium constant, K, activation energy, E_A, Arrhenius factor, A, and standard electrode potential, $E^{\ominus}$.

Significant figures

Whenever a measurement of a physical quantity is taken there will be a random uncertainty in the reading. The measurement quoted should include the first figure that is uncertain. This should include zero if necessary. Thus a reading of 25.30 °C indicates that the temperature was measured with a thermometer that is accurate to ±0.01 °C. If a thermometer accurate to only ±0.1 °C was used, then the temperature should be recorded as 25.3 °C.

Zeros can cause problems when determining the number of significant figures. Essentially, zero only becomes significant when it comes after (to the right of) a non-zero digit (1, 2, 3, 4, 5, 6, 7, 8, 9).

000123.4 0.0001234	1.0234 1.2340
zero not a significant figure	zero is a significant figure
values quoted to 4 s.f.	values quoted to 5 s.f.

Zeros after a non-zero digit but before the decimal point may or may not be significant, depending on how the measurement was made. For example, 123 000 might mean exactly one hundred and twenty-three thousand or one hundred and twenty-three thousand to the nearest thousand. This problem can be neatly overcome by using scientific notation.

1.23000×10^6	1.23×10^6
quoted to six significant figures	quoted to three significant figures

Calculations

1. When adding or subtracting, it is the number of decimal places that is important. Thus when using a balance that measures to ±0.01 g the answer can also be quoted to two decimal places, which may increase or decrease the number of significant figures.

7.10 g	+	3.10 g	=	10.20 g
3 s.f.		3 s.f.		4 s.f.
22.36 g	–	15.16 g	=	7.20 g
4 s.f.		4 s.f.		3 s.f.

2. When multiplying or dividing, it is the number of significant figures that is important. The number with the least number of significant figures used in the calculation determines how many significant figures should be used when quoting the answer.

   For example, when the temperature of 0.125 kg of water is increased by 7.2 °C, the heat required

   $= 0.125\,\text{kg} \times 7.2\,°\text{C} \times 4.18\,\text{kJ kg}^{-1}\,°\text{C}^{-1}$

   $= 3.762\,\text{kJ}$

   Since the temperature was recorded to only two significant figures, the answer should strictly be given as 3.8 kJ.

Random uncertainties and systematic errors

Quantitative chemistry involves measurement. A measurement is a method by which some quantity or property of a substance is compared with a known standard. If the instrument used to take the measurements has been calibrated wrongly or if the person using it consistently misreads it, then the measurements will always differ by the same amount. Such an error is known as a **systematic error**. An example might be always reading a pipette from the sides of the meniscus rather than from the middle of the meniscus.

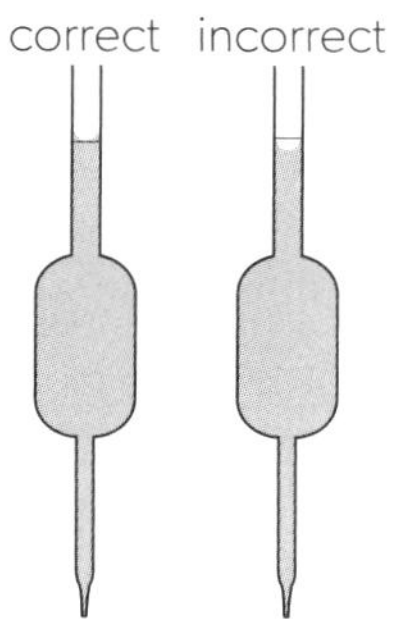

a systematic error will be introduced if a pipette is read incorrectly

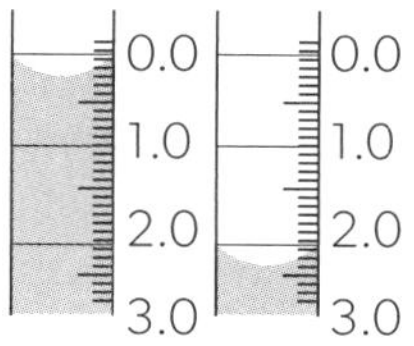

systematic errors may cancel out when a difference in two readings is taken: $\Delta V = 2.0\ cm^3$ whether or not the burette is read incorrectly

Random uncertainties occur if there is an equal probability of the reading being too high or too low from one measurement to the next. These might include variations in the volume of glassware due to temperature fluctuations or the decision about exactly when an indicator changes colour during an acid–base titration.

Precision and accuracy

- **Precision** refers to how close several experimental measurements of the same quantity are to each other.
- **Accuracy** refers to how close the readings are to the true value. This may be the standard value, or the literature or accepted value.

A measuring cylinder used to measure exactly 25 cm^3 is likely to be much less accurate than a pipette that has been carefully calibrated to deliver exactly that volume. Note that it is possible to have very precise readings that are inaccurate due to a systematic error. For example, all the students in a class may obtain the same or very close results in a titration (precise), but if the standard solution used in all the titrations had been prepared wrongly beforehand the results would be inaccurate due to the systematic error.

Systematic errors cannot be reduced by repeated readings because they are always either too high or too low. However, random errors can be reduced by repeated readings because there is an equal probability of them being high or low each time the reading is taken.

When taking a measurement, it is usual practice to report the reading from a scale as the smallest division or the last digit capable of precise measurement, even though it is understood that the last digit has been rounded up or down so that there is a random error or uncertainty of ±0.5 of the last unit.

Absolute and percentage uncertainties

When making a single measurement with a piece of apparatus, the absolute uncertainty and the percentage uncertainty can both be stated relatively easily. For example, consider measuring 25.0 cm^3 with a 25 cm^3 pipette which measures to ±0.1 cm^3. The absolute uncertainty is 0.1 cm^3 and the percentage uncertainty is equal to

$$\frac{0.1}{25.0} \times 100 = 0.4\%$$

If two volumes or two masses are simply added or subtracted, then the absolute uncertainties are added. For example, suppose two volumes of 25.0 cm^3 ± 0.1 cm^3 are added. In one extreme case the first volume could be 24.9 cm^3 and the second volume 24.9 cm^3, which would give a total volume of 49.8 cm^3. Alternatively, the first volume might have been 25.1 cm^3 which, when added to a second volume of 25.1 cm^3, gives a total volume of 50.2 cm^3. The final answer therefore can be quoted between 49.8 cm^3 and 50.2 cm^3, that is, 50.0 cm^3 ± 0.2 cm^3.

When using multiplication, division, or powers, percentage uncertainties should be used during the calculation and then converted back into an absolute uncertainty when the final result is presented. For example, during a titration, there are generally four separate pieces of apparatus, each of which contributes to the uncertainty. For example, when using a balance that weighs to ±0.001 g the uncertainty in weighing 2.500 g will equal

$$\frac{0.001}{2.500} \times 100 = 0.04\%$$

Similarly, a pipette measures 25.00 cm^3 ± 0.04 cm^3. The uncertainty due to the pipette is thus

$$\frac{0.04}{25.00} \times 100 = 0.16\%$$

Assuming that the uncertainties due to the burette and the volumetric flask are 0.50% and 0.10%, respectively, the overall uncertainty is obtained by summing all the individual uncertainties:

$$\text{overall uncertainty} = 0.04 + 0.16 + 0.50 + 0.10$$

$$= 0.80\% \simeq 1.0\%$$

Hence, if the answer is 1.87 mol dm^{-3}, the uncertainty is 1.0% or 0.0187 mol dm^{-3}.

The answer should be given as 1.87 ± 0.02 mol dm^{-3}.

If the generally accepted "correct" value (obtained from the data book or other literature) is known, then the total error in the result is the difference between the literature value and the experimental value divided by the literature value and then expressed as a percentage. For example, if the "correct" concentration for the concentration determined above is 1.90 mol dm^{-3} then:

$$\text{the total error} = \frac{(1.90 - 1.87)}{1.90} \times 100 = 1.6\%$$

Graphical techniques

By plotting a suitable graph to give a straight line or some other definite relationship between the variables, graphs can be used to predict unknown values and illustrate trends. There are various methods to achieve this. They include measuring the intercept, measuring the gradient, extrapolation, and interpolation. **Interpolation** involves determining an unknown value within the limits of the values already measured. **Extrapolation** (see example on page 74 to compensate for heat loss) requires extending the graph to determine an unknown value which lies outside the range of the values measured.

If possible, try to manipulate the raw data to produce a straight-line graph. For example, when investigating the relationship between pressure and volume for a fixed mass of gas a plot of P against V gives a curve whereas a plot of P against $\frac{1}{V}$ will give a straight line. Once the graph is in the form of $y = mx + c$, then the values for both the gradient (m) and the intercept (c) can be determined.

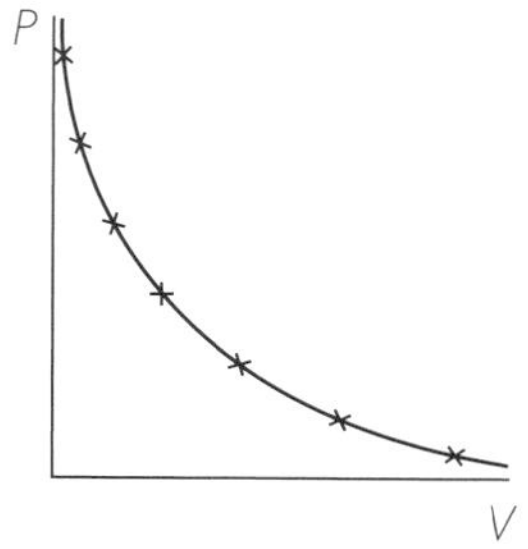

▲ Sketch graph of pressure against volume for a fixed mass of gas at a constant temperature

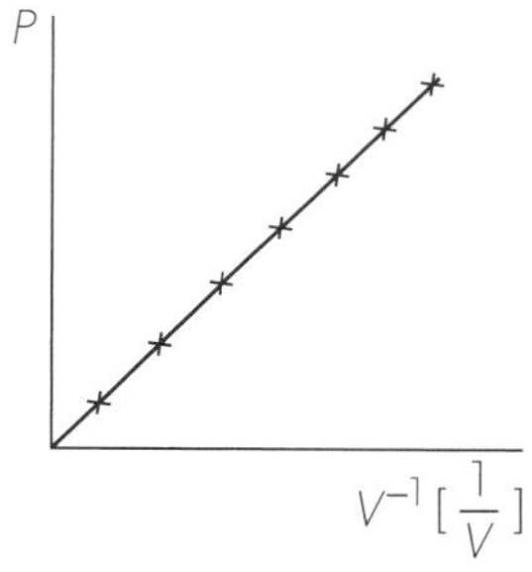

▲ Sketch graph of pressure against the reciprocal of volume for a fixed mass of gas at a constant temperature

Note that a sketched graph has labelled but unscaled axes and is used to show qualitative trends. Drawn graphs have labelled and scaled axes and are used in quantitative measurements.

The following points should be observed when drawing a graph.

- Plot the independent variable on the horizontal axis and the dependent variable on the vertical axis.
- Choose appropriate scales for the axes.
- Use SI units wherever possible.
- Label each axis and include the units.
- Draw the line of best fit.
- Give the graph a title.

Measuring a gradient from a graph

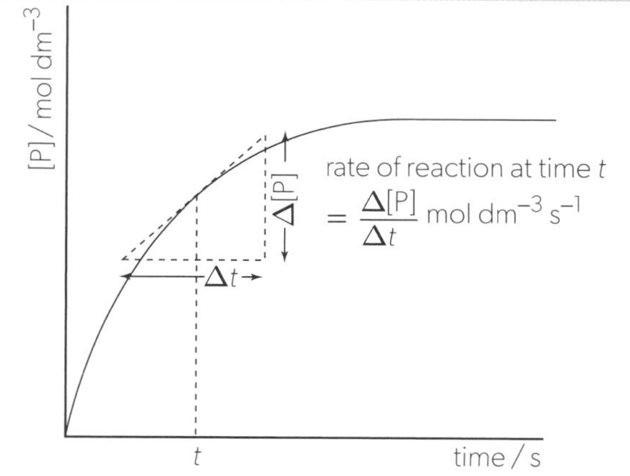

▲ A graph showing how the concentration of product P changes with time

Coefficient of determination, R^2

The coefficient of determination, also known as the R-squared value, R^2, is used to evaluate the goodness of fit of a trend line, i.e. how closely the data conforms to a linear relationship. The closer the value of R^2 is to 1, the closer the fit. For example, the graph of $\frac{PV}{n}$ against T to find the value of the gas constant (see page 147) has a coefficient of determination of 0.97. This shows that the trend line obtained from plotting the five data points is a very close fit.

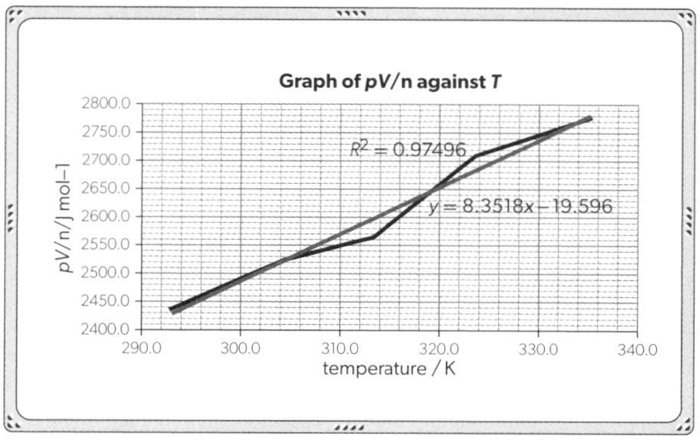

Multiple-choice questions—Tools for chemists

1. A 25.0 cm^3 sample of a basic solution of unknown concentration is to be titrated with a solution of acid of known concentration. Which of the following technique errors would give a value for the concentration of the base that is too high?

I. The pipette that is used to deliver the basic solution is rinsed only with distilled water before delivering the sample to be titrated.

II. The burette that is used to measure the acid solution is rinsed with distilled water but not with the solution of the titration.

A. **I** only **C.** Both **I** and **II**
B. **II** only **D.** Neither **I** nor **II**

2. In a school laboratory, which of the items listed below has the greatest relative uncertainty in a measurement?

A. A 50 cm^3 burette when used to measure 25 cm^3 of water

B. A 25 cm^3 pipette when used to measure 25 cm^3 of water

C. A 50 cm^3 graduated cylinder when used to measure 25 cm^3 of water

D. An analytical balance when used to weigh 25 g of water

3. A piece of metallic indium with a mass of 15.456 g was placed in 49.7 cm^3 of ethanol in a graduated cylinder. The ethanol level was observed to rise to 51.8 cm^3. From these data, the best value one can report for the density of indium is

A. 7.360 $g\,cm^{-3}$ **C.** 1.359×10^{-1} $g\,cm^{-3}$
B. 7.4 $g\,cm^{-3}$ **D.** 32.4 $g\,cm^{-3}$

4. A mixture of sodium chloride and potassium chloride is prepared by mixing 7.35 g of sodium chloride with 6.75 g of potassium chloride. The total mass of the salt mixture should be reported to __________ significant figures, the mass ratio of sodium chloride to potassium chloride should be reported to __________ significant figures, and the difference in mass between sodium chloride and potassium chloride should be reported to __________ significant figures.

The numbers required to fill the blanks above are, respectively,

A. 4, 3, 2 **C.** 3, 3, 1
B. 4, 2, 2 **D.** 4, 3, 1

5. Repeated measurements of a quantity can reduce the effects of

A. both random and systematic errors
B. neither random nor systematic errors
C. only systematic errors
D. only random errors

6. A 50.0 cm^3 pipette with an uncertainty of 0.1 cm^3 is used to measure 50.0 cm^3 of 1.00 ± 0.01 $mol\,dm^{-3}$ sodium hydroxide solution. The amount in moles of sodium hydroxide present in the measured volume is

A. 0.0500 ± 0.0010 **C.** 0.0500 ± 0.0012
B. 0.0500 ± 0.0001 **D.** 0.0500 ± 0.0006

7. Consider the following three sets each of five measurements of the same quantity; the quantity has an accurate value of 20.0.

I.	II.	III.
19.8	19.2	20.0
17.2	19.1	19.9
18.3	19.3	20.0
20.1	19.2	20.1
18.4	19.2	20.0

Which results can be described as precise?

A. **I**, **II**, and **III** **C.** **II** and **III**
B. **II** only **D.** **III** only

8. A thermometer with an accuracy of ±0.2 °C was used to record an initial temperature of 20.2 °C and a final temperature of 29.8 °C. The temperature rise was

A. 9.6 ± 0.4 °C **C.** 10 °C
B. 9.6 ± 0.2 °C **D.** 9.6 ± 0.1 °C

9. An experiment to determine the molar mass of solid hydrated copper(II) sulfate, $CuSO_4.5H_2O$, gave a result of 240 g. The experimental error was

A. 0.04% **C.** 10%
B. 4% **D.** 50%

10. Which sketch graph shows interpolation to find an unknown value?

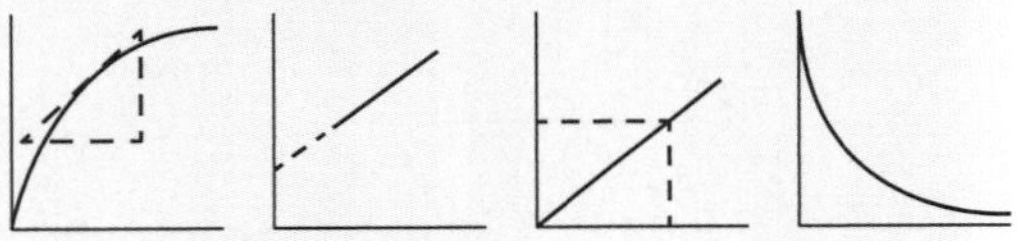

A. **B.** **C.** **D.**

11. Which is one of the seven SI base units of measurement?

A. mole, mol **C.** volts, V
B. pascal, Pa **D.** joule, J

12. What is the logarithm to base ten of 0.004? ($\log_{10} 4 = 0.60$)

A. −3.40 **B.** −3.60 **C.** −2.60 **D.** −2.40

13. An organic compound is prepared from ethanol by a four-step synthesis. Each step gives a yield of 70%. What will be the yield of the organic compound based on the initial amount of ethanol?

A. 24% **B.** 28% **C.** 34% **D.** 70%

14. Which is the correct symbol for rate constant?

A. K **B.** k **C.** *k* **D.** *K*

Practice with modelling

Modelling exercises

You can do these exercises using either physical models or digital models, or preferably both.

1. Build models of the first four members of the alkane homologous series to show that there is free rotation about the C–C single bond and that only butane can exist as structural isomers.

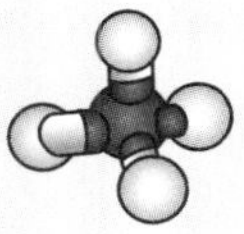

methane

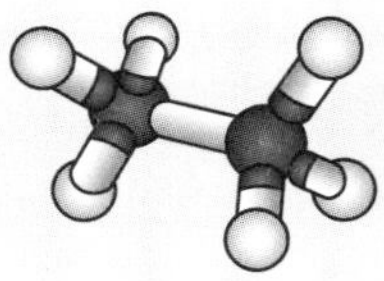

ethane

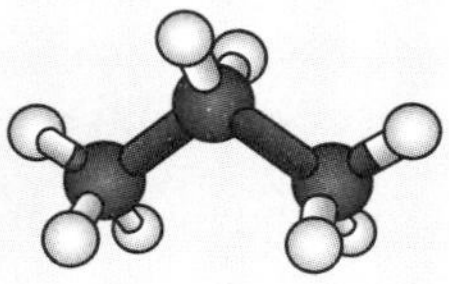

propane

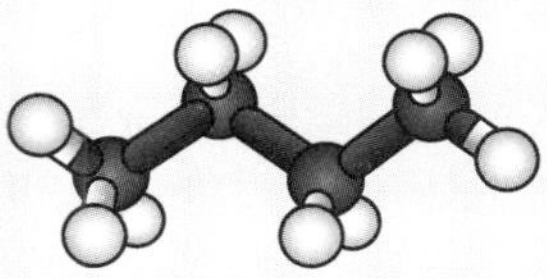

butane

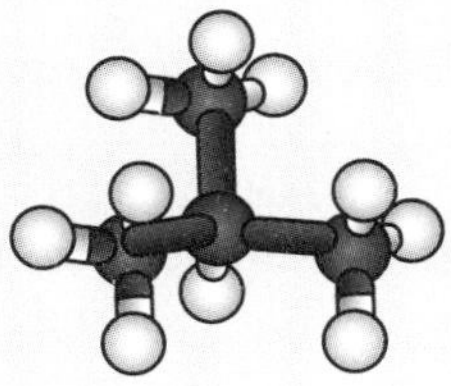

2-methylpropane

2. Make models to illustrate all the structural isomers of pentane.
3. Build models of ethane and ethene to show that there is no free rotation about a C=C double bond. Then replace two of the hydrogen atoms with chlorine atoms to show that 1,1-dicholoroethene does not show geometrical isomerism but 1,2-dichloroethene can exist either as the *cis* isomer or the *trans* isomer.

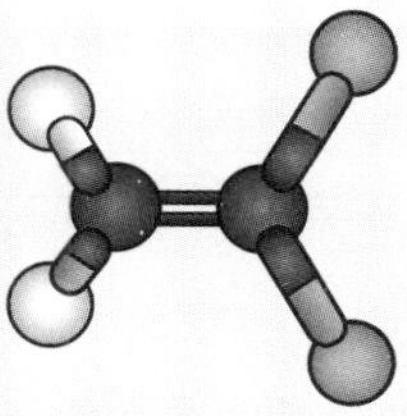

1,1-dichloroethene

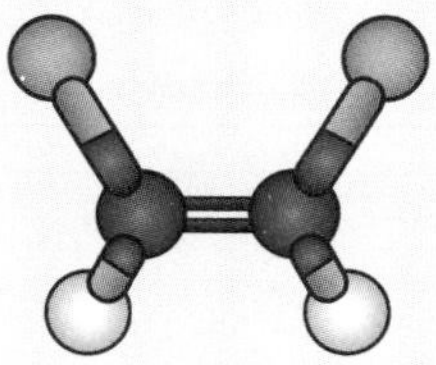

cis-1,2-dichloroethene

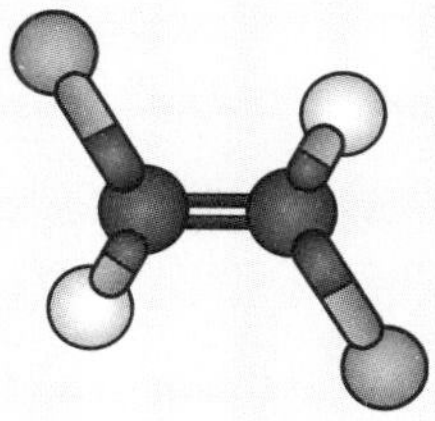

trans-1,2-dichloroethene

4. Build models of all the isomers of $C_4H_{10}O$ to show the importance of functional groups. How many different isomers of alcohols and ethers with the molecular formula $C_4H_{10}O$ can you make? Identify the alcohols as primary, secondary, or tertiary. You can repeat this exercise to find all the structural isomers and different functional groups possible for C_4H_8O. Did you remember to include cyclic structures?
5. Use one black ball and the same four different colours together with the connectors to make a tetrahedron with the colours around the central black ball. See whether the other students in your class all produce the same molecule as you or whether some are mirror images of the others. Then identify which alcohol with the molecular formula $C_4H_{10}O$ can show optical activity and make models of its two enantiomers.
6. Build models of these molecules/ions: CO_2, HCN, NH_3, NH_4^+, BF_3, and NO_3^-.(For HL only, also build models of XeF_4, SF_6, ICl_4^+, and SF_4).

Nature of science

Nature of science and theory of knowledge

The theory of knowledge (TOK) course considers 12 different concepts. In TOK classes you examine the strengths and weaknesses of these concepts and apply them to different areas of knowledge, one of which is the natural sciences. Put simply, the nature of science (NOS) is very much related to this part of TOK, i.e. TOK as applied to the area of knowledge that is natural sciences and, for this course, chemistry in particular.

The *IB Chemistry Guide* (which you can obtain from your teacher) contains a section describing the nature of science. It is well worth reading this as it could be helpful to you when you come to write your TOK essay or create your TOK exhibition. Essentially, it covers some key questions. For example:

1. What do we want to know in science?
2. How do we do science?
3. What type of knowledge do scientists produce?
4. What is the impact of scientific knowledge?

It also attempts to distinguish between the nature of science and theory of knowledge as it is applied to the natural sciences. Whereas TOK seeks to think critically and more broadly about the concepts that underpin knowledge production, NOS is more specific. An example it uses to illustrate this is peer review. In NOS, the process of peer review might be described as supporting objectivity in scientific literature. In TOK, the limitations of the process of peer review might be considered and a comparison made as to how objectivity in the natural sciences compares with objectivity in other areas of knowledge.

As you go through the two-year chemistry course, it is instructive to see how specific chemistry topics relate to these concepts. Different sub-topics exemplify different aspects of the concepts and some examples are given below to illustrate this. If you know and understand these you will be in a good position to answer the very few questions involving the nature of science on the chemistry exam papers. You will also be in a strong position when it comes to writing your TOK essay. This is because TOK examiners tend to give credit for relevant specific examples taken from subjects you study to back up your arguments. Too often they just see students using the typical examples provided by TOK class teachers who, of course, cannot be experts in all the different disciplines you study.

Examples of some key aspects

Changing theories

Theories change to accommodate new information and understanding as chemistry develops. The different theories of acids provide a good example of this. In Roman times, an acid was defined as a sour substance, then (Lavoisier, 1780s) as the oxide of a non-metal in water, then as a substance that donates protons (Lowry and Brønsted, 1923), before being defined as a substance that accepts a pair of electrons (Lewis, also in 1923). An even later definition (Usanovich, 1930s) defines an acid as a substance that accepts negative species or donates positive species.

Occam's razor

This states that simple explanations are, other things being equal, generally better than more complex ones. For example, collision theory is very simple but, based on models of reacting species, it explains kinetic theory and the factors affecting the rate of chemical reactions.

Falsification

Karl Popper, in the 1950s, maintained that it is impossible to prove something by doing an experiment, as you would need to do an infinite number of experiments to cover every possible permutation. However, if you try to disprove a theory, you only need one successful experiment to disprove it. He maintained that a theory is only scientific if it is capable of being falsified. $pV = nRT$ is only true for an ideal gas; real gases do occupy some volume and do have some weak intermolecular forces of attraction. Lavoisier's theory of acids was falsified when scientists realized that HCN and HCl are acids but do not contain oxygen.

Paradigm shift

Thomas Kuhn, in his 1962 book *The Structure of Scientific Revolutions*, proposed that scientific progress works through paradigms. A paradigm is an established model accepted by the scientific community. As more becomes known, the paradigm has to accommodate to fit the new knowledge. Eventually, it becomes unwieldy and a new model becomes accepted; this is a paradigm shift.

The classic example in early chemistry is phlogiston, thought of as a substance that was given off by everything when it burned. Even when Priestly discovered oxygen he called it "dephlogisticated air", as substances readily gave up phlogiston to it. It took the genius of Lavoisier to explain that combustion occurs when substances combine with oxygen rather than giving off a substance.

A more modern paradigm in chemistry is simple covalent bonding using the octet rule. Sharing a pair of electrons (one from each atom) to form a share in an inert gas structure works for simple substances such as hydrogen, methane, carbon dioxide, etc. The octet rule has to be stretched to include coordinate bonding and resonance hybrids but cannot explain substances such as SF_6 or NO.

A new paradigm is molecular orbital theory or valence bond theory, which takes account of the fact that electrons are in different orbitals and energy levels and also explains why diatomic oxygen is paramagnetic. Another example of a paradigm shift is the change from the understanding that atoms are indivisible to the paradigm in which they can be broken into many different sub-atomic particles.

Serendipity

Serendipity is the accidental discovery of something useful when not looking for it. Legend has it that glass was discovered when Phoenician sailors cooked a meal on a sandy beach. Liquid crystals were discovered by Friedrich Reinitzer when he was doing experiments with cholesteryl benzoate, William Perkin discovered azo dyes when he was trying to synthesize quinine, and Alexander Fleming is credited with discovering penicillin when he was working with staphylococci bacteria. Other examples include the discovery of Teflon (poly(tetrafluoroethene)) and superglue.

Models

Chemists use a variety of molecular models to represent the structure of molecules (e.g. ball and stick, space filling) and they use more sophisticated computer modelling to represent systems in which there are many different variables, such as climate change. Many potential drugs are first made virtually and modelled to see whether they might be effective before synthesizing those which look as if they may have some potential to test *in vitro* and then *in vivo*.

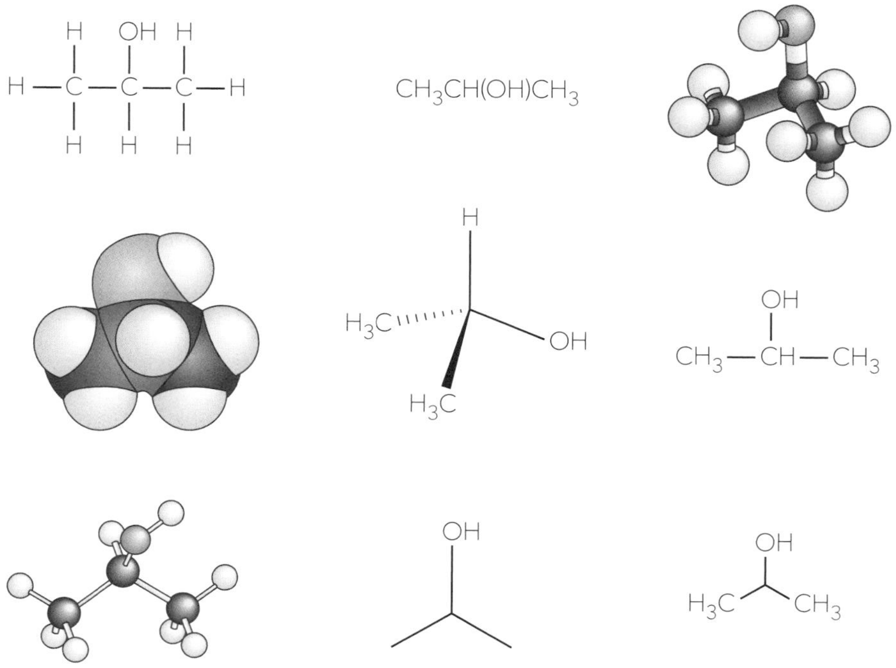

▲ Some of the different models that can be used to represent the structure of propan-2-ol

Use of concepts

Chemists often use concepts to work out values that cannot be determined directly. Energy cycles are a good example of this because they are based on the first law of thermodynamics – energy can neither be created nor destroyed. It is easy to determine the enthalpies of combustion of carbon, hydrogen, and methane practically. It is impossible to determine the enthalpy of formation of methane directly as carbon and hydrogen can react together to form many different compounds. However, by using an energy cycle the value for the enthalpy of formation can be readily obtained indirectly.

Assumptions

Sometimes, chemistry is based upon assumptions, even though they are not true, in order to provide a useful model. For example, to determine the oxidation numbers of elements in a molecule such as ammonia, you assume that it is ionic, with the "anion" being the element with the higher electronegativity, in this case nitrogen, so the oxidation number of nitrogen is −3 and the oxidation number of hydrogen is +1. For the simple octet rule and to determine shapes using VSEPR theory, it is assumed that all valence electrons are the same – the fact that there are s and p electrons in different energy levels is ignored. Oxidation is commonly defined as the loss of electrons and yet when carbon burns in oxygen neither carbon nor oxygen loses electrons.

Predictions

A good scientific theory enables scientists to make predictions. For example, theory explains that the lines in the visible emission spectrum of hydrogen are due to excited electrons dropping from higher energy levels to the $n = 2$ level. If this is true, one can predict that there should be another series of lines at higher energy corresponding to electrons dropping to the lower $n = 1$ level. This cannot be seen by the naked eye but the series is there if you use an ultraviolet spectrometer. Similarly, there are more series at lower energy in the infrared region due to electrons dropping to the $n = 3$ and $n = 4$ levels, etc.

Ethical implications

Fritz Haber won the Nobel Prize for Chemistry in 1918 for discovering how to fix nitrogen. This process allows the synthesis of artificial fertilizers to feed the world but also to provide nitrogen for explosives. Haber, a German chemist, also worked on chlorine as a poison gas in World War 1. He is a classic illustration of the ethical problems facing chemists.

Energy is needed by society, but almost all the ways in which it is generated are also bad for society. Green chemistry is one way in which chemists try to act responsibly towards society and yet still make scientific advances and supply goods, such as drugs and pesticides, which are helpful to society.

Instrumentation

Modern instrumentation has revolutionized the way chemists work. For example, it is now possible to measure the very small quantities of performance-enhancing drugs in athletes who cheat, to catch criminals from DNA residues, and to manipulate the addition of precise amounts of metals during the production of alloys to achieve desired properties. It has also enabled chemists to quickly and unambiguously assign structures to new compounds.

International mindedness

Introduction

Scientific knowledge has always tended to be freely available; the scientific method incorporates peer review, open-mindedness, and freedom of thought.

Chemistry clearly has a very large international dimension. Once gases are released (whether polluting or not) they do not remain in one country. Oil and other raw feedstocks are moved across oceans as well as across continents. In one way, even the elements are international. Not only are some of them distributed unevenly on the planet but they can also have slightly different relative atomic masses depending on their origin.

IUPAC

The International Union of Pure and Applied Chemistry (IUPAC) was formed in 1919. It is an international, non-governmental body consisting of chemists from industry and academia that has the aim of fostering worldwide communication in chemistry.

Currently, about 1000 chemists throughout the world are engaged on a voluntary basis working for IUPAC. One of the greatest achievements of IUPAC has been to bring in a logical and accepted way of naming compounds.

International cooperation

There are many examples of chemists cooperating both with other chemists and with other scientists and international bodies. These include international attempts to deal with climate change. In 1987, the Montreal Protocol set in motion ways to deal with the threat to the ozone layer by banning the use of CFCs. In the twenty-first century, the Kyoto Protocol paved the way for combatting global warming by reducing and minimizing the release of greenhouse gases. Other examples of international cooperation include the International Space Station and CERN in Geneva, both of which involve scientists from many different countries.

International symbols and units

Whatever their mother tongue, chemists can communicate with each other through the use of a recognized system of symbols and units. Look at a periodic table written in a language unfamiliar to you. You will still be able to use it, as the elements have the same symbols and the units for their properties are also international. Similarly, in any text book, you will see chemical equations written in the same format. Chemists use the International System of Units (SI), derived from the French *Le Système international d'unités*. It is true that some countries still cling to their traditional units – the UK has miles and pints, the US has Fahrenheit, and the French have millilitres – but in scientific papers chemists will use metres (m) , kelvin (K) (or still sometimes °C), centimetres cubed (cm^3), and decimetres cubed (dm^3). Gone, too, are the days when pressure was measured in millimetres of mercury or atmospheres; now pascals (Pa or $N\,m^{-2}$) are used internationally.

International legacy

Chemists communicate mainly by publishing in peer-reviewed journals. When doing research, they will make searches from journals published from around the world, many of which are now available online. All chemists recognize the work that others have done or are doing, and build upon it. Chemists also build on the international legacy of words. *Acidus* means sour in Latin and the Germans and Norwegians still use the words *sauer* and *syre*, respectively, for "acid". *Alkali* is derived from the Arabic word for calcined ashes and *oxygene* is a Greek word meaning "acid forming".

International wealth

A few countries, such as Bhutan, define their national wealth in terms of GNH (Gross National Happiness); most of the others define it in terms of GNP (Gross National Product). A country's wealth depends upon many factors but one of them is the availability of natural resources and the means to exploit them. This can change over time. Many states have grown rich on their oil deposits. Rare-earth metals, which are a very limited resource and are spread unevenly around the world, are now in high demand as they are needed in the manufacture of many hi-tech products. They can be difficult to extract and are now being stockpiled or controlled by some countries even though they are used by many.

Life expectancy is related to wealth. Life expectancy has increased dramatically in the developed world due to the contributions from chemists in areas such as the provision of safe drinking water, good sanitation, and the availability of effective drugs, pesticides, insecticides, and artificial fertilizers.

Making links between topics (1)

A holistic example of links between all the topics

The linking questions in the syllabus provide ideas of links to other parts of the syllabus. You are encouraged to further your inquiry skills by making your own links between topics. One way to do this is to take each topic in turn and think of actual examples as to how it can relate to all the other parts of the syllabus. As well as covering all the links given in the subject guide, this can be a really good way to review your knowledge and understanding at the end of the course before you take your final exams.

An example of this is to place "Models of bonding and structure" (Chapter 4) in the centre and then think of ways in which the chemistry covered in Chapter 4 can be related, in turn, to all the other topics covered in Chapters 1–12 and also to nature of science, international mindedness, inquiry skills, and tools for chemists. You can place another one of the topics in the centre and make relationships between that and all the other topics and then repeat the exercise until each of the topics has had its turn in the middle. The example provided below is just for Standard Level but you can include the AHL as well if you are taking Higher Level.

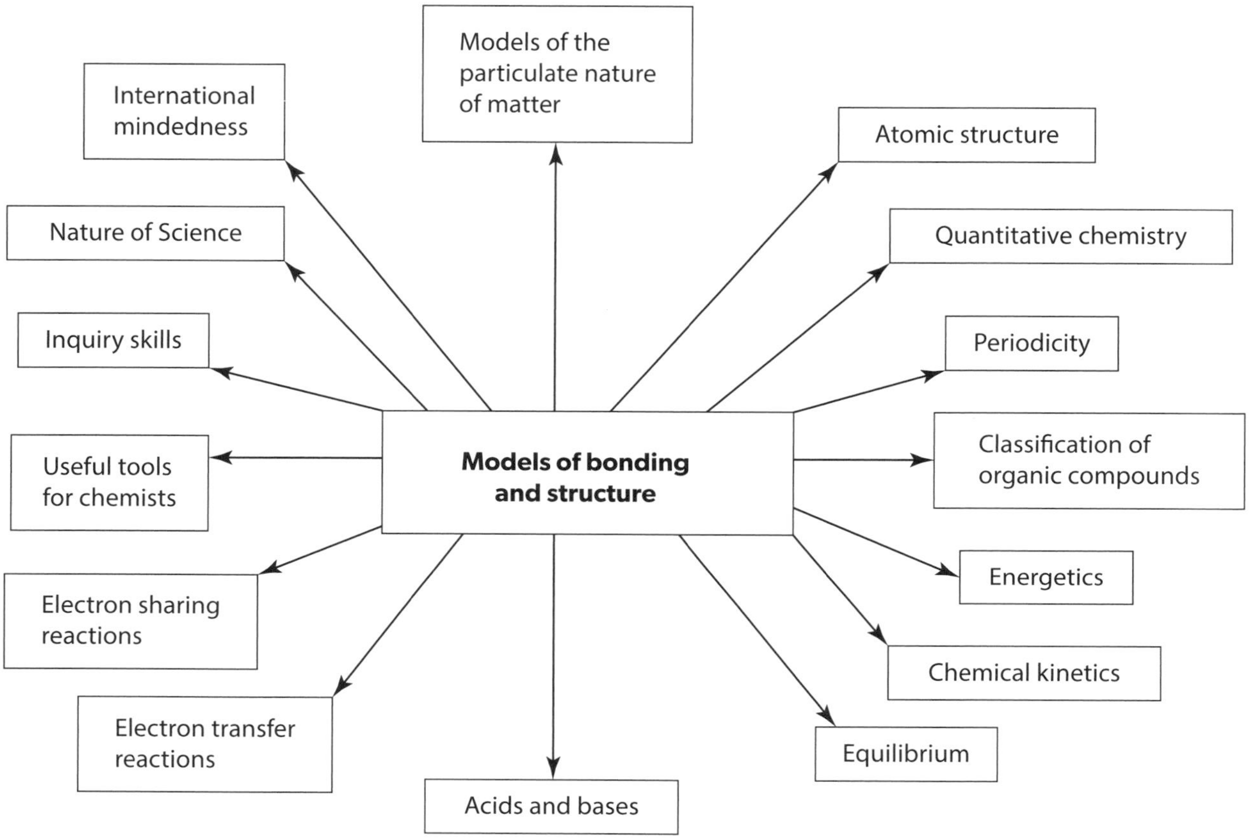

- **Models of the particulate nature of matter**
  Different types of bonding affect the properties of substances, including changes of state.
- **Atomic structure**
  Ionic compounds are formed as the result of electron transfer. The electrons that are transferred result in the ions formed having the same electron arrangement as a noble gas.
- **Quantitative chemistry**
  When comparing the strengths of single, double, and triple covalent bonds between atoms, molar quantities are used so the values are in $kJ\ mol^{-1}$.
- **Periodicity**
  To predict whether a compound formed between two elements will be covalent or ionic, their position in the periodic table and their electronegativities need to be taken into account.

Making links between topics (2)

- **Energetics**
  To be able to explain the relationship between the number of bonds and bond strength, it is necessary to be able to calculate the enthalpy changes associated with breaking and making bonds.
- **Chemical kinetics**
  The rate of a reaction increases as the temperature is increased because the extra energy increases the likelihood of the shared pair of electrons in a covalent bond having the necessary activation energy to split apart when molecules collide.
- **Equilibrium**
  When comparing boiling points to give an indication of the strength of intermolecular forces of attraction, the liquid is in dynamic equilibrium with the vapour. The boiling point is the temperature at which the vapour pressure is equal to the external pressure.
- **Acids and bases**
  When weak acids dissociate in aqueous solution, a covalent bond needs to be broken to form a hydronium ion, H_3O^+, and the acid radical.
- **Electron transfer reactions**
  The formation of ionic compounds (such as NaCl or MgO) from their elements involves the transfer of electrons, so it can always be classified as a redox reaction. The species that has lost electrons is oxidized and the species that has gained electrons is reduced.
- **Electron sharing reactions**
  Nucleophiles are electron-rich species that contain a non-bonding pair of electrons that they donate to an electron-deficient carbon. The donated pair of electrons form a coordinate bond.
- **Tools for chemists**
  The relative polarity of bonds can be predicted from electronegativity values. These values are not exact and there are different scales of measurement. Pauling's scale gives the values to one decimal place, which, for most values, is two significant figures.
- **Inquiry skills**
  The ability to identify and explain patterns is required to understand the graph of boiling points versus period for the hydrides of groups 14, 15, 16, and 17 in relation to hydrogen bonding.
- **Nature of science**
  When using VSEPR theory, the assumption is made that all the valence electrons are equal. The theory ignores the fact that they can be in different energy levels, as some are in s orbitals and some are in p orbitals.
- **International mindedness**
  Two Americans, Richard Smalley and Robert Curl, and one British chemist, Harold Kroto, were awarded the Nobel Prize in Chemistry in 1996 for working together in the discovery of buckminsterfullerene, C_{60}.

1. Zinc reacts with copper according to the following equation:

$$Zn(s) + CuSO_4(aq) \rightarrow ZnSO_4(aq) + Cu(s)$$

2.93 g of zinc powder was added to 50.0 cm³ of 0.250 mol dm⁻³ copper(II) sulfate solution in a calorimeter.

a) (i) Determine the limiting reagent in this reaction [2]

(ii) The mass of copper obtained experimentally was 0.679 g. Calculate the percentage yield of copper. [2]

b) (i) The maximum temperature rise of the solution was 11.1 °C.

Calculate the experimentally obtained value for the enthalpy change, ΔH, of the reaction, in kJ mol⁻¹, assuming that all the heat evolved in the reaction was transferred to the solution. [2]

(ii) Identify another assumption that you have made in b)(i). [1]

(iii) The major uncertainty in the experimental method used is the measure of the temperature rise. Assuming that this is the only uncertainty, determine the absolute uncertainty in the value of ΔH obtained experimentally if the uncertainty in the temperature rise was ±0.5 °C. [2]

c) (i) Sketch a graph of the concentration of zinc(II) sulfate, $ZnSO_4$, against time as the reaction proceeds. [2]

(ii) Show how the initial rate of reaction can be determined from the graph in part c)(i). [2]

(iii) Explain why replacing the zinc powder with a piece of zinc of the same mass lowers the rate of the reaction. [2]

2. a) Ethane-1,2-diol, also known as ethylene glycol, is fully miscible with water and is used as "anti-freeze". It can be manufactured by reacting dimethyl oxalate, $C_4H_6O_4$, with hydrogen according to the equation

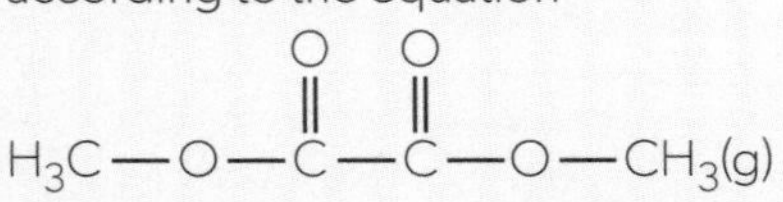

$$H_3C{-}O{-}\overset{\overset{O}{\|}}{C}{-}\overset{\overset{O}{\|}}{C}{-}O{-}CH_3(g) + 4H_2(g) \rightleftharpoons$$

$$HOCH_2CH_2OH(g) + 2CH_2OH(g)$$

(i) State the equilibrium constant expression, K, for this reaction. [1]

(ii) Deduce how increasing the pressure of the reaction mixture at a constant temperature will affect the value of K. [2]

(iii) Use section 12 of the data booklet to determine the enthalpy change, ΔH (in kJ), for this reaction. [3]

b) Ethane-1,2-diol ($M_r = 62$) and butane ($M_r = 58$) have similar relative formula masses.

Explain why the boiling point of ethane-1,2-diol is significantly greater than that of butane. [2]

c) Ethane-1,2-diol can be oxidized first to ethanedioic acid, $(COOH)_2$, and then to carbon dioxide and water. Use the changes in the oxidation state of carbon to outline that these two steps are oxidation reactions. [2]

d) Ethanedioic acid is a weak acid. Distinguish between a weak acid and a strong acid. [1]

e) Outline why acidity is usually expressed using the pH scale rather than using the hydrogen ion concentration in mol dm⁻³. [1]

f) 4.71 g of crystals of a slightly impure sample of hydrated ethanedioic acid, $(COOH)_2 \cdot 2H_2O$, was dissolved in water and the solution made up to 1.00 dm³ in a volumetric flask. 20.0 cm³ samples of this solution were titrated against 0.100 mol dm⁻³ sodium hydroxide solution using a suitable acid–base indicator.

$$(COOH)_2(aq) + 2NaOH(aq) \rightarrow (COONa)_2(aq) + 2H_2O(l)$$

The volume of the NaOH(aq) solution required to react with all the acid was 14.6 cm³.

(i) Determine the amount, in mol, of sodium hydroxide in 14.6 cm³ of a 0.100 mol dm⁻³ NaOH solution. [1]

(ii) Calculate the amount, in mol, of ethanedioic acid in each 20.0 cm³ sample. [1]

(iii) Determine the percentage purity of the sample of hydrated ethanedioic acid. [4]

3. Ammonium nitrate, NH_4NO_3, is a rich source of nitrogen, and so is a good fertilizer.

a) Calculate the percentage by mass of nitrogen in ammonium nitrate using section 7 of the data booklet. [2]

b) State the number of electron domains around the central nitrogen atom in the ammonium ion and in the nitrate ion and deduce the actual shapes (ion geometries) of both ions, applying VSEPR theory. [4]

c) Ammonium nitrate can be manufactured by reacting calcium nitrate with ammonia and carbon dioxide in the presence of water.

$$Ca(NO_3)_2(aq) + 2NH_3(g) + CO_2(g) + H_2O(l) \rightarrow 2NH_4NO_3(aq) + CaCO_3(s)$$

(i) Assuming that the calcium carbonate is discarded, calculate the atom economy of this reaction. [1]

(ii) Determine the maximum mass of ammonium nitrate that could be obtained from 40.0 kg of calcium nitrate. [2]

d) When calcium nitrate is heated strongly it decomposes to form nitrogen(IV) oxide, oxygen, and calcium oxide.

(i) Deduce the equation for this reaction, including the state symbols. [2]

(ii) Identify the element that is oxidized and the element that is reduced during this reaction. [2]

e) Ammonium nitrate needs to be handled and stored with care as it is potentially explosive. It decomposes when heated. At temperatures above 300 °C the reaction is exothermic and the products are mainly nitrogen, oxygen, and water.

$2NH_4NO_3(s) \rightarrow 2N_2(g) + O_2(g) + 4H_2O(g)$

(i) Suggest why ammonium nitrate is potentially explosive. [2]

(ii) Ammonium nitrate is very soluble in water. During the process, the temperature of the water decreases as the ionic lattice of the ammonium nitrate breaks down and the ions become hydrated. Compare and contrast the relative strengths of the lattice energy and the hydration energy. [2]

AHL

4. Butanone can be prepared from but-1-ene in several steps.

$$C_4H_8 \xrightarrow{\text{Step 1}} C_4H_9Br \xrightarrow{\text{Step 2}} C_4H_{10}O \xrightarrow{\text{Step 3}} C_4H_8O$$

a) Consider Step 1, the conversion of but-1-ene to C_4H_9Br.

(i) Identify the name of the mechanism for this type of reaction. [1]

(ii) State the IUPAC name of the major product. [1]

(iii) Outline why it is the major product. [2]

b) An experiment was carried out to determine the order of the reaction for step 2 between C_4H_9Br and aqueous sodium hydroxide. The following results were obtained.

Experiment	$[C_4H_9Br]$ / $mol\,dm^{-3}$	$[OH^-]$ / $mol\,dm^{-3}$	Initial rate / $mol\,dm^{-3}\,s^{-1}$
1	0.10	0.10	8.6×10^{-4}
2	0.20	0.20	3.4×10^{-3}
3	0.30	0.10	2.6×10^{-3}

(i) Deduce the overall order of the reaction and hence the rate equation from these results. [3]

(ii) Deduce the type of mechanism for the reaction of step 2 between C_4H_9Br and aqueous sodium hydroxide. [1]

(iii) Sketch the mechanism using curly arrows to represent the movement of electrons. [4]

(iv) If the product from step 1 is separated into optically active isomers and just the form that rotates plane-polarized light to the left is used in step 2, deduce what type of optical activity, if any, will be shown by the product, $C_4H_{10}O$. [2]

c) Consider step 3, the conversion of $C_4H_{10}O$ to C_4H_8O.

(i) State the necessary conditions and reagents required to bring about this reaction. [2]

(ii) Describe how the number of signals and the integration trace in the ^1H NMR spectrum of C_4H_8O will differ from the ^1H NMR spectrum of $C_4H_{10}O$. [4]

d) Identify, with an explanation, which of the products, C_4H_9Br, $C_4H_{10}O$, or C_4H_8O, has the following infrared spectrum. [2]

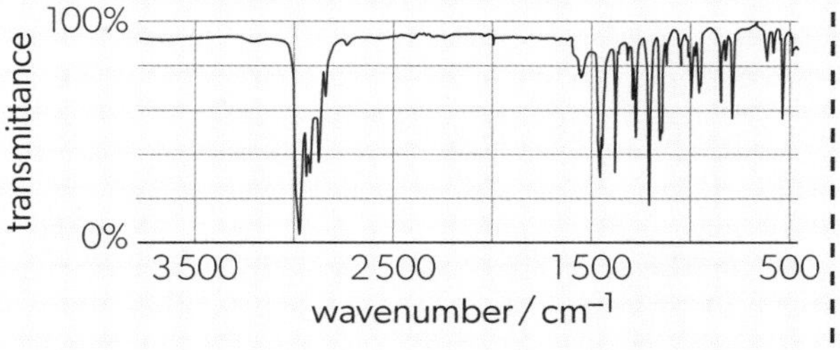

5. Calcium carbide, CaC_2, reacts with water to form calcium hydroxide and ethyne, C_2H_2. Ethyne burns in air with a sooty flame but in oxygen it burns with a very hot blue flame which can be used to weld metals.

a) State the equation for the reaction between calcium carbide and water. [1]

b) (i) Draw an energy cycle to show the relationship between the standard enthalpy of formation of ethyne and the standard enthalpies of combustion of carbon, hydrogen, and ethyne. [1]

(ii) Use the relevant enthalpies of combustion given in section 14 of the data booklet to determine the standard enthalpy of formation of ethyne. [1]

(iii) Compare your answer to **b)(ii)** with the value given in section 13 of the data booklet and suggest why the values are different. [1]

(iv) Use the values given in section 13 of the data booklet to determine the temperature, in °C, above which the formation of ethyne from its elements becomes spontaneous. [3]

AHL

c) (i) Draw the Lewis formula (electron dot structure) for ethyne. [1]

(ii) State the hybridization of the two carbon atoms in ethyne and show how the bonding can be explained using sigma and pi bonds. [2]

(iii) Explain how the shape of an ethyne molecule can be deduced using **(I)** VSEPR theory and **(II)** hybridization. [2]

d) Ethyne undergoes an addition reaction with methanol in the presence of a catalyst to form methoxyethene, $H_2C{=}CHOCH_3$:

$C_2H_2(g) + CH_3OH(g) \rightarrow H_2C{=}CHOCH_3(g)$

(i) Explain why the ^1H NMR spectrum of methoxyethene shows two doublets close together due to the $=CH_2$ protons. [2]

(ii) Methoxyethene can undergo addition polymerization. Represent the repeating unit of the polymer. [1]

(iii) Methoxyethene can also undergo an electrophilic addition reaction with hydrogen bromide. Draw the structural formula of the major product formed in this reaction. [1]

Inquiry process

In addition to requiring tools to understand and apply chemistry, chemists also need to develop skills of inquiry. These skills can be laid out in an inquiry cycle. They are examined, particularly in the internally assessed component of the final assessment, but they are also relevant throughout the whole of your chemistry course.

Exploration

Young children are naturally curious about their surroundings and it is good to try to maintain that approach as you mature into an adult. The concepts and content in the chapters covering Structure and Reactivity can seem like factual information that it is necessary to learn to pass written examinations. However, remember that it has all come from the innate curiosity of scientists over the centuries. Rather than just accept what you read and are taught, try to show independent thinking and explore the concepts for yourself. Think about what you are studying and find examples in the IB syllabus where contradictions seem to occur. Is something you learn in one topic ignored or treated differently in another topic or even within the same topic? For example, the ionic bonding of sodium chloride is often explained by a sodium atom donating an electron to a chlorine atom but the actual reaction to form sodium chloride is between sodium metal, in which the electrons are already delocalized, and a chlorine molecule, not a chlorine atom. When covering acids and bases, you learn that the pH scale goes from 0 to 14 and that $pH = -log_{10}[H^+(aq)]$, so what is the pH of 2.0 mol dm^{-3} HCl(aq)? The usual reason for these discrepancies is that a deeper knowledge of chemistry than IB Diploma level is required. However, you can explore the subject by asking searching questions, reading widely from a variety of sources, and selecting sufficient and relevant information to address problem areas. You can show initiative by formulating inquiry questions to research and by making predictions based on scientific knowledge and the insight you have gained.

Designing

Chemistry is an experimental science. Sometimes practical work has a specific aim, e.g. to synthesize in the laboratory a particular substance that occurs in nature from simple starting materials. At other times it can be a more open-ended investigation, e.g. to see how altering just one variable can affect a particular aspect of a reaction while all the other factors that could affect that aspect are kept constant. This second type of experiment is likely to form the basis of your scientific investigation. Having formulated a research question, you will need to consider possible ways in which you can investigate it, i.e. the methodology of the investigation. You will need to identify all the variables, select the dependent and independent variables, justify why you have selected them, and show how all the other variables listed can be controlled. You can show creativity both in the design and implementation of your investigation. When designing, you will need to decide whether you will obtain primary data through hands-on practical work or whether you will obtain secondary data through a variety of possible sources (such as databases or modelling systems through simulations), or whether you will try to obtain a combination of both primary and secondary data. You can show initiative by altering established methods or by designing the apparatus or simulations yourself. Once you have settled on your methodology, it is wise to pilot it first, i.e. do a trial run, to check that it works, and, if necessary, make any adjustments. You can then ascertain and justify the range and quantity of measurements you will need to be able to address your inquiry question fully.

Controlling variables

Having decided which variable you are going to manipulate (the independent variable) and which variable you are going to measure and how you are going to measure it (the dependent variable), you need to decide how you are going to control all the other variables and how this control will be monitored. If the controlled variables do change during the investigation, you cannot be certain that the only factor bringing about change to the dependent variable is the independent variable. For this reason, it is important to monitor all the variables throughout the process. For example, chemical reactions are either exothermic or endothermic and may involve considerable heat change, which affects the temperature. Unless temperature is the dependent or independent variable, then the temperature of the reaction vessel and any other surrounding equipment needs to be kept constant. One way of doing this is using a water bath and taking the temperature of the water before, during and immediately after any reaction takes place. If temperature is the dependent variable (e.g. in calorimetry experiments), then you need to insulate the system to prevent heat loss/gain to the surroundings. Sometimes, where it may be difficult to physically control a variable, you will need to make assumptions. For example, provided that your reaction vessel is open to the atmosphere, it is reasonable to assume that the atmospheric pressure remains constant throughout, but you should still identify that the pressure is controlled.

Make sure you also consider the controls necessary to make accurate measurements. For example, pH meters must be calibrated using buffered solutions before they are used, and calibration curves will be needed for colorimetry investigations where concentration is determined by the absorbance of coloured solutions at a fixed wavelength (λ_{max}). When making up standard solutions, use the most appropriate equipment, e.g. an accurate balance, pipettes, burettes and volumetric flasks, rather than kitchen scales and measuring cylinders.

Collecting and recording data

Raw data may be both qualitative and quantitative and is often a combination of both. Qualitative data in chemistry are the physical changes detected by your senses. These include smell, colour changes, effervescence when a gas is evolved, heat being given out or taken in, etc. Qualitative data should be identified and recorded. Quantitative data is obtained by measuring a physical quantity. For your investigation, you need to record raw quantitative data, much of which will then be processed. When recording quantitative data, include the value to the correct number of significant figures or decimal places, the units and the uncertainty associated with the measuring instrument. You also need to record sufficient readings so that a justifiable conclusion can be reached. Don't forget to include all the data you obtain to monitor the control variables, even if there is no need to process it. One of the best ways to record data that consists of a series of readings is by placing it in a table where the headings include the units and uncertainties. One advantage of writing the uncertainty followed by a slash (which means divide by) before the units in each heading is that you can then leave the uncertainties and units out of all the values in the columns beneath. Here is an example.

Time ± 0.01 / m	Temperature ± 0.2 / °C
0	21.3
0.50	23.6
1.00	26.9
1.50	30.1

Processing data

The reason for processing quantitative data is to put the raw data into a format that will identify patterns, trends, and relationships that are relevant to the research question. How you process clearly depends upon the type of data collected. For example, with repeat titration results that should give identical values, you should calculate the average volume used. Usually, however, to find trends, the raw data should be processed and then presented graphically. The direct variable may not actually be the prime variable of importance, so the first step might be to calculate the variable required, such as enthalpy values from a temperature rise or concentration from absorbance values. This may even require more steps so that, for example, once a rate equation has been obtained from the concentrations, further processing can lead to values for the rate constant at different temperatures. All the processing should be done accurately and it should be clear to the reader how it has been done so that, if necessary, the results could be checked. For repeat calculations of the same type, it is only necessary to show the working once and the processed results can then be presented in tabular form.

Interpreting results

Qualitative data should be explained, for example "the colour changed from orange to green during the reaction as Cr(VI) was reduced to Cr(III)". Quantitative data is almost always best interpreted graphically. Required graphing techniques have already been covered in Tools for chemists on page 155. Graphs can provide considerable information through the use of tangents, interpolation and extrapolation. If possible, try to plot a straight-line graph, which may require further processing, e.g. taking reciprocals or logarithms. Straight-line graphs lead directly to clear and quantifiable relationships from their shape, where they pass through the axes and from the equation in the form of $y = mx + c$. There are basically four different straight-line graphs that can be considered.

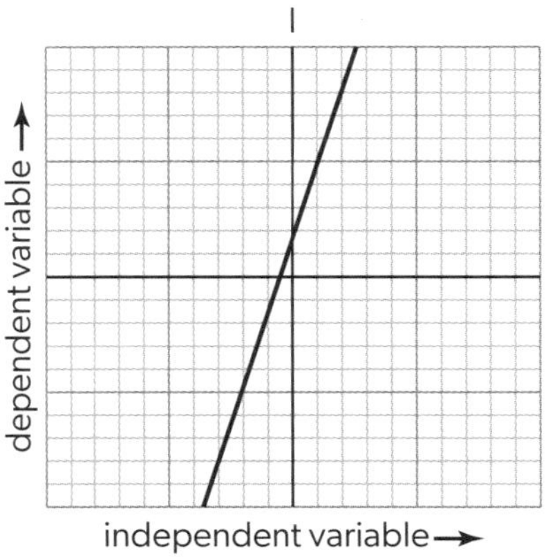

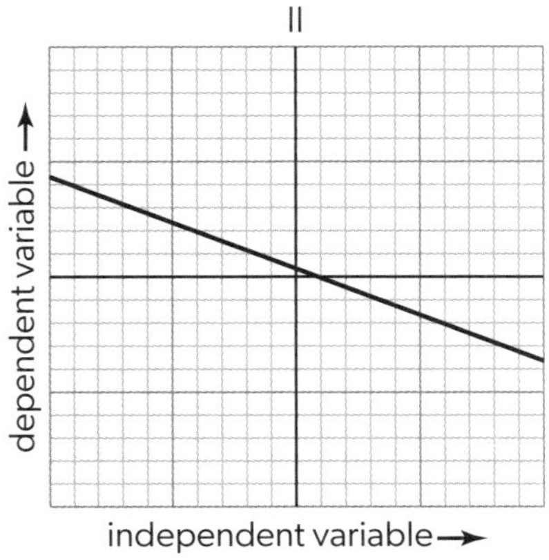

Graphs I and II show the relationship is directly proportional as the graphs pass through the origin. Graph I ($y = mx$) is positively directly proportional and the graph passes through the origin; as one variable increases the other variable increases by a constant ratio. Graph II ($y = -mx$) is negatively directly proportional and the graph passes through the origin; as one variable decreases the other variable decreases by a constant ratio.

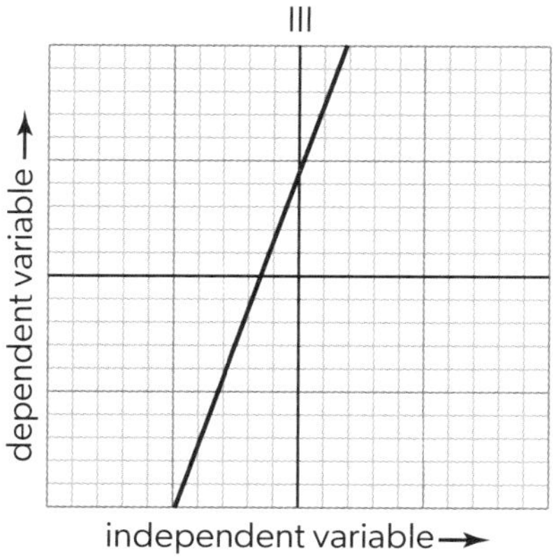

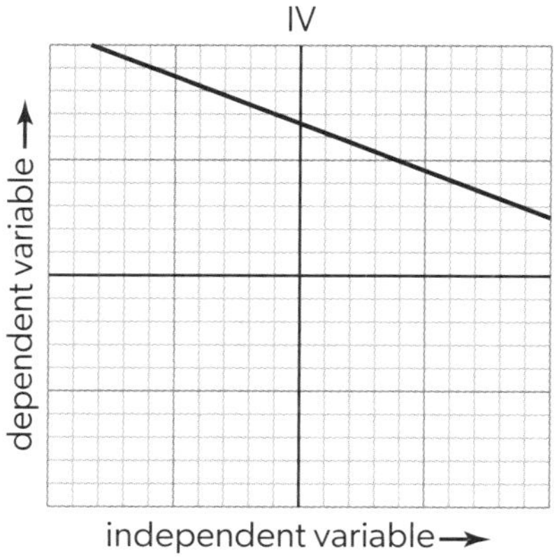

Graphs III and IV show that the relationships are just linear (not directly proportional) as neither graph passes through the origin. Graph III ($y = mx + c$) has a positive gradient; as one variable increases the other increases by a constant amount. Graph IV ($y = -mx + c$) has a negative gradient; as one variable increases the other decreases by a constant amount.

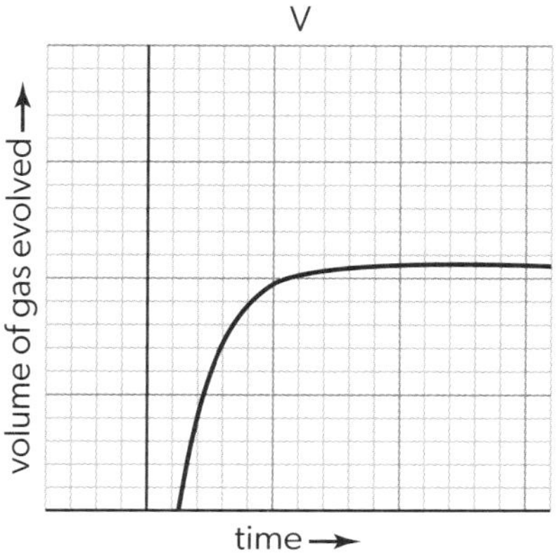

If a straight-line graph cannot be obtained, then a curved graph can be used, but it may be that this can only be described more generally. For example, as time increases on Graph V the rate of the reaction (obtained from the gradient) decreases until eventually the slope of the graph becomes horizontal, showing that the reaction has reached completion.

When interpreting results you should assess and comment on:

- their precision – how close are measurements of the same value to each other?
- their accuracy – how close are they to their true or accepted value? Inaccurate values may be due to a systematic error that affects all the results.
- their reliability – will repeating the procedure produce the same results? Reliability may be affected by random errors.
- their validity – how well do the results relate to the inquiry question? Their validity may be affected by failure to properly control other variables.

Dealing with outliers

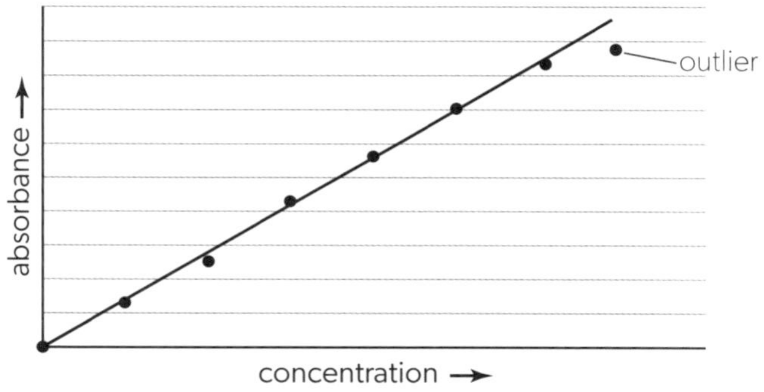

The trend line of the graph should pass through the error bars associated with each plotted point on the graph. If a point lies outside the trend line it is known as an "outlier" as it does not fit the trend. There can be different reasons for outliers. The obvious reason is that a mistake has been made during its measurement and the reading can be repeated to see if it is different. However, sometimes an outlier is actually a valid point and needs explaining. One good example is when a calibration curve is plotted of absorbance against known concentrations so that the graph can be interpolated to find an unknown concentration. This straight-line relationship is based on the Beer–Lambert law, but it is only valid for *dilute* concentrations. As the concentration increases the trend breaks down, so outliers to the best fit straight-line will occur at higher concentrations.

Concluding

Your conclusion must relate directly to your research question, must be based on the data you have generated or gathered and must be consistent with the arguments you have put forward following the correct processing of the data. If your conclusion results in you finding one or more final quantitative values, then you should include the total uncertainty and express it as an absolute value (rather than as a percentage) with the correct units. If the value(s) you determine are already published or known from elsewhere, then you should compare your value(s) with these literature value(s) and calculate the percentage error. Determine whether your values, together with their associated uncertainties, lie within the calculated percentage error and discuss the impact that these uncertainties had on your final result. If there are no literature values to be found, then you should still try to compare your outcome(s) with the accepted scientific context and look critically at your data to see whether any alternative conclusion could be reached within the limits of your uncertainties.

Evaluating

When considering all the variables in the exploration phase to help decide upon the methodology, it can be useful to classify all the variables by listing them in a table. This same table can be used when it comes to evaluating the effect that each variable had on the outcome. Identify which is responsible for the greatest uncertainty and how each may have contributed to random and systematic errors. Consider too the effect of any assumptions made on the reliability and validity of your methodology. This should enable you to identify and report on any weaknesses and lead you to consider how your methodology could be improved. Make sure that your suggestions to improve the methodology are relevant and realistic. Do not simply state that more accurate equipment, such as grade A glassware rather than the cheaper grade B glassware usually found in schools, should be used. One way of achieving this is by looking carefully at percentage uncertainties rather than absolute uncertainties. When using an analytical balance to weigh a stoppered flask filled with air, a reading such as 756.437 ± 0.001 g has almost negligible absolute and percentage uncertainties. If it is filled with a different gas and gives a new reading of 756.485 ± 0.001 g, again both uncertainties in the actual reading are negligible, but the difference in mass is 0.048 ± 0.002 g. The absolute uncertainty of the mass difference is still small, but the percentage uncertainty is now 0.002 × 100 divided by 0.0481 = 4.2%. Rather than state that an even more accurate balance weighing to ±0.0001 g is required, a sensible and realistic improvement would be to use a larger flask to contain the gas.

Approaches to learning (1)

The five main learning skills

During the two years you study for the IB it is well worth reflecting on *how* you learn. You should endeavour to build up your learning skills, not only to achieve a good final grade in Diploma Chemistry, but also to help you excel in your further education studies and in the world of work. The focus is on getting you to think for yourself, to question critically and to take responsibility for your own learning. The five main learning skills are covered below.

Thinking skills

Thinking skills can be listed in order of increasing complexity. There are six main thinking skills that are generally recognized. These are: Remember; Understand; Apply; Analyse; Evaluate; and Create.

The skills are listed in order of a hierarchy. The first three, which involve knowledge acquisition, comprehension and application, are known as lower-level thinking skills, whereas the ability to analyse, evaluate and create are known as higher-level thinking skills.

The key assessment objectives of IB Diploma Chemistry relate directly to these six thinking skills. The written examination questions are set so that approximately 50% of the marks are awarded to the lower-level skills and 50% to the higher-level thinking skills.

In summary, the lower-level skills are covered by two objectives:

1. **State** a definition or fact; this covers both remember and understand.
2. **Apply** this knowledge in a straightforward situation.

The higher-level skills are covered by one objective:

3. **Analyse**, **evaluate** and **create** how to solve a problem by selecting and applying the relevant information or method.

It is useful to be able to distinguish between these three objectives because you cannot implement Objective 3 without the knowledge and understanding gained through Objectives 1 and 2.

For example, consider the thinking skills involved when using an acid–base titration to solve problems.

Progress of thinking skills required

What are acids and bases?	***Remember*** different definitions
Which quantities to use?	***Remember*** amount, volume, concentration, etc.
Which are the correct units?	***Remember*** mol, cm^3, mol dm^{-3}, pH, etc.
How does titration work?	***Understand*** the stoichiometric relationship between amounts and concentrations to reach the end point
How to solve titration problems?	***Apply*** knowledge
Which indicator should be used for a specific titration?	***Analyse*** a novel situation
Perform an experiment to determine the amount of aspirin in an analgesic tablet	***Evaluate*** the method used and the results obtained
Plan an investigation to determine whether the shell of eggs from free-range chickens contains a higher percentage of calcium carbonate than from battery-reared chickens	***Create*** an experiment to solve an unknown problem, evaluate the results and put them into context

Approaches to learning (2)

Communication skills

The ability to communicate clearly, concisely, and unambiguously is an important life skill and one that will prove useful throughout your whole working life, and beyond. Communication in chemistry requires the general skills of communication applicable to all areas of life *plus* the understanding and ability to use the very specific language of chemistry, which is covered on page 174.

Remember that communication is a two-way process and the ability to listen is considered to be an important communication skill. So, too, is the ability to weigh up all the evidence presented in an argument or statement to determine its authenticity, i.e. the ability to spot "fake news". This ability to question authenticity will become ever more important as the use of artificial intelligence increases.

If you are taking your diploma in a language that is not your first language, then this may add an extra dimension to the communication skills you require. If necessary, ask for help and guidance from your language department and try to team up with a native speaker during practical sessions or go over lesson notes together to improve your language skills. Make sure you know and understand the following command terms used by the IB.

Command terms

Command terms are the imperative form of specific verbs that are used in examination questions. Although these are the terms that will normally be used, other terms may be used. They are important as they direct you to answer a question in a specific way. For example, *describing* what happens when hydrochloric acid is added to magnesium will require a very different answer to *explaining* what happens when hydrochloric acid is added to magnesium. Make sure you are familiar with the exact definition of each of the eighteen command terms used by the IB. These can be found in the subject guide, which you can obtain from your teacher.

Social skills

Social skills involve the interactions between you and your teachers and also between you and other students. There is considerable evidence that developing good social skills helps you to learn well. This includes the use of social media and the Internet as well as face-to-face contact. Good social skills involve making good eye contact, listening to others, encouraging others by praise rather than "putting people down", and the ability to accept criticism and learn from your mistakes. You will need to work as a team when you do the 10-hour collaborative sciences project, but there will be many other times when working with other students will benefit you and the others in the group. This may be formally arranged during normal lesson times, particularly for some practical work, but also for group discussions. You should also try to make informal work groups with a small number of friends as you can learn much from each other.

If you are in an international school, then students (and your teachers) may come from many different countries. Even in a local school there are likely to be students in your class from different ethnic backgrounds. Be aware that what is socially acceptable (possibly the social norm) in one culture may well be socially unacceptable and may even cause offence in another culture.

Approaches to learning (3)

Research skills

Good research skills are required, particularly for the internally assessed component of chemistry and for your extended essay. Research skills are related to the inquiry cycle and some of the ways of implementing specific required research skills are covered separately in the next few pages, but it can be helpful to have the general progression of steps followed for any type of research in a list.

Stages of the research process

1. Determine an area of interest
2. Identify and locate possible sources of information
3. Peruse and select likely resources of interest
4. Refine your choice of resources
5. Formulate a question
6. Extract, gather and record relevant information
7. Process, synthesize and analyse your gathered information
8. Reach a conclusion and evaluate the process
9. Communicate your findings to others

You should get practice at developing your research skills in all your subjects. This will give you a head start over many non-IB students if you go on to study at university. Remember to always attribute the work of others by using a standard referencing system.

Self-management skills

Self-management skills are essentially organization skills and affective skills. Organization skills involve time management, goal setting, etc., whereas affective skills concern the emotions and state of mind. Possessing and practising good self-management skills can make a considerable difference to your academic performance, both for your Diploma and in your future studies and career. Essentially, during the two-year IB course, you should increasingly be taking responsibility for your own learning.

Organization skills

Different students do work efficiently and effectively in different ways and you will need to determine how you work best. However, it is sensible to plan your time carefully and complete assignments by the set deadlines. Many students will have a personal tutor who can help with this. It is helpful to draw up a timetable for each term with all the key deadlines such as when your draft EE and internally assessed coursework for each subject are due as well as regular homework and test slots. This should help you to plan your time efficiently so that you are not suddenly faced with a large number of deadlines in a short space of time. If you do find yourself in difficulty timewise, then seek help rather than let it all get on top of you.

Affective skills help you to have control over your own learning. These include resilience, self-motivation, and the ability to concentrate.

Resilience means learning from your mistakes. Being a risk taker and being prepared to fail is one of the best ways of increasing your knowledge and understanding; you can learn from your mistakes. Be prepared to move out of your comfort zone, and learn to reflect and benefit from both your positive and negative experiences when you do so. A resilient student will bounce back from "failure".

Self-motivation is often linked to perseverance. You need to want to succeed and be willing to put in the necessary effort to ensure this. Nice though it is, don't worry if you are not the "best student in the class"; what matters is your own self-esteem and self-worth. Rather than competing against other students, compete against yourself and stretch your own horizons. If you know what you want to do, e.g. study medicine at university for which you need a grade 6 or 7 in HL chemistry, then focus on achieving this rather than worrying about being better or worse than others.

Concentration on a specific task for more than a brief period of time is a skill that needs practice in an era of multi-tasking and the use of multi-media. Relaxation techniques can help you to keep your attention focused on the task in hand and to avoid distractions.

Language of chemistry

Chemical terminology

Sometimes when students have problems answering a question in chemistry the reason is not because they do not understand the chemistry but because they do not understand the question. The language of chemistry is complex but it is an important tool as it enables efficient and effective communication between chemists. Although some aspects of chemical language are covered explicitly in the syllabus, there is much that is assumed. You are just expected to pick this up by some sort of "osmosis" as you are going along.

The syllabus covers IUPAC rules, so you should be familiar with the naming of compounds, such as 1,1-dibromopropane and pentan-2-one. You should also know how to name compounds with variable oxidation states, such as iron(III) sulfate and manganese(IV) oxide. The use of symbols such as ΔH and $E^\ominus$ has also been emphasized, on page 151. It is worth going through the following list carefully. It will help to ensure that you will be able to focus on the chemistry in a question rather than wondering what the question actually means.

Formulas of substances

Elements containing two atoms in a molecule (diatomic) are written as such. However, if there are more than two atoms in a molecule of the element (polyatomic), the element is often written as if only one atom is present, e.g.

$S + O_2 \rightarrow SO_2$

In fact, $S + 2O \rightarrow SO_2$ is more consistent and $S_8 + 8O_2 \rightarrow 8SO_2$ is more correct.

Order of elements in a compound

Usually, the more electropositive element comes first, e.g. NaCl and H_2O. Ammonia and methane have the formulas NH_3 and CH_4, but logically you might expect them to be H_3N and H_4C, respectively. For organic compounds, you give C, then H and then the other elements in alphabetical order.

Physical constants

Should be written in italics, e.g. R is the gas constant; N_A is Avogadro's constant.

Shorthand notation

[X] is shorthand for "the concentration of X", although actually it is the activity of X and has no units. This causes a problem when calculating equilibrium constants for the IB, because, if X is in mol dm^{-3}, then the equilibrium constant may have units, whereas in reality it does not have units.

Different meanings of words in English and chemistry

Words such as "strong", "spontaneous", and "reduce" have very specific meanings in chemistry that are different when compared with everyday English. Other examples include "degenerate", "weak", "mole", "inductive" (effect), "element", "oil", "orbital", "phase", "salt", "Contact" (the process), "saturated", "shell", and "volatile". Make sure you know their meaning in chemistry.

Words with different meanings within chemistry

"Stable" can mean *thermodynamically stable* or it can mean *kinetically stable* and so "stable" should not be used on its own. For example, diamond is thermodynamically unstable but the reaction between carbon and oxygen has a high activation energy so at room temperature diamonds are very stable kinetically. Diamonds do not suddenly burst into flames.

The Greek alphabet

It is assumed that you know the Greek alphabet, as Greek letters with chemical meanings are frequently used. For example, change, Δ; small positive charge, $\delta+$; different types of bond, π and σ; wavelength, λ; sum of, Σ; and electron, β^- particle.

Roman numerals

Oxidation states use Roman numerals, so you should know at least I, II, III, IV, V, VI, and VII.

Representation of radicals

A chlorine atom is represented by Cl but a chlorine radical (which is also a chlorine atom) is represented by Cl or Cl•. A methyl radical, which is neutral, is represented by CH_3, CH_3•, or CH_3– even though "–" normally means a pair of electrons.

Reciprocal units

Concentration is expressed as mol dm^{-3} rather than mol/dm^3 or mol per dm^3. When putting data in a table, reciprocal units can also be given at the top of the column so that the data can just be given as numbers. For example 0 cm^3, 10 cm^3, 20 cm^3, 30 cm^3 can be written as 0, 10, 20, 30 in one column of the table if "volume / cm^3" is written at the top of the column.

Oxidation states and formula mass

When determining oxidation states, chemists assume that covalent compounds are ionic, e.g. CH_4 (C = –4; H = +1). However, when referring to "molar molecular mass", ionic compounds cannot be assumed to be molecular, so the term molar molecular mass cannot be used for ionic compounds; "formula mass" is used instead.

Drawing organic structures

Often angles of 90° are used when drawing the structures of alkanes, even though alkanes are tetrahedral in shape, with bond angles of 109.5°. Wedges and dotted lines are used to illustrate a 3D structure in two dimensions. Know too the use of skeletal formulas, as shown on page 57.

Using tautology

The initiation step in free radical substitution reactions involves "*homolytic fission*" – this translates literally as "same breaking breaking".

The difference between oxidation state and oxidation number

In Cr_2O_3, for example, the oxidation state of Cr is +3 and the oxidation number of Cr is (III).

Numbering organic compounds

You can read from right to left or left to right when numbering organic compounds. $CH_3CH(OH)CH_2CH_3$ and $CH_3CH_2CH(OH)CH_3$ are both butan-2-ol.

Use of upper and lower case for variables and constants

T is temperature; t is time. K is equilibrium; k is rate constant.

Symbols with different meanings within chemistry

The use of square brackets, [ ], can have completely different meanings depending upon the context in which they are used. For example, [CH_3COO^-(aq)] means the concentration or activity of ethanoate ions, [Ar] means the electron configuration of argon, $[Mn(H_2O)_6]^{2+}$ represents the hexahydrated manganese(II) complex ion, and [O] can be used when writing organic equations to show oxidation.

Study methods

This book has been written to provide you with all the information you need to gain the highest grade in chemistry, whether at Standard level or at Higher Level. It is not intended as a "teach yourself" book and is not a substitute for a good teacher nor for the practical work to support the theory. There is no magic solution that will compensate for a lack of knowledge or understanding, but here are some pieces of advice that should ensure that you achieve to the best of your ability.

During the course

The IB course for both SL and HL is scheduled to last for two years, although some schools do attempt to cover the whole course in one year. There is a tendency for some students to take it easy in the first year as the final exams seem a long way off. Don't be tempted to do this as it will be harder to catch up later. Equally, do not try to simply remember all the information given about each topic. The exam does not particularly test recall, but is more about how to apply your knowledge in different situations. Although some facts must be learned, much of chemistry is logical. Knowledge about the subject tends to come much more from understanding than from "rote learning". During each lesson, concentrate on trying to understand the content. Try to relate it to what you already know as this will challenge you to think. At the end of the lesson or in the evening, go over your notes, add to them or rearrange them to ensure that you have fully understood everything. If there are parts you are not clear about, then ask your teacher to explain them again or research them online or in textbooks, to increase your understanding. You can also benefit much by talking and working through problems with other students. You will only really know if you understand something if you have to explain it to someone else. You can test your understanding by attempting the problems at the end of each chapter in this book.

Some of the topics do require you to perform basic calculations. If you have problems, persevere and see if you can identify exactly what the difficulty is and seek help. Most students find that, as the course progresses and more examples are covered, their confidence to handle numerical problems increases considerably. If you ensure that you do understand everything during the course, then you will find that, by the time it comes to the exam, learning the essential facts to support your understanding is much easier.

It is worth having some understanding of the inquiry process and the approaches to learning that you should be developing during the two years you study for the IB Diploma. They will stand you in good stead not only for when it comes to the final IB assessment in chemistry but will also help to set you up to be a "lifelong learner".

The final examinations

Preparing for the examinations

Hopefully, for much of the course, the emphasis has been on enjoying learning and understanding chemistry rather than always worrying about grades. Towards the end of the course, however, it does make sense to prepare yourself for the final exam. Examiners are human and mark positively, which means that they look to give credit rather than to penalize mistakes. You have to help them by being clear in your answers and addressing the particular question(s) asked.

- **Know what it is you have to know**

Ask your teacher for a copy of the current syllabus. If you are taking Higher Level, make sure it also includes all the Additional Higher Level (AHL) material. Go through the syllabus carefully and make sure that you recognize and have covered all the points listed for each topic and sub-topic. Make sure you understand all the contents of this book as it applies to your particular level and that you have worked through the relevant questions and answers at the end of each chapter.

- **Be familiar with key command terms**

Each question in the exam will normally contain a key command term. If a question asks you to *describe* a reaction then a very different answer is required than if the question had asked you to *explain* a reaction. Examiners can only award marks for the correct answers to the question asked for. Not paying careful attention to the correct command term may cost you marks unnecessarily.

- **Practice with past papers**

Most schools will give their students a "mock" or "trial" exam. This is helpful as it enables you to judge the correct amount of time to spend on each question. Make your mistakes in the mock exam and then learn from them. Of course, the IB questions are different each year but they do tend to follow a similar pattern. It helps to have seen similar questions before and know what level to expect.

- **Organize your notes**

As you review your work it is often helpful to rewrite your notes. Concentrate on just the key points – they should trigger your memory. This book already contains the important points in a fairly condensed form. Condense them even more to make your own set of review notes. Each time you review a topic try to condense the notes even more. By the time you are ready to take the exam all your personal review notes should ideally fit onto a single page!

- **Be familiar with using the IB data booklet**

You should get into the habit of using this throughout the course so that you are completely familiar with its contents and how to use them by the time of the exams.

- **Know the format of the exam papers**

Both HL and SL students take two exam papers. Paper 1 contains multiple-choice questions in Section A and one data-based question and some questions on experimental work in Section B. Paper 2 contains short-answer and extended-response questions. Both papers cover the whole of the syllabus and all the questions are compulsory. You can use your calculator and will be provided with the IB data booklet for both papers.

- **Know the dates of the exams**

Plan your review timetable carefully in advance. Remember that you will have exams in other subjects and that you may not have much time for a "last minute" review.

Taking the examinations

Try to ensure that the night before you are able to take some time to relax and get a good night's sleep.

Take all you need with you to the examination room, i.e. pens, pencils, ruler, and a simple translating dictionary if you are not taking the exams in your first language. You will also need your calculator for both papers – remember to include a spare battery.

For Paper 1, work through the multiple-choice questions in Section A methodically. The SL paper has 30 questions, which should take about 45 minutes; whereas the HL paper has 40 questions, which should take about 1 hour. Make sure you leave enough time to fully complete Section B (SL about 45 minutes, HL about 1 hour). If you get stuck on a question, move on and then come back to it if you have time at the end. Make a note of those questions you are unsure about. You can then come back to these at the end rather than going through all of the questions again. Make sure you give one answer for each multiple-choice question. You are not penalized for wrong answers, so if you run out of time make an educated guess rather than leave any questions unanswered.

You will have five minutes reading time before you are allowed to write your answers. You must attempt to answer all of the questions on both papers, so use the reading time to gather your thoughts and get an overview of what is on the paper. Read each question very carefully. Make a mental note of the key command term used so that you give the required answer.

You must write your answers to Section B on Paper 1 and all of Paper 2 only within the required space as your answers are scanned and marked digitally. Write as legibly as you can. For questions involving calculations do not round up too early but make sure that your final answer is given to the correct number of significant figures. Always include the correct units. If you change your mind, then clearly cross out whatever you do not want to be marked. If you need extra space, put a note in the answer box that your answer is continued on a separate sheet of answer paper which is then attached to the booklet.

Attempt all the questions. If you do not attempt a question you can receive no marks. For sequential numerical questions, even if you get the first part wrong, continue as you will not be marked wrong twice for the same mistake. For this reason, it is essential that you show your working. Leave yourself time to read through what you have written to correct any mistakes. Ensure that you have filled in the front of the paper correctly, including the number of attached extra pages (if any) before leaving the examination room.

Internal assessment (1)

Introduction

You are expected to spend 40 hours (SL) or 60 hours (HL) during the two years on the experimental programme. This is essentially time spent in the laboratory or on simulations. Chemistry is an experimental science and practical work is an important component of the course. Your teacher should devise a suitable practical programme for you to follow. Practical work can have many different aims: for example, to improve your skills at different techniques, to reinforce the theoretical part of the course and to give you experience of planning your own investigations. Hopefully, it will make studying chemistry much more challenging and rewarding and also fun. Throughout the practical course, you are expected to understand and implement safe practice and also to respect the environment.

Internal assessment: the facts

The internal assessment component contributes 20% towards the final mark, with the external examinations contributing 80%. The assessment is exactly the same for both SL and HL. Most of the practical work you do will not be assessed, as the assessment will only be on *one* individual scientific investigation taking about 10 hours and its subsequent write-up, which must be no more than 3000 words. This will be marked out of 24, which will then be scaled to a mark out of 20. It will be marked by your teacher but moderated externally by the IB. The scientific investigation can cover a wide range of activities: for example, a hands-on laboratory investigation, fieldwork, using a spreadsheet for analysis and modelling, extracting and analysing data from a spreadsheet, a hybrid of spreadsheet/database work with a traditional hands-on investigation, or using a simulation provided it is interactive and open-ended.

Although the rest of the experimental programme (whether hands-on or virtual) does not count towards the 20% of the internal assessment mark, it is tested to some extent on Section B in Paper 1. In order that students have some common understanding, the programme lists certain practical techniques which you should understand and be familiar with. There are, however, no mandatory experiments, as your teacher is free to determine which experiments to choose to cover these techniques. All of these techniques are listed in Chapter 13 tools for chemists. In addition, you are required to spend 10 hours on the collaborative sciences project, but this does not count towards the final internal assessment mark.

Grading of internal assessment

You will only gain good marks for your scientific investigation if you address each criterion fully. Although your IA report is marked by your teacher, it may be moderated later by the IB. Both your teacher and the moderators mark according to the descriptors, which are laid out in the chemistry subject guide. The marker decides how closely you meet the descriptors to be awarded the mark. The following summarizes what you need to show in your IA report to gain the maximum mark of 6 for each of the four criteria upon which you are assessed.

Research design

You must state your research question clearly and show that it is an appropriate area of chemistry to investigate and is capable of being addressed in 10 hours. You should describe the methodology you have chosen and provide sufficient detail so that it could be reproduced by others. You should explain how the method used can produce sufficient relevant data to answer the research question and discuss the advantages and disadvantages of the method compared with other methods that could have been used to obtain relevant data.

Data analysis

You must record all your relevant raw data and its subsequent processing clearly and succinctly and include all the correct units and related uncertainties. All the processing of your raw data must be carried out accurately and the appropriate processing method(s) used. You should make it clear how the data you have processed relates to your research question.

Conclusion

You must state your conclusion clearly and show that it is based on the evidence you have presented and that it relates directly to your research question. You must also show that your conclusion is justified by comparing it with information from other scientifically accepted sources.

Evaluation

You must identify any weaknesses in the method(s) you used and show the impact they may have on your conclusion. You should also suggest and explain any realistic ways in which your methodology could be improved to overcome or reduce the effect of any weaknesses or limitations.

Internal assessment (2)

Maximizing your internal assessment marks

The summary on the previous page explains how your IA will be graded and gives a brief outline of what is needed to gain the highest marks for each of the four individual criteria. So, how can you achieve this?

General points

- Before you undertake your scientific investigation, familiarize yourself thoroughly with the detailed internal assessment criteria set out in the chemistry subject guide.
- Make sure you know and can apply correctly all the tools covered in Chapter 13 and the skills covered in the inquiry process in Chapter 15.
- Look at examples of excellent past scientific investigations (available from your teacher).
- For ideas for your own investigation you could look at interesting developments from experiments you have already done, or base it on something you have read in a newspaper article, a journal or have seen online. Keep a note, if, at any time during a lesson on a particular topic, your teacher mentions something that could make an interesting investigation for your IA.
- Determine the precise wording of your sharply focused research question and discuss it with your teacher. Ideally, you should have identified all the variables so that your research question is concerned with how manipulating the independent variable affects the dependent variable while all the other variables are kept constant, i.e. controlled.
- Ensure that your independent variable is a continuous variable.
- Make sure that your identified dependent variable is the variable that responds to the changing independent variable. For example; time, absorbance, voltage, mass and volume are all dependent variables, as they can be measured directly. A derived variable that may appear in your research question, such as rate of reaction, equilibrium constant, enthalpy change, etc., is calculated from the dependent variable. Some students make this clear by wording their research question in the form of "How does the rate of the (specified) reaction depend upon the concentration of reactants A and B as determined by the volume of gaseous product evolved over time?"
- Explain how you will control and monitor all the other variables.
- Make sure that you have covered all the safety issues and the environmental impact of your methodology.
- Before proceeding to obtain your data, check with your teacher that your projected methodology is feasible in terms of time, safety and resources and has the potential to achieve a successful outcome.
- Record all your work as you proceed, including precise details of references.
- Record all measurements accurately to the correct number of significant figures and include all units. Remember to include all the uncertainties and assumptions made.
- For hands-on experimental work, record all observations. Include colour changes, solubility changes, whether heat was evolved or taken in, etc.
- Draw up a checklist to cover each criterion being assessed. As you write up your individual investigation, check that each criterion is addressed fully.
- Remember that academic honesty is paramount. You must always acknowledge the ideas of other people. If you have collaborated in any way with other students to obtain data, then this must be acknowledged but the individual research question, the recording of data, and subsequent report must be all your own work.
- Limit your complete report to a maximum of 3000 words using Arial font size 11. Do not include a contents page and do not include an appendix. The subject guide gives advice as to what counts as a word in the word count.

Primary or secondary raw data?

The raw data you need to investigate your research question can either be primary data (i.e. generated by you) or secondary data (generated by others or artificially), or a mixture of both.

For a scientific investigation in chemistry, primary data is most likely to be obtained from hands-on practical work in a laboratory or other setting where scientific apparatus can be used and controlled by you. In the past, this was the methodology chosen by the majority of students but with the closure of many schools or restricted access to laboratories in the early 2020s, more students relied upon obtaining secondary data. If you do obtain all or part of your data from hands-on experimental work, then make sure that you record precise details of all the equipment you use, e.g. a balance weighing to ±0.001 g, a thermometer measuring from −10 to +110 °C to an accuracy of ±0.1 °C or a 25.00 cm^3 pipette measuring to ±0.04 cm^3. Also record precise details of any chemicals used, e.g. copper(II) sulfate pentahydrate, $CuSO_4.5H_2O(s)$, and if it is a solution include the concentration, e.g. 0.100 mol dm^{-3} NaOH(aq).

Secondary data can essentially be obtained in two different ways. You can either use genuine data that has been produced experimentally by other scientists and published in reputable sources, such as journals, books or databases, or you can use programs to produce simulated data. If you use data generated by others, then you need to find several different sources so that you can compare values take mean values, and consider the veracity of the sources and the associated uncertainties. Ideally, you should be looking at a minimum of five different sources. Remember: you will need to use the data in a new way to address your specific research question, you cannot simply repeat the conclusion(s) already stated by others.

It is possible to obtain good secondary data from simulations but it is not generally easy to do at IB diploma level. Many simulation programs are very basic. For example, they may involve manipulating variables such as mass, concentration or temperature to see how the rate or pH is affected for simple reactions where the chemistry is already well known. If you have the ability to write your own simulation program(s), can make use of AI or can understand how to use some of the more advanced simulation programs available, then it is possible to investigate some interesting chemistry. However, be sure that your investigation is of sufficient complexity, i.e. it also includes the uncertainties associated with the collected simulated data and is interactive and open-ended, can be covered in 10 hours and that you can understand all the underlying chemistry theory. You should take relevant screenshots to provide evidence to whoever marks your report to ensure that they could reproduce the data.

The collaborative sciences project

Aim of the project

All diploma science students must work together in the interdisciplinary collaborative project to address a common topic or problem. The rationale is to give you experience of working in a group with students from different science subjects, where the emphasis is on the process rather than the product. In large schools, there may be more than one collaborative topic. However, in many schools, small groups of students will work on the same topic, which may be determined by the students or by the school. The topic should be scientific or technological and be associated with the 17 United Nations sustainable development goals. The project covers many of the science aims, in particular aims 7, 8 and 9, i.e. "develop technology skills in a scientific context", "develop the ability to communicate and collaborate effectively" and "develop awareness of the ethical, environmental, economic, cultural and social impact of science". It also is very relevant to aim 5, "design and model solutions to local and global problems in a scientific context". The international aspect is inherent in the sustainable development goals of the UN but can be further enhanced by collaborating with students from different countries within your own school or by collaborating with students in schools from other parts of the world. The collaborative sciences project may also help you to better understand the limitations of scientific study, for example, the shortage of appropriate data and/or the lack of resources.

Stages of the project

The 10 hours devoted to the project are effectively spread over three stages. Note that if you are studying two science subjects, then you do only one collaborative sciences project. Even students who are just doing chemistry as their science subject do not necessarily need to be involved in the chemistry aspects of the topic.

Planning (approximately 2 hours)

You will meet with all the other students in an ideas session, either initially to come up with a central topic or, if this has already been decided, to then break the topic down into different activities that can be carried out by different groups. At this stage, if the project is to be experimentally based, you should specify what apparatus will be required so that there is no delay when it comes to carrying out the next stage. You may also wish to make contact with other schools if a joint venture has been agreed.

Action (approximately 6 hours)

This will take place sometime after the planning stage. Different schools have different ways of providing the time for this. Some do it during normal lesson time, others allocate a specific day for it, and others will perhaps go away on a field trip over a weekend. Your group can consist of students studying mixed science subjects or they may all be chemists – there is no hard and fast rule. If you are involved in hands-on practical work, then pay attention to safety, ethical, and environmental issues. You should aim to collaborate fully with the other students in your group during this action phase.

Evaluation (approximately 2 hours)

During this stage, you should share the findings of your group with the other groups, focusing on both the successes and failures, and aim to present the findings. There are many ways in which the findings can be presented. Some schools devote an afternoon or evening to sharing the findings with other students, teachers and even parents by giving brief presentations. Other ways are by making posters to place around the school, putting together an online presentation or holding a science fair, etc.

There is no formal assessment of the collaborative sciences project and, although it is a required part of your diploma, you do not need to provide any evidence that you have participated in the project, except to write a short reflective statement. It may be of some benefit to you to carry out a self-assessment, i.e. reflect on how you performed, and to give a short questionnaire to the other members of your group to see how closely their assessment of you agrees or disagrees with your own self-assessment.

Extended essay (1)

What is an extended essay?

To fulfil the requirements of the IB, all diploma candidates must submit an extended essay in an IB subject of their own choice. The essay is an in-depth study of a limited topic within a subject. The purpose of the essay is to provide you with an opportunity to engage in independent research. Approximately 40 hours should be spent in total on the essay. Each essay must be supervised by a competent teacher. The length of the essay is restricted to a maximum of 4000 words and it is assessed according to a carefully worded set of criteria. The marks awarded for the extended essay are combined with the marks for the theory of knowledge course to give a maximum of three bonus points.

Extended essays in chemistry

Although, technically, any IB Diploma student can choose to write their essay in chemistry, it does help if you are actually studying chemistry as one of your six subjects! Most essays are from students taking chemistry at Higher Level but there have been some excellent essays submitted by Standard Level students. All essays must have a sharply focused research question. Essays may be just library based or may also involve individual experimental work. Although it is possible to write a good essay containing no experimental work, it is much harder to show personal input and rarely do such essays gain high marks. The experimental work is best done in a school laboratory, although the word "laboratory" can be interpreted in the widest sense and includes the local environment. It is usually much easier for you to control, modify or redesign the simpler equipment found in schools than the more sophisticated (and expensive) equipment found in university or industrial research laboratories.

Choosing the research question

Choosing a suitable research question is really the key to the whole essay. The best essays are almost always submitted by students who identify a particular area or chemistry problem that they are interested in and, together with the supervisor, formulate a precise and sharply focused research question. A title such as "A study of analysis by chromatography" is far too broad to complete in 4000 words. A focused title might be "An analysis of [a named red dye] present in [a specified number of] different brands of tomato ketchup by thin-layer chromatography". It is more usual to choose a topic and then decide which technique(s) might be used to solve the problem. An alternative way is to look at what techniques are available and see what problems they could address.

Different techniques

The list below shows some examples of how standard techniques or equipment available in a school laboratory can be used to solve some general research questions. For precise research questions, these exemplars may need to be more sharply focused and involve two or more of these techniques.

Redox titration
Do different (specified) varieties of seaweed contain different amounts of iodine?

Acid–base titration
How do storage time and temperature affect the vitamin C content of (specified) fruit juices?

Chromatography
Do strawberry jellies from (specified) different countries contain the same red dye(s)?

Calorimetry
How efficient is dried cow dung as a fuel compared with fossil fuels?

pH meter
Can (specified) different types of chewing gum affect the pH of the mouth and prevent tooth decay?

Steam distillation
What is the amount of aromatic oil that can be extracted from (a specified) plant species?

Refinement of a standard practical
How can the yield be increased in the laboratory preparation of 1,3-dinitrobenzene?

Microwave oven
What is the relationship between temperature increase and dipole moment for [specified substances]?

Polarimetry
Is it possible to prepare the different enantiomers of butan-2-ol in a school laboratory?

Data logging probes
What is the rate expression for [a specified reaction]?

Visible spectrometry
What is the percentage of copper in different ores found in [a specified area]?

Gravimetric analysis
Do (specified) "healthy" pizzas contain less salt than normal pizzas?

Extended essay (2)

Researching the topic

Once the topic has been chosen, research the background to the topic thoroughly before planning the experimental work. Information can be obtained from a wide variety of sources: a library, the Internet, personal contacts, questionnaires, newspapers, etc. Make sure that each time you record some information you make an accurate note of the source, as you will need to refer to this in the bibliography. Treat information from the Internet with care. If possible, try to determine the original source. Articles in journals are more reliable as they have been vetted by experts in the field. Together with your supervisor, plan your laboratory investigation carefully. Your supervisor should ensure that your investigation is safe, capable of producing results (even if they are not the expected ones) and lends itself to a full evaluation.

The laboratory investigation

Make sure you understand the chemistry that lies behind any practical technique before you begin. Keep a careful record of everything you do at the time that you are doing it. If the technique "works", then try to expand it to cover new areas of investigation. If it does not "work" (and most do not the first time), then try to analyse what the problem is. Try changing some of the variables, such as increasing the concentration of reactants, changing the temperature or altering the pH. It may be that the equipment itself is faulty or unsuitable. Try to modify it. Use your imagination to design new equipment in order to address your particular problem (modern packaging materials from supermarkets can often be used imaginatively to great effect). Because of the time limitations, it is often not possible to get reliable repeatable results, but attempt to if you can. Remember that the written essay is all that the external examiner sees, so leave yourself plenty of time to write the essay.

Writing the essay

Before starting to write the essay, make sure you have read and understood the assessment criteria. It may be useful to look at some past extended essays to see how they were set out. Almost all essays are word-processed and this makes it easier to alter draft versions, but they may be written by hand. You will not be penalized for poor English but you will be penalized for bad chemistry, so make sure that you do not make simple word-processing errors when writing formulas, etc.

Start the essay with a clear introduction and make sure that you set out the research question clearly and put it into context. The rest of the essay should then be very much focused on addressing the research question. Some of the marks are gained simply for fulfilling the criteria (e.g. numbering the pages, including a list of contents). These may be mechanical but you will lose marks if you do not do them. Give precise details of any experimental techniques and set out the results clearly and with the correct units and correct number of significant figures. If you have many similar calculations, then show the method clearly for one and set the rest out in tabular form. Numerical results should give the limits of accuracy and a suitable analysis of uncertainties should be included. Relate your results to the research question in your discussion and compare them with any expected results and with any secondary sources of information you can locate. State any assumptions you have made and evaluate the experimental method fully. Suggest possible ways in which the research could be extended if more time were available. Throughout the whole essay, show that you understand what it is that you are doing and demonstrate personal input and initiative.

When you have drafted the whole of the essay, give it to your supervisor for comment. Your final version should then take on board the feedback from your supervisor. Before handing in the final version, go through the checklist on the next page very carefully. If you can honestly answer "yes" to every question, then your essay will be at least satisfactory and hopefully much better than this.

Reflections on planning and progress – form EE/RPPF

In addition to the finished essay (the product), some of the assessment is also based on the extended essay process. During the course of your extended essay work, you will have three formal meetings with your supervisor. These are for you to reflect on the planning and progress of the essay. The first will take place near the start of the process, when you will discuss approaches and strategies. The second meeting (the interim reflection session) will take place after you have attempted to refine the research question and have recorded some relevant evidence and data. The final session takes place after the final version of the essay has been handed in, and you will be asked to reflect on the whole process. After each meeting, you must record your reflections on Form EE/RPPF. You should show how you wwhave responded to any setbacks and how you have engaged in the research process. Through your reflections (which should not exceed 500 words in total), you should also show that your work is authentic and demonstrates intellectual initiative and creativity. Your supervisor will also write their own comments at the end of the process and the completed Form EE/RPPF will be sent to the external assessor along with the final version of your essay for assessment.

Extended essay (3)

Extended essay checklist

To gain the maximum credit possible for your extended essay, it is crucial that you can answer YES to the following questions before you finally submit the final version of your essay and the completed Reflections on Planning & Progress form.

Before starting, check that you have the correct assessment criteria for your current examination session.

The maximum number of marks available for each criterion is given in brackets.

A: Focus & method (6)

Is the research question (RQ) outlined and clearly stated in the introduction?
Is the RQ focused and capable of being addressed in 4000 words?
Is the purpose and focus of the RQ set into context of background knowledge and understanding of chemistry?
Have you shown that a range of appropriate different sources/methods were considered?
Have you provided evidence of how you selected effective and appropriate sources/method(s)?
Have you shown how the RQ was arrived at from the sources gathered?
Does the whole essay remain focused on the RQ?

B: Knowledge & understanding (6)

Is correct chemical terminology used consistently and appropriately throughout the essay?
Have you shown that you understand the chemistry behind the sources/method(s) used?
Have the sources/method(s) chosen throughout the essay been used effectively to address the RQ?

C: Critical thinking (12)

Is the research appropriate to the RQ and its application consistently relevant?
Have you critically analysed the sources/method(s) used?
Have you developed an effective and reasoned argument from your research?
Is your argument well structured?
Are all your conclusions effectively supported by the evidence and relevant to the RQ?
Have you analysed your research effectively and stated any limitations and/or counter arguments?

D: Formal presentation (4)

Is your essay within the 4000 word limit?
Does your essay include all the required elements (title page, table of contents, introduction, discussion, conclusion, and bibliography)?
Is all illustrative material (graphs, tables, chemical structures, etc.) clearly and accurately labelled?
Does the bibliography include all, and only, those works that have been consulted?
Is the bibliography set out in a standard format that is consistently applied?
Is all the work of others clearly acknowledged?
Are all the pages numbered?
Are all pages double-spaced and formatted using Arial font size 12?
If you have included an appendix, does it only contain information necessary to support the essay?

E: Engagement (6)

Have you engaged fully in discussions with your supervisor regarding the planning and progress of your essay?
Have you shown how your reflections enabled you to refine the research process?
Have you shown how you responded to setbacks and challenges during the research process?
Have you shown initiative, creativity, and personal input throughout the research process?
Have you made suggestions as to how you can improve your own working practice?

Answers

Models of the particulate nature of matter: multiple choice (page 6)

1. B **2.** D **3.** D **4.** B **5.** C **6.** C **7.** A **8.** C
9. D **10.** A **11.** B **12.** D

Atomic structure: multiple choice (page 13)

1. C **2.** A **3.** B **4.** A **5.** B **6.** A **7.** D **8.** D
9. C **10.** B **11.** D **12.** C **13.** A **14.** C **15.** A
16. B

Atomic structure: short answers (page 14)

1. a) The weighted mean mass of all the naturally occurring isotopes of the element, relative to one-twelfth of the mass of a carbon-12 atom. **[1]**;
b) $37x+35(100-x)=100\times35.45=3545$, so $2x=45$ and $x=22.5$. Hence $^{37}Cl=22.5\%$ and $^{35}Cl=(100-22.5)=77.5\%$. **[2]**; c) i) $1s^22s^22p^63s^23p^5$ **[1]**; ii) $1s^22s^22p^63s^23p^6$ **[1]**; d) They do not differ as chemical properties are determined by the electron configuration and both isotopes have the same configuration. **[2]**

2. a) The weighted average of the sum of protons and neutrons for Co ($Z=27$) is greater than for Ni ($Z=28$) even though nickel atoms contain one more proton. **[1]**;
b) 27 protons, 25 electrons **[1]**;
c) i) $1s^22s^22p^63s^23p^64s^23d^7$ or $[Ar]4s^23d^7$ (or $1s^22s^22p^63s^23p^63d^74s^2$ or $[Ar]3d^74s^2$) **[1]**;
ii) $1s^22s^22p^63s^23p^63d^7$ or $[Ar]3d^7$ **[1]**

3. a) i) Atoms of the same element that contain the same number of protons but have a different number of neutrons in their nucleus. **[1]**; ii) 56 **[1]**; iii) It emits radiation, which can potentially damage cells. **[1]**;
b) i) Both contain 6 protons and 6 electrons, carbon-12 contains 6 neutrons and carbon-14 contains 8 neutrons. **[2]**;
ii) The length of time since death can be determined by looking at the ratio of ^{12}C to ^{14}C as it will increase at a uniform rate as the amount of ^{14}C halves every 5 300 years. **[2]**

4.

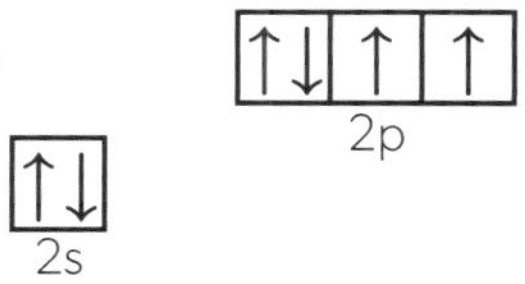

[1]

5

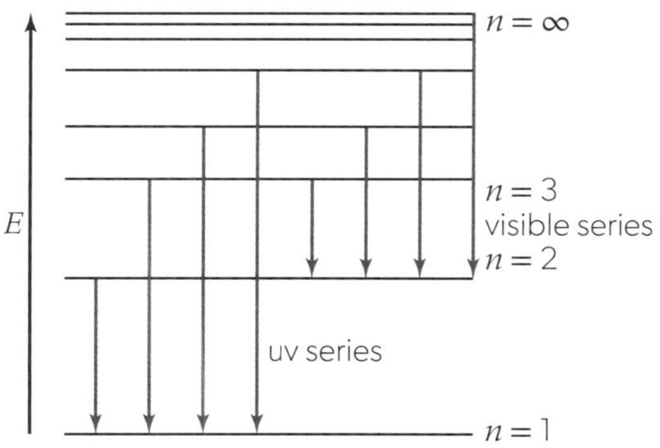

Showing y-axis labelled as energy/E/labelling at least two energy levels **[1]**, showing a minimum of four energy levels/lines with convergence;**[1]**, showing jumps to $n = 1$ for ultraviolet series;**[1]**, showing jumps to $n = 2$ for visible light series. **[1]**

6. a) The electron configuration of argon, i.e. $1s^22s^22p^63s^23p^6$ **[1]**; b) $x=1$, $y=5$ **[1]**;

c)

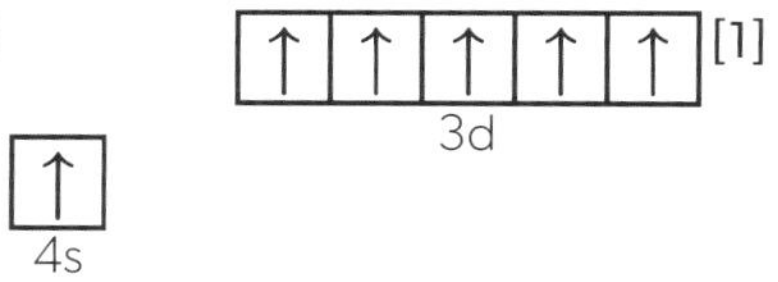

Accept 4s box higher than 3d box.

7. a) The minimum energy required to remove a mole of electrons **[1]** from a mole of gaseous atoms to form a mole of univalent cations in the gaseous state. **[1]**;
b) i) Electrons are being added to the same main energy level but the number of protons in the nucleus increases thus attracting the electrons more strongly as the atomic radius decreases. **[2]**; ii) The outermost electron in sodium is the $3s^1$ electron, which is much further from the nucleus than the 2p electrons in the outer energy level of neon. **[2]**; iii) The outer 2p sub-level in boron ($1s^22s^22p^1$) is higher in energy than the 2s outer sub-level in beryllium ($1s^22s^2$). **[2]**; iv) Phosphorus ($[Ne]3s^23p^3$) has three unpaired electrons, the pairing of two electrons in one of the 3p orbitals in oxygen ($[Ne]3s^23p^4$) causes repulsion between the electrons making it easier to remove one of them. **[2]**; c) The repeating pattern has shifted one place to the right (i.e. the plot would need to be shifted to the left by one atomic number to retain the same pattern against atomic number) **[1]**; the energy values are all higher **[1]**; the peaks in each period will now be given by Li^+, Na^+, and K^+, and the troughs by Be^+, Mg^+, and Ca^+ etc. **[1]**

8. Emission spectra consist of discrete lines representing transitions between the levels, if electrons could be anywhere the spectra would be continuous **[2]**; the convergence of lines in the spectra show that successive levels get closer in energy **[1]**; graphs of successive ionization energies give evidence for the number of electrons occupying each main energy level **[1]**; the irregularities in the graph of 1st ionization energies against atomic number (e.g. B and Be, and Mg and Al) give evidence for sub-levels. **[1]**

9. E for one electron $=\dfrac{(1\,312\times1000)}{(6.02\times10^{23})}=2.179\times10^{-18}\,J$ **[1]**;

$v=\dfrac{E}{h}=\dfrac{(2.179\times10^{-18})}{(6.63\times10^{-34})}=3.29\times10^{15}\,s^{-1}$ **[1]**;

$\lambda=\dfrac{c}{v}=\dfrac{(3.00\times10^{8})}{(3.29\times10^{15})}=9.12\times10^{-8}\,m$ (or 91.2 nm) **[1]**

Quantitative chemistry: multiple choice (pages 22 and 23)

1. D **2.** C **3.** B **4.** C **5.** D **6.** B **7.** D **8.** D
9. A **10.** B **11.** B **12.** A **13.** C **14.** B **15.** C
16. A **17.** A **18.** D **19.** B **20.** D **21.** A
22. C **23.** C **24.** B **25.** D **26.** C **27.** A
28. A

Quantitative chemistry: short answers (page 24)

1. a) Amount of ethanoic anhydride $= \frac{15.0}{102.1} = 0.147$ mol [1], amount of 2-hydroxybenzoic acid $= \frac{15.0}{138.13} = 0.109$ mol [1], 2 mol of 2-hydroxybenzoic acid required to react with 1 mol of ethanoic anhydride so 2-hydroxybenzoic acid is the limiting reagent. [1]; b) M_r(aspirin) $= [(9\times12.01)+(8\times1.01)+(4\times16.00)] = 180.17$ [1], 0.109 mol of 2-hydroxybenzoic acid produces 0.109 mol of aspirin so maximum mass of aspirin $= 0.109\times180.17 = 19.6$ g [1]; c) Percentage yield $= (13.7/19.6)\times100 = 69.9\%$ [1]

2. a) $M_r(BaSO_4) = 137.33+32.07+(4\times16.00) = 233.4$ [1]; amount of $BaSO_4 = \frac{9.336}{233.4} = 0.0400$ mol [1]; b) 0.0400 mol [1]; c) $M_r(M_2SO_4) = \frac{14.48}{0.0400} = 362$ [1]; d) $M_r(M_2SO_4) = 2\times A_r(M)+32.07+(4\times16.00) = 362$ so A_r for M $= 133$ [1]. Since M has an A_r of 133 and forms a unipositive cation, M is caesium. [1]

3. a) $Mg(s) + 2HCl(aq) \rightarrow MgCl_2(aq) + H_2(g)$ [1]; b) Amount of Mg $= \frac{(7.40\times10^{-2})}{24.31} = 3.04\times10^{-3}$ mol [1], amount of HCl $= \left(\frac{15.0}{1000}\right)\times2.00 = 3.00\times10^{-2}$ mol [1], for all the HCl to react would require 1.50×10^{-2} mol of Mg so Mg is the limiting reagent [1]; c) i) Theoretical yield of $H_2 = 3.04\times10^{-3}$ mol [1]; ii) 1 mol of gas occupies 22 700 cm^3 at 273 K, 1.00×10^5 Pa so at 293 K volume occupied by 3.04×10^{-3} mol of $H_2 = 3.04\times10^{-3}\times22700\times\frac{293}{273} = 74.1\ cm^3$ (74.1 cm^3 can also be obtained by using $pV = nRT$) [2]; d) ***Any two from:*** hydrogen is not an ideal gas, the syringe sticks, the magnesium is impure, the hydrogen dissolves in the solution, uncertainties associated with the concentration of the acid. [2]

4. a) i) Ratio of Pb : C : H $= \left(\frac{64.052}{207.2}\right) : \left(\frac{29.703}{12.01}\right) : \left(\frac{6.245}{1.01}\right)$ $= 0.309 : 2.47 : 6.18$ simplest ratio is 1 : 8 : 20 so empirical formula is PbC_8H_{20} [3]; ii) 1 mol of PbC_8H_{20} contains 1 mol of Pb so molecular formula is PbC_8H_{20} [1]; iii) $PbC_8H_{20} + 14O_2 \rightarrow PbO_2 + 8CO_2 + 10H_2O$ [2]; b) *Local:* carbon monoxide or volatile organics or nitrogen oxide or unburned hydrocarbons or particulates [1], *global:* carbon dioxide or nitrogen oxide. [1]

5. Temperature = 292 K;

Amount of gas in flask $= \frac{(1.01\times10^5\times4.043\times10^{-3})}{(8.31\times292)}$ $= 0.168$ mol [2];

M_r of air $= \frac{[(80\times28)+(20\times32)]}{100} = 28.8$ [1];

Mass of air in flask $= 28.8\times0.168 = 4.84$ g, Mass of gas in flask $= 742.10-734.66 = 7.44$ g [1];

M_r of gas $= \frac{7.44}{0.168} = 44.3$ [1]

6. a) Amount of $Cu_2O = \frac{10000}{[(2\times63.55)+16.00]}$ $= 69.89$ mol [1],

amount of $Cu_2S = \frac{5000}{159.17} = 31.41$ mol [1],

Cu_2S requires 2 × 31.41 mol of Cu_2O to react so Cu_2S is the limiting reagent [1]; b) Max amount of Cu = 6 × 31.41 = 188.46 mol [1], maximum mass = 188.46 × 63.55 = 11 976 g = 12.0 kg [1];

c) Atom economy $= \frac{381.3}{445.37}\times100 = 85.6\%$ [3]

7. ***Any four from:*** some of the product escaped when the lid was lifted, the Mg may have combined with nitrogen in the air, the Mg may not have been pure, not all the Mg may have burned, the crucible might have also reacted. [4]

8. a) C:H $= \frac{85.6}{12.01} : \frac{14.4}{1.01} = 7.13 : 14.3 = 1:2$, empirical formula is CH_2 [2];

b) i) $n = \frac{PV}{RT} = \frac{(1.00\times10^5\times0.405\times10^{-3})}{8.314\times273} = 1.784\times10^{-2}$ mol,

$M = \frac{1.00}{0.01784} = 56.1\ g\ mol^{-1}$ [2];

ii) Empirical formula mass $= 12.01+(1.01\times2) = 14.03$, $\frac{56.1}{14.03} = 4$ so molecular formula is C_4H_8 [2]; c) Carbon monoxide is produced, which can combine irreversibly with the iron in haemoglobin in the blood, or carbon particulates are formed, which can cause problems with the lungs. [2]

Bonding and structure: multiple choice (pages 40 and 41)

1. C 2. A 3. A 4. D 5. D 6. A 7. C 8. B
9. B 10. C 11. C 12. C 13. A 14. B 15. D
16. B 17. C 18. D 19. A 20. D 21. B
22. D 23. A 24. B 25. C 26. D 27. C
28. D 29. D 30. B

Bonding and structure: short answers (page 42)

1. Electron domain geometry for all three species is tetrahedral as they all have four electron domains. [2] Molecular shapes:

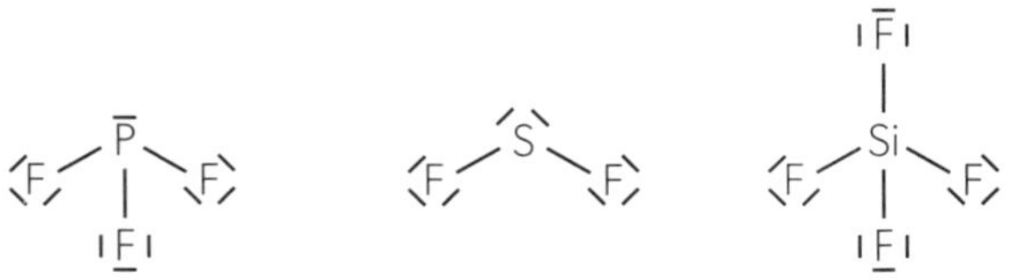

trigonal pyramid [2] bent or V-shaped [2] tetrahedral [2]

2. a) i) 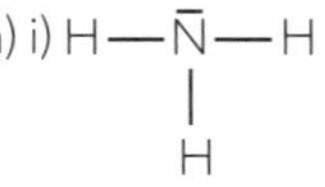

[1]; trigonal pyramid [1]; 107° [1]; the non-bonding pair repels more than the three bonding pairs. [1]; ii) Boiling points increase going down the group [1]; M_r/number of electrons/molecular

size increases down the group [1]; greater London dispersion forces/van der Waals' forces [1]; NH_3 has a higher boiling point than expected due to the hydrogen bonding between the molecules. [1];

b) 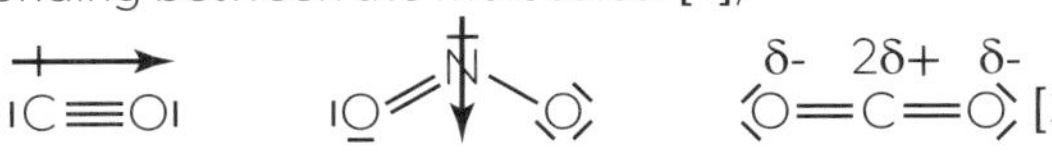

[3];

O is more electronegative than C in CO, NO_2 is bent and the C=O dipoles cancel out in the linear CO_2 [2]

3. a) 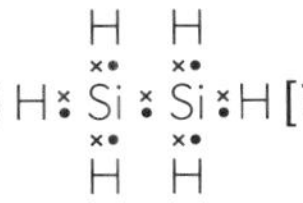 [1]

b) 109.5° [1], four equal electron domains around central C atom [1] c) C–H [1], greater difference in electronegativity values [1]; d) Both molecules are non-polar [1] as they are symmetrical [1]; e) Stronger London dispersion forces [1] due to greater mass/more electrons. [1]

4. a) Methoxymethane [1] as the strongest attraction between molecules is dipole–dipole [1] whereas between the alcohol molecules there is stronger hydrogen bonding. [1]; b) Propan-1-ol is more soluble [1] as the non-polar hydrocarbon chain is shorter. [1]; c) Graphite forms layers of flat hexagonal rings, each C atom is bonded strongly to three other C atoms, layers held by weak attractive forces so can slide over each other with delocalized electrons between layers. [3] In diamond all C atoms are strongly bonded to four other C atoms, giant tetrahedral structure with strong covalent bonds and no delocalized electrons. [3]

5. a) $1s^2 2s^2 2p^6 3s^2 3p^5$ [1]; $[Ne]3s^2 3p^5$ [1]

b) 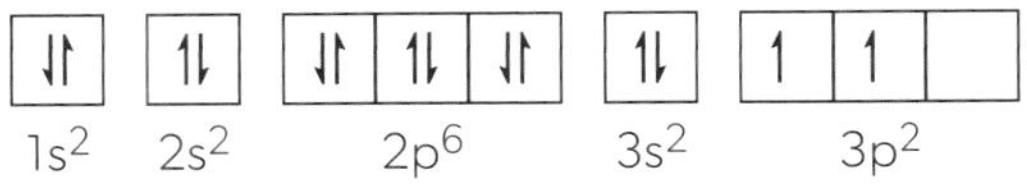

[2];

c) There is a large difference in electronegativity values between Cl and Na and only a small difference between Cl and Si so an electron is completely transferred when NaCl is formed and electrons are shared when $SiCl_4$ is formed. [2]

6. a) i) 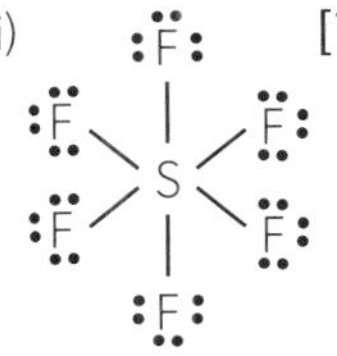 [1]

ii) S has readily available empty 3d orbitals which can be utilized, in O the d orbitals are too high in energy to be used. [1]; iii) O in ozone has three electron domains so trigonal planar with actual shape bent or V-shaped, S has six electron domains and six pairs of electrons so both are octahedral. [2]; iv) Ozone: <120° (actual value 117°), SF6 90° and 180° [2]; b) CF_2Cl_2 contains four electron domains around the central C atom. As they are all bonding pairs, it will be tetrahedral. [2]

7. Structure I O(LHS)=6−6−1=−1, N=5−0−4=+1, O(RHS)=6−2−3=+1 [2], structure II O=6−4−2=0, N=5−0−4=+1 [1], structure II favoured as formal charges lower. [1]

8. a) Triple covalent bond (one of which is a coordination bond with electron pair donated by O to C) made up of one σ and two π bonds. [2]; b) Spread of π electrons over more than two nuclei giving equal bond strengths and greater stability. [3]; c) Combination of two or more atomic orbitals to form new orbitals with lower energy [1], CO_2 sp, diamond sp^3, graphite sp^2, CO_3^{2-} sp^2 [4]; d) i) Molten Na_2O conducts as ions are mobile in liquid state, SO_3 has neutral molecules and no mobile ions or electrons so it does not conduct electricity. [2]; ii) $Na_2O(s) + H_2O(l) \rightarrow 2NaOH(aq)$ [1], $SO_3(l) + H_2O(l) \rightarrow H_2SO_4(aq)$ [1], both conduct as they react with water to form ions. [1]

9. a) ICl_4^+: 5 domains, 4 bonding, 1 non-bonding [1], ICl_4^-: 6 domains, 4 bonding, 2 non-bonding [1], I_3^-: 5 domains, 2 bonding, 3 non-bonding [1], BrF_3: 5 domains, 3 bonding, 2 non-bonding [1]; b) ICl_4^+: seesaw [1], ICl_4^-: square planar [1], I_3^-: linear [1], BrF_3: T-shaped. [1]

Periodicity: multiple choice (pages 51 and 52)

1. B 2. B 3. D 4. D 5. A 6. A 7. A 8. C 9. C 10. D 11. B 12. C 13. D 14. A 15. B 16. D 17. A 18. B 19. D 20. C 21. C 22. A 23. A 24. D 25. C 26. B 27. A 28. C 29. C 30. D

Periodicity: short answers (page 53)

1. a) Elements in the same group have similar outer electron configurations, in this case ns^2np^2, [1] in the same period the elements have a different number of electrons in the same outer energy level. [1]; b) p-block [1]; c) The outer 3p electron in Si is higher in energy than the outer 2p electron in C so is easier to remove. [2]; d) Attempt to pass electricity through the elements using a DC battery, leads and a multimeter. Diamond does not conduct (graphite is unusual for a non-metal in that it does conduct), silicon, a metalloid, is a semiconductor and tin, a metal, is a good conductor. [3]

2. a) The levels are split into sub-levels. The 4s sub-level is lower in energy than the 3d sub-level so fills before the 3d sub-level. [2]; b) The 4f sub-level is being filled for the lanthanides and the 5f sub-level for the actinides. [2]

3. a) From basic (Na_2O, MgO) through amphoteric (Al_2O_3) to acidic (all non-metal oxides) [3]; b) i) $Na_2O(s) + H_2O(l) \rightarrow 2NaOH(aq)$ [1]; ii) $CaO(s) + H_2O(l) \rightarrow Ca(OH)_2(aq)$ [1]; $SO_3(g) + H_2O(l) \rightarrow H_2SO_4(aq)$ [1]; c) Both are acidic oxides and dissolve in rain water to form acid rain, which reacts with calcium carbonate in building materials. e.g. $SO_2(g) + H_2O(l) \rightarrow H_2SO_3(aq)$, $3NO_2(g) + H_2O(l) \rightarrow 2HNO_3(aq) + NO(g)$, $CO_3^{2-}(s) + 2H^+(aq) \rightarrow H_2O(l) + CO_2(g)$ [4]

4. a) $1s^2 2s^2 2p^6 3s^2 3p^6$ [1]; b) Both have the same electron configuration but S has one more proton so has a greater attraction to the outer electrons. [2]; c) Br has more protons (35 compared to K's 19) so the outer energy level (which is the same for both) is attracted more strongly to the nucleus. [2]; d) Atomic radius is measured by dividing the distance between the two atoms in a molecule, Ne does not combine with another Ne atom. [1]

5. a) i) Atomic number **[1]**; ii) Increase in number of electrons in outer energy level, smaller atoms/ increase in positive nuclear charge **[2]**, do not form bonds easily with other elements **[1]**; b) i) The energy (in kJ mol^{-1}) required to remove an electron from an atom in the gaseous state **[2]**; ii) Increasing number of protons causes decreasing radius and lower outer energy level as electrons closer to nucleus so harder to remove. **[2]**; iii) The electron in the outer 2p sub-level in B ($1s^2 2s^2 2p^1$) is higher in energy than the electrons in the outer 2s sub-level in Be ($1s^2 2s^2$). **[2]**; c) Na is a metal and contains delocalized electrons, phosphorus consists of atoms covalently bonded in P_4 molecules in which there are no delocalized electrons. **[2]**

6. Less particulates/C/CO/VOCs and SO_2 produced **[2]**, particulates, CO, VOCs and SO_2 are toxic or SO_2 causes acid rain. **[1]**

7. a) Fe^{2+} acts as a Lewis acid and accepts one non-bonding pair of electrons from each water molecule, which act as Lewis bases. **[2]**; b) Fe^{3+} has one less electron than Fe^{2+} so the attraction of the nucleus on the remaining d electrons is stronger—this affects the splitting of the d orbitals in the complex ion and hence the wavelength of light absorbed. **[2]**; c) Iron metal contains unpaired electrons, which align parallel to each other in domains irrespective of whether an external magnetic or electric field is present **[1]**, CN^- is higher in the spectrochemical series than H_2O so causes greater splitting of the d orbitals **[1]**, in $[Fe(H_2O)_6]^{2+}$ there are four unpaired electrons as each of the five d orbitals is occupied (two electrons in one of the lower orbitals and one in each of the other four orbitals), $[Fe(CN)_6]^{4-}$ contains no unpaired electrons as the six electrons are spin-paired in the three lower d orbitals. **[2]**; d) As the reaction is exothermic, increasing the temperature causes a lower yield **[1]** so a catalyst speeds it up at a lower temperature, thus reducing costs **[1]**, iron is abundant and a cheap metal to use as a catalyst. **[1]**

8. a) $[CuC_{10}H_{12}O_8N_2]^{2-}$ = 351.8 g mol^{-1} **[2]**; b) 6, octahedral **[2]**; c) It 'wraps' around the metal ions using six non-bonding pairs of electrons to form coordinate bonds with Cu^{2+}, which is acting as a Lewis acid. **[3]**

9. a) Three of the d orbitals lie between the axes and two lie along the axes. As the ligands approach they repel the d orbitals that lie along the axes more. More electron-dense ligands cause greater repulsion/splitting. **[2]**; b) $[Cu(H_2O)_6]^{2+}$ absorbs orange light so transmits blue light, as the ligand changes to NH_3, ΔE increases so the absorbed colour shifts to a smaller wavelength (yellow) and the complementary transmitted colour is purple. **[3]**; c) Sc^{3+} contains no d electrons so no transitions between split d levels can occur. **[2]**

Classification of organic compounds: multiple choice (pages 70 and 71)

1. B **2.** C **3.** B **4.** D **5.** C **6.** A **7.** B **8.** D **9.** A **10.** C **11.** A **12.** A **13.** D **14.** D **15.** A **16.** D **17.** B

Classification of organic compounds: short answers (page 72)

1. a) i) ***Any one of:*** C1 to C6 **[1]**; ii) C7 **[1]**; iii) C8 or C9 **[1]**; b) C8 to O3 is a single bond, C8 to O4 is a double bond **[1]**, less shared electron pairs so single bond is longer than double bond. **[1]**; c) C1 to C6 is part of benzene ring so bond length between that of single and double bond, and shorter than single bond between C1 and C7. **[2]**

2. a) i) Methylpropene ***or*** 2-methylpropene ***or*** 2-methylprop-1-ene **[1]**; ii) C_nH_{2n} **[1]**; iii) $-CH_2-C(CH_3)_2-CH_2-C(CH_3)_2-CH_2-C(CH_3)_2-$ **[1]**; b) Functional group isomerism **[1]**; c) Both are non-polar and have weak London dispersion attractive forces between the molecules **[1]**, these are easy to break so the compounds have low boiling points, as they are non-polar they are not attracted to polar water molecules. **[1]**

3.

a)

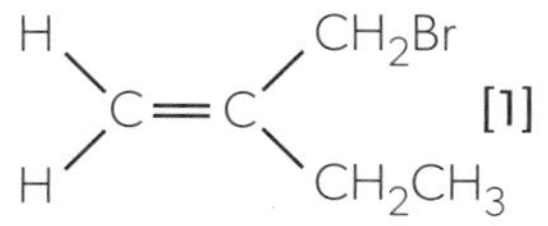

b)

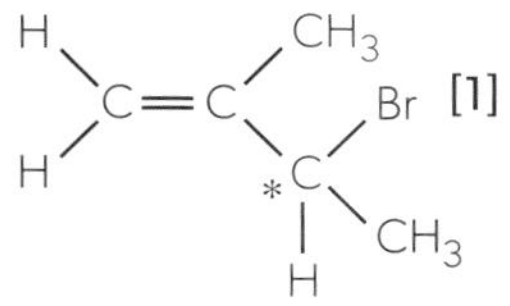

c)

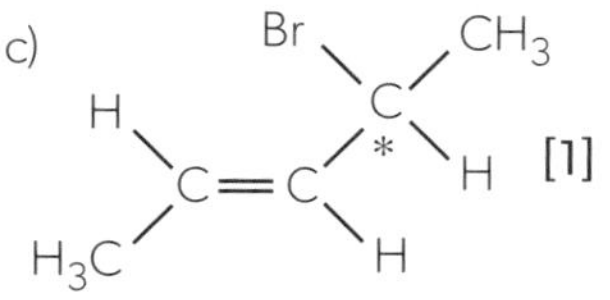

d)

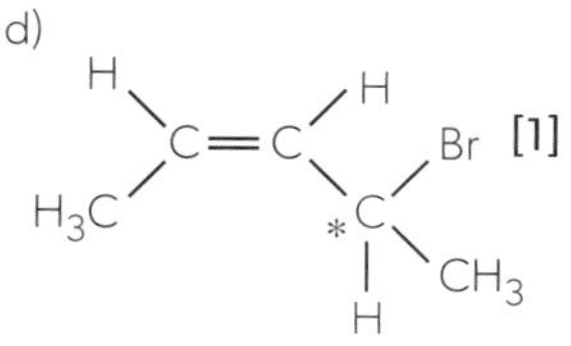

e)

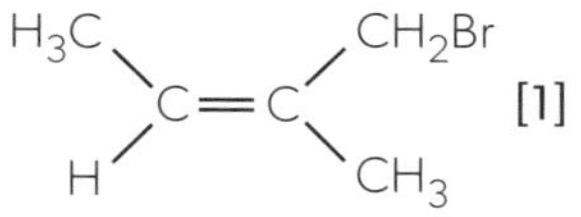

f)

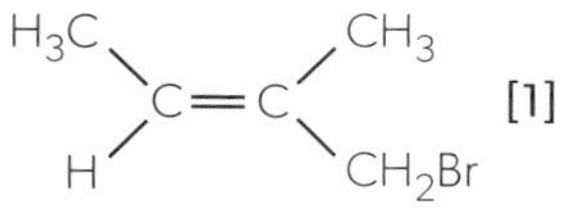

4. a) As a reference **[1]**; b) Quartet **[1]**; c) 3:3:2 **[1]**; d) $RCOOCH_2R$ **[1]**, no protons due to phenyl group present in spectrum or other structure has hydrogen atoms in only two different chemical environments. **[1]**; e) A: C–H **[1]**, B: C=O **[1]**, C: C–O **[1]**; f) 88: $C_4H_8O_2^+$ **[1]**, 73: $C_3H_5O_2^+$ or $(M - CH_3)^+$ **[1]**, 59: $C_2H_3O_2^+$ or $(M - C_2H_5)^+$ **[1]**; g) Ethyl ethanoate **[1]**, $CH_3COOC_2H_5$. **[1]**

Energetics: multiple choice (pages 86–88)

1. D **2.** B **3.** A **4.** A **5.** C **6.** D **7.** B **8.** C **9.** A **10.** B **11.** D **12.** A **13.** D **14.** A **15.** C **16.** C **17.** C **18.** D **19.** B **20.** C **21.** B

Energetics: short answers (page 88 and 89)

1. a) $100 \times 4.18 \times 35.0 = 14\,630\,J = 14.6\,kJ$ **[2]**;

b) Amount of ethanol $= \dfrac{1.78}{46.08} = 0.0386\,mol$ **[1]**,

$\Delta H_c = \dfrac{-14.6}{0.0386} = -378\,kJ\,mol^{-1}$ **[1]**;

c) *Any two from:* heat loss, incomplete combustion, heat absorbed by calorimeter not included. [2]

2. a) i) 100 g ethanol, 900 g octane [1]; ii) 2.17 mol of ethanol, 7.88 mol of octane [1]; iii) E from ethanol = $(2.17 \times 1367) = 2966$ kJ, E from octane = (7.88×5470) = 43 104 kJ, *total energy* = 4.61×10^4 kJ [3]; b) Greater as fewer intermolecular forces to break or vaporization is endothermic or gaseous fuel has greater enthalpy than liquid fuel. [2]

3. a) *Any two from:* all heat transferred to copper sulfate solution, specific heat capacity of zinc negligible, density of solution same as density of pure water, specific heat capacity of solution same as for pure water [2]; b) i) 48.2 °C [2]; ii) Temperature decreases at uniform rate [1]; iii) 10.1 kJ [1]; c) Amount of Zn = amount of $CuSO_4$ $= \frac{(1.00 \times 50.0)}{1000} = 5.00 \times 10^{-2}$ mol [1]; d) -201 kJ mol^{-1} [1]

4. a) $\Delta H = \frac{1}{2}$ Equation 1 $- \left(\frac{1}{2}\text{ Equation 2}\right) -$ (Equation 3) = +137 kJ [4]; b) Positive as number of moles of gas increasing. [2]; c) At low T, ΔH is positive and ΔG is positive, at high T, factor $T\Delta S$ predominates and ΔG is negative [2]; d) Energy in due to C–C and 2C–H = 1174 kJ mol^{-1}, energy out due to C=C and H–H = 1050 kJ mol^{-1}, $\Delta H = +124$ kJ mol^{-1} [3]; (e) Bond enthalpy values are average values. [1]

5. a) At 298 K, $\Delta G = \Delta H - T\Delta S = 210 - (298 \times 0.216) = +146$ kJ, positive value so non-spontaneous. [2]; b) When $\Delta G = 0$, $T = \frac{210}{0.216} = 972$ K [2]

Chemical kinetics: multiple choice (pages 94–96)

1. A **2.** A **3.** D **4.** B **5.** A **6.** B **7.** D **8.** D **9.** C **10.** D **11.** A **12.** A **13.** D **14.** A **15.** A **16.** D **17.** A **18.** A **19.** D **20.** C **21.** B **22.** C **23.** D

Chemical kinetics: short answers (page 97)

1. a) i)

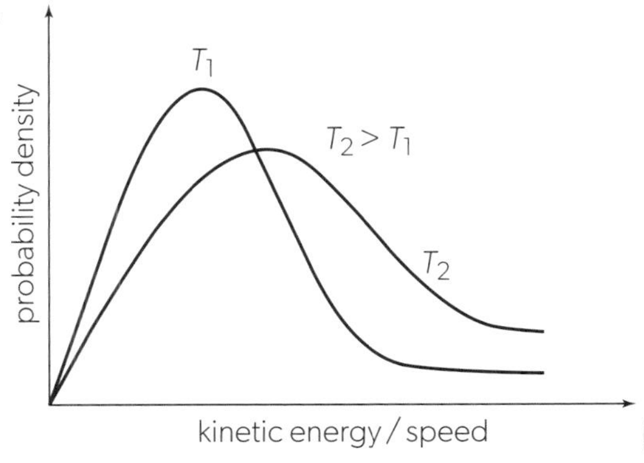

[2]

ii) Minimum energy required for the reaction to proceed [1]; iii) Increases rate of reaction by lowering the activation energy [2]

b) i)

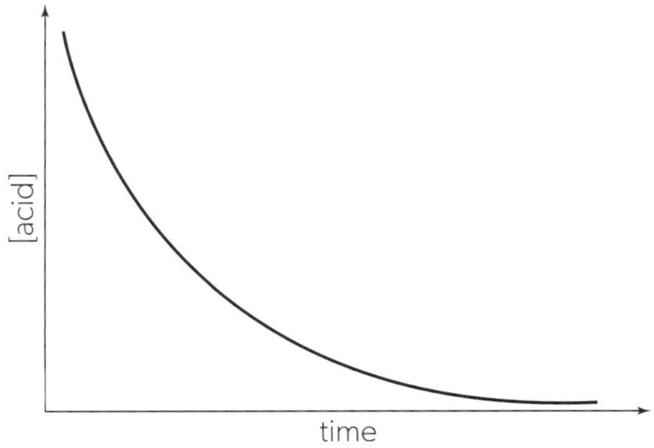

[1]

ii) Slope decreases [1]; iii) Rate decreases as fewer collisions per unit time. [2]

2. a) Reaction is complete so no more O_2 evolved [1] b) Rate = gradient of the tangent to the graph at 120 s = 0.017 mm s^{-1} [3]

c) i)

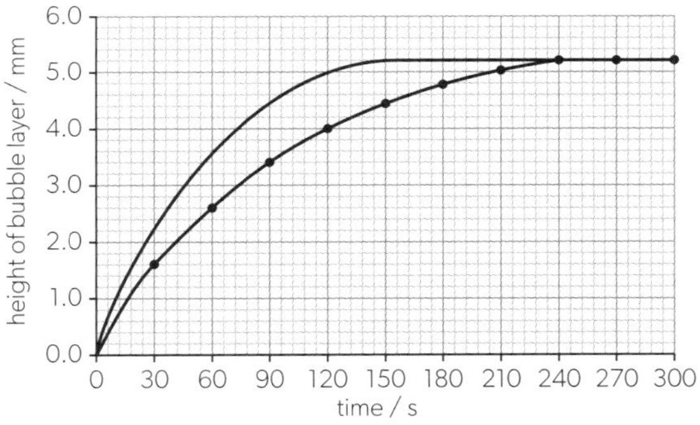

[1]

ii) Catalyst provides an alternative pathway with a lower activation energy [1] so more molecules have energy greater than or equal to activation energy. [1]

3. a) Doubling $[H_2]$ doubles the rate [1]; b) 2 [1], (using experiments 1 and 4) as [NO] is halved, rate goes down to $\frac{1}{4}$ [1]; c) rate = $k[H_2(g)][NO(g)]^2$ [1];

d) Experiment 3 rate $= 1.2 \times 10^{-2}$ mol dm^{-3} s^{-1} [1], Experiment 5 rate $= 2.5 \times 10^{-4}$ mol dm^{-3} s^{-1} [1];

e) $k = \frac{4.0 \times 10^{-3}}{(2.0 \times 10^{-3})(4.0 \times 10^{-3})^2} = 1.3 \times 10^5$ [1], mol^{-2} dm^6 s^{-1} [1];

f) e.g. NO + NO $\rightleftharpoons$ N_2O_2 (fast), $N_2O_2 + H_2 \rightarrow H_2N_2O_2$ (slow), $H_2N_2O_2 + H_2 \rightarrow 2H_2O + N_2$ (slow) [2]; g) A substance that increases the rate and is in a different phase to the reactants. [1];

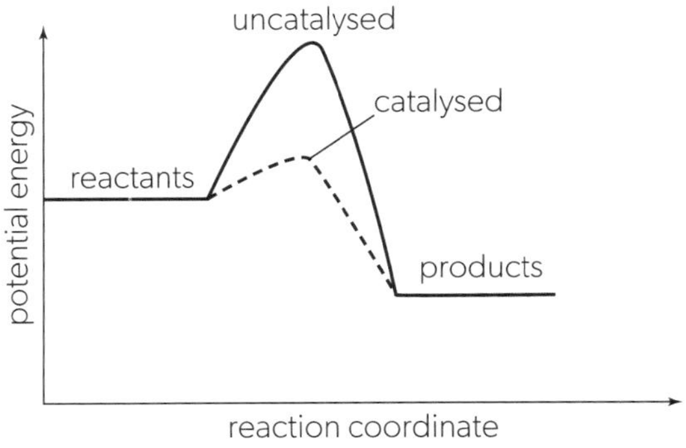

[2]

4. a) i) Rate = $k[NO(g)]^2[Cl_2(g)]$ **[1]**; ii) Rate of reaction will decrease by a factor of 4, no effect on the rate constant **[2]**; b) Zero-order reaction **[1]**, all concentrations are 1.0 mol dm^{-3} **[1]**

Equilibrium: multiple choice (page 103)

1. C **2.** B **3.** D **4.** B **5.** C **6.** A **7.** D **8.** C **9.** D **10.** C **11.** D

Equilibrium: short answers (page 104)

1.a) $K_c = \frac{[C_2H_5OH(g)]}{[C_2H_4(g)]\times[H_2O(g)]}$ **[1]**;

b) i) Favours reactants (shifted to the left) **[1]**; ii) ΔH negative **[1]** as forward reaction is exothermic **[1]**, heat is absorbed when equilibrium moves to left. **[1]**; c) Rate of reaction increased **[1]**, increased collision frequency **[1]**, equilibrium shifted to right **[1]** fewer moles of gas on right. **[1]**

2. a) $K_c = \frac{[NH_3(g)]^2}{[N_2(g)]\times[H_2(g)]^3}$ **[1]**;

b) Shifts to the right (products) **[1]**, 4 mol decreases to 2 mol, equilibrium moves to the side with fewer molecules **[1]**; c) K_c decreases **[1]**, forward reaction is exothermic. **[1]**; d) Lowers the activation energy of both the forward and backward reactions equally. **[1]**

3. a) $K_c = \frac{[NO(g)]^4\times[H_2O(g)]^6}{[NH_3(g)]^4\times[O_2(g)]^5}$ **[1]**;

b) i) Right **[1]**; ii) Right **[1]**; iii) Right **[1]**; iv) No change **[1]** c) Minimum energy needed by colliding particles to react. **[1]**

4. a) Reactants and products in same phase **[1]**, rate of forward reaction = rate of reverse reaction **[1]**;

b) $K_c = \frac{[HI(g)]^2}{[H_2(g)]\times[I_2(g)]}$ **[1]**;

c) No change to position of equilibrium or to K_c **[2]**
d) Reaction is exothermic **[1]**;

e) $K_c{}' = \frac{1}{160} = 6.25\times10^{-3}$ **[1]**

5. a) $Br_2(g) \rightleftharpoons Br_2(l)$ **[1]**, $Br_2(g) + H_2(g) \rightleftharpoons 2HBr(g)$ **[1]**; b) i) Increase in volume of liquid and no change in colour of vapour. **[1]**; ii) Shift to the right (towards products). **[1]**; iii) No effect as same amount of moles on both sides. **[2]**;

c) i) $K_c = \frac{[HBr(g)]^2}{[H_2(g)]\times[Br_2(g)]}$ **[1]**; ii) No effect **[1]**

6. a) $\Delta S^\ominus = (\Sigma S^\ominus \text{products}) - (\Sigma S^\ominus \text{reactants})$
$= (2\times192) - [193 + (3\times131)] = -202\ \text{J K}^{-1}\,\text{mol}^{-1}$ **[2]**;

b) $\Delta G = \Delta H - T\Delta S = (-92\times1000) - 298\times(-202) =$ $-31\,804$ J (31.8 kJ) **[2]**; c) As the temperature increases $T\Delta S$ becomes greater and eventually ΔG becomes positive and the reaction becomes non-spontaneous **[2]**; d) $\Delta G = -RT\ln K$, $-31\,804 = -8.31\times298\times\ln K$, $K = e^{12.84} = 3.77\times10^5$ **[3]**;

e) $K_c = \frac{0.060^2}{[0.17\times0.11^3]} = 16$ **[3]**;

f) The value for K_c is lower at temperature T_2 so T_2 must be higher than 298 K as the reaction is exothermic. **[2]**

Proton transfer reactions: acid–base behaviour: multiple choice (pages 115 and 116)

1. A **2.** B **3.** D **4.** C **5.** B **6.** A **7.** D **8.** D **9.** A **10.** B **11.** C **12.** D **13.** D **14.** A **15.** C **16.** C **17.** C **18.** B **19.** D **20.** D **21.** B **22.** A **23.** B **24.** B **25.** C **26.** D

Proton transfer reactions: acid–base behaviour: short answers (page 117)

1. a) i) A species that can accept a proton **[1]**; ii) HCl/Cl^- and H_3O^+/H_2O **[2]**; b) i) A strong acid is fully dissociated, a weak acid is only partially dissociated. **[2]**; ii) $CH_3COOH(aq) + NH_3(aq) \rightleftharpoons CH_3COO^-NH^{4+}(aq)$ **[1]**; iii) Both react to give the same amount of hydrogen **[1]** and form a salt **[1]** but the hydrochloric acid will react faster **[1]** as the hydrogen ion concentration is greater. **[1]**

2. a) i) $[H^+(aq)] = 1.00\times10^{-2}$ mol dm^{-3} **[1]**, pH = 2 **[1]**; ii) 4 **[2]**; b) $H_2SO_4(aq) + 2NaOH(aq) \rightarrow Na_2SO_4(aq) + 2H_2O(l)$ **[1]**; c) i) One drop will cause the colour of the solution to change from pink to colourless. **[2]**; ii) Amount of $OH^-(aq)$ in 25.0 cm^3 of NaOH(aq) $= \frac{25.0}{1000}\times1.00\times10^{-4} = 2.50\times10^{-6}$ mol.

Amount of 5.00×10^{-5} mol dm^{-3} H_2SO_4 required to give $= 1.25\times10^{-6}$ mol, volume = 25.0 cm^3 **[2]**

3. a) $HCl(aq) + NaHCO_3(aq) \rightarrow NaCl(aq) + H_2O(l) + CO_2(g)$ **[2]**; b) i) $CO_3^{2-}(aq)$ **[1]**; ii) $H_2CO_3(aq)$ or $H_2O(l)/CO_2(g)$ **[1]**; c) i) $2HCl(aq) + CuO(s) \rightarrow CuCl_2(aq) + H_2O(l)$ **[1]**, ii) $2HCl(aq) + Na_2CO_3(aq) \rightarrow 2NaCl(aq) + H_2O(l) + CO_2(g)$ **[1]**

4. a) Rain water contains dissolved $CO_2(g)$, which can give it a pH as low as 5.6 so acid rain, which contains other dissolved acids, must have a pH below 5.6. **[2]**; b) $N_2(g) + O_2(g) \rightarrow 2NO(g)$ **[1]**, $2NO(g) + O_2(g) \rightarrow 2NO_2(g)$ **[1]** then either $2NO_2(g) + H_2O(l) \rightarrow HNO_3(aq) + HNO_2(aq)$ or $4NO_2(g) + O_2(g) + 2H_2O(l) \rightarrow 4HNO_3(aq)$ **[2]**; c) The $CaCO_3$ reacts with the acid to form soluble salts, $CaCO_3(s) + 2H^+(aq) \rightarrow Ca^{2+}(aq) + CO_2(g) + H_2O(l)$ **[2]**; d) The hydroxide ions neutralize the hydrogen ions to form water, $OH^- + H^+(aq) \rightarrow H_2O(l)$ **[2]**

5. a) $H_2O(l) \rightleftharpoons H+(aq) + OH-(aq)$, endothermic as K_w increases with an increase in temperature **[2]**;
b) At 90 °C $K_w \approx 38\times10^{-14}$, $[H^+(aq)] = [OH^-(aq)]$ $= (38\times10^{-14})^{\frac{1}{2}} = 6.16\times10^{-7}$ mol dm^{-3} **[2]**, pH = 6.2 **[1]**

6. a) It contains a chiral carbon atom **[1]**;

b) $K_a = 1.38\times10^{-4} = \frac{[H^+]\times[CH(CH_3)(OH)COO^-]}{[CH(CH_3)(OH)COOH]}$

$\approx \frac{[H^+]^2}{0.100}$ **[1]**; $[H^+] = (1.38\times10^{-5})^{\frac{1}{2}} = 0.00371$ mol dm^{-3} **[1]**, pH = 2.43 **[1]**; c) M_r(lactic acid) = (3 × 12.01) + (6 × 1.01) + (3 × 16.00) = 90.1 and 2.00 g of NaOH =

$$\frac{2}{(22.99 + 16.00 + 1.01)} = 0.0500 \text{ mol } [1],$$

$$K^{9} = J^{\cdot}38 \times J0_{-4} = \frac{[CH(CH^{3})(OH)COOH]}{[H_{+}] \times [CH(CH^{3})(OH)COO_{-}]} \text{ and}$$

pH = 4.00

$$\text{so } \frac{[CH(CH3)(OH)COO^{-}]}{[CH(CH^{3-})(OH)COOH]}$$

$$= \frac{1.38 \times 10^{-4}}{10^{-4}} = 1.38 \text{ } [1],$$

$[CH(CH_3)(OH)COO^-] = [NaOH] = 0.100 \text{ mol dm}^{-3}$ so

$[CH(CH_3)(OH)COOH] = \frac{0.100}{1.38} = 0.0725 \text{ mol dm}^{-3}$ [1],

mass required in 500 cm^3

$$= \left[\left(\frac{0.0725}{2}\right) + 0.0500 \text{ (to react with the NaOH)}\right] \times 90.1$$

= 7.77 g. [1]

7. a) i) $C_2H_5COOH(aq) + H_2O(l) \rightleftharpoons C_2H_5COO^-(aq) + H_3O+(l)$ [1], $K_a = [C_2H_5COO^-(aq)][H^+(aq)]/[C_2H_5COOH(aq)]$ [1]; ii) $[H^+(aq)] = (2.00 \times 10^{-3} \times 10^{-4.87})^{1/2} = 1.64 \times 10^{-4}$ mol dm^{-3}, pH = 3.8 [3]; iii) The temperature is 25 °C as pK_a is measured at 25 °C [1], the concentration of the acid at equilibrium is the same as the undissociated acid. [1]; b) i) $Na^+(aq)$, $C_2H_5COO^-(aq)$, $C_2H_5COOH(aq)$, $H^+(aq)$ or $H_3O^+(aq)$, $OH-(aq)$, $H_2O(l)$ [2]; ii) Additional OH^- ions react with H^+ ions to form water but more of the acid dissociates to replace the H^+ ions so the concentration of H^+ ions remains almost constant. [2]

Electron transfer reactions: oxidation–reduction behaviour: multiple choice (pages 129 and 130)

1. C **2.** D **3.** A **4.** B **5.** B **6.** A **7.** B **8.** A **9.** D **10.** A **11.** C **12.** C **13.** B **14.** C **15.** A **16.** D **17.** A **18.** C **19.** A **20.** C **21.** C **22.** C **23.** B **24.** D **25.** D **26.** C **27.** A **28.** C

Electron transfer reactions: oxidation–reduction behaviour: short answers (page 131)

1. a) $5Fe^{2+}(aq) + MnO^{4-}(aq) + 8H^+(aq) \rightarrow Mn^{2+}(aq) + 5Fe^{3+}(aq) + 4H_2O(l)$ [2]; b) $Fe^{2+}(aq)$ [1];

c) $\frac{22.50}{1000} \times 2.152 \times 10^{-2} = 4.842 \times 10^{-4}$ mol [2];

d) $5 \times 4.842 \times 10^{-4} = 2.421 \times 10^{-3}$ mol [2];

e) $\left(\frac{55.85 \times 2.421 \times 10^{-3}}{3.682 \times 10^{-1}}\right) \times 100 = 36.72\%$ [2]

2. a) The electrons flow from the Mg half-cell to the Fe half-cell, showing that Mg is reducing $Fe^{2+}(aq)$. [2]; b) Fe [1]; c) i) $Fe^{2+}(aq) + 2e^- \rightarrow Fe(s)$ [1]; ii) $Mg(s) + Fe^{2+}(aq) \rightarrow Fe(s) + Mg^{2+}(aq)$ [2]; d) Greater as Cu is below Fe in the activity series so Cu^{2+} is more readily reduced by Mg. [2]

3. a) i) A cell showing the container, liquid, electrodes, and power supply (as shown on page 123), (+) electrode: Cl_2, (−) electrode Na(l). [2]; ii) $2Cl^-(aq) \rightarrow Cl_2(g) + 2e^-$, $Na^+(l) + e^- \rightarrow Na(l)$, $2NaCl(l) \rightarrow 2Na(l) + Cl_2(g)$ [2]; b) There are no free electrons and the ions are not able to move. [1]; c) Al forms a protective layer or does not rust or is less dense. [1]

4. a) Oxidation states change: I from 0 to −1 and S from +2 to +2.5 [2]; b) i) In SO_4^{2-} the oxidation state of S is +6 and O is −2. Since an O atom has been replaced by an S atom, the two S atoms are +6 and −2 in $S_2O_3^{2-}$ but all S atoms are assumed to be the same when calculating their oxidation state in an ion so the average is +2. [2]; ii) In $S_4O_6^{2-}$ where the oxidation state of S works out to be 2.5 the man-made concept of oxidation states breaks down as the S atoms cannot have an oxidation state that is not a whole number and suggests that not all four S atoms are in the same chemical environment. [3]; c) Addition of oxygen and increase in oxidation state both fit as definitions of oxidation but removal of hydrogen and loss of electrons do not fit as the carbon atom is surrounded by eight shared outer electrons in both diamond itself and in carbon dioxide. [4]

5. a) $Cl_2(g) + 2Ag+(aq) \rightarrow 2Ag(s) + 2Cl^-(aq)$ [2]; b) from the chlorine half-cell to the silver half-cell [1]; c) 0.56 V [1]; d) $\Delta G = nFE = -2 \times 96500 \times 0.56 = 1.08 \times 10^5$ J, energy produced = 108 kJ. [2]

6. a) i) (+) (mainly) $O_2(g)$, (−) $H_2(g)$ and ii) (+) (mainly) $Cl_2(g)$, (−) $H_2(g)$ [3]; b) Both give $H_2(g)$ and $O_2(g)$ at the (−) and (+) electrodes, respectively, in the ratio of 2:1. [3]; c) Make the spoon the (−) electrode (cathode) and pass a current of electricity through a solution of silver ions (e.g. $AgNO_3(aq)$). [2]

Electron sharing reactions: multiple choice (page 141)

1. D **2.** B **3.** D **4.** A **5.** D **6.** B **7.** A **8.** C **9.** D **10.** C **11.** C **12.** B **13.** C **14.** D **15.** D **16.** C

Electron sharing reactions: short answers (page 142)

1. a) i) $CH_3CH{=}CH_2 + Br_2 \rightarrow CH_3CHBrCH_2Br$ [1], 1,2-dibromopropane [1]; ii) Electrophilic addition [1]; iii) The oxidation state of bromine has changed from (0) to (−1). [2]; b) i) $CH_3CH_2CH_3 + Br_2 \rightarrow CH_3CH_2CH_2Br + HBr$ [1], 1-bromopropane [1] ***or*** $CH_3CH_2CH_3 + Br_2 \rightarrow CH_3CH_{Br}CH_3 + HBr$ [1], 2-bromopropane [1]; ii) Free radical substitution [1]; iii) ***Initiation***: $Br_2 \rightarrow 2Br\bullet$ [1], ***propagation***: $Br\bullet + C_3H_8 \rightarrow C_3H_7\bullet + HBr$ and $C_3H_7\bullet + Br_2 \rightarrow C_3H_7Br + Br\bullet$ [2], ***termination***: $C_3H_7\bullet + Br\bullet \rightarrow C_3H_7Br$ [1]; c) Shake with bromine water in the dark. It will be decolourised by propene as 1,2-dibromopropane is colourless but there will be no colour change with propane as it needs UV light to react [2];

d) H_2BrC 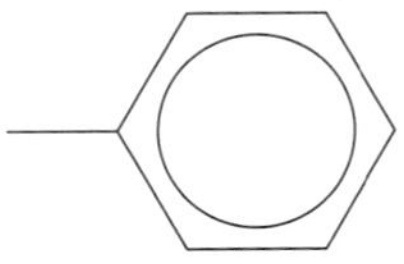 [1] and H−Br [1]

2. a) A is secondary as the halogen atom is bonded to a carbon atom with two R groups [1], B is tertiary as the halogen atom is bonded to a carbon atom with 3 R groups [1]; b) i) Nucleophile [1]; ii) Butan-2-ol [1] 2-methyl-butan-2-ol [1]; iii) The colour will change from orange to green as the butan-2-ol is oxidized to butan-2-one and there will be no change with 2-methyl-butan-2-ol as it is a tertiary alcohol and not oxidized by acidified dichromate(VII). [2];

d) i) 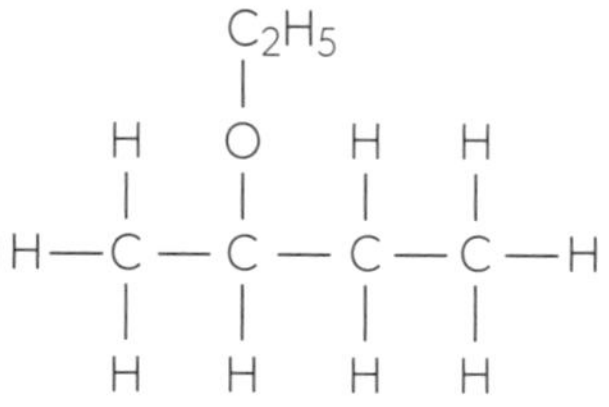 ether [1]

ii) 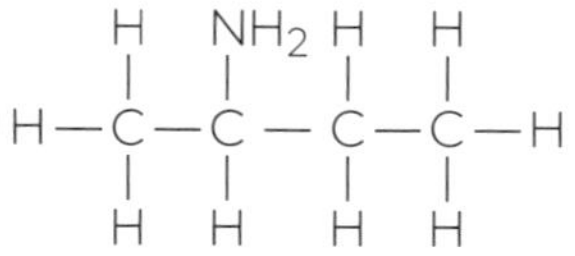 amine [1]

3. a) The carbon atom has a small positive charge (δ^+) as the C–Br bond is polar due to bromine being more electronegative than carbon; this attracts the OH^- nucleophile. [1]; b) Rate = k[R–Br][OH^-] [1], S_N2 [1];

c)

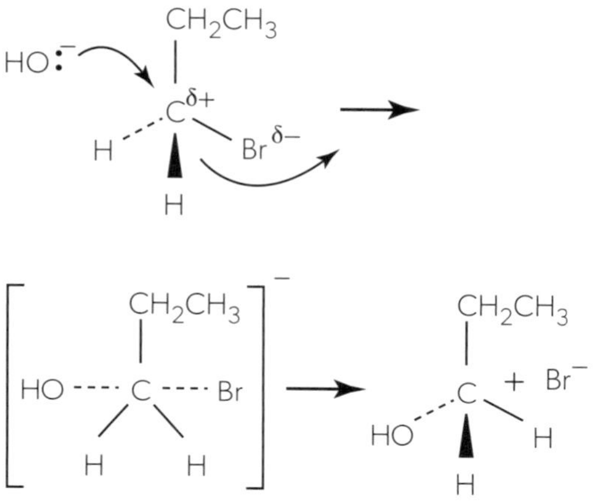

[4]

d) Slower rate [1] as the C–Cl bond is stronger than the C–Br bond so harder to break. [1]

4. H_2SO_4 acts as a catalyst [1]. It protonates the nitric acid to form the NO_2^+ electrophile [1]. $HNO_3 + H_2SO_4 \rightarrow H_2NO_3^+ + HSO_4^-$ [1], $H_2NO_3^+ \rightarrow H_2O + NO_2^+$ [1]. After the NO_2^+ has reacted with benzene to form a positive intermediate the HSO_4^- ion extracts a proton to form nitrobenzene and regenerate the sulfuric acid [1], $C_6H_6NO_2^+ + HSO_4^- \rightarrow C_6H_5NO_2 + H_2SO_4$ [1]

Tools for chemists: multiple choice (page 156)

1. B 2. C 3. B 4. A 5. D 6. D 7. C 8. A
9. B 10. C 11. A 12. D 13. A 14. C

Underlying philosophy: holistic short answers (pages 164–166)

1. a) i) Amount of Zn $= \frac{2.93}{65.38} = 0.0448$ mol and amount of $CuSO_4 = \left(\frac{50.0}{1000}\right) \times 0.250 = 0.0125$ mol [1], $CuSO_4$ is the limiting reagent. [1]; ii) Theoretical yield of Cu $= 0.0125 \times 63.55 = 0.794$ g [1],

percentage yield $= \left(\frac{0.679}{0.794}\right) \times 100 = 85.5\%$ [1];

b) i) Heat evolved $= 50.0 \times 4.18 \times 11.1 = 2.32 \times 10^3$ J

$= 2.32$ kJ [1], $\Delta H = \frac{-2.32}{0.0125} = -1.86 \times 10^2$ kJ mol^{-1} [1]

ii) ***Either*** density of solution = 1.00 g cm^{-3} ***or*** specific heat capacity of solution is 4.18 J g^{-1} K^{-1}/same as pure water ***or*** reaction goes to completion [1]; iii) Percentage

uncertainty $= \left(\frac{0.5}{11.1}\right) \times 100 = 4.5\%$ [1], absolute uncertainty

$= \pm(0.045 \times 1.86 \times 10^2) = \pm 8.4$ kJ mol^{-1} [1];

c) i)

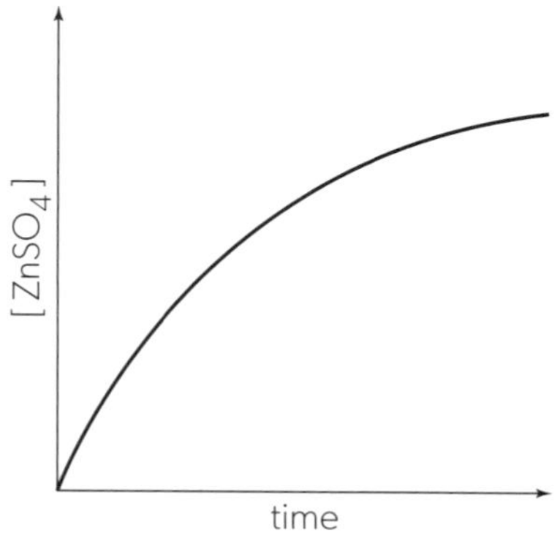

initial concentration zero and concentration increases with time [1], decreasing gradient as reaction proceeds [1]; ii) draw a tangent to the curve at time, t = 0 [1], rate = gradient or slope of the tangent [1]; iii) piece has smaller surface area [1], lower frequency of collisions. [1].

2. a) i) $K = \frac{[HOCH_2CH_2OH] \times [CH_3OH]^2}{[C_4H_6O_4] \times [H_2]^4}$ [1];

ii) No change in value of K [1], as at a fixed temperature K is a constant. [1]; iii) Energy in to break 6(C–H) + 4(C–O) + 2(C=O) + C–C + 4(H–H) bonds

$= (6 \times 414) + (4 \times 358) + (2 \times 804) + 346 + (4 \times 436) =$

7614 kJ [1], energy out to form 4(C–O) + 4(O–H) + 10(C–H) + C–C bonds

$= (4 \times 358) + (4 \times 463) + (10 \times 414) + 346 = 7770$ kJ [1],

$\Delta H = 7614 - 7770 = -156$ kJ [1]; b) Ethane-1,2-diol can form hydrogen bonds and butane cannot [1], hydrogen bonds are stronger attractive forces between molecules than London dispersion forces. [1]; c) 1st step increases from +1 to +3 [1], 2nd step increases from +3 to +4 [1]; d) Weak acids are only slightly dissociated whereas strong acids are fully dissociated in water. [1]; e) Converts exponential expression into linear scale with simple numbers. [1]; f) i) Amount of NaOH

$= \left(\frac{14.6}{1000}\right) \times 0.100 = 1.46 \times 10^{-3}$ mol [1]; ii) Amount of

ethanedioic acid $= 0.5 \times 1.46 \times 10^{-3} = 7.30 \times 10^{-4}$ mol [1]; iii) Amount of pure hydrated ethanedioic acid in

1.00 dm^3 $= \left(\frac{1000}{20.0}\right) \times 7.3 \times 10^{-4} = 3.65 \times 10^{-2}$ mol [1],

M_r of pure hydrated ethanedioic acid

$=(2\times12.01)+(61.01)+(6\times16.00)=126.1$ [1], mass of pure hydrated ethanedioic acid in sample $=(3.65\times10^{-2})\times126.1=4.60$ g [1], percentage purity $=\left(\frac{4.60}{4.71}\right)\times100=97.7\%$ [1]

3. a) $M(NH_4NO_3)=(2\times14.01)+(4\times1.01)+(3\times16.00)$ $=80.06$ g mol^{-1} [1], percentage of N $=\left(\frac{28.02}{80.06}\right)\times100=35.0\%$ [1]; b) NH_4^+: 4 [1], NO_3^-: 3 [1], molecular geometry: NH_4^+: tetrahedral [1], NO_3^-: trigonal planar [1]; c) i) Total mass of products = (2×80.06) + 100.09 = 260.2, atom economy = (160.12 ÷ 260.2)×100 = 61.5% [1]; ii) M_r $Ca(NO_3)_2$ $=40.08+(2\times14.01)+(6\times16.00)=164.1$, amount in 40.0 kg $=\frac{(40.0\times10^3)}{164.1}=243.8$ mol [1], maximum amount of NH_4NO_4 formed $=2\times243.8=487.6$ mol, mass of NH_4NO_4 $=487.6\times80.06=3.90\times10^4$ g = 39.0 kg [1]; d) i) $2Ca(NO_3)_2(s) \rightarrow 2CaO(s) + 4NO_2(g) + O_2(g)$ [2]; ii) N is reduced from +5 to +4 [1], O is oxidized from −2 to 0 [1]; e) i) 2 mol of solid NH_4NO_3 produces 7 mol of gas [1] so if the reaction goes too fast there is a very large rapid increase in volume. [1]; ii) Breaking down the lattice requires energy so is endothermic, hydrating ions is exothermic [1], the overall reaction is endothermic (as the temperature of the water decreases) so the lattice energy is greater than the hydration energy. [1]

4. a) i) Electrophilic addition [1]; ii) 2-Bromobutane [1]; iii) Two possible carbocations could be formed as an intermediate as the H$^+$ electrophile adds to the pi bond [1], secondary carbocation intermediate is more stable than primary carbocation. [1]; b) i) rate $=k[C_4H_9Br][OH^-]$ [1], first order with respect to $[C_4H_9Br]$ as when $[OH^-]$ is kept constant and $[C_4H_9Br]$ is tripled the rate is tripled [1], first order with respect to $[OH^-]$ as when both $[OH^-]$ and $[C_4H_9Br]$ are doubled the rate quadruples. [1]; ii) S_N2 [1];

iii)

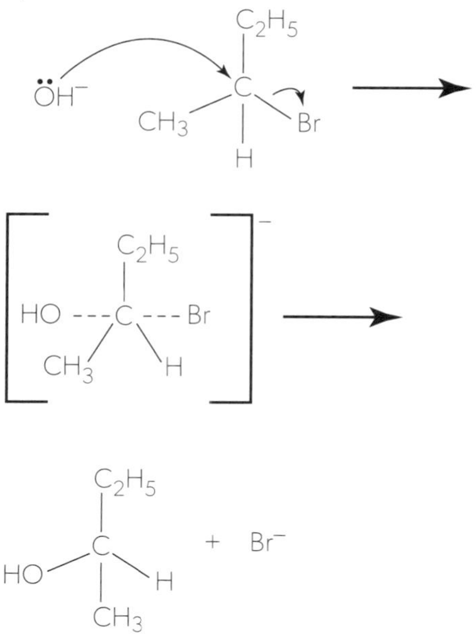

Curly arrow from lone pair on O/negative charge on OH^- to C [1], curly arrow showing C−Br bond breaking [1], transition state showing negative charge square brackets and partial bonds [1], formation of $CH_3CH(OH)C_2H_5$ and Br^- [1]; iv) It will rotate the plane of plane-polarized light to the right/opposite direction [1], OH− attacks from the opposite side to the Br atom so a mirror image is formed at the chiral carbon atom/Walden inversion [1]; c) i) ***Either*** $Cr_2O_7^{2-}$ and H$^+$ ***or*** MnO_4^- and H$^+$ [1], warm/heat [1]; ii) C_4H_8O: three signals as H atoms in three different chemical environments [1], in the ratio 3:3:2 [1], $C_4H_{10}O$: five signals [1] in the ratio 3:1:1:2:3 [1]; d) C_4H_9Br [1], no absorptions due to C=O at 1700–1750 cm^{-1} or due to O−H at 3200–3600 cm^{-1}. [1]

5. a) $CaC_2(s) + 2H_2O(l) \rightarrow Ca(OH)_2(aq) + C_2H_2(g)$ [1];

b) i)

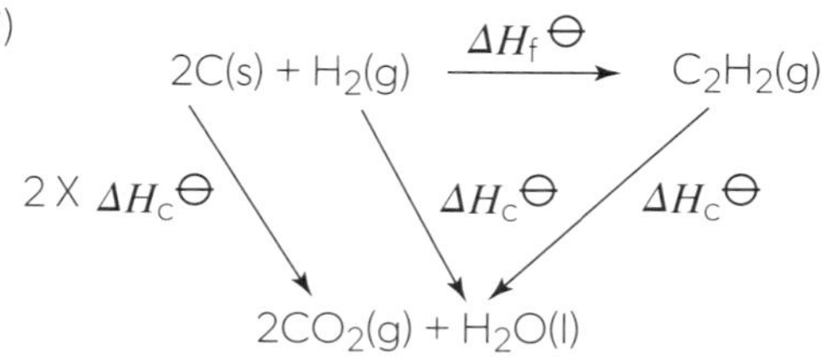

[1];

ii) $\Delta H_f^{\ominus}(C_2H_2)=(2\times-394)+(-286)-(1301)=+227$ kJ mol^{-1} [1]; iii) The values should be identical but it is +228 kJ mol^{-1}, this difference of 1 kJ mol^{-1} is most likely due to rounding up all the values to whole numbers. [1]; iv) Standard entropy of elements = zero so $\Delta S_f^{\ominus}$ = +201 J K^{-1} mol^{-1} = 0.201 kJ K^{-1} mol^{-1} [1], for the reaction to be spontaneous $T\Delta S_f^{\ominus}$ must be greater than $\Delta H_f^{\ominus}$ [1], $\Delta G_f^{\ominus}$ = 0 when $T=\frac{228}{0.201}=1134\ K=861\ °C$ [1];

c) i) H:C⋮C:H [1]; ii) sp [1], sigma bonds between the C and H atoms, one sigma and two pi bonds between the two C atoms [1]; iii) (I) Two domains of bonding pairs of electrons around each C atom so molecule is linear. [1], (II) the two sp orbitals are at 180° to each other so the molecule is linear. [1]; d) i) the two $=CH_2$ atoms give separate signals as they are not in the same chemical environment as there is no free rotation around the C=C bond [1], each signal is split into a doublet as there is one H atom on the adjacent carbon atom [1];

ii)

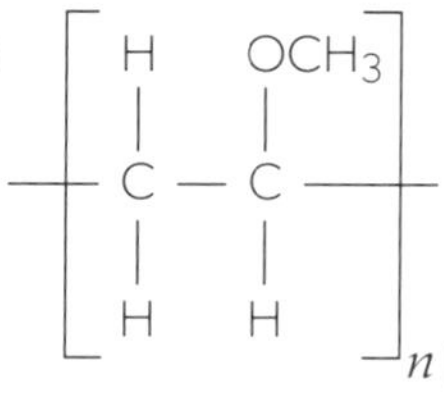

[1]

iii)

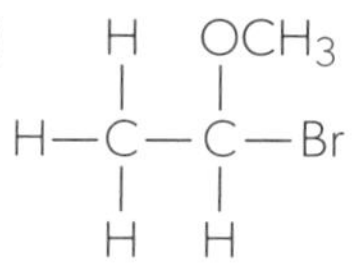

[1]

Index

Page numbers in *italics* refer to question sections

The periodic table

alkali metals

s-block

group

d-block

Non-metals

Metalloids

Metals

period n =	1	2	3	4	5	6	7	8
1	1 H 1.01							
2	3 Li 6.94	4 Be 9.01						
3	11 Na 22.99	12 Mg 24.31						
4	19 K 39.10	20 Ca 40.08	21 Sc 44.96	22 Ti 47.87	23 V 50.94	24 Cr 52.00	25 Mn 54.94	26 Fe 55.85
5	37 Rb 85.47	38 Sr 87.62	39 Y 88.91	40 Zr 91.22	41 Nb 92.91	42 Mo 95.96	43 Tc [98]	44 Ru 101.07
6	55 Cs 132.91	56 Ba 137.33	57 La † 138.91	72 Hf 178.49	73 Ta 180.95	74 W 183.84	75 Re 186.21	76 Os 190.23
7	87 Fr [223]	88 Ra [226]	89 Ac ‡ [227]	104 Rf [267]	105 Db [268]	106 Sg [269]	107 Bh [270]	108 Hs [269]

f-block

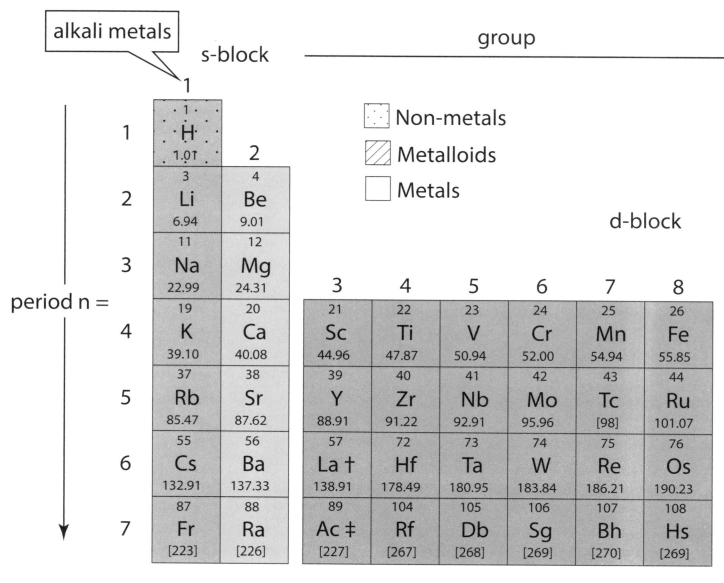

†lanthanoids	58 Ce 140.12	59 Pr 140.91	60 Nd 144.24	61 Pm [145]	62 Sm 150.36
‡actinoids	90 Th 232.04	91 Pa 231.04	92 U 238.03	93 Np [237]	94 Pu [244]

Atomic number
Element
Relative atomic mass

p-block

halogens (group 17)

noble gases (group 18)

9	10	11	12	13	14	15	16	17	18
									2 He 4.00
				5 B 10.81	6 C 12.01	7 N 14.01	8 O 16.00	9 F 19.00	10 Ne 20.18
				13 Al 26.98	14 Si 28.09	15 P 30.97	16 S 32.06	17 Cl 35.45	18 Ar 39.95
27 Co 58.93	28 Ni 58.69	29 Cu 63.55	30 Zn 65.38	31 Ga 69.72	32 Ge 72.63	33 As 74.92	34 Se 78.96	35 Br 79.90	36 Kr 83.80
45 Rh 102.91	46 Pd 106.42	47 Ag 107.87	48 Cd 112.41	49 In 114.82	50 Sn 118.71	51 Sb 121.76	52 Te 127.60	53 I 126.90	54 Xe 131.29
77 Ir 192.22	78 Pt 195.08	79 Au 196.97	80 Hg 200.59	81 Tl 204.38	82 Pb 207.20	83 Bi 208.98	84 Po [209]	85 At [210]	86 Rn [222]
109 Mt [278]	110 Ds [281]	111 Rg [281]	112 Cn [285]	113 Nh [286]	114 Fl [289]	115 Mc [288]	116 Lv [293]	117 Ts [294]	118 Og [294]

63 Eu 151.96	64 Gd 157.25	65 Tb 158.93	66 Dy 162.50	67 Ho 164.93	68 Er 167.26	69 Tm 168.93	70 Yb 173.05	71 Lu 174.97
95 Am [243]	96 Cm [247]	97 Bk [247]	98 Cf [251]	99 Es [252]	100 Fm [257]	101 Md [258]	102 No [259]	103 Lr [262]